Zero Coupon Bonds Pay Phantom Interest (Ch. 14)
Mutual Funds or Indexed Funds? (Ch. 15)
Invest Only Fun Money Aggressively (Ch. 15)
Check Your Stockbroker's Background (Ch. 16)
How to Collect Retirement Benefits and Social Security from a
   Divorced Spouse (Ch. 18)
Think Smart About Retirement Savings (Ch. 18)
Apply Sound Principles for Managing Your Retirement Accounts
   (Ch. 18)
Ten Things Every Spouse Must Know About Financial, Estate,
   Tax, and Investment Planning (Ch. 19)

Tax Considerations and Consequences

Saving for Children's College (Ch. 3)
How to Reduce Income Taxes: An Example (Ch. 4)
Buying Housing (Ch. 9)
Health Care Planning (Ch. 11)
Life Insurance Planning (Ch. 12)
Bonds (Ch. 14)
Mutual Funds (Ch. 15)
Buying and Selling Securities (Ch. 16)
An Income-Producing Real Estate Investment (Ch. 17)
Retirement Planning (Ch. 18)
Use of a Charitable Remainder Trust to Boost Current Income
   (Ch. 19)

Decision-Making Worksheets

Choosing Between Low-Interest-Rate Dealer
   Financing and a Rebate on a New Vehicle (Ch. 8)
Comparing Automobile Financing and Leasing (Ch. 8)
Should You Buy or Rent? (Ch. 9)
Should You Refinance Your Mortgage? (Ch. 9)
Buying Automobile Insurance (Ch. 10)
Determining Disability Income Insurance Needs (Ch. 11)
The Needs Approach to Life Insurance (Ch. 12)
Estimating Your Retirement Savings Goal in Today's Dollars (Ch. 18)

Decision-Making Cases

Reasons to Study Personal Finance (Ch. 1)
Budgeting Advice for Two Young Men (Ch. 2)
A Couple Creates an Educational Savings Plan (Ch. 3)
Budget Control for a Recent Graduate (Ch. 3)
A New Family Calculates Income and Tax Liability (Ch. 4)
Taxable Versus Nontaxable Income (Ch. 4)
A Lobbyist Considers Her Checking Account Options (Ch. 5)
A Delayed Report of a Stolen Credit Card (Ch. 6)
Debt Consolidation as a Debt Reduction Strategy (Ch. 7)
Clauses in a Car Purchase Contract (Ch. 7)
A Dispute over New-Car Repairs (Ch. 8)
Grant and Richard Weigh the Benefits and Costs of Buying Versus
   Renting (Ch. 9)
Patricia Chooses Among Alternative Mortgage Options (Ch. 9)
Abigail Contemplates a New Homeowner's Insurance Policy (Ch. 10)
A Student Buys Insurance for a Used Car (Ch. 10)
An Argument About the Value of Insurance (Ch. 10)
A CPA Selects a Health Insurance Plan (Ch. 11)

Life Insurance for a Newly Married Couple (Ch. 12)
Investing a Gift of Cash (Ch. 13)
Two Brothers' Attitudes Toward Investments (Ch. 14)
A College Student Ponders Investing in the Stock Market (Ch. 14)
Matching Mutual Fund Investments to Economic Projections
   (Ch. 15)
Selection of Mutual Fund as Part of a Retirement Plan (Ch. 15)
From Real Estate to Options and Futures (Ch. 17)
Estimating Early and Normal Retirement Benefits (Ch. 18)
Calculation of Annual Savings Needed to Meet a Retirement Goal
   (Ch. 18)
A Couple Considers the Ramifications of Dying Intestate (Ch. 19)

Money Matters Continuing Cases

Victor and Maria Hernandez Analyze Their Financial
   Statements (Ch. 2)
The Johnsons' Financial Statements (Ch. 2)
Victor and Maria Hernandez Think About Their Budget (Ch. 3)
The Johnsons Have Some Budget Problems (Ch. 3)
Victor and Maria Reduce Their Income Tax Liability (Ch. 4)
The Johnsons Calculate Their Income Taxes (Ch. 4)
Victor and Maria Hernandez Need to Save Money Fast (Ch. 5)
How Should the Johnsons Manage Their Cash? (Ch. 5)
Victor and Maria Have a Billing Dispute (Ch. 6)
The Johnsons Attempt to Resolve Their Credit and Cash-Flow
   Problems (Ch. 6)
Victor and Maria Advise Their Niece (Ch. 7)
The Johnsons' Credit Questions (Ch. 7)
Victor and Maria Hernandez Buy a Third Car (Ch. 8)
The Johnsons Decide to Buy a Car (Ch. 8)
Victor and Maria Hernandez Learn About Real Estate Agents
   (Ch. 9)
The Johnsons Decide to Buy a Condominium (Ch. 9)
The Hernandezes Consider Additional Liability Insurance
   (Ch. 10)
The Johnsons Decide How to Manage Their Risks (Ch. 10)
The Herandezes Face the Possibility of Long-Term Care (Ch. 11)
The Johnsons Consider Buying Disability Insurance (Ch. 11)
Victor and Maria Hernandez Contemplate Switching Life
   Insurance Policies (Ch. 12)
The Johnsons Change Their Life Insurance Coverage (Ch. 12)
Victor and Maria Hernandez Try to Catch Up on Their
   Investments (Ch. 13)
The Johnsons Start an Investment Program (Ch. 13)
Victor and Maria Hernandez Wonder About Investing (Ch. 14)
The Johnsons Want Greater Yields on Investments (Ch. 14)
Victor and Maria Invest for Retirement (Ch. 15)
The Johnsons Decide to Invest Through Mutual Funds (Ch. 15)
The Hernandez Family Has Some Investment Questions (Ch. 16)
The Johnsons Want to Invest in Stock (Ch. 16)
Victor and Maria Consider Hedging an Investment with Puts
   (Ch. 17)
The Johnsons Consider a Real Estate Investment (Ch. 17)
Victor and Maria's Retirement Plans (Ch. 18)
The Johnsons Consider Retirement Planning (Ch. 18)
Victor and Maria Update Their Estate Plans (Ch. 19)
Belinda Johnson Helps Her Uncle Plan His Estate (Ch. 19)

Personal Finance

Personal Finance

EIGHTH EDITION

E. Thomas Garman

VIRGINIA TECH UNIVERSITY

Raymond E. Forgue

UNIVERSITY OF KENTUCKY

Houghton Mifflin Company

BOSTON   NEW YORK

Publisher: Charles Hartford
Editor-in-Chief: George Hoffman
Associate Editor: Julia M. Perez
Editorial Assistant: Kira Robinson-Kates
Project Editor: Andrea Cava
Senior Art and Design Coordinator: Jill Haber
Senior Composition Buyer: Sarah Ambrose
Manufacturing Coordinator: Renee Ostrowski
Executive Marketing Manager: Steven W. Mikels
Senior Marketing Manager: Todd Berman
Marketing Associate: Lisa Boden

Cover images: © Gen Nishino / Getty Images, woman in elevator; © Elizabeth Simpson / Getty Images, tax forms; © Michael Denora / Getty Images, credit card; © Richard Price / Getty Images, New England house; © Terry Husebye / Getty Images, retired couple; © Nancy R. Cohen / Getty Images, mother and child

Printed in the U.S.A.

Library of Congress Control Number: 2004110350

ISBN: 0-618-47142-1

23456789-DOW-09 08 07 06 05

Brief Contents

Part One

Financial Planning

| Chapter 1 | The Importance of Personal Finance | 2 |
| Chapter 2 | Financial Planning | 29 |

Part Two

Money Management

Chapter 3	Budgeting and Cash-Flow Management	58
Chapter 4	Managing Income Taxes	90
Chapter 5	Management of Monetary Assets	127
Chapter 6	Credit Use and Credit Cards	153
Chapter 7	Installment Credit	179
Chapter 8	Automobiles and Other Major Purchases	203
Chapter 9	The Housing Expenditure	229

Part Three

Income and Asset Protection

Chapter 10	Risk Management and Property/Liability Insurance	266
Chapter 11	Health Care Planning	301
Chapter 12	Life Insurance Planning	324

Part Four

Investments

Chapter 13	Investment Fundamentals	360
Chapter 14	Investing in Stocks and Bonds	391
Chapter 15	Investing Through Mutual Funds	421
Chapter 16	Buying and Selling Securities	447
Chapter 17	Real Estate and Speculative Investments	479

Part Five

Retirement and Estate Planning

| Chapter 18 | Retirement Planning | 502 |
| Chapter 19 | Estate Planning | 541 |

Appendixes

| A | Present and Future Value Tables | A-2 |
| B | Estimating Social Security Benefits | A-12 |

Contents

Preface   xxi

Part One

Financial Planning

1   The Importance of Personal Finance   2

Why You Should Study Personal Finance   4

GOLDEN RULES OF
Personal Finance   4

The Six Key Steps to Personal Finance Success   5
How the Economic Environment Will Affect Your
  Personal Finances   7
  Know the State of the Economy   8
  Predict Future Directions for the Economy   9
  Predict Future Directions of Prices and Inflation   9

ADVICE FROM AN EXPERT
*How Inflation Affects Borrowing, Saving,
and Investing   12*

  Estimate Future Interest Rates   12
Economic Considerations That Affect Decision
  Making   12
  Opportunity Costs and Trade-offs in Decision
    Making   13
  Marginal Analysis in Decision Making   13

ADVICE FROM AN EXPERT
Seven Money Mantras for a Richer Life   14

  Income Taxes in Decision Making   14
The Time Value of Money in Decision Making   16

DID YOU KNOW? . . .
*Lottery Officials Use Time Value of Money
Calculations   17*

  Calculating Future Values   18
  Present Value Calculations   20
Career-Related Money Decisions   21
  Comparing Salary and Living Costs in Different
    Cities   21
  Employer-Sponsored Tax-Sheltered Flexible Spending
    Accounts   22
  Employer-Sponsored Qualified Retirement Plans   23
  How to Maximize the Benefits from a Tax-Sheltered
    Retirement Plan   24

Summary   26
Key Terms   26

Chapter Review Questions   26
Group Discussion Issues   27
Decision-Making Cases   27
Financial Math Questions   27
What Would You Recommend Now?   28
Exploring the World Wide Web   28

2   Financial Planning   29

GOLDEN RULES OF
Financial Planning   31

Setting the Stage for Successful Personal Financial
  Planning   31
  Values Provide the Base for Financial Planning   31
  Financial Goals Follow from Values   33

DID YOU KNOW? . . .
Life Planning Issues When You Tie the Knot   34

  Financial Strategies Guide Financial Behavior   35
Developing Your Initial Financial Statements   35
  The Balance Sheet Reveals Your Net Worth   36

HOW TO . . .
Increase Your Net Worth   38

  The Cash-Flow Statement Tracks Your Income and
    Expenses   39

HOW TO . . .
Obtain Information for Your Financial Statements   41

Financial Ratios Assess Your Financial Strength and
  Progress   44
  Basic Liquidity Ratio   44
  Asset-to-Debt Ratio   44
  Debt Service-to-Income Ratio   45
  Debt-Payments-to-Disposable-Income Ratio   45
  Investment Assets-to-Total Assets Ratio   46
  Savings Ratio   46
  Other Ways to Assess Financial Progress   46

DID YOU KNOW? . . .
*It Is Helpful to Use a Computer to Manage Your
Finances   47*

Financial Recordkeeping Saves Time and Money 47
Where to Seek Professional Financial Planning Advice 49
How Are Financial Planners Compensated? 49
Planners Should Have the Appropriate Professional Designations and Credentials 50

ADVICE FROM AN EXPERT
How to Choose a Financial Planner 51

Summary 52
Key Terms 52
Chapter Review Questions 52
Decision-Making Cases 53
Financial Math Questions 53
Money Matters Continuing Cases 54
What Would You Recommend Now? 56
Exploring the World Wide Web 56

Part Two

Money Management

3   Budgeting and Cash-Flow Management 58

GOLDEN RULES OF
Budgeting and Cash-Flow Management 60

The Relationships Among Financial Planning, Budgeting, and Financial Goals 60
The Relationship Between Financial Planning and Budgeting 60
Budgeting and Financial Goals 61

TAX CONSIDERATIONS AND CONSEQUENCES
Saving for Children's College 62

HOW TO . . .
Effectively Achieve Your Financial Goals 63

The Organization Phase of Budgeting 66
Select an Appropriate Recordkeeping Format 66
Use the Cash or Accrual Basis 69
Select Appropriate Budget Classifications 69
Select Appropriate Time Periods 69
The Decision-Making Phase of Budgeting 70
Consider Inflation 70
Make Realistic Budget Estimates 70
Reconciling Budget Estimates 72

HOW TO . . .
Set Up a Budget from Scratch 72

The Implementation Phase of Budgeting 74
Recording Actual Income and Expenditures 74
Managing with a Cash-Flow Calendar 74
Utilizing a Revolving Savings Fund 75
Calculating Time-Period Totals 76
The Control Phase of Budgeting 77
Reasons for Budget Controls 77
Seven Budget Control Measures 77

ADVICE FROM AN EXPERT
Crisis Steps to Take if Budget Deficits Occur Repeatedly 80

The Evaluation Phase of Budgeting 80
Compare Estimated and Actual Amounts 81
Decide How to Handle Balances 81

DID YOU KNOW? . . .
What to Do with Extra Money 81

Assess Progress Toward Goals 82
The Personal Side of Money 82
Money Management and Financial Decision Making for Couples 82
People Ascribe Strong Emotions to Money 83
Talking about Financial Matters Effectively 83
Complications Brought by Remarriage 84

HOW TO . . .
Determine if You and Your Partner Are Financially Compatible 85

HOW TO . . .
Develop Money Sense in Children 86

Summary 87
Key Terms 87
Chapter Review Questions 87
Group Discussion Issues 87
Decision-Making Cases 88
Financial Math Questions 88
Money Matters Continuing Cases 88
What Would You Recommend Now? 89
Exploring the World Wide Web 89

4   Managing Income Taxes   90

GOLDEN RULES OF
Managing Income Taxes   92

Progressive Income Taxes and the Marginal Tax Rate   92
The Progressive Nature of the Federal Income Tax   93
The Marginal Tax Rate Is Applied to the Last Dollar Earned   93
Determining Your Federal Marginal Tax Rate   96
Your Effective Marginal Tax Rate Is Higher   96
The Marginal Tax Rate Affects Your Financial Decisions   96
Your Average Tax Rate Is Lower   96

Filing a Tax Return   96

Ways to Pay Income Taxes   97
Method One: Payroll Withholding   98
Method Two: Estimated Taxes   98

Eight Steps in Calculating Your Incomes Taxes   99
1. Determine Your Total Income   99
2. Determine and Report Gross Income by Subtracting Exclusions   102
3. Subtract Adjustments to Income   103

ADVICE FROM AN EXPERT
A Sideline Business Can Reduce Your Income Taxes   104

4. Subtract the Standard Deduction for Your Tax Status or Itemize Your Deductions   104
5. Subtract the Value of Your Personal Exemptions   107
6. Determine Your Tax Liability   108
7. Subtract Appropriate Tax Credits   109
8. Calculate the Balance Due or the Amount of Your Refund   111

Avoid Taxes Through Proper Planning   111
Practice Legal Tax Avoidance, Not Tax Evasion   111
A Dollar Saved from Taxes Is Really Two Dollars— or More   112
Strategy: Seek Tax-Sheltered Returns on Investments   112
Strategy: Reduce Taxable Income via Your Employer   113

DID YOU KNOW? . . .
Cafeteria Plans Offer Tax-Free Employee Benefits   113

Strategy: Use Tax-Sheltered Investments   115

TAX CONSIDERATIONS AND CONSEQUENCES
How to Reduce Income Taxes: An Example   116

HOW TO . . .
Compare Taxable and After-Tax Yields   118
Strategy: Shift Income to Children   119

ADVICE FROM AN EXPERT
Buy a Home to Reduce Taxes   120

Strategy: Postpone Income   121
Strategy: Bunch Deductions   121
Strategy: Take All of Your Legal Tax Deductions   121
Strategy: Buy and Manage a Real Estate Investment   122
Strategy: Keep Your Tax Records a Long Time   122

Summary   123
Key Terms   123
Chapter Review Questions   123
Group Discussion Issues   123
Decision-Making Cases   124
Financial Math Questions   125
Money Matters Continuing Cases   125
What Would You Recommend Now?   126
Exploring the World Wide Web   126

5   Management of Monetary Assets   127

GOLDEN RULES OF
Managing Monetary Assets   129

What Is Monetary Asset Management?   129
The Four Tools of Monetary Asset Management   129
Who Provides Monetary Asset Management Services?   130

Electronic Banking   132
You Can Do Your Banking with an Automatic Teller Machine   133
You Can Purchase at Point-of-Sale Terminals Using a Debit Card   133
Smart Cards and Stored-Value Cards   134
Direct Deposits and Preauthorized Payments   134
Consumer Protection Regulations   134

Monetary Asset Management: Tool #1— Interest-Earning Checking Accounts   135
Types of Checking Accounts   135
Checking Account Charges, Fees, and Penalties   136

DID YOU KNOW? . . .
What Happens When You Write a Check   137

Monetary Asset Management: Tool #2— Savings Accounts   138

ADVICE FROM AN EXPERT
Endorse Your Checks Properly   139

ADVICE FROM AN EXPERT
Protect Yourself from Checking Account Overdraft Fees 140

How to Save 140

HOW TO . . .
Reconcile Your Bank Accounts 141

DID YOU KNOW? . . .
About Payment Instruments for Special Needs 142

Savings Account Interest 142

Monetary Asset Management: Tool #3—Money Market Accounts 143

Super NOW Accounts 143

DID YOU KNOW? . . .
How Ownership of Accounts (and Other Assets) Is Established 144

Money Market Deposit Accounts 145
Money Market Mutual Funds 145
Asset Management Accounts 145

Monetary Asset Management: Tool #4—Long-Term Savings Instruments 146

DID YOU KNOW? . . .
The Interest Rates for Short-Term Monetary Asset Management Opportunities 146

Certificates of Deposit 147
U.S. Government Savings Bonds 148

Summary 149
Key Terms 149
Chapter Review Questions 149
Group Discussion Issues 150
Decision-Making Cases 150
Financial Math Questions 150
Money Matters Continuing Cases 151
What Would You Recommend Now? 151
Exploring the World Wide Web 151

6 Credit Use and Credit Cards 153

Reasons For and Against Using Credit 154

GOLDEN RULES OF
Credit Use and Credit Cards 155

Why People Use Credit 155
The Downside of Credit Usage 156

HOW TO . . .
Guard Your Privacy 158

Obtaining Credit and Building a Good Credit Reputation 158

The Credit Approval Process 159

DID YOU KNOW? . . .
Certain Forms of Credit Discrimination Are Unlawful 159

DID YOU KNOW? . . .
About FICO Scores 160

Your Credit Reputation 161

DID YOU KNOW? . . .
The Effects of Divorce on Your Credit 163

Types of Consumer Credit and Credit Card Accounts 163

Types of Consumer Credit 163
Credit Card Accounts 164

HOW TO . . .
Close a Credit Card Account 166

Common (But Not Always Beneficial) Aspects of Credit Card Accounts 167

Teaser Rates and Default Rates 167
Preapproved Credit Card Offers 169
Annual and Transaction Fees 169
Liability for Lost or Stolen Cards 169
Late-Payment, Bounced Check, and Over-the-Limit Fees 170
Credit Card Insurance 170

Managing Credit Cards Wisely 170

Credit Statements 170

ADVICE FROM AN EXPERT
Avoid the Minimum Payment Trap 173

Correcting Errors on Your Credit Card Statement 173
Computation of Finance Charges 174

DID YOU KNOW? . . .
How Credit Card Balances Are Calculated 175

Summary 176
Key Terms 176
Chapter Review Questions 176
Group Discussion Issues 176
Decision-Making Cases 177
Financial Math Questions 177
Money Matters Continuing Cases 177
What Would You Recommend Now? 178
Exploring the World Wide Web 178

7 Installment Credit   179

You Should Set Your Own Debt Limits   180

GOLDEN RULES OF
Installment Credit   181

Debt Payments-to-Disposable Income Method   181
Ratio of Debt-to-Equity Method   183
Continuous-Debt Method   184

ADVICE FROM AN EXPERT
Managing Student Loan Debt   184

Setting Debt Limits for Dual-Earner Households   185
Understanding Consumer Loans   185
Calculating an Installment Loan Payment   185
Installment Loans Can Be Unsecured or Secured   186
Purchase Loan Installment Contracts   187
Sources of Consumer Loans   187
Depository Institutions Loan Money to Their Banking
  Customers   187
Sales Finance Companies Loan Money to Buy
  Consumer Products   188
Consumer Finance Companies Make Small Cash
  Loans   188
Stockbrokers Loan Money to Their Clients   189

DID YOU KNOW? . . .
About Alternative Lenders   189

Insurance Companies Loan Money to Their
  Customers   190
**Calculating Finance Charges and Annual Percentage
  Rates   190**
APR Calculations for Single-Payment Loans   191
APR Calculations for Installment Loans   191
Dealing with Overindebtedness   194
Ten Signs of Overindebtedness   194
Federal Law Regulates Debt Collection Practices   195

DID YOU KNOW? . . .
*The Effect of Using Voluntary Repossession to Get Out
of Debt   195*

Steps to Take to Get Out from Under Excessive
  Installment Debt   196

ADVICE FROM AN EXPERT
Control and Reduce Your Credit Card Debt   197

Bankruptcy as a Last Resort   198

Summary   199
Key Terms   199
Chapter Review Questions   199
Group Discussion Issues   200
Decision-Making Cases   200
Financial Math Questions   201

Money Matters Continuing Cases   201
What Would You Recommend Now?   202
Exploring the World Wide Web   202

8 Automobiles and Other Major
      Purchases   203

Guidelines for Planned Buying   204
Control Buying on Impulse   204

GOLDEN RULES OF
Automobiles and Other Major Purchases   205

Pay Cash   205
Buy at the Right Time   205
Don't Pay Extra for a "Name"   206
Recognize the High Price of Convenience   206
Steps Taken Before Interacting with the Seller   206
Prioritize Your Wants   206
Conduct the Necessary Preshopping Research   208

ADVICE FROM AN EXPERT
Tips for Buying On-line   210

Fit the Expenditure into Your Budget   211

DECISION-MAKING WORKSHEET
*Choosing Between Low-Interest-Rate Dealer Financing
and a Rebate on a New Vehicle   212*

Comparison Shopping   214

DID YOU KNOW? . . .
The Keys to a Safe Car   215

Compare Prices   215
Compare Financing Options   215
Consider Leasing Instead of Buying   216

DECISION-MAKING WORKSHEET
Comparing Automobile Financing and Leasing   217

Compare Warranties   218
Service Contracts Are Overpriced   219
Negotiate and Decide on the Best Deal   219
Successful Negotiators Are Armed with
  Information   220
Make the Decision   221

ADVICE FROM AN EXPERT
How to Buy a Used Vehicle   222

Evaluate Your Decision   223

Summary   225
Key Terms   225
Chapter Review Questions   225
Group Discussion Issues   225
Decision-Making Cases   226
Financial Math Questions   226

Money Matters Continuing Cases **226**
What Would You Recommend Now? **227**
Exploring the World Wide Web **227**

9 The Housing Expenditure — 229

Deciding Whether to Rent or Buy Your Home 230

GOLDEN RULES OF
The Housing Expenditure *231*

Rented Housing *231*

HOW TO . . .
Make Sure Your Security Deposit Is Returned 232

Owned Housing *233*
Who Pays More—Renters or Owners? *234*
The Steps of Home Buying 234

DECISION-MAKING WORKSHEET
Should You Buy or Rent? 235

TAX CONSIDERATIONS AND CONSEQUENCES
Buying Housing 236

Getting Your Finances in Order *236*
Prequalifying for a Mortgage *237*

DID YOU KNOW? . . .
The Income Needed to Qualify for a Mortgage 237

DID YOU KNOW? . . .
*The Impact of Your Existing Debt on Your Ability
to Qualify for a Mortgage 238*

Negotiating a Purchase *239*

DID YOU KNOW? . . .
The Role of Real Estate Agents 240

Applying for a Mortgage Loan *240*

DID YOU KNOW? . . .
*Your Credit Score Affects the Mortgage Rate You
Will Pay 241*

Signing Your Name on Closing Day *241*

Financing a Home **241**
Mortgage Loans 242
Factors Affecting the Monthly Payment on a
Mortgage 243

DECISION-MAKING WORKSHEET
Should You Refinance Your Mortgage? 246

The Conventional Mortgage Loan 247
The Adjustable-Rate Mortgage Loan 247
Alternative Mortgage Loans 248

DID YOU KNOW? . . .
About Second Mortgage Loans 250

What Does It Cost to Buy a Home? 251
Principal and Interest 251
Taxes and Insurance 251
Mortgage Insurance 253

ADVICE FROM AN EXPERT
*Don't Wait Too Long to Drop Private Mortgage
Insurance 254*

Points 254
Title Insurance 255
Home Warranty Insurance 255
The Services of an Attorney 256
Miscellaneous Costs 256
Selling a Home 257
Should You List with a Broker or Sell a Home
Yourself? 257
Selling Carries Its Own Costs 257
Be Wary of Seller Financing 258

Summary 258
Key Terms 258
Chapter Review Questions 259
Group Discussion Issues 259
Decision-Making Cases 259
Financial Math Questions 260
Money Matters Continuing Cases 261
What Would You Recommend Now? 262
Exploring the World Wide Web 262

Part 3

Income and Asset Protection

10 Risk Management and Property/ Liability Insurance — 266

Risk and Risk Management 267

GOLDEN RULES OF
*Risk Management and Property/Liability
Insurance 268*

The Nature of Risk   268
The Risk-Management Process   268
Understanding How Insurance Works   272
Hazards Make Losses More Likely to Occur   272

HOW TO . . .
Read Your Insurance Policies   273

Only Certain Losses Are Insurable   273
The Principle of Indemnity Limits Insurance
   Payouts   274
An Insurable Interest Must Exist to Purchase
   Insurance   274
Factors That Reduce the Cost of Insurance   274

ADVICE FROM AN EXPERT
Apply the Large-Loss Principle   275

The Essence of Insurance   276

DID YOU KNOW? . . .
*How Companies Select Among Insurance
Applicants   276*

Who Sells Insurance   277
Homeowner's Insurance   277
Coverages   277
Types of Homeowner's Insurance   278
Buying Homeowner's Insurance   279
Automobile Insurance   283
Losses Covered   283
Buying Automobile Insurance   287

DID YOU KNOW? . . .
The Best Way to Own Vehicles   287

HOW TO . . .
Apply Automobile Insurance to an Accident   288

DECISION-MAKING WORKSHEET
Buying Automobile Insurance   290

**Protection for Other Property and Liability Loss
Exposures   291**
Comprehensive Personal Liability Insurance   291
Professional Liability Insurance   291
Umbrella Liability Insurance   291

HOW TO . . .
Save Money on Insurance   292

Floater Policies   294

DID YOU KNOW? . . .
What's Covered While You Are Away at College   294

**How to Collect on Your Property and Liability
Losses   295**
Contact Your Insurance Agent   295
Document Your Loss   295

File Your Claim   296
Sign a Release   296

Summary   296
Key Terms   296
Chapter Review Questions   297
Group Discussion Issues   297
Decision-Making Cases   297
Financial Math Questions   298
Money Matters Continuing Cases   299
What Would You Recommend Now?   300
Exploring the World Wide Web   300

11   Health Care Planning   301

GOLDEN RULES OF
Health Care Planning   303

Sources of Health Care Benefits   303

HOW TO . . .
*Avoid Duplication of Employee Health Care
Benefits   304*

Health Maintenance Organizations   305
Traditional Health Insurance   305
Government Health Care Plans   306
Making Sense of Your Health Plan Benefits   307
General Terms and Provisions   307

TAX CONSIDERATIONS AND CONSEQUENCES
Health Care Planning   308

Payment Limitations   308
Coverage Limitations   310

ADVICE FROM AN EXPERT
Maintain Your Health Care Plan Between Jobs   311

**What Medical Costs Are Covered by Health Care
Plans?   311**
Hospital Coverage   312
Surgical Coverage   312
Medical Expense Coverage   312

DID YOU KNOW? . . .
Who Pays if You Are Hurt on the Job   312

Major Medical Expense Insurance   313
Comprehensive Health Insurance   313
Dental Expense and Vision Care Insurance   313
Accident and Dread Disease Health Insurance   314

ADVICE FROM AN EXPERT
*Shop Carefully for a Private and Individual Health Care
Plan   314*

Long-Term Health Care Insurance   315
Disability Income Insurance   317
  Level of Need   317
DECISION-MAKING WORKSHEET
  Determining Disability Income Insurance Needs   318
  Important Disability Income Insurance Policy
    Provisions   318

Summary   320
Key Terms   320
Chapter Review Questions   320
Group Discussion Issues   321
Decision-Making Cases   321
Financial Math Questions   322
Money Matters Continuing Cases   322
What Would You Recommend Now?   323
Exploring the World Wide Web   323

12 Life Insurance Planning   324

Why Do People Need Life Insurance?   325
GOLDEN RULES OF
  Life Insurance Planning   326
  Income-Replacement Needs   326
  Final-Expense Needs   326
  Readjustment-Period Needs   326
  Debt-Repayment Needs   327
  College-Expense Needs   327
  Other Special Needs   327
  Government Benefits Can Reduce the Level
    of Need   327
  Existing Insurance and Assets Reduce the Level
    of Need   328
Calculating Your Need for Life Insurance   328
  The Multiple-of-Earnings Approach Is an Inaccurate
    Method   328
  The Needs Approach Is a Better Method   329
DECISION-MAKING WORKSHEET
  The Needs Approach to Life Insurance   330
The Two Basic Types of Life Insurance   332
  Term Life Insurance   332
HOW TO . . .
  Layer Your Term Insurance Policies   334

Cash-Value Life Insurance   334
  Interest-Sensitive Life Insurance Is a Form
    of Cash-Value Life Insurance   338
Understanding Your Life Insurance Policy   340
  Insurance Policies Are Organized into Five
    Sections   340
DID YOU KNOW? . . .
  About Life Insurance Sales Commissions   340
  Policy Terms and Provisions Unique to Life
    Insurance   341
  Settlement Options Allow the Beneficiary to Decide
    How to Receive the Death Benefit   343
  Policy Features Unique to Cash-Value Life
    Insurance   344
Step-by-Step Strategies for Buying Life Insurance   346
  First Ask Whether Your Life Should Be Insured
    at All   346
  If Yes, Choose the Right Type of Life Insurance for
    You   347
  Then Properly Integrate Your Life Insurance into Your
    Overall Financial Planning   347
  And Adjust Your Life Insurance and Investment Plan
    Over Your Life Cycle   347
ADVICE FROM AN EXPERT
  Buy Term and Invest the Rest   348
  Choose a Financially Strong Company   350
TAX CONSIDERATIONS AND CONSEQUENCES
  Life Insurance Planning   350
  Choose an Agent   351
  Compare Costs Among Policies   351

Summary   354
Key Terms   354
Chapter Review Questions   354
Group Discussion Issues   355
Decision-Making Cases   355
Financial Math Questions   355
Money Matters Continuing Cases   356
What Would You Recommend Now?   357
Exploring the World Wide Web   357

Part Four

Investments

13 Investment Fundamentals 360

Why You Should Establish an Investment Program and How to Get Started 362
Why People Invest 362

GOLDEN RULES OF
Investment Fundamentals 362

Prerequisites to Investing 363
An Investment Plan 364

HOW TO . . .
Get Money to Save and Invest 364

Investment Returns 364
Discover Your Own Approach to Investing 366
How Do You Handle Investment Risk? 366
Ultraconservative "Investors" Are Really Just "Savers" 366
What Is Your Investment Philosophy? 367
Should You Take an Active or Passive Investing Approach? 368
Identify the Types of Investments You Want to Make 368
Do You Want to Lend or Own? 369
Do You Want to Make Short-Term or Long-Term Investments? 369
Which Types of Investments Are Best Given Your Investment Goals? 370
Factors That Affect the Rate of Return on Different Investments 371
Investment Risk 371
Leverage 374
Income Taxes 376
Commissions and Transaction Costs 376
Inflation 377
The Strategies of Long-Term Investors 377

HOW TO . . .
Calculate the Real Rate of Return (After Taxes and Inflation) on Investments 377

Investors Understand Market Movements 378
Inverstors Understand That Trying to Time the Market Is Too Difficult to Accomplish 378
Strategy: Buy-and-Hold Anticipates Long-Term Economic Growth 379
Strategy: Portfolio Diversification Reduces Portfolio Volatility 379

Strategy: Asset Allocation Keeps You in the Right Investment Categories at the Right Time 380
Strategy: Modern Portfolio Theory Evolves from Asset Allocation 380
Strategy: Dollar-Cost Averaging Buys at "Below-Average" Costs 381
Steps to Take for Effective Long-Term Investing 384

ADVICE FROM AN EXPERT
Buy Shares of Stock Directly Using a Dividend-Reinvestment Plan 385

ADVICE FROM AN EXPERT
When to Sell an Investment 386

Summary 386
Key Terms 387
Chapter Review Questions 387
Group Discussion Issues 387
Decision-Making Cases 387
Financial Math Questions 388
Money Matters Continuing Cases 388
What Would You Recommend Now? 389
Exploring the World Wide Web 389

14 Investing in Stocks and Bonds 391

GOLDEN RULES OF
Investing in Stocks and Bonds 393

Stocks and Bonds and How They Are Used 393
Common Stock 393
Preferred Stock 394
Bonds 395
An Illustration: Running Paws Cat Food Company 396
Numeric Measures of Stock Performance That Influence Investment Decisions 397
Cash Dividends 397
Dividend Payout Ratio 398
Dividends per Share 398
Dividend Yield 398
Book Value 398

DID YOU KNOW? . . .
How Stock Dividends and Stock Splits Work 399

Book Value per Share 399
Price-to-Book Ratio 399
Earnings per Share 400

Price/Earning Ratio   400
Price-to-Sales Ratio   400
Beta   401

The Classifications of Stocks   401
Income Stocks   401

DID YOU KNOW? . . .
Shareholders Have Voting and Preemptive Rights   402

Growth Stocks   402
Speculative Stocks   402

DID YOU KNOW? . . .
How Most Investors Pick Stocks   403

Other Characterizations for Common Stocks   403

HOW TO . . .
Use the Internet to Help You Invest in Stocks and Bonds   405

Characteristics of Bonds   405
Bonds Are Either Secured or Unsecured   406
Bonds Are Registered and Issued in Book-Entry Form   406
Bonds Are Callable   406
Corporate, U.S. Government, and Municipal Bonds   407

DID YOU KNOW? . . .
You Can Buy New Treasury Securities Only from the Government   409

ADVICE FROM AN EXPERT
Zero-Coupon Bonds Pay Phantom Interest   411

Evaluate Bond Prices and Returns   411
Interest-Rate Risk Results in Variable Value   411
Premiums and Discounts   411
Current Yield   411

DID YOU KNOW? . . .
How Far Bond Prices Will Move When Interest Rates Change   413

HOW TO . . .
Estimate the Selling Price of a Bond After Interest Rates Have Changed   414

Yield to Maturity   414
Decisions Bond Investors Must Make   415

TAX CONSIDERATIONS AND CONSEQUENCES
Bonds   416

Summary   416
Key Terms   417
Chapter Review Questions   417
Group Discussion Issues   417
Decision-Making Cases   418

Financial Math Questions   418
Money Matters Continuing Cases   419
What Would You Recommend Now?   420
Exploring the World Wide Web   420

15 Investing Through Mutual Funds   421

What Investors Expect from Mutual Funds   423

GOLDEN RULES OF
Investing Through Mutual Funds   424

Investors Expect Mutual Fund Dividend Income   425
Investors Expect Capital Gains Through Price Appreciation   425

Mutual Funds Have Different Investment Objectives   426
Funds with an Income Objective   426
Funds with a Balanced Objective   427
Funds with a Growth Objective   427
Funds with a Growth and Income Objective   428

Unique Features of Mutual Funds   429
Easy Purchase and Sale   429

DID YOU KNOW? . . .
The Total Long-Term Returns for Various Types of Stock Mutual Funds Are Roughly the Same   429

ADVICE FROM AN EXPERT
Mutual Funds or Index Funds?   430

Check Writing and Wiring of Funds   431
Automatic Investment   431
Automatic Reinvestment   431
Switching Privileges Within a Mutual Fund Family   431
Recordkeeping and Help with Taxes   432
Beneficiary Designation   432
Easy Establishment of Retirement Plans   433
Withdrawal Plans   433

Mutual Fund Fees   433
Mutual Fund Transaction Fees   433
Mutual Fund Expense Charges   435

DID YOU KNOW? . . .
Commissions on Load Funds Depend on Share Class   436

Disclosure of Fees   436
What's Best: Load or No-Load? Low-Fee or High-Fee?   436

How to Evaluate Mutual Funds in Which to Invest   437
Match Your Investment Philosophy and Financial Goals to a Mutual Fund's Objectives   437
Read Prospectuses and Annual Reports   437

Locate Sources of Comparative Performance
Data   438
Interpret Comparative Performance Information
over Time   439

TAX CONSIDERATIONS AND CONSEQUENCES
Mutual Funds   440

ADVICE FROM AN EXPERT
Invest Only Fun Money Aggressively   442

Summary   443
Key Terms   443
Chapter Review Questions   443
Group Discussion Issues   443
Decision-Making Cases   444
Financial Math Questions   444
Money Matters Continuing Cases   445
What Would You Recommend Now?   445
Exploring the World Wide Web   446

16   Buying and Selling Securities   447

GOLDEN RULES OF
Buying and Selling Securities   449

Securities Markets and Brokerage Firms   449
Primary Markets   449
Secondary Markets   450
Organized Stock Exchanges   451

DID YOU KNOW? . . .
About Securities Markets Regulation   453

How to Select a Brokerage Firm   453

ADVICE FROM AN EXPERT
Check Your Stockbroker's Background   455

**Ordering Securities Transactions and Reading
Newspaper Price Quotations   455**
The Process of Trading Stocks   455
Matching or Negotiating Stock Prices   455
Types of Stock Orders   456
Buying and Selling Mutual Funds   457
Reading Newspaper Price Quotations   458
Obtaining and Using Investment Information   460
Securities Market Indexes   461
General Economic Conditions and Financial
News   462
Facts About Industry Trends   462
Information about Specific Companies and
Funds   464
Extensive Investment Information Is Available
On-line   465

**Determine Whether an Investment Has a Sufficient
Potential Rate of Return   466**
Investors Should Begin with the Return on U.S.
Treasury Bills   467
Use Beta to Estimate the Risk of the Investment   467
Estimate the Market Risk   467
Calculate the Required Rate of Return   468
Calculate the Potential Rate of Return on the
Investment   468
Compare the Required Rate of Return with the
Potential Rate of Return on the Investment   470
**Margin Buying and Selling Short Are Risky Trading
Techniques   470**
Margin Trading Is Buying Stocks on Credit   470

TAX CONSIDERATIONS AND CONSEQUENCES
Buying and Selling Securities   471

Selling Short Is Selling Stocks Borrowed from Your
Broker   473

HOW TO . . .
Determine a Margin Call Stock Price   473

Summary   474
Key Terms   475
Chapter Review Questions   475
Group Discussion Issues   475
Decision-Making Cases   475
Financial Math Questions   476
Money Matters Continuing Cases   477
What Would You Recommend Now?   478
Exploring the World Wide Web   478

17   Real Estate and Speculative
Investments   479

GOLDEN RULES OF
Real Estate and Speculative Investments   481

**Direct and Indirect Ownership Investments
in Real Estate   481**
Direct Ownership Investments in Real Estate   481
Indirect Ownership Investments in Real Estate   483
What Should You Pay for a Real Estate Investment?   484
**Advantages and Disadvantages of Real Estate
Investments   484**
Advantages of Real Estate Investments   485
Disadvantages of Real Estate Investments   488
Collectibles and Precious Metals and Stones   489

TAX CONSIDERATIONS AND CONSEQUENCES
An Income-Producing Real Estate Investment   490

Options and Futures Contracts   492

Options Allow You to Buy or Sell an Asset
at a Predetermined Price   492

HOW TO . . .
Make Sense of Option Contracts   493

ADVICE FROM AN EXPERT
Calculate Break-Even Prices for Option Contracts   495

Futures Contracts Focus on Market Price Changes
in Certain Types of Commodities   496

Summary   497
Key Terms   497
Chapter Review Questions   498
Group Discussion Issues   498
Decision-Making Cases   498
Financial Math Questions   498
Money Matters Continuing Cases   499
What Would You Recommend Now?   500
Exploring the World Wide Web   500

Part Five

Retirement and Estate Planning

18   Retirement Planning   502

Retirement Planning Is Your Responsibility   504

GOLDEN RULES OF
Retirement Planning   504

**Understanding Your Social Security Retirement Income
Benefits   506**

DID YOU KNOW? . . .
About Women and Retirement Planning   506

Your Contributions to Social Security   507
How You Can Become Qualified for Social Security
Benefits   507
How to Estimate Your Social Security Retirement
Benefits   508
Check the Accuracy of Your Social Security
Statement   510

ADVICE FROM AN EXPERT
*How to Collect Retirement Benefits and Social Security
from a Divorced Spouse   510*

**How to Calculate Your Estimated Retirement Needs
in Today's Dollars   511**
Projecting Your Annual Retirement Expenses and
Income   511
A Retirement Needs Illustration   511

DECISION-MAKING WORKSHEET
*Estimating Your Retirement Savings Goal in Today's
Dollars   512*

**Invest Your Retirement Money in Tax-Sheltered
Retirement Accounts   514**
Contributions May Be Tax-Deductible   514
Earnings Are Tax-Deferred   514
Withdrawals Might Be Tax-Free   515
Much More Money Can Be Accumulated   515

You Have Greater Flexibility   516
You Have Ownership and Portability   516
**The Three Major Types of Employer-Sponsored
Retirement Plans   516**

DID YOU KNOW? . . .
*Retirement Plan Contribution Tax Credit for Low-
Income and Moderate-Income Savers   517*

Defined-Contribution Retirement Plan—Today's
Standard   517

ADVICE FROM AN EXPERT
Think Smart About Retirement Savings   518

Defined-Benefit Retirement Plan—Yesterday's
Standard   520
Cash-Balance Plan—The Newest Retirement
Deal   521
Additional Employer-Sponsored Plans   522

DID YOU KNOW? . . .
*What Questions to Ask About Your Employer's
Retirement Plan   523*

**You Can Also Contribute to Personal Retirement
Accounts   524**
Individual Retirement Accounts   524
Keoghs and SEP-IRAs   525

DID YOU KNOW? . . .
*Congress Is Considering Establishing Some New Retire-
ment Accounts   526*

**Suggestions for the Do-It-Yourself Retirement Investor
Including Monte Carlo Simulations   526**
Avoid the Big Mistakes in Retirement Planning   527
What if No Employer-Sponsored Retirement Plan
Is Available?   527

How Much Should You Save? 528

Start to Save Early in Your Career and Save as Much
as You Can 528

Use Long-Term Investment Strategies 528

ADVICE FROM AN EXPERT
*Apply Sound Principles for Managing Your Retirement
Accounts 529*

Use Monte Carlo Simulations to Help Guide Your
Retirement Investment Decisions 529

DID YOU KNOW? . . .
*How to Avoid Rollover Penalties When Changing
Employers or Retiring 530*

**Withdrawing Money Early from a Tax-Sheltered
Retirement Account 532**

Withdrawals That May Avoid the 10 Percent IRS
Penalty 532

Withdrawals Cause Bad Things to Happen to Your
Retirement Accounts 532

**Living in Retirement Without Running Out of
Money 533**

Figure Out How Many Years Your Money Will Last
in Retirement and Make Monthly Withdrawals
Accordingly 533

TAX CONSIDERATIONS AND CONSEQUENCES
Retirement Planning 534

Buy an Annuity and Receive Monthly Checks 534
Consider Working Part-Time 535

Summary 536
Key Terms 536
Chapter Review Questions 536
Group Discussion Issues 537
Decision-Making Cases 537
Financial Math Questions 538
Money Matters Continuing Cases 538
What Would You Recommend Now? 539
Exploring the World Wide Web 540

19 Estate Planning 541

GOLDEN RULES OF
Estate Planning 543

Appropriate Ways to Transfer Your Estate 543
Having a Valid Will Is a Smart Way to Transfer
Your Assets 544
It Is Smart to Avoid Probate 546
**Use of Trusts to Transfer Assets and Reduce
Estate Taxes 547**
Living Trusts 548

DID YOU KNOW? . . .
Spouses Have Legal Rights to Each Other's Estates 548

Testamentary Trusts 549
**Prepare Advance Directive Documents in Case You
Become Incapacitated 550**

TAX CONSIDERATIONS AND CONSEQUENCES
*Use of a Charitable Remainder Trust to Boost Current
Income 550*

ADVICE FROM AN EXPERT
*Ten Things Every Spouse Must Know About Financial,
Estate, Tax, and Investment Planning 551*

Estate and Inheritance Taxes 552

Summary 552
Key Terms 553
Chapter Review Questions 553
Group Discussion Issues 553
Decision-Making Cases 554
Financial Math Questions 554
Money Matters Continuing Cases 554
What Would You Recommend Now? 555
Exploring the World Wide Web 555

**Appendix A   Present and Future Value
Tables   A-2**

**Appendix B   Estimating Social Security
Benefits   A-12**

Index   I-1

Preface

Your happiness in life will be affected by many factors, including your career choice and your personal relationships. It will also be affected by your personal financial success. Fortunately, as a college graduate, the coming years will bring you many opportunities for financial success. You will be able to capitalize on those opportunities, however, only if you can avoid the potential pitfalls and navigate some significant financial challenges.

Within 10 years after college graduation, the typical college graduate will purchase two or three vehicles for more than $25,000 each; spend several thousand dollars for expensive household items such as furniture and a television; shell out a few thousand dollars in interest on credit cards; hand over to the Internal Revenue Service many thousands of dollars in income and Social Security taxes; buy a life insurance policy; contribute $2000 to $4000 annually to an employer-sponsored tax-sheltered retirement plan; and save enough money to make a $15,000 to $30,000 down payment to purchase a home valued at more than $200,000 or $300,000.

And there will be even more finance-related activities during middle age and beyond. During your lifetime, you will be personally responsible for saving $1 million, $2 million, or even more for retirement. That will likely be your most significant financial management challenge!

You cannot get from here . . . to there . . . without a solid understanding of the concepts and principles of personal finance. *Personal Finance*, eighth edition, provides a clear and thorough examination of the principles of personal financial planning. It offers virtually all the key strategies and tactics that you need to successfully confront life's financial challenges.

You will find that *Personal Finance* is logically organized, clearly presented, highly substantive, interesting, and, perhaps most importantly, inherently practical. This book and the academic course for which it was adopted will be one of your most important collegiate experiences. No other textbook or course is so fundamentally about you and for you.

Your first requirement for achieving financial success is a simple one—spend less than you earn. (Yes, this *can* happen and *Personal Finance* will show you how.) Next, you must develop the knowledge and skills necessary to take best advantage of the income you earn, the credit you require, the insurance protection available for your assets and income, and the world of investing that will be the key to your long-term financial security. This book is not about "snapshots," "headlines," or "highlights." Rather, it is designed to help you achieve genuine financial success.

Goals and Features of the Book

Competence and *confidence* were our two broad goals in writing *Personal Finance*. To develop competence in personal finance, you need a text with a wide scope. We have endeavored to make *Personal Finance* the most comprehensive and thorough textbook available. To help you become a skillful lifelong manager of personal finances, we take a *how-to approach*, explaining, for example, how to manage cash, establish personal credit limits, reduce income taxes, buy a car, obtain an affordable home mortgage loan, select an insurance agent, choose a life insurance policy, select a stockbroker, compare mutual fund investments, calculate the anticipated return on an investment, and determine how to diversify your retirement investments.

We also outline *step-by-step procedures* for the more complex financial activities, such as developing a comprehensive personal financial plan, planning and reconciling a 12-month budget, calculating personal income taxes, choosing between low-interest-rate dealer financing and a rebate on a new vehicle, determining how much life insurance is needed, estimating how much money will be needed for your retirement in today's dollars, and calculating how to spend down your retirement dollars at a rate that will not deplete the funds too rapidly.

To develop confidence in the area of personal finance, the reader needs to be led through—not simply pointed toward—the material. We aim to acquaint the reader with the subject matter logically and to offer no surprises. For students who have little background in finance, economics, or mathematics, this book offers clear explanations and instructions. Numerical examples are always explained parenthetically, and both the benefits and the costs of a multitude of personal finance decisions are examined closely. Key words and concepts—which are printed in boldface type—are clearly and completely defined when they first occur and often redefined in later chapters. Instructors who assign chapters out of sequence will find this feature particularly convenient.

This book has become highly popular with students because of its informal writing style and with instructors because of its readability, which enhances the likelihood that students come to class prepared. We have again aimed with the eighth edition to keep the narrative conversational, yet clear and concise.

Among the many helpful features of *Personal Finance* are more than 120 tables, charts, and illustrations to support the narrative, including facsimiles of forms that are used in personal finance, such as budgets, income tax tables, and Monte Carlo investment simulations. Beginning-, middle-, and end-of-chapter pedagogical materials are all designed to develop the reader's confidence in personal finance.

Every aspect of the design of *Personal Finance* aims to get the reader to think deeply about the subject, to consider appropriate alternatives, and to make tentative decisions about the best courses of action in money matters to take throughout one's lifetime. In short, the goal is to help the reader truly learn the subject of personal finance.

We want readers to internalize all of the best concepts and principles and to make smart personal finance decisions early in life. We want readers to understand and follow what we call the "Golden Rules of Personal Finance"—because if they do, they will be successful in their personal financial lives.

As an aside, Houghton Mifflin is pleased to report that *Personal Finance* is the required text for the first part of the two-part examination process for the certification program, Accredited Financial Counselor™, sponsored by the Association for Financial Counseling and Planning Education.* Also, this book is recommended by the Certified Financial Planner Board of Standards, Inc.,† as a resource for those studying for the CFP™ or Certified Financial Planner™ Professional designation.

New in the Eighth Edition

The single word that best describes the eighth edition of *Personal Finance* is *quality*. To be the very best college textbook in personal finance requires paying great attention to

---

*For more information, contact Association for Financial Counseling and Planning Education, 2112 Arlington Avenue, Suite H, Upper Arlington, Ohio 43221-4339; telephone (614) 485-9650; fax (614) 485-9621; e-mail: chite@afcpe.org; Internet: www.afcpe.org.

†For more information, contact Certified Financial Planner Board of Standards, Inc., 1670 Broadway, Suite 600, Denver, Colorado 80202-4809; telephone 303-830-7500; fax 303-860-7388; e-mail: initialcert @CFP-Board.org; Internet: www.cfp.org.

detail, and we believe we have succeeded in doing so with this edition. *Personal Finance* has been rigorously revised to increase the effectiveness of the text for student learning. It is up-to-date and covers all of the concepts fundamental to understanding our economic environment and succeeding in personal finance.

We have thoroughly enjoyed the process of updating and revising *Personal Finance*. It is challenging work for us, but it is very satisfying work, too. We continuously seek to stay abreast of the rapidly changing world of personal finance and then figure out the best way to communicate this information to student readers. Our motto is "Use continuous improvements to get a concept across better than before."

To create the eighth edition, we listened to the comments and suggestions of many reviewers—both users and nonusers. Accordingly, we have made dozens of substantive changes to increase the effectiveness of the text for student learning. Chapter 19, Estate Planning, is new, for example. It concisely covers the basics as well as focuses on all the right actions that newly employed college graduates should take to sensibly own their assets and plan the transfer of their estates. Chapter 4, Managing Income Taxes, has been completely updated to reflect the 30-plus recent tax law changes affecting individual taxpayers, including numerous tax credits that can be used to reduce almost anyone's income tax liability.

We added more topics, re-sequenced subject matter, shortened sentences, rewrote the first paragraph following each major section head, identified numerous new Internet websites, updated all tables and figures, created several new graphics, reworded all chapter summaries, and added more than 50 new key terms (including "financial responsibility," "financial happiness," "health savings account," and "universal default.") In addition, we created new end-of-chapter cases and updated the entire contents of all chapters.

New Material on Up-to-Date Topics

Additional learning material has been added to every chapter. Examples include the following:

- The importance of sacrificing some current spending to invest toward one's future lifestyle
- How to reduce income taxes by subtracting appropriate credits
- How to reduce taxable income via your employer with a flexible spending account
- Tips for setting a debt limit
- How the economic environment will affect your personal finances
- Suggestions for getting out of debt
- How ownership of accounts (and other assets) is established
- How to build a credit history and navigate common (but not always beneficial) aspects of credit card accounts
- Techniques for using the Web to assess home costs in any U.S. market
- Ways to maintain health care coverage when changing jobs
- Determining how a marginal tax rate will affect your financial decisions
- Steps to take for effective long-term investing
- Things to consider when assessing a mutual fund's volatility
- Investing in collectibles
- Trading in high-risk options and futures contracts
- How to invest wisely for your retirement using Monte Carlo simulations
- Smart ways to avoid probate
- Buying an immediate annuity and receiving monthly checks

New Features

New "Golden Rules of Personal Finance."   This feature consists of 19 new "big-picture" boxes that appear on the second page of every chapter. Each list of "Golden Rules" provides concise advice about what a college graduate needs to do when managing his or her personal finances. Following these effective, practical suggestions all but guarantees that your lifetime of personal finances will be smooth and successful. Why did the authors decide to create this feature? We wanted to lead the reader to the basic truths—the most important personal finance knowledge and ideas to be applied in real life. The "Golden Rules" suggestions, when followed, will help readers by guiding them to make the right personal finance decisions early in and throughout life and to avoid mistakes made by others.

New "Advice from an Expert."   This series of 31 boxes is co-authored by some of the United States' best personal finance experts. Each has shared some of the specialized and unique knowledge gained through years of practice in the field. Topics include:

- Seven Money Mantras for a Richer Life
- How Inflation Affects Borrowing, Saving, and Investing
- Crisis Steps to Take if Budget Deficits Occur Repeatedly
- Avoid the Minimum Payment Trap
- Control and Reduce Your Credit Card Debt
- Apply the Large-Loss Principle
- Think Smart About Retirement Savings
- Ten Things Every Spouse Must Know About Financial, Estate, Tax, and Investment Planning

New Group Discussion Issues.   This end-of-chapter activity is designed to bring the classroom together. The five issues offer students an opportunity to share some of their own personal finance experiences with their classmates.

New Figures and Tables.   All tables and figures have been updated, redrawn for more precise visual impact and comprehension, and appear in the most appropriate places within the narrative. Some new tables and figures include the following:

- Phases of the Business Cycle
- The Relationships Among the Three Types of Goals
- Sample Budget Classifications and Expense Guidelines
- How Your Income Is Really Taxed
- Credit Card Disclosure Information
- What It Costs to Borrow Money
- Changes in Principal and Interest Components of the Monthly Payment on a $100,000 Mortgage Loan at 8% for 30 Years
- Changes in Loan Balance and Owner's Equity for a Home Purchased with 20% Down at 8% for 30 Years
- Comparison of Premium Dollars for Life Insurance
- Life Insurance and Investment Program Over the Life Cycle
- Ten Best- and Worst-Performing Industries
- Balancing Risk and Returns on Mutual Funds
- Illustrative Diversified Investment Portfolios
- The Wisdom of Automatic Reinvestment of Income and Capital Gains Dividends for 20 Years
- Monte Carlo Simulation

Pedagogical Features That Enhance Learning

To provide a complete perspective on personal finance, this book emphasizes comprehensive treatment of the subject and carefully designed pedagogical features to strengthen the learning opportunities for students. Each feature is designed to communicate vital information meaningfully and to maintain student interest. In addition to the new features highlighted earlier, the following features appear wherever appropriate throughout the text.

Time Value of Money.   Students need to thoroughly understand the concept of the time value of money. Recognizing that fact, our explanations in Chapter 1 and the applications of these techniques in subsequent chapters are simple and clear, and well within the grasp of college students.

Graphics, Color, and Real Examples.   The sophisticated graphics and color scheme in the text are meant to heighten interest in the topics and focus the reader's attention on the most important concepts. The use of a full spectrum of colors is new to this eighth edition. Personalized examples are used throughout the text to show how the topic at hand translates into *real* life for individuals and couples throughout the life cycle. Many examples are mathematical in nature, and they illustrate the critical importance of achieving long-term financial goals through investing.

Visual Format That Reinforces Thinking.   Every chapter begins with the same topical and visual format. On the first page, the student sees the chapter title and learning objectives. The next page presents a concise personal finance case about an individual or couple, "What Would You Recommend?." It is followed by questions that the reader should keep in mind while learning about the key personal finance concepts introduced in that chapter. The chapter's introductory paragraphs first explain *why* this personal finance content is important, and then preview the organization of the chapter. On the next page, the reader's eye is drawn to the box titled the "Golden Rules of Personal Finance." Thus, in less than two minutes, the student is purposefully provided multiple messages that reinforce what and how to think about the most important concepts contained in the chapter.

Pretest/Post-test Chapter Opening Case: What Would You Recommend?
This realistic case is presented at the beginning of each chapter and is intended to introduce the relevant chapter content to the reader. It is followed by four to eight leading questions tied to the most important fundamental concepts in the chapter. This unusual style of case is really a unique pretest/post-test for readers. At first the case acts as a pretest, because students will be able to offer only simplistic, experience-based opinions and suggestions to answer the questions. This initial exercise should communicate to students how much they have to learn from reading the chapter. A parallel exercise—the post-test—appears as part of the end-of-chapter pedagogy. At that point, student responses should be informed, practical, and action oriented. Instructors are encouraged to lead a class conversation about the case questions when initiating a discussion of a chapter as well as to spend a few moments at the end of the chapter's coverage revisiting them.

Learning Objectives.   The learning objectives are listed and highlighted at the beginning of each chapter. They are highlighted again at the beginning of each major section of the chapter, one more time in the end-of-chapter summary, and yet again in the margin notes.

Margin Notes.   Each major section in a chapter begins with a margin note that restates the appropriate learning objective to help the reader focus precisely on the anticipated content to be learned.

Key Terms.   All key terms appear in bold type and are defined clearly and concisely. They are also listed in bold type in the end-of-book index.

Six Types of Boxes.   Six types of boxes are found in *Personal Finance:* "Golden Rules of Personal Finance," "Decision-Making Worksheet," "How to . . . ," "Did You Know? . . .", "Tax Considerations and Consequences," and "Advice from an Expert." The content in each box is absolutely relevant to student understanding of personal finance concepts and principles. The boxes are not fluff; they are purposeful in nature. New to this edition, the "Golden Rules of Personal Finance" boxes concisely list the "right kind of advice" for readers desiring success in their personal finances throughout their lives. Examples of tips found in these boxes include paying yourself first by spending less than you earn, establishing a year-long revolving savings fund and evaluating its success as time passes, fully funding your 401(k) retirement account and taking full advantage of any employer matching contributions, and making a list of five important money topics that you should discuss with a significant other. Another new series of boxes, called "Advice from an Expert," was written by some of the nation's very best personal finance experts. Their expert, real-world advice focuses on, among other topics, managing student loan debt, getting out of credit card debt, opening a sideline business to reduce income taxes, buying on-line, buying a used car, and buying retirement on the layaway plan.

End-of-Chapter Pedagogy.   The end-of-chapter pedagogy carefully directs student learning of the concepts and principles key to success in personal finance.

- **Summary.** Two to four sentences review the chapter content in an order matching each of the chapter objectives.
- **Key Terms.** This list of 20 of the most important terms and concepts in the chapter gives the page numbers where their definitions can be found.
- **Chapter Review Questions.** This list of 10 questions is intended to help readers assess their knowledge of the most important ideas and principles covered in the chapter.
- **Group Discussion Issues.** Students are given an opportunity to converse about their personal experiences related to the chapter by addressing these questions. Their answers can be quickly and easily shared in a classroom discussion.
- **Decision-Making Cases.** Students must apply key concepts when analyzing "typical" personal financial problems, dilemmas, and challenges that face individuals and couples. The series of case questions requires data analysis and/or critical thinking, and this effort reinforces mastery of chapter concepts.
- **Financial Math Questions.** These questions allow the reader to apply the relevant quantitative mathematical calculations utilized in personal finance decision making. Some exercises emphasize using the time value of money tables in the appendix.
- **Money Matters Continuing Cases.** These cases ask students to apply personal finance concepts to changing life situations. Students read the popular Harry and

Belinda Johnson case study, which follows a young married couple, as well as the Victor and Maria Hernandez case study, which focuses on a family moving from mid-life into retirement. These cases can be analyzed in a logical series from chapter to chapter as the families deal with changing needs and priorities. Because the cases are designed to be both continuous *and* independent of the other chapters' cases, each case can be analyzed by itself.

- **What Would You Recommend Now?** The same leading questions pertaining to the case at the beginning of the chapter are repeated in this section. At this point, however, instructors can anticipate high-quality responses and a deeper level of understanding because the questions are posed from the perspective of "Now that you have read the chapter. . . ." Because the "answers" are not found in a single paragraph in the chapter, students must "dig" into the chapter material to develop appropriate responses to the questions. Good responses will require reflection, contemplation, and critical thinking, resulting in correct conclusions from a first-textbook-in-personal-finance level of thinking. Suggested answers appear in *The Instructor's Resource Manual with Test Bank.*

- **Exploring the World Wide Web.** Internet-based exercises, cases, and focused questions let the student research and apply chapter concepts while finding the answers. Students are encouraged to use on-line calculators and other Web resources. The Internet is thoroughly integrated throughout *Personal Finance,* eighth edition. We also continue to feature specific Web links throughout the text.

Organization and Topical Coverage of the Eighth Edition

The contents of the eighth edition have been arranged so that as each new topic is introduced, it is fully explained and its fundamental underpinnings are thoroughly examined before commencing further study. For example, Chapter 13, Investment Fundamentals, precedes chapters on specific types of investments. In addition, not only does each chapter follow an overall logical sequence, but each is also a complete entity. The chapters can therefore be rearranged to follow any instructor's developmental sequence without endangering students' comprehension.

Part 1, **Financial Planning,** provides a two-chapter introduction to financial planning. Chapter 1, The Importance of Personal Finance, discusses what students will gain from the study of personal finance, describes the goals of financial planning, and helps the reader understand the economic environment so he or she can succeed financially by forecasting the state of the economy and understanding how work decisions affect success in personal finance. In Chapter 2, Financial Planning, we explain how to plan financially over a lifetime, and we review the types of financial records and statements that are pertinent to success in effective personal financial management, such as tax records and documents, balance sheets, and cash-flow statements. This chapter provides an example of a *complete financial plan*—"Financial Plans, Goals, and Objectives"—for a young couple starting out financially.

Part 2, **Money Management,** comprising seven chapters, examines the specifics of managing all major personal expenditures. The student will learn that one can succeed in personal finance fairly quickly by not paying too much in income taxes, not throwing money away on a high-interest credit card, not wasting money when purchasing a vehicle, and not investing in high-fee mutual funds. First, however, Chapter 3, Budgeting and Cash-Flow Management, introduces the cash-flow approach to budgeting, including the tasks of goal setting, organizing, decision making, and implementing, controlling, and evaluating one's financial decisions. This chapter illustrates the wisdom of making a cash-flow calendar and utilizing a revolving savings account. In addition, it outlines seven budget control measures and provides detailed illustrative budgets.

Chapter 4, Managing Income Taxes, takes the student through all phases of personal income taxation. This chapter is unique among personal finance textbooks in that it properly emphasizes and explains the strategies and tactics to legally avoid taxes. It also offers updated information on Coverdell education savings accounts and the qualified tuition (Section 529) programs.

Chapter 5, Monetary Asset Management, examines the concept of cash management, which involves making effective use of today's changing financial services industry to earn maximum interest on all one's money while still maintaining liquidity, safety, and convenience. Chapter 6, Credit Use and Credit Cards, focuses on smart reasons to use credit and practical tips for employing today's ubiquitous credit cards, including new legal protections for borrowers. Chapter 7, Installment Credit, treats the subjects of the planned use of credit, non-credit-card borrowing, and the ramifications of becoming overextended using credit. Chapter 8, Automobiles and Other Major Purchases, covers automobiles and other expensive purchases, discusses ways to save money when purchasing goods and services, details the several steps in the planned buying process, with an emphasis on automobile purchases, and shows how to compare leasing with financing. Chapter 9, The Housing Expenditure, tackles all aspects of the home-buying process, including the newest methods of financing, as well as the topic of renting because renting is sometimes the wiser choice. It also provides information on both refinancing and selling a home.

Part 3, Income and Asset Protection, includes the three most comprehensive chapters in any personal finance college textbook, and it focuses on risk management and planning for both health care and life insurance needs. Chapter 10, Risk Management and Property/Liability Insurance, thoroughly explains the concepts fundamental to understanding risk management, insurance, and purchasing coverage. It emphasizes automobile and home-related property and liability coverage. Chapter 11, Health Care Planning, takes a new approach to health care planning by acknowledging that most people's health insurance is really a health care plan; for this reason, we have strengthened the book's coverage of health maintenance organizations, preferred provider organizations, and managed care systems. Chapter 12, Life Insurance Planning, covers the key concepts in term and cash-value life insurance, including single-premium life insurance and variable life insurance.

Part 4, Investments, contains five chapters on investments. Because this broad subject is too complex to treat superficially, this chapter-by-chapter breakdown offers instructors flexibility in deciding which topics to teach. Importantly, Chapter 13, Investment Fundamentals, provides a comprehensive overview for instructors who have time to teach only one chapter on investments. All of the long-term strategies for successful investing are explained in detail. Chapter 14, Investing in Stocks and Bonds, offers a thorough explanation of this key topic. Chapter 15, Investing Through Mutual Funds, offers sufficient detail for the reader to decide which funds are most suitable; this consideration is particularly important because mutual funds are the most commonly available choice with 401(k) retirement accounts. Chapter 16, Buying and Selling Securities, provides a streamlined how-to approach to trading stocks, bonds, and mutual funds. It also presents specific guidelines for determining when each investment should be sold. Chapter 17, Real Estate and Speculative Investments, examines real estate, collectibles, and other tangibles from their perspective as investment opportunities.

Part 5, Retirement and Estate Planning, includes two chapters that are vital to all students of personal finance. Chapter 18, Retirement Planning, is unquestionably the most thorough chapter on retirement issues found in any college-level personal finance textbook. It is designed to convince readers of the wisdom of beginning as soon as possible to invest wisely for retirement. Along the way, it illustrates ways to develop and implement a plan for a secure retirement. Chapter 19, Estate Planning, provides an overview of the key steps that need to be taken at an early age of adulthood to properly protect and transfer one's estate.

Students will find the appendixes accompanying *Personal Finance* useful both during and beyond the course. Appendixes A and B can be found in the main text. Appendix A, Present and Future Value Tables, offers 24 math-oriented illustrations on how to correctly use the present and future value tables. The calculators behind the tables appear on the book's website so students can perform all time-value-of-money mathematics. Appendix B, Estimating Social Security Benefits, permits students to estimate the three types of Social Security benefits: retirement, survivor's, and disability. The calculators for Appendixes A and B are on the book's website as well as two additional appendixes: Careers in Personal Financial Planning and Counseling, written by the authors, and How to Use a Financial Calculator, written by Professor Jing-Jang Xiao (University of Rhode Island).

Personal Finance also provides an end-of-book index that contains several hundred entries. Each of the key terms in the chapters appears in bold type in the index, making them easy to find.

Complete Instructor Support

The instructor teaching package for the eighth edition of *Personal Finance* includes the *Instructor's Resource Manual with Test Bank, HMClassPrep/HMTesting Instructor CD,* a set of color transparencies, PowerPoint slides, the *Garman/Forgue Personal Finance* textbook website, and the Blackboard Course Cartridge, WebCT e-Pack.

- The *Instructor's Resource Manual with Test Bank.* Written by Rosemary Carlson of Morehead State University, this ancillary includes a variety of useful components: suggested course outlines to emphasize a general, insurance, or investments approach to personal finance; a summary overview, learning objectives, teaching suggestions, and detailed lecture outline for each chapter; answers and solutions to all end-of-chapter questions and problems; and outside research projects and class assignments. The manual also includes a test bank containing more than 2200 questions, with the correct answers identified as well as a listing of textbook pages on which the responses can be found.
- *HMClassPrep/HMTesting Instructor CD.* This instructor support CD offers electronic versions of much of the IRM material, PowerPoint slides, and supplemental material designed to aid in class preparation and instruction. In addition, the CD includes a computerized version of the *Test Bank.* This program is very user-friendly and permits editing of test questions and generation of class exams.
- **Color Transparencies.** These transparencies—which include selected tables, figures, formulas, and boxed features from the text—illustrate the most commonly taught concepts in personal finance.
- **PowerPoint Slides.** Two sets of downloadable slides are available for this program. The Basic PowerPoint slides contain chapter outlines that follow the text, including a selection of the text art. The Premium slides include all of the content found in the Basic slides, along with supplemental art and worksheets. Instructors can select which set best suits their in-classroom presentation needs.
- **Instructor Website.** The instructor website that accompanies *Personal Finance* provides a wealth of supplemental materials to enhance learning and aid in course management. Features of the site include Basic and Premium PowerPoint slides,

downloadable *Instructor Resource Manual* files, an Updated Content section that highlights changes in personal finance, personal finance on-line calculators and Web links, and much more.

■ *Blackboard Course Cartridge, WebCT e-Pack.* This course cartridge allows flexible, efficient, and creative ways to present learning materials and opportunities. In addition to course management benefits, instructors may make use of an electronic gradebook, receive papers from students enrolled in the course via the Internet, and track student use of communication and collaboration functions.

Complete Student Support

■ **Student Website.** The student website accompanying *Personal Finance* contains many useful materials. For example, among other assets, it repeats the "Exploring the World Wide Web" exercises from the text with links to the appropriate external websites, the "Decision-Making Worksheets," the end-of-chapter exercises with links to on-line calculators, and the ACE self-test quizzes (with immediate feedback). The website also includes *Study Guide* material, flashcards for students to test their comprehension of major personal finance concepts, and much more.

■ *My Personal Financial Planner* **Worksheets.** This new workbook prepared by the authors comes packaged with all *new* copies of *Personal Finance*, eighth edition. It includes most of the "Decision-Making Worksheets" from the book as well as dozens of other original forms and worksheets. Students can use these materials to record their thoughts, plans, decisions, and other important personal financial information and to create key parts of their overall personal financial plan. These forms are not intended as "busywork for students." Rather, they represent the nuts and bolts of a student's own personal financial plan. You can build your whole financial life around the topics covered in the *My Personal Financial Planner.*

Acknowledgments

We would like to thank our reviewers and other experts, who offered helpful suggestions and criticisms to this and previous editions. This book is their book, too. We especially appreciate the assistance of the following individuals:

Gary Amundson, *Montana State University–Billings*

Dori Anderson, *Mendocino College*

Robert E. Arnold, Jr., *Henry Ford Community College*

Bala Arshanapalli, *Indiana University Northwest*

Hal Babson, *Columbus State Community College*

Anne Bailey, *Miami University*

Rosella Bannister, *Bannister Financial Education Services*

Richard Bartlett, *Muskingum Area Technical College*

Anne Baumgartner, *Navy Family Service Center–Norfolk*

John J. Beasley, *Georgia Southern University*

Kim Belden, *Daytona Beach Community College*

Pamela J. Bennett, *University of Central Arkansas*

Daniel A. Bequette, *Hartwell College*

Peggy S. Berger, *Colorado State University*

David Bible, *Louisiana State University–Shreveport*

George Biggs, *Southern Nazarene University*

Robert Blatchford, *Tulsa Junior College*

Susan Blizzard, *San Antonio College*

Dean Brassington, *Financial Educator*

Anne Bunton, *Cottey College*

Paul L. Camp, *Galecki Financial Management*

Chris Canellos, *Stanford University*

Andrew Cao, *American University*

Diana D. Carroll, *Carson-Newman College*

Gerri Chaplin, *Joliet Junior College*

Steve Christian, *Jackson Community College*

Ron Christner, *Loyola University*

Charlotte Churaman, *University of Maryland*

Carol N. Cissel, *Roanoke College*

Thomas S. Coe, *Xavier University of Louisiana*

Edward R. Cook, *University of Massachusetts–Boston*

Patricia Cowley, *Omni Travel*

Kathy Crall, *Des Moines Area Community College*

Sheran Cramer, *University of Nebraska–Lincoln*

Ellen Daniel, *Harding University*

Jocl J. Dauten, *Arizona State University*

Carl R. Denson, *University of Delaware*

Dale R. Detlefs, *William M. Mercer, Inc.*

A. Terrence Dickens, *California State University*

Charles E. Downing, *Massasoit Community College*

Alberto Duarte, *InCharge Education Foundation*

Sidney W. Eckert, *Appalachian State University*

Jacolin P. Eichelberger, *Hillsborough Community College*

Gregory J. Eidleman, *Alvernia College*

Richard English, *Augustana College*

Evan Enowitz, *Grossmont College*

Don Etnier, *University of Maryland–European Division*

Judy Farris, *South Dakota State University*

Vicki Fitzsimmons, *University of Illinois*

Fred Floss, *Buffalo State College*

Paula G. Freston, *Colby Community College*

H. Swint Friday, *University of South Alabama*

Caroline Fulmer, *University of Alabama*

Wafica Ghoul, *Davenport University*

Joel Gold, *University of South Maine*

Elizabeth Goldsmith, *Florida State University*

Joseph D. Greene, *Augusta State University*

Jeri W. Griego, *Laramie County Community College*

Michael P. Griffin, *University of Massachusetts–Dartmouth*

David R. Guarino, *Standard & Poor's*

Hilda Hall, *Surry Community College*

Patty Hatfield, *Bradley University*

Andrew Hawkins, *Lake Area Technical Institute*

Janice Heckroth, *Indiana University of Pennsylvania*

Diane Henke, *University of Wisconsin–Sheboygan*

Roger P. Hill, *University of North Carolina–Wilmington*

Jeanne Hilton, *University of Nevada*

Laura Horvath, *University of Detroit Mercy*

David Houghton, *Northwest Nazarene College*

George Hruby, *University of Akron*

Roger Ignatius, *University of Maine–Augusta*

James R. Isherwood, *Community College of Rhode Island*

Naheel Jeries, *Iowa State University*

Karen Jones, *SWBC Mortgage Corporation*

Marilyn S. Jones, *Friends University*

Ellen Joyner, *Liberty National Bank–Lexington*

Peggy D. Keck, *Western Kentucky University*

Dennis Keefe, *Michigan State University*

Haejeong Kim, *Central Michigan University–College Park*

Jinhee Kim, *University of Maryland*

Eloise J. Law, *State University of New York–Plattsburgh*

Andrew H. Lawrence, *Delgado Community College*

Charles J. Lipinski, *Marywood University*

Janct K. Lukens, *Mississippi State University*

Ruth H. Lytton, *Virginia Tech University*

Kenneth Marin, *Aquinas College*

Kenneth Mark, *Kansas Community College*

Julia Marlowe, *University of Georgia*

Billy Moore, *Delta State University*

John R. Moore, *Navy Family Services Center–Norfolk*

Diane R. Morrison, *University of Wisconsin–La Crosse*

Steven J. Muck, *El Camino College*

Randolph J. Mullis, *WEATrust*

Donald Neuhart, *Central Missouri State University*

Oris L. Odom II, *University of Texas–Tyler*

William S. Phillips, *Memphis State University*

Carl H. Pollock, Jr., *Portland State University*

Angela J. Rabatin, *Prince George's Community College*

Gwen M. Reichbach, *Dealers' Financial Services*

Mary Ellen Rider, *University of Nebraska*

Eloise Lorch Rippie, *Iowa State University*

Edmund L. Robert, *Front Range Community College*

Clarence C. Rose, *Radford University*

David E. Rubin, *Glendale Community College*

Michael Rupured, *University of Georgia*

Peggy Schomaker, *University of Maine*

Barry B. Schweig, *Creighton University*

Elaine D. Scott, *Bluefield State University*

James Scott, *Southwest Missouri State University*

Wilmer E. Seago, *Virginia Tech University*

Marilyn K. Skinner, *Macon Technical Institute*

Rosalyn Smith, *Morningside College*

Horacio Soberon-Ferrer, *University of Florida*

Edward Stendard, *St. John Fisher College*

Mary Stephenson, *University of Maryland–College Park*

Eugene Swinnerton, *University of Detroit Mercy*

Lisa Tatlock, *The Master's College*

Francis C. Thomas, *Port Republic, New Jersey*

Stephen Trimby, *Worcester State College*

John W. Tway, *Amber University*

Dick Verrone, *University of North Carolina–Wilmington*

Jerry A. Viscione, *Boston College*

Stephen E. Wagner, *Attorney at Law, Blacksburg, Virginia*

Rosemary Walker, *Michigan State University*

Grant J. Wells, *Michigan State University*

Jon D. Wentworth, *Southern Adventist University*

Dorothy West, *Michigan State University*

Gloria Worthy, *State Technical Institute–Memphis*

Rui Yau, *South Dakota State University*

Alex R. Yguado, *L.A. Mission College*

Robert P. Yuyuenyongwatana, *Cameron University*

Martha Zenns, *Jamestown Community College*

Larry Zigler, *Highland College*

Virginia S. Zuiker, *University of Minnesota*

This eighth edition also has benefited from the contributions of some of the United States' best personal finance experts, who have shared some specialized expertise by contributing to a series of new boxes titled "Advice from an Expert":

Dennis R. Ackley, *Ackley & Associates*

M. J. Alhabeeb, *University of Massachusetts–Amherst*

Jan D. Andersen, *California State University–Sacramento*

Anthony J. Campolo, *Columbus State Community College*

Martin Carrigan, *The University of Findlay, Ohio*

Brenda J. Cude, *University of Georgia*

Lorraine R. Decker, *Decker & Associates, Inc.*

Elizabeth Dolan, *University of New Hampshire*

Jonathan Fox, *Ohio State University*

Jordan E. Goodman, *MoneyAnswers.com*

Gail M. Gordon, *University of Wyoming*

Linda Gorham, *Berklee College of Music*

Sue Alexander Greninger, *University of Texas at Austin*

Reynolds Griffith, *Stephen F. Austin State University*

John P. Hewlett, *University of Wyoming*

Holly Hunts, *Montana State University*

Alena C. Johnson, *Utah State University*

Ronald R. Jordan, *New Mexico State University*

Constance Y. Kratzer, *New Mexico State University*

Frances C. Lawrence, *Louisiana State University*

Jean M. Lown, *Utah State University*

Allen Martin, *California State University–Northridge*

Joan Koonce Moss, *University of Georgia*

Cora Newcomb, *Technical College of the Lowcountry, South Carolina*

Eve Pentecost, *University of Alabama*

Aimee D. Prawitz, *Northern Illinois University*

Kathleen Prochaska-Cue, *University of Nebraska–Lincolon*

Michelle Singletary, *The Washington Post*

Donald Stuhlman, *Wilmington College, Delaware*

Robert O. Weagley, *University of Missouri–Columbia*

David Wray, *Profit Sharing/401(k) Council of America*

We definitely wish to thank the many students who had the opportunity to read, critique, and provide input for various components of the *Personal Finance* project. Please keep sending us your e-mails. Jing-Jang Xiao (University of Rhode Island) prepared the financial calculator appendix found on the website.

This edition of *Personal Finance* benefited enormously from the editorial efforts of Andrea Cava. In addition to being a fine manager and editor, she brought much insight, creativity, intelligence, and wisdom to the project. We would also like to thank Rosemary Carlson for her contributions to the *Instructor's Resource Manual* and Amy Forgue for efforts on the PowerPoint slides.

A project of this dimension would never have been completed without the patience, support, understanding, and sacrifices of our friends and families during the book's development, revision, and production. Tom Garman, Fellow and Professor Emeritus at

Virginia Tech University, and his wife Lucy, live in Orlando, Florida, and they stay in contact with their children and their spouses and significant others: Dana, Julia, Scott, David, Alieu, Isatou, Kumba, Alimatou, and Ousman. Thanks are owed to all. Tom also credits the mentors in his life—Ron West, Bill Boast, Bill McDivitt, and John Binnion—for guiding him along the way, particularly through their many noble examples of compassion, commitment, and excellence. Ray Forgue, a professor at the University of Kentucky, lives in Lexington, where he proudly watches over son Matthew and daughter Amy as they wind up their college lives and commence their working careers. Ray wishes to thank his mother, Mary, and brothers Bob, Gary, Joe, and Dave for their patience over the years as he spent time during vacation and holiday visits working on this book. Special thanks to Snooky, whose assistance on the first edition of *Personal Finance* continues to shine through to this current edition.

Finally, we wish to say "thank you" to the hundreds of personal finance instructors around the country who have generously shared their views, in person and by letter and e-mail, on what should be included in a high-quality textbook and ancillary materials. You demand the best for your students, and we've listened. *Personal Finance* is your book! The two of us and all the people at Houghton Mifflin have tried very hard to meet your needs in every possible way. We hope we have exceeded your expectations. Why? Because we share the belief that students need to study personal finance concepts thoroughly and learn them well so that they will be truly successful in their personal finances.

E. Thomas Garman
tgarman@bellsouth.net

Raymond E. Forgue
rforgue@uky.edu

P.S. Dear Students: If you are going to save any of your college textbooks, be certain to keep this one because the basic principles of personal finance are everlasting. Also, you might want to present the book as a gift to a significant other, spouse, or parent.

Personal Finance

Part One

Financial Planning

CHAPTER 1   The Importance of Personal Finance

CHAPTER 2   Financial Planning

Chapter 1

The Importance of Personal Finance

LEARNING OBJECTIVES

After reading this chapter, you should be able to:

1 **List** the benefits of studying personal finance.

2 **Summarize** the six key steps in successful personal financial planning.

3 **Understand** the current economic environment and forecast the state of the economy, inflation, and interest rates over the next few years.

4 **Explain** fundamental economic considerations that affect decision making in personal finance.

5 **Make** use of time value of money calculations when making financial decisions.

6 **Recognize** how employer-related money decisions can affect success in personal finance.

Lawrence Crawford, age 23, recently graduated with his bachelor's degree in Library and Information Sciences. He is about to take his first professional position as an archivist with a civil engineering firm in a rapidly expanding area in the U.S. Southwest. While in school, Lawrence worked part-time, earning about $8000 per year. For the last two years he has managed to put $1000 each year into an individual retirement account (IRA). Lawrence owes $5000 in student loans on which he must now begin making payments. His new job will pay $45,000. Lawrence may begin participating in his employer's 401(k) retirement plan immediately and he can contribute up to 6 percent of his salary to the plan.

What would you recommend to Lawrence on the importance of personal finance regarding:

1. Factoring the current state of the economy into his personal financial planning?

2. Understanding the effects of income taxes on his income and financial decisions?

3. Participating in his employer's 401(k) retirement plan?

4. Using time value of money considerations to project what his IRA might be worth at age 63?

5. Using time value of money considerations to project what his 401(k) plan might be worth at age 63 if he were to participate fully?

Your **financial literacy** is your knowledge of facts, concepts, principles, and technological tools that are fundamental to being smart about money. Being financially literate will enhance your economic well-being by allowing you to make informed decisions. It will enhance your ability to handle day-to-day financial matters and will help you avoid or reduce the negative consequences of poor financial decisions that otherwise might take years to overcome.

Financial literacy is not widespread among Americans. Obstacles to financial literacy include a lack of knowledge about personal finance, the complexity of financial life today, being overburdened with numerous choices in financial decision making, and a lack of time for learning about personal finance. To make matters worse, most workers today face the challenge of saving, investing, and managing their own retirement funds. It is no wonder that many adults feel less than competent, a bit confused, and a little anxious about financial matters. Even successful business people sometimes express these concerns—after all, it is one thing to know how to manage a company's finances, but quite another thing to manage one's own money.

A lack of financial literacy can result in a person falling prey to investment scams, buying the wrong kind of life insurance, incurring excessive levels of consumer debt, paying too much interest on debt, spending money unconsciously or frivolously, delaying saving for retirement, and ultimately being unable to reach his or her financial objectives. If you are a financially responsible person, you will not want to make such mistakes! **Financial responsibility** means that you are accountable for your future financial well-being and that you strive to make the best possible decisions in personal finance.

The goal of this book is to educate you so that you will be able to make the best decisions about spending, managing money, maintaining creditworthiness, purchasing insurance, and saving and investing to control your personal financial destiny. Like everyone else, you will inevitably make some mistakes in financial matters. Studying this book will help you to make fewer personal finance errors and will help you to become a financially responsible manager of your personal finances for the rest of your life. Learning more about personal finance is empowering. It helps you make informed and confident personal money decisions. The more you know about personal finances and yourself the more quickly you will act on what you have learned. Such efforts will put you firmly on the road to greater self-reliance and financial security, thus enabling you to achieve your financial and lifestyle goals.

This chapter begins by examining what you will gain by studying personal finance and by reviewing the relationships among an individual's standard of living and the six key steps in personal financial planning. Finding success in financial matters requires an understanding of the economic environment so that you can be aware of how the state of the economy, inflation, and interest rates will affect your ability to achieve financial goals. It is also useful to recognize the fundamental economic considerations in financial decision making, including opportunity costs, marginal analysis, and income taxes. Of particular importance is the concept of the time value of money. The following section provides an overview of how decisions at work can affect success in personal finance. Finally, we examine the objectives and key steps to achieving your personal financial objectives.

Why You Should Study Personal Finance

1 List the benefits of studying personal finance.

You probably recognize that managing your life sometimes can be difficult and that it will become even more complicated as you grow older. You will make many complex decisions—some related to your education, your career, and your personal lifestyle, and many that affect your financial success.

Although the decision-making process may be accompanied by some anxious and uncomfortable moments, you will become prepared to choose more wisely as you gain experience and education.

Personal finance is the study of personal and family resources considered important in achieving financial success; thus, it involves how people spend, save, protect, and invest their financial resources. Topics in personal finance include budgeting, tax management, cash management, use of credit cards, borrowing, major expenditures, risk management, investments, retirement planning, and estate planning. A solid under-

Golden Rules of

Personal Finance

Financial success comes from learning the Golden Rules of personal finance and then putting what you have learned into practice. Make the following your money habits in personal finance:

1. Pay yourself first by spending less than you earn.
2. Stay up-to-date about current economic conditions.
3. Use marginal and opportunity costs and time value of money calculations when making financial decisions.
4. Map your financial future by establishing goals and realistic plans to achieve them.
5. Take advantage of opportunities to tax-shelter some income through your employer's benefits program, including fully funding your 401(k) retirement account.
6. Develop expertise in financial matters and heed your own advice because you are responsible for your own financial success.

standing of personal finance topics will offer you a better chance of success in facing the financial challenges, responsibilities, and opportunities of life. Such successes might include paying minimal credit costs, not paying too much in income taxes, purchasing automobiles at low prices, financing housing on excellent terms, buying appropriate and fairly priced insurance, selecting successful investments that match your needs, planning for a comfortable retirement, and passing on your estate with minimal transfer costs.

Closely associated with personal finance is the topic of **personal financial planning**—the development and implementation of coordinated and integrated long-range plans to achieve financial success. This book focuses on providing you with the "nuts and bolts"—the knowledge, skills, tools, strategies, and tactics necessary for you to plan effectively and achieve personal financial success.

Many people do not learn about personal financial planning until they become mired in financial problems—that is, they "learn from bad experience." Simply put: "A failure to plan is a plan for failure." Studying personal finance now will help you avoid such difficulties and show you how to take advantage of financial opportunities. At the beginning of each chapter, we provide a short case vignette entitled "What Would You Recommend?" Each case focuses on the important financial challenges that can be experienced by someone who has not learned about the material in that chapter. You will be asked to think about what advice you might give the person as you study the chapter. Then, at the end of each chapter, you will again be asked to provide more informed advice based on what you have learned.

The Six Key Steps to Personal Finance Success

2 Summarize the six key steps in successful personal financial planning.

Many people think that being wealthy is a function of how much you earn or inherit. In reality, it is much more closely related to your ability to understand trade-offs and make decisions that generate wealth for you. A **trade-off** is giving up one thing for another. You have to do only a few things right in personal finance during your lifetime, as long as you don't do too many things wrong. Personal finance is not rocket science. You can succeed very well in your personal finances by making appropriate plans and taking actions to implement those plans. First, recognize that financial objectives are rarely achieved without forgoing or sacrificing current **consumption** (spending on goods and services). This restraint is accomplished by putting money into **savings** (income not spent on current consumption) for use in achieving future goals. Some savings are actually **investments** (assets purchased with the goal of providing additional income from the asset itself). By saving and investing, people are much more likely to have funds available for future consumption.

SAVINGS

Effective financial management often separates the "Haves" from the "Have Nots." The Haves, observes Virginia Tech professor Celia Hayhoe, are those who learn to live on less than they earn and are the savers and investors of society. The Have Nots are the spenders who live paycheck to paycheck, usually with high consumer debt.

Saving for future consumption represents a good illustration of the human desire to achieve a certain **standard of living.** This standard is what an individual or group earnestly desires and seeks to attain, to maintain if attained, to preserve if threatened, and to regain if lost. At any particular time, individuals actually experience their **level of living.** In essence, your standard of living is where you would like to be and your level of living is where you actually are.

FIN SAT:
achievement of
fin. aspirations

fin.Hap:
satisfaction felt

Financial success is the achievement of financial aspirations that are desired, planned, or attempted. Success is defined by the individual or family that seeks it. Some people define financial success as being able to actually live according to one's standard of living. Many people seek **financial security,** which provides the comfortable feeling that your financial resources will be adequate to fulfill any needs you have as well as most of your wants. Others want to be **wealthy** and have an abundance of money, property, investments, and other resources. A fundamental truth of personal finance is that you cannot build financial security or wealth unless you spend less than you earn. As a result, you cannot reach your standard of living without somewhat restricting your level of living as you save and invest.

Financial happiness encompasses a lot more than just making more money. It is the satisfaction you feel about money matters. People who are happy about their finances are likely to be in control of their money, and this happiness spills over in a positive way to feelings about their overall enjoyment of life. Financial happiness is in part a result of practicing good financial behaviors—the subject of this book. Examples of such behaviors include paying bills on time, spending less than you earn, knowing where your money goes, and investing some money for retirement. The more good financial behaviors you practice, the greater your financial happiness. In fact, just making progress toward achieving financial goals contributes to financial happiness.

Today's marketplace provides a constant barrage of messages suggesting that you can spend and borrow your way to financial success, security, and wealth. These messages are very enticing for those starting out in their financial lives. In truth, overspending and overuse of consumer credit *impede* financial success!

Bridging the gap between one's level of living and one's desired standard of living involves six steps. These steps provide the blueprint for the remainder of this book, as illustrated in Figure 1.1. The six steps are

① PLANNING

1. Financial planning, focusing on establishing and achieving long-term goals through planning and budgeting,

② MANAGEMENT

2. Money management, centering on minimizing income taxes and efficient utilization of cash and credit,

③ EXPENDITURES

3. Managing expenditures, especially for "big ticket" items such as vehicles and housing,

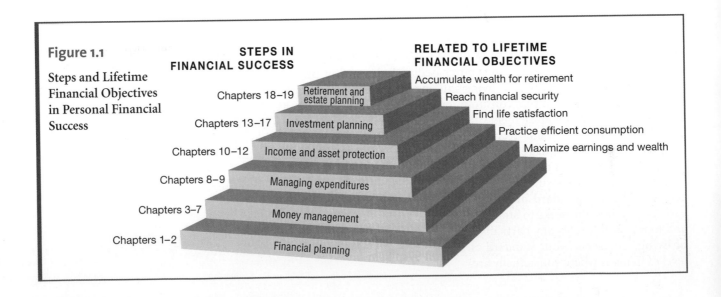

Figure 1.1

Steps and Lifetime
Financial Objectives
in Personal Financial
Success

STEPS IN FINANCIAL SUCCESS

Chapters 18–19 — Retirement and estate planning
Chapters 13–17 — Investment planning
Chapters 10–12 — Income and asset protection
Chapters 8–9 — Managing expenditures
Chapters 3–7 — Money management
Chapters 1–2 — Financial planning

RELATED TO LIFETIME FINANCIAL OBJECTIVES

Accumulate wealth for retirement
Reach financial security
Find life satisfaction
Practice efficient consumption
Maximize earnings and wealth

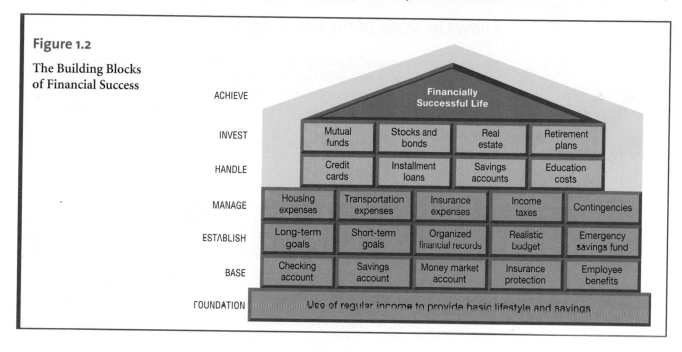

Figure 1.2

The Building Blocks
of Financial Success

4. Income and asset protection through insurance, so that hard-earned resources and assets are not placed at undue risk,

④ INSURANCE

5. Investment planning, with its focus on selecting the appropriate investment vehicles based on the objectives at hand and the relative levels of investment risk, and

⑤ INVESTMENTS

6. Retirement and estate planning, with the ultimate goal of being able to live off of one's financial nest egg and plan for transfer of assets to heirs.

⑥ RETIREMENT

Figure 1.2 shows how the building blocks of a financially successful life fit together, and all of these factors are examined in the remainder of the text.

How the Economic Environment Will Affect Your Personal Finances

3 Understand the current economic environment and forecast the state of the economy, inflation, and interest rates over the next few years.

Your success in personal finance partly depends on how well you understand and use information to cope with the economic environment. This effort includes knowing the state of the economy, predicting future directions for the economy, and predicting future directions of prices and inflation.

Forecasting involves predicting, estimating, or calculating in advance. You need to be able to forecast the state of the economy, inflation, and interest rates so that you can have advance warning of the direction and strength of changes in economic trends, as they will definitely affect your personal finances. Your planning should identify methods for accomplishing a personal finance objective given certain assumptions.

FORECASTING

Know the State of the Economy

An **economy** is a system of managing the productive and employment resources of a country, state, or community. The U.S. federal government attempts to regulate the country's overall economy to maintain stable prices (low inflation) and stable levels of employment (low unemployment). In this way, the government seeks to achieve sustained **economic growth,** which is a condition of increasing production (business spending) and consumption (consumer spending) in the economy—and hence increasing national income. Government policies also affect the economy. For example, tax cuts put money into consumers' pockets, which they are then likely to spend. Tax increases, in contrast, depress consumer demand.

Growth in the U.S. economy varies over time. The **business cycle** (also called the **economic cycle**) is a wavelike pattern of rising and falling economic activity, in which the same pattern occurs again and again over time. As depicted in Figure 1.3, the phases of the business cycle are expansion (when the economy is increasing), peak (the end of an expansion and the beginning of a contraction), contraction (when the economy is falling), and trough (the end of a contraction and beginning of an expansion).

The preferred stage of the economic cycle is the **expansion** phase, where production is at high capacity, unemployment is low, retail sales are high, and prices and interest rates are low or falling. Under these conditions, consumers find it easier to buy homes, cars, and expensive goods on credit, and businesses are encouraged to borrow to expand production to meet the increased consumer demand. The stock market also rises because investors expect higher profits. As the demand for credit increases, short-term interest rates rise because more borrowers want money. Consumers and businesses purchase more goods, exerting upward pressure on prices. Eventually, prices and interest rates climb high enough to stifle consumer and business borrowing, send stock prices down, and choke off the expansion. The result is negligible economic growth or even a decline.

In such situations, the economy often moves toward a **recession.** The federal government's Business Cycle Dating Committee officially defines a recession as "a recurring period of decline in total output, income, employment and trade, usually lasting from six months to a year and marked by widespread contractions in many sectors of the economy." During recessions, consumers become pessimistic about their future buying plans. The typical U.S. recession is marked by an average economic decline of

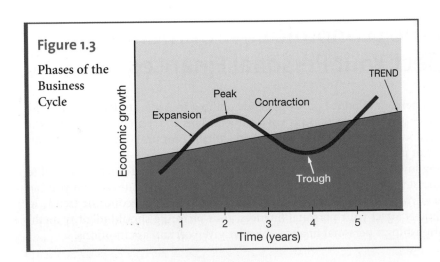

Figure 1.3

Phases of the Business Cycle

2 percent that lasts for ten months with an average unemployment rate exceeding 6 percent.

Eventually the economic contraction ends, and consumers and businesses become more optimistic. The economy then moves beyond the trough toward expansion, where levels of production, employment, and retail sales begin to improve (usually rapidly), allowing the overall economy to experience some growth from its previously weakened state. The entire business cycle normally takes four to five years.

To make sound financial decisions, you need to know both the current state of the economy and the direction in which it is headed in the next few years. For example, when the economy begins to show clear signs of a slowdown, it may be a good time to invest in fixed-interest securities because interest rates are sure to fall as the government lowers its own interest rates to boost the economy. A point at which the economy is in the trough of a recession may be an excellent time to invest in stocks because the economy will soon expand and stock prices will rise.

Predict Future Directions for the Economy

Tracking at least two statistics may help you understand the direction of the economy: the nation's gross domestic product and the index of leading economic indicators. **Gross domestic product (GDP)** is the value of all goods and services produced by workers and capital located in the United States, regardless of ownership. It provides the broadest measure of the economic health of the nation because it reports how much economic activity has occurred within the U.S. borders. The government regularly announces the annual rate at which the GDP has grown during the previous three months. An annual rate of less than 2 percent is considered low growth; 4 percent or more is considered vigorous growth.

The **index of leading economic indicators (LEI)** is a composite index, reported monthly by the Conference Board, which suggests the future direction of the U.S. economy. The LEI averages 21 components of growth from different segments of the economy, such as new orders for consumer goods and materials, new business formation, new private housing starts, average weekly claims for initial unemployment insurance, and growth of the money supply. Taken together, these measures generally offer a relatively reliable prediction about future directions in the economy. A falling index for three or more consecutive months has been associated with slower economic growth in the months ahead; in contrast, three or more monthly increases in the LEI index suggest robust economic growth in the future.

Information on the economic projections made by government and private economists can be obtained in numerous periodicals on personal finance (such as *Kiplinger's Personal Finance Magazine, Smart Money,* and *Money*) and business (such as *Business Week* and *Forbes*), as well as in news magazines (such as *U.S. News & World Report, Time,* and *Newsweek*) and daily newspapers. After considering their views, you can form your own projections and then make financial decisions accordingly.

Predict Future Directions of Prices and Inflation

Inflation is a steady rise in the general level of prices; **deflation** involves falling prices. Inflation is measured by the changing cost over time of a "market basket" of goods and services that a typical household might purchase. Inflation occurs when the supply of money (or credit) rises faster than the supply of goods and services available for purchases. It also may be attributed to excessive demand or sharply increasing costs of production.

Inflation can be self-perpetuating. Workers may ask for higher wages, thereby adding to the cost of production. In response to the increases in the costs of labor and raw materials, manufacturers will charge more for their products. Lenders, in turn, will require higher interest rates to offset the lost purchasing power of the loaned funds. In addition, consumers will lessen their resistance to price increases because they fear even higher prices in the future. In times of moderate to high inflation, buying power declines rapidly, and people on fixed incomes suffer the most.

How Inflation Affects Income and Consumption.   When prices are rising, an individual's income must rise at the same rate to maintain its **purchasing power,** which is a measure of the goods and services that one's income will buy. From an income point of view, inflation has significant effects. Consider the case of Scott Marshall of Chicago, a single man who took a job in retail management three years ago at a salary of $32,000 per year. Since that time, Scott has received annual raises of $800, $900, and $1000, but he still cannot make ends meet because of inflation. Although Scott received raises, his current income of $34,700 ($32,000 + $800 + $900 + $1000) did not keep pace with the annual inflation rate of 4.0 percent ($32,000 × 1.04 = $33,280; $33,280 × 1.04 = $34,611; $34,611 × 1.04 = $35,996). If Scott's cost of living rose at the same rate as the general price level, in the third year he would be $1296 ($35,996 − $34,700) short of keeping up with inflation. He would need $1296 more in the third year to maintain the same purchasing power that he enjoyed in the first year.

Personal incomes rarely keep up in times of high inflation. Your **real income** (income measured in constant prices relative to some base time period) is the more important number. It reflects the actual buying power of the **nominal income** (also called money income) that you have to spend as measured in current dollars. Rising nominal income during times of inflation creates the illusion that you are making more money, when in reality that may not be true.

To compare your annual wage increase with the rate of inflation for the same time period, you must first convert your dollar raise into a percentage, as follows:

$$\text{Percentage change} = \frac{\text{nominal income after raise} - \text{nominal income last year}}{\text{nominal income last year}} \times 100 \qquad \textbf{(1.1)}$$

For example, imagine that John Bedoin, a single parent and assistant manager of a convenience store in Columbia, Missouri, received a $1600 raise to push his $37,000 annual salary to $38,600. Using Equation (1.1), John calculated his percentage change in personal income as follows:

$$\frac{(\$38,600 - \$37,000)}{\$37,000} \times 0.043 \times 100 = 4.3\%^*$$

After a year during which inflation was 4.0 percent, he did better than the inflation rate because his raise amounted to 4.3 percent. Measured in real terms, John's raise was 0.3 percent (4.3 − 4.0). In dollars, his real income after the raise can be calculated by dividing his new nominal income by 1.0 plus the previous year's inflation rate (expressed as a decimal):

---

*This equation shows how the percentage change is calculated for any difference between two measurements. Divide the difference between measurement 1 and measurement 2 by the value of measurement 1. For example, a stock selling for $65 per share on January 1 and for $76 on December 31 of the same year would have risen 16.92 percent during the year: ($76 − $65) ÷ $65 = 0.1692 or 16.92 percent.

$$\text{Real income} = \frac{\text{nominal income after raise}}{1.0 + \text{previous inflation rate}} \qquad (1.2)$$

$$\frac{\$38,600}{1 + 0.040} = \$37,115$$

Clearly, a large part of the $1600 raise John received was eaten up by inflation. To John, only $115 ($37,115 − $37,000) represents real economic progress, while $1485 ($1600 − $115) was used to pay the inflated prices on goods and services. Note that the $115 real raise is equivalent to 0.31 percent ($115 ÷ $37,000) of his previous income, reflecting the difference between John's percentage raise in nominal dollars and the inflation rate.

How Inflation Is Measured.   The U.S. Bureau of Labor Statistics measures inflation on a monthly basis using the **consumer price index (CPI)**. The CPI is a broad measure of changes in the prices of all goods and services purchased for consumption by urban households. The prices of more than 400 goods and services (a "market basket") sold across the country are tracked, recorded, weighted for importance in a hypothetical budget, and totaled. In essence, the CPI is a cost of living index. The index has a base time period—or starting reference point—from which to make comparisons. The 1982–1984 time period represents the base period of 100. For example, if the CPI were 190 on January 1, 2005, the cost of living would have risen 90.0 percent since the base period [(190 − 100) ÷ 100 = 0.90 or 90%]. Similarly, if the index rises from 190 to 195 on January 1, 2006, then the cost of living will have increased by 2.63 percent over the year (195 − 190 ÷ 190 = 0.0263 or 2.63%).

When prices rise, the purchasing power of the dollar declines, but not by the same percentage. Instead, it falls by the *reciprocal amount* of the price increase (the counterpart ratio quantity needed to produce unity). In the preceding example, prices rose 90 percent since the base period, whereas the purchasing power of the dollar declined 47.4 percent over the same period. [The base-year index of 100 divided by the index of 190 equals 0.526; the reciprocal is 0.474 (1 − 0.526), or 4.74 percent.]

Inflation pushes up the costs of the products and services we consume. If automobile prices rose 20 percent over the past five years, for example, then it will take $24,000 now to buy a car that once sold for $20,000. Conversely, the purchasing power of the car-buying dollar has fallen to 83.3 percent of its original power ($20,000 ÷ $24,000) five years ago. Of course, if your market basket of goods and services differs from that used to calculate the CPI, you might have a very different **personal inflation rate** (the rate of increase in prices of items purchased by a particular person).

How You Can Estimate Future Inflation.   Projections about future inflation rates are made by the U.S. government's Office of Management and Budget (OMB), as well as by a number of economists and private organizations. Projections are reported in popular newspapers and magazines, including the *Wall Street Journal, Barron's, Business Week,* and *Kiplinger's Personal Finance Magazine.* To make sound financial decisions in the future, you need to make your own inflation estimates, both for the near term and for some years to come.

Your views on future inflation might be affected by how successfully you think that the Federal Reserve Board (an agency of the federal government commonly referred to as the *Fed*) will hold down inflation. In addition, unanticipated world events, such as war, political upheaval, and supply cutbacks by the oil-producing countries, could affect inflation estimates. You should be able to project inflation relatively accurately over the near term, perhaps for the next one or two years. Inflation pushes up the cost of borrowing, so monthly car payments and mortgages increase when inflation rises.

Advice from an Expert

How Inflation Affects Borrowing, Saving, and Investing

Interest is the price of money. During times of high inflation, interest rates on new loans for cars, homes, and credit cards rise. Even though nominal interest rates for savers rise as well, the increases do not provide "real" gains if the inflation rate is higher than the interest rate on savings accounts or certificates of deposit. In fact, savers will be worse off after they pay income taxes on their interest earnings. Likewise, stock market investors can be negatively affected, as inflation reduces the value of future corporate earnings and depresses stock prices. Throughout your financial life, you will want to factor the impact of inflation into your financial decisions so as to avoid its negative effects on purchasing power. The remainder of this book explains how you can spend, borrow, save, invest, and donate in ways that beat inflation.

Eve Pentecost
University of Alabama

Estimate Future Interest Rates

Your estimate of the rates of interest for borrowing at some point in the future should affect the return you anticipate from your savings and investments. The degree of risk is higher for long-term lending (5 or 20 years, for example) than for short-term lending (a year, for example), because the likelihood of estimating error increases when lots of time is involved. As a result of this factor, long-term interest rates are generally higher than short-term interest rates. Rising interest rates depress the value of stock investments for three reasons: (1) Businesses must pay more when they borrow, thereby reducing their profits; (2) earnings will not be worth as much in the future as they are today; and (3) stock investors may be lured away to interest-paying investments that promise higher rates of return, such as bonds.

You can forecast interest rates by paying attention to changes in the **federal funds rate,** which is the rate that banks charge one another on overnight loans. Because it is set by the Fed and regularly reported by the news media, the federal funds rate provides an early indication of Fed policy and trends for longer-term interest rates.

Prices, inflation, and interest rates typically move in the same direction. In general, short-term interest rates on conservative and moderate-risk investments are 1 to 2 percent higher than the inflation rate, while long-term interest rates are 2 to 6 percent higher than inflation.

4 Explain fundamental economic considerations that affect decision making in personal finance.

Economic Considerations That Affect Decision Making

Your understanding of a number of basic economic considerations will certainly affect your financial success in life. Important among these factors are opportunity costs, marginal analysis, and income taxes.

Opportunity Costs and Trade-offs in Decision Making

The **opportunity cost** of a decision is the value of the next best alternative that must be forgone. This measure allows you to address the personal consequences of choices, because every decision inevitably involves trade-offs. For example, suppose that instead of reading this book you could have gone to a movie or watched television, but most of all you wanted to sleep. Therefore, the lost benefit of that sleep—the next best alternative—is the opportunity cost when you choose to read. Knowing the opportunity cost of alternatives aids decision making because it indicates whether the decision made is truly the best option.

In personal finance, opportunity cost reflects the best alternative of what one could have done instead of choosing to spend, save, or invest money. For example, by deciding to put $2000 into a stock mutual fund for retirement rather than keeping the funds readily available in a savings account, you are giving up the option of using the money for a down payment on a new automobile. Of course, keeping the money in a savings account has the opportunity cost of the higher return on investment that the stock mutual fund might pay. This opportunity to earn a higher rate of return is a primary consideration when making low-risk investment decisions.

A significant opportunity-cost decision that some people face involves the choice of returning to college for a graduate degree (see partners.financenter.com/kiplinger/calculate/us-eng/college02.fcs.). Another difficult decision might relate to the opportunity cost of renting an apartment versus buying a home. If these costs are underestimated, then decisions will be based on faulty information, and judgments may prove wrong. Properly valuing the costs and benefits of alternatives represents a key step in rational decision making. The opportunity cost mathematics of the rent versus buy decision is illustrated later in Chapter 9.

Marginal Analysis in Decision Making

Utility is the ability of a good or service to satisfy a human want. A key task in personal finance is to determine how much utility you will gain from a particular decision. For example, if you decide to spend $70 on a ticket to a concert, you might begin by thinking about what you might gain from the expenditure. Perhaps you'll enjoy a nice evening, good music, and so on. **Marginal utility** is the extra satisfaction derived from having one more incremental unit of a product or service. **Marginal cost** is the additional (marginal) cost of one more incremental unit of some item. When known, this cost can be compared with the marginal utility received. Thinking about marginal utility and marginal cost can help in decision making because it reminds us to compare only the most important variables. It requires that we examine what we will gain if we also experience a certain extra cost.

To illustrate this idea, assume that you consider spending $100 instead of $70 (an additional $30) to obtain a front-row seat at the concert. What marginal utility will you gain from that decision? Perhaps an ability to see and hear more or the satisfaction of having one of the best seats in the theater. You would then ask yourself whether those extra benefits are worth 30 extra dollars. In practice, people are inclined to seek additional utility as long as the marginal utility exceeds the marginal cost.

In another example, imagine that two new automobiles are available on a dealership lot in Ferndale, Michigan, where retired engineer Charles Hicks and his wife, Pamela, are trying to make a purchase decision. Both vehicles are similar models, but one is a

Advice from an Expert

Seven Money Mantras for a Richer Life

1. It's not an asset if you are wearing it!
2. Is this a need or is it a want?
3. Sweat the small stuff.
4. Cash is better than credit.
5. Keep it simple.
6. Priorities lead to prosperity.
7. Enough is enough!

Michelle Singletary
Nationally syndicated Washington Post *columnist*
("The Color of Money") and author of 7 Money
Mantras for a Richer Life: How to Live Well
with the Money You Have

Reprinted with permission of the author.

Mercury and the other is a Ford. The Mercury, with a sticker price of $25,100, has a moderate number of options; the Ford, with a sticker price of $26,800, has numerous options. Marginal analysis suggests that Charles and Pamela do not need to consider all of the options when comparing the vehicles. Instead, the concept of marginal cost says to compare the benefits of the additional options with the additional costs—$1700 in this instance ($26,800 − $25,100). Charles and Pamela need decide only whether the additional options are worth $1700.

Income Taxes in Decision Making

Effective personal finance managers should regularly consider the economic effects of paying income taxes when making decisions. Of particular importance is the **marginal tax rate,** which is the tax rate at which your last dollar earned is taxed. As income rises, taxpayers pay progressively higher marginal income tax rates. Most financially successful people must pay U.S. federal income taxes at the 25 percent, or higher, marginal tax rate. For example, if Juanita Martinez, an unmarried office manager working in Atlanta, Georgia, has a taxable income of $66,000 and receives a $1000 bonus from her employer, she must pay an extra $250 in taxes on the bonus income ($1000 × 0.25 = $250). Juanita must also pay state income taxes of 6 percent, or $60 ($1000 × 0.06 = $60), and Social Security taxes of 7.65 percent, or $76.50 ($1000 × 0.0765 = $76.50). Thus, Juanita pays an *effective marginal tax rate* of nearly 40 percent (25% + 6% + 7.65% = 38.65%), or $ 386.50, on the extra $1000 of earned income.

People who pay high marginal tax rates sometimes can do better by making tax-exempt investments, such as buying bonds issued by various agencies of states and municipalities. For example, Serena Miller, a married chiropractor with two children

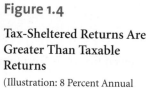

Figure 1.4

Tax-Sheltered Returns Are Greater Than Taxable Returns

(Illustration: 8 Percent Annual Return and $2000 Annual Contribution)

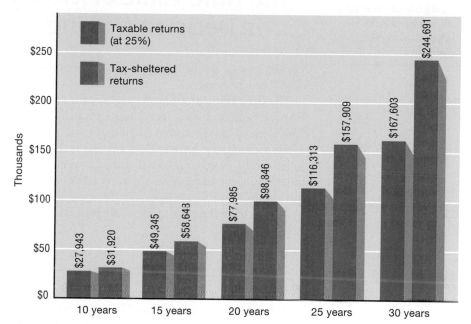

The mathematics assumes that all funds were deposited/invested at the beginning of each year. Note that income taxes must be paid on both the earnings and the previously tax-exempt investment contributions when the funds are eventually withdrawn. This topic is examined in more detail in Chapters 4 and 18.

from Cleveland, Ohio, currently has $5000 in utility stocks earning 5 percent, or $250 ($5000 × 0.05), annually. She pays $62.50 in federal income tax on that income at her 25 percent marginal tax rate ($250 × 0.25), leaving her with $187.50 after taxes. Alternatively, a tax-exempt $5000 state bond paying 4 percent will provide Serena with a better after-tax return, $200.00 instead of $187.50. That is, she would receive $200.00 tax-free from the state bond ($5000 × 0.04) compared with $187.50 ($250 − $62.50) after taxes on the income from the stocks.

As this discussion implies, the very best kind of income is **tax-exempt income,** which is income that is totally and permanently free of taxes. By legally avoiding paying one dollar in income taxes, you gain by not paying that dollar in taxes and, therefore, you receive the alternative use for that dollar. You also benefit by not having to earn another dollar to replace the one that might have been paid in taxes.

The second best kind of income for individuals is **tax-sheltered income**—that is, income that is exempt from income taxes in the current year but which will be subject to taxation in a later tax year. As demonstrated in Figure 1.4, tax-sheltered returns on savings and investments provide much greater returns than returns on which income taxes must be paid, because more money remains available to be invested. In addition, tax-sheltered funds grow more rapidly because compounding (the subject of the next section in this chapter) is enhanced when larger dollar amounts grow during the last years of an investment. You should realize that eventually one must pay income taxes on the income deferred.

5 Make use of time value
of money calculations
when making financial
decisions

The Time Value of Money
in Decision Making

A dollar in your pocket today is worth more than a dollar received five years from now. Why? Time is money.

The **time value of money** is perhaps the single most important concept in personal finance. It adjusts for the fact that dollars to be received or paid out in the future are not equivalent to those received or paid out today. It is easy to understand that a dollar received today is worth more than a dollar received five years from now, because today's dollar can be saved or invested and in five years you expect it to be worth more than a dollar. Thus, the time value of money involves two components: future value and present value.

To illustrate the time value of money, two questions in personal finance are commonly asked:

1. What will an investment (or a series of investments) be worth after a period of time? This question asks for a future value.

2. How much must be put away today (or as a series of investments) to provide some dollar amount in the future? This question asks for a present value.

As you can see from these two questions, comparisons between time periods cannot be made without making adjustments to money values. Accordingly, time value of money calculations compare future and present values by taking into account the interest rate (or investment rate of return) and the time period involved.

Calculations involving the time value of money are based on basic interest calculations. The calculation of interest involves (1) the dollar amount, called the *principal*, (2) the rate of interest earned on the principal, and (3) the amount of time the principal is invested. One way of calculating interest is called simple interest and is illustrated by the *simple interest formula* where

$$i = prt \text{ where} \tag{1.3}$$
$$p = \text{the } principal \text{ set aside}$$
$$r = \text{the } rate \text{ of interest}$$
$$t = \text{the } time \text{ in years that the funds are left on deposit}$$

Thus, if someone saved or invested $1000 at 8 percent for four years, that person would recieve $320 in interest ($1000 $\times$ 0.08 $\times$ 4) over the four years.

But something is missing here. The simple interest formula assumes that the interest is withdrawn each year and only the $1000 stays on deposit for the entire four years. Most people do *not* invest this way. Instead, they leave the interest earned in the account so that it will earn additional interest. This earning of interest on interest is referred to as **compound interest.**

Earning compound interest (or **compounding**) is the best way to build investment values over time. Because of compound interest, money grows much faster when the income from an investment is left in the account. In fact, the deposit of $1000 in our example would grow to $4,661 after 20 years (the calculation is described below). Most of the techniques for building wealth that we describe in this book are based on compounding. The way to build wealth is to make money on your money, not simply to put money away. Yes, you need to put money away first. But compounding over time is what really builds wealth.

Did You Know? . . .

Lottery Officials Use Time Value of Money Calculations

How often have you heard or seen reports of lottery jackpots reaching extremely high amounts? Does the lottery actually pay out these amounts? Not really. Let's assume a lucky ticket holder wins a jackpot of $100 million. The announced jackpot is based on the assumption that the winner will receive the amount in a series of 20 annual payments of $5 million each, adding up to the $100 million advertised total. In fact, the lottery will invest a lump sum right away to fund the annual payments made over the 20 years. It needs to invest only $57,349,500 at 6 percent to fund the stream of $5 million payments ($5 million × 11.4699 from the 6 percent column and 20-year row of Appendix Table A.4). Alternatively, lottery winners may be permitted to take a "cash option" instead of the annual payments. In this case, a winner of a $100 million jackpot who chooses the cash option would receive only $57,349,500. The winner would also have to pay federal, and perhaps state and city, income taxes on this amount, resulting in an after-tax jackpot of closer to $35 million.

Compounding serves as the basis of all time value of money considerations. To see how this works, let us look again at our example where $1000 is invested at 8 percent for four years. Here is how the amount invested (or **principal**) would grow using compounding:

At the end of year 1, the $1000 would have grown to $1080 [$1000 + ($1000 × 0.08)].
At the end of year 2, the $1080 would have grown to $1166.40 [$1080 + ($1080 × 0.08)].
At the end of year 3, the $1166.40 would have grown to $1259.71 [$1166.40 + ($1166.40 × 0.08)].
At the end of year 4, the $1259.71 would have grown to $1360.49 [$1259.71 + ($1259.71 × 0.08)].

Due to the effects of compounding, this investor would have earned an additional $40.49 ($360.49 − $320). While this amount might not seem like much, realize that a $1000 investment for a longer period—say, 40 years—earning 8 percent interest would grow to $21,724.52, providing $20,724.52 in interest over that time period. Simple interest would have resulted in only $3200 in interest ($1000 × 0.08 × 40). The benefit of compounding over that time period is an additional $17,524.52 in interest ($20,724.52 − $3200).

The results are even more dramatic if $1000 is invested at the end of *each year* for 40 years. The total at the end of 40 years would be $259,056, with $219,056 representing the interest on the invested funds. This illustration suggests one of the cardinal rules of personal financial planning: Getting rich is not a function of investing a lot of money, but rather a result of investing regularly for long periods of time.

Essentially there are two types of time value of money calculations: (1) converting present values to future values (as illustrated in the preceding example) and (2) converting future values to present values. Within each type, the calculations differ slightly depending on whether a lump sum is involved or whether a series of payments (an **annuity**) is involved.

Calculating Future Values

Future value (*FV*) is the valuation of an asset projected to the end of a particular time period in the future. You can calculate the future value of a lump sum or the future value of a series of deposits.

Future Value of a Lump Sum.   Equation (1.4) can be used to calculate the future value of a lump sum:

$$FV = (\text{Present value of sum of money}) \, (i + 1.0)^n \qquad \textbf{(1.4)}$$

where i represents the interest rate and n represents the number of time periods. Applying this formula to our earlier example of investing $1000 at 8 percent for four years, we obtain

$$\$1360.49 = (\$1000)(1 + 0.08)^4$$

or

$$\$1360.49 = (\$1000)(1.08)(1.08)(1.08)(1.08)$$

While mathematically correct, these calculations can be cumbersome when using long time periods. Table 1.1 provides a quick and easy way to determine the future dollar value of an investment. For the preceding example, use the table in the following manner: Go across the top row to the 8 percent column. Read down the 8 percent column to the row for four years to locate the factor 1.3605 (at the intersection of the green column and row). Multiply that factor by the present value of the cash asset ($1000) to arrive at the future value ($1360.50).

Appendix Table A.1 provides an even more complete table for calculating the future value of lump-sum amounts. Figure 1.5 demonstrates the effects of various compounded returns on a $10,000 investment. The $10,000 will grow to $57,435 in 30 years with an interest rate of 6 percent. Compounding $10,000 at 10 percent yields $174,494 over the same time period; at 14 percent, it yields a whopping $509,502! For practice you might want to confirm these results using Appendix Table A.1.

A handy formula for figuring the number of years it takes to double the principal using compound interest is the **rule of 72.** You simply divide the interest rate that the money will earn *into* the number 72. For example, if interest is compounded at a rate of 7 percent per year, your principal will double in 10.3 years (72/7); if the rate is 6 percent, it will take 12 years (72/6). The rule of 72 (see Figure 1.6) also works for deter-

Table 1.1 Future Value of $1 After a Given Number of Periods

Periods	1%	2%	3%	4%	5%	6%	7%	8%	9%	10%
1	1.0100	1.0200	1.0300	1.0400	1.0500	1.0600	1.0700	1.0800	1.0900	1.1000
2	1.0201	1.0404	1.0609	1.0816	1.1025	1.1236	1.1449	1.1664	1.1881	1.2100
3	1.0303	1.0612	1.0927	1.1249	1.1576	1.1910	1.2250	1.2597	1.2950	1.3310
4	1.0406	1.0824	1.1255	1.1699	1.2155	1.2625	1.3108	1.3605	1.4116	1.4641
5	1.0510	1.1041	1.1593	1.2167	1.2763	1.3382	1.4026	1.4693	1.5386	1.6105
6	1.0615	1.1262	1.1941	1.2653	1.3401	1.4185	1.5007	1.5869	1.6771	1.7716
7	1.0721	1.1487	1.2299	1.3159	1.4071	1.5036	1.6058	1.7138	1.8280	1.9487
8	1.0829	1.1717	1.2668	1.3686	1.4775	1.5938	1.7182	1.8509	1.9926	2.1436
9	1.0937	1.1951	1.3048	1.4233	1.5513	1.6895	1.8385	1.9990	2.1719	2.3579
10	1.1046	1.2190	1.3439	1.4802	1.6289	1.7908	1.9672	2.1589	2.3674	2.5937

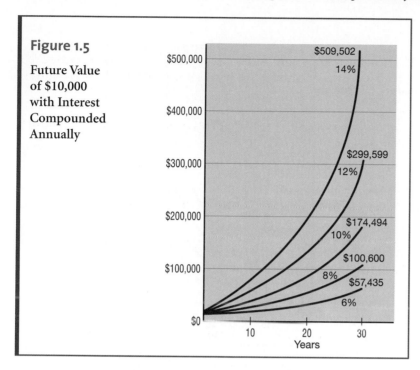

Figure 1.5

Future Value
of $10,000
with Interest
Compounded
Annually

mining how long it would take for the price of something to double given a rate of increase in the price. For example, if college tuition costs were rising 8 percent per year, the cost of a college education would double in just over nine years. In addition, the rule of 72 can be used to calculate the number of years before prices will double given a certain inflation rate. Just divide the inflation rate into 72.

Future Value of an Annuity.   Most people save for long-term goals by putting away a series of payments. Appendix Table A.3 provides a complete table for calculating the future value of a stream of deposited amounts, referred to as an annuity. Figure 1.7 (page 20) graphically demonstrates the effects of various compounded returns on a $2000 annual investment made at the end of each year. The $2000 will grow to $91,524 in 20 years (read across the interest rate row in Appendix Table A.3 to 8 percent and then down the

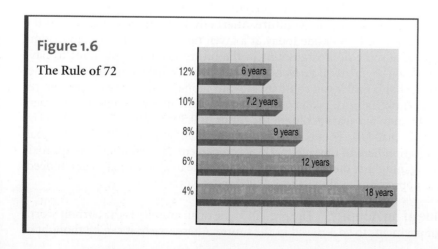

Figure 1.6

The Rule of 72

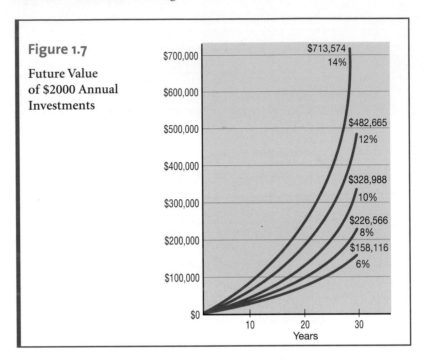

Figure 1.7

Future Value of $2000 Annual Investments

$700,000

$600,000

$500,000

$400,000

$300,000

$200,000

$100,000

$0

$713,574
14%

$482,665
12%

$328,988
10%

$226,566
8%

$158,116
6%

10   20   30
Years

column to 20 years to obtain the factor of 45.762 to multiply by $2000) and to $226,566 in 30 years at an 8 percent rate. Compounding $2000 at 10 percent yields $114,550 in 20 years and $328,988 over 30 years; at 14 percent, it becomes $713,574 after 30 years! For practice you might want to confirm these results using Appendix Table A.3.

Present Value Calculations

Present value (or **discounted value**) is the current value of an asset (or stream of assets) that will be received in the future. You can calculate the present value of a lump sum to be received in the future or the present value of a series of payments to be received in the future.

Present Value of a Lump Sum.   The present value of a lump sum is the current worth of an asset to be received in the future. Alternatively, it can be thought of as the amount you would need to set aside today at a given rate of interest for a given time period so as to have some desired amount in the future. Suppose you want to have $20,000 for the down payment on a new home in ten years. What would you need to set aside today to reach this goal if you could invest your money and receive a 7 percent return? Using Appendix Table A.2 you could look across the interest rate rows to 7 percent and then down to ten years to obtain the factor of 0.5083. Multiplying $20,000 by this factor reveals that $10,166 set aside today would allow you to reach your goal. (Note the connection here to the rule of 72: Seven percent divided into 72 is approximately 10.28, meaning that the investment would double in about 10.28 years. Indeed, $10,166 would approximately double to $20,000 in ten years.)

Present Value of an Annuity.   The present value of an annuity is the current worth of a stream of payments to be received in the future. Alternatively, it can be thought of as the amount you would need to set aside today at a given rate of interest for a given time period so as to receive that stream of payments. Suppose you want to have $30,000 per year for 20 years during your retirement. What amount would you need to have invested at retirement to reach this goal if you could invest your money and receive a 7 percent return? Using Appendix Table A.4 you could look across the interest rate rows to 7 percent and then down to 20 years to obtain the factor of 10.5940. Multiplying $30,000 by this factor reveals that $317,820 (10.5940 × $30,000) set aside at retirement would fund this stream of payments. Note the beauty of compound interest in this result. It takes only $317,820—not $600,000—to fund a $30,000 per year retirement for 20 years if you can earn 7 percent on your financial nest egg.*

Career-Related Money Decisions

 6 Recognize how employer-related money decisions can affect success in personal finance.

A number of career-related money decisions will affect your success in personal finance. Smart decisions can increase your actual income by thousands of dollars each year. For this reason, you should know how to compare salary offers from employers in regions with varying costs of living. Also, you need to be able to calculate the tax-sheltered aspects of employee benefits, such as flexible spending accounts and retirement plans.

It is vital to make effective use of the employee benefits offered through an employer. An **employee benefit** is compensation for employment that does not take the form of wages, salaries, commissions, or other cash payments. Examples include paid holidays, health insurance, and a retirement plan. Some employee benefits are tax-sheltered, such as flexible spending accounts and retirement plans. *Tax-sheltered* in this situation means that the employee avoids paying current income taxes on the value of the benefits received from the employer. In addition, the taxes may be postponed, or deferred, until a later date (usually a good idea)—perhaps until retirement, when the individual's income tax rate might be lower. Smart decisions on employee benefits can increase your actual income by thousands of dollars each year. (See www.bestplaces.com.)

Comparing Salary and Living Costs in Different Cities

Most workers older than age 25 change jobs every five years, and many of them move to distant cities in pursuit of employment. Comparing salary offers from employers located in different cities can be difficult without sufficient information on the approximate cost of living in each community. Sometimes those costs vary drastically. Information from Sperling's Best Places reveals, for example, that life in a high-cost city such as Boston is, on average, 30 percent more expensive than life in a lower-cost city such as Portland, Oregon. The data are reported in index form, with the "average cost" community being given a rating of 100.

The following example demonstrates how to compare salary offers in two cities. In a recent year, the index was 144 for Boston (city 1) and 173 for San Francisco (city 2). Assume you want to compare the buying power of a salary offer of $48,000 in Boston with a $55,000 offer in San Francisco. The costs can be compared using Equations (1.5) and (1.6).

*If you are using a financial calculator for time value of money calculations, see "How to Use a Financial Calculator" on the *Garman/Forgue* website, or you can use the present and future value calculator found on the *Garman/Forgue* website, college.hmco.com/business.students.

$$\text{Salary in city 1} \times \frac{\text{index city 2}}{\text{index city 1}} = \text{equivalent salary in city 2} \quad \text{(1.5)}$$

$$\text{Boston's } \$48,000 \times \frac{173}{144} \text{ is equivalent to } \$57,667 \text{ in San Francisco}$$

Thus, the $48,000 Boston salary offer would buy $57,667 of goods and services in San Francisco—an amount more than the $55,000 San Francisco salary offer. All things being equal (and they are both nice cities), the Boston offer is better.

To compare the buying power of salaries in the other direction, reverse the formula:

$$\text{Salary in city 2} \times \frac{\text{index city 1}}{\text{index city 2}} = \text{equivalent salary in city 2} \quad \text{(1.6)}$$

$$\text{San Francisco's } \$55,000 \times \frac{144}{173} \text{ is equivalent to } \$45,780 \text{ in Boston}$$

Thus, the $55,000 San Francisco salary offer can buy only $45,780 of goods and services in Boston—an amount lesss than the $48,000 Boston salary offer. All things being equal, the Boston offer is still better.

You may compare salary figures and the cost of living in different communities on the Web. Visit the website www.bestplaces.com to do so.

Employer-Sponsored Tax-Sheltered Spending Accounts

One example of a tax-sheltered employee benefit is the **flexible spending account (FSA).** These government-approved, employer-sponsored accounts allow selected employee-paid expenses for medical or dependent care to be paid with employee's pretax dollars rather than after-tax income. Under a typical FSA, the employee agrees to have a certain amount deducted from each paycheck that is then deposited in a separate account called a flexible spending account. As qualified expenses are incurred, the employee requests and receives reimbursements from the account. FSA accounts can be used to pay for two types of expenses: dependent care or medical care. Funds in a dependent care account may be used to pay for the care of a dependent younger than age 13 or the care of another dependent who is physically or mentally incapable of caring for himself or herself and who resides in the taxpayer's home. Funds in a health care account may be used to pay for qualified, unreimbursed out-of-pocket expenses for health care. Examples of the last kind of expenses include copayments, deductibles, orthodontia, flu shots, chiropractic care, acupuncture, counseling, eyeglasses, contact lenses, laser eye surgery, and some over-the-counter medicines.

The tax advantage of an FSA occurs because the amounts deducted from the employee's salary avoid federal income tax, Social Security taxes, and, in most states, state income taxes, thereby allowing selected personal expenses to be paid with pretax (rather than after-tax) income. Paying the expenses with **pretax dollars** (money income that has not been taxed by the government) lowers taxable income, decreases take-home pay, and increases effective take-home pay because of the reimbursements. The resulting tax savings can be close to 40 percent of the amount placed in the account for someone in the 25 percent federal and 6 percent state marginal tax brackets when the 7.65 percent Social Security and Medicare taxes saved are included (25% + 6% + 7.65% = 38.65%).

Before enrolling in an FSA, it is important to estimate your expenses carefully so that the amount in the FSA does not exceed anticipated expenses. Internal Revenue

Service (IRS) regulations do not allow the plan to return unused amounts at the end of the plan year, and money cannot be transferred from one account to another, or from one plan year to another. Thus, unused amounts are forfeited and are not returned to the employee—a condition called the "use it or lose it" rule. A nominal monthly fee is assessed to participate in these programs. The maximum annual contribution limits are usually $5000 for dependent-care FSA and $2000 to $3000 for medical-care FSA. Many employers offer debit cards that withdraw money directly from an employee's FSA.

The newest type of tax-free account is the **health savings account (HSA).** This special savings account is intended for people who have health insurance policies with annual deductibles (the amount paid to cover expenses before benefits begin) of at least $1000 for individuals and $2000 for families. Individuals and/or employers can make tax-free contributions of no more than $2600 per year for individuals and $5150 for families. Withdrawals can be used to pay for most medical expenses, including expenses for Medicare and nursing-home premiums and long-term health care services.

Employer-Sponsored Qualified Retirement Plans

More than half of all workers are covered by an employer-sponsored **qualified retirement plan,** also called a **tax-sheltered retirement plan.** The most popular of the plans is the 401(k) plan offered by private companies, although similar 403(b) and 457 plans are available for other workers. These retirement plans have been approved (qualified) by the IRS as vehicles in which to deposit tax-sheltered contributions. They offer tax advantages that can reduce a person's current income taxes and increase his or her financial nest egg for retirement. Employer-sponsored qualified retirement plans provide two distinct advantages.

First Advantage: Tax-Deductible Contributions.   Tax-sheltered retirement plans provide tremendous tax-deductibility benefits compared with ordinary savings and investment plans. Because pretax contributions to qualified plans reduce income, the current year's tax liability is lowered. The money saved in taxes can then be used to partially fund a larger contribution, which creates even greater returns. In effect, says financial expert Steve Lansing, "the employer's 401(k) plan can be viewed as an interest-free loan from the government, via the income taxes saved, to help finance a retirement plan."

As Table 1.2 illustrates, you can save substantial sums for retirement with minimal effects on your monthly take-home pay. For example, a single person with a monthly taxable income of $4000 in the 25 percent marginal tax bracket who forgoes consumption and instead places $500 into a tax-sheltered retirement plan every month reduces monthly take-home pay from $3175 to $2800, or $375—that is certainly not an enor-

Table 1.2 The Value of Tax-Sheltered Contributions			
Monthly Salary	$4000	Monthly Salary	$4000
Pretax retirement plan contribution	0	Pretax retirement plan contribution	500
Taxable income	4000	Taxable income	3500
Federal taxes*	825	Federal taxes*	700
Monthly take-home pay	3175	Monthly take-home pay	2800
You put away for retirement	0	Cost to put away $500 per month ($3175 − $2800)	375
		You put away for retirement	6000

*From Chapter 4; 25 percent income tax rate, single.

mous amount. The net effect is that it costs that person only $375 to put away that $500 per month into a retirement plan. The immediate "return on investment" equals a fantastic 25 percent ($125 ÷ $500). In essence, the taxpayer puts $375 into his or her retirement plan and the government contributes $125. (Without the plan, the taxpayer would pay the $125 directly to the government.) A taxpayer paying a higher marginal tax rate realizes even greater gains. Because a substantial part of your contributions to a tax-sheltered retirement plan comes from money that you would have paid in income taxes, it costs you less to save more.

Second Advantage: Tax-Deferred Growth.   Because interest, dividends, and capital gains from qualified plans are taxed only after funds are withdrawn from the plan, investments in tax-sheltered retirement plans grow tax-free. The benefits of tax deferral can be substantial.

For example, if a person in the 25 percent tax bracket invests $2000 at the beginning of every year for 30 years and the investment earns an 8 percent taxable return compounded annually, the fund will grow to $167,603 at the end of the 30-year period. If the same $2000 invested annually was instead compounded at 8 percent within a tax-sheltered program, it would grow to $244,691! The higher amount results from compounding at the full 8 percent and not paying any income taxes. (Figure 1.4 on page 15 illustrates these differences in returns.) Indeed, when the funds are finally taxed upon their withdrawal some years later, the taxpayer may be in a lower marginal tax bracket.

How to Maximize the Benefits from a Tax-Sheltered Retirement Plan

1. Start Early to Boost Your Retirement.   Recall the rule of 72, which can be used to calculate the number of years it would take for a lump-sum investment to double. A 9 percent rate of return doubles an investment every eight years. Thus, waiting eight years to begin saving results in the loss of one doubling. Unfortunately, it is the *last* doubling that is lost, as illustrated in Table 1.3. In that example, $48,000 ($96,000 − $48,000) is lost due to a hesitancy to invest $3000. That is quite an opportunity cost.

The opportunity costs are even greater when the start of regular, continuing deposits is delayed. For example, a worker who starts saving $25 per week in a qualified retirement plan at age 23 will have about $616,390 by age 65, assuming an annual rate

Table 1.3 How Starting Just Eight Years Later Will Affect Investment Growth				
Starting Earlier			**Starting Later**	
Age	**$ Value**		**Age**	**$ Value**
23	$ 3,000		23	$ 0
31	6,000		31	3,000
39	12,000		39	6,000
47	24,000		47	12,000
55	48,000		55	24,000
63	$ 96,000		63	$ 48,000

Starting to save $3000 eight years later (age 31 instead of 23) costs the investor $48,000 ($96,000 − $48,000) in compound growth assuming $3000 is invested annually at 9 percent.

of return of 9 percent. Waiting until age 33 to start saving, instead of beginning at age 23, results in a retirement fund of *only* about $242,230. The cost of delay is nearly $375,000 ($616,390 − $242,230), even though ten years' worth of delayed deposits would have totaled only $13,000. Again, this effect occurs because most of the power of compounding appears in the last years of growth.

2. Plan to Be a Millionaire.   Becoming a millionaire is not as difficult as it might seem. Investing $214 per month in a tax-sheltered retirement plan earning 9 percent for 40 years will yield slightly more than $1 million. Setting aside $214 each month may seem like a difficult task at first, but this amount can include employer contributions into the plan. Plus, as your income grows, you will be able to deposit larger amounts, resulting in a financial nest egg of perhaps $2 or $3 million. The best time to start saving for retirement is when your income first jumps significantly. College graduates could start with their very first paycheck from a full-time job. Once you start living on the higher level of income, cutting back is difficult, so start to save right away.

3. Saving Just 1 Percent More of Your Pay Makes a Big Difference.   Most workers do not save the maximum amount allowed under their employers' qualified retirement plans. A 23-year-old worker earning $30,000 who saves just 1 percent more of his or her pay (only an extra $300 per year) will see a boost in the retirement fund at age 65 of $121,058 (assuming an annual rate of return of 9 percent).

4. Never Make a Hardship Withdrawal from a Tax-Sheltered Retirement Plan.
The tax sheltering of funds in a qualified plan actually represents a deferment of taxes rather than a permanent avoidance of them. Income taxes must be paid when the funds are withdrawn. If money is withdrawn prior to a certain age—usually 59½—a 10 percent penalty is likely to be assessed as well as the usual income tax. After paying the penalty (10%) and the income tax (probably 25%) due on funds withdrawn from a retirement plan, the worker loses the opportunity cost associated with keeping the funds invested. For example, assume that Ramsey Marshalla, a legal assistant from San Jose, California, makes a hardship withdrawal of $5000 from his employer-sponsored retirement plan. Such withdrawals are permitted for medical expenses, funeral costs, home eviction or foreclosure, college expenses, and purchase of a home. As a result, Ramsey will not accumulate the $61,338 (investment return) that he would have earned on this money over the next 30 years, assuming an annual rate of return of 9 percent. When faced with a financial problem, you should borrow from a credit union or bank (see Chapter 7) before requesting a hardship withdrawal of money from a retirement plan. When changing jobs, if you take possession of money in a tax-sheltered retirement plan, you will owe the penalty and tax. Instead, leave your money in the account, transfer the funds to an account at your new employer, or make a tax-free rollover to an individual retirement account (IRA), which is discussed in Chapters 4 and 18.

Summary

1. Personal finance is the study of personal and family resources considered important in achieving financial success; thus, it involves how people spend, save, protect, and invest their financial resources. A solid understanding of personal finance topics offers people a better chance of success in facing the financial challenges, responsibilities, and opportunities of life. Such successes might include paying minimal credit costs, not paying too much in income taxes, and selecting successful investments that match your needs.

2. Financial success is the achievement of financial aspirations that are desired, planned, or attempted. There are six key steps to achieve financial success: financial planning, money management, managing expenditures, income and asset protection through insurance, investment planning, and retirement and estate planning.

3. Your success in personal finance partly depends on how well you understand and use information to cope with the economic environment. This ability includes knowing the state of the economy, predicting future directions for the economy, and predicting future directions of prices and inflation.

4. Your understanding of a number of basic economic considerations will certainly affect your financial success in life. Important among these factors are opportunity costs, marginal analysis, and income taxes.

5. Time is money. The time value of money is perhaps the single most important concept in personal finance. It can be referred to as interest because it adjusts for the fact that dollars to be received or paid out in the future are not equivalent to those received or paid out today. A dollar received today is worth more than a dollar received a year from now, because today's dollar can be saved or invested; thus, by next year you expect it to be worth more than a dollar. The time value of money involves two components: future value and present value. The four basic time value of money calculations involve finding the future value of a lump sum, the future value of an annuity, the present value of a lump sum, and the present value of an annuity.

6. A number of career-related money decisions will affect a person's success in personal finance. Smart decisions can increase your real income by thousands of dollars each year. You should be able to compare salary offers from employers located in cities that have different costs of living. You should also calculate the tax-sheltered aspects of employee benefits, such as flexible spending accounts and retirement plans.

Key Terms

business (economic) cycle, 8
compound interest, 16
employee benefit, 21
federal funds rate, 12
financial literacy, 3
financial success, 6
flexible spending account (FSA), 22
future value (*FV*), 18
inflation, 9
interest, 12
marginal tax rate, 14
opportunity cost, 13
personal finance, 4
present value, 20
pretax dollars, 22
purchasing power, 10
qualified retirement plan, 23
rule of 72, 18
tax-sheltered income, 15
time value of money, 16

Chapter Review Questions

1. What is financial success? Give some examples of it.

2. Summarize why people studying personal finance need to understand economic growth and the business cycle.

3. Define "opportunity cost" and give an example of how opportunity costs might affect your financial decision making.

4. Explain and give an example of how marginal analysis makes some financial decisions easier.

5. Describe and give an example of how income taxes can affect financial decision making.

6. What are the two components used when figuring the time value of money?

7. Explain the difference between simple interest and compound interest, and describe why that difference is important.

8. Explain why the same dollar amount of salary offered by employers in two different cities may not allow you to achieve the same standard of living.

9. How do contributions to a flexible spending account work to benefit the finances of the employee?

10. List two ways you can maximize the benefits from a tax-sheltered retirement program.

Group Discussion Issues

1. Where is the United States in the economic cycle now, and where does it seem to be heading? List some indicators that suggest in which direction it may move (e.g., GDP growth, unemployment, inflation). If everyone in the group does not agree on the direction, explain why.

2. What are some common mistakes that people make in personal finance? List ten such mistakes. Which three are the worst, and why?

3. People regularly make decisions in personal finance that have opportunity costs. List five financial decisions you have made recently and identify the opportunity cost for each.

4. The cost of living varies across the country. List five cities in which it would be very expensive to live, and five cities in which life would be relatively inexpensive. Comment on what one's lifestyle would be like in the most expensive city and in the least expensive city, assuming an income of $60,000.

Decision-Making Cases

▶ Case 1
Reasons to Study Personal Finance

Patricia Bailey of Gulfport, Mississippi, is a senior in college, majoring in sociology. She anticipates getting married a year or so after graduation. Patricia has only one elective course remaining and must choose between another advanced class in sociology and one in personal finance. As Patricia's friend, you want to persuade her to take personal finance. Give some examples of how Patricia might benefit from the study of personal finance.

▶ Case 2
A Closer Look at Lifetime Financial Objectives

You have been asked to give a brief speech on the lifetime financial objectives of most people and their relationship to steps in successful management of personal finances. Make an outline of the points in your speech.

Financial Math Questions

1. As a graduating senior, Gwen Reishman of Manhattan, Kansas, is eager to enter the job market at an anticipated annual salary of $34,000. Assuming an average inflation rate of 5 percent and an equal cost-of-living raise, what will Gwen's salary be in 10 years? In 20 years? (Hint: Use Appendix Table A.1 or calculations on the *Garman/Forgue* website.) To make real economic progress, how much of a raise (in dollars) must Gwen receive next year?

2. Kathryn Berry, a freshman nutrition major at the University of Minnesota, has some financial questions for the next three years of school and beyond. Answers to these questions can be obtained by using Appendix Table A or the *Garman/Forgue* website.

   (a) If Kathryn's tuition, fees, and expenditures for books this year total $8000, what will they be during her senior year (three years from now), assuming costs rise 6 percent annually? (Hint: Use Appendix Table A.1 or the *Garman/Forgue* website.)

   (b) Kathryn is applying for a scholarship currently valued at $3000. If she is awarded it at the end of next year, how much is the scholarship worth in today's dollars, assuming inflation of 5 percent? (Hint: Use Appendix Table A.2 or the *Garman/Forgue* website.)

   (c) Kathryn is already looking ahead to graduation and a job, and she wants to buy a new car not long after her graduation. If after graduation she begins a savings program of $2400 per year in an investment yielding 6 percent, what will be the value of the fund after three years? (Hint: Use Appendix Table A.3 or the *Garman/Forgue* website.)

   (d) Kathryn's Aunt Karroll told her that she would give Kathryn $1000 at the end of each year for the next three years to help with her college expenses. Assuming an annual interest rate of 6 percent, what is the present value of that stream of payments? (Hint: Use Appendix Table A.4 or the *Garman/Forgue* website.)

3. Using the present and future value tables in Appendix A, the appropriate calculations on the *Garman/Forgue* website, or a financial calculator, calculate the following:

   (a) The future value of $400 in two years that earns 5 percent.

   (b) The future value of $1200 saved each year for ten years that earns 7 percent.

   (c) The amount a person would need to deposit today with a 5 percent interest rate to have $2000 in three years.

   (d) The amount a person would need to deposit today to be able to withdraw $6000 each year for ten years from an account earning 6 percent.

(e) A person is offered a gift of $5000 now or $8000 five years from now. If such funds could be expected to earn 8 percent over the next five years, which is the better choice?

(f) A person wants to have $3000 available to spend on an overseas trip four years from now. If such funds could be expected to earn 7 percent, how much must be invested in a lump sum to realize the $3000 when needed?

(g) A person who invests $1200 each year finds one choice that is expected to pay 9 percent per year and another choice that may pay 10 percent. What is the difference in return if the investment is made for 15 years?

(h) A person invests $50,000 in an investment that earns 6 percent. If $6000 is withdrawn each year, how many years will it take for the fund to run out?

4. You win a contest. The prize is cash, and you are offered several alternative payment plans. Which plan should you choose? Assume you can earn 5 percent on your money and ignore inflation.

(a) $30,000 today

(b) $40,000 in five years

(c) $10,000 one year from today and $25,000 two years later

(d) $4000 per year starting today for the next ten years

5. Using the rule of 72, calculate how quickly $1000 will double to $2000 at interest rates of 2 percent, 4 percent, 6 percent, 8 percent, and 10 percent.

What Would You Recommend Now?

Now that you have read the chapter on the importance of personal finance, what would you recommend to Lawrence in the case at the beginning of the chapter regarding:

1. Factoring the current state of the economy into his personal financial planning?

2. Understanding the effects of income taxes on his income and financial decisions?

3. Participating in his employer's 401(k) retirement plan?

4. Using time value of money considerations to project what his IRA might be worth at age 63?

5. Using time value of money considerations to project what his 401(k) plan might be worth starting at age 63 if he were to participate fully.

Exploring the World Wide Web

To complete these exercises, go to the *Garman/Forgue* website at college.hmco.com/business/students. Under General Business, select the title of this text. Click on the Internet Exercises link for this chapter, and answer the questions that appear on the Web page.

1. Visit the Bureau of Labor Statistics Consumer Price Index home page, and link to information for various areas of the country and metropolitan areas of various sizes. Describe how prices have been changing for your area and city size during the past year.

2. Visit the website for the Conference Board, where you will find the latest information on the consumer confidence index and the index of leading economic indicators. What do the indexes say about the direction of the economy over the next six months to one year?

3. Visit the website for the Federal Reserve Board, where you will find a summary of economic information provided on the Web by the Fed. Select three websites that you feel would be especially useful for people seeking information on economic trends to help them with their personal financial planning.

4. Visit the website for WageWeb, where you will find the results of salary surveys in numerous career areas. Explore the information for careers related to your college major. Does the information confirm what you had expected or did it open your eyes to a differing reality?

5. Visit the website for *Kiplinger's Personal Finance Magazine*. There you will find a link to a long list of calculators that could be used in various present and future value calculations. Select four that you feel would be particularly useful in the aspects of personal financial planning that were discussed in this chapter.

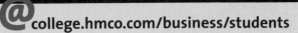

Chapter 2

Financial Planning

LEARNING OBJECTIVES

After reading this chapter, you should be able to:

1 **Explain** the elements of successful financial planning.

2 **Describe** the balance sheet and the cash-flow statement.

3 **Use** financial ratios to evaluate your financial strength and progress.

4 **Know** which financial records to maintain and where to keep them.

5 **Understand** which factors to consider when choosing a professional financial planner.

What Would You Recommend?

Brian and Marlene Patterson, both age 26, have been married for four years. They have no children. Brian is a licensed electrician earning $33,000 per year, and Marlene earns $31,000 annually as a middle-school teacher. Brian would like to go to half-time on his job and return to school on a part-time basis; he is one year short of finishing his bachelor's degree in engineering. His education expenses would be about $10,000 per year, which could be partially covered by student loans. He has not yet discussed his plans with Marlene.

Brian and Marlene have recently started saving for retirement through their employment and have set aside some savings for emergencies. They have substantial credit card debt and are still paying off their student loans. The couple rents a two-bedroom apartment. Brian always thought it important to save all of their receipts, bank statements, and other financial documents. His system for organizing their records is very simple; each month he puts everything in a manila envelope and then puts the 12 envelopes into a box at the end of the year.

Brian knows that his educational plans will have financial implications for the couple. He wants to factor these financial issues into his discussion with Marlene about his plans. To this point, they have never developed financial statements or explicit financial goals.

What would you recommend to Brian for his talk with Marlene on the subject of financial planning regarding:

1. Determining what the couple owns and owes?

2. Better understanding the family's income and expenditures?

3. Using the information in Brian's newly prepared financial statements to summarize the family's financial situation?

4. Setting up an organized recordkeeping system so that he and Marlene can have easier access to accurate information when needed?

5. Who they might contact to obtain professional financial advice?

Most people develop a pattern of financial behavior through trial and error. They want to be financially successful but typically lack clear goals for the future. For this reason, their decision making is often flawed. Instead of simply muddling through your financial life, it is important that you engage in explicit financial planning.

This chapter begins with an explanation of *financial planning*—what it is and how it can be important to you. We then examine two financial statements: the balance sheet and the cash-flow statement. The next section considers how to use information from those financial statements to calculate financial ratios that will allow you to evaluate your financial strength and progress. Next, we provide a detailed overview of recordkeeping to help you establish your own financial recordkeeping system. The chapter concludes by offering information on using a computer in personal financial planning and on the professional financial planning assistance available in today's marketplace.

20 pgs

Golden Rules of

Financial Planning

Financial success comes from learning the Golden Rules of personal finance and then putting what you have learned into practice. Make the following your money habits in financial planning:

1. Develop your own balance sheet and update it annually.
2. Develop your own cash-flow statements monthly or quarterly and compile them into an annual statement each year.
3. Calculate your financial ratios periodically and use them to assess your financial progress.
4. Develop a list of your financial goals. Start with the shorter-term goals and then expand your list to longer-range goals. Update and revise your goals annually.
5. Develop specific financial strategies so you can always keep a balance between spending and saving.
6. Start an uncomplicated personal financial recordkeeping system that meets your needs.

Setting the Stage for Successful Personal Financial Planning

1 Explain the elements of successful financial planning.

Financial planning is the process of developing and implementing a coordinated series of financial plans to achieve financial success. Financial planning is unique to each individual or family. It should take into consideration all aspects of financial activity as the individual or family moves through life.

Figure 2.1 (page 33) provides an overview of effective personal financial planning, and Table 2.1 (page 32) illustrates one couple's financial plan. Note that the couple has made plans in 15 specific areas spread across three broad categories: spending, risk management, and capital accumulation. Most people ignore certain areas (retirement planning is a common example) and act with only partial knowledge in other areas (relying on their employers' often inadequate disability income insurance, for example). Yet, achieving success in financial matters requires effective financial planning in all 15 specific areas. Subsequent chapters in this book will examine personal finance topics in enough detail so that you will feel confident and competent as you implement your financial plans.

Values Provide the Base for Financial Planning

Your **values** are your fundamental beliefs about what is important, desirable, and worthwhile. They serve as the basis for your goals. All of us differ in the ways we value education, spiritual life, health, employment, credit use, family life, and many other factors. Personal financial goals grow out of these values because we inevitably consider some things more important or desirable than others. We express our values, in part, by

Table 2.1 Financial Plans, Goals, and Objectives for Harry (Age 23) and Belinda (Age 22) Johnson Prepared in February, 2005

Financial Plan Areas	Long-Term Goals and Objectives	Short-Term Goals and Objectives
For Spending		
Evaluate and plan major purchases	Purchase a new car in two years.	Begin saving $200 a month for a down payment for a new car.
Manage debt	Keep installment debt under 10 percent of take-home pay.	Pay off charge cards at end of each month and do not finance any purchases of appliances or other similar products.
For Risk Management		
Medical costs	Avoid large medical costs.	Maintain employer-subsidized medical insurance policy by paying $135 monthly premium
Property and casualty losses	Always have renter's or homeowner's insurance Always have maximum automobile insurance coverage.	Make semi-annual premium payment of $220 on renter's insurance policy. Make premium payments of $440 on automobile insurance policy.
Liability losses	Eventually buy $1 million liability insurance.	Rely on $100,000 policy purchased from same source as automobile insurance policy.
Premature death	Have adequate life insurance coverage for both as well as lots of financial investments so the survivor would not have any financial worries.	Maintain employer-subsidized life insurance on Belinda. Buy some life insurance for Harry. Start some investments.
Income loss from disability	Buy sufficient disability insurance.	Rely on sick days and seek disability insurance through private insurers.
For Capital Accumulation		
Tax fund	Have enough money for taxes (but not too much) withheld from monthly salaries by both employers to cover eventual tax liabilities.	Confirm that employer withholding of taxes is sufficient. Have extra money withheld to cover additional tax liability because of income on trust from Harry's deceased father.
Revolving savings fund	Always have sufficient cash in local accounts to meet monthly and annual anticipated budget expense needs.	Develop cash-flow calendar to ascertain needs. Put money into revolving savings fund to build it up quickly to the proper balance. Keep all funds in interest-earning accounts.
Emergency fund	Build up monetary assets equivalent to three months' take-home pay.	Put $150 per month into an emergency fund until it totals one month's take-home pay.
Education	Maintain educational skills and credentials to remain competitive. Have employer assist in paying for Belinda to earn a master's in business administration (MBA). Have Harry complete a master's of fine arts (MFA), possibly a Ph.D. in interior design.	Both take one graduate class per term.
Savings	Always have a nice-size savings balance. Regularly save to achieve goals. Save a portion of any extra income or gifts. Save $26,000 for a down payment on a home to be bought within five years.	Save enough to pay cash for a good-quality digital video disc (DVD) player. Pay off Visa credit card balance of $390 soon. Begin saving $400 per month for a down payment on a new home.
Investments	Own substantial shares of a conservative mutual fund that will pay dividends equivalent to about 10 percent of family income at age 45. Own some real estate and common stocks.	Start investing in a mutual fund before next year.
Retirement	Retire at age 60 or earlier on income that is the same as the take-home pay earned just before retirement.	Establish individual retirement accounts (IRAs) for Harry and Belinda before next year. Contribute the maximum possible amount to employer-sponsored retirement accounts.
Estate planning	Provide for surviving spouse.	Each spouse makes a will.

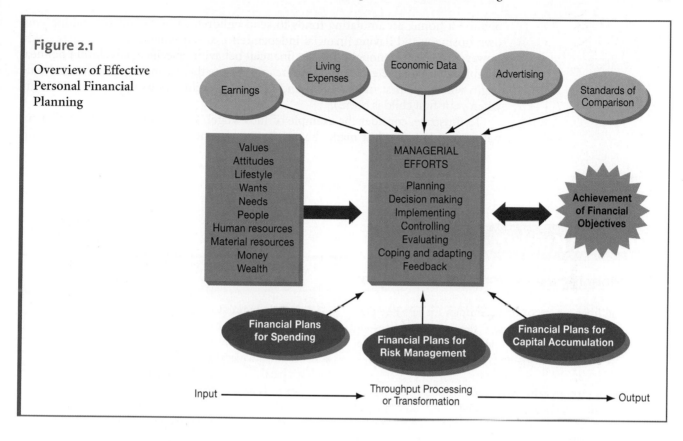

Figure 2.1

Overview of Effective
Personal Financial
Planning

the ways we spend, save, and invest our money. For example, parents who value education would want to start a college savings fund when their children are young.

You set the stage for financial planning by examining your values as they relate to your finances. Your values provide the underlying support and rationale for your financial and lifestyle goals. Successful financial planning includes the following elements that guide behavior: (1) specified values that underlie the plans; (2) explicitly stated financial goals; and (3) logical and consistent financial strategies. Only after this value-development process is complete do you take actions to achieve the goals. In other words, planning comes before action.

Financial Goals Follow from Values

Financial goals are the specific long- and short-term objectives to be attained through financial planning and management efforts. Financial and lifestyle goals should be consistent with your values. To serve as a rational basis for financial actions, they must be stated explicitly. Financial goals should be specific in terms of both dollar amounts and the projected dates by which they are to be achieved.

Setting goals helps you visualize the gap between your current financial status and where you want to be in the future. Examples of general financial goals include finishing a college education, paying off debts (including education loans), taking a vacation, owning a home, accumulating funds to send children through college, owning your own business, and having financial independence at retirement. None of these goals, however, is specific enough to guide financial behavior. Specific goals should be measurable, attainable, relevant, and time-related. (Note that saving for retirement should begin with your first full-time job and saving for children's education should begin when your first child is born.)

To illustrate, consider the example of Judy Vogel, a dance instructor from Cincinnati, Ohio. Judy has just made the last $347 payment on her four-year car loan. She

Did You Know? . . .

Life Planning Issues When You Tie the Knot

Personal finances are complex enough for just one person, but when two people join their financial lives together in marriage there are important actions to take. Here are some key things newlyweds should do:

- Change your beneficiaries. Life insurance policies, retirement accounts, and mutual fund accounts all have beneficiaries (the people who will receive the funds at your death) named when you set them up. With marriage, it is time to put your partner's name first. (See Chapters 12, 15, and 18.)
- Coordinate your employee benefits. Most couples have two incomes today, so each has a menu of employee benefits from which to choose. As a result, one spouse may drop a benefit that is being received via the other's plan. For example, if one partner receives family coverage for health care for free or at a low monthly cost, perhaps the other can drop that aspect of his or her own plan. One spouse might then be able to add another benefit at no cost, such as paid education expenses. Your employee benefits officer can help you decide which options to select.
- Update your life insurance coverage. Focus on term life insurance for the bulk of your needs. (See Chapter 12.)
- Review auto and homeowner's insurance coverages and inventory your personal property. (See Chapter 10)
- Get out of debt. One or both of you may bring debts into the new family. Because a couple can live together a little more cheaply than two individuals who live apart, funds can be freed up to pay off credit card, student, and other loans. Maybe you could put some of your wedding gift money toward this purpose.

This debt reduction has an added benefit: It sets the stage for getting a mortgage to buy your first home. (See Chapters 6 and 7.)

- Update your government program names. If one or both partners' names are changed as a result of your new status, you need to notify the Social Security Administration and driver's licensing office of that change. You will need to show your marriage certificate as proof of the change.
- Save for retirement separately. As both of you will likely be wage earners for a large proportion of your lives together, you will come to rely on both incomes and become accustomed to the lifestyle you achieve together. Day-to-day living expenses will go down somewhat when you team up as a couple. Use some of that money to allocate additional amounts to your retirement plans. (See Chapter 18.)
- Update your estate transfer plans. With a new number one in your life, you should change (or set up) your will, durable power of attorney, living will, and health care surrogate designations. (See Chapter 19 for more information on these documents.)
- Close redundant bank and credit accounts that each partner brings into the marriage. Reducing the number of accounts can save money on account fees. Decide which accounts should be yours, mine, or ours. Having excess credit cards can reduce your credit scores and exposes you to the potential for overuse. (See Chapters 5 and 6 for more on managing accounts.)
- Manage your money together. All of the topics in this chapter on financial planning should be undertaken as a team. (See Chapter 3 for more ways to more effectively discuss money matters.)

does not like being in debt, so she does not want to take out such a large loan again. Judy would like to put at least part of the money she has been paying monthly for the loan into a savings account, which would allow her to replace her current vehicle in five years. Judy figures that it would take about $22,500 to buy a similar vehicle in five years. She assumes she could earn a 3 percent return on her savings and, using Appendix Table A.3, has determined that she would need to save $4238 per year ($22,500 ÷ 5.3091 for five years at 3 percent interest from Appendix Table A.3), or roughly $353 per month.

Judy's thinking offers a good example of how financial goal setting works. She recognized the value she put on staying out of debt and proceeded to the general goal of paying cash for her next car. After determining an overall dollar amount needed, she broke that amount down into first annual and then monthly amounts. For only $6 more per month than she has been paying on her loan ($353 − $347), Judy will be able to pay cash for her next car. This is a sacrifice she is willing to make to avoid using credit to buy a vehicle in the future.

Financial Strategies Guide Financial Behavior

Financial strategies are preestablished plans of action to be implemented in specific situations. Judy Vogel implemented a very effective strategy in the preceding example. That is, when a loan has been repaid, start a savings program with the same monthly payment amount. Judy's strategy will work out even better if she arranges to have the money transferred automatically each month from her checking into her savings account. Another effective strategy is to arrange for one-half of every raise to go into savings before you become accustomed to the additional income. Strategies such as this one will be presented throughout this book, as they help you keep a balance between spending and saving.

Note that Judy's actions have nothing to do with her earning more money. Many people think that being wealthy is a function of how much you earn or inherit. In reality, accumulating wealth is much more related to your ability to understand trade-offs and make the sacrifices that will save money and generate wealth for you. In Judy's case, all that remains for her to do is put the strategy into action. She can then review her strategy annually and adjust it as necessary to keep pace with her shifting circumstances.

Developing Your Initial Financial Statements

2 Describe the balance sheet and the cash-flow statement.

Financial statements are compilations of personal financial data designed to communicate information on money matters. They are used—often along with other financial data—to indicate the financial condition of an individual or family. The two most useful statements are the balance sheet and the cash-flow statement.

A **balance sheet** (or **net worth statement**) describes an individual's or family's financial condition on a specified date (often January 1) by showing assets, liabilities, and net worth. It provides a current status report and includes information on what you own, what you owe, and what the net result would be if you paid off all of your debts.

A **cash-flow** (or **income and expense**) **statement** lists and summarizes income and expense transactions that have taken place over a specific period of time, such as a month or a year. It tells you where your money came from and where it went.

The Balance Sheet Reveals Your Net Worth

Your first step to a better financial life ought to be an assessment of where you are on the wealth-building scale—that is, your net worth. If you are indeed serious about your financial success, then you need to sit down soon with pencil and paper or at your computer to see exactly where you stand. You do so by preparing your balance sheet, which summarizes the value of what you own minus what you owe. Your balance sheet should be updated at least once each year, so that you can compare your progress from one year to the next. For most people, net worth grows slowly. However, if you are successful in your career and follow the basic principles outlined in this book, there is no reason why you cannot have a net worth of more than $2 million later in your life. For most people, net worth peaks in their mid-sixties and declines thereafter as they live off their financial nest egg in retirement.

Components of the Balance Sheet.   A balance sheet consists of three parts: assets, liabilities, and net worth. Your **assets** include everything you own that has monetary value. Your **liabilities** are your debts—what you owe to others. Your **net worth** is the dollar amount left when what is owed is subtracted from the dollar value of what is owned—that is, when liabilities are subtracted from assets.

What Is Owned—Assets.   The assets section of the balance sheet identifies things valued at their **fair market value**—what a willing buyer would pay a willing seller, not the amount originally paid. It is useful to classify assets as monetary, tangible, or investment assets.

  Monetary assets (also known as **liquid assets**) include cash and near-cash items that can be readily converted to cash. They are primarily used for maintenance of living expenses, emergencies, savings, and payment of bills.

  Tangible (or **use**) **assets** are physical items that have fairly long lifespans and could be sold to raise cash, but whose primary purpose is to provide maintenance of one's lifestyle (for example, a car). Tangible assets generally depreciate in value over time.

  Investment assets (also known as **capital assets**) include tangible and intangible items acquired for the monetary benefits they provide, such as generating additional income and increasing in value. Successful financial planning generally requires diversification of investment assets by putting money into a variety of investments (such as real estate, stocks, bonds, and mutual funds). If one investment does not perform well, gains in others will then be available to maintain the overall value of the portfolio. Investment assets generally appreciate and are dedicated to the maintenance of one's future level of living.

  Following are some examples of each kind of asset.

Monetary Assets
- Cash (including cash on hand, checking accounts, savings accounts, savings bonds, certificates of deposit, and money market accounts)
- Tax refunds due
- Money owed to you by others

Tangible Assets
- Automobiles, motorcycles, boats, bicycles
- House, mobile home, condominium
- Household furnishings and appliances
- Personal property (jewelry, furs, tools, clothing)
- Other "big ticket" items

Investment Assets
- Stocks, bonds, mutual funds, gold, partnerships, art, IRAs
- Life insurance and annuities (cash values only)
- Real estate investments
- Personal and employer-provided retirement accounts

What Is Owed—Liabilities.   The liabilities section of the balance sheet summarizes debts owed, including both personal and business-related debts. The debt could be either a **short-term** (or **current**) **liability,** an obligation to be paid off within one year, or a **long-term liability,** an obligation to be paid off in a time period longer than one year. To be accurate, you must include all debt obligations at their current payoff amounts. This is usually *not* simply the total of all remaining payments, because future payments include interest that will not be owed if the loan were to be paid off. Following are some examples of items to include in the liabilities section of a balance sheet, with some suggested subheadings.

Short-Term Liabilities
- Personal loans (owed to other persons)
- Credit card charge accounts, travel and entertainment credit cards
- Professional services unpaid (doctors, dentists, chiropractors, lawyers)
- Taxes unpaid

don't need to know specific liabilities

Long-Term Liabilities
- Automobile and other installment loan balances
- Home mortgage balance
- Home equity (second mortgage) loan balance
- Education loan balance
- Personal loan balance

Net Worth—What Is Left.   Net worth is determined by subtracting liabilities from assets, as indicated in the *net worth formula:*

$$\text{Net worth} = \text{assets} - \text{liabilities} \qquad\qquad (2.1)$$

or

$$\text{Net worth} = \text{what is owned} - \text{what is owed}$$

This formula assumes that if you converted all assets to cash and paid off all liabilities, the remaining cash would be your net worth. Calculating your net worth will give you a reading on where you stand and point out any trouble spots on your balance sheet. The only way to increase your net worth is to spend less than your income. To get ahead in your personal finances, then, you must save and invest.

Sample Balance Sheets.   The balance sheet serves as a statement of the assets and liabilities of a family, individual, or a business on a specified date. The total assets on a balance sheet must equal the total liabilities plus the net worth. Thus, both sides must balance, which is the source of the name "balance sheet." The amount of detail shown on a balance sheet depends on the person or family for whom it is prepared. Accuracy and sufficiency are the key considerations. You must decide how much to include so as to show your financial condition accurately on a given date.

The balance sheets shown in Tables 2.2 (page 38) and 2.3 (page 39) reflect the degree of detail that might be included for a traditional college student and a couple with two children, respectively. Notice that Table 2.2 includes very few items. This pattern is

How to . . .

Increase Your Net Worth

One strategy to increase net worth is to increase assets. Surely anyone can cut back spending by just $5 a week, and any decrease in spending leaves money in the bank as an asset. Reducing expenses on high-cost items like housing and transportation will have an even larger impact on assets. Another tactic is to earn more income and save most of it, rather than using the added money to up your lifestyle.

A second strategy to increase net worth is to decrease liabilities. Paying off debt, especially high-interest credit card balances, can quickly boost your net worth. Avoiding taking on new debt can help maintain your net worth. Reducing your federal income tax liability will keep more of your money available to save or invest, so your net worth can increase.

typical of single persons who have not acquired many objects of value. Observe also the excess of liabilities over assets. This situation is not unusual for college students, for whom debts often seem to grow much faster than assets do. In this case, the person is technically **insolvent** because he or she has a negative net worth. When students graduate and take on full-time jobs, typically their balance sheets change dramatically after a few years. The balance sheet in Table 2.3 shows greater detail and more items, reflecting the increasing financial complexity that typically occurs at later stages in a person's life.

Table 2.2 Balance Sheet for a College Student—Bill Soshnik, January 1, 2006

	Dollars		Percent
ASSETS			
Cash on hand	$ 85		1.07
Checking account	335		4.21
Savings account	800		10.05
Personal property*	3140		39.45
Automobile	3600		45.23
Total Assets		**$7960**	100.00
LIABILITIES			
Telephone bill past due	$ 70		0.88
Bank loan—automobile	3130		39.32
College loan	1000		12.56
Government educational loan	4500		56.53
Total Liabilities		**$8700**	109.30
Net Worth		**($740)**	−9.30
Total Liabilities and Net Worth		**$7960**	100.00

*At fair market value, list includes clothing, $400; dresser, $50; television, $150; chair, $30; table, $40; desk, $120; cooking/dining items, $50; and computer equipment, $2300.

Table 2.3 Balance Sheet for a Couple with Two Children—Victor and Maria Hernandez, January 1, 2006			
	Dollars		**Percent**
ASSETS			
Monetary Assets			
Cash on hand	$ 260		0.08
Savings account	1,500		0.48
Victor's checking account	600		0.19
Maria's checking account	700		0.23
Tax refund due	700		0.23
Rent receivable	660		0.21
Total monetary assets		$ 4,420	1.43
Tangible Assets			
Home	$176,000		56.79
Personal property	9,000		2.90
Automobiles	11,500		3.71
Total tangible assets		$196,500	63.40
Investment Assets			
Fidelity mutual funds	$ 4,500		1.45
Scudder mutual fund	5,000		1.61
General Motors stock	2,800		0.90
New York 2016 bonds	1,000		0.32
Life insurance cash value	5,400		1.74
IRA	6,300		2.03
Real estate investment	84,000		27.10
Total investment assets		$109,000	35.17
Total Assets		$309,920	100.00
LIABILITIES			
Short term liabilities			
Dentist bill	$ 120		0.04
Credit card debt	1,545		0.50
Total short-term liabilities		$ 1,665	0.54
Long-term liabilities			
Sales finance company: automobile	7,700		2.48
Savings and loan: real estate	92,000		29.69
Total long-term liabilities		$ 99,700	32.17
Total Liabilities		$101,365	32.71
Net Worth		$208,555	67.29
Total Liabilities and Net Worth		$309,920	100.00

The Cash-Flow Statement Tracks Your Income and Expenses

The cash-flow (or income and expense) statement is very different from a balance sheet. Whereas the balance sheet shows your financial condition at a single point in time, the cash-flow statement summarizes the total amounts that have been received and spent over a period of time, usually one month or one year. The cash-flow statement, therefore, shows whether you were able to live within your income during that time period.

A cash-flow statement includes three sections: **income** (total income received), **expenses** (total expenditures made), and **surplus** (or **net gain** or **net income**), where total income exceeds total expenses, or **deficit** (or **net loss**), where expenses exceed income.

Income.   You may think of income as simply what is earned from salaries or wages. In fact, many other types of income exist that you should also include on a cash-flow statement. The following are some examples:

- Bonuses and commissions
- Child support and alimony
- Public assistance
- Social Security benefits
- Pension and profit-sharing income
- Scholarships and grants
- Interest and dividends received (from savings accounts, investments, bonds, or loans to others)
- Income from the sale of assets
- Other income (gifts, tax refunds, rent, royalties, capital gains)

Expenses.   All expenditures made during the period covered by the cash-flow statement should be included in the expenses section. The number and type of expenses shown will vary for each individual and family. Many people categorize expenses according to whether they are fixed or variable.

    Fixed expenses are usually paid in the same amount during each time period; they are often contractual. Examples of such expenses include rent payments and automobile installment loans. It is usually difficult—but not impossible—to reduce a fixed expense.

    Variable expenses are expenditures over which an individual has considerable control. Food, entertainment, and clothing are variable expenses, for example. Note that some categories, such as savings, can be listed twice, as both fixed and variable expenses. The following are examples of fixed and variable expenses that you might include in a cash-flow statement:

Fixed Expenses
- Savings and investments
- Retirement contributions (employer's plan, IRA)
- Housing (rent, mortgage, loan payment)
- Automobile (installment payment, lease)
- Insurance (life, health, liability, disability, renter's, homeowner's, automobile)
- Installment loan payments (appliances, furniture)
- Taxes (federal income, state income, local income, real estate, Social Security, personal property)

Variable Expenses
- Meals (at home and away)
- Utilities (electricity, water, gas, telephone)
- Transportation (gasoline and maintenance, licenses, registration, public transportation, tolls)
- Medical expenses
- Child care (nursery, baby-sitting)
- Clothing and accessories (jewelry, shoes, handbags, briefcases)
- Snacks (candy, soft drinks, other beverages)
- Education (tuition, fees, books, supplies)
- Household furnishings (furniture, appliances, curtains)
- Cable television (beyond basic services)
- Personal care (beauty shop, barbershop, cosmetics, dry cleaner)
- Entertainment and recreation (hobbies, socializing, health club, tapes/CDs, videotape/DVD rentals, movies)

- Charitable contributions (gifts, church, school, charity)
- Magazine subscriptions
- Vacations and long weekends
- Credit card payments
- Savings and investments
- Miscellaneous (postage, books, magazines, newspapers, personal allowances, domestic help, membership fees)

There is no rigid list of categories to be used in the expenses section, but you do need to classify all of your expenditures in some way. Rather than just use fixed and variable expenses categories, you might also separate expenditures into savings/investments, debts, insurance, taxes, and household expenses. The more specific your categories, the deeper your understanding of your outlays.

Surplus (Deficit).   The surplus (deficit) section shows the amount remaining after you have itemized income and subtracted expenditures from income, as illustrated by the following calculations of the *surplus/deficit formula*. (A business would call this amount its net profit or net loss.)

$$\text{Surplus (deficit)} = \text{total income} - \text{total expenses} \qquad (2.2)$$

or

$$\$1100 \text{ surplus} = \$12{,}500 - \$11{,}400$$
$$(\$800 \text{ deficit}) = \$14{,}900 - \$15{,}700$$

How to . . .

Obtain Information for Your Financial Statements

Preparing your first balance sheet and cash-flow statement may seem like guesswork, but much of the information is readily available.

For the Balance Sheet

Your checkbook, savings account records, and statements for your various bank, investment, and credit accounts are good sources from which to begin. You may have to estimate dollar values for household furnishings, jewelry, and personal belongings. Remember to value such items at their fair market value. The dollar values of homes and automobiles can be based on what similar items are selling for currently. The degree of precision used to determine the values of assets depends on the purpose and use of a balance sheet. Many people find it useful to make a detailed list or schedule of items summarized on the balance sheet (as illustrated in the footnote to Table 2.2).

For the Cash-Flow Statement

Every check written, every receipt received, every payment made, and every earnings payment received represents a source of information for the cash-flow statement. Of course, if you keep poor records and save few documents, it will be difficult to prepare a sufficiently detailed cash-flow statement. If so, it might be best to keep detailed records for a month before preparing your first statement. To do so, purchase a small spiral notepad and write down each purchase as it is made (or at the end of each day). Use categories such as those in Table 2.5 as headings for the pages in the notebook. Each time you have an expenditure in a particular category, you can then record it on the appropriate page. At the end of the month, the total for each page will be the total for that category.

It is important to strive to have a surplus rather than a deficit. A surplus demonstrates that you are managing your financial resources successfully and do not have to use savings or borrow money to make financial ends meet. When the calculation shows a surplus, that amount is then available (in your checking and savings accounts) to spend, save, or invest.

Sample Cash-Flow Statements.   Tables 2.4 and 2.5 show the cash-flow statements for a college student and a couple with two children, respectively. Table 2.5 vividly highlights the additional income needed to rear children and shows the increased variety of expenditures that characterize a family's (rather than an individual's) lifestyle. As a person earns more income, the cash-flow statement usually becomes more involved and detailed.

Table 2.4 Cash-Flow Statement for a College Student—Bill Soshnik
January 1–December 31, 2005

	Dollars	Percent
INCOME		
Wages (after withholding)	$4,650	39.71
Scholarship	1,750	14.94
Government grant	2,500	21.35
Government loan*	2,600	22.20
Tax refund	210	1.79
Total Income	**$11,710**	**100.00**
EXPENSES		
Room rent (includes utilities)	$1,500	12.81
Laundry	216	1.84
Food	1,346	11.49
Automobile loan payments	1,292	11.03
Automobile insurance	778	6.64
Books and supplies	932	7.96
Tuition	3,160	26.99
Telephone	282	2.41
Clothing	475	4.06
Gifts	300	2.56
Automobile expenses	600	5.12
Health insurance	102	0.87
Recreation and entertainment	360	3.07
Personal expenses	300	2.56
Total Expenses	**$ 11,643**	**99.43**
Surplus (deficit)	**$ 67**	**0.57**

*Technically, loans are not income. Bill plans to be a teacher and his loan will be forgiven should he go into teaching and remain in the profession for five years.

Table 2.5 Cash-Flow Statement for a Couple with Two Children— Victor and Maria Hernandez

January 1, 2004–December 31, 2004

	Dollars		Percent
INCOME			
Victor's gross salary	$43,180		65.42
Maria's salary (part-time)	12,500		18.94
Interest and dividends	1,800		2.73
Bonus	600		0.91
Tax refunds	200		0.30
Net rental income	7,720		11.70
Total Income		$66,000	100.00
EXPENSES			
Fixed Expenses			
Mortgage loan payments	$12,000		18.18
Real estate taxes	$2,400		3.64
Homeowner's insurance	760		1.15
Automobile loan payment	4,400		6.67
Automobile insurance and registration	1,191		1.80
Life insurance premiums	1,200		1.82
Medical insurance (employee portion)	2,980		4.52
Savings at credit union	1,260		1.91
Federal income taxes	6,800		10.30
State income taxes	3,100		4.70
City income taxes	720		1.09
Social Security taxes	4,260		6.45
Personal property taxes	950		1.44
Retirement IRAs	4,000		6.06
Total fixed expenses		$46,021	69.73
Variable Expenses			
Food	$4,900		7.42
Utilities	2,100		3.18
Gasoline, oil, maintenance	3,100		4.70
Medical expenses	1,245		1.89
Medicines	750		1.14
Clothing and upkeep	1,950		2.95
Church	1,200		1.82
Gifts	900		1.36
Personal allowances	1,160		1.76
Children's allowances	960		1.45
Miscellaneous	500		0.76
Total variable expenses		$18,765	28.43
Total Expenses		$64,786	98.16
Surplus (deficit)		$ 1,214	1.84

3   Use financial ratios to evaluate your financial strength and progress.

Financial Ratios Assess Your Financial Strength and Progress

Financial ratios are numerical calculations designed to simplify the process of assessing your financial condition. Ratios can serve as yardsticks to help manage financial resources more effectively and to develop spending and credit-use patterns consistent with your goals. The first ratio that we will discuss pertains to liquidity, the next three provide insight into the burden of debt, and the last two ratios highlight progress toward building wealth. Evaluate each ratio in light of the particulars of each individual's and family's circumstances, considering such factors as stage in the life cycle, marital status, and financial goals. Calculators for these ratios can be found on the *Garman/Forgue* website.

Basic Liquidity Ratio

Liquidity is the speed and ease with which an asset can be converted to cash. You can use the **basic liquidity ratio** to determine the number of months that you could continue to meet your expenses using only your monetary assets should all income cease. For example, compare the monetary assets on the balance sheet for Victor and Maria Hernandez in Table 2.3 ($4420) with their monthly expenses in Table 2.5 ($64,786 ÷ 12 = $5399) using Equation (2.3):

$$\text{Basic liquidity ratio} = \frac{\text{monetary (liquid) assets}}{\text{monthly expenses}} \qquad \textbf{(2.3)}$$

$$= \frac{\$4420}{\$5398}$$

$$= 0.82$$

This financial ratio suggests that the Hernandezes may have insufficient monetary assets, unable to support them for even one month (0.82) if they faced a loss of income. According to researchers at the University of Texas, experts recommend that people should have monetary assets equal to three months' expenses in emergency cash reserves. Of course, the exact amount of monetary assets necessary depends on your family situation and your job. A smaller amount may be sufficient for your needs if you have adequate income protection through an employee benefit program, are employed in a job that is definitely not subject to layoffs, or have a spouse who works outside the home. Households dependent on the income from a self-employed person with fluctuating income need a larger emergency cash reserve. In the Hernandezes' case, their rental income would be a plus.

Asset-to-Debt Ratio

The **asset-to-debt ratio** compares total assets with total liabilities. It provides you with a broad measure of your financial liquidity. This ratio measures solvency and ability to pay debts, as shown in Equation (2.4). Calculations based on the figures in the Hernandezes' balance sheet (Table 2.3) show that the couple has ample assets compared with their debts because they own items worth more than three times what they owe. (Reversing the mathematics shows that they owe less than one-third of what they own.)

$$\text{Asset-to-debt ratio} = \frac{\text{total assets}}{\text{total debt}} \qquad (2.4)$$

$$= \frac{\$309{,}920}{\$101{,}365}$$

$$= 3.057$$

If you owe more than you own, then you are technically insolvent. While your current income may be sufficient to pay your current bills, you still do not have enough assets to cover all of your debts. Many people in such situations seek credit counseling, and some eventually declare bankruptcy. (These topics are discussed in Chapter 7, Installment Credit.)

Debt Service-to-Income Ratio

The **debt service-to-income ratio** provides a view of your total debt burden by comparing the dollars spent on gross annual debt repayments (including housing costs; rent or mortgage payments) with gross annual income. (It is similar to the back-end ratio used to determine the affordability of a mortgage discussed in Chapter 9.) Using data in Table 2.5, Equation (2.5) shows that the Hernandezes' $16,400 in annual loan repayments ($12,000 for the mortgage loan and $4400 for the automobile loan) amount to 24.85 percent of their $66,000 annual income. A ratio of 0.36 or less indicates that gross income is adequate to make debt repayments, including housing costs, and implies that you usually have some flexibility in budgeting for other expenses. This ratio should decrease as you grow older.

$$\text{Debt service-to-income ratio} = \frac{\text{annual debt repayments}}{\text{gross income}} \qquad (2.5)$$

$$= \frac{\$16{,}400}{\$66{,}000}$$

$$= 24.85\%$$

Debt Payments-to-Disposable Income Ratio

The **debt payments-to-disposable income ratio** divides monthly disposable personal income (not gross income) into monthly debt repayments (excluding mortgage debt). **Disposable personal income** is the amount of your income remaining after taxes and withholding for such purposes as insurance and union dues. Thus, it accurately estimates funds available for debt repayment. A debt payments-to-disposable income ratio of 16 percent or more is considered to be problematic because the person is overindebted and would be in serious financial trouble if a disruption in income occurred.

In the Hernandezes' case, their disposable monthly income from Table 2.5 is $3932.50 [($66,000 − $2980 − $6800 − $3100 − $720 − $4260 − $950) ÷ 12]. Their monthly debt repayments from Table 2.5 are $366.67 ($4400 ÷ 12). The result using Equation (2.6) is a debt payments-to-disposable income ratio of 9.32 percent.

Debt payments-to-disposable income ratio $= \dfrac{\text{monthly nonmortgage debt repayments}}{\text{disposable income}}$ (2.6)

$$= \dfrac{\$\ 366.67}{\$3932.50}$$

$$= 9.32\%$$

Investment Assets-to-Total Assets Ratio

The **investment assets-to-total assets ratio** compares the value of your investment assets with your net worth. This ratio reveals how well an individual or family is advancing toward their financial goals for capital accumulation, especially as related to retirement. Inserting the data from their balance sheet in Table 2.3 into Equation (2.7) shows that the Hernandezes have a ratio of 0.352 or 35.2 percent. As you can see, a little more than one-third of their total assets is made up of investment assets, a typical proportion for this stage in their lives. According to researchers at the University of Texas, experts recommend a ratio that is 50 percent or higher. Younger people often have an investment assets-to-net worth ratio of less than 20 percent, primarily because they have few investments.

Investment assets-to-total assets ratio $= \dfrac{\text{investment assets}}{\text{total assets}}$ (2.7)

$$= \dfrac{\$109{,}000}{\$309{,}920}$$

$$= 0.352$$

Savings Ratio

As noted earlier, the only way to build net worth is to spend less than your income. Simply put, you must save. How do you know if you are saving enough, or even what you are saving? The **savings ratio** compares your dollars saved to your after-tax income. For the Hernandez family, their savings (from Table 2.5) add up to $6474 ($1260 + 4000 + $1214) and their after-tax income totals $50,170 ($66,000 − $6800 − $3100 − $720 − $4260 − $950). Thus, their savings ratio is 12.9 percent, an acceptable rate.

Savings ratio $= \dfrac{\text{annual savings}}{\text{after-tax income}}$ (2.8)

$$= \dfrac{\$\ 6474}{\$50{,}170}$$

$$= 0.129$$

Other Ways to Assess Financial Progress

In addition to calculating financial ratios, you can use data from your balance sheet and cash-flow statement to analyze your finances. Consider the assets listed on the balance sheet for Victor and Maria Hernandez in Table 2.3. Do they have too few monetary assets compared with tangible and investment assets? Many experts recommend that 15

Did You Know? . . .

It Is Helpful to Use a Computer to Manage Your Finances

Using your computer to help manage your personal finances offers many benefits. Laborious calculations are sharply reduced, banking transactions can be performed with automatic updating of financial records, the balance sheet and cash-flow statements are automatically updated when transactions occur, and financial plans can be developed.

Quicken and Microsoft Money are the most popular vendors of personal finance software. Both provide complete financial planning systems. Several other programs focus primarily on income tax preparation, including TurboTax. In addition, many financial services companies (banks, mutual funds, and stock brokerages) have placed financial planning tools and calculators on their respective websites. Among the more popular are money.com, troweprice.com, kiplinger.com, brm.com, bankrate.com, and financenter.com. The Garman/Forgue website also has a number of templates, calculators, and worksheets that you can use in your own personal financial planning.

to 20 percent of your assets be in monetary form, and that this proportion increase as you near retirement. Do you have too much invested in one asset, or have you diversified, like the Hernandezes? Have your balance sheet figures changed in a favorable direction since last year? And, of course, are you making progress toward achieving your financial goals?

Examine your income figures to see what proportion comes from labor compared with the share that comes from investments. As demonstrated in Table 2.5 for the Hernandezes, most people desire to have a growing proportion of income from investments. Twenty percent is an achievable goal for many persons.

In the expense area, it is vital to ask, "Am I spending money where I really want to?" In which categories could you reduce expenses? In which categories could you increase income? The Hernandezes, for example, might consider setting aside additional monies for a year or so to build up sufficient monetary assets to improve their basic liquidity ratio.

Financial Recordkeeping Saves Time and Money

4 Know which financial records to maintain and where to keep them.

Your financial records will help determine where you are, where you have been, and where you are going in a financial sense. They enable you to review the results of financial transactions as well as permit other family members to find them in your absence. Having accessible, organized, and complete financial records is a prerequisite for effective financial management. In addition, organized records permit easier fact gathering when it is time to file income taxes.

Some of your records will be original, legal documents that record a particular financial activity. Debit and credit card receipts, canceled checks and receipts from bank deposits, individual retirement account (IRA) documents, insurance policies, and photocopies of filed income tax returns are examples. Other records are the lists and financial statements that you develop in the course of your financial planning. Examples are budgets, lists of goals, and balance sheets.

Table 2.6 (page 48) shows categories of financial records and the contents that might be included in each. Some records may be safely stored at home in a fire-resistant file

Table 2.6 Financial Records: Categories and Contents

Category	Contents	
	In Home Files	**In Safe-Deposit Box**
Financial plans/ budgeting	Copies of written financial plans, goals, and budgets Balance sheets and income and expense statements List of safe-deposit box contents Names and addresses of financial advisors	Names and addresses of financial advisors Copy of written financial plans, goals, and budgets
Financial services and investments	Checkbook and unused checks List of locations and account numbers for all bank accounts Bank account statements Locations and access numbers for safe-deposit boxes Account transaction receipts Retirement plan quarterly and annual reports Copies of trust documents (originals with trustees/attorney)	List of locations and account numbers for all bank accounts Certificates of deposit
Insurance	Original insurance policies List of insurance policies with premium amounts and due dates Premium payment receipts Calculation of life insurance needs Insurance claims forms Medical records for family	List of all insurance policies with company and agent names and addresses and policy numbers Listing with photographs or videotape of personal property
Housing, vehicles, and personal property	Copies of legal documents (leases, mortgage, deeds, titles) Property appraisals and inspection reports Warranty records Vehicle repair receipts	Original legal documents (leases, mortgage, deeds, titles) Copies of property appraisals Vehicle purchase contracts (until vehicle is sold)
Contributions	Receipts for all donations of cash or property Log of volunteer expenses	
Taxes	Copies of all income tax returns, both state and federal, for the past three years, including all supporting documentation and receipts Copies of all retirement plan transactions	Copies of all income tax filings, both state and federal, for the past three years Copies of all retirement plan transactions Records of securities purchased and sold
Personal	Copies of birth certificates and marriage license Copies of Social Security cards Copies of divorce decrees, property settlements, and custody agreements Receipts for alimony and child support payments Copies of advanced directives (wills, living wills, medical powers of attorney, durable powers of attorney with originals with attorney)	Passports while not being used Originals of birth certificates and marriage license Originals of Social Security cards Originals of divorce decrees, property settlements, and custody agreements

cabinet or a safe. Other records should be kept in a safe-deposit box. Safe-deposit boxes are secured lockboxes available for rent ($50 to $250 per year) in banks. Two keys must be used to open such a box. The customer keeps one key, and the bank holds the other. Many people keep duplicates of important records with relatives, because the likelihood of records at both locations being stolen or destroyed simultaneously is very small.

Where to Seek Professional Financial Planning Advice

5 Understand which factors to consider when choosing a professional financial planner.

At some point in their lives, most people rely on the advice of a professional to make financial plans and decisions. Quite often this consultation is done on a haphazard basis and focuses on a narrow area of their finances. These professionals, such as a family lawyer, tax preparer, insurance agent, credit counselor, or stockbroker, can be helpful within their specific area of expertise. Unfortunately, they may not have the broad education required to develop a thorough financial plan. Indeed, virtually anyone can call himself or herself a financial planner. All too often this person is really a salesperson for a narrow band of financial services and has a conflict of interest.

A true financial planner should be able to analyze a family's total needs in such areas as investments, taxes, insurance, education goals, and retirement and pull all of the information together into a cohesive plan. The planner may help a client select and prioritize goals and then rearrange assets and liabilities to fit the client's lifestyle, stage in the life cycle, and financial goals. In addition, financial planners should be problem solvers and coordinators. If necessary, they can make referrals to outside advisers, such as attorneys, accountants, trust officers, real estate brokers, stockbrokers, and insurance agents.

How Are Financial Planners Compensated?

Financial planners can be classified into four groups:

1. **Commission-only financial planners** live solely on the commissions they receive on the financial products (such as investments or insurance) they sell to their clients. In this case, the plan will be "free," but a commission will be paid to the advisor by the source of the financial product, such as an insurance company or mutual fund.

2. **Fee-only financial planners** earn no commissions and work solely on a fee-for-service basis—that is, they charge a specified fee (typically $50 to $200 per hour or 1 percent of the client's assets annually) for the services provided. They usually need five or more one-hour appointments to analyze a client's financial situation and to present a thorough plan. Fee-only planners do not sell financial products, such as stocks or insurance. Finding a true fee-only financial planner is difficult. Many offer fee-only services to clients who desire that approach but also sell commission products to other customers. Thus advertisements touting "fee only" may have no meaning whatsoever.

3. **Fee-based financial planners** charge an up-front fee for providing services and charge a commission on any securities trades or insurance purchases that they conduct on your behalf. Thus, they may appear less costly than fee-only planners but add to their up-front fee with commissions earned.

4. **Fee-offset financial planners** charge an annual or hourly fee. However, that fee will be reduced by any commissions earned off the purchase of financial products sold to the client.

Planners Should Have the Appropriate Professional Designations and Credentials

You should expect that persons calling themselves professionals will have an accredited educational background, have significant professional experience, be licensed by the appropriate government regulatory agency, and exhibit a commitment to helping others. Many financial planners have voluntarily undergone training and satisfied various qualifications for particular professional certifications to respond to these desires. Most certification examinations require three years of work experience prior to sitting for the examination.

A number of certifications and designations exist:

1. The **certified financial planner (CFP)** is perhaps the best-known certification in the field of financial planning. CFPs have been certified as having completed a comprehensive program of study approved by the International Board of Standards and Practices for Certified Financial Planners. To become a CFP, a planner must pass a two-day examination, have three years of work experience in the field, agree to adhere to a code of ethics, and continuously update his or her financial planning knowledge. The Financial Planners Association, a trade group, will provide a list of planners in your area [(800) 322-4237; www.fpanet.org]. The National Association of Personal Financial Advisors [(888) FEE-ONLY; www.feeonly.org] will provide names of fee-only planners in your area.

2. A **chartered financial consultant (ChFC)** has passed a financial services curriculum sponsored by the American College of Bryn Mawr, Pennsylvania, with an emphasis on life insurance. Closely related is the chartered life underwriter (CLU), who has received training in life insurance.

3. A **certified public accountant (CPA)** has passed a rigorous examination in accountancy under the auspices of the American Institute of Certified Public Accountants (AICPA; www.aicpa.org). Most CPAs focus on tax matters for individuals, small businesses, and corporations. Many CPAs who focus on financial planning have also qualified for the Personal Financial Specialist credential conferred by the AICPA.

4. An **accredited financial counselor (AFC)** has passed two examinations, one in personal finance and one in financial counseling, and subscribes to the AFC code of professional ethics. This program is offered through the Association for Financial Counseling and Planning Education (www.afcpe.org).

Advice from an Expert

How to Choose a Financial Planner

When considering hiring a financial planner, you should ask the following questions:

1. What credentials do you have to practice financial planning?
2. How long have you been in financial planning and related fields?
3. How long have you resided in the community, and who can vouch for your professional reputation?
4. Will you provide references from three or more clients you have counseled for at least two years?
5. Will you or an associate be involved in evaluating and updating the plan you suggest?
6. May I see examples of plans and monitoring reports that you have drawn up for other investors?
7. To what financial planning trade organizations do you belong?
8. If you earn commissions, from whom do you earn them?

In addition, you should check the background of the planner you are considering. Government agencies and self-regulatory organizations are available to help.

- The CFP Board of Standards [(888) 237-6275; www.cfp.net] keeps records on planners holding its credential.
- The National Association of State Insurance Commissioners [(816) 842-3600; www.naic.org] directs inquiries to the appropriate state agency where you can check on planners who also sell insurance products.
- The National Association of Securities Dealers Regulation [(800) 289-9999; www.nasdr.com] oversees securities brokers.
- The Securities and Exchange Commission [(800)732-0330; www.sec.gov] regulates investment advisers and all securities dealers.

Joan Koonce Moss
University of Georgia

5. A **mutual fund chartered counselor (MFCC)** has passed a nine-part education program and a final examination on topics ranging from mutual funds to ethics and professional conduct. This designation is conferred by the National Endowment for Financial Education and the Investment Company Institute.

6. A **registered investment adviser (RIA)** has registered with your state officials or the Securities and Exchange Commission (www.sec.gov) because he or she gives investment advice to more than five people each year. The RIA designation means simply that the person is registered; it does not mean that the adviser has met any government professional standards or passed any tests.

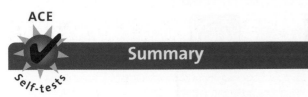

Summary

1. Most people need to undertake some form of financial planning to achieve their financial objectives. Financial planning should reflect an individual's or family's values and life-cycle circumstances and include appropriate objectives in three broad areas: plans for spending, plans for risk management, and plans for capital accumulation. Success in financial planning requires an understanding of one's values, explicitly stated financial goals, certain assumptions about the economy, and logical and consistent financial strategies.

2. Financial statements are compilations of personal financial data designed to furnish information about the way in which money has been used and about the financial condition of the individual or family. The balance sheet provides information on what you own, what you owe, and what the net result would be if you paid off all of your debts. The cash-flow statement lists income and expenditures over a specific period of time, such as the previous month or year.

3. Financial ratios can be used to assess your financial condition and progress so that you can better manage your financial resources and develop spending and credit-use patterns consistent with your goals.

4. Having accessible, organized, and complete financial records is a prerequisite to effective financial management. Your financial records are useful in preparing financial statements that can help you to evaluate where you are, where you have been, and where you are going in a financial sense.

5. When choosing a financial planner, you should recognize that many professional designations are meaningful in this field, such as CFP and ChFC. Costs may be charged on a fee-only, commission-only, fee-based, or fee-offset basis.

Key Terms

accredited financial counselor (AFC), 50
assets, 36
balance sheet (net worth statement), 35
cash-flow (income and expense) statement, 35
certified financial planner (CFP), 50
disposable personal income, 45
expenses, 39
fair market value, 36

fee-only financial planner, 49
financial goals, 33
financial planning, 31
financial ratios, 44
financial strategies, 35
fixed expenses, 40
income, 39
insolvent, 38
liabilities, 36
net worth, 36
values, 31
variable expenses, 40

Chapter Review Questions

1. Define and describe financial planning.

2. Give two examples of specific financial goals.

3. Distinguish between the two principal financial statements.

4. Why must assets be listed on a balance sheet at their fair market value?

5. Differentiate between monetary, tangible, and investment assets.

6. Differentiate between fixed and variable expenses.

7. Describe one change in a cash-flow statement that would affect net worth.

8. Explain how you can use financial ratios to help to evaluate your financial progress. Give an example.

9. What are the benefits of keeping good financial records?

10. Explain the four methods that financial planners use to charge for their services.

Group Discussion Issues

1. What are your three most important personal values? Give three examples of how those values might influence your financial plans.

2. What would you expect to see from the data included in the typical college student's balance sheet? Do you feel that your balance sheet is typical or atypical? Why?

3. College students often do not have much income or many expenses. Does this reduce or increase the impor-

tance of completing a cash-flow statement on a monthly basis?

4. Of the six financial ratios described in this chapter, which two are most revealing for the typical college student? Which two are the most revealing for a retiree?

5. What are the benefits and costs of using a financial planner? How do these differ depending on the way the planner is compensated? If you were to become a planner, in which professional designation(s) would you be most interested?

Decision-Making Cases

▶ **Case 1**
Budgeting Advice for Two Young Men

Bill Bailey, a poultry scientist from Little Rock, Arkansas, thinks that his two sons, who live at home, need budgeting advice. Ralph, age 19, works as a sales representative for an electronics manufacturer and regularly spends all of his $2400 monthly income. Wilfred, 24, is a midlevel manager in a psychological testing company. He has completed three evening classes toward a master's degree and usually saves about 10 percent of his monthly salary of $3400. Wilfred is also contemplating marriage. Bill would like you to offer suggestions to his sons about financial management.

(a) What advice would you offer Ralph regarding life's opportunities?

(b) Realizing that Wilfred is contemplating marriage, what advice would you offer him regarding life's opportunities? How might his goals differ from Ralph's goals?

(c) Use the data in the balance sheets for Bill Soshnik and Victor and Maria Hernandez (Tables 2.2 and 2.3) to advise Wilfred on how his financial life will change when he marries and beyond.

▶ **Case 2**
Manipulation of a Cash-Flow Statement

Using the cash-flow statement developed by Bill Soshnik (see Table 2.4), enter the data from the Garman/Forgue website. The program will calculate the totals.

(a) Print the cash-flow statement, and compare the results with the text for accuracy.

(b) What original source records might Bill have used to develop his cash-flow statement?

(c) Use the data in the cash-flow statements for Bill (Table 2.4) and for Victor and Maria Hernandez (Table 2.5) to advise Bill on how his financial life will change as he becomes older.

Financial Math Questions

1. Review the financial statements of Victor and Maria Hernandez (Tables 2.3 and 2.5) and respond to the following questions:

(a) Using the data in the Hernandezes' balance sheet, calculate an investment assets-to-net worth ratio. How would you interpret the ratio? The Hernandez family appears to have too few monetary assets compared with tangible and investment assets. How would you suggest that they remedy that situation over the next few years?

(b) Comment on the couple's diversification of their investment assets.

(c) Calculate the asset-to-debt ratio for Victor and Maria. How does this information help you understand their financial situation? How do their total assets compare with their total liabilities?

(d) The Hernandezes seem to receive most of their income from labor rather than investments. What actions would you recommend for them to remedy that imbalance over the next few years?

(e) The Hernandezes want to take a two-week vacation next summer, and they have only eight months to save the necessary $1200. What reasonable changes in expenses and income should they consider to increase net income and make the needed $150 per month?

2. Bob Green has been a retail salesclerk for six years. At age 35, he is divorced with one child, Amanda, age 7. Bob's salary is $36,000 per year. He regularly receives $250 per month for child support from Amanda's mother. Bob invests $100 each month ($50 in his mutual fund and $50 in U.S. savings bonds). Using the following information, construct a balance sheet and a cash-flow statement for Bob.

ASSETS	Amount
Vested retirement benefits	$3000
(no employee contribution)	
Money market account	5000
(includes $150 of interest earned last year)	
Mutual fund	4000
(includes $200 of reinvested dividend income from last year)	
Checking account	1000
Personal property	5000
Automobile	3000
U.S. savings bonds	3000

LIABILITIES	Outstanding Balance
Dental bill	$ 450
(pays $25 per month and is included in uninsured medical/dental)	

Visa (pays $100 per month)	1500
Student loan (pays $100 per month)	7500

ANNUAL EXPENSES	Amount
Auto insurance	$ 780
Rent	9100
Utilities	1200
Phone	680
Cable	360
Food	3000
Uninsured medical/dental	1000
Dry cleaning	480
Personal care	420
Gas, maintenance, license	2120
Clothes	500
Entertainment	1700
Vacations/visitation travel	1300
Child care	3820
Gifts	400
Miscellaneous	300
Taxes	6400
Health insurance	2440

Money Matters Continuing Cases

Throughout this book we will present a continuing narrative about two couples: Victor and Maria Hernandez and Harry and Belinda Johnson. A brief description of the lives of these two couples follows.

Victor and Maria Hernandez

Victor and Maria, both in their late thirties, have two children: John, age 13 and Joseph, age 15. Victor has had a long sales career with a major retail appliance store. Maria works part-time as a dental hygienist. The Hernandezes own two vehicles and their home, on which they have a mortgage. They will face many financial challenges over the next twenty years, as their children drive, go to college, and leave home and go out in the world on their own. Victor and Maria also recognize the need to further prepare for their retirement and the challenges of aging.

Victor and Maria Hernandez Analyze Their Financial Statements

Victor and Maria Hernandez spent some time making up their first balance sheet, which is shown in Table 2.3. Using the data in their balance sheet, complete the following calculations and interpret the results.

1. Victor and Maria are a bit confused about how various financial activities can affect their net worth. Assume that their home is now appraised at $192,000 and the value of their automobile has dropped to $9500. Calculate and characterize the effects of these changes on their net worth.

2. If Victor and Maria take out a bank loan for $1545 and pay off their credit card debts totaling $1545, what effects would these changes have on their net worth?

3. If Victor and Maria sell their New York 2016 bond and put the cash into their savings account, what effects would this move have on their net worth and their basic liquidity ratio?

Harry and Belinda Johnson

Harry graduated with a bachelor's degree in interior design last spring from a large midwestern university near his hometown. Belinda has a degree in business finance from a university on the West Coast. Harry and Belinda both worked on their school's student newspapers and met at a conference during their junior year in college. They were married last June and live in an apartment in Kansas City. They currently own one car and Belinda uses public transportation to commute to work. Harry and Belinda look forward to advancing in their careers, buying their own home, and having children.

The Johnsons' Financial Statements

Harry and Belinda both found jobs in the same city. Harry works at a small interior design firm and earns a gross salary of $2500 per month. He also receives $3000 in interest income per year from a trust fund set up by his deceased father's estate; the trust fund will continue to pay that amount until 2012. Belinda works as a salesperson for a regional stock brokerage firm. She earns $3000 per month, and when she finishes her training program in another two months, her gross salary will increase $300 per month. Belinda has many job-related benefits, including life insurance, health insurance, and a credit union. The Johnsons live in an apartment located approximately halfway between their places of employment. Harry drives about ten minutes to his job, and Belinda travels about 15 minutes via public transportation to reach her downtown job. Harry and Belinda's apartment is very nice, but small, and it is furnished mostly with furniture given to them by their families. Soon after starting their first jobs, Harry and Belinda decided to begin their financial planning. Each had taken a college course in personal finance, so after initial discussion, they worked together for two evenings to develop the two financial statements presented on page 55.

1. Briefly describe how Harry and Belinda probably determined the fair market prices for each of their tangible and investment assets.

2. Using the data from the cash-flow statement developed by Harry and Belinda, calculate a basic liquidity ratio, asset-to-debt ratio, debt service-to-income ratio, debt payments-to-disposable income ratio, and investment assets-to-net worth ratio. What do these ratios tell you about the Johnsons' financial situation? Should Harry and Belinda incur more debt?

Balance Sheet for Harry and Belinda Johnson— January 1, 2005

	Dollars	Percent
ASSETS		
Monetary assets		
Cash on hand	$ 1,178	5.48
Savings (First Federal Bank)	890	4.14
Savings (Far West Savings and Loan)	560	2.60
Savings (Smith Brokerage Credit Union)	160	0.74
Checking account (First Federal Bank)	752	3.50
Total monetary assets	**$ 3,540**	16.45
Tangible Assets		
Automobile (3-year-old Toyota)	$11,000	51.13
Personal property	2,300	10.69
Furniture	1,700	7.90
Total tangible assets	**$15,000**	69.72
Investment Assets		
Harry's retirement account	$ 1,425	6.62
Belinda's retirement account	1,550	7.20
Total investment assets	**$ 2,975**	13.83
Total Assets	**$21,515**	100.00
LIABILITIES		
Short-term liabilities		
Visa credit card	$ 390	1.81
Sears card	45	0.21
Dental bill	400	1.86
Total short-term liabilities	**$ 835**	3.88
Long-term liabilities		
Student loan (Belinda)	$ 3,800	17.66
Automobile loan (First Federal Bank)	8,200	38.11
Total long-term liabilities	**$12,000**	55.78
Total Liabilities	**$12,835**	59.66
Net Worth	**$ 8,680**	40.34
Total Liabilities and Net Worth	**$21,515**	100.00

Cash-Flow Statement for Harry and Belinda Johnson July 1–December 31, 2004 (First Six Months of Marriage)

	Dollars	Percent
INCOME		
Harry's gross income ($2500 x 6)	$15,000	41.64
Belinda's gross income ($3000 x 6)	18,000	49.97
Interest on savings account	24	0.07
Harry's trust fund	3,000	8.33
Total Income	**$36,024**	100.00
EXPENSES		
Fixed expenses		
Rent	$ 5,400	14.99
Renter's insurance	220	0.61
Automobile loan payment	1,710	4.75
Automobile insurance	420	1.17
Medical insurance (withheld from salary)	750	2.08
Student loan payments	870	2.42
Life insurance (withheld from salary)	54	0.15
Cable television	540	1.50
Health club	300	0.83
Savings (withheld from salary)	900	2.50
Harry's retirement plan (6% of salary)	900	2.50
Belinda's retirement plan (4% of salary)	720	2.00
Federal income taxes (withheld from salary)	4,600	12.77
State income taxes (withheld from salary)	1,600	4.44
Social Security (withheld from salary)	2,520	7.00
Automobile registration	90	0.25
Total fixed expenses	**$21,594**	59.94
Variable Expenses		
Food	$ 2,300	6.38
Utilities	750	2.08
Telephone	420	1.17
Gasoline, oil, maintenance	700	1.94
Doctor's and dentist's bills	710	1.97
Medicines	345	0.96
Clothing and upkeep	1,900	5.27
Church and charity	800	2.22
Gifts	720	2.00
Christmas gifts	350	0.97
Public transportation	720	2.00
Personal allowances	1,040	2.89
Entertainment	980	2.72
Vacation (holiday)	700	1.94
Vacation (summer)	600	1.67
Miscellaneous	545	1.51
Total variable expenses	**$13,580**	37.70
Total Expenses	**$35,174**	97.64
Surplus (deficit)	**$ 850**	2.36

What Would You Recommend Now?

Now that you have read the chapter on financial planning, what would you recommend to Brian Patterson in the case at the beginning of the chapter regarding:

1. Determining what the couple owns and owes?

2. Better understanding the family's income and expenditures?

3. Using the information in Brian's newly prepared financial statements to summarize the family's financial situation?

4. Setting up an organized recordkeeping system so that he and Marlene can have easier access to accurate information when needed?

5. Who they might contact to obtain financial advice?

Exploring the World Wide Web

To complete these exercises, go to the *Garman/Forgue* website at college.hmco.com/business/students. Under General Business, select the title of this text. Click on the Internet Exercises link for this chapter, and answer the questions that appear on the Web page.

1. Visit the website of the Financial Planning Association. Read over its answer to the question, Ten Questions to Ask When Choosing a Financial Planner.

2. Visit the website for SRI Consulting, where you will find the VALS questionnaire. This short questionnaire will help you identify your values in the context of the values of other members of American society.

3. Visit the website of the Financial Planning Association. Read through the code of ethics for members of the organization. What does the code tell you about the members?

4. Visit the website set up to accompany this text, where you will find a balance sheet template that you can use to determine your net worth. Is your net worth at the level that you expected for this point in your life? What are the prospects for change in your net worth over the next three years?

5. Visit the website set up to accompany this text, where you will find a cash-flow statement template that you can use to determine your surplus or loss over the past month. What changes might you put into effect for the next month to avert a deficit or enhance your surplus?

Visit the Garman/Forgue website . . .

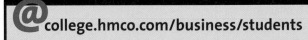 college.hmco.com/business/students

Under General Business, select *Personal Finance 8e*. There, among other valuable resources, you will find a complete glossary, ACE questions, links to help you complete the chapter exercises, and links to other personal finance sites.

Part Two

Money Management

CHAPTER 3   Budgeting and Cash-Flow Management

CHAPTER 4   Managing Income Taxes

CHAPTER 5   Management of Monetary Assets

CHAPTER 6   Credit Use and Credit Cards

CHAPTER 7   Installment Credit

CHAPTER 8   Automobiles and Other Major Purchases

CHAPTER 9   The Housing Expenditure

Chapter 3

Budgeting and Cash-Flow Management

LEARNING OBJECTIVES

After reading this chapter, you should be able to:

1 **Describe** how financial planning and budgeting are the keys to achieving long- and short-term financial goals.

2 **Organize** your personal budget.

3 **Explain** how the decision-making phase of budgeting resolves conflicting financial needs and wants.

4 **Describe** how to implement a budget.

5 **List** techniques to keep income and expenditures within planned budget totals.

6 **List** three ways to evaluate a budget.

7 **Give** details about how people can discuss money matters effectively.

Recall the case of Brian and Marlene Patterson from Chapter 2. Brian decided to take Marlene out to a nice restaurant to discuss his plans for going back to school. He waited until dessert and then mentioned his desires—but in vague terms, leaving out the financial implications. The discussion did not go well. Marlene was upset that he wasn't thinking about her plans. She reminded Brian that she needed to finish her master's degree within six years of starting her teaching career. She used the expensive dinner as an example to illustrate how the couple tended to overspend. Marlene asked many financial questions that Brian could not answer because he did not bring the financial statements he had prepared.

Both Brian and Marlene were silent during their ride home, but started discussing the topic again once they arrived at their apartment. Marlene began to understand Brian's desire to finish his degree but remained concerned about the couple's finances. The two had other goals that needed to be discussed, such as buying a home, having children, planning for their children's education, and saving for their own retirements. Brian's plans had opened up a significant number of previously unresolved issues related to their finances. Marlene wanted to discuss Brian's educational plans in the context of all of their financial objectives.

What would you recommend to Brian and Marlene on the subject of budgeting regarding:

1. Developing a series of financial goals and prioritizing them?

2. Getting organized to set up a budget if Brian does go back to school?

3. Controlling spending once their budget is established?

4. Periodically assessing their progress?

5. Discussing their finances comfortably and successfully?

The old saying, "If you fail to plan, you plan to fail," applies to success in money matters, too. Achieving financial success requires that you actually implement your financial plans. This invariably involves budgeting in some way. Budgeting helps you make intelligent financial decisions that are consistent with your values and goals. You might view budgeting as painful or difficult, but there is no way around it.

This chapter outlines the budgeting process in sufficient detail for you to be able to make budgeting work for you. To start our discussion, we examine the relationship between personal financial planning and budgeting. This discussion prepares the way for coverage of the six phases of budgeting: establishing specific financial goals, organizing, decision making, implementing, controlling, and evaluating. We end the chapter by describing how families can effectively talk about money, which is a topic many people find difficult to discuss.

Golden Rules of

Budgeting and Cash-Flow Management

Financial success comes from learning the Golden Rules of personal finance and then putting what you have learned into practice. Make the following your money habits in budgeting and cash-flow management.

1. Take time to list your financial goals, along with a realistic plan for achieving them, and update both once a year.
2. Spend less than you earn by paying yourself first and using a budget to control spending.
3. Establish a year-long revolving savings fund and evaluate its success as time passes.
4. Before committing to a significant expenditure or credit purchase, determine whether it really fits into your budget and financial plans.
5. Regularly make a list of five important money topics that you should discuss with a significant other, and do so.

---

1 Describe how financial planning and budgeting are the keys to achieving long- and short-term financial goals.

The Relationships Among Financial Planning, Budgeting, and Financial Goals

Knowing the relationships among financial planning, budgeting, and your financial goals is crucial to realizing success in personal finance. In Chapter 2, we identified *financial planning* as the process of developing and implementing a coordinated series of financial plans to achieve financial success. This process includes the preparation of financial statements, such as the cash-flow statement and the balance sheet. **Budgeting** is the process of projecting, organizing, monitoring, and controlling future income and expenditures (cash and credit purchases as well as savings).

The Relationship Between Financial Planning and Budgeting

Figure 3.1 illustrates how to think about budgets and financial statements. The cash-flow statement focuses on *where you have been* financially, the balance sheet shows *where you are* financially at the present time, and the budget indicates *where you want to go* in the future. Your personal values are always the starting point in financial planning and budgeting. **Values** are fundamental beliefs about what is important, desirable, and worthwhile. Your values serve as the basis for your financial goals. Once you identify your current financial position by examining information from your balance sheet and your cash-flow statement, you can develop plans for spending, risk management, and capital accumulation. Your financial goals evolve from plans, and both general and specific goals drive the creation of budgets.

A **budget** is a document or set of documents used to record both projected and actual income and expenditures over a period of time. The budgeting process represents

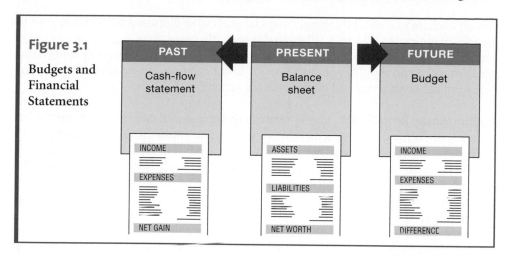

Figure 3.1

Budgets and Financial Statements

the major mechanism through which financial plans are carried out and goals are achieved. Budgeting is narrower in scope than financial planning, because it is primarily concerned with projecting future income and expenditures for a month or a year and reconciling the two with your short- and long-term financial goals.

Budgeting forces you to think about what is important in your life, what things you want to own, how you want to live, what it will take to do that, and, more generally, what you want to achieve in life. The process gives you control over your finances, and it empowers you to achieve your financial goals while simultaneously (and successfully) confronting any unforeseen events. The six-phase budgeting process illustrated in Figure 3.2 can be adapted to suit your needs while giving you the competence and confidence to manage your financial affairs successfully—year after year.

Budgeting and Financial Goals

Goal setting demands that you take a realistic look at your future income and the amounts needed to reach your established goals. It requires careful and reasoned thinking; it is

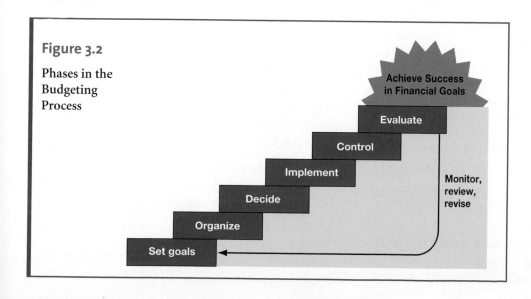

Figure 3.2

Phases in the Budgeting Process

not an exercise in wishful thinking. Financial goals were discussed in the context of financial planning in Chapter 2, although the goals discussed there were more general in nature and were tied directly to values. Here, in the **goal-setting phase of budgeting,** goals must be specific. They should contain dollar-amount targets (both for the long term and the short term) and target dates for achievement.

Setting Long-Term Goals.   **Long-term goals** are financial targets or ends that an individual or family desires to achieve more than 1 year in the future—perhaps 2, 5, or even 30 years hence. Such goals provide direction for overall financial planning as well as shorter-term budgeting. For example, a long-term goal might be to save $22,500 within 5 years for a down payment on a home. Other goals might be more general, such as to have sufficient common stock investments by age 50 to receive dividends equivalent to 20 percent of your salary income.

If you have a small income or large debts, it may be unrealistic to think of long-term goals until any current financial difficulties are resolved. You may be unable to do much more than take care of immediate necessities, such as housing expenses, food, and util-

Tax Considerations and Consequences

Saving for Children's College

A long-term goal of many families is saving for their children's college education. To encourage such saving, the U.S. Congress and many state governments have established mechanisms whereby people can lower their income tax bills while they save for this purpose.

Put Money for College in the Child's Name. Parents and others may save on income taxes by giving cash or other assets to children. For children younger than age 14, all income earned on assets placed in a Uniform Gifts to Minors Act (or Uniform Transfers to Minors Act, depending on the state of residence) **custodial account** above an annually adjusted earnings level is taxable at the child's (presumably lower) income tax rate, not the parent's income tax rate. Also, the first $800 of **unearned income** (the income from an investment) that the child receives is tax-free. Unearned income in excess of $1600 is taxed at the parent's (likely higher) rate. Starting at age 14, when income earned on the fund may have grown sufficiently to be taxed, the federal income taxes are figured at the child's lower rate (often 10 percent).

Put Money in an IRA. Money invested in a traditional or Roth IRA retirement plan (explained in Chapters 4 and 18) can be withdrawn and used to pay for a child's college education.

Save Through a Coverdell Education Savings Account. Contributions up to a maximum of $2000 per

year may be made to a Coverdell education savings account (also known as an education savings account and formerly known as an education IRA) to pay the future education costs for a child younger than age 18. The money and earnings on the account can be used later to pay for public, private, or religious school expenses, from kindergarten through trade school or college, including tuition, fees, tutoring, uniforms, home computers, educational computer games, transportation, and extended day care.

Put Money in a Section 529 College Savings Plan. Named after the related section of the Internal Revenue Service Code, many states have established a Section 529 college savings plan. Withdrawals may be used to pay qualified higher-education expenses, including tuition, room, and board.

Contribute to a Prepaid Tuition Plan. A state-sponsored prepaid tuition plan allows parents, relatives, and friends to purchase a child's future college education at today's prices by guaranteeing that today's payment will be used for the future tuition payments at an approved institution of higher education in a particular state. The funds may only be used to pay for tuition—not for room, board, or supplies.

ity bills. In such instances, you need to focus on short-term efforts to improve your financial situation.

Target dates may serve as checkpoints in your progress toward reaching long-term goals or as deadlines to indicate when a goal should be achieved. Nonetheless, long-term goals need to remain somewhat flexible given the length of time involved in achieving them. In addition, some goals may need to be changed if they prove unrealistic. As your circumstances change, you should review and make adjustments or deletions to your goals. Likewise, as desired financial outcomes are achieved or changed, you can add new goals to your overall financial plans. An annual review of your progress made in achieving your long-term goals is a good idea.

Developing Short-Term Goals from Long-Term Goals.   **Short-term goals** are financial targets or ends that can be achieved in a year or less. They should be consistent with the general direction of long-term goals and objectives. For example, if a long-term goal is to be debt-free in three years, a short-term objective might be to pay off a particular credit card balance within six months. Short-term goals provide the key input for the budget-making process. The task is to design a budget (perhaps covering one month at a time) that projects future expenditures and that, if followed, will permit you to reach your short-term goals.

You should explicitly express both long- and short-term goals when possible. The worksheet examples in Figure 3.3 (page 64) provide rough estimates of how much must be saved to reach both types of goals. In particular, short-term goals must be stated clearly, or you will never know when you have achieved them. "To save enough for a down payment on an automobile," for example, is too vague. Instead, the short-term goal is more clear when it is stated as "to save $2400 by December of this year for a down payment on a new Ford Mustang."

Some short-term goals are ends in themselves because they can be fully achieved within one year. When placing dollar amounts on goals as far as one or two years in the

How to . . .

Effectively Achieve Your Financial Goals

The goal-setting process has seven steps:

1. Identify the goal as specifically as possible.
2. Set a clear deadline to reach the goal and put intermediate target dates on long-term goals, thereby creating short-term goals.
3. List specific obstacles to the goal's achievement and devise strategies to overcome them.
4. List your skills, knowledge, and other people who will help you reach the goal.
5. List the benefits to yourself that will occur when you reach the goal. You are most likely to achieve a goal when you are convinced that it really is "your goal," when you make an emotional commitment to the goal, when short-term goals lead to long-term goals, and when you can visualize yourself receiving its benefits.
6. Establish an automatic savings plan by using payroll withholding or electronic transfers from checking to savings accounts.
7. Tell others about the goal you set because they can help keep you motivated to achieve it.

Figure 3.3

Goals Worksheet for Harry and Belinda Johnson

Date worksheet prepared ___Feb. 20, 2005___

1 LONG-TERM GOALS	2 AMOUNT NEEDED	3 MONTH & YEAR NEEDED*	4 MONTHS TO SAVE	5 DATE START SAVING	6 MONTHLY AMOUNT TO SAVE (2 ÷ 4)
European vacation	$3,000	Aug. 2007	30	Feb. '05	$100
Down payment on new auto	5,000	Oct. 2008	45	Jan. '05	111
Down payment on home	26,078	Dec. 2010	60	Jan. '05	435

Date worksheet prepared ___Feb. 20, 2005___

1 SHORT-TERM GOALS	2 AMOUNT NEEDED	3 MONTH & YEAR NEEDED*	4 MONTHS TO SAVE	5 DATE START SAVING	6 MONTHLY AMOUNT TO SAVE (2 ÷ 4)
Partial down payment on new auto	$1,332	Dec. '05	12	Jan. '05	$111
House fund	4,815	Dec. '05	12	Jan. '05	401
Christmas vacation	700	Dec. '05	12	Jan. '05	58
Summer vacation	600	Aug. '05	6	Mar. '05	100
Anniversary party	250	June '05	5	Feb. '05	50

*Goals requiring five years or more to achieve require consideration of investment return and after-tax yield, which will be presented in later chapters.

future, it is generally fair to assume that interest earned on savings will offset inflationary increases. Thus you can simply divide the dollar amount of the long-term goal measured in today's price by the number of short-term time periods needed to determine the short-term goals.

For a time period exceeding one or two years, consider the example of Belinda and Harry Johnson. Belinda and Harry are newlyweds who hope to buy their own home someday. They have decided to establish a five-year savings plan to purchase their first home. After studying the real estate market in their area, the couple figures that they will need 15 percent of the purchase price of the home for a down payment (10 percent) and moving expenses and initial decorating costs (5 percent). Condominiums that they would like and that seem to be affordable for first-time buyers are currently selling for approximately $150,000 in their area. Simple division would indicate that $22,500 would be necessary in five years. Belinda and Harry are sharp enough to realize, however, that housing costs have been rising about 3 percent per year in their community. Using Appendix Table A.1, they calculate that the type of housing they are considering will cost $173,850 ($150,000 × 1.159 from Appendix Table A.1) and require a financial nest egg of $26,078 ($173,850 $\times$ 0.15) in five years.* The Johnsons also know that their savings will earn interest that can be used to reach their goal. Using Appendix Table A.3, they calculate they would need to save $4815 per year ($26,078 $\div$ 5.416 from Appendix Table A.3) if they could earn 4 percent on their savings. As the Johnsons budget monthly, they have set a monthly goal of saving $401.25 ($4815 $\div$ 12) to achieve their first-year short-term goal (as indicated in Figure 3.3) on the way to buying their first home.†

Precautionary Goals.   Not all savings are earmarked for specific purposes. You should also set aside savings to be able to withstand irregular and unexpected expenses. An example would be an emergency fund sufficient to cover two to three months of lost income due to a job change or illness. In addition, you should set aside savings to cover certain bills that do not come in every month—insurance bills, for example. Similarly, you should have a revolving savings fund (discussed later in this chapter) that can help you get through months when your income is lower or your expenses are higher than normal. Figure 3.4 shows the interrelationships among long-term, short-term, and precautionary goals.

Prioritizing Goals.   Many people become discouraged in the goal-setting phase of budgeting because they quickly realize that they cannot achieve all of their goals immediately. For this reason, it makes sense to attack the most important financial goals

Figure 3.4

The Relationships Among the Three Types of Goals

TYPE OF GOAL	PURPOSE
Long-Term Goals	Retirement Children's college fund Purchase of a first home or vacation residence Vehicle purchase Start a business
Short-Term Goals	Interim steps for the achievement of long-term goals Vacations Specials events such as weddings Holiday gifts Birth of a child
Precautionary Goals	Emergency fund Revolving savings fund Insurance or nonmonthly and irregular bills

*You may wish to review the time value of money material from Chapter 1.
†Note that their savings each month would also earn interest resulting in monthly, rather than annual, compounding. Appendix Table A.3 cannot be used to make such fine distinctions. Using a financial calculator, we can more accurately calculate a monthly savings amount of $398.34. While the difference is minor here, when long time horizons are involved, frequent compounding can mean additional thousands of dollars.

first. But what are the most important goals? One guideline is to pay off high-interest credit cards as soon as possible. Another is to contribute as much as possible to one's retirement plan. Don't be lured into following everyone else's approach. Many college graduates buy a new car soon after getting their first job because such a vehicle signifies having "made it." Give careful consideration to your priorities and recall that every action carries not only the dollar cost of the action taken, but also the opportunity cost of the alternatives forgone. The key is to recognize trade-offs when prioritizing your goals. In some cases, to achieve your long-term goals, you may have to defer some of your short-term desires.

The Johnsons decided that their new car and European vacation would have to wait. Instead, they will concentrate on building an emergency fund and saving for a home, their Christmas and summer vacations, and an anniversary party.

The Organization Phase of Budgeting

2 Organize your personal budget.

The **organization phase** of budgeting involves establishing the structural aspects of your budget. Getting organized entails choosing a recording format, selecting the cash or accrual basis of budgeting, determining which budgeting classifications are appropriate for you, and identifying the time period of your budget. Table 3.1 (page 68) offers both simple and complex budget classifications, and Table 3.2 (page 71) shows five sample budgets that you may consider using for your own budget.

Select an Appropriate Recordkeeping Format

Recordkeeping is the process of recording the sources and amounts of dollars earned and spent. Its primary value derives from its ability to provide detailed information about what happened financially during any given period of time. Recording the estimated and actual amounts for both income and expenditures will help you monitor your money flow. Keeping track of income and expenses may seem an uninteresting task, but it is the only way to collect sufficient information to evaluate how close you are to achieving your financial objectives.

A **ledger** is a sheet of paper, form, booklet, or computer file for maintaining income and expenditure records. You can create your own ledgers or you can purchase forms that satisfy your needs. Figure 3.5 shows four samples of self-prepared budget ledgers that vary in complexity. In a later section of this chapter, you will learn how budget data are recorded.

To keep even better records, you can purchase a computer software program designed specifically for budgeting or use a more general spreadsheet program such as Microsoft Excel. Computerized ledgers have many advantages, especially the ability to make adjustments, corrections, and updates. Quicken and Microsoft Money are two popular software programs that are excellent for budgeting. The *Garman/Forgue* website provides a budget template and several financial calculators that might also be useful for your budgeting needs.

Figure 3.5

Recordkeeping Formats

Food Budget: $90			
DATE	ACTIVITY	AMOUNT	BALANCE
2-6	Groceries	$20	$70
2-9	Dinner out	18	62
2-14	Groceries	11	

(a) Simple form for each budget classification

(b) More complex form for each classification

(c) Simple form for all expense classifications

DATE	ACTIVITY	AMOUNT BUDGETED	EXPENDITURES	BALANCE
2-1	Budget estimate	$90		$90
2-6	Groceries		$20	70
2-9	Dinner out		18	52
2-14	Groceries		11	41
2-20	Groceries		25	16
2-28	February Totals	$90	$74	$16

DATE	ACTIVITY	Food Budget: $90	Clothing Budget: $30	EXPENDITURES Auto Budget: $60	Rent Budget: $275	Savings Budget: $60	Utilities Budget: $40	TOTAL Budget: $680	REMARKS
2-1	Gasoline			10				10	
2-6	Groceries	20						20	Had friends over
2-8	Gasoline			17				17	Good price
2-9	Dinner out	18						18	
2-14	Groceries	11						11	Pepsi on sale
2-15	Subtotals	/49		/27				/76	

(d) More complex form for all income and expenditure classifications

			INCOME Salary	Other	TOTAL	EXPENDITURES Food	Clothing	Auto	Rent	Savings	Utilities	TOTAL	REMARKS
		Estimates	700	40	740	90	30	60	275	60	40	680	
		Balance forwarded from January	—	—	—	6	—	14	—	—	2	28	
		Sum	700	40	740	96	30	74	275	60	42	708	
DATE	ACTIVITY	CASH IN											
2-1	Paycheck	700	700										
2-1	Texaco-gasoline							10				10	
2-6	Safeway-groceries					20						20	Had friends over
2-8	7/11-gasoline							17				17	Good price
2-9	Dinner out-pizza					18						18	
2-14	Giant-groceries					11						11	Pepsi on sale
2-15	Subtotals	/700				/49		/17				/76	
2-16	Cell phone										41	41	
2-28	Totals	700		40	740	83	28	17	275	60	41	660	Good month

Table 3.1 Sample Budget Classifications and Expense Guidelines

	Income	Fixed Expenses*	Variable Expenses*
Simple	Salary Nonsalary	Housing and utilities (25–45%) Insurance (2–10%) Savings and investments (6–20%) Taxes (8–20%)	Food (12–30%)† Transportation (3–10%) Clothing (1–10%) Health care (2–8%) Entertainment/vacations (2–10%) Personal/miscellaneous (2–5%) Credit payments (0–15%) Gifts and contributions (1–10%)
Complex	Salary Rent Interest Dividends Captial gains Tax refunds Loans Other	Retirement contributions Individual retirement account Home mortgage loan Life insurance Health insurance Disability insurance Homeowner's insurance Automobile insurance Cable television Church Other contributions Christmas gifts Automobile loan or lease Loan 1 Loan 2 Dues and club memberships Savings (withheld from salary) Federal income taxes State income taxes Social Security taxes Real estate property taxes Personal property taxes Mutual fund investment Monthly investment plan Child support/alimony	Revolving budget savings fund Other savings Food at home Food away from home Electricity and gas Water Telephone Gasoline and oil Automobile maintenance/repairs Automobile license renewal Automobile registration Public transportation Home maintenance/renovations Gifts Doctors and dentists Medicines and drugs Hospital bills Veterinary costs Legal advice Child care Domestic help Clothing and accessories Hobby supplies Sports equipment CDs, DATs, tapes, DVDs, and records Books Newspaper/magazine subscriptions Tobacco products Alcoholic beverages Education and tuition School books and supplies Furnishings and appliances Personal care products Entertainment/recreation Vacations/long weekends Credit card 1 Credit card 2 Investments—other

*The percentages represent the range of expenses of various family units.
†The U.S. Department of Agriculture reports that more than half of all meals are eaten outside the home.

Use the Cash or Accrual Basis

You can use either of two systems of financial recording in your budgeting process. **Cash-basis budgeting** recognizes earnings and expenditures when money is actually received or paid out. **Accrual-basis budgeting** recognizes earnings and expenditures when money is earned and expenditures are incurred, regardless of when money is actually received or paid. Most people employ the cash basis in the budgeting process because it is easier to use. Either method will work as long as you use it consistently.

Select Appropriate Budget Classifications

There are two broad budgeting classifications: income (money earned or received) and expenditures (money spent). Each can be subdivided into more detailed classifications.

Table 3.1 lists both simple and complex budget classifications for income and expenses. Even though the simple budgeting classifications illustrated in the table include only 12 expense items, they represent a suitable format for many people. (Some computer programs offer more than 100 budget classifications.) You can subdivide any extraordinarily broad categories into more detailed classifications when more specificity is warranted. You should have sufficient classifications so that very few of your expenditures (less than 5 percent of total spending) are classified as miscellaneous.

Savings can be categorized in four ways: (1) savings withheld from a paycheck and deposited directly to a savings account; (2) savings as a fixed expenditure; (3) savings as a variable expenditure; and (4) savings as what is left over after all other expenditures are paid. The first two methods embody the concept of "pay yourself first"—saving and investing before you pay other expenses—one of the major precepts of personal financial planning. The problem with relying solely on the last two methods of saving is that you might not save at all. Therefore, before paying bills and other financial obligations, set aside an affordable amount each month in accounts designated for long-range goals and unexpected emergencies.

Select Appropriate Time Periods

Most people who budget create a plan to cover income and expenses for one month at a time. Using a one-month timeframe enables you to identify and control your financial activities and to maintain accurate records. These monthly budgets can be combined into an annual budget and used to create financial statements (net worth and cash flow) that are also usually compiled on an annual basis.

3 Explain how the decision-making phase of budgeting resolves conflicting financial needs and wants.

The Decision-Making Phase of Budgeting

The **decision-making phase of budgeting** focuses on the financial aspects of budgeting and the decisions about the sources of your funds as well as their destinations. As a financial manager, you should consider examining the anticipated effects of inflation and economic conditions on your budget. Next, you should make realistic budget estimates for income and expenditures. Finally, you should resolve conflicting needs and wants or desires by revising estimates as necessary.

Consider Inflation

Inflation is perhaps the single most influential factor for budgets because it affects the prices you must pay for the expenditure items identified in your budget. If food prices are rising 5 percent per year, a food budget of $250 per month would need to increase to $262.50 after just 12 months. If you anticipate inflationary increases, you will be less likely to be caught unprepared by necessary changes in your budget.

An increase in interest rates can have a serious effect on budgeting, for example, because the amount allocated for credit purchases may need to be increased. Suppose it is January and you are planning to buy a $200,000 home with a $40,000 down payment; at that time you may obtain a 30-year mortgage loan at 7 percent for the balance. By July, the interest rates may have risen (or fallen). If you must wait until July to buy the home and interest rates have increased by just one percentage point, you may have a monthly mortgage payment of $1174 instead of $1064. Chapter 1 offered suggestions on how to predict inflation and other economic factors.

Make Realistic Budget Estimates

Budget estimates are the projected dollar amounts in a budget that one plans to receive or spend during the period covered by the budget. Most people begin by estimating either their total gross income from all sources or their disposable income. **Disposable income** was defined in Chapter 2 as your income remaining after taxes and withholding for such purposes as insurance and union dues. It represents the money available for spending, saving, and investing. It is important to focus also on your **discretionary income.** This income includes the money left over once the necessities of living are covered. It is usually the money that is really controllable and often makes up the bulk of your variable expenses. Bear in mind that a budget is a working tool. As such, it should remain flexible. Do not treat a budget as if it were engraved in stone. Instead, make and use a budget to fulfill your changing needs, wants, and goals.

Everyone's budgeted expenses are different because people's lives are different. Nonetheless, it is useful to review how other people allocate their money when planning your own budget. Table 3.2 presents budget estimates for a college student, a single working person, a young married couple, a married couple with two young children, and a married couple with two college-age children. Note that the college student's budget given in Table 3.2 requires monthly withdrawals of previously deposited savings to make ends meet. The single working person's budget allows for an automobile loan, but not much else. The young married couple's budget permits one automobile loan,

Table 3.2 Sample Monthly Budgets for Various Family Units

Classifications	College Student	Single Working Person	Young Married Couple	Married Couple with Two Young Children	Married Couple with Two College-Age Children
INCOME					
Salary	$ 300	$2800	$2200	$3500	$4400
Salary	0	0	2100	860	1600
Interest and dividends	5	15	15	15	80
Loans/scholarships	300	0	0	0	0
Savings withdrawals	570	0	0	0	500
TOTAL INCOME	**$1175**	**$2815**	**$4315**	**$4375**	**$6580**
EXPENSES					
Fixed Expenses					
Retirement contributions	$0	$20	$ 360	$ 180	$ 340
IRA	0	20	160	180	200
Savings (withheld)	0	20	20	10	100
Housing	350	750	900	1100	1300
Health insurance	0	0	60	150	140
Life and disability insurance	0	0	20	60	40
Homeowner's or renter's insurance	0	0	40	60	80
Automobile insurance	0	80	90	60	140
Automobile payments	0	280	345	220	0
Loan 1 (TV and stereo)	0	80	80	40	0
Loan 2 (other)	0	40	40	0	50
Federal and state taxes	30	455	715	600	710
Social Security taxes	23	210	330	305	385
Real estate taxes	0	0	0	0	40
Investments	0	0	60	100	300
Total fixed expenses	**$ 403**	**$1955**	**$3220**	**$3065**	**$3825**
Variable Expenses					
Other savings	$ 0	$ 60	$ 150	$ 0	$ 0
Food	180	230	270	340	350
Utilities	40	80	90	140	145
Automobile gas, oil, maintenance	0	90	110	90	100
Medical	10	30	40	70	50
Child care	0	0	0	260	0
Clothing	20	50	60	50	40
Gifts and contributions	10	20	40	60	80
Allowances	20	75	60	100	180
Education	400	0	0	0	1500
Furnishing and appliances	10	10	30	20	20
Personal care	10	45	25	30	30
Entertainment	40	120	100	60	120
Vacations	17	30	40	30	60
Miscellaneous	15	20	80	60	80
Total variable expenses	**$ 772**	**$ 860**	**$1095**	**$1310**	**$2755**
TOTAL EXPENSES	**$1175**	**$2815**	**$4315**	**$4375**	**$6580**

an investment program, contributions to individual retirement accounts, and significant spending on food and entertainment. The budget of the married couple with two young children allows for only an inexpensive automobile loan payment; note that one spouse has a part-time job to help with the finances. In contrast, the budget of the married couple with two college-age children permits a home mortgage payment, ownership of two paid-for automobiles, savings and investment programs, and a substantial contribution for college expenses.

To make realistic estimates of your income and expenses, you must have reliable financial information. The more accurate the estimates, the more effective the budget. Information on several prior months of cash flows (described in Chapter 2) is a good resource for making estimates, for example. Most people begin by making budget estimates for one pay period and then multiply that result by the number of pay periods per year to obtain annual budget figures. Although accuracy is important, rounding figures to the nearest dollar (or sometimes even $5) is usually sufficient.

It is essential to make reasonable estimates for things you already have planned. If you have seven Christmas gifts to buy and expect to spend $50 for each, it's easy to make an estimate of $350. If you want to go out to dinner once each week at $50 per meal, you might estimate an expense of $200 per month. Avoid using unrealistically low figures because these low estimates can prove very frustrating when higher expenditures occur in reality. Simply be fair and honest in your estimates. The next step is to add up your total budget estimates for monthly or annual income and expenses.

Reconciling Budget Estimates

People are sometimes shocked when their initial expense estimates far exceed their income estimates in their budget. Only three choices are available in such cases: (1) earn more income; (2) cut back on expenses; or (3) try a combination of more income and less expenses. While sometimes uncomfortable, the process of reconciling needs and wants is a healthy exercise. It helps identify your priorities by telling you what is important in your life at the present time. It also suggests sacrifices that you might make.

Extra income, of course, is usually difficult to find. Therefore, the immediate task is to focus on expenditures. You must reconcile conflicting wants to revise your budget

How to . . .

Set Up a Budget from Scratch

Setting up a family's first budget can be a bit difficult. It is wise to base the budget on previous cash flows. Sometimes, however, it helps to know what similar families might spend as a guide for determining one's own budget. One place to look is on the Web at www.epinet.org/content.cfm/datazone_fambudget_budget. There you will find a calculator that can be used to obtain budget estimates for various family sizes in approximately 400 communities in the United States. Be aware that the budgets are basic. That is, they make no provisions for savings, insurance, restaurant meals, or funds for emergencies. Those expenses would need to be added in by the individual family.

Table 3.3   Annual Budget Estimates for 2005 for Harry and Belinda Johnson

	Jan.	Feb.	Mar.	Apr.	May	June	July	Aug.	Sept.	Oct.	Nov.	Dec.	Yearly Total	Monthly Average
INCOME														
Harry's salary	$2,500	$2,500	$2,500	$2,500	$2,500	$2,500	$2,575	$2,575	$2,575	$2,575	$2,575	$2,575	$30,450	$2,537.50
Belinda's salary	3,000	3,000	3,300	3,300	3,300	3,300	3,300	3,300	3,300	3,300	3,300	3,300	39,000	3,250.00
Interest	24	24	24	25	26	27	27	28	30	31	33	33	332	27.67
Trust	0	0	0	0	0	0	0	0	3,000	0	0	0	3,000	250.00
TOTAL INCOME	**$5,524**	**$5,524**	**$5,824**	**$5,825**	**$5,826**	**$5,827**	**$5,902**	**$5,903**	**$8,905**	**$5,906**	**$5,908**	**$5,908**	**$72,782**	**$6,065.17**
EXPENSES														
Fixed Expenses														
Rent	$ 900	$ 900	$ 900	$ 900	$ 900	$ 900	$ 950	$ 950	$ 950	$ 950	$ 950	$ 950	$11,100	$ 925.00
Health insurance	135	135	135	135	135	135	135	135	135	135	135	135	1,620	135.00
Life insurance	9	9	9	9	9	9	9	9	9	9	9	9	108	9.00
Home purchase fund	400	400	400	400	400	400	400	400	400	400	400	400	4,800	400.00
Renter's insurance	0	0	0	0	0	220	0	0	0	0	0	0	220	18.33
Automobile insurance	0	0	0	0	0	440	0	0	0	0	0	440	880	73.33
Auto loan payment	285	285	285	285	285	285	285	285	285	285	285	285	3,420	285.00
Student loan	145	145	145	145	145	145	145	145	145	145	145	145	1,740	145.00
Savings/emergencies	24	24	70	150	85	150	150	28	150	150	150	150	1,281	106.75
Harry's retirement plan	150	150	150	150	150	150	154	154	154	154	154	154	1,824	152.00
Belinda's retirement	120	120	132	132	132	132	132	132	132	132	132	132	1,560	130.00
Health club	50	50	50	50	50	50	50	50	50	50	50	50	600	50.00
Cable television	35	35	35	35	35	35	35	35	35	35	35	35	420	35.00
Federal income taxes	767	767	848	848	848	848	854	854	854	854	854	854	10,050	837.50
State income taxes	266	266	284	284	284	284	289	289	289	289	289	289	3,402	283.50
Social Security	421	421	444	444	444	444	450	450	450	450	450	450	5,318	443.17
Total fixed expenses	**$3,707**	**$3,707**	**$3,887**	**$3,967**	**$3,902**	**$4,627**	**$4,038**	**$3,916**	**$4,038**	**$4,038**	**$4,038**	**$4,478**	**$48,343**	**$4,028.58**
Variable Expenses														
Savings/investments	$ 0	$ 0	$ 0	$ 0	$ 0	$ 0	$ 0	$ 0	$3,000	$ 0	$ 0	$ 0	$ 3,000	$ 250.00
Revolving savings fund	140	140	140	140	140	0	250	0	215	190	0	0	1,355	112.92
Food	350	350	350	350	350	350	350	350	350	350	350	350	4,200	350.00
Utilities	150	150	150	150	100	100	100	100	100	125	125	150	1,500	125.00
Telephone	70	70	70	70	70	70	70	70	70	70	70	90	860	71.67
Auto expenses	115	115	115	115	115	115	115	115	115	115	115	115	1,380	115.00
Medical	100	100	100	100	100	100	100	100	100	100	100	100	1,200	100.00
Clothing	180	180	180	180	180	180	180	180	180	180	180	180	2,160	180.00
Church and charity	100	100	100	100	175	100	100	100	100	100	100	100	1,275	106.25
Gifts	80	80	160	75	120	20	20	60	60	60	60	20	815	67.92
Christmas gifts	0	0	0	0	0	0	0	0	0	0	400	300	700	58.33
Public transportation	60	60	60	60	60	60	60	60	60	60	60	60	720	60.00
Personal allowances	200	200	200	200	200	200	200	200	200	200	200	200	2,400	200.00
Entertainment/meals	240	240	240	240	240	240	240	240	240	240	240	240	2,880	240.00
Automobile license	0	0	0	0	0	40	0	0	0	0	0	0	40	3.33
Vacation (Christmas)	0	0	0	0	0	0	0	0	0	0	0	700	700	58.33
Vacation (summer)	0	0	0	0	0	0	0	600	0	0	0	0	600	50.00
Anniversary party	0	0	0	0	0	250	0	0	0	0	0	0	250	20.83
Miscellaneous	32	32	72	78	74	75	79	62	77	78	75	75	809	67.42
Total variable expenses	**$1,817**	**$1,817**	**$1,937**	**$1,858**	**$1,924**	**$1,900**	**$1,864**	**$2,237**	**$4,867**	**$1,868**	**$2,075**	**$2,680**	**$26,844**	**$ 2,237**
TOTAL EXPENSES	**$5,524**	**$5,524**	**$5,824**	**$5,825**	**$5,826**	**$6,527**	**$5,902**	**$6,153**	**$8,905**	**$5,906**	**$6,113**	**$7,158**	**$75,187**	**$6,265.58**
Difference (available for spending, saving, and investing)	$0	$0	$0	$0	$0	−$700	$0	−$250	$0	$0	−$205	−$1,250	−$2,405	
Revolving savings withdrawals						700		250			205	200	1355	
Uncovered shortfall	$0	$0	$0	$0	$0	$0	$0	$0	$0	$0	$0	−$1,050	−$1,050	

until total expenses do not exceed income. This process is known as **reconciling budget estimates.** First, review the fixed expenditures to see whether they are accurate and truly necessary. Next, look at each of the variable expenditures and change some "must have" items to "maybe next year" purchases. Perhaps you might keep some quality items but reduce their quantity. For example, instead of $160 for four meals at restaurants each month, consider dining out twice each month at $60 per meal. You'll save $40 and still have two really nice meals.

Table 3.3 presents the annual budget for Harry and Belinda Johnson and reflects their efforts to reconcile their budget estimates until the total planned expenses fall below the total planned income. Note that Harry and Belinda are "paying themselves first," in the amount of $400 per month, to save to buy their own home.

4 Describe how to implement a budget.

The Implementation Phase of Budgeting

In the **implementation phase of budgeting,** you put the budget into effect. Specifically, you record expenditures made and income received during the budget time period, manage cash-flow problems, determine totals for the time period, and prepare financial statements.

Recording Actual Income and Expenditures

An **expenditure** is an amount of money that has been spent. You may plan for a budgetary expense but, when the money has been spent, it becomes an actual expenditure. It is important to keep an accurate and up-to-date record of expenditures. Keeping this information handy may remind you to record expenditures frequently. If you have a good memory or keep a notepad in your pocket or purse for that purpose, expenditures can be formally recorded every few days.

When writing data in the "activity" column in your record, be descriptive (as shown in Figure 3.5 on page 67) because you may need the information later. Many people also write comments in a "remarks" column in their records for the same reason, as shown in parts (c) and (d) of Figure 3.5. Use a pencil to facilitate making corrections or revisions.

Managing with a Cash-Flow Calendar

For most people, income remains somewhat constant month after month, but planned expenses can rise and fall sharply. As a result, people occasionally complain that they are "broke, out of money, and sick of budgeting." As you will see, this problem can be anticipated by the creation of a cash-flow calendar and eliminated through the use of a revolving savings fund.

The budget estimates for monthly income and expenses in Table 3.3 have been re-cast in summary form in Table 3.4, providing a **cash-flow calendar** for the Johnsons. Annual estimated income and expenses are recorded in this calendar for each budget-ing time period in an effort to identify surplus or deficit situations. In the Johnsons' case, planned annual income exceeds expenses. The couple starts out the year with many expenses, resulting in deficits for the next six months. Later in the year, income usually exceeds expenses, but they are still faced with a deficit at year's end.

Effective management of cash flow can involve curtailing expenses during months with financial deficits, increasing income, using savings, or borrowing. If you borrow money and must pay finance charges, the credit costs will further increase your monthly expenses. For this reason, it is better to borrow from yourself by using a re-volving savings fund.

Utilizing a Revolving Savings Fund

In its simplest form, a **revolving savings fund** is a variable expense classification in budgeting into which funds are allocated in an effort to create savings that can be used to balance the budget later so as to avoid running out of money. Establishing such a fund involves planning ahead—much like a college student does when saving money all summer (creating a revolving savings fund) to draw on during the school months. Most people need to establish a revolving savings fund for two purposes: (1) to accu-mulate funds for large irregular expenses, such as automobile insurance premiums, medical costs, Christmas gifts, and vacations; and (2) to meet occasional deficits due to income fluctuations.

Table 3.4 Cash-Flow Calendar for Harry and Belinda Johnson

Month	1 Estimated Income	2 Estimated Expenses	3 Surplus/Deficit (1 - 2)	4 Cumulative Surplus/Deficit
January	$ 5,524	$ 5,524	$ 0	$ 0
February	5,524	5,524	0	0
March	5,824	5,824	0	0
April	5,825	5,825	0	0
May	5,826	5,826	0	0
June	5,827	6,527	−700	−700
July	5,902	5,902	0	−700
August	5,903	6,153	−250	−950
September	8,905	8,905	0	−950
October	5,906	5,906	0	−950
November	5,908	6,113	−205	−1,155
December	5,908	7,158	−1,250	−2,405
Total	**$72,782**	**$75,187**		**−$2,405**

Table 3.5 shows the Johnsons' revolving savings fund in worksheet format. When preparing their budget, the Johnsons realized that in June, August, November, and December they were going to have significant deficits. They decided to begin setting aside $140 per month to cover the June deficit. To do so, they decided to wait to start building their emergency fund. By June they had $700 in their revolving savings fund to cover the June deficit. Continued use of the revolving savings fund helped them meet the August and November deficits as well.

The Johnsons will still be $1050 short in December, however. Lacking that much money, the couple has three alternatives: (1) use some of Harry's trust fund money to cover the deficit, (2) dip into their emergency savings in December, or (3) cut back on their expenses enough throughout the year to create sufficient surpluses. Ideally, the Johnsons should have sufficient emergency funds by the end of the year to establish their revolving savings fund for the next year. Thus, cutting back on expenses may be their best option.

Calculating Time-Period Totals

After the budgeting period has ended—usually at the beginning of a new month—you need to add up the actual income received and expenditures made during that period. You can perform this calculation on a form for each budget classification, as shown in parts (a) and (b) of Figure 3.5 (page 67), or on a form with all income and expenditure classifications, as in parts (c) and (d) of Figure 3.5. Such calculations indicate where you may have overspent within your budget categories. If you are new at budgeting, do not be too concerned about overspending; it occurs in some classifications almost always, only to be balanced by underspending in other categories. Use such information to refine your budget estimates in the future. In three or four months, you should be able to estimate your expenses much more accurately.

Table 3.5 Revolving Savings Fund Worksheet for Harry and Belinda Johnson

Month	Large Expenses	Amount Needed	Deposit into Fund	Withdrawal from Fund	Fund Balance
January		$ 0	$ 140	$ 0	$ 140
February		0	140	0	280
March		0	140	0	420
April		0	140	0	560
May		0	140	0	700
June	Party and insurance premiums	700	0	700	0
July		0	250	0	250
August	Vacation	250	0	250	0
September		0	215	0	215
October		0	190	0	405
November	Holiday gifts	205	0	205	200
December	Holiday gifts and vacation	1250	0	200	0
Total		**$2405**	**$1355**	**$1355**	**−$1050**

The Control Phase of Budgeting

5 List techniques to keep income and expenditures within planned budget totals.

In the **control phase of budgeting,** an individual or family uses various methods and techniques to keep income and expenditures within the planned budget totals. The control phase occurs simultaneously with the implementation phase, because the best time to control spending is *during* the budget time period.

Reasons for Budget Controls

Budget controls tell you whether you are on target and how well you are progressing on a financial level; they also alert you to such problems as errors, overspending, emergencies, and exceptions or omissions. For example, when Postal Service employee Barbara Smith of New Smyrna, Florida, examined her budget figures for the month of May, she discovered that her "cash out" column equaled $1596 while all other expenditure columns totaled only $1532. The two figures should be the same if she had recorded all transactions and added all figures correctly. Thus, this cross-check serves as a built-in control. It is futile to try to account for every single dollar because some cash is bound to "slip away" every month. However, a difference of $64 ($1596 – $1532) indicates that something is wrong. Most likely, Barbara omitted some expenditure item.

Comparison of totals represents a valuable control built into the recording process. The controls used should not, of course, be treated as absolute mandates with penalties should errors occur. Instead, they simply inform you that you need to reexamine your budgeting practice and remedy any missteps.

Seven Budget Control Measures

Suggestions for controlling a budget include the following: (1) use a checking account; (2) employ a credit controlsheet; (3) check accuracy; (4) monitor unexpended balances; (5) justify exceptions; (6) set up subordinate budgets; and (7) use the envelope system.

Use a Checking Account.   If you use cash frequently instead of checks, you may have trouble tracking the amount you spend. You must retain many receipts and write the purpose of each expense on the back of each receipt; you should also keep a daily log that includes expenditures for which you obtained no receipt. In contrast, checks provide a record of the business or person with whom you did business, and each check contains a space to record the purpose, as shown in Figure 3.6 (page 78). It is also a good control measure to deposit all checks received to your checking account without receiving a portion in cash; if you need cash, write a check.

It is easy to write a check in haste without recording its purpose on the front of the check. The check stub or register (also shown in Figure 3.6) provides a handy place to record explanations of expenditures. A special concern arises with people who use automatic teller machines (ATMs) frequently to withdraw cash or who use debit cards to pay for day-to-day expenditures. These withdrawals should be recorded in the check register *immediately.* In addition, the budget expenditure category for which the funds were used must be recorded so that the budget balance can be appropriately adjusted. You should establish a habit of safeguarding ATM and debit card receipts by always

Figure 3.6

Check with Explanation Space

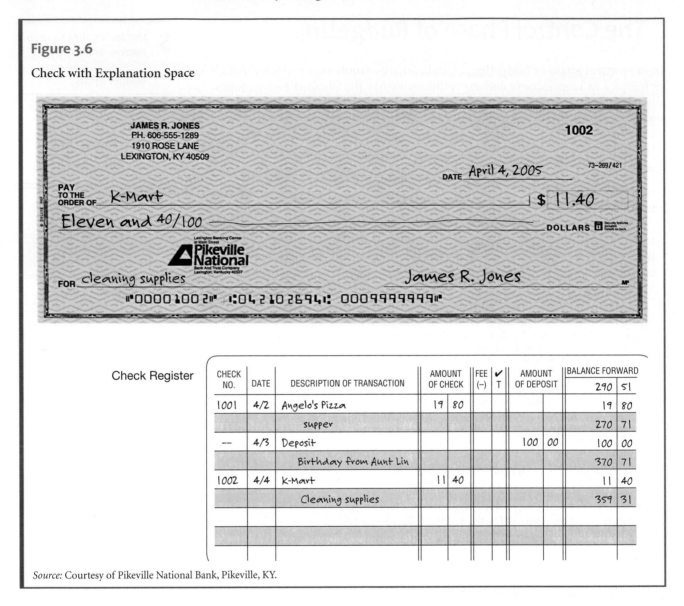

Check Register	CHECK NO.	DATE	DESCRIPTION OF TRANSACTION	AMOUNT OF CHECK		FEE (–)	✔ T	AMOUNT OF DEPOSIT		BALANCE FORWARD	
										290	51
	1001	4/2	Angelo's Pizza	19	80					19	80
			supper							270	71
	—	4/3	Deposit					100	00	100	00
			Birthday from Aunt Lin							370	71
	1002	4/4	K-Mart	11	40					11	40
			Cleaning supplies							359	31

Source: Courtesy of Pikeville National Bank, Pikeville, KY.

putting them in the same place in your wallet or handbag and then filing them safely when you return home.

Employ a Credit Controlsheet.   Figure 3.7 shows a sample **credit controlsheet** that can be used to monitor credit use, amounts owed, and parties to whom debts are owed. This form can keep you abreast of outstanding credit obligations and allows you to cross-check easily the credit-flow check sheet with credit statements received in the mail.

People who keep budgets on a cash basis sometimes do not track credit transactions until they receive a statement noting the amount due. While this system works well for some people, others continue to buy on credit and fail to recognize the detail and amount of their indebtedness until they receive a statement. People who make credit purchases also need to keep the receipts for future reference so charges listed on a statement can be verified and any errors challenged (see Chapter 6). A credit controlsheet

Figure 3.7

Credit Controlsheet

DATE	PURPOSE FOR CREDIT	VISA Chg (Pay)	VISA Balance	MASTERCARD Chg (Pay)	MASTERCARD Balance	AMES Dept. Store Chg (Pay)	AMES Dept. Store Balance	SUMMARY All Creditors Chgs	Paid	Balance
1-2	Gas for car	14.95	14.95					14.95		14.95
1-2	Clothing					32.00	32.00	32.00		46.95
1-15	Paid Visa	(14.95)	- 0 -						14.95	32.00
1-27	New desk			320.00	320.00			320.00		352.00
2-12	Gas for car	20.00	20.00					20.00		372.00
2-28	Paid Ames					(32.00)	- 0 -		32.00	340.00

Credit flow for _____Jan.—Mar._____

allows you to record each credit transaction when it occurs; if you misplace a receipt, you still have a record available for verification.

Check Accuracy.   Another way to control a budget is to double-check the accuracy of financial records. Many people increase the accuracy of their records by using a computer, a word processor, or a calculator. Accuracy in recordkeeping builds confidence in handling financial affairs.

Monitor Unexpended Balances.   The best method to control overspending is to **monitor unexpended balances** in each budget classification. You can accomplish this task by using a budget design that keeps a declining balance, as illustrated by parts (a) and (b) of Figure 3.5 (page 67). Other budget designs, such as those shown in parts (c) and (d) of Figure 3.5, need to be monitored differently. As illustrated in parts (c) and (d) of the figure, simply calculate subtotals every week or so, as needed, during a monthly budgeting period.

Justify Exceptions.   **Budget exceptions** occur when budget estimates in various classifications differ from actual expenditures, with discrepancies usually taking the form of overexpenditures. Exceptions may also occur in the over- or under-receipt of earnings. Allowing for exceptions keeps your budget flexible, although you still need to monitor them. Of course, to remain within your budget allocations, you must balance—or offset—overexpenditures with extra earnings received or with reductions in spending elsewhere.

Set Up Subordinate Budgets.   A **subordinate budget** is a detailed listing of planned expenses within a single budgeting classification. For example, an estimate of $1200 for a week-long vacation could be supported by a subordinate budget as follows: motel, $700; restaurants, $300; and entertainment, $200. Subordinate budgets help you control spending within a category more effectively.

Use the Envelope System.   The **envelope system** of budgeting gets its name from the fact that exact amounts of money are placed into envelopes for purposes of strict

Advice from an Expert

Crisis Steps to Take if Budget Deficits Occur Repeatedly

If you always run out of money before the month is over, you may need to take some drastic steps to get your finances under control. Those steps may include the following:

1. Stop or significantly reduce spending on luxuries such as eating out, clothing, and entertainment.
2. Switch items from your "need" list to your "luxury" list and do without them, at least temporarily. These items may include cell phone services, memberships, hobbies, clothing, CDs and DVDs, expanded cable channels, and going to the movies.
3. Stop making ATM withdrawals and getting cash back from purchases to use for pocket money.
4. Stop using credit cards. Spend only cash or money that is in your checking account.
5. Sell an asset, especially one that requires additional expenses, such as a second car.
6. Consider moving to lower-cost housing.
7. Take steps to increase income by working overtime, finding a second job, or paying off high-interest debt.

Alena C. Johnson,
Utah State University

budgetary control. If you decide to use the envelope system, simply place money equal to the budget estimate for the various expenditure classifications in envelopes at the start of a budgeting period. Write the classification name and the budget amount on the outside of each envelope. As expenditures are made, record them on the appropriate envelope and remove the proper amounts of cash. When an envelope is empty, funds are exhausted for that classification. This technique works well in controlling expenditures for variable expenses such as entertainment, personal allowances, and food. It may also provide a good way for younger children to learn to budget their allowances. Of course, the envelopes must be safeguarded against theft.

6 List three ways to evaluate a budget.

The Evaluation Phase of Budgeting

Evaluation is the crucial final step in the budgeting process. In addition, the **evaluation phase of budgeting** provides feedback for the next budget cycle. In plain language, the purpose of evaluation is to determine whether the earlier steps in the budgeting process have worked. Although evaluation is a continuous process, the formal evaluation phase occurs at the end of each budgeting cycle. At that point, you compare actual amounts with budgeted amounts, decide whether the budget objectives have been met, and judge the success of the overall process of budgeting. Evaluation includes comparing your estimated and actual income and expenditures, deciding how to handle any leftover balances, and assessing progress toward your short- and long-term goals.

Compare Estimated and Actual Amounts

Making comparisons is important if you want to understand why expenditures were higher or lower than your estimates. This **variance analysis** involves comparing the budgeted and actual amounts in the various budget classifications at the end of each month. In some budget expenditure classifications, the budget estimates rarely agree with the actual expenditures—particularly in variable expenses. The remarks column, as illustrated in parts (c) and (d) of Figure 3.5, can help clarify why discrepancies occur.

Decide How to Handle Balances

At the end of the budgeting time period, some budget classifications may still have a positive balance. For example, perhaps you estimated the electric bill at $50, but it was only $45 in reality. You may then ask, "What do I do with the balance?" You also may ask, "What happens to budget classifications that were overspent?"

People often deposit the **net surplus** (the amount remaining after all budget classification deficits are subtracted from those with surpluses) in a savings account, such as their revolving savings fund account, or put the money toward paying off their highest-interest credit card accounts. Others treat it like "mad money" and spend it. Still others leave the funds in a checking account and carry the surpluses forward, thereby providing larger budget estimates for the following month. The budgeting form in part (d) of Figure 3.5 allows for carrying forward balances to the next period. Some people carry forward deficits, with the hope that having less available in a budgeted classification the following month will motivate them to keep expenditures low. Because variable expense estimates are usually averages, it is best not to change the estimate based on a variation that occurs over just one or two months. If estimates are too high or low for a longer period, however, you will want to make adjustments.

Be aware of any over- or underestimates for earnings or expenditures. Overages on a few expenditures may cause little concern. If excessive variances have prevented you

---

Did You Know? . . .

What to Do with Extra Money

A common fear in budgeting is that spending will exceed income. But what if the opposite happens, and income regularly exceeds budgeted expenditures? This situation can happen if you get a raise, if your projections for expenses were too high, or simply if you are frugal. If you have money left over at the end of the month, you might consider taking the following steps:

■ Pay down your credit card debt. Paying on these high-interest loans will result in even lower expenditures in the future as interest charges diminish.

■ Put the money in your employer-sponsored retirement plan. Because these plans are tax-sheltered,

you save on taxes at the same time that you add to your financial nest egg.

■ Invest in a mutual fund. Investing is a habit that is difficult to start but easier to continue. Starting when funds are readily available will help continue the pattern when money is tighter.

■ Pay down a mortgage or other loan. Putting additional amounts toward monthly loan payments will get them paid off earlier and reduce overall interest expenses.

from achieving your objectives or making the budget balance, however, then take some action. New controls might have to be instituted or current controls tightened. Reflective thinking during this type of evaluation will ensure an improved budgeting process in the future.

Assess Progress Toward Goals

Whatever your goals, it is exciting to know that some or all of them have been achieved or that you have made progress toward those ends. A successful budget reflects on the person behind it. Even though achieving such objectives as staying within the budget estimates, paying off a small debt, or saving a few dollars within the budget period may seem unimpressive to some people, it allows you to say, "I achieved my goals because I made a plan and implemented it successfully."

If you did not achieve some of your objectives, you can use the evaluation process to determine why and then adjust your budget and objectives accordingly. Suppose the Johnsons find that they are unable to set aside the planned $400 for their new home. By evaluating their budget, they might find that unexpected medical expenses and an out-of-state trip to visit a sick relative led them to dip into their savings. Under these circumstances, they can easily understand why the objective was not achieved and they can set their sights on reaching the goal during the next budgeting time period.

Evaluation of your progress toward reaching savings goals is especially important. As noted in Chapter 2, your net worth can grow only when you spend less than your income. Success comes when savings goals are being met. If this is not the case, the budgeter must establish mechanisms to force savings to occur. Payroll deductions and automatic transfers from checking to savings accounts, for example, may aid this process by making saving automatic. Such mechanisms are especially helpful for first-attempt savers who are simply trying to build the three months emergency fund that is recommended for most people.

7 Give details about how people can discuss money matters effectively.

The Personal Side of Money

A common cause of marital tension is conflict over money. Sometimes one person in a relationship will make a crucial financial decision without consulting the other person, thereby creating resentment and perhaps setting the stage for a series of retaliatory actions. Some couples seem unable to work together to perform the fundamental tasks of managing money, such as reconciling the checking account, creating a workable budget, and paying bills on time. It is not uncommon for at least one spouse to bring a great deal of debt to a marriage. Other couples get into financial trouble after marriage because they use credit too often. Mutual trust in money matters can be developed—and must be—to have happy interpersonal relationships and achieve financial success.

Money Management and Financial Decision Making for Couples

Managing money and making decisions about money matters are two different processes. Managing money includes such tasks as handling the checkbook, overseeing the budget, and doing the day-to-day shopping. Some couples also split money management chores. For example, one spouse might handle the checkbook and pay the bills, while the other might keep track of the budget, complete forms for health insurance claims, and fill out income tax returns. While managing family money is an important responsibility, decision making is where disagreements typically arise in this area.

Decision making can be unilateral, shared, or divided. Couples typically share decision making to some extent. The two partners talk with each other and decide how much to spend on major purchases, such as appliances, jewelry, and recreation activities. They also share decision-making power on more expensive planned financial activities, such as buying automobiles and housing, as well as on key topics such as estate planning and investments. Families can divide financial decision making equally or by mutual agreement based on their respective knowledge, interest, and experience in personal financial matters.

Financial experts recommend that each person in a relationship keep some money of his or her own. This could be accomplished by setting up three checking accounts for most dual-earner couples: a discretionary account for each individual (two accounts) and a third joint account. The budget categories related to each account should be clearly and jointly specified. Each partner can then feel that he or she has access to money that the other partner does not control. These feelings of autonomy encourage independence and self-control in a relationship rather than dependency on the other person.

People Ascribe Strong Emotions to Money

People often ascribe a number of emotions to money, including freedom, trust, self-esteem, guilt, indifference, envy, security, comfort, power, and control. It is important to recognize the importance of these emotions. Many people consider their way of handling money to be a deeply private and personal matter. They may want to hold on to their fiscal autonomy as long as possible, and they may be embarrassed to inquire about how much others—even loved ones—spend, earn, or owe. For many people, money is a dark little area of self-suspected incompetence, and it is a difficult subject to discuss. Judith Viorst, author of *Necessary Losses,* suggests that becoming responsible and adept at managing one's financial matters represents a true passage into adulthood. This evolution involves communicating effectively with others on money matters.

Talking about Financial Matters Effectively

Discussions about money matters are not always easy because they often reflect deeply held values that are difficult to change. Some people who are entirely rational about most things in life can prove unpredictable or even careless in money matters. While unrealistic values should be identified and discussed, adults need to accept that honest differences may exist among people and that these values must be respected. The following techniques should help you discuss money with more confidence and candor.

Get to Know Yourself and Your Partner.   The first step in learning to talk with others about financial matters is to understand your own approach to money. Consider the emotions described earlier to help get you started. Use the "financial compatibility" checklist on page 85 to consider your individual perspective before discussing matters together. It will be constructive to discuss any differences in how you view yourself as compared with how your partner views you.

Learn to Manage Financial Disagreements.　Give all family members time to express their views when discussing financial matters. Each family member also needs to listen to what others are saying and feeling. If talking proves too difficult, have each person separately write down his or her concerns. By swapping notes, ideas and concerns can be shared. Schedule a time and place for financial talks, decide on agenda items, and leave other conflicts outside the door. When necessary, agree to disagree or postpone difficult decisions until a later time—but do so consciously and not simply out of procrastination.

Avoid "You" Statements.　"You" statements are blaming statements, such as "You always . . . ," "You never . . . ," "You are acting like . . . ," "You should forget that idea . . . ," and "If you don't, I will . . . ." These statements have a high probability of being condescending to other people, of making them feel guilty, and of implying that their needs and wants are not as important as yours.

Use "I" Statements.　Use such phrases as "I think" and "I feel" when discussing money. Messages focusing on "I" describe the behavior in question, the feelings you experienced because of the behavior, and any tangible effect on you. For example, a spouse might say, "I feel upset when we use credit cards, because I do not know where we will find the money to pay the bills at the end of the month." "I" messages say three things: what (the behavior), I feel (feelings), because (reason). Using "I" messages helps build stronger relationships because they tell the other person that "I trust you to decide what change in behavior is necessary." Beware of "I" statements that end with "I need you to . . . ." These statements may be seen as attempts to exert power.

Focus on Commonalities.　Successful communication about money requires that the effort be aimed toward agreeing on common goals and reaching a consensus of opinion without substantially compromising the views of family members.

Be Honest.　Achieving consensus requires that each person be honest when talking about money matters. It further demands that family members regularly talk about finances, particularly when money decisions are not pressing. Be prepared to compromise. When you make decisions together, act on them. People learning to discuss money matters often focus their attention on current financial activities and short-term issues to the exclusion of long-term financial planning. Recall, however, that values, financial plans, and long-term goals form the bases for short-term goals and issues. Therefore, you should try to use these discussions to forge overall long-term strategies for dealing with your family finances. Once the proper base has been established, short-term issues are more likely to fall into place.

Complications Brought by Remarriage

Remarriage merges financial histories, values, and habits as well as households. Some remarried couples will have substantial combined incomes bolstered by child-support payments from a former spouse. In many cases, at least one spouse may be paying (instead of receiving) alimony and child support. When "his," "her," and "our" children are included in the household, living expenses can be quite steep. Special concerns for blended families include determining who assumes financial responsibility for biological offspring without neglecting or offending spouses and stepchildren, handling resentment over alimony and child-support payments, and managing unequal assets, incomes, responsibilities, and debts. Even gift giving can become a quandary.

How to ...

Determine if You and Your Partner Are Financially Compatible

Couples should discuss each partner's values and attitudes prior to making long-term commitments. These discussions should focus on several areas that will significantly affect a family's finances. It might help if each person writes down his or her views on the following topics. Then the views can be compared.

Employment. How do you feel about dual-career arrangements? Are you satisfied with your careers? Are you earning enough money? Are you willing to move for your spouse's advancement?

Day-to-Day Money Management. Should you pool all of your money and spend out of one "pot"? Or should you have separate accounts and divide up certain of your expenses? Who should manage the accounts, balance the checkbook, and take care of insurance claims?

Childbearing. How many children do you want to have? How soon? Will both of you want to work full-time while raising the children?

Clothing. How important is clothing to you? Are you satisfied with the amount, quality, and prestige value of clothing that you have?

Food. Is the food you are eating at home the quality you really want? Who should do the cooking and shopping for food? Do you want to eat out more often? Where?

Debt. How comfortable are you using credit to buy now, thereby committing future earnings?

Housing. How much do you want to spend on home furnishings? Do you really want to buy a home, or is renting acceptable? Where would you like to live?

Transportation. Could you cope by using mass transportation and by having just one automobile? Could one car be an inexpensive vehicle that gets high mileage? If so, who would drive it? Do you associate status with the car you drive?

Recreation. Would you be satisfied spending less (or more) money on recreational activities?

Vacations. What do you really want to do on vacations? Should you consider separate vacations? Do you prefer one long vacation each year or more frequent long-weekend breaks?

Future Security. How important are savings and investments? Will your retirement plan actually provide you with a decent (or high) level of living? What would happen financially if you became disabled or died?

How was money handled when you were a child? Was it discussed openly or kept private? Was money used as a reward—or punishment? Do you mirror your parents' style of handling money—or did you rebel against it?

Many remarried people use "his" and "hers" funds and require the legally responsible parent owing financial support to a previous spouse or to children to make such payments out of his or her own money. Professor Jean Lown of Utah State University suggests that, "What is best is what the couple can agree on." Some couples choose to sign a **prenuptial agreement,** a contract specifying what (if any) share of each person's assets the other will be entitled to during marriage or in case of divorce. Another useful device is a **postnuptial agreement,** a contractual agreement signed after marriage that spells out each spouse's financial responsibilities.

How to . . .

Develop Money Sense in Children

Parents can help children develop money sense by providing them with opportunities to manage their own money while still young and guiding this behavior toward appropriate patterns. Five suggestions follow.

1. **Give children access to money.** Even children as young as five years old should have some money of their own. An allowance and an opportunity to earn additional money ("pay") around the house should be the source of these funds in the preteen years. Later, work outside the home may be an option. The amounts of allowance and pay should fit the family income level. Allowances should not be viewed as pay for performing routine household chores but are, instead, a means for teaching money management.
2. **Give children the freedom to save as well as to spend their money.** Children should have autonomy over at least some of their own money. Consider requiring that the child deposit one-half of his or her allowance in a savings account. The remainder could be available for discretionary spending in certain categories jointly determined by the parent and the child.
3. **Allow children the freedom to fail.** Parents should not stop children from "wasting their money." Advice is fine, but kids still need to feel the pain of a purchase gone bad. Similarly, kids should not be bailed out from every mistake. We sometimes learn best from experience, not from what someone else tells us is best. Note that item 4 is designed to keep these mistakes from being too devastating.
4. **Teach responsibility through increasingly complex activities.** The dollar amounts and the areas of discretionary spending can increase as the child becomes older. A seven-year-old might be allowed to spend his or her own money on toys, snacks, and gifts to charity at church or school. A 14-year-old might be allowed to buy meals and clothing as well. More responsibility and autonomy should be given only as the child exhibits the ability to handle previous, less complicated tasks.
5. **Talk about family finances with children.** In many families, money matters are a taboo subject. Children need to see that parents must work at managing the family finances. They should know what it costs to raise a family and how difficult it can be to make ends meet sometimes. Otherwise, kids will grow up with unrealistic expectations and behaviors that will be passed on to their children.

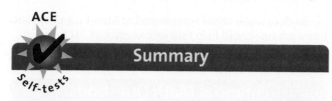

Summary

1. Your personal values are the starting point in financial planning and budgeting. Budgeting is a process of projecting, organizing, monitoring, and controlling future income and expenditures (cash and credit purchases as well as savings). The purpose of budgeting is to reach financial goals. In the goal-setting phase of budgeting, goals must be specific. In particular, they should contain dollar amounts and target dates for achievement.

2. In the organization phase of budgeting—which focuses on the structural and mechanical aspects of budgeting—you choose a recording format, select either the cash or accrual basis of accounting, choose various budget classifications, and select the time period for the budget. It is important to maintain a positive attitude toward budgeting and to maintain flexibility.

3. The decision-making phase of budgeting requires you to make realistic budget estimates for income and expenditures as well as to resolve conflicting needs and wants by revising estimates as needed.

4. In the implementation phase of budgeting, you put the budget into effect, primarily by recording actual income and expenditures. You then manage cash flow and calculate time-period totals.

5. The control phase of budgeting includes the potential use of seven means of control. Using a checking account, checking accuracy, and monitoring unexpended balances are popular controls. Formal budgeting controls include the credit controlsheet and the envelope system.

6. In the evaluation phase of budgeting, you compare actual amounts with budgeted amounts, decide how to handle balances, and assess progress made toward your goals.

7. Many people find it difficult to talk with others about money and the tough financial decisions they must make. A number of useful strategies can be used to improve communications about money matters, including the use of "I" statements.

Key Terms

budget, 60
budget controls, 77
budget estimates, 70

cash-basis budgeting, 69
cash-flow calendar, 75
credit controlsheet, 78
custodial account, 62
discretionary income, 70
disposable income, 70
envelope system, 79
expenditure, 74
ledger, 66
monitoring unexpended balances, 79
net surplus, 81
prenuptial agreement, 86
recordkeeping, 66
revolving savings fund, 75
short-term goals, 63
subordinate budget, 79
variance analysis, 81

Chapter Review Questions

1. Concisely describe the relationships among the following terms: values, financial planning, budgeting, and financial goals.

2. List and explain the six phases of budgeting.

3. Briefly explain how inflation affects budgeting.

4. Describe how a cash-flow calendar works.

5. Outline how a revolving savings fund works.

6. What purposes do budget controls serve?

7. Explain how the envelope system helps to control a budget.

8. How can a subordinate budget be used on a vacation?

9. What should be done during the evaluation phase of budgeting?

10. List three financial questions that couples and families face.

Group Discussion Issues

1. Suggest three typical financial goals for a recent college graduate, three financial goals for a family with young children, and three financial goals for a couple whose children have now ventured out on their own.

2. Do you have a budget? Why not? What do you think are the reasons why people do not make formal budgets?

3. What advice can you offer people about using credit cards when they are interested in better controlling their budget?

4. What is the biggest budget-related mistake that you have made? What would you do differently?

5. Did your parents talk about money with you when you were a child? Why do you think they did or did not?

6. What ideas do you have for how to make it easier for young couples to talk frankly and honestly about money issues before blending their finances?

Decision-Making Cases

▶Case 1
A Couple Creates an Educational Savings Plan

Stanley Marsh and Wendlene Testaburger of Gary, Indiana, have two young children and have been living on a tight budget. Their monthly budget is illustrated in Table 3.2 as the "married couple with two young children." Wendlene and Stanley are nervous about not having started an educational savings plan for their children. Wendlene has just begun working on a part-time basis at a local accounting firm and earns about $860 per month; this income is reflected in the Marsh-Testaburgers' budget. They have decided that they want to save $200 per month for the children's education, but Wendlene does not want to work more hours away from home.

(a) Review the family's budget and make suggestions about how to modify various budget estimates so that they could save $200 per month for the education fund.

(b) Briefly describe the effect of your recommended changes on the Marsh-Testaburgers' lifestyle.

(c) What factors should the couple remember as they attempt to discuss and resolve this important financial issue for their family?

▶Case 2
Budget Control for a Recent Graduate

Marvin Jackson, a political scientist from Tucson, Arizona, graduated from college eight months ago and is having a terrible time with his budget. Marvin has a regular monthly income from his job and no really large bills, but he likes to spend. He exceeds his budget every month, and his credit card balances are increasing. Choose three budget control

methods that you could recommend to Marvin, and explain how each one could help him gain control of his finances.

Financial Math Questions

1. Sharon and Dick DeVaney of West Lafayette, Indiana, have decided to start a family next year, so they are looking over their budget (illustrated in Table 3.2 as the "young married couple"). Sharon thinks that she can go on half-salary ($1050 instead of $2100 per month) in her job as a graduate assistant for about 18 months after the baby's birth; she will then return to full-time work.

(a) Looking at the DeVaneys' current monthly budget, identify categories and amounts in their $4315 budget where they realistically might cut back $1050. (Hint: Federal and state taxes should drop about $290 as their income drops.)

(b) Assume that Sharon and Dick could be persuaded not to begin a family for another two to three years until Sharon finishes graduate school. What specific budgeting recommendations would you give them for handling (i) their fixed expenses and (ii) their variable expenses to prepare financially for an anticipated $1050 loss of income for 18 months as well as the expenses for the new baby?

(c) If the DeVaneys' gross income of $4315 rises 6 percent per year in the future, what will their income be after five years? (Hint: See Appendix Table A.1 or the *Garman/Forgue* website.)

Money Matters Continuing Cases

Victor and Maria Hernandez Think About Their Budget

Victor and Maria Hernandez have begun the transition from being parents with children at home to being a couple without live-at-home children. As their children grow older and prepare to go away to college, Victor and Maria have been considering several issues related to their children's money matters. They could use some advice.

1. Explain five ways that the Hernandezes might create money sense in their children.

2. Use the sample budgets in Table 3.2 to explain to the couple how their budget might change when their children go to college.

The Johnsons Have Some Budget Problems

The Johnsons enjoy a high income because both work at well-paying jobs. They cannot believe that less than a year ago they were living the stressful financial lives of college students. Times have changed for the better. The Johnsons have spent parts of three evenings over the past several days discussing their financial values and goals together. As shown in the upper portion of Figure 3.3, they have established three long-term goals: $3000 for a European vacation to be taken in 2 ½ years, $5000 needed in October 2008 for a down payment on a new automobile, and $26,078 for a down payment on a home to be purchased in December 2010. As shown in the lower portion of the figure, the Johnsons did some calculations to determine how much they had to save for each goal—over the short term—to stay on schedule to reach their long-term goals as well as pay for two vacations and an anniversary party. After developing their balance sheet and cash-flows (shown on page 55), the Johnsons made a budget for the year (shown in Table 3.3). They then reconciled various conflicting needs and wants until they found that total annual income exceeded expenses. Next, they created a revolving savings fund (Table 3.5) in which they were careful to include enough money each month to meet all of their short-term goals. When developing their cash-flow calendar for the year (Table 3.4), however, they noticed a problem: substantial cash deficits during four months of the year. In fact, despite their projected high income, they anticipate a deficit for the year. To meet this problem, they do not anticipate increasing their income, using savings, or borrowing. Instead, they are considering modifying their needs and wants to reduce their budget estimates to the point where they would have a positive balance for the year.

1. Make specific recommendations to the Johnsons on how they could make reductions in their budget estimates. Do not offer suggestions that would alter their new lifestyle drastically, as the couple would reject these ideas.

What Would You Recommend Now?

Now that you have read the chapter on budgeting, what would you recommend to Brian and Marlene Patterson in the case at the beginning of the chapter regarding:

1. Developing a series of financial goals and prioritizing those goals?

2. Getting organized to set up a budget if Brian does go back to school?

3. Controlling their spending once their budget is established?

4. Periodically assessing their progress?

5. Discussing their finances comfortably and successfully?

Exploring the World Wide Web

To complete these exercises, go to the *Garman/Forgue* website at college.hmco.com/business/students. Under General Business, select the title of this text. Click on the Internet Exercises link for this chapter, and answer the questions that appear on the Web page.

1. Visit the website for Healthy Cash. There you will find a series of short questionnaires designed to identify your spending style. What does that information tell you about potential problems you might have in achieving your financial goals and what you might want to discuss with loved ones?

2. Visit the website for the U.S. Bureau of Labor Statistics, where you will find information on expenditure patterns for a typical family. Compare this information with both the absolute dollar amounts you spend and the percentages spent in each category.

3. Visit the Colorado State University Cooperative Extension website, where you will find an article on the cost of raising children. How does the information compare with what you have done or seen other young families do as they prepare for a new arrival?

4. Visit the website for this book, where you will find a budget spreadsheet set up for your use. Create a budget for yourself for the next month. Track your income and spending for the month to see how well you are able to keep within the budgeted amounts.

5. Visit the website for CareerJournal.com, where you will find an article addressing the question of whether two incomes are better than one for couples. What three issues are raised in the article that support the notion that two incomes are not always better?

Visit the Garman/Forgue website . . .

@ college.hmco.com/business/students

Under General Business, select *Personal Finance 8e.* There, among other valuable resources, you will find a complete glossary, ACE questions, links to help you complete the chapter exercises, and links to other personal finance sites.

Chapter 4

Managing Income Taxes

LEARNING OBJECTIVES

After reading this chapter, you should be able to:

1 **Explain** the nature of progressive income taxes and the marginal tax rate.

2 **Determine** whether you should file an income tax return.

3 **Describe** the two ways of paying taxes: payroll withholding and estimated taxes.

4 **Identify** the eight steps involved in calculating federal income taxes.

5 **Understand** strategies to legally avoid overpayment of income taxes.

What Would You Recommend?

Sean Hutchinson and Nicole Martin have set a wedding date in two years. Sean earns $44,000 per year managing a national franchise fast-food restaurant. He also earns roughly $10,000 to $12,000 per year selling jewelry that he designs at shows held monthly in various nearby cities. Right after they get married, Sean is planning on going back to college full-time to finish the last year of his undergraduate degree. Nicole earns $58,000 annually working as an institutional sales representative for an insurance company. Both Sean and Nicole contribute $100 per month each to their employer-sponsored 401(k) retirement accounts. Sean has little additional savings, but Nicole has accumulated $18,000 that she wants to use for a down payment on a home. Nicole owns 300 shares of stock in an oil company that she inherited four years ago when the price was $90 per share; now the stock is worth $130 per share. Sean and Nicole live in a state where the state income tax is 6 percent.

What would you recommend to Sean and Nicole on the subject of managing income taxes regarding:

1. Using tax credits to help pay for Sean's college expenses?

2. If Nicole pays federal income taxes at the 25 percent rate, understanding how much money she will realize if she sells the stocks?

3. Buying a home?

4. Increasing contributions to their employer-sponsored retirement plans?

5. Establishing a sideline business for Sean's jewelry operation?

Managing your money effectively includes efforts to avoid paying unnecessary sums to the government in taxes. This strategy will provide you with more money to spend, save, donate, and invest. Of course, you should pay your income tax liabilities in full, but that's all—there is no need to pay a dime extra. To achieve this goal, you need to adopt a **tax planning** perspective designed to reduce, defer, or eliminate some income taxes. To get started, you should recognize that you pay personal income taxes only on your **taxable income.** This amount is determined by subtracting your allowable exclusions, adjustments, exemptions, and deductions from your gross income, with the result being the income upon which the tax is actually calculated. We will provide details on this calculation later. For now, simply remember that the key idea in managing income taxes is to legally reduce your taxable income as much as possible, which, in turn, reduces your tax liability.

This chapter examines the principles of income taxation in the United States and the impacts of those taxes on your disposable income. It then discusses who must pay taxes and how those taxes are paid—through payroll withholding and estimated tax payments. Next, the chapter details the eight-step process, with examples, of calculating federal income taxes, from the determination of gross income through the computation of one's tax liability and the resulting balance owed or refund due. Finally, the chapter presents several excellent strategies that you can use to reduce your tax liability.

Golden Rules of

Managing Income Taxes

Financial success comes from learning the Golden Rules of personal finance and then putting what you have learned into practice. Make the following your money habits in managing your income taxes:

1. Sign up for tax-free and tax-advantaged employee benefits at your workplace such as premium conversion, cafeteria plans, and flexible spending accounts for health and dependent care.
2. Save and invest the maximum amount possible in your employer-sponsored 401(k) retirement plan or at least up to the amount of your employer's matching contribution. Invest additional money for retirement in tax-sheltered accounts.
3. Buy a home so you can record the interest and property taxes as itemized tax deductions along with many previously non-itemized deductions. Later, when you sell, you can reap the benefit of the enormous capital gains exclusion.
4. Consider buying and managing real estate as an investment and/or open a sideline business for the possible tax advantages it can bring.
5. Do your own tax return so you can learn more about how to reduce your income tax liability. No one except you can think of how to save money on your own income taxes.

1 Explain the nature of progressive income taxes and the marginal tax rate.

Progressive Income Taxes and the Marginal Tax Rate

Taxes are compulsory charges imposed by a government on its citizens and their property. To learn how to manage taxes effectively, you should know how taxes are administered and classified. Taxes are administered at all levels of government. This chapter focuses primarily on the federal personal income tax. Three-fourths of all Americans pay federal income taxes. The U.S. **Internal Revenue Service (IRS)** is the agency charged with the responsibility of collecting federal income taxes based on the legal provisions in the **Internal Revenue Code.** This code represents the major tax laws written by the U.S. Congress.

In addition, the IRS itself issues regulations, which interpret and make specific the tax laws passed by Congress. These regulations have the force and effect of law; they are printed in thick volumes available in some public libraries. Finally, dozens of IRS rulings are issued each year; these decisions are related to specific tax cases and are based on the IRS's interpretations of both the Internal Revenue Code and the IRS regulations. Tax rulings provide guidance on how the IRS may act in similar situations. The courts also issue decisions giving the judicial interpretation of the tax laws that Congress passes and the regulations and decisions of the Internal Revenue Service.

The Progressive Nature of the Federal Income Tax

Taxes can be classified as progressive or regressive. A **progressive tax** takes a larger percentage—not just dollar amount—of income from high-income taxpayers than from low-income taxpayers. In the United States, the federal personal income tax is progressive because the tax rate increases as a taxpayer's income (and thus implied ability to pay) increases. As Table 4.1 shows, the higher portions of a taxpayer's income are taxed at increasingly higher rates under the federal income tax.* A **regressive tax** operates in the opposite way. That is, as income rises, the tax demands a decreasing proportion of a person's income as income increases. Such taxes are not based on ability to pay. An example of a regressive tax is a state sales tax.

The Marginal Tax Rate Is Applied to the Last Dollar Earned

A **marginal tax bracket (MTB)** is one of the six income-range segments that are taxed at increasing rates as income goes up. These segments and their corresponding marginal tax rates are shown in the tax-rate schedules (see Tables 4.1 and 4.2, page 94). Recall from Chapter 1 that the **marginal tax rate** is applied to your last dollar of earnings. Depending on their income, taxpayers fit into one of these tax brackets (as shown in Table 4.2) and, accordingly, pay at one of those marginal tax rates: 10 percent, 15 percent, 25 percent, 28 percent, 33 percent, or 35 percent. Each year the taxable income levels for the tax brackets are adjusted to reduce the effects of inflation, a process called **indexing.** Indexing keeps taxpayers from being unfairly forced to pay more taxes as they receive raises simply to keep up with inflation.

Your marginal tax rate is perhaps the single most important concept in personal finance. It tells you the portion of any extra taxable earnings—from a raise, investment income, or money from a second job—you must pay in income taxes. Correspondingly, it measures the tax reduction benefits of a tax-deductible expense that allows you to reduce your taxable income.

As an example, consider Susan Bassett, from Syracuse, New York (see Figure 4.1, page 94). Susan is in the 25 percent marginal tax bracket because the *last* dollar that she earned is taxed at that level. Part of her $60,000 gross income ($3100 + $4850) is not taxed, the next $7150 of income is taxed at 10 percent, the next $21,900 is taxed at 15 percent, and the remaining $23,000 of Susan's income is taxed at 25 percent. Thus, Susan is in the 25 percent marginal tax bracket. The mathematics shown in Figure 4.1 is

Table 4.1 The Progressive Nature of the Federal Income Tax	
Segment of Taxable Income	**Tax Rate***
First $7,150	10%
Over $7,150 but not over $29,050	15%
Over $29,050 but not over $70,350	25%
Over $70,350 but not over $146,750	28%
Over $146,750 but not over $319,100	33%
Over $319,100	35%
*Tax rates are for a single taxpayer for income earned in 2004.	

*All tax rates cited in this chapter are for income earned in 2004 for tax returns filed in 2005.

Table 4.2 Tax-Rate Schedules

If Taxable Income Is	The Tax Is	Plus	This Percent	Of Amount Over
Single Return				
Not over $7,150	$ 0	+	10%	$ 0
Over $7,150 but not over $29,050	715.00	+	15	7,150
Over $29,050 but not over $70,350	4,000.00	+	25	29,050
Over $70,350 but not over $146,750	14,325.00	+	28	70,350
Over $146,750 but not over $319,100	35,717.00	+	33	146,750
Over $319,100	92,592.50	+	35	319,100
Married Filing Jointly				
Not over $14,300	$ 0	+	10%	$ 0
Over $14,300 but not over $58,100	1,430.00	+	15	14,300
Over $58,100 but not over $117,250	8,000.00	+	25	58,100
Over $117,250 but not over $178,650	22,787.50	+	28	117,250
Over $178,650 but not over $319,100	39,979.50	+	33	178,650
Over $319,100	86,328.00	+	35	319,100

based on the **tax-rate schedules** in Table 4.2; these tax brackets must be used by persons with a taxable income of $100,000 or more. Another depiction of the income tax brackets appears in the IRS's **tax tables.** These tables, which are used to look up one's tax liability, were designed to save computational time for taxpayers with taxable incomes of less than $100,000. The tax tables and tax-rate schedules yield nearly equal tax liabilities (differing by less than $10 because of rounding) if used for the same taxable income. Segments of the tax tables are provided in Table 4.3. The tax tables and tax-rate schedules are found in *Publication 17* at the IRS website (www.irs.ustreas.gov/) by inputting the title into the search function.

Figure 4.1

How Your Income Is Really Taxed (Example: Susan Bassett with a $60,000 Gross Income)

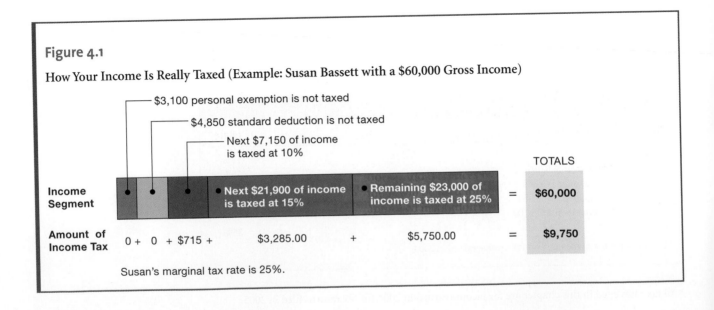

Susan's marginal tax rate is 25%.

Table 4.3 Illustrations of Segments of Tax Tables*

If Taxable Income Is		And You Are Filing	
At Least	But Less Than	Single	Joint
		Your Tax Is	
$20,000	$20,050	$2,646	$2,289
20,050	20,100	2,654	2,296
20,100	20,150	2,661	2,304
20,150	20,200	2,669	2,311
20,200	20,250	2,676	2,319
20,250	20,300	2,684	2,326
20,300	20,350	2,691	2,334
20,350	20,400	2,699	2,341
25,600	25,650	3,486	3,129
25,650	25,700	3,494	3,136
25,700	25,750	3,501	3,144
25,750	25,800	3,509	3,151
26,000	26,050	3,546	3,181
26,050	26,100	3,554	3,189
26,100	26,150	3,561	3,196
26,150	26,200	3,569	3,204
27,700	27,750	3,801	3,444
27,750	27,800	3,809	3,451
27,800	27,850	3,816	3,459
27,850	27,900	3,824	3,466
30,500	30,550	4,369	3,864
30,550	30,600	4,381	3,871
30,600	30,650	4,394	3,879
30,650	30,700	4,406	3,887
53,000	53,050	9,994	7,239
53,050	53,100	10,006	7,246
53,100	53,150	10,019	7,254
53,150	53,200	10,027	7,261
74,100	74,150	15,382	12,006
74,150	74,200	15,396	12,019
74,200	74,250	15,410	12,031
74,250	74,300	15,424	12,044
90,000	90,050	19,834	15,981
90,050	90,100	19,848	15,994
90,100	90,150	19,862	16,006
90,150	90,200	19,876	16,019
90,200	90,250	19,890	16,631
90,250	90,300	19,904	16,044
90,300	90,350	19,918	16,056
90,350	90,400	19,932	16,069

*Derived from the tax schedules in Table 4.2.

Determining Your Federal Marginal Tax Rate

You can use the tax-rate schedules in Table 4.2 to find your marginal tax rate. First, you must estimate your taxable income. You can start by looking at last year's tax return for the line labeled "taxable income" and then adding or subtracting an estimate of how much higher or lower your income will be this year. Next, you simply look at the income brackets presented and find the percentage rate. For example, a single person whose taxable income is $40,125—that is, more than $29,050 but less than $70,350—falls within the 25 percent marginal tax bracket.

Your Effective Marginal Tax Rate Is Higher

In reality, most of us pay effective marginal tax rates that are higher than 15 or 25 percent. The **effective marginal tax rate** describes a person's true marginal tax rate on income after including federal, state, and local income taxes as well as Social Security and Medicare taxes. To determine your effective marginal tax rate on income, add all of these other taxes to your federal marginal tax rate. For example, a taxpayer might have a federal marginal income tax rate of 25 percent, a combined Social Security and Medicare tax rate of 7.65 percent, a state income tax rate of 6 percent, and a city income tax rate of 4 percent. These taxes result in an effective marginal tax rate of 43 percent (25 + 7.65 + 6 + 4 = 42.65, rounded to 43). Thus, many employed taxpayers pay an effective marginal tax rate of 43 percent or higher.

The Marginal Tax Rate Affects Your Financial Decisions

The marginal tax rate can affect many financial decisions that you make. Consider, for example, what happens if you are in the 25 percent marginal tax rate and you make a $100 tax-deductible contribution to a charity. The charity receives the $100, and you deduct the $100 from your taxable income. This deduction results in a $25 reduction in your federal income tax ($100 × 0.25). In effect, you give $75 and the government "gives" $25 to the charity.

Your Average Tax Rate Is Lower

Your **average tax rate** is a calculated figure showing your tax liability as a percentage of your total income. Because your total income is not fully taxed by the federal government, your average tax rate is always less than your marginal tax rate. For example, as shown in Figure 4.1, Susan Bassett's average tax rate on total income is 16.25 percent ($9750 ÷ $60,000). The average federal tax rate for all U.S. taxpayers is approximately 15 percent.

Filing a Tax Return

2 Determine whether you should file an income tax return.

Citizens and residents of the United States and Puerto Rico must file federal income tax returns if they have sufficient **earned income** (compensation for performing personal services, such as salaries, wages, tips, and net earnings from self-employment). To **file** simply means to report formally to the IRS any income earned and your tax liability for the year. In general, the minimum levels of income that require filing a return are $7950 for single individuals and $15,900 for married people filing jointly. These numbers represent the sum of the value of the personal exemption and the standard deduction for taxpayers of the appropriate filing status. The law also requires you to file a return (even if you owe no taxes) when someone (such as your parent) can claim you as a dependent and you have **unearned income** (investment returns in the form of rents, dividends, capital gains, interest, or royalties) exceeding $800, or if you have earned income greater than $4850 (the value of a standard deduction).

There are several other cases in which it is wise to file a tax return, even though it is not required:

1. **To get a refund of any federal income taxes withheld.** People who have had federal income taxes withheld from paychecks but who did not receive enough income to be required to file should submit a return to obtain a refund. If you moved and never received a filed-for deserved refund, submit IRS Form 8822, the official change-of-address notification, and the agency will forward you a check.

2. **To get a refund if you neglected to file for refunds in the past.** If you have neglected to file for refunds in the past, you can complete the appropriate tax form for the year in question: 1040EZ (which the IRS calls its "very short form"), 1040A (short form), or 1040 (the long form).

3. **To get a refund if you overpaid your taxes in the past three years.** You may file an amended return for a refund on Form 1040-X to correct returns filed in error during the past three years. For example, you might have overpaid your tax on your original return because you neglected to take all allowable deductions or credits (details are given later in this chapter) or you might need to correct a mistake on an original or previously amended return.

4. **To get a refund if you can qualify for a refundable tax credit.** You also may qualify for the earned income credit or "additional" child tax credit. Claiming a credit may allow you to get money from the government even though you owed no income taxes for the year. (More information about credits is found on pages 109–110.)

Ways to Pay Income Taxes

When taxpayers complete their tax returns for mailing to the Internal Revenue Service by the April 15 deadline,* they go through a number of steps to determine their **tax liability**, the amount of tax that must be paid based on income received during the previous year. Note, however, that the federal income tax is a "pay as you go" tax. Accordingly, taxpayers are required to use one of two methods to pay their tax liability gradually during the year prior to filing: payroll withholding or estimated taxes.

3 Describe the two ways of paying taxes: payroll withholding and estimated taxes.

*If you are unable to mail your tax return on time, you may avoid a penalty for late filing by (1) completing Form 4868 to obtain an automatic four-month extension, and (2) paying by the regular due date the amount you estimate you owe to the IRS. You may complete and mail Form 4868, use it as a guide for a letter containing the same information, or telephone (888) 796-1074. Have your previous year's tax return available to verify certain key facts. A second extension for two months is also available. Approximately 8 million taxpayers get extensions every year.

Method One: Payroll Withholding

In **payroll withholding,** an employer takes a certain amount from an employee's income as a prepayment of an individual's tax liability for the year and sends that amount to the IRS, where it is credited to that particular taxpayer's account. The amount withheld is based on the amount of income earned, the number of exemptions reported to the employer by the employee on Form W-4 (the Employee's Withholding Allowance Certificate), and other factors.

You may be exempt from payroll withholding (for example, if you are a student who works only summers) if you meet three tests:

1. You had no income tax liability last year and were entitled to a full refund of any tax withheld.

2. You expect to owe no tax in the current year on an income of $800 or less.

3. You are not claimed as an exemption on another person's tax return.

If you satisfy these criteria, request a Form W-4 from your employer and write the word "exempt" in the appropriate place. If you do not satisfy all three tests, you must file a tax return after the end of the year to obtain a refund of the money withheld. Withholding for Social Security and Medicare taxes occurs regardless of whether you are exempt from income tax withholding.

Overwithholding occurs when employees have their employers withhold more in estimated taxes than the tax liability ultimately due the government. Approximately four-fifths of all taxpayers practice overwithholding, which is a form of forced savings. These taxpayers receive their refunds (which averaged more than $2200 last year) approximately six weeks after filing their income tax returns. The IRS does not pay interest on such refunded monies. If you anticipate that your tax liability will be lower than the federal government's withholding schedule, you can file a new W-4 form with your employer to decrease the amount withheld, which will in turn increase the amount of your take-home income.

Method Two: Estimated Taxes

Many people are self-employed or receive substantial income from an employer that is not required to practice payroll withholding. Lawyers, accountants, consultants, movie actors, and owners of rental property are examples of such workers. Under the "pay as you go" requirements, such taxpayers must estimate their tax liability and pay it in quarterly installments on April 15, June 15, September 15, and the following January 15. **Estimated taxes** represent the advance payments of one's current tax liability based on estimated tax liability. Form 1040-ES, Declaration of Estimated Tax for Individuals, must be filed if the estimated tax is $1000 or more and if all other withholdings will total less than 90 percent of the current year's tax.

Eight Steps in Calculating Your Income Taxes

4 Identify the eight steps involved in calculating federal income taxes.

There are eight basic steps in calculating federal income taxes:

1. Determine your total income.

2. Determine and report gross income by subtracting exclusions.

3. Subtract adjustments to income.

4. Subtract the IRS's standard deduction amount for your tax status or list your itemized deductions.

5. Subtract the value of your personal exemptions.

6. Determine your tax liability.

7. Subtract appropriate tax credits.

8. Calculate the balance due the IRS or the amount of your refund.

Figure 4.2 (page 100) graphically depicts these eight steps in the overall process of federal income tax calculation. Our discussion here will remain general so that you can grasp the "big picture" of federal income taxation. Although we highlight a number of details, limitations, and qualifications throughout this chapter, we do not examine these points in depth. The wise financial manager will call the IRS at (800) TAX-1040 to obtain Publication 17, *Your Federal Income Tax: For Individuals,* for the current year, or download it from the IRS at www.irs.gov/. All federal income tax forms can be obtained by telephoning the IRS at (800) TAX-3676. IRS information (such as forms, regulations, guides, and answers to common questions) may be accessed from the World Wide Web at www.irs.gov/. A visit to a bookstore will also give you an opportunity to purchase privately produced tax guides that offer advice on how to reduce income taxes and computer software to assist in filling out your return.*

When studying income taxes, keep in mind that a number of terms used have very precise meanings, even though people often get them mixed up. The idea is to legally reduce your income so that you pay the smallest amount possible in income taxes. You do so by reducing total income by removing nontaxable income and then subtracting exclusions, deductions, exemptions, and tax credits, as indicated in the unshaded boxes in Figure 4.2. Definitions follow as appropriate.

1. Determine Your Total Income

Practically everything you receive in return for your work or services and any profit from the sale of assets is considered income, whether the compensation is paid in cash, property, or services. Listing these earnings will reveal your **total income**—compensation from all sources—and most of it, but not all, will be subject to income taxes.

---

*The best and most readable tax guide is the annual *J. K. Lasser's Your Income Tax* (New York: Simon & Schuster). *The Ernst & Young Tax Guide* is detailed and authoritative. Popular computer software programs to help prepare income tax returns include Quicken TurboTax (www.turbotax.com), H. D. Vest Financial Planning (www.hdvest.com), TAXACT (www.taxact.com), and H&R Block's Kiplinger TaxCut (www.taxcut.com).

Figure 4.2

The Process of Income Tax Calculation

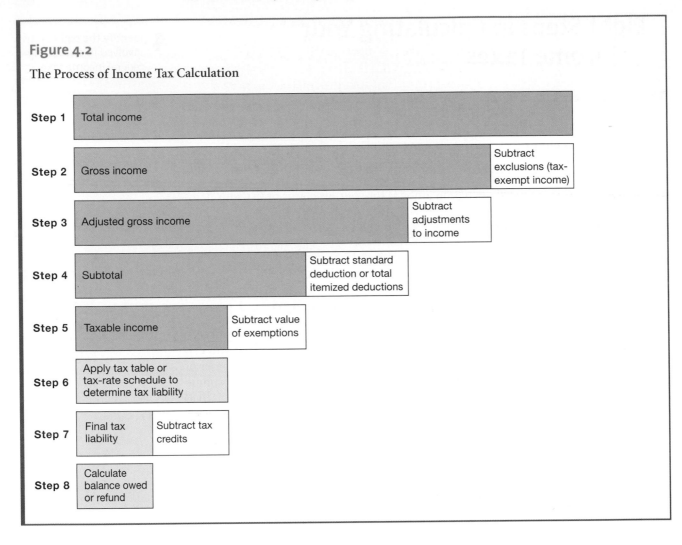

Income to Include.   For most people, earned income is reported to them annually on a Form W-2, Wage and Tax Statement. Employers must provide W-2 information by January 31 of the next year. If you receive income from interest or dividends or other sources, those sources may send you a Form 1099. That information is also provided to the IRS.

The following types of income are included when you report your income to the IRS:

- Wages and salaries
- Commissions
- Bonuses
- Professional fees earned
- Income from stock options
- Tips earned
- Alimony received
- Scholarship and fellowship income spent on room, board, and other living expenses
- Grants and the value of tuition reductions that pay for teaching or other services
- Annuity and pension income received
- Distributions from retirement accounts and tax-deferred annuities
- Military retirement income

- Social Security income (a portion is taxed above certain income thresholds)
- Disability payments received if you did not pay the premiums
- Damage payments from personal injury lawsuits (punitive damages only)
- Value of personal use of employer-provided car
- Withdrawals and disbursements from retirement accounts, such as an individual retirement account (IRA) or 401(k) retirement plan (discussed in Chapter 18, Retirement Planning)
- State and local income tax refunds (only if the taxpayer itemized deductions during the previous year)
- Fair value of anything received in a barter arrangement
- Employee productivity awards
- Awards for artistic, scientific, and charitable achievements unless assigned to a charity
- Prizes, contest winnings, and rewards
- Gambling and lottery winnings
- All kinds of illegal income
- Fees for serving as a juror or election worker
- Unemployment benefits
- Partnership income or share of profits
- Net rental income
- Royalties
- Investment, business, and farm profits
- Interest income (this includes credit union dividends)
- Dividends from mutual funds (including capital gains distributions even though they are reinvested)
- Dividend income from corporations (This income is specially taxed at a maximum rate of 15 percent—at the same rates as capital gains, as discussed in the next section—and the rate is only 5 percent for taxpayers in the lowest two brackets.

Include Capital Gains and Losses in Total Income.   An **asset** is property owned by a taxpayer for personal use or as an investment. Examples of assets include stocks, mutual funds, bonds, land, art, gems, stamps, and coins typically held for investment as well as vehicles and homes. A **capital gain** is the net income received from the sale of an asset above the costs incurred to purchase and sell it. A **capital loss** results when the sale of an asset brings less income than the costs of purchasing and selling the asset. Capital gains and losses on investments must be reported on your tax return. Capital gains from the sale or exchange of property held for *personal use,* such as on a vehicle or vacation home, must be reported as income, but losses on such property are not deductible.

There is no tax liability on any capital gains until the stock, bond, mutual fund, real estate, or other investment is sold. When you sell such an investment, the gain or loss is calculated by comparing how much you have invested in the asset sold to the sales proceeds, net of commissions and transaction fees.

A **short-term gain** (or **loss**) occurs when you sell an asset that you owned for one year or less; it is taxed at the same rates as ordinary income. A **long-term gain** (or **loss**) occurs when you sell an asset that you owned for more than one year (at least a year and a day); it is taxed at more favorable special rates. Long-term capital gains from corporations are taxed at a maximum rate of 15 percent, for example, and the rate is only 5 percent for taxpayers in the lower two brackets. Long-term capital gain tax rates for collectibles are 28 percent.

Capital losses may be used first to offset capital gains. If there are no capital gains, or if the capital losses are larger than the capital gains, you can deduct the capital loss against your other income, but only up to a limit of $3000 in one year. If your overall capital loss is more than $3000, the excess carries forward to the next tax year, up to an annual $3000 maximum.

2. Determine and Report Gross Income by Subtracting Exclusions

Gross income consists of all income (both earned and unearned) received in the form of money, goods, services, and property that a taxpayer is required to report to the IRS. To determine gross income, you need to determine which kinds of income are not subject to federal taxation and, therefore, need not be reported as part of gross income. These amounts are called **exclusions.**

Income to Exclude.   Some of the more common exclusions (sometimes subject to limits) are as follows:

- Inherited money or property
- Income from a car pool
- Income from items sold at a garage sale for a sum less than what you paid
- Cash rebates on purchases of new cars and other products
- Scholarship and fellowship income spent on course-required tuition, fees, books, supplies, and equipment (degree candidates only)
- Distributions from state-sponsored Section 529 Plans (prepaid tuition and savings) used for education.
- Prizes and awards made primarily to recognize artistic, civic, charitable, educational, and similar achievements
- Federal income tax refunds
- State and local income tax refunds for a year in which you claimed the standard deduction
- Interest received on Series EE and Series I bonds used for college tuition and fees
- Child support payments received
- Property settlement in a divorce
- Compensatory damages in physical injury cases
- Return of money loaned
- Withdrawals from medical savings accounts used for qualified expenses
- Earnings accumulating within annuities, cash-value life insurance policies, Series EE bonds, and qualified retirement accounts
- Interest income received on tax-exempt government bonds issued by states, counties, cities, and districts
- Life insurance benefits received
- Combat zone pay for military personnel
- Gifts
- Welfare, black lung, worker's compensation, and veterans' benefits
- Value of food stamps
- First $500,000 ($250,000 if single) gain on the sale of a principal residence
- Disability insurance benefits if you paid the insurance premiums
- Social Security benefits (except for high-income taxpayers)
- Up to 14 days of rental income from a vacation home
- Tuition reduction, if not received as compensation for teaching or service
- First $5000 of death benefits paid by an employer to a worker's beneficiary
- Travel and mileage expenses reimbursed by an employer (if not previously deducted by the taxpayer)

- Employer-provided per diem allowance covering only meals and incidentals
- Amounts paid by employers for premiums for medical insurance, worker's compensation, and Social Security taxes
- Contributions by employers to provide coverage for health and accident insurance policies and long-term care services
- Moving expense reimbursements received from an employer (if not previously deducted by the taxpayer)
- Employer-provided commuter highway vehicle transportation and transit passes (up to $100 per month for both)
- Employer-provided parking (up to $190 per month)
- Value of premiums for first $50,000 worth of group-term life insurance provided by an employer
- Employer payments (up to $5000) for dependent care assistance (for children and parents)
- Benefits from employers that are impractical to tax because they are so modest, such as occasional supper money and taxi fares for overtime work, company parties, holiday gifts (not cash), and occasional theater or sporting events
- Employee contributions to flexible spending accounts
- Reimbursements from flexible spending accounts
- Reimbursements for medical expenses from health reimbursement accounts funded solely by employer contributions
- Employer-provided educational assistance payments for undergraduate and graduate classes (up to $5250 annually)

3. Subtract Adjustments to Income

In the process of determining your taxable income, you make **adjustments to income** (or **adjustments**). These allowable subtractions from gross income include items such as contributions to qualified personal retirement accounts [such as to IRA, SEP, and 401(k) accounts] and Health Savings Accounts, moving expenses to a new job location (including college graduates who move to take their first job), alimony payments, interest penalties for early withdrawal of savings certificates of deposit, higher education expenses for tuition and fees (up to $3000), student loan interest for higher education ($2500 maximum), business expenses, net operating losses, capital losses (up to $3000), and certain expenses of self-employed persons (such as health insurance premiums). Adjustments are called **above-the-line deductions** because they may be subtracted from gross income even if itemized deductions are not claimed. Thus, adjustments may be taken regardless of whether the taxpayer itemizes deductions or takes the standard deduction amount (these procedures are explained later in this section). Adjustments are subtracted from gross income to determine **adjusted gross income (AGI).** In addition to reducing your AGI directly, they help you qualify for other AGI-based write-offs, such as for some itemized deductions. Subtracting adjustments to income from gross income results in a subtotal.

To illustrate the value of adjustments to income, consider a person with a gross income of $41,000 who contributes $1000 to certain types of **qualified retirement accounts** (plans that the IRS has approved to encourage saving for retirement). The adjustment reduces gross income to $40,000 and, therefore, saves $250 in income taxes (calculated using Table 4.2). (Contributions to retirement plans are covered later in this chapter and in Chapter 18.)

Advice from an Expert

A Sideline Business Can Reduce Your Income Taxes

Did you realize that a sideline business can open many doors to tax deductions and income-shifting techniques? That's right! While we would never recommend spending money for a tax deduction, if you're going to spend the money anyway, you should do everything you can to make it tax-deductible.

By having your own business, every dollar you spend in your attempts to make a profit becomes tax-deductible. Even better, it's deductible "above the line," saving you federal, state, local, and even self-employment taxes! These are very high-powered deductions. You can deduct auto expenses, in-home office expenses, office equipment (e.g., desk, chair, computer), contributions to self-funded retirement accounts, health insurance premiums, educational expenses, entertainment, business gifts, and more. You can deduct salaries of employees, even if they are your children, other relatives, or friends. The list goes on!

The business does not even have to be your primary employment. In fact, if you lose money on such a business, you can deduct those losses from your other income. The IRS says that you must do what a "reasonable business person" would do to make a profit. If you do not meet that test, the IRS will classify the operation as a hobby business, require you to report the income, and disallow the deductions.

In summary, it's a good idea to start your own business doing something you enjoy. Keep detailed records, and take advantage of your deductions.

Anthony J. Campolo
Columbus State Community College

4. Subtract the Standard Deduction for Your Tax Status or Itemize Your Deductions

Over the years, Congress has allowed a number of day-to-day personal living expenses to be deducted from adjusted gross income. Taxpayers may, therefore, reduce adjusted gross income by the amount of the standard deduction or by the total of their itemized deductions, whichever is larger. The **standard deduction** is a fixed amount that all taxpayers (except some dependents) who do not choose to itemize deductions may subtract from their adjusted gross income. In effect, it consists of the government's legally permissible estimate of any likely tax-deductible expenses these taxpayers might have. For example, the standard deduction amounts are $4850 for single individuals and twice as much, $9700, for married people filing jointly.

Persons who are age 65 or older and/or blind may claim an extra amount for their standard deduction. Taxpayers whose total itemized deductions would not exceed the amount permitted for the standard deduction may, instead, use the appropriate standard deduction.

About one-fourth of all taxpayers have itemized deductions that total more than the standard deduction amount for their **filing status**—the description of family status that determines the taxpayer's tax bracket and rate at which income is taxed. A return can be filed with a status of a single person, a married person (filing separately or jointly), or a head of household.

Taxpayers whose tax-deductible expenses exceed the standard deduction amount may forego the standard deduction and list their **itemized deductions** instead. These items are part of the total expenditures of a person that can be deducted from adjusted gross income in determining taxable income. For example, a single person might list all of his or her possible tax deductions and find that they total $5000, which is more than the standard deduction amount of $4850 permitted for single taxpayers. In that case, the taxpayer should deduct the larger amount, $5000, instead of taking the $4850 standard deduction amount. Some deductions are subject to limits based on your adjusted gross income. The tax form lists the following classifications of itemized deductions, and many are subject to certain limits:

- Medical and Dental Expenses
- Taxes You Paid
- Interest You Paid
- Gifts to Charity
- Casualty and Theft Losses
- Job Expenses and Most Other Miscellaneous Deductions

Examples of legitimate deductions in each of these categories follow.

Medical and Dental Expenses (Not Paid by Insurance)
in Excess of 7.5 Percent of Adjusted Gross Income
Medicine and drugs
Medical insurance premiums, including those for long-term insurance for the chronically ill and for insurance on contact lenses
Medical services (doctors, dentists, nurses, hospitals, long-term health care)
Sterilizations, legal abortions, and prescription contraceptives
Costs of a physician-prescribed course of treatment for obesity
Expenses for prescription drugs/programs to quit smoking
Medical equipment and aids (contact lens, eyeglasses, hearing devices, orthopedic shoes, false teeth, wheelchair lifts)
Fees for childbirth preparation classes
Costs of sending a mentally or physically challenged person to a special school
Home improvements made for the physically handicapped (ramps, railings, widening doors)
Transportation costs to and from locations where medical services are obtained, using a standard flat mileage allowance
Travel and conference registration fees for a parent to learn about a child's disease

Taxes You Paid
Real estate property taxes (such as on a home or land)
Personal property taxes (such as on an automobile or boat when any part of the tax is based on the value of the asset)
State and local income taxes or state and local taxes

Interest You Paid
Interest paid on first and second home mortgage loans
"Points" treated as a type of prepaid interest on the purchase of a principal residence
Interest paid on home-equity loans
Interest paid on loans used for investments
Education loan interest ($2500 maximum) on borrowed funds used for higher education

Gifts to Charity

Cash contributions to qualified organizations, such as churches, schools, and other qualifying charities (receipt required for $250 or more)

Noncash contributions (such as personal property) at **fair market value** (what a willing buyer would pay to a willing seller); a receipt is required for contributions of more than $500

Mileage allowance for travel and out-of-pocket expenses for volunteer charitable work

Charitable contributions made through payroll deduction

Casualty and Theft Losses (Not Paid by Insurance) in Excess of 10 Percent of Adjusted Gross Income

Casualty losses (such as from storms, vandalism, and fires) in excess of $100

Theft of money or property in excess of $100 (a copy of the police report provides good substantiation)

Mislaid or lost property if the loss results from an identifiable event that is unexpected or unusual (such as catching a diamond ring in a car door and losing the stone)

Job Expenses and Most Other Miscellaneous Deductions in Excess of 2 Percent of Adjusted Gross Income (Partial Listing Only)

Union or professional association dues and membership fees

Subscriptions to magazines, journals, and newspapers used for business or professional purposes

Books and software for use in a profession

Tools and supplies for use in a profession

Cost of computers and cell phones required as a condition of your job

Clothing and uniforms not suitable for off-the-job usage as ordinary wearing apparel (protective shoes, hats, safety goggles, gloves, uniforms), laundering and cleaning

Unreimbursed employee business expenses (but only a portion of the cost of meals and entertainment), including long-distance telephone calls, cleaning and laundry, and car washes (of business vehicle)

Investment-related expenses (e.g., computer software, fees for on-line trading, adviser fees, investment club expenses, IRA fees [if paid directly rather than from the account itself], safe-deposit box rental, subscriptions to investment magazines and newsletters)

Tax preparation fees

Legal fees that pertain to tax advice in a divorce or to the details of alimony payments

Travel costs between two jobs, using a flat mileage allowance

Job-related car expenses (but not commuting to a regular job), using a flat mileage allowance or actual expenses

Commuting costs to a temporary workplace

Commuting costs that qualify as a business or education expense

Medical examinations required (but not paid for) by an employer to obtain or keep a job

Appraisal fees for charitable donations or casualty losses

Education expenses if required to keep your job or improve your job or professional skills (but not if the training readies you for a new career)

Job-hunting expenses for typing, printing, résumé advice, career counseling, want ads, telephone calls, employment agency fees, mailing costs, and travel for seeking a job in your present career field

Transportation, food, and entertainment costs for job hunting (which does not have to be successful) in your present career

Cost of contesting a tax, including federal income taxes

Other Miscellaneous Deductions Allowed at 100 Percent
Gambling losses (but only to offset reported gambling income)
Business expenses for handicapped workers

Given the considerable number of deductions listed here and numerous others for which you might qualify, it makes sense to estimate your possible deductions very carefully. If the estimated total exceeds the standard deduction amount or is even close, go back and itemize deductions more carefully and then deduct the larger amount.

5. Subtract the Value of Your Personal Exemptions

An **exemption** (or **personal exemption**) is a legally permitted deduction from adjusted gross income based on the number of persons supported by the taxpayer's income. An exemption may be claimed for the taxpayer and qualifying dependents, such as a spouse (if filing jointly), children, parents, and other dependents earning less than a specific income and for whom the taxpayer provides more than half of their financial support. A person can serve as an exemption on only one tax return—his or her own or another person's (usually a parent). Each exemption reduces taxable income by $3100. The value of an exemption is phased out for higher-income taxpayers.

Claiming Another Person as an Exemption.   To claim someone else as a dependent for tax purposes and, therefore, that person's exemption value, the dependent must meet five criteria:

1. The dependent must be a relative or, if unrelated, must have resided in your home as a member of your household.

2. If the person was younger than age 19 or was a full-time student younger than age 24, his or her income does not matter. A person not meeting this age and student status requirement must have received less than $3100 in gross income for the year to be claimed as a dependent.

3. More than half of the dependent's total support must have been provided by you. (Exceptions include children of divorced parents, who generally can be claimed only by the custodial parent.)

4. The dependent must be a U.S. citizen or a legal resident of the United States, Canada, or Mexico.

5. The dependent must not have filed a joint return with his or her spouse. If the person and the person's spouse file a joint return only to obtain a refund, you may claim him or her if the other criteria apply.

What If You Are Claimed as an Exemption?   If you are claimed as a dependent on someone else's return or are eligible to be claimed, you may not claim a personal exemption for yourself, as only one person receives the exemption. For dependents who are claimed as an exemption by another person but who must still file a return, the amount permitted for that taxpayer's standard deduction is limited to the amount of income earned on a job up to the amount of the standard deduction ($4850).

6. Determine Your Tax Liability

The steps detailed to this point have explained how to determine your taxable income. Taxable income is calculated by taking the taxpayer's gross income, subtracting the adjustments to income, subtracting either the standard deduction or total itemized deductions, and subtracting the amount permitted for the number of exemptions allowed. The amount of taxable income is then used to determine the taxpayer's tax liability via the tax tables or tax-rate schedules combined with the appropriate filing status (such as single or married filing jointly). Each filing status has a separate tax-rate table or schedule, which you then use to find your tax liability.* Table 4.3 on page 95 shows segments from the tax tables.

The following examples show how to determine tax liability.

1. A married couple filing jointly has a gross income of $47,025, adjustments of $5350, itemized deductions of $4285, and two exemptions. They take the standard deduction of $9700 because their itemized deductions do not exceed that amount.

Gross income	$47,025
Less adjustments to income	− 5,350
Adjusted gross income	41,675
Less standard deduction for married couple	− 9,700
Subtotal	31,975
Less value of two exemptions	− 6,200
Taxable income	25,775
Tax liability (from Table 4.3)	$ 3,151

2. A single person has a gross income of $47,300, adjustments of $5220, itemized deductions of $8400, and one exemption. He or she subtracts his or her total itemized deductions because the amount exceeds the $4850 permitted standard deduction value.

Gross income	$47,300
Less adjustments to income	− 5,220
Adjusted gross income	42,080
Less itemized deductions	− 8,400
Subtotal	33,680
Less value of one exemption	− 3,100
Taxable income	30,580
Tax liability (from Table 4.3)	$ 4,381

3. A married couple with a gross income of $137,000 has adjustments of $3400, itemized deductions of $9800, and two exemptions. The itemized deductions are taken because they exceed the standard deduction value of $9700 for a married couple.

Gross income	$137,000
Less adjustments to income	− 3,400
Adjusted gross income	133,600
Less itemized deductions	− 9,800
Subtotal	123,800
Less value of two exemptions	− 6,200

*Instead of paying income taxes at the standard tax rates, about 3 million high-income taxpayers must pay a higher **alternative minimum tax (AMT)**. The AMT rate (26 or 28 percent) is triggered for people with excessive deductions. Examples include taxpayers who have several children and income from tax-exempt sources. When the value of those benefits is added back to your income, it results in an AMT amount that may exceed your regular tax.

Taxable income	117,600
Tax liability	$22,886*

*The tax liability here is calculated from the tax-rate schedules in Table 4.2 because the taxable income exceeds $100,000, which is the maximum for the tax tables. The tax liability is computed as follows: $117,600 − $117,250 = $350 × 0.28 = $98 + $22,787.50 = $22,885.50, rounded to $22,886.

7. Subtract Appropriate Tax Credits

You also may be able to lower your tax liability through tax credits. A **tax credit** (or **credit**) is a dollar-for-dollar subtraction from your tax liability that yields your "final" tax liability. A credit directly reduces your tax liability, as opposed to deductions that reduce the income subject to tax. For example, if you have calculated your tax liability to be $4200 and you qualify for $800 in tax credits, you simply subtract the $800 from the $4200 to obtain a final tax liability of $3400 ($4200 − $800), which is the amount owed after subtracting tax credits. You may take tax credits regardless of whether you itemize deductions. A **nonrefundable tax credit** may reduce your tax liability to zero; if the credit is more than your tax, however, the excess is not refunded to you. A **refundable tax credit** is treated as a payment and is added to the federal income tax withheld and estimated tax payments made. If this total is more than the total tax liability, the excess will be refunded to the taxpayer. Most credits are subject to income limits, meaning that high-income taxpayers may not be eligible for the credit.*

Hope Scholarship Credit.   A nonrefundable **Hope Scholarship credit** to the parent or student may be claimed in the amount of 100 percent of the first $1000 you spend and 50 percent of the next $1000, for a maximum credit of $1500 for each qualifying student. The money must have been spent for the qualified tuition and expenses for books, supplies, equipment, and student activity fees if required as a condition of enrollment. The credit can be claimed in two taxable years (but not beyond the year when the student completes the first two years of college) for individuals enrolled on at least a half-time basis during any part of the year. Both the Hope Scholarship credit and the lifetime learning credit (discussed next) may not be claimed for the same student expenses for the same tax year.

Lifetime Learning Credit.   The nonrefundable **lifetime learning credit** may be claimed every year for tuition and related expenses paid for all years of postsecondary education undertaken to acquire or improve job skills. The expenses for one or more courses may be for yourself, your spouse, or your dependents. The student need not be pursuing a degree or other recognized credential. This credit amounts to 20 percent of the first $10,000 paid, for a maximum of $2000 for *all* eligible students in a family. There is no limit on the number of years the credit may be taken for the same eligible student. The lifetime learning and Hope Scholarship credits may not be claimed for the same student expenses for the same tax year.

Earned Income Credit.   The refundable **earned income credit** (**EIC**) may be claimed not only by workers with a qualifying child, but also, in certain cases, by childless workers.

*Most states impose state income taxes, and they may offer residents opportunities to claim a number of tax credits (e.g., first-time homebuyers and renters). You might save hundreds or even thousands of dollars on your state income taxes by carefully checking into allowable tax credits. Alaska, Florida, Nevada, South Dakota, Texas, Washington, and Wyoming do not impose state income taxes; New Hampshire and Tennessee tax only interest and dividends.

It is a special income subsidy that the government pays to low-income working people. This credit is available for joint filers whose earned income and adjusted gross income are less than about $35,000. The maximum credit is $4300 for a family with two children, $2604 for a family with one child, and $390 for a family with no qualifying children. Note that college students may qualify for the EIC. Anyone who was eligible for the credit may file to receive a credit retroactively for the previous three tax years (Form 1040-X).

Child Tax Credit.   You may claim a nonrefundable $1000 **child tax credit** for each qualifying child younger than age 17 claimed as a dependent. (This credit amount will be lower in 2006.)

Additional Child Tax Credit.   Because the formula for calculating the child tax credit results in some low-income taxpayers not qualifying for the entire credit, Congress created the additional tax credit for them. This credit is refundable.

Child and Dependent Care Credit.   The nonrefundable **child and dependent care credit** may be claimed by workers who pay employment-related expenses for care of a child or other dependent if that care gives them the freedom to work, seek work, or attend school full-time. Depending on your income, the maximum credit is 35 percent of qualifying care expenses up to a $1050 maximum credit for one dependent and a maximum credit of $2100 for two or more dependents. Taxpayers may claim both a dependent care tax credit and a child tax credit.

Adoption Credit.   A nonrefundable **adoption tax credit** of up to $10,390 is available for the qualifying costs of an adoption.

Mortgage Interest Credit.   A nonrefundable **mortgage interest tax credit** of up to $2000 for mortgage interest paid may be claimed under special state and local government programs that provide a "mortgage credit certificate" for people who purchase a principal residence or borrow funds for certain home improvements. Generally, the home must not cost more than 90 to 110 percent of the average area purchase price. This credit is designed to help low-income families purchase homes.

Retirement Savings Contribution Credit.   Singles with adjusted gross incomes of $25,000 or less and joint filers earning $50,000 or less can claim a nonrefundable **retirement savings contribution credit** (also known as a **saver credit**) ranging from 10 to 50 percent of every dollar they contribute to an IRA or employer-sponsored retirement plan, up to $2000. Married couples filing jointly qualify for the 50 percent credit if their AGI is $30,000 or less, for a 20 percent credit if their AGI is between $30,001 and $32,500, and for a 10 percent credit if their AGI is between $32,501 and $50,000. For singles, the income limits are $15,000 or less for the 50 percent credit, $15,001 to $16,250 for the 20 percent credit, and $16,251 to $25,000 for the 10 percent credit.

Electric Vehicle Credit.   If you placed a qualified electric vehicle in service during the year, you may qualify for a nonrefundable **electric vehicle credit.** It generally amounts to 10 percent of the cost of the vehicle.

Elderly or Disabled Tax Credit.   Individuals who are age 65 or older or who are permanently and totally disabled may claim a nonrefundable federal tax credit that can be as much as $1125.

8. Calculate the Balance Due or the Amount of Your Refund

Next, you should examine the Form W-2 for the year that summarizes your federal income tax withheld. If the amount withheld plus any estimated tax payments you made is greater than your final tax liability, then you should receive a tax refund. If the amount is less than your final tax liability, then you have a tax balance due. In such a case, you must send the government a check or money order made out to the U.S. Treasury for the money owed. If you pay by credit card, the IRS will impose a "convenience fee" of 2.5 percent of the amount charged. Many taxpayers file their returns by mail, although you may qualify for Internet filing for free. Visit www.irs.gov/efile for more information.

If you have no money with which to pay your full tax liability, do not try to hide. Interest and penalties will follow you forever! You should always file your return on time to avoid a penalty. You then have two options: (1) borrow to pay the taxes or (2) contact the IRS about setting up an installment plan that will repay the debt within three years. Taxpayers generally hear from the IRS within three weeks if they have failed to sign the return, neglected to attach a copy of the Form W-2, made an error in arithmetic, or used the wrong tax tables or tax-rate schedules.

Avoid Taxes Through Proper Planning

5 Understand strategies to legally avoid overpayment of income taxes.

If you are knowledgeable about tax laws and regulations, keep reasonably good records, and are assertive in your planning, you can avoid overpayment of taxes. While the U.S. tax laws are strict and punitive about compliance (although the IRS audits fewer than 0.5 percent of all returns), they remain neutral about whether the taxpayer should take advantage of every "break" and opportunity possible. As Judge Learned Hand said many years ago, "There is nothing sinister in so arranging one's affairs as to keep taxes as low as possible." In a similar vein, economist John Maynard Keynes said, "The avoidance of taxes is the only intellectual pursuit that carries any reward." The strategies described here will enable you to reduce your tax liability.

Practice Legal Tax Avoidance, Not Tax Evasion

Tax evasion involves deliberately and willfully hiding income, falsely claiming deductions, or otherwise cheating the government out of taxes owed. It is illegal. A waiter who does not report tips received and a baby-sitter who does not report income are both evading taxes, as is a person who deducts $150 in charitable contributions but who fails to actually make the donations. **Tax avoidance,** on the other hand, means reducing tax liability through legal techniques. It involves applying knowledge of the tax code and regulations to personal income tax planning. Tax evasion results in penalties, fines, interest charges, and a possible jail sentence. In contrast, tax avoidance boosts your income because you pay less in taxes; as a result, you will have more money available for spending, saving, donating, and investing.

2. Long-term capital gains are usually taxed at a special marginal tax rate of 15 or 5 percent. What is your opinion on the fairness of these lower capital gains tax rates as compared to the marginal rates applied to income earned from employment that range as high as 35 percent?

3. Many college students (and other people, as well) earn money that is paid to them in cash and is not reported to the IRS and thus subject to employer withholding. Many then do not include this cash income when they file their tax returns. What are your views of this practice? What problems are these people causing for themselves when they do not report this income?

4. Identify three examples of possible sideline businesses that you might engage in to reduce your income tax liability after college graduation.

5. Name four tax credits that a college student might take advantage of while still in college or during the first few years after obtaining full-time employment.

6. Give five examples of strategies to reduce income tax liability that you will likely take advantage of during the first few years after graduating and obtaining full-time employment.

Decision-Making Cases

▶Case 1
A New Family Calculates Income and Tax Liability

Holly Bender and her two children, Austin and Alexandra, recently moved into the home of her new husband, Glenn Sandler, in Summit, Mississippi. Holly is employed as a union organizer, and her husband manages a vegetarian food store. The Bender-Sandler family income consists of the following: $40,000 in Holly's salary; $42,000 in Glenn's salary; $10,000 in life insurance proceeds from a deceased aunt; $140 in interest savings; $4380 in alimony from Holly's ex-husband; $4200 in child support from her ex-husband; $500 cash as a Christmas gift from Glenn's parents; $90 from a friend who rides to work in Holly's vehicle; $60 in lottery winnings gained from playing the lottery at $5 every week; $170 worth of dental services traded for a quilt Holly gave to the dentist; and a $1600 tuition-and-books scholarship Holly received to go to college part-time last year.

(a) What is the total of the Bender-Sandlers' reportable gross income?

(b) If Holly and Glenn put $2800 into qualified retirement plan accounts last year, what is their adjusted gross income?

(c) How many exemptions can the family claim, and how much is the total value allowed the household?

(d) How much is the allowable standard deduction for the household?

(e) Holly and Glenn have listed their itemized deductions, which total $10,200. Should they itemize or take the standard deduction?

(f) What is their family's taxable income?

(g) What is their final federal income tax liability? (For your calculations, use Table 4.2 or the *Garman/Forgue* website.)

(h) If Holly's and Glenn's employers withheld $14,000 for income taxes, do the couple owe money to the government or do they get a refund? How much?

▶Case 2
Taxable Versus Tax-Exempt Bonds

Art Williams, radio station manager in Franklin County, New Jersey, is in the 25 percent federal marginal tax bracket and pays an additional 8 percent in taxes to the state of New Jersey. Art currently has more than $20,000 invested in corporate bonds bought at various times that are earning differing amounts of taxable interest: $10,000 in ABC earning 5.9 percent; $5000 in DEF earning 5.5 percent; $3000 in GHI earning 5.8 percent; and $2000 in JKL earning 5.4 percent. His stockbroker has suggested that Art consider investing these same sums into tax-exempt municipal bonds, which currently pay a tax-free yield of 3.2 percent. What is your advice? Use the *Garman/Forgue* website to calculate your answers, or use the after-tax yield formula (or the reversed formula) on page 118.

▶Case 3
Taxable Versus Nontaxable Income

Identify each of the following items as either taxable income or an exclusion from taxable income for Jenny Lynn Wells and Bob Smithfield, a married couple from Denton, Texas:

(a) Bob earns $45,000 per year.

(b) Bob receives a $1000 bonus from his employer.

(c) Jenny Lynn receives $40,000 in commissions from her work.

(d) Jenny Lynn receives $300 in monthly child support.

(e) Bob pays $200 each month in alimony.

(f) Bob contributes $2000 to his retirement account.

(g) Jenny Lynn inherits a car from her aunt that has a fair market value of $3000.

(h) Bob receives a $5000 gift from his mother.

Financial Math Questions

1. What would be the tax liability for a single taxpayer who has a gross income of $33,975? (Hint: Use Table 4.2, and don't forget to first subtract the value of a standard deduction and one exemption.)

2. What would be the marginal tax rate for a single person who has a taxable income of (a) $20,210, (b) $27,800, (c) $26,055, and (d) $90,230? (Hint: Use Table 4.2.)

3. Ramona Peterson determined the following tax information: gross salary, $39,400; interest earned, $90; qualified retirement plan contribution, $1000; personal exemption, $3100; and itemized deductions, $3950. Calculate Ramona's taxable income and tax liability. (Hint: Use Table 4.2.)

4. Brandy and Dusty Timberline determined the following tax information: gross salaries, $234,000 and $222,500, respectively; interest earned, $11,140; qualified retirement plan contributions, $60,000; personal exemptions, $6200; and itemized deductions, $26,150. Calculate the Timberlines' taxable income and tax liability. (Hint: Use Table 4.2.)

5. Don Clark determined the following tax information: gross salary, $143,750; interest earned, $1140; personal exemption, $3100; itemized deductions, $7200; qualified retirement plan contribution, $7000. Calculate Don's taxable income and tax liability. (Hint: Use Table 4.2.)

6. Using Table 4.2, find the tax liabilities based on the taxable income of the following people:

   (a) A married couple earning a total of $74,125

   (b) A married couple earning a total of $53,077

   (c) A single person earning $27,880

   (d) A single person earning $53,000

Money Matters Continuing Cases

Victor and Maria Reduce Their Income Tax Liability

The year before last, Victor earned $51,000 from his retail management position and Maria earned $45,000 as a dental hygienist. After they took the standard deduction and claimed four exemptions (themselves plus their two children), their federal income tax liability totaled close to $15,000. After learning from friends that they were paying too much in taxes, the couple vowed to try and never again pay that much. Therefore, the Hernandezes embarked on a year-long effort to reduce their income tax liability. This year, they tracked all of their possible itemized deductions, and both made contributions to qualified retirement plans at their places of employment.

1. Calculate the Hernandezes' income tax liability for this year as a joint return (using Table 4.2) given the following information: gross salary income (Victor, $55,000; Maria $49,000); state income tax refund ($400); interest on checking and savings accounts ($250); car pool income from Maria's coworkers ($240); contributions to qualified retirement accounts ($6000); itemized deductions (real estate taxes, $4000; mortgage interest, $6000; charitable contributions, $1700); and exemptions for themselves and their two children.

2. List any other strategies to reduce tax liability that Victor and Maria might have missed.

The Johnsons Calculate Their Income Taxes

Harry and Belinda are both working hard and earning good salaries. They believe, however, that they are paying too much in federal income taxes. The Johnsons' total income last year included Harry's salary of $30,000, Belinda's salary of $36,000, $48 interest on savings and checking, and $3000 interest income from the trust that is taxed in the same way as interest income from checking and savings accounts.

1. What is the Johnsons' reportable gross income?

2. Assuming that the Johnsons file a joint federal income tax return, what is the total value of their exemptions?

3. How much is the standard deduction for the Johnsons?

4. The couple has $6400 in itemized deductions. Should they itemize or take the standard deduction?

5. What is the Johnsons' taxable income?

6. Assuming the Johnsons have no tax credits, what is their tax liability (using Table 4.2)?

7. Assuming they had a combined $10,500 in federal income taxes withheld, how much of a refund will the Johnsons receive?

8. What is their marginal tax rate?

9. Based on gross income, what is their average tax rate?

10. Even though they are renters, assume the Johnsons were buying a home with monthly payments of $800, or $9600 for the year. Of this amount, the sum of $8400 might go for interest and real estate property taxes, both of which are tax-deductible. The couple would then

have $14,800 ($8400 + $6400) in itemized deductions. Using these numbers and Table 4.2, calculate their taxable income and tax liability, assuming $14,800 in itemized deductions instead of taking the standard deduction.

11. What might be your advice to the Johnsons about the tax wisdom of purchasing a home instead of renting?

12. List four additional ways that the Johnsons could reduce their tax liability next year.

What Would You Recommend Now?

Now that you have read the chapter on managing income taxes, what advice can you offer Sean Hutchison and Nicole Martin in the case at the beginning of the chapter regarding:

1. Using tax credits to help pay for Sean's college expenses?

2. If Nicole pays income taxes at the 25 percent rate, understanding how much money she will realize if she sells the stocks?

3. Buying a home?

4. Increasing contributions to their employer-sponsored retirement plans?

5. Establishing a sideline business for Sean's jewelry operation?

Exploring the World Wide Web

To complete these exercises, go to the *Garman/Forgue* website at college.hmco.com/business/students. Under General Business, select the title of this text. Click on the Internet Exercises link for this chapter, and answer the questions that appear on the Web page.

1. Do you know the state income tax rates for your home state? Visit the website for the Federal Tax Administrators. Click on "state comparisons." There you will find a table with tax rates for all states that levy an income tax. Based on what you found, what is your combined federal and state marginal tax rate?

2. Visit the website for the Internal Revenue Service. There you will find a copy of *Publication 501—Exemptions, Standard Deduction, and Filing Information*. Use *Publication 501* to determine (1) whether you must file a return, (2) who can claim you as an exemption, and (3) how much your standard deduction is.

3. Visit the website for *Kiplinger's Personal Finance Magazine*. Click on "taxes" in "your finances." There you will find recent articles. Which of the suggestions might have the greatest impact on your personal taxes?

4. Visit the website for the Internal Revenue Service. There you will find information on the Hope Scholarship credit and the lifetime learning credit. How might these two credits help you lower your overall federal income tax bill?

5. Visit the *Tax Prophet's* Frequently Asked Questions Web page. Select two FAQs and their answers that are most applicable to your tax situation.

Visit the Garman/Forgue website . . .

college.hmco.com/business/students

Under General Business, select *Personal Finance 8e*. There, among other valuable resources, you will find a complete glossary, ACE questions, links to help you complete the chapter exercises, and links to other personal finance sites.

Chapter 5

Management of Monetary Assets

LEARNING OBJECTIVES

After reading this chapter, you should be able to:

1 **List** and define the tools of monetary asset management and describe the various providers of financial services.

2 **Understand** the key aspects of electronic banking and the legal protections available.

3 **Describe** the different types of checking accounts.

4 **Identify** the key aspects and benefits of a savings account.

5 **Explain** the importance of placing excess funds in an appropriate money market account.

6 **List** the benefits of putting money into longer-term savings instruments.

Clarence Cline and Amanda Adams are to be married in two months. Both are employed full-time and currently have their own apartments. Once married, they will move into Amanda's apartment because it is larger. They plan to use Clarence's rent money to begin saving for a down payment on a home to be purchased in four or five years. Clarence has a checking account at a branch of a large regional commercial bank near his workplace where he deposits his paychecks. He also has three savings accounts—one at his bank and two small accounts at a savings and loan association near where he went to college. Clarence pays about $30 per month in fees on his various accounts. In addition, he has a $10,000 certificate of deposit (CD) from an inheritance; this CD will mature in five months. Amanda has her paycheck directly deposited into her share draft account at the credit union where she works. She has a savings account at the credit union as well as a money market account at a stockbroker that was set up when her father gave her 300 shares of stock. She also has $4300 in an individual retirement account invested through a mutual fund.

What would you recommend to Amanda and Clarence on the subject of monetary asset management regarding:

1. Their use of electronic banking in the future?
2. Their checking accounts?
3. Their savings accounts, including saving for a home?
4. The use of a money market account for their monetary asset management?
5. Monetary asset management using longer-term savings instruments?

Think back to your first experiences in handling money. Perhaps you received an allowance from your parents. Did you worry about losing the money? Were you encouraged (or pressured) to save some of it? Did you put the cash in a box or a piggy bank at home? Did you realize that you could earn interest if you opened a savings account at a bank? Did you open a checking account when you got your first job or went off to college? Did you understand that you might have to pay bank fees depending on how you handled the account?

All of these questions relate to managing monetary assets. Recall from Chapter 2 that monetary assets are defined as cash and near-cash items that can be readily converted to cash. You probably answered yes to most of the questions posed here. In other words, you managed your monetary assets even at a young age. If you are a typical college student, your monetary assets are the largest component of your net worth and probably are the major focus of the activities you consider "personal finance."

This chapter begins with a general discussion of ways to manage your monetary assets with the goal of maximizing your interest earnings at the lowest possible cost. This discussion includes an overview of the providers of today's financial services so you can better understand where to get help managing your monetary assets. Then because today's financial services industry increasingly relies upon computers to conduct business, we discuss how electronic funds transfers are used to manage monetary assets. The remainder of the chapter focuses on the four tools you can use to manage your monetary assets: (1) interest-earning checking accounts, (2) savings accounts, (3) money market accounts, and (4) various longer-term savings instruments.

Golden Rules of

Managing Monetary Assets

Financial success comes from learning the Golden Rules of personal finance and then putting what you have learned into practice. Make the following your money habits in management of monetary assets:

1. Choose an interest-earning checking account for your checking account needs and reconcile the bank statement monthly.
2. Minimize ATM fees by making fewer large withdrawals rather than more frequent small withdrawals.
3. Monitor your bank fees and, if necessary, change financial institutions to avoid fees.
4. Build and maintain an emergency fund sufficient to cover three months of expenses and keep those funds in higher-interest accounts.
5. Start saving regularly when you are young: The sooner you start, the more funds you will amass over time.

What Is Monetary Asset Management?

1 List and define the tools of monetary asset management and describe the various providers of financial services.

Monetary asset (cash) management encompasses how you handle all of your monetary assets, including cash on hand, checking accounts, savings accounts, money market accounts, other short-term investment vehicles, and longer-term savings instruments. The goal is to maximize interest earnings and to minimize fees while keeping funds safe and readily available for living expenses, emergencies, and saving and investment opportunities. The accounts into which such funds are placed are called **cash equivalents** for two reasons: because they retain a constant or nearly constant value and because they have ready liquidity. Successful monetary asset management allows you to earn interest on your money while maintaining reasonable liquidity and safety. **Liquidity** refers to the speed and ease with which an asset can be converted to cash; **safety** is freedom from financial risk.

The Four Tools of Monetary Asset Management

As illustrated in Figure 5.1 (page 130), monetary asset management relies on four major tools:

1. You need a low-cost, interest-earning checking account from which to pay monthly living expenses.

2. You might want to maintain a small savings account in a local financial institution. A savings account will earn interest and provides an easily accessible source of emergency cash.

3. When income begins to exceed expenses regularly, you can consider opening a money market account. These accounts pay higher interest rates than checking and savings accounts. Many people place funds in such accounts for safekeeping while considering other investment options.

4. Your monetary asset management plan is complete when you transfer some funds into longer-term savings instruments (such as certificates of deposit and government savings bonds) because you want to earn even higher returns and still maintain safety. With this option, you commit the amounts for longer time periods (sacrificing some liquidity for higher interest). Such a monetary asset management strategy allows you to build up larger amounts to be used for later spending, saving, or investing.

Who Provides Monetary Asset Management Services?

Providers of monetary asset management services are collectively referred to as the **financial services industry.** The firms in this industry offer one or more of the following services to individuals and families: checking, savings, traveler's checks, credit, insurance, stocks and bonds, real estate, credit and budget counseling, financial planning, and legal advice on financial matters. They include depository institutions, mutual funds, and stock brokerage firms. Table 5.1 matches these various types of firms with the financial products and services that they sell. In recent years, it has become increasingly common for banks to also offer mutual fund and stock brokerage (and even insurance) services. Conversely, many mutual funds and stock brokerages now offer banking services. The lines that separate the members of the financial services industry are blurring rapidly.

Banks and Depository Institutions.   **Depository institutions** are organizations licensed to take deposits from and make loans to consumers, firms, or governments. They all can offer some form of government account insurance on their customers' deposits and are government regulated. They offer a wide range of financial services. Examples of depository institutions are banks, savings banks, and credit unions. Although each is a distinct type of institution, people often call them all simply "banks."

Commercial banks are corporations chartered under federal and state regulations. They offer numerous consumer services, such as checking, savings, loans, safe-deposit boxes, investment services, financial counseling, and automatic payment of bills. Accounts in a federally chartered bank are insured against loss by the **Bank Insurance Fund (BIF)** of the **Federal Deposit Insurance Corporation (FDIC),** which is an agency

---

Figure 5.1

Four Tools of Monetary Asset Management (with Illustrative Interest Rates Earned on Funds)

Interest-earning checking account (0.7–0.9%)	Savings account in a financial institution (1.0–1.2%)	Money market account (1.9–2.1%)	Other low-risk, longer-term savings instruments (3.0–5.0%)
• NOW checking account	• Statement savings account	• Super NOW account • Money market deposit account • Money market mutual fund • Asset management account	• Certificate of deposit • Government savings bonds

Table 5.1 Today's Providers of Monetary Asset Management Services	
Providers	**What They Sell**
Depository institutions (banks, mutual savings banks, savings and loan associations, and credit unions)	Checking, savings, lending, credit cards, investments, and trust advice
Mutual funds	Money market mutual funds, tax-exempt funds, bond funds, and stock funds
Stock brokerage firms	Stocks, bonds, mutual funds, and real estate investment trusts
Financial services companies	Checking, savings, lending, credit cards, real estate, investments, insurance, accounting and legal advice, and financial planning

of the federal government. Accounts in state-chartered banks are usually insured by the FDIC's BIF program or a private insurance program.

Savings and loan associations (S&Ls) focus primarily on accepting savings and providing mortgage and consumer loans. They offer checking services through interest-earning NOW accounts (discussed later in this chapter). S&Ls generally pay depositors an interest rate about 0.10 to 0.20 percentage points higher than the rate found at commercial banks. The FDIC insures accounts in all federally chartered S&Ls and some state-chartered S&Ls; the insurance is provided through the FDIC's **Savings Association Insurance Fund (SAIF).**

A **mutual savings bank (MSB)** is similar to an S&L in that it also accepts deposits and makes housing and consumer loans. These banks are legally permitted in only 17 states, primarily those in the eastern United States. They are called "mutual" because the depositors own the institution and share in the earnings. Generally, MSBs have the FDIC's BIF coverage. Like S&Ls, they offer interest-earning NOW accounts to checking customers.

A **credit union (CU)** is a not-for-profit cooperative venture that pools the deposits of its member-owners, which are then invested or lent to those member-owners. The members of the credit union all share some common bond, such as the same employer, church, union, or fraternal association. Persons in the immediate family of a member are also eligible to join. Federally chartered credit unions have their accounts insured through the **National Credit Union Share Insurance Fund (NCUSIF),** which is administered by the **National Credit Union Administration (NCUA);** it provides the same safety as deposits insured by the FDIC. State-chartered credit unions are often insured by NCUSIF, and most others participate in private insurance programs. Credit unions accept deposits and make loans for consumer products; the larger institutions also make home loans. They typically use payroll deductions to receive deposits and loan repayments, and they often offer free insurance to pay off a loan in the event of death or disability. In addition, many offer free financial counseling. Credit unions usually pay higher interest rates and charge lower fees than commercial banks, S&Ls, or MSBs.

Deposits in depository institutions are insured against loss of both the amount on deposit and the accrued interest by various insurance funds. This **deposit insurance** for your deposits at any one institution works as follows:

1. The maximum insurance on all of your single-ownership accounts (held in your name only) is $100,000.

2. The maximum insurance on all of your joint accounts held with other individuals is $100,000.

3. The maximum insurance on all of your retirement accounts is $100,000.

4. A maximum of $100,000 in insurance per beneficiary is payable on "death accounts" (accounts set up so that the funds go to a spouse, child, parent, or sibling upon the death of the account holder).

Thus, a person might have several $100,000 increments of insurance for his or her accounts at any one institution. Funds on deposit at other institutions will also have these same limits.

Mutual Funds.   A **mutual fund** is an investment company that raises money by selling shares to the public and then invests that money in a diversified portfolio of investments. Many of these companies have created mutual fund accounts that can be used for monetary asset management purposes. For example, cash management accounts in mutual funds provide a convenient and safe place to keep money while awaiting alternative investment opportunities. Note that money deposited in a mutual fund is not insured by the federal government, although some mutual fund companies purchase private insurance to cover potential losses. Mutual funds are the subject of Chapter 15.

Stock Brokerage Firms.   A **stock brokerage firm** is a licensed financial institution that specializes in selling and buying stocks, bonds, and other investment alternatives. Such firms provide advice and assistance to investors and earn commissions based on the buy and sell orders that they process for their clients. Stock brokerage firms typically offer money market mutual fund accounts (operated by mutual funds) into which clients may place money while waiting to make investments. In this way, they provide monetary asset management services.

Electronic Banking

2 Understand the key aspects of electronic banking and the legal protections available .

Electronic banking occurs whenever banking transactions are conducted via computers without the customer using paper documents or having face-to-face contact with financial services personnel. It includes services such as direct deposit of paychecks and other income sources, checking account transactions, transfer of funds among accounts, and automatic bill payment, among many others. Most of these activities involve **electronic funds transfers (EFTs),** in which funds are shifted electronically (rather than by check or cash) among various bank accounts.

Most major banks now provide access to their banking services via websites. Customers can make payments, transfer funds among their accounts, buy and sell stocks and mutual funds, and gain access to financial information and advice. In fact, some banks, known as "Internet banks," operate entirely on-line. Because they have no offices or branches, these banks often have lower fees and pay higher rates of interest. They offer a full range of banking services. Examples include Netbank.com, Etradebank.com, and RBC Centura (www.centura.com). In addition, a number of Internet-based bill-paying services (such as CheckFree. com and PiggyBills.com) are available to automate your bill paying. With these services, bills can be both received and paid on-line. Customer services include payment reminders and summary statements of all bills paid.*

This section profiles the most widely recognized aspects of electronic banking: automated teller machines (ATMs), point-of-sale (POS) terminals and debit cards, smart cards, stored-value cards, and direct deposits and preauthorized payments. Also dis-

---

*Quicken, Microsoft Money, and other computer software programs available for managing your personal finances all have templates for managing your accounts and processing payments on-line.

cussed are government regulations that protect consumers who use electronic funds transfers.

You Can Do Your Banking with an Automatic Teller Machine

An **automated teller machine (ATM;** sometimes called a **cash machine**) is a computer terminal located on the premises of a financial institution or elsewhere through which customers may make deposits (usually restricted to your own bank's ATMs), make withdrawals, and complete other financial transactions just as they would through a human bank teller. Most major depository institutions belong to international networks; you can use any bank's ATM that is part of the same network as your own. To conduct a transaction, you must enter your **personal identification number (PIN),** which confirms that you are, in fact, authorized to access the account. Some ATM security systems "read" your face, fingerprint, or iris of your eye to confirm your identity.

An **ATM transaction fee** may be assessed for using an ATM. Fees may be levied by your financial institution as well as by the institution that provides the ATM if you are using an ATM linked to a national network. For example, you might pay your institution $1–$3 and another $1–$3 (or more) to the machine provider. Note that the average ATM withdrawal is $60, with the most common amount withdrawn being just $20. A $2 ATM fee is 10 percent of a $20 withdrawal but just 1 percent of a $200 withdrawal. As you see, making frequent, small withdrawals can be expensive.

You Can Make Purchases at Point-of-Sale Terminals Using a Debit Card

A **point-of-sale (POS) terminal** is a computer terminal located at a store or other merchant location that allows the customer to make purchases electronically via a debit card or credit card (covered in Chapter 6). A **debit** (or **check**) **card** is a plastic card that provides instant access to your checking account; it is issued by the financial institution where the user maintains his or her checking account. It differs from a credit card in that use of the debit card does not borrow money but rather takes funds directly out of your account. In this way, debit cards eliminate the need for check writing. Debit cards are also very helpful when traveling internationally, as the currency exchange fees are usually lower than can be obtained from retailers and currency exchange offices.

You will have two choices when you use a debit card at a POS terminal. First, you can use a PIN to authorize the transaction, which instantly transfers funds from your account to the merchant's account. Note that some banks charge a transaction fee when you use a PIN to authorize a debit-card transaction. Alternatively, you can conduct an off-line transaction in which you sign a receipt (rather than use a PIN) to authorize the transaction. In this case, the funds are transferred from your account within one or two days, much like what happens when you write a check.

Debit-card PINs basically "unlock" your account. For safety reasons, they should be written down and memorized, with the written version being stored in a safe place at home. You should never keep your written PIN in your checkbook or wallet. Users also need to be clear about which type of debit-card arrangement (on-line or off-line) applies with a particular purchase. These distinctions are important because the protections for fraudulent transactions differ for the various types of cards and their usages.

kept in an accompanying **check register.** In addition, the canceled check provides proof of payment and a tax record. Similarly, using an ATM or POS terminal provides a written receipt that should be kept with other checking documents.

We will use the traditional term *checking* from this point forward to include demand deposits, negotiable orders of withdrawal, and share drafts. When a check is written, it becomes a **negotiable instrument,** which is an unconditional written promise to pay a specified sum of money as of a specific date to a specified payee or bearer.

Traditional checking accounts at commercial banks are technically known as **demand deposits.** That is, a financial institution must withdraw funds and make payments whenever demanded to do so by the checking account depositor. Only commercial banks may offer demand deposits. While these accounts permit unlimited checking, they also pay no interest.

The rules will vary for checking accounts that do not pay interest. Some accounts require a monthly service charge (perhaps $5 or $10) or assess a fee for each check or transaction (perhaps $0.50); they may also restrict the maximum number of transactions allowed each month before additional fees kick in. Most frequently, checking accounts are assessed a monthly fee only if the balance in the account drops below some minimum (as discussed in the next section).

A **lifeline banking account** offers access to certain minimal financial services that every consumer needs—regardless of income—to function in our society. An applicant's income and net worth determine acceptance into a lifeline program. (College students generally do not qualify because their parents' assets and income are often considered part of the resources available to them.) The cost of lifeline banking accounts is extremely low, often about $3 per month.

All depository institutions can offer some form of **interest-earning checking account,** which is simply a checking account that pays interest to the depositor. Commercial banks, S&Ls, and mutual savings banks may offer a **negotiable order of withdrawal (NOW) account.** This checking account earns interest or dividends as long as minimum-balance requirements are satisfied. A NOW account can be described as an "interest-earning checking account." When the financial institution receives the negotiable order of withdrawal (or "check"), the funds on deposit are used to make the payment.

A **share draft account** is the credit-union version of a NOW account. Its name arises because members of the credit union actually own the organization and their deposits are called shares. Technically, share draft accounts earn dividends instead of interest; for tax purposes, however, the earnings are dubbed "interest income." Costs for a share draft account are often lower than for those for a checking account at a bank or savings and loan association.

Usually, NOW accounts pay nearly the same interest rate as savings accounts. Sometimes they may pay higher interest rates on larger balances (such as $1000), but the amount up to the minimum earns only the base interest rate. The combination of a base rate and a higher rate is called a **tiered interest rate.**

Checking Account Charges, Fees, and Penalties

Depository institutions often assess their checking account customers a number of charges, fees, and penalties. For example, many institutions have monthly service fees, per-check charges, and EFT transaction charges. In addition, charges and penalties may be assessed for violating the rules of the account, such as writing a check for insufficient

Did You Know? . . .

What Happens When You Write a Check

When you write a check, you are ordering your depository institution to take money from your account and make it available to someone else. But what happens to the actual check? Years ago the check itself was sent from institution to institution and ultimately was returned to you as a **canceled check.** That rarely happens anymore, as checks are now processed electronically. Instead, you simply are sent a listing of the checks you have written that have been paid, or cleared, by the depository institution. This alternative to receiving a canceled check is called **check truncation.** As a substitute for canceled checks, some banks send customers monthly **image statements** that show miniature computer pictures of their checks.

Typically when you write a check, you simultaneously make a copy that serves as your record that the check was written. These copies (and image statements) may or may not be accepted as accurate proof of payment, depending on the policies of the entity to which you wrote the check. For greater protection, you could sign up (for a fee) for a checking account that offers **sub-** **stitute checks** that the bank warrants are an acceptable version of the original check written by you. Under the Check Clearing for the 21st Century Act your bank must quickly correct any errors in the processing of your check if you have chosen the substitute check feature for your account.

Another aspect of electronic check processing relates to stop-payment orders. A **stop-payment order** tells your bank not to honor a check when it's presented for payment. To issue such an order, you can telephone your bank and stop payment on the check. In any event, a stop-payment order works only if the check has not yet cleared. And with electronic processing, check clearing can occur in a matter of minutes, once your check is scanned by the retailer or bank that receives it. Further, many people are unaware that if the verbal stop-payment order is not followed up with a written instruction to the bank, the person or merchant to whom the check was written can cash the check after 14 days. Even with a written request, the check can be cashed after six months unless the order has been renewed.

---

funds. Fees may also kick in if the customer does not maintain a minimum balance in an account. Because of these fees, customers pay, on average, $15 to $20 each month to maintain a checking account. People interested in getting their money's worth in banking would be wise to avoid as many of the charges shown in Table 5.2 (page 138) as possible.

Check users must consider the amount of interest that the account will earn and the portion of it that will be offset by any occasional imposition of fees. A NOW account with no balance requirement is preferable. Decision making becomes more difficult when the institution offers a NOW account in combination with either a minimum- or average-balance requirement.

With a **minimum-balance account,** the customer must keep a certain amount (perhaps $500 or $700) in the account throughout a specified time period (usually a month or a quarter) to avoid a flat service charge (usually $5 to $15). A fee is assessed whenever the triggering event occurs—that is, when the balance drops below the specified minimum. With an **average-balance account,** a service fee is assessed only if the average daily balance of funds in the account drops below a certain level (perhaps $800 or $1000) during the specified time period (usually a month or a quarter). Many financial institutions offer no-fee checking accounts to customers who have their paychecks electronically sent from their employer via direct deposit.

asset accounts, AMAs are offered through depository institutions, stock brokerage firms, financial services companies, and mutual funds. Such an account enables you to conduct all of your financial business with one institution. Typically, $10,000, spread across all subaccounts, is required to open an AMA. Some AMAs assess an annual fee, usually $100.

Institutions that offer AMAs use computer programs to manage the funds in these accounts. Daily or weekly, the program checks the various subaccounts and **sweeps** funds in and out of the MMMF to ensure that the highest interest rates apply to the funds. AMAs usually have other features that attract investors as well—for example, free credit and debit cards, a rebate of 1 percent on credit card purchases, free traveler's checks, inexpensive term life insurance, and a free investment advisory newsletter.

6 List the benefits of putting money into longer-term savings instruments.

Monetary Asset Management: Tool #4— Long-Term Savings Instruments

If you are an effective manager of your personal finances, you will have established a NOW checking account, a savings account, and a money market account; you will be earning interest on all funds until they are expended. The fourth tool of monetary asset management involves placing money into longer-term savings instruments that allow you to earn even higher returns in exchange for giving up some liquidity. These opportunities require that you commit some of this money for specific time periods—

Did You Know? ...

The Interest Rates for Short-Term Monetary Asset Management Opportunities

If you want to put your money in a safe "parking" place for a short period, consider the alternatives listed here. The interest rates show relationships during a time of low inflation (1 to 3 percent). During times of higher inflation, these rates would be commensurately higher.

Type of Account	Interest Rate
NOW checking account	0.5
Statement savings account	1.2
Super NOW account	0.8
Money market deposit account	1.4
Asset management account	1.5
Money market mutual fund	1.6
Three-month bank certificate of deposit	1.5
Six-month certificate of deposit	1.6
One-year certificate of deposit	2.2
Two and one-half year certificate of deposit	2.8
Five-year certificate of deposit	4.0

from six months to two years, or perhaps even longer. Obligating amounts for longer time periods permits you to earn high returns while accumulating amounts to be used for later spending, saving, or investing.

Savings instruments of this type include certificates of deposit and U.S. government savings bonds. In addition, funds could be placed into certain higher-yielding, short-term Treasury issues (discussed in Chapter 14). Note, however, that the minimum purchase requirements for these Treasury issues range from $100 to $10,000.

Certificates of Deposit

A **certificate of deposit (CD)** is an interest-earning savings instrument purchased for a fixed period of time. The required deposit amounts range from $100 to $100,000, while the time periods range from seven days to eight years. The interest rate in force when the CD is purchased typically remains fixed for the entire term of the deposit. Depositors collect their principal and interest at the end of the specified time period (although sometimes on a monthly basis). Certificates of deposit are insured through the FDIC or the NCUSIF if purchased through an insured depository institution.

Interest rates on longer-term CDs are usually higher than the comparable rates on shorter-term instruments. This difference is meant to reward savers for accepting higher risk: The longer they remain locked into a CD, the greater the chance that inflation will force interest rates to rise. If interest rates rise, savers will have missed out on earning even greater returns; if interest rates fall, they will benefit from the excellent return locked in.

Variable-rate certificates of deposit (sometimes called **adjustable-rate CDs**) are also available. These instruments pay an interest rate that is adjusted (up or down) periodically. Typically, savers are allowed to "lock in," or fix, the rate at any point before their CDs mature. Of course, this variability detracts from the main virtue of the fixed-rate CD—predictability. The best variable-rate CDs have a guaranteed minimum interest rate. **Bump-up CDs** allow savers to bump up the interest rate once to a higher market rate, if available, and to add up to 100 percent of the initial deposit whenever desired.

Money withdrawn from a CD before the end of the specified time period is subject to interest penalties. On certificates held less than one year, the depositor may lose a minimum of one month's interest; on certificates held more than a year, the depositor may lose a minimum of three months' interest. If the penalty exceeds the interest amount, you will get back less than you deposited. Consequently, before putting money into a CD, make sure that it is appropriate to tie up your funds in this way.

Because you do not make deposits and withdrawals after initially investing in a CD, you have no reason to restrict yourself to a nearby institution when searching for the highest yields. An extra 0.05 percent yield amounts to $50 on a $10,000 CD every year! Lists of institutions paying the highest yields on CDs are published monthly by *Kiplinger's Personal Finance Magazine* and *Money*. Alternatively, you can search for high-rate CDs at www.bankrate.com. You might also check with a stockbroker for high yields, because brokerage firms often buy CDs in volume to resell to individuals; these instruments are called **brokered certificates of deposit.** All types of CDs are excellent tools for managing monetary assets, and as banking deposits, they enjoy the added protection of federal deposit insurance. In reality, some so-called CDs are actually "investment certificates." They are not insured and can be recalled by the financial institution and reissued at a lower interest rate prior to their maturity.

U.S. Government Savings Bonds

U.S. government savings bonds represent loans to the U.S. government and are used to finance the national debt. These bonds are backed by the full faith and credit of the U.S. government, so they are very safe places to invest savings. Savings bonds can be purchased through employer payroll deduction plans and from many federally insured financial institutions (without any fees, charges, or commissions). Six in ten U.S. households own government savings bonds.

There are two types of U.S. Savings bonds: Series EE savings bonds and Series I bonds (new Series HH bonds are no longer sold). (For more on U.S. savings bonds, go to the website www.savingsbonds.gov.) Both types will earn interest for up to 30 years. You cannot redeem a bond until one year after purchase, however, and you will forfeit three months of interest if you redeem the bond within five years.

Savings bonds offer several tax advantages. For example, the semiannual interest accrued on a savings bond is exempt from all state and local income taxes. Federal income taxes may be deferred until the bond is redeemed and the money is actually received. Alternatively, the owner may choose to report interest annually on his or her income tax return. This option is usually best when bonds are held in the name of a child who has little or no other taxable income. The interest on savings bonds may be *exempt* from federal income taxes if the bonds are redeemed to pay for education expenses for the bonds' purchaser, for his or her spouse, or for an IRS-defined dependent. The purchaser must be at least 24 years old and have an adjusted gross income below a certain threshold (approximately $75,000 for singles and $120,000 for married couples).

Series EE savings bonds are U.S. government savings instruments, available in denominations ranging from $25 to $10,000, that are purchased for 50 percent of their face value. Thus, a $100 Series EE bond would be purchased for $50 and redeemed at maturity for $100. Such a bond is an example of a **discount bond**—that is, a bond sold at less than its face value. The difference between the discount bond's purchase price and its value at maturity represents the interest earned. This explains why Series EE bondholders do not receive interest payments while they hold the bond.

Newly issued Series EE bonds earn a return equal to 90 percent of the six-month average yield on five-year **Treasury security issues** (another type of debt instrument issued by the federal government). For example, if the Treasury rate is 2.50 percent, the bond rate would be approximately 2.25 percent ($2.5\% \times 0.90$). To find out the current rate, call (800) 487-2663. The maturity date at which your investment will double depends on what happens to interest rates. A bond earning an average of 5 percent interest would reach its face value in about 14½ years, whereas one earning 6 percent would reach its face value in 12 years. (The maximum maturity in recent years has ranged from 12 to 24 years with corresponding interest rates varying from 6 to 3 percent.)

A variation on the Series EE bond is the **Series I savings bond.** Series I bonds are not discount bonds but instead are purchased at their face value. A fixed interest rate (perhaps 2 percent) is set when the bond is purchased. An inflation rate is then added that is tied to changes in the consumer price index (CPI) rather than to the average rate for Treasury security issues. This type of bond sometimes produces a higher return than Series EE bonds do, which gives the holder some protection against inflation.

Treasury Inflation-Protected Securities (TIPS) are similar to savings bonds. They are the only Treasury security whose value increases as inflation occurs, so they guarantee that the investor's return will outpace inflation. The principal is adjusted every six months according to the rise and fall of the Consumer Price Index (CPI). TIPS are sold in terms of 5, 10, and 20 years and interest is paid to TIPS owners every six month until it matures.

ACE

Summary

Self-tests

1. Monetary asset management is the task of maximizing interest earnings and minimizing fees on all of your funds kept readily available for day-to-day living expenses, emergencies, and savings and investment opportunities. The four major tools of monetary asset management include an interest-earning checking account, a savings account at a local financial institution, a money market account, and various longer-term savings instruments. The four primary providers of monetary asset management services are depository institutions (including commercial banks, savings and loan associations, mutual savings banks, and credit unions), mutual funds, stock brokerage firms, and financial services companies.

2. Electronic banking occurs whenever banking transactions are conducted via computers without the customer using paper documents or having face-to-face contact with financial services personnel. The most widely recognized forms of electronic banking are automatic teller machines (ATMs), point-of-sale (POS) terminals using debit cards, smart cards, and direct deposits and preauthorized payments. The Electronic Funds Transfer Act protects consumers who use debit and ATM cards.

3. The first tool of monetary asset management should be an interest-earning checking account that is used to pay monthly living expenses. In choosing a financial institution at which to set up such an account, you should consider such criteria as charges, fees, and penalties.

4. The second tool of monetary asset management is a local savings account. Savers can use the APY interest rate to compare savings options when considering various account fees.

5. The third tool of monetary asset management is a money market account. When income begins to exceed expenses on a regular basis, it is wise to move excess funds into such an account, which typically pays a higher interest rate. The funds can be left in the account while you consider later investment options. Money market accounts include super NOW accounts, money market deposit accounts, money market mutual funds, and asset management accounts.

6. The fourth tool of monetary asset management consists of longer-term savings instruments that allow you to earn even higher returns, but safely. Funds for this part of monetary asset management primarily come from

amounts building up in your money market account. The available choices are certificates of deposit and U.S. government savings bonds.

Key Terms

annual percentage yield (APY) , 143
asset management (central asset) account (AMA) , 145
automatic funds transfer agreement, 140
certificate of deposit (CD) , 145
checking account, 135
debit (check) card, 133
depository institution, 130
direct deposit, 134
electronic banking, 132
joint tenancy with right of survivorship, 144
minimum-balance account, 137
monetary asset (cash) management, 129
money market mutual fund (MMMF), 145
negotiable order of withdrawal (NOW) account, 136
periodic statement, 134
Series EE savings bonds, 148
signature card, 144
statement (passbook) savings account, 139
stop-payment order, 137
tiered interest rate, 136

Chapter Review Questions

1. What are the benefits of effective monetary asset management?

2. List the four tools of monetary asset management. Which two generally pay the highest interest rates?

3. Differentiate among the following depository institutions: commercial banks, savings and loan associations, mutual savings banks, and credit unions.

4. What legal safeguards apply to lost or stolen debit cards?

5. Give some examples of unusual checking and savings account transactions that result in assessment of costs or penalties.

6. Compare and contrast an automatic funds transfer agreement with an automatic overdraft loan agreement.

7. Distinguish between joint tenancy with right of survivorship and tenancy by the entirety.

8. Who might benefit most from having a money market account and why?

9. Summarize how an asset management account works.

10. What is a certificate of deposit? Who might want to purchase one?

Group Discussion Issues

1. When did you open your first bank account? How did you feel about turning your money over to an institution?

2. Do you use electronic banking? Why or why not? Do you think electronic banking usage varies by age?

3. Do you regularly reconcile your checking and savings account balances with your monthly statements? Why do you think some people avoid completing this task? Is going on-line frequently to check your accounts a reasonable substitute?

4. Have you ever overdrawn your checking account? What fees did you have to pay? Do you feel the amount of the fees was justified?

Decision-Making Cases

▌Case 1
A Lobbyist Considers Her Checking Account Options

Jane Sheharky, a lobbyist for the textile industry living in Springfield, Virginia, has maintained a checking account at a commercial bank for three years. The bank requires a minimum balance of $100 to avoid an account charge, and Jane has always maintained this balance. Recently, she heard that a nearby savings and loan association is offering NOW accounts paying 3 percent interest on the average daily balance of the account. This institution requires a minimum balance of only $300, but a forfeiture of monthly interest occurs if the account falls below this minimum. Given her past habits at the commercial bank, Jane feels that the $300 minimum would not be too difficult to maintain. She is seriously thinking about moving her money to the NOW account.

(a) What is the main reason Jane should move her checking account?

(b) What should Jane know about the differences among NOW accounts offered at various financial institutions?

(c) If Jane maintained an average balance of $350 in a NOW checking account earning 3 percent, how much interest

would she have earned on her money after one year? (Hint: Use Appendix Table A.1 or visit the *Garman/Forgue* website. Do not forget to subtract Jane's initial lump-sum deposit from the derived answer.)

(d) How much more would Jane have earned in one year if she decided to invest in a money market mutual fund paying 4 percent interest instead of the NOW account? (Hint: Use Appendix Table A.1 or visit the *Garman/Forgue* website.)

▌Case 2
Use of a Computer Banking Service

Trent Searle, a service station owner from Roy, Utah, pays a $25 monthly fee for a computerized home banking service. His friend Brad Simpson feels that Trent is wasting his money on the service. Trent has a net income of $3000 per month, plus other earnings from some investments. In addition, he is part-owner of an apartment complex, which gives him approximately $1000 per month in income. He always tries to put his excess earnings into solid investments so that they might bring future income and security.

(a) What specific computer banking services would help a person such as Trent?

(b) Justify Trent's paying the $25 monthly fee for computer banking.

(c) Recommend to Trent a combination of the four monetary asset management tools that will offer some alternative money management services. Defend your answer to Trent, making sure to consider factors such as convenience, cost, services, and safety.

Financial Math Questions

1. Twins Barbara and Mary are both age 22. Beginning at age 22, Barbara invests $2000 per year for eight years and then never sets aside another penny. Mary waits ten years and then invests $2000 per year for the next 30 years. Assuming they both earn 8 percent, how much will each twin have at age 65? (Hint: Use Appendix Tables A.1 and A.3 or visit the *Garman/Forgue* website.)

2. You need to amass $20,000 in the next ten years to help with a relative's college expenses. You have $10,000 available to invest. What annual percentage rate must be earned to realize the $20,000? (Hint: Use Appendix Table A.1 or visit the *Garman/Forgue* website.)

3. You want to create a college fund for a child who is now three years old. The fund should grow to $30,000 in 15 years. If a current investment yields 7 percent, how much must you invest in a lump sum now to realize the $30,000 when needed? (Hint: Use Appendix Table A.2 or visit the *Garman/Forgue* website.)

4. How many years of investing $2000 annually at 8 percent will it take to reach a goal of $20,000? (Hint: Use Appendix Table A.3 or visit the *Garman/Forgue* website.)

5. You plan to retire in 22 years. To provide for your retirement, you initiate a savings program of $6000 per year yielding 7 percent. What will be the value of the retirement fund at the beginning of the twenty-third year? (Hint: Use Appendix Table A.3 or visit the *Garman/Forgue* website.)

Money Matters Continuing Cases

Victor and Maria Hernandez Need to Save Money Fast

The Hernandez family is experiencing some financial pressures, even though the couple has a combined income of $66,000. Also, their eldest son, Joseph, will start college in only three years. Maria is contemplating going to work full-time to add about $15,000 to the family's annual income.

1. If Maria begins working full-time, how much federal income and Social Security tax will the couple pay on this amount if their marginal tax rate is 25 percent rate and the Social Security and Medicare tax rate is 7.65 percent?

2. How much should they save annually for the next three years if they want to build up Joseph's college fund to $20,000, assuming a 7 percent rate of return and ignoring taxes on the interest? (Hint: Use Appendix Table A.1 or visit the *Garman/Forgue* website.)

3. Given their 25 percent marginal tax rate, what is the Hernandezes' after-tax return and how would that affect the amount they would need to save each year?

4. What savings options are open to the Hernandezes that could reduce or eliminate the effects of taxes on their savings program?

How Should the Johnsons Manage Their Cash?

In January, Harry and Belinda Johnson had $3540 in monetary assets (see page 55): $1178 in cash on hand; $890 in a statement savings account at First Federal Bank earning 1.5 percent interest compounded daily; $560 in a statement savings account at the Far West Savings and Loan earning 1.5 percent interest compounded semiannually; $160 in a share account at the Smith Brokerage Credit Union earning

a dividend of 1.6 percent compounded quarterly; and $752 in their non-interest-earning regular checking account at First Interstate.

1. What specific recommendations would you give the Johnsons for selecting a checking account and savings account that will enable them to effectively use the first and second tools of monetary asset management?

2. Their annual budget, cash-flow calendar, and revolving savings fund (see Tables 3.3, 3.4, and 3.5 on pages 73–76) indicate that the Johnsons will have additional amounts to deposit in the coming year. You probably have some recommendations for the Johnsons on using the third and fourth tools of monetary asset management.

   (a) What type of money market account would you recommend that they open? Why?

   (b) What long-term savings instrument would you recommend for their savings, given their objective of saving enough to purchase a new home? Support your answer.

3. If the Johnsons could put most of their cash on hand ($1000) into a money market account earning 3 percent, how much would they have in the account after one year? (Hint: Use Appendix Table A.1 or visit the *Garman/Forgue* website.)

What Would You Recommend Now?

Now that you have read the chapter on monetary asset management, what would you recommend to Clarence Cline and Amanda Adams in the case at the beginning of the chapter regarding:

1. Their use of electronic banking in the future?

2. Their checking accounts?

3. Their savings accounts, including saving for a home?

4. The use of a money market account for their monetary asset management?

5. Monetary asset management using longer-term savings instruments?

Exploring the World Wide Web

To complete these exercises, go to the *Garman/Forgue* website at college.hmco.com/business/students. Under General Business, select the title of this text. Click on the Internet

Exercises link for this chapter, and answer the questions that appear on the Web page.

1. Visit the website for *Economic Review,* published by the Federal Reserve Bank of Kansas City, where you will find an article (scroll down) on electronic payment mechanisms in retail trade. What is the major reasoning behind the contention in the article that such forms of payment are more evolutionary than revolutionary?

2. Visit the website for BanxQuote, where you will find a wealth of information about rates of return on certificates of deposit. What is the best rate for a one-year CD and a five-year CD in a large city near your home (look in the state, then the city)? How do these rates compare to the average rates nationally and the highest rates nationally?

3. Visit the website for Federal Reserve Bank of Chicago, where you will find information about Internet banking. After reading the information, make a list of important positive and negative aspects of Internet banking. Is Internet banking right for you?

4. Visit the website for Bank Rate Monitor to find information about checking accounts. After reading the information, what type of checking account seems best for your needs?

5. Do you own any savings bonds or have you given savings bonds to others? Visit the website for the U.S. Department of the Treasury, where you will find information about the various types of U.S. savings bonds. Which would you be most likely to use?

Visit the Garman/Forgue website . . .

@college.hmco.com/business/students

Under General Business, select *Personal Finance 8e.* There, among other valuable resources, you will find a complete glossary, ACE questions, links to help you complete the chapter exercises, and links to other personal finance sites.

Chapter 6

Credit Use and Credit Cards

LEARNING OBJECTIVES

After reading this chapter, you should be able to:

1   **Explain** reasons for and against using credit.

2   **Describe** how people obtain and build a good credit reputation.

3   **Compare** and contrast the types of consumer credit and credit card accounts.

4   **Recognize** the impact of common (but not always beneficial) aspects of credit card accounts.

5   **Manage** your credit card and charge accounts to avoid fees and finance charges.

Darrell Cochrane, a 31-year-old dental technician in Tampa, Florida, made $42,000 last year. Darrell avoided using credit and credit cards until he was 28 years old. At that time, he missed three months of work due to a water skiing accident. He responded to the financial challenges brought on by his unemployment by applying for several credit cards. Two of these cards were bank credit cards that, due to his lack of a credit history, carry 19.6 and 24 percent annual percentage rates (APRs). Darrell now has 11 credit card accounts open: 5 bank cards and 6 retail cards. He uses them regularly, pulling out of his wallet the first card he comes to that a store will honor. Currently, he owes $13,000 on the 19.6 percent APR card and $4400 on the 24 percent APR card. Darrell has been late making his payments on the high-APR card three times in the last six months. His other bank cards carry APRs of 11 percent,

12 percent, and 15 percent, and he owes $500–$700 on each one. For the past year, Darrell has been making only the minimum payments on his bank cards. His retail cards all carry APRs in excess of 21 percent. Although he has managed to keep from running a balance on those cards during most months, occasionally these accounts have balances as well.

What would you recommend to Darrell on the subject of credit use and credit cards regarding:

1. His approach to using credit cards, including the number of cards he has?

2. How he might lower his interest expense each month?

3. Determining whether his credit history has been damaged this past year?

L ike many people, you probably have conflicting feelings about the use of credit. On the one hand, you may be attracted to the ease of using a credit card to pay for a vacation or some of your college expenses. Perhaps you might like to take out a loan to buy a vehicle. On the other hand, you may have vivid memories of a friend or relative who fell deeply into debt by overusing credit and ended up being pressured by creditors or even going bankrupt. A recent survey revealed that one in three U.S. households truly fears becoming overextended on credit, and more than one-half are concerned about making their monthly credit card payments.

Your lifetime of financial success hinges on your ability to make the sacrifices necessary to spend less than you earn and to avoid the use of excessive amounts of consumer credit. Otherwise, your personal finances can and will likely go amiss—perhaps terribly so. This chapter shows you how to use charge accounts and credit cards wisely. First, it explores a number of positive reasons for using credit as well as some negative aspects of credit. Next, the focus turns to the important topic of how lenders select the borrowers to whom they are willing to loan money and how you can build a good credit reputation. The discussion then addresses the types of credit accounts available, with an emphasis on open-ended credit accounts such as credit cards. The chapter concludes with information on how you can manage your credit card accounts properly.

1 Explain reasons for and against using credit.

Reasons For and Against Using Credit

Credit is a term used to describe any situation in which goods, services, or money are received in exchange for a promise to pay a definite sum of money at a future date. In essence, credit represents a form of trust established between a lender and a borrower. If the lender believes that a prospective borrower has both the ability and the willingness to repay money, then credit will be extended. The borrower is expected to live up

Golden Rules of

Credit Use and Credit Cards

Financial success comes from learning the Golden Rules of personal finance and then putting what you have learned into practice. Make the following your money habits in using credit and credit cards:

1. Protect your credit reputation just as you would guard your personal reputation.
2. Obtain copies of your credit bureau reports every year, and challenge all errors or omissions on them.
3. Obtain the lowest APRs possible when opening credit accounts. If necessary, move credit card balances to lower-cost accounts.
4. Pay your credit cards off each month. Never make convenience purchases on bank credit cards on which you carry a balance.
5. Always check your monthly billing statements against your receipts to ensure their accuracy. Challenge all discrepancies.

to that trust by repaying the lender. For the privilege of borrowing, a lender typically requires that a borrower pay interest and some other charges, such as processing fees.

In recent years, the use of consumer credit has exploded in the United States. Unfortunately, with this growth have come unprecedented levels of overindebtedness, financial distress and bankruptcies. At times, using credit may be a good decision. On other occasions, credit may be an inappropriate choice because of its costs and other disadvantages. Many people distinguish between good and bad uses of credit. Among the good uses are mortgage loans to buy a home, loans to open a business, and student loans. These uses are seen as wise choices because the funds are invested to have a long-term payoff. Bad uses of credit include using a credit card to support a lifestyle that you could not otherwise afford and taking out loans to buy overly expensive and otherwise unaffordable vehicles.

Why People Use Credit

Credit can be used in very positive ways to enhance personal financial planning. Some of the reasons why people use credit are summarized in the following list:

1. **For convenience.** Using credit—and credit cards in particular—simplifies the process of making many purchases. It provides a record of purchases, and it can be used as leverage if disputes later arise over purchases. This type of convenience use of credit is growing. For example, the use of credit cards at grocery stores has increased greatly in recent years. Convenience use is justified *only* if the card balance is paid in full each month, however. After all, you do not want to be paying for today's restaurant meal for months or years in the future.

2. **For emergencies.** Consumers may use credit to pay for such unexpected expenses as emergency medical services or automobile repairs.

3. **For identification.** For many activities, such as reserving a hotel room or renting an automobile, consumers may need to show a bank credit card to verify their identities.

Merchants are not allowed to charge a bad check amount against a customer's bank credit card, and putting your card account number on your check increases the possibility of fraudulent use of your charge account.

4. **To make reservations.** Most motels, hotels, and car rental agencies require some form of deposit to hold a reservation. A credit card number usually will serve as such a deposit, allowing guaranteed reservations to be made over the telephone. Note, however, that a hotel might notify the credit card issuer to put a hold on your account for the anticipated total amount of the charge; this process is called **credit card blocking.**

5. **To consume expensive products sooner.** Buying "big ticket" items such as a computer or automobile on credit allows the consumer to enjoy immediate use of the product. Many expensive items would not be purchased (or would be bought only after several years of saving) without the opportunity to pay for them over time. Note, however, that the product should last at least as long as the repayment period on the debt.

6. **To enjoy the good life.** An increasing number of people are using credit as a way to raise their current lifestyle in anticipation of higher incomes in the future. As a result, they can enjoy a rate of consumption today that is higher than their current income seemingly would permit. Unfortunately, this strategy for using credit gets many people into financial trouble.

7. **To take advantage of free credit.** Merchants sometimes offer "free" credit for a period of time as an inducement to buy. Known as "same as cash" plans, these programs allow the buyer to pay later without incurring finance charges. Typically, the free credit lasts for a defined time period, such as 90 days or six months. Be careful when using such plans, as interest may be owed for the entire time period if the buyer pays even one day after the allotted free-credit period ends. One financial strategy is to use a cash advance or convenience check from a bank credit card (discussed later in this chapter) to "pay" the debt just before the deadline, thereby obtaining several months of free credit before finance charges begin.

8. **To consolidate debts.** Many consumers who have difficulty making credit repayments resort to a **debt-consolidation loan,** through which the debtor exchanges several smaller debts with varying due dates and interest rates for a single large loan. Even when the debt-consolidation loan has a higher interest rate, the new payment is usually smaller than the combined payments for the other debts because the term of the new loan is longer than the terms of the old ones.

9. **For protection against rip-offs and frauds.** Mail-order and telephone purchases made on a credit card can be contested with the credit card issuer under the guidelines of the Fair Credit Billing Act (discussed later).

10. **To obtain an education.** The rising cost of higher education has forced many students to borrow to pay their tuition. This application may be one of the better uses of credit, as the borrower is investing in himself or herself to raise the quality of life and/or income in the future.

The Downside of Credit Usage

Reasons for not using credit include interest costs, the potential for overspending, credit's negative effect on your financial flexibility, and concerns about privacy.

Interest Is Costly.　**Interest** represents the price of credit. When stated in dollars, interest makes up part of the **finance charge,** which is the total dollar amount paid to use credit (including interest and any other required charges such as a loan application fee). The Truth in Lending Act requires lenders to state the finance charge both in dollars and as an **annual percentage rate (APR);** the APR expresses the cost of credit on a yearly basis as a percentage rate. For example, a single-payment, one-year loan for $1000 with a finance charge of $140 has a 14 percent APR. Knowing the APR simplifies making comparisons among loans: The lower the APR, the lower the true cost of the credit. Thus, the APR can be used to compare credit contracts with different time periods, finance charges, repayment schedules, and amounts borrowed. Note that some credit cards carry **variable interest rates** that will go up and down (perhaps monthly) to reflect interest rate changes in the economy as a whole.

The Fair Credit and Charge Card Disclosure Act (FCCCDA) has also made it easier to shop for the best credit card. This law requires that key pieces of information be disclosed in direct-mail advertising and on applications for credit cards. Such information includes the APR, the APR's method of calculation if it is a variable rate, all fees (including fees for late payments), the length of the grace period, and the method used to calculate the account balance (these topics are discussed later in this chapter). To search for the best offers on credit cards, you can visit www.bankrate.com or www. cardtrack.com.

Many states have **usury laws** (sometimes called **small loan laws**) that establish the maximum loan amounts, interest rates, and credit-related fees for different types of loans from various sources. These maximum rates can vary from 18 percent to as much as 54 percent. Note that the laws of the state in which the lending institution is located apply, rather than the laws of the state in which the borrower lives. These regulations would apply to the annual fee, late payment fee, and other fees charged on a bank credit card.

It Is Tempting to Overspend.　A major disadvantage of credit is that its use often leads to overspending. Buying $425 worth of new clothes on a charge account for $25 per month for 20 months (for a $75 finance charge) may appear easier than paying cash for a planned $300 worth of new clothes. It is even easier to buy more clothes on credit the next month, especially if you have more than three or four cards—as is typical for U.S. credit card holders.

Overindebtedness can present a real problem for credit users. If a consumer has monthly nonmortgage debt repayments amounting to 16 percent of monthly take-home pay, then he or she is considered to be seriously in debt. Instead of working at a job and spending the income, the consumer slaves at a job to pay the bills. Life feels like "paying on Visa forever" instead of "paying off Visa." Misusing credit and not paying bills on time can give a consumer a poor credit reputation, damage employment prospects, and sometimes result in the loss of items purchased.

Use of Credit Reduces Financial Flexibility.　Perhaps the greatest disadvantage of credit use comes from the loss of financial flexibility in personal money management. If your installment debts claim 10 percent of your after-tax income, then you have lost the opportunity to spend those dollars for some other purpose. Credit use also reduces your future buying power, as the money you pay out on a loan includes a finance charge as well as the principal. In fact, credit can be seen as a promise to work for the creditor in the future to pay off the debt.

Establish both a checking account and a savings account. Lenders see people who can handle these accounts as being more likely to manage credit usage properly.

Have your telephone and other utilities billed in your name. The fact that you can maintain a good payment pattern on your utility bills indicates that you can manage your money wisely and will do the same with your credit repayments.

Request, acquire, and use an oil-company credit card. These cards are not difficult to obtain. Should one company refuse, simply apply to another company, as companies' scoring systems differ. Use the credit sparingly and repay the debt promptly.

Apply for a bank credit card. Most bank card issuers have a program of test credit for people who lack an extensive credit history. The credit limit may be low (perhaps $500), but at least the opportunity exists to establish a credit rating. Later, you can request an increase in the credit limit.

Ask a bank for a small short-term cash loan. Putting these funds into a savings account at the bank will almost guarantee that you will make the required three or four monthly payments. In addition, the interest charges on the loan will be partially offset by the interest earned on the savings.

Pay off student loans. Many people have their first exposure to credit through the student loans they use to attend college. Paying off these loans quickly through a series of regular monthly payments can show prospective lenders that you are a responsible borrower.

Managing Your Credit Bureau File.   Federal law requires credit bureaus to provide consumers with their credit reports upon request. You can obtain one report for free each year from each of the national credit bureaus. In addition, consumers must be notified if merchants plan to report negative information to a credit bureau.

You should request a report periodically (perhaps every year) or whenever you move, have a change in family status (marry, get divorced, or become widowed), or resolve any credit billing errors or disputes (to ensure that negative information was not added to your file). To obtain a report, contact one or more of the three major credit reporting bureaus: Equifax (www.econsumer.equifax.com), TransUnion (www.transunion.com) and Experian (www.experian.com/consumer/index.html).*

When you obtain your report, thoroughly inspect it for accuracy. The **Fair Credit Reporting Act (FCRA)** requires that reports contain accurate, relevant, and recent information, and that only bona fide users be permitted to review a file for approved purposes. (One in five complaints to the Federal Trade Commission involves credit bureaus.) FCRA is partially enforced by consumers.

If you find an error or omission, you should immediately take steps to correct the information. Here's how:

1. Notify the credit bureau that you wish to exercise your right to a reinvestigation under FCRA. Specifically, you should ask the bureau to "reaffirm" the item. If the credit bureau responds by stating that the information is accurate, you have the right to challenge the item with the lender involved.

2. The bureau must reinvestigate the information within 30 days. If it cannot complete its investigation within 30 days, it must drop the information from your credit file.

---

*These bureaus often sell lists of consumer names in their files (albeit not the specific credit history information) for credit card marketing purposes. To have your name withheld for two years from this practice, call (888) 567-8688.

Did You Know? . . .

The Effects of Divorce on Your Credit

Besides the obvious emotional toll exacted by divorce, the breakup of a marriage affects the creditworthiness of both partners. The Federal Trade Commission makes the following suggestions for individuals seeking a divorce.

Pay careful attention to credit accounts held jointly, including mortgages, second mortgages, and credit cards. The behavior of one divorcing spouse will continue to affect the other individual as long as the accounts are held in both names. One party could make credit card charges, for example, and refuse to pay the debt, leaving the financial burden on the other party. Accordingly, where possible ask creditors to close joint accounts and reopen them as individual accounts. Never accept a creditor's verbal assurance, either over the telephone or in person, that an account has been closed. Al-

ways insist on written confirmation, including the effective date of the account closure.

When debts were accumulated in both names, divorce decrees have no legal effect on who technically owes which debts. Creditors can legally collect from *either* of the divorcing parties. If the person absolved of responsibility for the debt under the divorce decree is forced by a creditor to pay off the account, he or she must then go to court to seek enforcement of the divorce decree and collect reimbursement from the former spouse.

Both before and after a divorce, get a copy of your credit report. Check it for accuracy and challenge any problem areas, such as accounts that continue to be shown in both names.

3. If the information was erroneous, it must be corrected. If a report containing the error was sent to a creditor investigating your application within the past six months, a corrected report must be sent to that creditor.

4. If the credit bureau refuses to make a correction (perhaps because the information was "technically correct"), you may wish to provide your version of the disputed information (in 100 words or less) by adding a **consumer statement.**

5. Negative information in your file is generally not reportable after a period of seven years except for bankruptcy data, for which the time limit is ten years.

Types of Consumer Credit and Credit Card Accounts

3 Compare and contrast the types of consumer credit and credit card accounts.

Consumer credit is nonbusiness debt used by consumers for expenditures other than home mortgages. (Borrowing for housing has investment aspects that result in a separate classification; see Chapter 9.)

Types of Consumer Credit

There are two types of consumer credit: installment credit and noninstallment credit.

- With **installment credit,** the borrower must repay the amount owed in a specific number of equal payments, usually monthly. For example, a $18,000 automobile loan might require monthly payments of $380 for 60 months.

■ **Noninstallment credit** includes single-payment loans [such as a loan of $2000 at 12 percent interest with a single payment of $2240 ($2000 + $240 interest; $2000 × 0.12) due at the end of one year] and open-ended credit.

With **open-ended credit** (also called **revolving credit**), credit is extended in advance of any transaction, so that the borrower does not need to reapply each time credit is desired. Credit cards are an example of open-ended credit. Any amounts owed may be repaid in full in a single payment or via a series of equal or unequal payments, usually made monthly. The borrower makes any purchases and cash advances desired as long as the total does not exceed his or her **credit limit,** which is the preapproved maximum outstanding debt allowed on the credit account by the lender. Credit limits vary with the perceived creditworthiness of the borrower. Lenders may view having too many accounts or having high credit limits on your accounts in an unfavorable light, even if the balances owed on the accounts are low. This viewpoint is especially critical with mortgage lenders. The remainder of this chapter focuses open-ended credit, and Chapter 7 discusses installment credit.

Credit Card Accounts

Open-ended credit can be used to make purchases and, in some cases, to obtain cash advances. The most convenient type of credit, it is also the most abused. Open-ended credit includes bank credit cards, retail credit cards, travel and entertainment accounts (such as American Express's familiar "green card"), service credit, and other charge accounts. Many open-ended accounts—but not all—use a credit card. A **credit** (or **charge**) **card** is a plastic card identifying the holder as a participant in the charge account plan of a lender, such as a retailer or financial institution.

Charge accounts carry either fixed or variable interest rates. Variable interest rates fluctuate according to changes in interest rates in the economy as a whole as indicated for the account illustrated in Figure 6.1 on page 168.

Some open-ended accounts require that the entire balance be repaid each month; most, however, allow the borrower to carry a balance from month to month. If the latter payment scheme is selected, a **minimum payment** must be made each month to cover interest and a small payment on the amount owed (the **principal**). If at least the minimum payment is not received by the due date, the cardholder may be declared in **default** (the borrower has failed to make a payment of principal or interest when due or has not met another key requirement of a credit agreement). Most cardholders maintain balances and can do so for years even as other charges are added to the same account. As long as the total debt remains below the credit limit, the user may continue to make charges against the account. Thanks to their ease of use, credit cards are now the primary source of consumer debt other than home mortgages.

Bank Credit Cards.   A **bank credit card account** is an open-ended account at a financial institution (commercial bank, savings and loan association, or credit union) that allows the holder to make purchases almost anywhere. Visa, MasterCard, Discover, and Optima are the most commonly recognized bank card names. In reality, however, the actual lender is the financial institution. Visa, MasterCard, and the like are simply service providers that maintain the electronic network through which transactions are communicated. Participating merchants and financial institutions pay transaction fees to these service providers based on the dollar amounts charged. Virtually all financial institutions offer bank credit cards. So do a number of consumer-products companies, such as AT&T, General Motors, Allstate Insurance, and Verizon, which contract with Visa, MasterCard, and their counterparts to offer **co-branded credit cards.**

Cash advances may be obtained at any financial institution that issues the type of card (Visa, MasterCard, and so on) being used. A **cash advance** is a cash loan from a bank credit card account. A transaction fee is usually assessed for each cash advance, and cash advances often are subject to a higher APR than are purchases. Interest charges begin to accrue as soon as the cash advance is granted. In most cases, the borrower receives cash, such as from an ATM. Alternatively, the funds may be transferred automatically into the cardholder's bank account.

Many bank credit card issuers periodically send three to five **convenience checks** to their cardholders. Customers can use these checks as cash advances to make payments to others. If such a payment is used to make a payment on another credit card, it represents a **balance transfer.** Of course, these instruments are not genuine checks but simply a check-equivalent way to borrow money. If you receive convenience checks but do not want to use them, either put them in a safe place or destroy them immediately, as they easily could be used fraudulently by someone else. As indicated in Figure 6.1 on page 168, a transaction fee is often charged for receiving cash advances, using convenience checks, or making balance transfers.

Some bank cards are a form of **prestige card,** often with a precious metal in the brand name such as "gold," "silver," or "platinum." These accounts require that the user possess higher credit qualifications and offer enhancements such as free traveler's checks and higher credit limits. Prestige cards may carry higher annual fees. Most holders of regular bank credit cards do not realize that they could obtain a higher credit limit on their standard card just by requesting one from the issuer.

Some Visa and MasterCard credit cards are identified as **affinity cards**—that is, standard bank cards with the logo of a sponsoring organization imprinted on the face of the card. Typically, the issuing financial institution donates a portion of the annual fee and a small percentage of the amounts charged (perhaps 0.25, 0.5, or 1 percent) to the sponsoring organization. Sponsors may include charitable, political, sports, or other organized groups, such as the Sierra Club or Mothers Against Drunk Driving. Members of the sponsoring organization may be motivated to use an affinity card because their organization receives money from each transaction. Creditors rightly calculate that fewer delinquencies will occur among the particular group of people, so they can afford to transfer some dollars to the named organization.

Secured Credit Cards.   A **secured credit card** (also called a **collateralized credit card**) is backed by collateral in the form of a savings account opened at the financial institution that issues the card. Banks offering secured credit cards typically charge an application fee and require the applicant to make a deposit of $500 to $1000 into a savings account. The person then receives a credit limit equal to the same amount on a bank credit card, such as a Visa or MasterCard card. The savings balance cannot be withdrawn as long as the card is available for use. The deposit is refunded (with interest) when the balance is paid off and the account is closed. Most people do not need a secured credit card, but those who have no alternative should consider obtaining one from a reputable institution, as scams abound in this market.

Retail Credit Card Accounts.   A **retail credit card** allows a customer to make purchases on credit at any of the outlets of a particular retailer or retail chain. Examples of credit card accounts at retail stores include those offered by JCPenney, Best Buy, and Shell Oil. Today, it is common practice for a retailer to form an alliance with a financial institution to offer a bank credit card that carries the retailer's logo but that can be used anywhere the bank card can be used.

Some smaller retail establishments offer open-ended accounts that do not use a credit card as the vehicle for using the account. With these **retail charge accounts,** the customer simply asks to have the purchase put on his or her account for repayment at a later date.

Travel and Entertainment Cards.

Travel and entertainment (T&E) cards are similar to bank credit cards in that they allow holders to make purchases at numerous businesses. The entire balance charged must be repaid within 30 days, however. The best-known T&E cards are those issued by American Express, Diners Club, and Carte Blanche. Such cards are often used by business people for food and lodging expenses while traveling. They are somewhat more difficult to obtain than bank cards because applicants must have higher-than-average incomes to qualify for an account; in addition, applicants must pay an annual membership of $35 or more. T&E cards are not accepted at as many outlets as are bank credit cards.

Other Forms of Open-Ended Credit.

A **personal line of credit** is a lending arrangement that allows the borrower access to a prearranged revolving line of credit provided by the lender (usually a bank, savings and loan association, or brokerage firm). The essence of a line of credit is that borrowers can obtain a cash advance when needed and not reapply for a loan each time they need money. Like credit card accounts, a personal line of credit includes a credit limit and a flexible repayment schedule. Some people also use the equity in their home as collateral for a line of credit. This arrangement is referred to as a **home-equity line of credit.**

Service credit is granted to consumers by public utilities, physicians, dentists, and other service providers that do not require full payment when services are rendered. For example, your electric company allows you to use electricity all month and then

How to . . .

Close a Credit Card Account

Credit card accounts are open-ended credit and, therefore, can remain open for decades even if you never use the card or stop using it at some point. Accounts are not closed if you cut up the cards. Instead, the lender must be formally notified of your request before the account will be officially closed. Here's what to do:

1. Obtain the customer-service telephone number for the lender from your most recent monthly statement. If you do not have a recent bill, obtain a copy of your credit report, which will list the contact information for the lender.
2. Contact the lender to request the address to which you should send your cancellation request. It will not be same address to which you send your monthly payment.
3. Send a written request to close the account and request that the creditor send a confirmation that the account is, indeed, closed.
4. After 90 days, obtain copies of your credit reports from the three major national credit bureaus to confirm that the account is shown as closed on all of them.

Note that you cannot "close" an account on which you currently owe a balance. You can, however, ask the lender to no longer honor the card.

sends you a bill that may not be due for 10 to 15 days. Service credit usually carries no interest, although penalty charges may apply if payments are made slowly. Service may eventually be cut off for continued slow payment or nonpayment of the debt.

Common (But Not Always Beneficial) Aspects of Credit Card Accounts

4 Recognize the impact of common (but not always beneficial) aspects of credit card accounts.

Federal law requires credit card lenders to disclose all the rules governing the account to borrowers before they sign up for any card. Some of that information must be displayed in a uniform manner, as illustrated in the sample credit card disclosure box in Figure 6.1. The remainder of the information appears in the credit agreement (contract). Credit card issuers are free to change the rules on an account at any time, as long as they notify the account holder of the change. This notification is usually included as an insert in the monthly bill for the account and often appears in very small print. You can avoid any penalties imposed by the new rules by paying off the account or by closing it. If you cannot pay the bill in full, you will be obligated to adhere to the new rules until you close the account. This section outlines some of the more important aspects of credit card accounts.

Teaser Rates and Default Rates

Some cards carry a temporarily low **introductory** (or **teaser**) **rate** to entice borrowers to apply for an account. Teaser APRs of 0 to 3.9 percent are common, for example. In Figure 6.1, the teaser rate is 4.99 percent for purchases and 0.0 percent during the first six months the account is open. The APR typically reverts to a much higher fixed or variable interest rate after the introductory period ends. Some credit card borrowers take advantage of teaser rates by opening new accounts regularly and transferring the balances from other accounts to the new account to take advantage of the low introductory rate in spite of the high balance transfer fee that might exist. This technique can be used several times in succession by customers with a good credit history. It is important to close old accounts, however, or eventually the simple fact of having many credit card accounts may negatively affect your credit score. Further, lenders catch on to people who frequently take advantage of this technique and become reluctant to offer teaser rates to them.

Usually the teaser rate will be rescinded and the regular rate on the account will be applied if the borrower makes a late payment even once during the introductory period. A more serious downside to most credit card accounts is the assessment of a **default rate.** A default rate is a high APR that is assessed whenever a borrower fails to uphold certain rules of the account, such as making on-time payments or staying within the specified credit limit. The disclosure notice in Figure 6.1 indicates that if you are late making a payment even once during the introductory period, you will not only lose the teaser rate but also see a default rate of perhaps 27.99 percent APR [23.99 percent plus 4 percent (the current prime rate)].

It is probably understandable that a credit card company might want to raise the interest rate when a customer is having trouble paying on the account. In fact, many credit card companies now recheck their customers' credit reports on a regular basis after an account is opened. The purpose of this practice to look for *any* situation where a customer is having trouble with other accounts or has taken on significantly higher levels of debt. In such a situation, the credit card company can decide whether the borrower

Figure 6.1

Credit Card Disclosure Information

DETAILS OF RATE, FEE, AND OTHER COST INFORMATION	
As required by law, rates, fees, and other costs of this credit card offer are disclosed here. All account terms are governed by the Credit Card Agreement sent with the card. Account terms are not guaranteed for any period of time; all terms, including the APRs and fees, may change in accordance with the Agreement and applicable law.	
Annual Percentage Rate for purchases	The **introductory rate** (see notes below) is **4.99%** until the first billing after the sixth-month anniversary of the opening of the account. After that **9.99%** (variable rate).
Other APRs (all other APRs are variable)	**Balance Transfers:** The introductory rate is 0% until the first billing after the sixth-month anniversary of the opening of the account. After that **9.99%**. Cash Advances: **19.99%**. Default Rate: **27.99%** (see notes below).
Variable rate information	**Your APRs may vary** during each billing period. The rate for purchases and balance transfers is determined by adding 5.99% to the prime rate (see notes below). The rate for cash advances is determined by adding 15.99% to the prime rate but such rate will never be below 19.99%. The default is determined by adding no more than 23.99% to the prime rate.
Grace period for repayment of purchases	**Not less than 20 days** if you pay your total new balance in full each billing period by the due date. Payment must be received by 9 a.m. on the due date. There is **no grace period for balance transfers and cash advances.**
Method of computing the balance	**Average Daily Balance** (including new purchases).
Annual fee	$25
Minimum Finance Charge	$1.00
Miscellaneous fees	**Transaction fee for Cash Advances:** 3% of the amount of the transaction but not less than $20. **Transaction fee for Balance Transfers:** 3% of the amount of the transfer but not less than $50. There is no balance transfer fee during the six-month introductory period. **Late fee:** $15 on balances up to $500. $35 on balances over $500. **Over-the-limit fee:** $35. **Bounced check fee:** $35.
Notes	**Introductory rates:** Eligibility for introductory rate is subject to your maintaining good credit. Rates indicated in this offer are subject to change to reflect changes in the prime rate (see below) at the time of your application. **Default rate:** All of your APRs may increase if you default under any Card Agreement that you have with us because you fail to make a payment to us **or any other creditor** when due, you exceed your credit limit, or you make a payment to us that is not honored. Factors considered when determining your default rate may include the length of time your account with us has been open, the existence, seriousness, and timing of defaults under any Card Agreement you have with us; or other indications of account usage and performance on this or any other account you have with us **or any other creditor**. **Prime rate:** The prime rate (currently 4%) used to determine your APRs for each billing period is the U.S. prime rate published in the Wall Street Journal two business days prior to the billing date for that billing period.

is in **universal default** and, if so, apply the default rate. Note the words "or any other creditor" in bold in Figure 6.1—they indicate that this company utilizes the concept of universal default. Under universal default, you can be charged a default rate on an account that you are handling well simply because you are having trouble with other accounts. In fact, being late just once or twice on one account can trigger universal default on other accounts.

Preapproved Credit Card Offers

Companies interested in expanding their base of credit customers sometimes pay credit bureaus to prescreen their files and identify people who pass certain tests of creditworthiness. A company may then send applications for credit to the prescreened people. Some consumers will have been preapproved as part of this process, so they merely need to sign the notice to open the account. Note that being preapproved means only that you will be granted credit. Both the credit card debt limit and APR will be determined after you apply for an account.

Annual and Transaction Fees

Some bank credit card lenders assess **annual fees** ranging from $25 to $50 (or more). In addition, lenders may charge a **transaction fee** (a small charge levied each time a card is used). The card illustrated in Figure 6.1 assesses transaction fees for cash advances and balance transfers. Some lenders even charge a fee for printing the monthly credit bill. Most fees are not required to be included in the APR calculation because they cannot be known in advance. Thus an apparently low-rate card may turn into a high-cost card when all fees are considered.

Liability for Lost or Stolen Cards

The Truth in Lending Act limits a cardholder's **credit card liability** for lost or stolen credit cards. Under the law, if you notify the card issuer within two days of a loss or theft, you are not legally responsible for any fraudulent usage of the card. After two days, your maximum liability for fraudulent usage of the card (including telephone calling cards) prior to your notification is $50. You are not responsible for any fraudulent usage after you notify the issuer of the loss. Although your financial liability is low, some companies nevertheless specialize in selling credit card insurance (for an annual premium ranging from $15 to $49) that will pay creditors for the first $50 of unauthorized use of an insured person's lost or stolen credit cards. Such insurance is profitable for insurance companies—but an unnecessary expense for you. In addition, most homeowner's and renter's insurance policies pay for such losses (see Chapter 10 for details). Furthermore, as a gesture of goodwill, most credit card companies will waive the $50 fee for unauthorized use.

Late-Payment, Bounced Check, and Over-the-Limit Fees

Late-payment fees of $30 or more are often applied when the borrower fails to make a payment by the due date. In addition, most card issuers assess a similar charge if you write a bad check when making your monthly payment. Similarly, many credit card issuers charge a significant ($20 to $50) over-the-limit fee when the cardholder exceeds his or her credit limit. Each of these fees is much higher than necessary in terms of the actual cost to the lender for these rule violations. Indeed, they represent a significant source of profits for credit card issuers. The account illustrated in Figure 6.1 assesses a $35 fee for each of these offenses.

Credit Card Insurance

Many lenders encourage borrowers to sign up for **credit life insurance** that pays the unpaid balance of a loan—to the lender—in the event of the borrower's death. Credit life insurance is grossly overpriced and is one cost that can be avoided. The same can be said for **credit disability insurance,** which repays the outstanding loan balance if the borrower becomes disabled (with "disability" usually being very narrowly defined) and **credit unemployment insurance.** The only exception might be credit life insurance for people who cannot obtain life insurance through more traditional means.

Managing Credit Cards Wisely

5 Manage your credit card and charge accounts to avoid fees and finance charges.

Credit cards can be a positive tool in personal financial management—when used appropriately. The key, then, is to manage their use wisely. To do so, you must understand and monitor your credit statements, correct errors when appropriate, and also recognize how finance charges are computed. Your goal should be to use the credit card in a manner that avoids all fees, including finance charges. This means paying your balance in full every month.

Credit Statements

Active charge account holders receive a monthly **credit statement** (also called a **periodic statement**) that summarizes the charges, payments, finance charges, and other activity on the account. The significant features of credit statements are the billing date, due date, transaction and posting dates, grace period, payment minimum, and credit for merchandise returns and errors obtained. You also need to know how to correct errors in your credit statements. Figure 6.2 shows a monthly statement for a credit card.

Billing Date.   The billing date (sometimes called the **statement date** or **closing date**) is the last day of the month for which any transactions are reported on the statement. In Figure 6.2, this date is 5/22/05. Any transactions or payments made after this date will be recorded on the following month's credit statement. The statement is mailed to the cardholder a day or so after the billing date. The billing date is generally the same day of each month, and the time period between billing dates is referred to as the **billing cycle.**

Figure 6.2

Sample Statement for a Revolving Charge Account

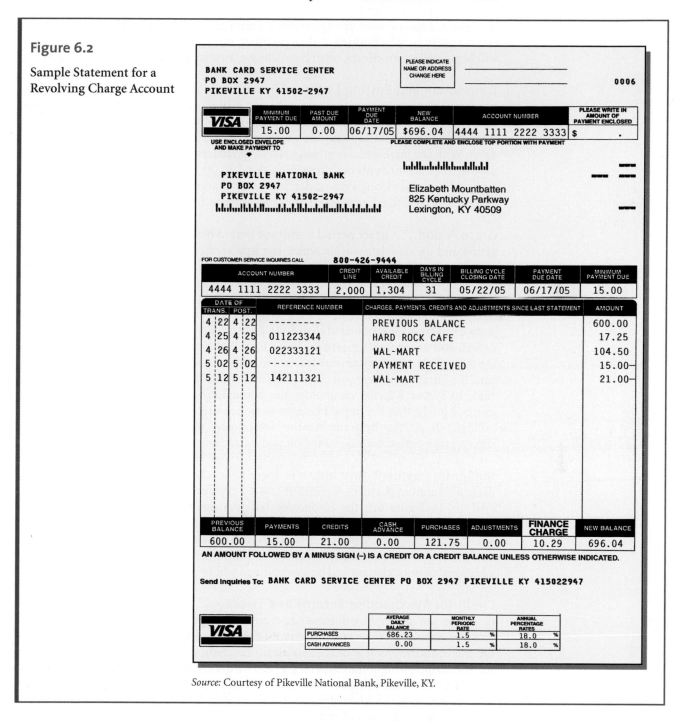

Source: Courtesy of Pikeville National Bank, Pikeville, KY.

Due Date. The due date is the specific day by which the credit card company should receive payment from you. In Figure 6.2, this date is 6/17/05. The period between the billing date and the due date—usually 20 to 25 days (with 20 days becoming more common)—represents the time allowed for statements and payments to be mailed and for the borrower to make arrangements to pay. Federal law states that bills must be mailed to cardholders at least 14 days before payments are due. The account illustrated in Figure 6.2 has a 25-day billing period. If payment is received later than the due date, a credit bureau may be notified of slow payment. If no payment is received, the company will begin collection efforts, often by mailing a "first notice" that a payment is overdue.

Transaction and Posting Dates.   The date on which a credit cardholder makes a purchase (or receives a credit, as described later in this chapter) is known as the **transaction date.** In the past, several days would pass before the credit card company was informed of the transaction and the charge was posted to the account (on the posting date). With the increased use of magnetic strip readers at retailers, however, these dates may be concurrent, with both matching the date on which the clerk or the customer "swipes" the card through the reader. Interest is charged from the posting date unless a grace period is offered; some lenders charge interest from the transaction date.

Grace Period.   A **grace period** is the time period between the posting date of a transaction and the due date, within which any new credit card purchases made during the billing cycle will avoid finance charges (also see Figure 6.1). Most cards provide a grace period only if the previous month's total balance was paid in full and on time. Approximately 30 percent of all cardholders pay their bills in full by the due date and receive, in effect, an interest-free loan on their new purchases during the next billing cycle. It is a smart move to use one credit card for convenience items that are paid in full each month and another credit card for items for which paying off the balance each month is not possible. Use a no-annual-fee card for the convenience purchases and a low-APR card for purchases where you carry a balance. Avoid cards that do not offer a grace period. In Figure 6.2, the cardholder has a previous unpaid balance, $600, and was charged interest on the unpaid balance as well as on the new charges made within the billing cycle, starting from the date they were posted to the account. Thus, this example lacks a grace period because of the unpaid balance on the card.

Minimum Payment Amount.   To meet his or her obligations, a borrower must make a minimum payment monthly that is no smaller than the amount required by the creditor. In Figure 6.2, the cardholder has two options: pay the total amount due ($696.04) or make at least the minimum payment of $15. If the borrower pays the full amount due, finance charges on new purchases in the next billing cycle generally can be avoided. If a partial payment, such as the "total minimum payment due" of $15, is made, additional finance charges will be assessed and will be payable the following month.

Credit for Merchandise Returns and Errors.   If you return merchandise bought on credit, the merchant will issue you a **credit receipt**—written evidence of the items returned that notes the specific amount of the transaction. In essence, the amount of the merchandise credit is charged back to the credit card company and eventually to the merchant. A credit may also be granted by the credit card company when a billing error has been made (discussed in the next section) or when an unauthorized transaction appears. Credits obtained in the current month should appear on the next monthly statement as a reduction of the total amount owed. The credit statement in Figure 6.2 shows a $21.00 credit.

Advice from an Expert

Avoid the Minimum Payment Trap

Two out of three college students have a credit card, with the average level of debt exceeding $2500. In fact, the first financial mistake many students make is signing up for too many credit cards. Their second mistake is typically using the card with no clear plan for how to repay the debt. Third, and most significantly, students often have no idea how much the interest will eventually cost them.

Do you currently have balances outstanding on your credit cards? If so, how long have you carried those balances? If you open an account in college and already have an unpaid balance of $2500 upon your graduation at age 22, you may find that the balance will not drop below $2500 for many years. This situation occurs when you continue to make purchases with the card but continue to send in only the required minimum payment amount. If $2500 is still owed on the account years later (perhaps when you reach age 37), then you have "permanent debt." In essence, you have never repaid the college charges. With an 18 percent APR, the finance charges on a principal of $2500 for 15 years will total $6750 (0.18 × $2500 × 15), almost three times as much as the debt itself!

The outlook is similarly bleak if you discontinue using the card for new purchases but still remit only the required minimum repayment amount. Credit card issuers often require a minimum monthly payment as low as 2 or 2½ percent of the outstanding balance. This tiny payment requirement is mathematically guaranteed to keep the user in debt for many, many years. To illustrate, a minimum payment of $50 (2 percent) on an outstanding balance of $2500 with a 1.6 percent monthly periodic rate results in only $10 going to reduce the actual debt (the principal). The other $40 ($2500 × 0.016 = $40) is used to pay the monthly interest. At this rate of repayment, it will take more than eight years to repay the $2500.

A ploy that card issuers frequently use is to allow cardholders to "skip a payment"—in essence, to make "a zero-dollar minimum payment"—if a sufficiently large repayment was made in the prior month. Of course, interest will continue accrue for the month during which no payment is made. This practice increases the total amount owed because the unpaid interest simply adds to the unpaid balance.

Such offers for a "low" or "zero-dollar" minimum payment perfectly illustrate the minimum payment trap. To avoid paying credit card charges for 8 to 15 years, or even longer, you must make much larger monthly payments that go toward retiring your credit card balances. Better still, ask yourself—no, ask yourself twice—"Do I really need to charge it?"

Donald Stuhlman
Wilmington College, Delaware

Correcting Errors on Your Credit Card Statement

The Fair Credit Billing Act (FCBA) helps people who wish to dispute billing errors on revolving credit accounts. In effect, the FCBA permits a **chargeback**—that is, the amount of the transaction is charged back to the business where the transaction originated. Withholding payment to a credit card company is permitted when the cardholder alleges that a mathematical error has been made in a billing statement, when fraudulent use of the card appears to have occurred, or when (within certain reasonable limitations) a **goods and services dispute** asserts that the charges were for faulty, damaged, shoddy, defective, or poor-quality goods and services and you made a good-faith effort to try to correct the problem with the merchant.*

You must make your billing error complaint within 60 days after the date on which the first bill containing the error was mailed to you. The lender then has 30 days to acknowledge your notification and, within 90 days, must either correct the error permanently, return any overpayment (if requested), or provide evidence of why it believes the bill to be correct (such as a copy of a charge slip you supposedly signed).

While the dispute is being investigated, creditors cannot assess interest on or apply penalties for nonpayment of the disputed amount, send **dunning letters** (notices that make insistent demands for repayment), or send negative information about your account to a credit bureau without stating that "some items are in dispute." A lender that does not follow the procedures correctly cannot collect the first $50 of the questioned amount, even if the bill was correct. Back interest and penalties may be charged if the disputed item is proved to be legitimately owed.

You should take several actions when disputing an item on a billing statement:

1. Send a written notice of the error to the credit card issuer. The notice must be in writing to qualify for the protections provided under the FCBA. Instead of sending the notice to the same address where repayments are normally remitted, examine the billing statement thoroughly, looking for an address under the heading "Send Inquiries to" or something similar.

2. Provide photocopies (not originals) of any necessary documentation. Keep the originals to challenge any finding by the company that no error occurred.

3. Withhold payment for disputed items. If possible, pay the remaining amount owed in full to isolate a disputed item. Under the provisions of the FCBA, the company must immediately credit your account for the amount in dispute.

4. After the dispute has been settled, review your credit bureau file to ensure that it does not include information regarding your refusal to repay the disputed amount.

Computation of Finance Charges

Companies that issue credit cards must tell consumers the APR applied as well as the method used to compute the finance charges. In addition, they must disclose the **periodic rate,** which is the APR for a charge account divided by the number of billing cycles per year (usually 12). For example, a periodic rate of 1.5 percent per month would result from an APR of approximately 18 percent (actually a bit higher because of compounding); both figures must be disclosed. Typically, the finance charge is calculated by first computing the **average daily balance**—the sum of the outstanding balances owed each day during the billing period divided by the number of days in the period. The periodic rate is then applied against that balance.

---

*For goods and services disputes, the FCBA applies only to charges of more than $50 made in your home state or within 100 miles of your current mailing address. Most lenders apply the spirit of the FCBA to any goods and services disputes, regardless of the geographic distances involved.

Did You Know? . . .

How Credit Card Balances Are Calculated

Four methods are commonly used to calculate the average daily balance on a credit card billing statement:

Average daily balance excluding new purchases. The cardholder pays interest only on any balance left over from the previous month.

Average daily balance including new purchases with a grace period. The balance calculation includes the balance from the previous month and any new charges made during the billing cycle. The grace period allows for the exclusion of new charges made during the billing cycle only if the balance from the previous billing cycle was zero.

Average daily balance including new purchases with no grace period. The balance from the previous month and any new charges made during the billing cycle are included in the balance calculation, even if the previous month's balance was paid in full.

Two-cycle average daily balance including new purchases. This method is the least favorable for con-sumers, especially as they pay down the credit card balance. It eliminates the grace period on new purchases made during the current billing cycle, and it retroactively eliminates the grace period for the previous month each time the account carries a balance. The two-cycle method effectively doubles the finance charges and is a device for advertising one interest rate and charging another. Unlike with the one-cycle systems, where each billing cycle stands alone, you must pay off your balance for at least two months to avoid finance charges.

The chart illustrates how cardholders can sometimes be horribly (and legally) overcharged. It demonstrates how finance charges vary for a hypothetical situation in which a borrower charges $1000 per month and pays only the minimum payment, except for every third month when the balance is paid in full. Executing this scheme four times over the course of a year would result in the finance charges shown in the table under the three most common ways of computing the average daily balance and for low-, average-, and high-interest cards.

	Annual Percentage Rate		
	12.0%	**17.3%**	**19.8%**
Average daily balance (excluding new purchases)	$ 40.00	$ 57.60	$ 66.00
Average daily balance (including new purchases)*	$ 80.00	$115.20	$132.00
Two-cycle average daily balance (including new purchases)	$120.00	$172.80	$198.00

*This is the most common method used by credit card issuers.

Summary

1. People borrow for a variety of reasons—for example, to deal with financial emergencies, to have goods immediately, and to obtain discounts in the future. Perhaps the greatest disadvantage of using credit is the ensuing loss of financial flexibility in personal money management. The annual percentage rate (APR) provides the best approximation of the true cost of credit.

2. In the process of opening a credit account, the lender investigates your credit history, obtains a credit score (such as a FICO score) from a credit bureau, and then determines whether to grant credit and under what conditions.

3. Borrowers can use both installment and noninstallment credit. Open-ended credit is an example of noninstallment credit. It permits the customer to gain repeated access to credit without having to fill out a new application each time money is borrowed. The consumer may choose either to repay the debt in a single payment or to make a series of payments of varying amounts. Bank credit card and travel and entertainment credit cards are the most commonly used open-ended credit accounts.

4. Credit card borrowers must adhere to all the rules of the account or risk being charged a number of punitive fees such as late-payment and bounced check fees. Borrowers also need to be wary of default rates, which may raise the APR on the account for any violation of the account rules. Some lenders apply default rates if the borrower falls behind in payments on other accounts, even if the borrower is in good standing on the lender's own account.

5. Credit card statements provide a monthly summary of credit transactions and the calculation of any finance charges. Credit card issuers compute finance charges by multiplying the average daily balance by the periodic interest rate.

Key Terms

annual percentage rate (APR), 157
average daily balance, 174
cash advance, 165
credit, 154
credit agreement, 160
credit bureau, 160
credit limit, 164
credit report, 160
credit (risk) scoring, 160
default, 164

default rate, 167
finance charge, 157
grace period, 172
interest, 157
introductory (teaser) rate, 167
minimum payment, 164
periodic rate, 174
principal, 164
tiered pricing, 161
variable interest rates, 157

Chapter Review Questions

1. According to the Truth in Lending Act, what two items of credit-cost information must lenders disclose to credit applicants?

2. Describe four disadvantages of using credit.

3. How are cardholders protected from losses resulting from unauthorized use of a lost or stolen credit card?

4. Name and describe briefly courses of action you can take to establish a good credit history.

5. What steps should you take to maintain the accuracy of your credit bureau files?

6. What factors are used in the calculation of a credit applicant's FICO score?

7. What is the effect of making only the minimum payments on your credit card accounts?

8. What types of information are provided on a credit card statement?

9. Summarize how you would go about correcting an error on your credit card statement.

10. Summarize the steps that creditors use when computing the monthly finance charges for a credit card account.

Group Discussion Issues

1. Is there such a thing as good debt? What types of debt do you consider to be "good"? What types do you consider to be "bad"?

2. What aspects of your financial life make you creditworthy? What aspects would make it difficult for you to obtain credit?

3. Do you know anyone who has gotten into financial difficulty because of overuse of credit cards? Is it too easy for college students to get credit cards?

4. How do you feel about the fact that the major national credit bureaus may have files containing information about you? How do you feel about the process required to correct errors in those files?

5. Some credit cards offer a 1 percent or higher rebate for all purchases made on the card. How would you feel about using such a card to get those rebates with the intention of paying the balance off in full each month?

Decision-Making Cases

▶Case 1
Preparation of a Credit-Related Speech

Fred Marchese, of Auburn, Alabama, is the credit manager for a regional chain of department stores. He has been asked to join a panel of community members and make a ten-minute speech to graduating high-school seniors on the topic "Using Credit Wisely." Fill in the following outline Fred has prepared with things that he can say:

(a) What is consumer credit?

(b) Why might graduates use credit?

(c) How can graduates use credit wisely?

▶Case 2
A Delayed Report of a Stolen Credit Card

Joan Craycraft of Fairbanks, Alaska, had taken her sister-in-law Julia Johnson out for an expensive lunch. When it came time to pay the bill, Joan noticed that her Visa credit card was missing, so she paid the bill with her MasterCard. While driving home, Joan remembered that she had last used the Visa card about a week earlier. She became concerned that a sales clerk or someone else could have taken it and might fraudulently charging purchases on her card.

(a) Summarize Joan's legal rights in this situation.

(b) Discuss the likelihood that Joan must pay Visa for any illegal charges to the account.

Financial Math Questions

1. Talika Sampson, an antiques dealer from Sarasota, Florida, received her monthly billing statement for April for her MasterCard account. The statement indicated that she had a beginning balance of $600, on day 5 she charged $150, on day 12 she charged $300, and on day 15 she made a $200 payment. Out of curiosity, Talika wanted to confirm that the finance charge for the billing cycle was correct.

(a) What was Talika's average daily balance for April without new purchases?

(b) What was her finance charge on the balance in part (a) if her APR is 19.2 percent?

(c) What was her average daily balance for April with new purchases?

(d) What was her finance charge on the balance in part (c) if her APR is 19.2 percent?

(e) What was her finance charge using the two-cycle average daily balance if her average daily balance for March was $800? (Hint: Add the March average daily balance to the April average daily balance, and then divide by 2 to obtain the two-cycle average daily balance.)

2. Elizabeth Mountbatten, a biologist from Baton Rouge, Louisiana, is curious about the accuracy of the average daily balance shown on her most recent credit card billing statement, which appears in Figure 6.2 on page 171. Use the posting dates for her account to calculate her average daily balance and compare the result to the amount shown on the statement.

Money Matters Continuing Cases

Victor and Maria Have a Billing Dispute

Maria Hernandez was reviewing her recent bank credit card account statement when she found two charges that she and Victor could not have made. The charges involved rental of a hotel room and purchase of a meal on the same day in a distant city. These charges totaled $219.49 out of the couple's $367.89 balance for the month.

1. What payment should Maria make on the account?

2. How should she notify her credit card issuer about the unauthorized use?

3. Once the matter is resolved, what should Maria do to ensure that her credit history is not negatively affected by this error?

The Johnsons Attempt to Resolve Their Credit and Cash-Flow Problems

Harry and Belinda have a substantial annual joint income—more than $70,000, in fact. Nevertheless, they expect to experience some cash-flow deficits during several months of the upcoming year (see Tables 3.3 and 3.4).

To resolve this difficulty, the couple opened two bank card accounts and then obtained a cash advance at an interest rate (APR) equal to about 19 percent. When the statement came for the cash advance on one card, they took out another cash advance on the other bank card to make the minimum payment. The Johnsons now have cash advance balances totaling more than $1400 outstanding on the two cards. Their budget for the upcoming months will not allow them to begin repaying these debts.

1. What are the advantages and disadvantages of the Johnsons opening more than one bank credit card account?

2. Comment on the costs involved in continually getting cash advances from one bank card to apply to amounts due on another bank card.

3. Harry and Belinda have considered applying for an installment loan to pay off the cash advance balances and to set up a regular payment pattern to pay off the $1400. Based on the factors used when setting credit scores (pages 160–161), write a paragraph evaluating the Johnsons' application for such a loan. To do so, you should review their financial statements in Chapters 2 and 3.

What Would You Recommend Now?

Now that you have read the chapter on credit use and credit cards, what would you recommend to Darrell Cochrane in the case at the beginning of the chapter regarding:

1. His approach to using credit cards, including the number of cards he has?

2. How he might lower his interest expense each month?

3. Determining whether his credit history has been damaged this past year?

Exploring the World Wide Web

To complete these exercises, go to the *Garman/Forgue* website at college.hmco.com/business/students. Under General Business, select the title of this text. Click on the Internet Exercises link for this chapter, and answer the questions that appear on the Web page.

1. Do you owe money on one or more credit cards? Visit the Financenter website, where you will find a calculator that will tell you how long it will take to pay off your balances.

2. Visit the website for one of the three major credit reporting firms. Order a copy of your credit report.

3. Visit the website for the Bank Rate Monitor, where you will find information on bank credit card interest rates around the United States. View the information for the lenders in a large city nearest your home. How does the information compare to the interest rates charged on your own credit card account(s)? How do the rates in the city you selected compare with those found elsewhere in the United States?

4. Privacy is a major issue in credit reporting. Visit the website for Equifax and review its privacy policy (click on "privacy policy").

5. Visit the website for the Federal Reserve Board. Locate its on-line copy of the *Consumer Handbook on Credit Protection Laws.* Identify one additional protection not discussed in this book that is provided by each of the following laws: the Fair Credit Billing Act, the Equal Credit Opportunity Act, and the Fair Credit Reporting Act.

6. Visit the website for Fair, Isaacs and Company. Read up on how credit scoring works and view a sample report. Identify three things that you could do to improve your credit score.

Visit the Garman/Forgue website . . .

college.hmco.com/business/students

Under General Business, select *Personal Finance 8e.* There, among other valuable resources, you will find a complete glossary, ACE questions, links to help you complete the chapter exercises, and links to other personal finance sites.

Chapter 7

Installment Credit

LEARNING OBJECTIVES

After reading this chapter, you should be able to:

1 **Establish** your own debt limit.

2 **Understand** three types of consumer loans.

3 **Describe** sources of consumer loans.

4 **Calculate** the annual percentage rate and finance charges on loans.

5 **Describe** signs of overindebtedness and know what options are available for people with excessive debts.

Carrie Savarin, age 25, is a nurse practitioner with the local health department. She makes $50,000 per year, with about $4000 of her income coming from overtime pay. Her employer provides a qualified tax-sheltered retirement plan to which Carrie contributes 4 percent of her salary and for which she receives an additional 4 percent matching contribution from her employer. (She could contribute up to 6 percent with an equal employer match.) Carrie has $19,000 in outstanding student loans on which she will pay $354 per month over the next five years, and her total credit card debt is $3000. Otherwise, she is debt-free. Carrie would like to purchase a new or late-model used car to replace the car she has been driving since her senior year in high school. She has about $2000 that she could use as a down payment on the replacement vehicle.

What would you recommend to Carrie on the subject of installment credit regarding:

1. Factors she should consider regarding her ability to take on additional debt?

2. Where she might obtain financing for a vehicle loan?

3. Whether she should get a simple-interest or add-on rate loan?

4. The effect of taking on an installment loan on her overall financial planning?

U sing credit requires deliberate thinking and planning before taking action. You need to consider whether it is right to borrow and decide in advance how you will repay any debt that you incur. This is especially true for installment credit used to purchase vehicles; to make home improvements; to buy furniture, computers, and major appliances; and to obtain personal loans. **Installment credit** (also called **closed-end credit**) requires that the consumer repay the amount owed plus interest in a specific number of equal payments, usually monthly. With installment credit, you determine how the loan will be used, from which lender you will borrow, how much to borrow, and how to manage repayment every time new installment credit is obtained.

In this chapter we begin by discussing the essential first step in planned borrowing: setting one's own debt limit. We then examine the important terminology of consumer loans. The many sources of consumer loans are described next so that you can determine which creditors are best for you. The chapter continues with an explanation of how finance charges on consumer loans are computed. This knowledge will help keep you from paying too much interest and fees when you use credit. We end by considering the topics of being overly indebted and who should consider bankruptcy.

1 Establish your own debt limit.

You Should Set Your Own Debt Limits

Recall from Chapter 6 that credit card issuers set a credit limit for each of their cardholders. In a similar fashion, you should set your own **debt limit,** which is the overall maximum you believe you should owe based on your ability to meet the repayment obligations. Most people's debt limit is, and should be, lower than what lenders are willing to tender. Lenders are willing to take chances that some borrowers will not repay. By contrast, you should not take such a chance when making your own credit decisions.

When considering a new loan, many people simply look at the monthly payment required. This view is very short-sighted, however, as it is easy to get a low monthly pay-

Golden Rules of

Installment Credit

Financial success comes from learning the Golden Rules of personal finance and then putting what you have learned into practice. Make the following your money habits in installment credit:

1. Calculate your own debt limits before taking on any installment loan.
2. Select loans that have the lowest possible fees and annual percentage rate.
3. Use student loans for direct education expenses only, rather than to maintain a good lifestyle.
4. Graduate from college with no debt other than student loans.
5. Never co-sign a loan for anyone, including relatives.
6. Always repay your debts in a timely manner so you will never have to pay a late fee.
7. If you ever find yourself in credit difficulty, stay in communication with your creditors and, if necessary, seek help from a not-for-profit credit counseling agency.

ment simply by lengthening the time period over which the loan will be repaid. You should assess your overall debt obligations. There are three useful ways to determine your debt limits.

- Debt payments-to-disposable income method
- Ratio of debt-to-equity method
- Continuous-debt method

Debt Payments-to-Disposable Income Method

To use the **debt payments-to-disposable income method,** you first need to decide the percentage of your disposable personal income that can be spent for regular debt repayments excluding the first mortgage loan on a home and credit card charges that are paid in full each month. **Disposable income** is the amount of your income remaining after taxes and withholding for such purposes as insurance and union dues. Table 7.1 (page 182) shows some monthly debt-payment limits expressed as a percentage of disposable personal income. As the table indicates, with monthly payments representing 16 to 20 percent of monthly disposable personal income, a borrower is seriously over-indebted and fully extended; taking on additional debt would be unwise. This means that someone with an average income and an expensive car loan might not be able to afford to carry any credit card balances that revolve from month to month.

Once you have decided the percentage that is appropriate for you, you can compare it to your debt payments-to-disposable income ratio as discussed in Chapter 2 (see page 45). In that chapter we calculated a debt payments-to-disposable income ratio for the Hernandez family of 9.32 percent. As indicated by Table 7.1, they could take on new debt—but only cautiously.

Table 7.2 (page 183) shows the effects of increasing debts on a budget. In the table, after deductions, disposable personal income amounts to $2200 per month. Current budgeted expenses (totaling the full $2200) are allocated in a sample distribution throughout the various categories. As you can see, increasing debt payments from $0 to $550 per

Table 7.1 Debt-Payment Limits as a Percentage of Disposable Personal Income*

Percent	Current Debt Situation†	Borrower's Feelings	Take on Additional Debt?
0	No debt at all	No stress about personal finances	Taking on some consumer debt is fine
10 or less	Little debt	Borrower feels no stress from debt repayment obligations	More debt could be undertaken cautiously
11 to 15	Safe debt limit but fully extended financially	Borrower is moderately stressed about pressure from debt repayment obligations	Should not acquire more debt, and a debt consolidation loan from a credit union may be a good option
16 to 20	Seriously over-indebted	Borrower starts to feel seriously stressed about debts and hopes no emergency arises	Absolutely positively should not take on more debt
21 to 25	Precariously over-indebted	Borrower feels overwhelming stress and is desperate about debts	Contact a non-profit credit counseling company
26 to 30	Excessively over-indebted	Borrower feels hopeless and is painfully stressed about debts	Contact a bankruptcy attorney
31+	Dangerously over-indebted	Borrower knows his or her debts are so large that he or she is doomed to financial failure	Contact a bankruptcy attorney

*Excluding home mortgage loan repayments and convenience credit card purchases to be repaid in full when the bill arrives.

†People with a 16 percent or higher debt-payment limit as a percentage of personal income are "seriously over-indebted." They may feel "seriously stressed" about their personal finances and begin to wonder if they are so overly indebted that they may never be able to get out of debt.

month (for example, to buy a new automobile or home entertainment system on credit) have dramatic effects on this budget. The financial manager must decide where to cut back to meet monthly credit repayments. As the debt load grows, each 5 percentage point increase makes it much more difficult to "find the money" and make the cutbacks. In this case, the borrower reduced expenditures on savings and investments immediately and then finally reduced the amount in this category to $50. Food was cut back, but only slightly. Utilities, automobile insurance, and rent are relatively fixed expenses; as a consequence, it is difficult to reduce these amounts without moving or buying a less expensive car. Entertainment expenses were steadily reduced, and newspapers and magazines were eliminated altogether. Trimming expenditures in other areas would seriously affect this individual's quality of life. Not only that, but the reductions in savings and investments will have long-term consequences. Recall from Chapter 1 that saving over long periods of time is the key to building wealth. People who take on excessive debts early in life will get behind and may never be able to catch up and become financially successful.

Are you curious about where you would have made reductions? Spend a few minutes changing the figures in Table 7.2—that exercise will give you an idea of your priorities and the size of the debt limit that you might establish. Note that the debt payments-to-disposable income method focuses on the amount of monthly debt repayment—not the total debt. As a result, it would be wise to consider the length of time that the severe financial situation caused by high debt payments might last. It could be years.

Table 7.2 Effects of Increasing Debt Payments on a Budget*					
Gross income	$34,000				
Deductions for taxes, 401(k), insurance	$ 7,600				
Disposable personal income	$26,400				
Monthly	$ 2,200				
	No Debt	**10% Debt**	**15% Debt**	**20% Debt**	**25% Debt**
Rent	$ 700	$ 700	$ 700	$ 700	$ 700
Savings and investments	250	**180**	**120**	**80**	**50**
Food	280	**250**	**240**	**220**	**210**
Utilities (telephone, electricity, heat)	130	130	130	**120**	120
Insurance (automobile, renter's, and life)	80	80	80	80	80
Transportation expenses	100	**90**	90	**80**	80
Charitable contributions	60	**50**	50	**40**	40
Entertainment	140	**120**	**110**	**100**	**80**
Clothing	50	**40**	**30**	**20**	20
Vacations and long weekends	60	**50**	**40**	40	**30**
Medical/dental expenses	60	**50**	50	50	50
Newspapers and magazines	40	**30**	30	30	**0**
Cable TV	50	50	**40**	40	**30**
Personal care	30	**20**	20	20	20
Gifts and holidays	40	**30**	30	30	30
Health club	60	60	60	60	60
Miscellaneous	70	**50**	50	50	50
Debt repayments	0	**220**	**330**	**440**	**550**
TOTAL	**$2,200**	**$2,200**	**$2,200**	**$2,200**	**$2,200**

*One person's decisions on where to cut back expenses to make increasing monthly debt payments.

Ratio of Debt-to-Equity Method

Another method of determining your debt limit involves calculating the ratio of your consumer debt to your assets. In Chapter 2, we performed such an analysis for the Hernandez family when we calculated their asset-to-debt ratio. The **ratio of debt-to-equity** is similar except that it uses the **equity** in a person's assets (the amount by which the value of those assets exceeds debts), excluding the value of a primary residence and the first mortgage on that home. This ratio recognizes that mortgage debt does not get people into trouble. In fact, mortgage debt is backed up by excellent collateral—one's own home.

From Table 2.3 (page 39), we see that the Hernandez family has assets of $133,920 ($4420—monetary assets; $20,500—tangible assets less the value of their home; and $109,000—investment assets). Their debts (excluding their home mortgage) total $9365 ($120 + $1545 + $7700). With $9365 in debts and $133,920 in assets, the Hernandezes have equity of $124,555 ($133,920 − $9365), or a debt-to-equity ratio of 0.08 ($9365 ÷ $124,555).

The ratio of debt-to-equity method provides a quick idea of one's financial solvency. The larger the ratio, the riskier the likelihood of repayment. A ratio in excess of 0.33 is considered high. The Hernandezes are well under that limit, unlike the result found by calculating their debt repayments-to-disposable income ratio. This contrast occurs primarily because of their real estate investment asset, on which they have no debt. Recent college graduates, who often bear the burden of large education loans, have high debt-to-equity ratios. If one's income rises quickly, the ratio will improve. But if the ratio does not improve in three to five years, a serious debt problem may exist.

Continuous-Debt Method

Another approach for determining when debts are too large is the **continuous-debt method.** If you are unable to get completely out of debt every four years (except for a

---

Advice from an Expert

Managing Student Loan Debt

It is wise to take on little or no student loan debt because repaying large debts early in one's working career makes it more challenging to succeed financially in life. The dollars spent repaying loans, for example, cannot be used to save for retirement. Borrowing to pay for education, is however, one of the best uses of credit because it is an investment in oneself. Here are some tips for managing student loan debt.

1. **Choose the most advantageous repayment pattern allowed.** The standard repayment plan for student loan debt calls for equal monthly installments paid over ten years. If you owe more than $12,000, it may be possible to stretch payments over longer time periods. Alternatively, you can establish a graduated repayment plan whereby the payments are lower in the early years but then increase in later years when income is expected to be higher. Finally, an income-contingent plan can be used to tie your debt repayments to the rise and fall of your income.

2. **Pay electronically.** In some loan programs, the graduate can make arrangements to have the monthly payment transferred electronically and automatically out of a checking account. As a reward for setting up such an arrangement, the graduate receives a one-quarter percentage point reduction in the interest rate.

3. **Be punctual with your repayments.** In some programs, if you make the first 48 payments on time, the interest rate will be reduced by two percentage points. This bonus is almost guaranteed when borrowers opt for electronic repayment. Failing to repay in a timely manner can have dire consequences, including having to pay the cost of collection efforts and becoming subject to forfeiture of federal and

state income tax refunds, as well as Social Security and veteran's benefits. These disadvantages are in addition to the normal negative impacts on your credit reputation when you fail to pay on time.

4. **Consolidate your student loans.** Consolidating your education loans means that your existing loans are paid off and one new loan is created. This strategy may allow for a much more convenient repayment schedule. The interest rate may be lower, the monthly payment is usually lower, and the amount of time for repayment may be longer under the new loan. Loan rates may be further reduced if you repay on time for 12 months or consolidate Stafford loans within six months of graduation. Loans can be consolidated through a private bank or through one of three government programs: College Funding Services (www.cfsloans.com), Sallie Mae (www.salliemae.com), or Federal Direct Consolidation Loans (www.loanconsolidation.ed.gov).

5. **Use on-line tools to help manage student loans.** A variety of resources are available on the Internet to help people manage their student loans. They offer the tools and information needed to set up a budget, review credit accounts, maintain a secure updated personal information file, and make electronic repayments. Many universities provide on-line assistance through their student financial aid offices. Other resources include American Education Service (www. aessuccess.org/index.html), Mapping Your Future (www.mapping-your-future.org), and National Student Loan Program (www.nslp.org/fmantool.htm).

Gail M. Gordon and John P. Hewlett
University of Wyoming

mortgage loan), you probably lean on debt too heavily. You could be developing a credit lifestyle, in which you will never eliminate debt and continuously pay out substantial amounts of income for finance charges—likely $1000 or more per year.

Setting Debt Limits for Dual-Earner Households

On top of the companionship and other emotional benefits provided, entering into a relationship can prove financially beneficial because it means joining incomes together. Two people, each of whom earns $27,000 per year, will gross $54,000, with a disposable personal income from this total of around $42,000, or $3500 monthly. Such an amount seemingly means the couple can afford a much higher level of debt than before the incomes were combined. While the guidelines given in Table 7.1 are realistic, they would allow a doubling of debt payments if the addition of a second earner doubled household earnings.

In reality, many young couples adopt a lifestyle based on two incomes. In other words, their spending grows in tandem with their rising incomes. After a while, they are spending and borrowing to the limit. This situation cannot go on forever, of course. Eventually such couples begin to feel financially stressed and wonder, "How can we be so broke when we make so much money?" When they have a child or a financial setback occurs, they may be in deep trouble. If one earner's income is reduced, perhaps because of a need to take care of family responsibilities, debts that had been manageable with two incomes quickly become burdensome or overwhelming. Couples should avoid taking on excessive debt. Instead, they should work toward building savings accounts and make investments early in their lives together that will protect their future financial security.

Understanding Consumer Loans

2 Understand three types of consumer loans.

Consumers obtain installment credit in two ways. A **cash loan** means that the borrower receives cash and then uses it to make purchases, pay off other loans, or make investments. With a **purchase loan** (also called **sales credit**), the consumer makes a purchase on credit with no cash transferring from the lender to the borrower. Instead, the funds go directly from the lender to the seller. For example, a car buyer might obtain a purchase loan from the General Motors Acceptance Corporation (GMAC) to buy a new Pontiac Grand Am. With some purchase loans, the lender *is* the seller. For all such loans, the borrower will sign a formal **promissory note** (a written installment loan contract) that spells out the terms of the loan.

Calculating an Installment Loan Payment

To help you figure out the required monthly payment for different loan amounts, Table 7.3 (page 186) shows various monthly installment payments used to repay a $1000 loan at commonly seen interest rates and time periods. For loans of other dollar amounts, divide the borrowed amount by 1000 and multiply the result by the appropriate figure from the table. For example, an automobile loan for $12,000, financed at 10 percent interest, might be repaid in 36 equal monthly payments of $387.24 ($32.27 × 12). A loan for $3550 at 16 percent for 24 months will require monthly payments of $173.81 ($48.96 × 3.550).

Table 7.3 Monthly Installment Payment (Principal and Interest) Required to Repay $1000*							
	Number of Monthly Payments						
APR†	**12**	**24**	**36**	**48**	**60**	**72**	**84**
5	$85.61	$43.87	$29.97	$23.03	$18.87	$16.10	$14.13
6	86.07	44.32	30.42	23.49	19.33	16.57	14.61
7	86.53	44.77	30.88	23.95	19.80	17.05	15.09
8	86.99	45.23	31.34	24.41	20.28	17.53	15.59
9	87.45	45.68	31.80	24.88	20.76	18.03	16.09
10	87.92	46.14	32.27	25.36	21.25	18.53	16.60
11	88.38	46.61	32.74	25.85	21.74	19.03	17.12
12	88.85	47.07	33.21	26.33	22.24	19.55	17.65
13	89.32	47.54	33.69	26.83	22.75	20.07	18.19
14	89.79	48.01	34.18	27.33	23.27	20.61	18.74
15	90.26	48.49	34.67	27.83	23.79	21.14	19.27
16	90.73	48.96	35.16	28.34	24.32	21.69	19.86
17	91.20	49.44	35.65	28.85	24.85	22.25	20.44
18	91.68	49.92	36.15	29.37	25.39	22.81	21.02
19	92.16	50.41	36.66	29.90	25.94	23.38	21.61
20	92.63	50.90	37.16	30.43	26.49	23.95	22.21

*To illustrate, assume an automobile loan of $14,000 at 8 percent for five years. To repay $1000 the monthly payment is $20.28; therefore, multiply $20.28 (8% row and 60-month column) by 14 to give a monthly payment of $283.92. For amounts other than exact $1000 increments, simply use decimals. For example, for a loan of $14,500, the multiplier would be 14.5.

†For fractional interest rates of 5.5, 6.5, 7.5, and so on, simply take a monthly payment halfway between the whole-number APR payments. For example, the payment for 48 months at 9.5 percent is $25.12 ($25.36 − $24.88 = $0.48 ÷ 2 = $0.24 + $24.88).

Installment credit typically comes with a **fixed interest rate,** meaning that the rate will not change over the life of the loan. It is becoming increasingly common for lenders to offer variable-rate loans as an alternative to borrowers. A **variable-rate loan** (also called an **adjustable-rate loan**) features a periodic rate that fluctuates according to some measure of interest rates in the economy.

Installment Loans Can Be Unsecured or Secured

Credit can either be unsecured or secured. An **unsecured loan** is granted solely based on the good credit character of the borrower. Sometimes unsecured loans are called **signature loans** because they are backed up by only the borrower's signature. Because unsecured loans carry higher risk than secured debts, the interest rate charged on them is substantially higher.

A **secured loan** requires a cosigner or collateral. A **cosigner** agrees to pay the debt should the original borrower fail to do so. Being a cosigner is a major responsibility, because a cosigner has the same legal obligations for repayment as the original borrower does. In case of default, a lender will go after the party—either the borrower or the cosigner—from whom it is more likely to collect the funds.

A loan secured with **collateral** means that the lender has a security interest in the property that is pledged as collateral. For example, the vehicle itself is the collateral on an automobile loan. The item of collateral does not necessarily need to be the property purchased with the loan. Typically, the lender records a lien in the county courthouse to make the security interest known to the public. A **lien** is a legal right to seize and dispose of (usually sell) property to obtain payment of a claim. When the loan is repaid, the lien will be removed. (The borrower should make sure this removal occurs.)

In the event that the borrower fails to repay the loan, the creditor can exercise the lien and seize the collateral through **repossession,** sometimes without notice. Almost all credit contracts contain an **acceleration clause** stating that after a specific number of payments are unpaid (often just one), the loan is considered in default and all remaining installments are due and payable upon demand of the creditor. These clauses protect the lender's interest, but can prove very difficult for borrowers. Don't be fooled if you miss a payment and the lender does not exercise the acceleration clause immediately: It can do so at any time after default occurs. Do not ignore a warning letter from a creditor!

When a lender repossesses property because the borrower defaults on a loan, the borrower may still owe on the debt due to a deficiency balance. A **deficiency balance** occurs when the sum of money raised by the sale of the repossessed collateral fails to cover the amount owed on the debt plus any repossession expenses (collection, attorney, and court costs) paid by the creditor. Deficiency balances are likely to occur whether repossession is voluntary or involuntary.

Purchase Loan Installment Contracts

Two kinds of contracts are used when purchasing goods with an installment loan:

- **Installment purchase agreements** (also called **collateral installment loans** or **chattel mortgage loans**), in which the title of the property passes to the buyer when the contract is signed
- **Conditional sales contracts** (also known as **financing leases**), in which the title does not pass to the buyer until the last installment payment has been paid

An installment purchase agreement provides a measure of protection for the borrower, as the creditor must follow all legal procedures required by state law when repossessing the property. Some state laws permit the lender to take secured property back as soon as the buyer falls behind in payments, possibly by seizing a car right in the person's driveway.

Sources of Consumer Loans

3 Describe sources of consumer loans.

Today's consumers have many sources of consumer loans from which to choose. Most consumer lending occurs through depository institutions and sales finance companies. Other popular sources include consumer finance companies, stockbrokers, and insurance companies. Table 7.4 (page 188) shows the interest rates charged and example payment amounts and finance charges from these various sources of consumer loans.

Depository Institutions Loan Money to Their Banking Customers

Depository institutions include commercial banks, mutual savings banks, savings and loan associations, and credit unions (see Chapter 5, pages 130–132, for more detailed

Table 7.4 What It Costs to Borrow Money

Lender	Annual Percentage Rate	Two-Year Loan		Five-Year Loan	
		Monthly Payment	Finance Charge	Monthly Payment	Finance Charge
Life insurance company	6	$44.32	$ 63.68	$19.33	$159.80
Sales finance company	8	45.23	85.52	20.28	216.80
Credit union	10	46.14	107.36	21.25	275.00
Commercial bank	12	47.07	129.68	22.24	334.40
Mutual savings bank	12	47.07	129.68	22.24	334.40
Savings and loan association	12	47.07	129.68	22.24	334.40
Bank credit card	21	51.38	233.25	27.05	623.20
Consumer finance company	24	52.87	268.88	28.77	726.20

Credit costs money. Just how much can be seen by considering the cost of borrowing $1000 for two years and for five years from various sources at various interest rates.

descriptions). They tend to make loans to their own customers and to noncustomers with good credit histories. For most loans, depository institutions offer highly competitive rates, partly because the funds loaned are obtained primarily from their depositors. The interest rate commonly ranges from 9 to 16 percent. Research indicates that many people who go elsewhere for loans actually meet the qualifications for depository institution lending and end up paying a higher interest rate than necessary.

Sales Finance Companies Loan Money to Buy Consumer Products

A **sales finance company** is a seller-related lender (such as General Motors Acceptance Corporation, Ford Motor Credit, and JCPenney Credit Corporation) whose primary business is financing the sales of its parent company. Such companies specialize in making purchase loans, with the item being purchased serving as the collateral for the loan. Because the seller often works in close association with the sales finance company, credit can be approved almost immediately.

Because sales finance companies require collateral and deal only with customers who are considered medium to good risks, their interest rates are often competitive with those offered by depository institutions. Furthermore, their interest rates may be lower than those offered by other sources if the seller subsidizes the rate to encourage sales—as with the special low-APR financing often offered on new cars, for example. Most new-car loans today are made by sales finance companies.

Consumer Finance Companies Make Small Cash Loans

A **consumer finance company** specializes in making relatively small loans and is, therefore, also known as a **small-loan company.** These lenders range from the well-recognized Household Finance Corporation (HFC) and Beneficial Finance Corporation (BFC) to many local neighborhood lenders. Such companies make both secured and unsecured loans and require repayment on an installment basis. The interest rates they charge are higher than those available from depository lenders because consumer finance companies focus on borrowers with low credit scores.

Approximately one-fifth of all loans granted by consumer finance companies are for the purpose of debt consolidation. Other common uses of such loans are for travel, vacations, education, automobiles, and home furnishings. Some small-loan companies specialize in making loans by mail. They advertise in newspapers and magazines and on the Internet to attract borrowers, who complete a credit application and receive approval via mail.

Stockbrokers Loan Money to Their Clients

Many people build significant assets in investment accounts that may be earmarked for their children's college education, their own retirement, or other specific needs. Although many people prefer not to tap into these funds directly, it may be possible to borrow from or against these accounts. For example, it is possible to borrow from certain employer-sponsored, tax-sheltered retirement accounts (see Chapter 18), depending on the rules of the plan. Alternatively, if you have a margin account (see Chapter 16), you can borrow from your stockbroker using your investments as collateral. In both cases, care must be taken to ensure that the loan plus interest is repaid lest the savings goal will go unmet. Furthermore, tax consequences may arise if retirement account loans are not repaid.

Did You Know? . . .

About Alternative Lenders

A number of avenues through which to obtain credit are available that may not look like credit. Credit may also come from unusual sources, including pay-day lenders, rent-to-own stores, and pawnshops.

Pay-day lenders (which are banned in some states) are businesses that grant credit when they honor a personal check but agree not to deposit the check for a week or longer. The fees for check cashing are sometimes 20 percent or more of the amount of the check, pushing the APR (if the check is held for later deposit) to several hundred percent or higher.

A **rent-to-own program** provides a mechanism for buying an item with little or no down payment by renting it for a period of time after which it is owned. Furniture, appliances, and electronic entertainment items are commonly sold via the rent-to-own approach. This form of credit is often used by persons who believe they cannot qualify for credit purchases. In reality, these programs have two big drawbacks for consumers. First, the renter does not own the item until the final payment is made. Paying late or stopping payments will cause the products

to be seized with no allowance being made for the previous "rental" payments. Second, the actual cost for renting items is often exorbitantly high. For example, a TV worth $300 might be rented for $15 per week for one year, producing a finance charge of $480 ($52 \times \$15 - \$300$).

A **pawnshop** is a lender that offers single-payment loans, often ranging from $100 to $500, for short time periods (typically one or two months), after the borrower turns over an item of personal property to the pawnshop. The dollar amount loaned is typically equal to one-third or less of the value of the item pawned. In most states, a borrower need merely turn over the item, present identification, and sign on the dotted line. The pawnshop owner can legally sell the item if the borrower fails to redeem the property by paying the amount due, plus interest, within the time period specified. The pawnshop typically charges an interest rate of about 5 percent per month plus a 2 percent monthly storage fee; thus, the annual combined "interest" amounts to 84 percent $[(5 + 2) \times 12]$. Clearly, pawnshops represent the lender of last resort for borrowers.

Insurance Companies Loan Money to Their Customers

It is becoming increasingly common for insurance companies, such as State Farm or Allstate, to offer car loans and credit cards to their policyholders. Some insurance companies make these loans out of their own funds; others have set up bank subsidiary companies to handle such loans. Insurance companies loan only to their customers with high credit scores. As a consequence, they can be a low-cost source from which to borrow money.

Policyholders who have cash-value life insurance policies can obtain loans based on the cash values built up in their policies. (This topic is examined in Chapter 12.) Note, however, that such cash-value policies may take many years to build up to an amount sufficient to borrow. An advantage to borrowing on a cash-value life insurance policy is that the interest rates are low, ranging from 4 to 6 percent. Policyholders actually borrow their own money. Many people fail to pay back such loans, however, because no fixed schedule of repayment is established and insurance companies do not pressure borrowers to repay the debt. Should the insured person die before repaying the loan, the insurance company will deduct the amount of the loan from the amount that would otherwise be paid on the policy. In reality, the insurance company incurs no risk, yet they still charge interest to borrow one's own money.

4 Calculate the annual percentage rate and finance charges on loans.

Calculating Finance Charges and Annual Percentage Rates

The federal **Truth in Lending Act** (**TIL**) requires lenders to disclose to credit applicants both the interest rate expressed as an annual percentage rate (APR) and the finance charge. As explained in Chapter 6, the APR is the relative cost of credit on a yearly basis expressed as a percentage rate. The finance charge is the cost of credit expressed in dollars. Any interest rate quoted by a lender must be the APR. Always inquire about the APR if it is not readily apparent and use it to compare rates from various sources to obtain the best deal.

The finance charge must include all mandatory charges to be paid by the borrower. In addition to interest, lenders may charge fees for a credit investigation, a loan application, or credit life, credit disability, or credit unemployment insurance. When fees are required, the lender must include them in the finance charge in dollars as part of the APR calculations. When the borrower elects these options voluntarily, the fees are not included in the finance charge and APR calculations, even though they raise the actual cost of borrowing.

Interest accounts for the greatest portion of the finance charge. Three methods are used to calculate interest on installment and noninstallment credit: the simple-interest method, the add-on interest method, and the discount method. The following discussion illustrates the calculation of the annual percentage rate for single-payment and installment loans using each of these methods.

APR Calculations for Single-Payment Loans

Two methods are employed to calculate interest on single-payment loans: the add-on interest method and the discount method. The APR reveals the difference in the effective cost of credit with each method.

The Add-On Interest Method.   With the **add-on interest method,** interest is calculated by applying an interest rate to the amount borrowed times the number of years. The add-on interest formula given in Equation (7.1) is used as follows:

$$I = PRT \qquad\qquad (7.1)$$

where

I = Interest or finance charges
P = Principal amount borrowed
R = Rate of interest (simple, add-on, or discount rate)
T = Time of loan in years

Suppose you took out a single-payment loan of $500 for two years at an add-on interest rate of 12 percent. Your interest charges would be $120 ($500 × 12% × 2 years), which would be "added on" to the debt, and you would make one payment of $620 at the end of two years.

To calculate the APR for a single-payment loan, divide the average outstanding loan balance ($500, as the full amount was owed during the entire loan period) into the average annual finance charge ($60, as $120 is the total for two years).

$$APR = \frac{\text{average annual finance charge}}{\text{average outstanding loan balance}} \qquad (7.2)$$

$$= \frac{\$60}{\$500}$$

$$= 12\%$$

In this example, the APR is 12 percent. When the add-on interest method is used for any type of loan, the add-on rate of interest and the APR are equivalent.

The Discount Method.   The **discount method** is often used for calculating the cost of single-payment loans. With this method, interest is paid up front and subtracted from the amount of the loan. The difference is the actual cash given to the borrower.

Using the same figures as in the last example, the denominator in Equation (7.2) changes. The average outstanding loan balance, or principal, is $380 [$500 − ($500 × 0.12 × 2)], which is the amount actually received. Dividing $380 into the average annual finance charge of $60 gives an APR of 15.8 percent, as compared with the discount rate of 12 percent. This higher APR reflects the fact that the borrower does not have full use of the $500 borrowed.

APR Calculations for Installment Loans

The simple-interest, add-on, and discount methods are all used to determine the interest on installment loans. The simple-interest method is widely used by credit unions to calculate interest. The add-on method predominates at banks, savings and loan associations, and consumer finance companies in installment loans for automobiles, furniture, and other credit requiring collateral.

The Simple-Interest Method.

With the **simple-interest method,** the interest assessed during each payment period (usually each month) is based on the outstanding balance of the installment loan. The lender initially designs a schedule (such as that given in Table 7.5) to have the balance repaid in full after a certain number of months. The borrower may vary the rate of repayment by making payments larger than those scheduled or may repay the loan in full at any time.

It is easy to illustrate the simple-interest method applied to an installment loan. As shown in Table 7.5, at the end of the first month, a periodic interest rate (the stated rate applied to the outstanding balance of a loan) of 1.5 percent (18 percent annually, divided by 12 months) is applied to the beginning balance of $1000, giving an interest charge of $15. Of the first monthly installment of $91.68, $76.68 goes toward payment of the principal and $15 goes toward the payment of simple interest. For the second month, the interest portion of the payment drops to $13.85, as the outstanding balance after the first month is $923.32 ($1000 − $76.68). Because the simple-interest method of calculating interest on installment loans applies the periodic interest rate to the outstanding loan balance, the APR and the simple interest rate will differ only if fees (such as an application fee) boost the finance charge. (This method of paying off a loan, called **amortization,** is discussed in Chapter 9 when we examine home mortgage loans.) Note that simple-interest loans carry no prepayment penalties.

The Add-On Method.

The add-on method is a widely used technique for computing interest on installment loans. With this method, the interest is calculated and added to the amount borrowed to determine the total amount to be repaid. Once again, Equation (7.1) is used to calculate the dollar amount of interest. (Note that the interest rate used in this equation for the add-on method is an add-on rate and should not be confused with the APR.)

For example, assume that Mary Ellen Broman of New York, New York, borrows $2000 for two years at 9 percent add-on interest to be repaid in monthly installments. Using Equation (7.1), her finance charge in dollars is $360 ($2000 × 0.09 × 2). Adding the finance charge ($360) to the amount borrowed ($2000) gives a total amount of

Table 7.5 Sample Repayment Schedule for $1000 Principal plus Simple Interest (1.5 Percent per Month)

Month	Outstanding Balance	Payment	Interest	Principal	Ending Balance
1	$1000.00	$91.68	$15.00	$76.68	$923.32
2	923.32	91.68	13.85	77.83	845.49
3	845.49	91.68	12.68	79.00	766.49
4	766.49	91.68	11.50	80.18	686.31
5	686.31	91.68	10.29	81.39	604.92
6	604.92	91.68	9.07	82.61	522.31
7	522.31	91.68	7.83	83.85	438.46
8	438.46	91.68	6.58	85.10	353.36
9	353.36	91.68	5.30	86.38	266.98
10	266.98	91.68	4.00	87.68	179.30
11	179.30	91.68	2.69	88.99	90.31
12	90.31	91.66	1.35	90.31	0

$2360 to be repaid. When this amount is divided by the total number of scheduled payments (24), we find that Mary Ellen must make 24 monthly payments of $98.33.

We know that the APR must be higher than the add-on rate of 9 percent, however, because monthly repayments mean that Mary Ellen does not have use of the total amount borrowed for the full two years. Equation (7.3) shows the **n-ratio method** of estimating the APR on an add-on loan.

$$\text{APR} = \frac{Y(95P + 9)F}{12P(P + 1)(4D + F)} \qquad \qquad (7.3)^*$$

$$= \frac{(12)(95 \times 24 + 9)(360)}{12(24)(24 + 1)[(4 \times 2000) + 360]}$$

$$= \frac{12(2289)(360)}{(288)(25)(8360)}$$

$$= \frac{9{,}888{,}480}{60{,}192{,}000}$$

$$= 16.4\%$$

where

$\quad$ **APR** = Annual percentage rate
$\quad$ Y = Number of payments in one year
$\quad$ F = Finance charge in dollars (dollar cost of credit)
$\quad$ D = Debt (amount borrowed or proceeds)
$\quad$ P = Total number of scheduled payments

Using Equation (7.3), the APR is 16.4 percent. Note that the APR is approximately double the add-on rate because, on average, Mary Ellen has use of only half of the borrowed money during the entire loan period.

Add-On Method Loans Have Prepayment Penalties.   Most installment loan contracts that use the add-on method include a **prepayment penalty**—a special charge assessed to the borrower for paying off a loan early. Prepayment penalties take into consideration the reality that borrowers should pay more in interest early in the loan period when they have the use of more money and increasingly less interest as the debt shrinks over time. With an add-on method loan, however, the interest is spread evenly across all payments rather than declining as the loan balance falls. If an add-on method loan is paid off early, the lender will use some penalty method to compensate for the lower interest component applied in the early months.

The **rule of 78s method** (also called the **sum of the digits method**) is the most widely used method of calculating a prepayment penalty. Its name derives from the fact that, for a one-year loan, the numbers between 1 and 12 for each month add up to 78 (12 + 11 + 10 + 9 + 8 + 7 + 6 + 5 + 4 + 3 + 2 + 1). For a two-year loan, the numbers between 1 and 24 would be added, and so on for longer time period loans.

To illustrate the use of the rule of 78s method, consider the case of Devin Grigsby from Berea, Kentucky. He borrowed $500 for 12 months plus an additional $80 finance charge, and is scheduled to pay equal monthly installments of $48.33 ($580 ÷ 12). Assume Devin wants to pay the loan off after only six months. He might assume—incorrectly—that he would owe only $250 more because after six months he had paid $250 (one-half) of the $500 borrowed and $40 (one-half) of the finance charge, for a

---

*Calculations involving Equation (7.3) can be performed on the *Garman/Forgue* website.

total of $290 in payments ($48.33 × 6). In reality, Devin still owes $268.46, including a prepayment penalty of $18.46. To calculate this amount using the rule of 78s method, the lender adds together all of the numbers between 12 and 7 (12 for the first month, 11 for the second, and so on for six months): 12 + 11 + 10 + 9 + 8 + 7 = 57. The lender assumes that during the first six months $58.46 [(57 ÷ 78) × $80]—not $40—of the finance charges was received from the $290 in payments Devin had made on the loan.* Consequently, only $231.54 ($290.00 − $58.46) was paid on the $500 borrowed, leaving $268.46 ($500.00 − $231.54) still owed, for a prepayment penalty of $18.46 ($268.46 − $250.00).

The Discount Method.   Occasionally, the discount method may be used to compute the interest on an installment loan. When this method is applied to our earlier example involving Mary Ellen Broman, she would receive only $1640 ($2000 − $360) at the beginning of the loan period. Using Equation (7.3), the APR would be 19.8 percent (the APR rises because only $1640 is borrowed while $2000 is repaid).

5 Describe signs of overindebtedness and know what options are available for people with excessive debts.

Dealing with Overindebtedness

People become **overindebted** when their excessive personal debts make repayment difficult and cause financial distress. Signs of overindebtedness are described next. If these signs appear, debtors can take steps such as getting credit counseling to improve their situation. Lenders, of course, will attempt to collect the debts, but they are required to adhere to the stipulations of the Fair Debt Collections Practices Act. As a last resort, some debtors choose, or are forced by creditors into, bankruptcy.

Ten Signs of Overindebtedness

1. **Exceeding debt limits and credit limits.** Are you spending more than 20 percent of your take-home pay on credit repayments? Do you sometimes reach the maximum approved credit limits on your credit cards?

2. **Running out of money.** Are you using credit cards on occasions when you previously used cash? Are you borrowing to pay insurance premiums, taxes, or other large, predictable bills? Are you borrowing to pay for regular expenses, such as food or gasoline? Do you try to borrow from friends and relatives to carry you through the month?

3. **Paying only the minimum amount due.** Do you pay the minimum payment—or just a little more than the minimum—on your credit cards instead of making larger payments to more quickly reduce the balance owed?

4. **Requesting new credit cards and increases in credit limits.** Have you applied for additional credit cards to increase your borrowing capacity? Have you asked for increases in credit limits on your present credit cards? Have you obtained a cash advance on one credit card to make the payment on another card?

---

*If the loan was paid off after one month, the amount of interest paid is assumed to be 12/78 of the $80 finance charge, or $12.31. For a loan paid in full after two months, the amount of interest paid is assumed to be 23/78 of the total (12/78 for month 1 plus 11/78 for month 2), or $23.59.

5. **Paying late or skipping credit payments.** Are you late more than once a year in paying your mortgage, rent, car loan, or utility bills? Do you frequently pay late charges? Are you juggling bills to pay the utilities, rent, or mortgage? Are creditors sending overdue notices?

6. **Not knowing how much you owe.** Have you lost track of how much you owe? Do you avoid reality by not adding up the total? Are you afraid to add up how much debt you have?

7. **Using debt-consolidation loans.** Are you borrowing, perhaps from a new source, to pay off old debts? Such action may temporarily reduce pressure on your budget, but it also indicates that you are using too much credit.

8. **Taking add-on loans.** Taking **add-on loans,** also called **flipping,** occurs when you refinance or rewrite a loan for an even larger amount before it has been completely repaid. Suppose that a loan of $1000 has been repaid down to $400. You decide to refinance the debt balance of $400 by borrowing $2000 and using the additional $1600 ($2000 − $400) for other purposes.

9. **Experiencing garnishment. Garnishment** is a court-sanctioned procedure by which a portion of the debtor's wages are set aside by one's employer to pay debts. Wages and salary income, including that of military personnel, can be garnished. The Truth in Lending Act prohibits more than two garnishments of one person's paycheck. The total amount garnished cannot represent more than 25 percent of a person's disposable income for the pay period or more than the amount by which the weekly disposable income exceeds 30 times the federal minimum wage (whichever is less). In addition, the law prohibits garnishment from being used as grounds for employment discharge.

10. **Experiencing repossession or foreclosure.** As noted earlier, repossession is a legal proceeding by which the lender seizes an asset (called **foreclosure,** if the property is a home) for nonpayment of a loan.

Federal Law Regulates Debt Collection Practices

The federal Fair Debt Collection Practices Act (FDCPA) prohibits third-party debt collection agencies from using abusive, deceptive, and unfair practices in the legitimate

Did You Know? . . .

The Effect of Using Voluntary Repossession to Get Out of Debt

Consider the tale of Betty Peterson, a corporal in the Army from San Diego, California, whose husband lost his job. In an attempt to reduce expenditures, Betty voluntarily turned her Chevrolet Camaro back to the finance company while still owing $11,000 on the debt. A month later, she was notified that the vehicle had been sold at auction for $7800; the proceeds were reduced to only $7100, however, due to collection and selling costs of $500 and attorney fees of $200. Betty was billed for a deficiency balance of $3900 ($11,000 − $7100). She would have been much better off had she sold the vehicle herself, as vehicles at auction usually sell for much less than their book values.

effort to collect past-due debts. **Debt collection agencies** are firms that specialize in making collections that could not be obtained by the original lender. In some cases, they assist the original lender (for a fee); in other cases, they take over (purchase) the debt and become the creditor. When a debtor offers to make payment for several debts, the FDCPA requires that the amount paid must be applied to whichever debts the debtor desires. Banks, dentists, lawyers, and others who make their own collections (second-party collectors) are exempt from the provisions of the FDCPA. Nevertheless, many states have enacted similar laws that govern these second-party collectors.

Collection agencies are prohibited from telephoning the debtor at unusual hours, making numerous repeated telephone calls during the day, not applying payments to amounts under dispute, using deceptive practices (such as falsely claiming that their representatives are attorneys or government officials), making threats, or using abusive language. They also cannot telephone a debtor's employer. Even with these limitations, collection agencies can be irritatingly persistent when collecting past-due accounts. If the collection effort is not successful, as a last resort the creditor may take the debtor to court to seek a legal judgment against the debtor; this judgment may be collected by repossessing some of the debtor's property or garnishing wages.

Steps to Take to Get Out from Under Excessive Installment Debt

Even the most well-meaning credit user can become overextended as a result of illness, unemployment, or divorce. What should you do if you realize that you are overly indebted?

1. **Determine your account balances and payments required.** Find out exactly what it would take to pay off your balances today. This amount is not the same as the total of your remaining payments and probably includes penalties and late charges if you have been unable to keep up with your payments. Also ask your lenders to give you a monthly payment dollar amount needed to pay off the debts by the date previously agreed.

2. **Focus your budget on debt reduction.** Calculate the percentage of your budget necessary to make the payments on your debts, and then add 5 percent. Use this extra money to help pay your creditors by applying the extra money to the debt with the highest APR. The sacrifices required will pay off in the long-run. Remember, paying off debts provides a better "rate of return" than putting money into savings and investments, so invest your money in debt repayment first.

3. **Contact your creditors.** Try to work out a new payment plan with your creditors. Many lenders, including those that finance automobiles, may let you skip a payment. They want to see you solve your financial problems so you can avoid bankruptcy. Creditors are more likely to work with borrowers who come to them first rather than after collection efforts begin.

4. **Take on no new credit.** Return your credit cards to the issuer or lock them up so that you cannot use them. Disciplined action to reduce debt should show results in only a few months. If progress does not occur, seek professional help.

5. **Refinance.** Determine whether some loans can be refinanced to obtain a lower interest rate, especially mortgage loans. (See Chapter 9 for details.) Even if you refinance, keep making the same payment so you will pay the new loan off more quickly. Obtaining a debt-consolidation loan might be appropriate for someone who acquired too much debt, but you should avoid the temptation to use this strat-

egy simply to lower your total monthly payments. However, it is smart to use debt consolidation to lower APRs.

6. **Find good help.** You may be able to obtain free budget and credit advice from your employer, credit union, or labor union. Also, many banks and consumer finance companies offer advice to help financially distressed debtors, as do nonprofit **credit counseling agencies (CCAs).** Such an agency can make arrangements with unsecured creditors to collect payments from overly indebted consumers to repay debts, and it can provide individuals with credit counseling, assistance with financial problems, educational materials on credit and budgeting, and a **debt management plan (DMP).** A DMP is an arrangement whereby the consumer provides one monthly payment (usually somewhat smaller than the total of previous credit payments) that is distributed to all creditors. Creditor concessions, such as reduced interest rates, may also allow debtors to repay what they owe more quickly than would otherwise be possible. Credit counseling services are provided at a nominal cost on a face-to-face basis on-line or via the telephone. You can obtain consumer information and a referral by contacting the Association of Independent Consumer Credit

---

Advice from an Expert

Control and Reduce Your Credit Card Debt

If your credit card debt rises to a hard-to-manage level, consider the following suggestions:

1. Immediately stop using your credit cards, and do not open new credit accounts or accept any new credit offers.
2. Evaluate all of your budgeted expenditures and plan to devote the largest possible amounts toward paying off your credit card balances.
3. Work overtime or take another job. Devote any extra income, such as a tax refund, toward paying these debts.
4. Gather your most recent credit card statements, sit down with pencil and paper, and write down the balance of each debt and the interest rate charged using a format similar to Figure 3.7 on page 79.
5. Use a credit card pay-off calculator to see what it will take to eliminate your credit card balances. (Visit bankrate.com or money.cnn.com to find this kind of calculator.)
6. Consider transferring existing balances on high-interest rate accounts to an account with a lower interest rate. Use caution, however, because brief introductory periods, transaction fees, and penalties may eliminate any potential savings.
7. Pay the minimum amount due on your low interest-rate cards, and pay as much as possible on the highest interest-rate cards. Continue to do so until all of your debts are paid off, recognizing that this endeavor may take a few years.
8. If after three to six months you are not making good progress toward paying off your credit card balances, consider seeking assistance from a nonprofit credit counseling agency. It can negotiate with your creditors to lower your payments and interest rates and to reduce or eliminate late fees and over-the-limit charges.

M. J. Alhabeeb
University of Massachusetts–Amherst

Counseling Agencies [(800) 450-1794; www.aiccca.org] or the National Foundation for Credit Counseling [(800) 388-2227; www.nfcc.org].

7. **Avoid bad help.** Many people claim that they want to help people in debt. Some are not so reputable, however. A **credit repair company** (also known as a credit clinic) is a firm that offers to help improve or fix a person's credit history for a fee; it typically requires a hefty advance payment (often $250 to $2000). In reality, no company can remove or "fix" accurate but negative information in anyone's credit history. You can improve your future credit history by making on-time repayments.

Bankruptcy as a Last Resort

When debts are so overbearing that life seems really bleak—a situation that may be aggravated by recent unemployment, illness, disability, death in the family, divorce, or small-business failure—many people consider filing a petition in federal court to declare bankruptcy. Attorneys typically charge $500 to $1000.

Bankruptcy is a constitutionally guaranteed right that permits people (and businesses) to ask a court to find them officially unable to meet their debts. When the bankruptcy court grants such a petition, most of the bankrupt person's assets are given over to a trustee. Any assets that serve as collateral for loans are turned over to the appropriate secured creditors. Most of the remaining assets are sold, and the proceeds of the sales are distributed to the unsecured creditors of the bankrupt person. Any leftover debt is usually **discharged** (forgiven or canceled) by the court when the debtor emerges from bankruptcy. State and federal laws govern what assets the debtor can keep. In general, bankrupt people are allowed to keep a small amount of equity in their homes, an inexpensive automobile, and limited personal property. Federal laws allow bankruptcy for consumers in two forms: Chapter 13 and Chapter 7. Some debts are never excused or exempted through either Chapter 13 or 7 bankruptcy, including education loans that have come due within the previous seven years, fines, alimony, child support, income taxes for the most recent three years, debts not listed on a bankruptcy petition, and debts for causing injury while driving under the influence of alcohol or drugs.

Chapter 13—Regular Income Plan.   **Chapter 13** of the Bankruptcy Act (also known as the **wage earner** or the **regular income plan**) is designed for individuals with regular incomes who might be able to pay off some or all of their debts given certain protections of the court. Under this plan, the debtor submits a debt repayment plan to the court that is designed to repay as much of the debt as possible, typically in three to five years. After the debtor files a petition for bankruptcy, the court issues an automatic **stay**—a court order that temporarily prevents all creditors from recovering claims arising from before the start of the bankruptcy proceeding. This action protects the debtor from collection efforts by creditors, including garnishments. Typically, no assets may be sold by the debtor or repossessed by the lender after a stay is granted.

After the court notifies all creditors of the petition for bankruptcy, a hearing is scheduled. With the help of a bankruptcy trustee (or U.S. trustee), who verifies the accuracy of a bankruptcy petition at a hearing and who distributes the assets according to a court-approved plan, the proposed repayment plan is reviewed (and modified, if necessary) and finally approved by the court. The debtor must then follow a strict budget while repaying the obligations. During this time, the bankrupt person cannot obtain any new credit without the permission of the trustee. If the debtor makes all scheduled payments, he or she is discharged of any remaining amounts due that could not be repaid within the repayment period.

Chapter 7—Immediate Liquidation Plan.   Chapter 7 of the Bankruptcy Act, also called **straight bankruptcy,** provides for an immediate liquidation of assets. This option is permitted when it would be highly unlikely that substantial repayment could ever be made. After filing a Chapter 7 petition, individuals who actually have the ability to repay some of their debts are sometimes required to transfer their case to a Chapter 13 program.

Bankruptcy should be used as a last resort rather than as a quick fix or cure-all for overuse of credit. Bankruptcy remains on one's credit record for ten years. Because employers, landlords, and creditors check credit reports, people who have declared bankruptcy typically face years of trouble when renting housing, obtaining home loans, and getting credit cards. A discharged debtor usually emerges with little, if any, debt and a much improved net worth but cannot use Chapter 7 again for at least six years. Therefore, some creditors will lend to bankrupt individuals, albeit at much higher interest rates than usual.

ACE

Summary

Self-tests

1. It is important to establish your own debt limit. Three methods can be used: the debt payments-to-disposable income method, the ratio of debt-to-equity method, and the continuous-debt method.

2. Consumer loans are classified as either installment or noninstallment credit. Borrowers must also distinguish between secured loans, which use collateral or a cosigner, and unsecured loans, which are riskier for the lender and, therefore, carry higher finance charges.

3. Major sources of consumer loans include depository institutions (commercial banks, savings and loan associations, and credit unions), sales finance companies, and consumer finance companies. Loans are also available through insurance companies and stockbrokers. Depository institutions typically offer the best interest rates, although sales finance companies sometimes offer low rates to increase sales of the products being financed. In any case, only those people with high credit scores qualify for the best rates from any source.

4. Both the simple-interest and add-on methods are used to calculate the interest on installment loans, although the annual percentage rate formula gives the correct rate in all cases. With simple-interest loans, the dollar amount of interest incorporated in each monthly payment declines as the loan balance declines.

5. Among the signals of being overly indebted are exceeding credit-limit guidelines and running out of money too often. People experiencing serious financial difficulties can obtain professional assistance through nonprofit

credit counseling agencies or by contacting an attorney about bankruptcy.

Key Terms

acceleration clause, 187
add-on method, 192
amortization, 192
bankruptcy, 198
cash loan, 185
collateral, 186
credit counseling agency (CCA), 197
debt collection agency, 196
debt limit, 180
deficiency balance, 187
disposable income, 181
installment (closed-end) credit, 180
lien, 187
prepayment penalty, 193
promissory note, 185
purchase loan (sales credit), 185
repossession, 187
sales finance company, 188
secured loan, 186
simple-interest method, 191
Truth in Lending Act (TIL), 190
variable-rate (adjustable-rate) loan, 186

Chapter Review Questions

1. Describe the major ways that consumers can set debt limits for themselves.

2. Distinguish between noninstallment credit and installment credit.

3. For the borrower, what are the advantages and the disadvantages of a variable-rate loan?

4. Distinguish between a secured loan and an unsecured loan.

5. What burden might an acceleration clause place on a borrower?

6. Compare and contrast an installment purchase agreement with a conditional sales contract.

7. Summarize why lenders impose the rule of 78s and describe how it works.

8. For installment loans, summarize how the simple-interest method of APR calculation works.

9. Describe three of the signals of credit overindebtedness.

10. Compare and contrast the two forms of bankruptcy, Chapter 13 and Chapter 7.

Group Discussion Issues

1. Because college students have very low incomes and few assets, the usual ratios for setting debt limits might not apply when considering student loan debt levels. How might students judge whether they are taking on too high a level of student loan debt?

2. Should young couples with two incomes consider taking on much less debt than might otherwise be appropriate for their level of income? Explain.

3. If you wanted to borrow money to buy a new or used car, where would you turn? What aspects of the deal would most interest you?

4. How do you feel about the fact that interest costs are higher in the early months of a simple-interest loan than they are in the later months?

5. How do you feel about bankruptcy? When might bankruptcy be justified in your opinion? When might it not be justified?

Decision-Making Cases

▶Case 1
Reducing Expenses to Buy a New Car

Terisha Bennett recently graduated from college and accepted a position in Manhattan, Kansas, as an assistant librarian in the public library. Terisha has no debts, and her budget is shown in the first column of Table 7.2. She now faces the question of whether to trade in her old car for a new one requiring a monthly payment of $330. Taking the role of a good friend of Terisha, suggest how Terisha might cut back on her expenses so that she can afford the vehicle.

(a) What areas might be cut back?

(b) How much in each area might be cut back?

(c) After finishing your analysis, what advice (and possibly alternatives) would you offer Terisha about buying the new car?

▶Case 2
Clauses in a Car Purchase Contract

Virginia Rowland is a dentist in Hattiesburg, Mississippi, who recently entered into a contract to buy a new automobile. After signing to finance $18,000, she hurriedly left the office of the sales finance company with her copy of the contract. Later that evening Virginia read the contract and noticed several clauses—an acceleration clause, a repossession clause, and a rule of 78s clause. When she signed the contract, Virginia was told these standard clauses should not concern her.

(a) Should Virginia be concerned about these clauses? Why or why not?

(b) Considering the rule of 78s clause, what will happen if Virginia pays off the loan before the regular due date?

(c) If Virginia had financed the $18,000 for four years at 7 percent APR, what would her monthly payment be, using the information in Table 7.3 or on the *Garman/Forgue* website?

▶Case 3
Debt Consolidation as a Debt Reduction Strategy

Isaac Granovsky, an assistant manager at a small retail shop in Las Vegas, Nevada, had an unusual amount of debt. He owed $5400 to one bank, $1800 to a clothing store, $2700 to his credit union, and several hundred dollars to other stores and individuals. Isaac also was paying more than $460 per month on the three other major obligations to pay them off when due in two years. He realized that his take-home pay of slightly more than $2100 per month did not leave him with much excess cash. Isaac discussed an alternative way of handling his major payments with his bank's loan officer. The officer suggested that he pool all of his debts and take out an $11,000 debt-consolidation loan for seven years at 14%. As a result, he would pay only $206 per month for all his debts. Isaac seemed ecstatic over the idea.

(a) Is Isaac's enthusiasm over the idea of a debt-consolidation loan justified? Why or why not?

(b) Why can the bank offer such a "good deal" to Isaac?

(c) What compromise would Isaac make to remit payments of only $206 as compared with $460?

(d) If you assume that the debt-consolidation loan will cost more in total interest, what would be a justification for this added cost?

Financial Math Questions

1. Rosemary Jensen and Janice Parker of East Lansing, Michigan, are both single. The pair share an apartment on the limited resources provided through Rosemary's disability check from Social Security and Janice's part-time job at a grocery store. The two grew tired of their old furniture and went shopping. A local store offered credit at an annual interest rate of 16 percent, with a maximum term of four years. The furniture they wish to purchase costs $2800, with no down payment required. Using Table 7.3 or the *Garman/Forgue* website, make the following calculations.

(a) What is the amount of their monthly payment if they borrow for four years?

(b) What are the total finance charges over that four-year period?

(c) How would the payment change if Rosemary and Janice reduced the loan term to three years?

(d) What are the total finance charges over that three-year period?

(e) How would the payment change if they could afford a down payment of $500 with four years of financing?

(f) What are the total finance charges over that four-year period given the $500 down payment?

(g) How would the payment change if they could afford a down payment of $500 with three years of financing?

(h) What are the total finance charges over that three-year period given the $500 down payment?

2. Jack Sprater of Bozeman, Montana, has been shopping for a loan to buy a new car. He wants to borrow $18,000 for four or five years. Jack's credit union offers a simple-interest loan at 9.1 percent for 48 months, resulting in a

monthly payment of $448.78. The credit union does not offer five-year auto loans for amounts less than $20,000, however. If Jack borrowed $18,000, this payment would strain his budget. A local bank offered him a five-year loan at a 9.34 percent APR, with a monthly payment of $376.62. This credit would not be a simple-interest loan. Because Jack is not a depositor in the bank, he would also be charged a $25 credit check fee and a $45 application fee. Jack likes the lower payment but knows that the APR is the true cost of credit, so he decided to confirm the APRs for both loans before making his decision.

(a) What is the APR for the credit union loan?

(b) Use the n-ratio formula to confirm the APR on the bank loan.

(c) What is the add-on interest rate for the bank loan?

(d) By how much would Jack lower the APR on the bank loan if he opened an account to avoid the credit check and application fees?

3. Elliott Carson of Bishop, California, obtained a two-year installment loan for $1500 to buy some furniture eight months ago. The loan had a 12.6 percent APR and a finance charge of $204.72. His monthly payment is $71.03. Elliott has made eight monthly payments and now wants to pay off the remainder of the loan. The lender will use the rule of 78s method to calculate a prepayment penalty.

(a) How much will Elliott need to give the lender to pay off the loan?

(b) What is the dollar amount of the prepayment penalty on this loan?

Money Matters Continuing Cases

Victor and Maria Advise Their Niece

Victor and Maria have always enjoyed a close relationship with Maria's niece Teresa, who graduated from college with a pharmacy degree. Teresa recently asked Maria for some assistance with her finances now that her education debts are coming due. She owes $19,000 in student loans and earns $44,000 per year in disposable income. Teresa would like to take on additional debt to furnish her apartment and buy a better car.

1. What advice might Maria give Teresa about managing her student loan debt?

2. If next year Teresa were to consolidate her loans into one loan at 8 percent interest, what advice might Maria give regarding Teresa's overall debt limit using both the debt repayment-to-disposable income method and the continuous-debt methods? (Hint: Use Table 7.3 or visit

the *Garman/Forgue* website to calculate monthly payments for various time periods.)

3. Evaluate Teresa's monthly payments for loan terms of three, four, and five years. Compare the results.

The Johnsons' Credit Questions

Harry and Belinda need some questions answered regarding credit. Their seven-year-old car has been experiencing mechanical problems lately. Instead of buying a new set of tires, as planned for in March, they are considering trading the car in for a newer used vehicle so that Harry can have dependable transportation for commuting to work. The couple still owes $3600 to the bank for their present car, or $285 per month for the remaining 18 months of the 48-month loan. The trade-in value of this car and $1000 that Harry earned from a free-lance interior design job should allow the couple to pay off the auto loan and leave $1250 for a down payment on the newer car. The Johnsons have agreed on a sales price for the newer car of $14,250. The money planned for tires will be spent for other incidental fees associated with the purchase.

1. Make recommendations to Harry and Belinda regarding where to seek financing and what APR to expect.

2. Using the *Garman/Forgue* website or the information in Table 7.3, calculate the monthly payment for a loan period of three, four, and five years at 8 percent APR. Describe the relationship between the loan period and the payment amount.

3. Harry and Belinda have a cash-flow deficit projected for several months this year (see Tables 3.3 and 3.4 on pages 73 and 75). Suggest how, when, and where they might finance the shortages by borrowing.

What Would You Recommend Now?

Now that you have read the chapter on installment credit what would you recommend to Carrie Savarin in the case at the beginning of the chapter regarding:

1. Factors she should consider regarding her ability to take on additional debt?

2. Where she might obtain financing for a vehicle loan?

3. Whether she should use a simple-interest or add-on rate loan?

4. The effect of taking on an installment loan on her overall financial planning?

Exploring the World Wide Web

To complete these exercises, go to the *Garman/Forgue* website at college.hmco.com/business/students. Under General Business, select the title of this text. Click on the Internet Exercise link for this chapter, and answer the questions that appear on the Web page.

1. A key to getting out of debt quickly and at the least cost is to determine which debts should be paid off first. Visit the website for Debt Analyzer. Either enter your own data or enter hypothetical data to determine the most efficient way to pay off debts. What three insights did you learn about debt repayment priorities?

2. Visit the website for the Consumer Information Center in Pueblo, Colorado. There you will find an on-line copy of *Fair Debt Collections*. Download or print the booklet. What five tips would you give to someone who feels overindebted?

3. Visit the website for Interest.com. There you will find a calculator that determines the monthly payment for any simple-interest loan given a specified time period, interest rate, and loan amount. Assume you wish to borrow $12,000 to buy a car. Vary the time period and interest rate of the loan to see how these variations affect your monthly payment.

4. Visit the website for Interest.com. Use their mortgage calculator to determine the monthly payment for a hypothetical loan of $170,000 at 6% interest for 30 years. Then use the amortization schedule feature to determine which portion of the first month's payment is allocated to principal and to interest.

Visit the Garman/Forgue website . . .

@**college.hmco.com/business/students**

Under General Business, select *Personal Finance 8e.* There, among other valuable resources, you will find a complete glossary, ACE questions, links to help you complete the chapter exercises, and links to other personal finance sites.

Chapter 8

Automobiles and Other Major Purchases

George and Emily Cosgrove of Tacoma, Washington, are in their early forties and have three children. They own three vehicles: an almost new mid-size sedan driven by Emily, a 5-year-old pickup truck driven by George, and an 11-year-old compact car driven by their 17-year-old daughter, Charise. Recently, their daughter's vehicle caught fire in their garage. George's vehicle was not at home at the time, but Emily's vehicle was destroyed in the blaze. The Cosgroves received an insurance settlement of $20,900 on Emily's vehicle, although the loan payoff amount was $21,800. Charise's vehicle was not insured for fire. The couple wants to obtain replacement vehicles that are similar to those destroyed.

What would you recommend to George and Emily on automobiles and other major purchases regarding:

1. How to search for two vehicles to replace those destroyed?

2. Whether to replace Emily's vehicle with a new or used vehicle?

3. Whether to lease or buy a vehicle?

4. How to decide between a rebate and a special low-APR financing opportunity should they decide to purchase a new vehicle for Emily?

5. How to negotiate with the sellers of the vehicles?

This chapter focuses on the principles of planned buying. You can use these principles anytime, but they are especially useful when you are purchasing vehicles and other expensive products. **Planned buying** uses seven distinct steps to lead you through a formal decision process that begins with needs and wants and ends with an evaluation of the decision reached. A learned skill, planned buying takes time and effort to perform. After reading this chapter, however, you should understand enough about this modeling process to be able to save money when buying expensive goods and still meet your needs and most of your wants.

The first section of the chapter provides some guidelines that you can use to save substantial amounts of money over your lifetime. Next, the steps in the buying process are examined and illustrated. The first three steps occur prior to interacting with sellers: determining your needs and wants, performing preshopping research, and fitting a purchase into your budget. The important topic of comparison shopping follows as the fourth step in the buying process. The next two steps—negotiating and making the decision—are then discussed with an emphasis on making the final decision at home. The seventh and final step—evaluation of the decision—is taken after making the purchase.

1 Describe guidelines for saving money on major purchases.

Guidelines for Planned Buying

The myriad ways that people waste money could fill the pages of dozens of books. Fortunately, the following simple guidelines can yield savings of 10 or more percent during the course of a year, equivalent to a nice tax-free increase in income.

Control Buying on Impulse

Simple restraint will help you avoid **impulse buying,** which is buying without fully considering priorities and alternatives. For example, you may have shopped carefully

Golden Rules of

Automobiles and Other Major Purchases

Financial success comes from learning the Golden Rules of personal finance and then putting what you have learned into practice. Make the following your money habits for automobiles and other major purchases:

1. Think through all of your major purchases by using the planned buying process.
2. When considering a new or used vehicle, check that model's repair ratings history in the April issue of *Consumer Reports* magazine.
3. Purchase late-model, high-quality, used vehicles and check their ownership history at www.carfax.com and any recall history at www.nhtsa.gov.
4. If you want a new vehicle, purchase it rather than use a lease, put at least 20 percent down, and do not finance the purchase for more than four years.
5. Obtain price information from at least three sources and aggressively negotiate prices and financing terms for major purchases. Never tell a seller what payment you can afford.
6. Promptly seek redress when dissatisfied with purchases or services.

by comparing various personal computers and then selected one at a discount store. While at the store, you impulsively pick up some games and entertainment software that you had not originally planned to buy. The extra $100 spent on an unplanned purchase ruins some of the benefits of the careful shopping for the computer itself.

Pay Cash

The desire to have all of life's comforts early in life is one reason why the average household headed by someone younger than age 25 spends 17 percent more than its disposable income. How? By using credit. Paying cash whenever possible can save money in two ways. First, it helps control impulse buying, which is always a risk when credit cards are used. Second, using credit can complicate financial planning by taking away financial flexibility and adding to the cost of items you buy. If you buy lots of things on credit, you certainly get the products you want. Of course, you also get the debt—often for 5 or 10 years, or even longer.

Buy at the Right Time

Paying attention to sales and looking for the right time to buy will save you money. Many items, such as sporting goods and clothing, are marked down near certain holidays and at the end of each climate season. Another $5 or $10 weekly can be saved on food simply by stocking up on advertised specials. New vehicles are least expensive at the end of the month and the model year (because of sales) and near the close of a retailer's promotion. Of course, you should always be certain that what you buy on sale is something you will really use.

Conduct the Necessary Preshopping Research

Preshopping research means gathering information about products or services before actually beginning to shop for them. Manufacturers, sellers, and service providers all represent important sources of information about products and services during preshopping research. Two other sources of information are friends and consumer magazines. If you know someone who drives an automobile you are considering buying, ask that person about his or her experience with the vehicle. You could also read about the vehicle in a consumer magazine, such as *Consumer Reports®,* which tests and reports on five to ten product categories each month. In addition, *Consumer Reports Buying Guide,* which is published every December, lists facts and figures for numerous products. Monthly issues of *Consumer Reports* generally provide a two- to five-page narrative analyzing the products and summarizing the information in chart form. Figure 8.3 provides an example of such a chart for PDAs. Each year, the April issue of *Consumer Reports* is devoted entirely to the buying of automobiles. All this and more can be seen at www.ConsumerReports.org.®

When shopping for any product, it may help to review publications on a more specific topic, such as *Photography, PC World, Car and Driver,* and *Stereo Review.* Keep in mind, however, that these trade magazines accept advertising for the products on which they report and thus are not likely to be as unbiased as *Consumer Reports,* which does not accept any advertising. Another unbiased source of information on wise buying (and many other personal finance topics) is the federal government's Consumer Information Center (Pueblo, Colorado 81009; www.pueblo.gsa.gov/staff/pa/cic/cic.htm).

The Internet has emerged as a valuable source of information for consumers in the preshopping phase. Virtually any product can now be researched and purchased online. Throughout this text we list websites that provide particularly pertinent information on a given topic. You can also look for websites yourself. Simply type the name of the product or service desired into your Web browser's search box, and you'll receive a list of hundreds of sites to review. Make sure that you distinguish between sites that are sales oriented and those that provide independent information.

Researching Price.   Advertising is a key source of information about prices. You can also obtain price information through catalogs, on the telephone, and over the Internet. While the prices of "big ticket" items such as furniture, appliances, and vehicles may be advertised, you may need to visit a showroom or dealership for prices on specific makes, models, and options. This first visit should not be a buying trip, but rather a mission to gather information only.

A key piece of price information is the **retail** or **manufacturer's suggested retail price (MSRP),** which simply consists of the initial asking price. On new automobiles, the MSRP—called the **sticker price**—appears on a window sticker in the vehicle. Usually, there is a **dealer sticker price** as well, which includes additional charges tacked on by the dealer; many of these are nothing more than attempts to generate additional revenue. The sticker prices should in no way be seen as the price that needs to be paid for a new vehicle or other big-ticket item. Instead, it should be viewed as a starting point for negotiations. You can research new and used vehicle retail prices by visiting the websites for Edmunds (www.edmunds.com), Kelley Blue Book (www.kbb.com), or the National Automobile Dealers Association (www.nadaguides.com).

Researching Trade-in Values.   You may be able to trade in an old model when buying a new one, especially with automobiles. In one common sales technique, called **high-balling,** a dealer offers a trade-in allowance that is much higher than the vehicle is worth. This apparent generosity is counterbalanced by charging more for the vehicle being purchased. Buyers need to know the true value of any item they will trade in.

Figure 8.3

Consumer Reports Ratings on Personal Digital Assistants

Ratings PDAs

• **Availability** Most models in stores until summer 2005.

Excellent ● Very good ◕ Good ○ Fair ◑ Poor ●

1 Sony 2 PalmOne 5 PalmOne 13 Toshiba

Within types, in performance order. Blue key numbers indicate Quick Picks; see box at right.

Key number	Brand & model	Price	Overall score	Ease of use	Battery life	Display	Convenience	Pocket-size	Memory (MB)	Expansion slot	Replaceable battery	Wireless connectivity	Display size (in.)	Office software	MP3 player
	PALM OS MODELS *For Macintosh compatibility, some need additional software ($30 to $40).*														
1	**Sony** Clié PEG-TH55	$400		◕	●	○	◑	•	29	MS		W	3.8	•	•
2	**PalmOne** Tungsten C	500		○	◕	◕	○		51	M		W	3.0	•	
3	**PalmOne** Tungsten T3	400		◕	○	◕	◕	•	52	M		B	3.8	•	•
4	**Sony** Clié PEG-TJ37 PEG-TJ27	300		○	○	○	◑	•	23	MS		W	3.0	•	•
5	**PalmOne** Tungsten E	200		○	○	◑	○	•	29	M			3.0	•	•
6	**Sony** Clié PEG-UX50	600		◕	◑	○	◑		16	MS		B,W	3.3	•	
7	**Garmin** iQue 3600	550		◕	◑	◕	○		23	M			3.7	•	•
8	**PalmOne** Zire 21	100		○	○	○	○	•	7	-			2.7		
	POCKET PC MODELS *For Macintosh compatibility, all need additional software ($30 to $50).*														
9	**Asus** MyPal A716	450		◕	◕	◕	●		56	CF, M	•	B,W	3.5	•	•
10	**Toshiba** e805 e800	600		◕	◕	◕	●	•	127	CF, M	•	W	3.9	•	•
11	**HP** iPaq h4355 h4350	500		○	◕	◕	◕	•	57	M	•	B,W	3.5	•	•
12	**Asus** MyPal A620BT A620	380		◕	◕	◕	◕	•	55	CF		B	3.5	•	•
13	**Toshiba** e405 e400	280		◕	○	◕	◕	•	62	M			3.5	•	•
14	**HP** iPaq h4155 h4150	450		○	○	◕	◕	•	57	M	•	B,W	3.5	•	•
15	**Dell** Axim X3 ▣ X30	200		○	○	○	◕	•	31	M	•		3.6	•	•
16	**HP** iPaq h2215 h2210	400		○	○	○	◕	•	57	CF, M	•	B	3.6	•	•

Similar models in small type, comparable to tested model. Notable exceptions (▸) are described below chart.

Overall score scale: 0 — 100 (P F G VG E)

▣ *Discontinued, but similar model is available. Price is for similar model.*

Guide to the Ratings

Overall score is based primarily on ease of use, battery life, and display. **Ease of use** considers overall design, navigation, and built-in software. **Battery life** is how long fully charged models lasted with continuous use. (For battery life and display, we scored monochrome and color models differently.) For color units: ● 15 hours or more; ◕ 8 to 15 hours; ○ 4 to 8 hours; ◑ less than 4 hours. **Display** is readability in low and normal room light and in sunlight. **Convenience** considers battery type, expansion capability, and software. **Expansion slot** indicates the type of removable media you can add: CompactFlash (CF), MultiMedia/SecureDigital Card (M), or Memory Stick (MS). **Wireless connectivity** indicates connection type: Bluetooth (B) or Wi-Fi (W). **Price** is approximate retail. ➤ The Sony Clié PEG-TJ27, similar to Sony (4), lacks Wi-Fi and an MP3 player. The Asus MyPal A620, similar to Asus (12), lacks Bluetooth.

Decision-Making Worksheet

Choosing Between Low-Interest-Rate Dealer Financing and a Rebate on a New Vehicle

It is not uncommon to see ads for new vehicles offering low APRs for dealer-arranged loans. For buyers who arrange their own financing or pay cash, a cash rebate of $1000 to $3000 (or more) off the price of the car is sometimes offered as an alternative to the low interest rate. If you intend to pay cash, then the cash rebate obviously represents the better deal. But which alternative is better when you can arrange your own financing? You can't simply compare the dealer APR to the APR that you arranged on your own.

To compare the two APRs accurately, you must add the opportunity cost of the foregone rebate to the finance charge of the dealer financing. The worksheet given here provides an example of this process. Suppose your dealer offers 2.9 percent financing for three years with a $907 finance charge; alternatively, you can receive a $3000 rebate if you arrange your own financing. The price of the car before the rebate is $22,000. Assume you can make a $2000 down payment and that you can get a 6.5 percent loan on your own. This worksheet can be found on the *Garman/Forgue* website, or you can find similar worksheets at www.bankrate.com (search for "calculators") or www.financenter. com (click on "calculators").

The lower of the values obtained in Steps 3 and 4 is the better deal. In this instance, the financing that you arranged on your own is more attractive. In fact, any loan you arrange that carries an APR lower than 12 percent compares favorably with the dealer-arranged financing in this case.

Step	Example	Your Figures
1. Determine the dollar amount of the rebate.	$3000	_____
2. Add the rebate amount to the finance charge for the dealer financing (dollar cost of credit).	+ $ 907	_____
3. Use the n-ratio APR formula from Chapter 7 [Equation (7.3) on page 193 and replicated here as Equation (8.1)] to calculate an adjusted APR for the dealer financing.		

$$APR = \frac{Y(95P + 9)F}{12P(P + 1)(4D + F)} \qquad (8.1)$$

where

APR = Annual Percentage Rate
Y = Number of payment periods in one year
F = Finance charge in dollars
D = Debt (amount borrowed)
P = Total number of scheduled payments

$$APR = \frac{(12)[(95 \times 36) + 9](\$3000 + \$907)}{(12 \times 36)(36 + 1)[(4 \times \$20,000) + (\$3000 + \$907)]} = 12\%$$

Step	Example	Your Figures
4. Write in the APR that you arranged on your own.	6.5%	_____

To see how this process works with a more expensive purchase, consider how Sharon Danes might fit a new car into her budget. She estimates that the base sticker price of the subcompact car she wants will be about $16,000. This price includes the five items she specified as her highest priority because she would not consider buying a car that lacked them. The second-priority options will likely add a total of $2300 to the sticker price: side-impact airbags, $700; air conditioning, $700; antilock brakes, $600; and cruise control, $300.

Buying a car with her first- and second-priority features might cost Sharon $19,500 ($16,000 + $2300 for the options + $1200 for sales tax and title registration). She can use $2500 from her savings account as a down payment, receive $2000 for trading in her old car, and borrow the remaining $15,000. The prices for the car and its options are Sharon's estimates from her preshopping research. The actual price she will pay for the car will depend on her ability to negotiate the final price down from the sticker price. From her research, Sharon knows that the dealer cost of new vehicles averages about 12 percent less than the sticker price. By multiplying the sticker price by 12 percent, she can make a rough estimate of her bargaining room. For example, Sharon might bargain to reduce the price of the car with the wanted options and taxes by 10 percent to $17,550 [$19,500 − ($19,500 × 0.10)], leaving the dealer with a modest profit margin.

The monthly payment that Sharon must fit into her budget will depend on five factors:

- The price she actually pays for the car
- The down payment she makes
- The time period for payback of the loan
- The amount she receives in trade for her old car
- The interest rate on the loan

For illustration, we will choose a down payment of $2500 and assume a 48-month time period (a common financing term). Sharon figures that she can get no more than $2000 for her old car. But what about the actual price and interest rate?

We will assume that Sharon has done a good job of estimating the price she might pay for the car. If she can reduce the price by 10 percent, she will need to borrow $13,050 ($17,550 − $2500 down − $2000 trade-in). This figure is merely an estimate, however, and may vary by as much as $1000 depending on her negotiating skills. If the loan amount is $13,050, Sharon would then need to use the likely APR figure from her preshopping research to determine a monthly payment. If she obtains a loan with an 8 percent APR, Sharon estimates that her monthly payment would be $318.55 (13.05 × 24.41, from Table 7.3 on page 186).

Table 8.1 (page 214) shows Sharon's monthly budget. Her monthly take-home pay of $1765 is totally committed. To buy the automobile with options, she will need $318.55 per month and will have to change her budget drastically. For example, she could cut food expenditures ($30 per month); spend less on clothing ($50); cut entertainment, gifts, personal care, and miscellaneous items ($50, $10, $10, and $20, respectively); and put $50 less in savings (she was saving to buy a vehicle). In addition, her transportation-related expenses would change as follows: gasoline, −$20; maintenance and repairs, −$50; and insurance costs, +$20. (You should always get an insurance quote before buying a vehicle.) In all, these efforts would raise only $270, still $48 short of the amount she needs for the car. Sharon's alternatives are to make more cutbacks in her budget, to work overtime, or to get a part-time job. She could also reduce her payments to $264.65 per month by taking out a longer, 60-month loan (13.05 × $20.28, from Table 7.3). She should be wary about having to operate on such a tight budget for five years, however. Sharon will pay much more in interest with a longer-term loan and might want to consider a less expensive new car or a used car.

Table 8.1 Fitting a Vehicle Payment into a Monthly Budget			
	Prior Budget	**Possible Cutbacks**	**New Budget**
Food	$ 250	$ − 30	$ 220
Clothing/laundry	120	− 50	70
Vehicle maintenance and repairs	75	− 50	25
Auto insurance	60	20	80
Gasoline	90	− 20	70
Housing	450		450
Utilities	80		80
Telephone	50		50
Entertainment	150	− 50	100
Gifts	50	− 10	40
Church and charity	60		60
Personal care	60	− 10	50
Savings	200	− 50	150
Miscellaneous	70	− 20	50
TOTAL	**$1765**	**$ − 270**	**$1495**
Car payment			318
TOTAL WITH CAR PAYMENT	**$1765**	**$ −270**	**$1813**

3 Describe the key aspects of comparison shopping.

Comparison Shopping

After completing the first three steps in planned buying, it is time to begin interacting with sellers by **comparison shopping**—the process of comparing products or services to find the best buy. A **best buy** is a product or service that, in the buyer's opinion, represents acceptable quality at a fair or low price for that level of quality. Purchasing the product with the lowest price does not necessarily assure a best buy; quality and features count, too. In comparison shopping, you visit different stores to gather specific information to expand upon your preshopping research.

Comparison shopping takes time and effort, but the payoff in both satisfaction and savings can be considerable. During the early steps in the comparison shopping process, a shopper should narrow his or her choices to specific makes and models and desired options. Then, he or she should visit the appropriate dealerships (or stores) again. This time, the shopper will be much closer to the decision to buy and will be ready to discuss details, although he or she should not buy at this point. When comparison shopping, tell the salesperson exactly what interests you and ask about price and any dealer incentives and rebates that apply. You should inquire about financing options, leasing, warranties, and service contracts. Finally, test-drive the vehicle.* The goal is to narrow the choice even further prior to negotiating for the very best deal, which is the next step in the buying process.

*Do not give out your Social Security number or allow the dealer to photocopy your driver's license. The dealer might use the information to obtain your credit bureau report while you are on the test-drive. The dealer can then estimate how much you can afford to pay for the vehicle and your ability to obtain low-rate financing elsewhere.

Did You Know? . . .

The Keys to a Safe Car

The following pointers may help you buy a safer new or used vehicle.

- **Check government safety test results.** The federal government crash-tests motor vehicles to analyze their safety. For results on various makes and models, call the National Highway Traffic Safety Administration (NHTSA) "auto hotline" at (800) 424-9393 or visit www.nhtsa.gov.
- **Check on recalls.** With more than 10 million new vehicles sold in the United States each year, it is understandable that some will be recalled for repairs to safety features. When buying a used car, call the NHTSA auto hotline to see whether the vehicle has been recalled. If so, confirm that the repairs have been made to the car you're considering; if not, buy elsewhere. Dealers are required to fix vehicles recalled for safety reasons for free.
- **Consider a model with additional airbags.** All new cars now have driver and passenger front-seat airbags. For added protection, consider new and used models that also provide side-impact airbags.
- **Look for antilock brakes.** Antilock brakes are believed to reduce the possibility of skidding during sudden stops. They are especially helpful in rain and inclement winter conditions.
- **Think about theft as well as accident safety.** Some makes and models of vehicles are much more attractive to thieves than others. These vehicles also require higher auto insurance premiums. Call the NHTSA auto hotline (or go to www.nhtsa.gov) to find information on new and used vehicle theft ratings.

Compare Prices

Prices on big-ticket items such as vehicles, furniture, appliances, and electronic equipment are rarely the same from seller to seller or even from week to week. Literally thousands of dollars can be saved by taking the time to search for the best prices. Experts recommend use of the "rule of three," which says to compare at least three alternatives before making any decision. As discussed later in this chapter, price is the first consideration in any negotiation, and comparison shopping arms you with the information you need to be successful in getting a best buy. When buying an automobile, for example, compare the prices you find at car dealers with the information provided at one of the websites devoted to vehicle prices (see page 208).

Compare Financing Options

Sellers are not the only source of financing. Your own bank or credit union will also be willing to loan money to make purchases. Your comparison shopping won't be complete, however, until you use websites such as www.bankrate.com.

Be on the lookout for "same as cash" offers on furniture, appliances, and electronics that allow you to delay interest or payment for, perhaps, 90 days to one year. If the product is paid off during this time period, you will not incur any finance charges. Be wary, however. Interest may be charged retroactively from day one if a payment is late or if the purchase isn't fully paid off during the required time period.

Consider Leasing Instead of Buying

Leasing a new vehicle is an increasingly attractive option to many people who are in the market for a car. About 20 percent of the new cars "sold" each year are actually leased. It is even possible to lease used cars. Is leasing a better deal than financing? You cannot answer this question until you understand some basics of leasing.

When **leasing** a vehicle or any other product, you are, in effect, renting the product while the ownership title remains with the lease grantor. Regulation M issued by the Federal Reserve Board governs lease contracts. A major requirement of this regulation is a mandatory disclosure of pertinent information about the lease that the consumer is considering. The disclosure form must summarize the offer of the lessee (leasing agency) to the lessor (consumer). The information in this form should be compared with the actual lease contract prior to signing to ensure that the lease signed is actually what was agreed upon verbally. Five terms are important in leasing:

1. The **gross capitalized cost** (**gross cap cost**) includes the price of the vehicle plus what the leasee paid to finance the purchase plus any other items you agree to pay for over the life of the lease, including insurance or a maintenance agreement.

2. **Capitalized cost reductions** (**cap cost reductions**) are moneys paid on the lease at its inception, including any down payment, trade-in value, or rebate.

3. The **adjusted capitalized cost** (**adjusted cap cost**) is determined by subtracting the capitalized cost reductions from the gross capitalized cost.

4. The **residual value** is the projected value of a leased asset at the end of the lease time period.

5. The **money factor** (or **lease rate** or **lease factor**) measures the rent charge portion of your payment. Although sometimes described by dealers as a figure for comparing leases, lease forms must carry the following disclosure about the money factor: "This percentage may not measure the overall cost of financing this lease."

Always negotiate a purchase price before discussing a lease. Leasing typically requires an initial outlay of cash to pay for the first month's lease payment and a security deposit. Payments are based on the capitalized cost of the asset minus any capitalized cost reductions and the residual value. This difference represents the cost of using the asset during the lease period; when divided by the number of months in the contract, it serves to establish the base for the monthly lease payment. (Some new vehicles are offered with single-payment leases in which the entire difference between the capitalized cost and residual value is paid up front.) With monthly payment leases, the payments are lower than monthly loan payments for equivalent time periods because you are paying for only the reduction in the asset's value—not its entire cost. To compare the costs of leasing versus buying, use the Decision-Making Worksheet, "Comparing Automobile Financing and Leasing."

A lease may be either open-end or closed-end. In an **open-end lease,** you must pay any difference between the projected residual value of the vehicle and its actual market value at the end of the lease period. When a vehicle depreciates more rapidly than expected, the holder of an open-end lease has to pay extra money when the lease expires. For example, a vehicle with an $11,000 residual value but a $10,250 market value would require an end-of-lease payment of $750 ($11,000 − $10,250). The Consumer Leasing Act limits this end-of-lease payment to a maximum of three times the average monthly payment.

In a **closed-end lease** (also called a **walkaway lease**), the holder pays no charge if the end-of-lease market value of the vehicle is lower than the originally projected residual value. Closed-end leases may carry some end-of-lease charges if the vehicle has greater

Decision-Making Worksheet

Comparing Automobile Financing and Leasing

The worksheet given here can be used to compare leasing and borrowing to buy a vehicle. Remember that the cost of credit is the finance charge—the extra that you pay because you borrowed. Leases also carry costs, but they are hidden in the contract. Indeed, some may remain unknown until the end of the lease period. These items, which are indicated by an asterisk (*), are negotiable and are defined in the text. Ask the dealer for the price of each item, as these fees must be disclosed by dealers. Then complete the worksheet and compare the dollar cost of leasing with the finance charge on a loan for the same time period.

To make the comparison accurately, you must know the underlying price of the car if you were purchasing it. Often you are not told this value with a lease arrangement, so you should negotiate a price for the vehicle before mentioning the lease option.

Always shop for a lease through several dealers and through independent leasing companies, because costs vary considerably. If you do choose a leasing option, your goal should be to lower your monthly cost rather than to buy more car. Otherwise, in just a few years, you will find that you have spent big bucks for a vehicle you no longer drive. This worksheet can be found on the *Garman/Forgue* website or you can find similar worksheets at www.bankrate.com (search for "calculators") or www.financenter.com (click on "consumer site").

Step	Example	Your Figures
1. Monthly lease payment (36 payments of $275, for example)	$ 9900	_____
2. Plus acquisition fee* (if any)	300	_____
Plus disposition charge* (if any)	300	_____
Plus estimate of excess mileage charges* (if any)	0	_____
Plus projected residual value of the vehicle	4500	_____
3. Amount for which you are responsible under the lease	15,000	_____
4. Less the capitalized cost* after taking capitalized cost reductions*	12,600	_____
5. Dollar cost of leasing to be compared with a finance charge if you purchased the vehicle	2400	_____

than normal wear or mileage, however. For example, a four-year closed-end lease might require a $0.20 per mile charge for mileage in excess of 55,000 miles. If you actually drove the vehicle 60,000 miles during the four years, you would be charged an extra $1000 [$0.20 × 5000 (60,000 − 55,000)]. With either an open- or closed-end lease, you may purchase the vehicle at the end of the lease period. With an open-end lease, you would pay the actual cash value. With a closed-end lease, you would pay the residual value.

Other charges are possible with a lease. An **acquisition fee** is either paid in cash or included in the gross capitalization cost. It pays for a credit report, application fee, and other paperwork. A **disposition fee** is assessed when you turn in the vehicle at the end of the lease and the lessor must prepare it for resale. An **early termination charge** may also be levied if you decide to end the lease prematurely. Be wary of a lease with an early termination charge, even if you do not plan to end the lease early, because termination also occurs when a leased vehicle is traded in or is totally wrecked or stolen. Make sure that you obtain a written disclosure of these charges well before you actually make your decision. The **early termination payoff** is the total amount you would need to repay if you end the lease agreement early; it includes both the early termination charge and the unpaid lease balance. In its early years, your lease may be financially upside-down, which means that you owe more on the vehicle than it is worth. (This situation is also likely to occur when you buy on credit and you only make a small down payment.)

You should be wary of several potential events in this market. First, be cautious if you talk about buying all through the negotiation process only to be offered a lease at the last minute. Because the monthly charge will be lower, you may be tempted to sign a deal that actually costs considerably more. Second, make sure that all oral agreements related to trade-in value, mileage charges, and rebates are included in the lease contract. Third, watch out for additional fees being assessed, especially near the very end of the negotiations or in the final written lease.

To make buying more attractive than leasing, many bank lenders have developed balloon automobile loans. With a **balloon automobile loan,** the last monthly payment equals the projected residual value of the vehicle at the end of the loan period. Thus, the amount borrowed represents the difference between the selling price and the vehicle's expected value at the end of the loan period. This arrangement effectively lowers all the other earlier monthly payments to make them more competitive with lease payments. When the final balloon payment is due, perhaps $1000–$7000, the borrower generally has three options:

1. Sell the car and pay the balloon payment with the proceeds (with luck, the vehicle will sell for a high enough amount).

2. Pay the balloon payment and keep the vehicle.

3. Return the vehicle to the lender to cover the balloon payment.

Compare Warranties

Warranties are an important consideration in comparison shopping. Almost all products have **warranties**—assurances by sellers that goods are as promised and that certain steps will be taken to rectify problems—even if only in the form of implied warranties. Under an **implied warranty,** the product sold is warranted to be suitable for sale (a **warranty of merchantability**) and to work effectively (a **warranty of fitness**) whether or not a written warranty exists. Implied warranties are required by state law. To avoid them, the seller can state in writing that the product is sold **as is.** If you buy any product "as is," you have no legal recourse should it fail to perform, even if the salesperson made verbal "promises" to take care of any problems. Used cars are often sold "as is."

Written and oral warranties are called **express warranties.** Companies that offer written express warranties must do so under the provisions of the federal Magnuson-Moss Warranty Act if the product is sold for more than $15. This law provides that any written warranty offered must be classified as either a full warranty or a limited warranty. A **full warranty** includes three stringent requirements:

1. A product must be fixed at no cost to the buyer within a reasonable time after the owner has complained.

2. The owner will not have to undertake an unreasonable task to return the product for repair (such as ship back a refrigerator).

3. A defective product will be replaced with a new one or the buyer's money will be returned if the product cannot be fixed after a reasonable number of attempts.

A **limited warranty** includes less than a full warranty. For example, it may offer only free parts, not labor. Note that one part of a product could be covered by a full warranty (perhaps the engine on a lawnmower) and the rest of the unit by a limited warranty. Read all warranties carefully, and note that both full and limited warranties are valid for only a specified time period.

Service Contracts Are Overpriced

A **service contract** is an agreement between the contract seller (a dealer, manufacturer, or independent company) and the buyer of a product to provide repair services to covered components of the product for some specified time period. Service contracts are sometimes given names such as "extended warranty," "maintenance agreement," or "buyer protection plan." These contracts are purchased separately from the product itself (such as a vehicle, appliance, or electronics equipment). The cost is paid by the purchaser either in a lump sum or in monthly payments. Service contracts are very similar to insurance. For example, a 25-inch television priced at $600 could have a service contract that promises to fix anything that goes wrong during the third and fourth years of ownership; the manufacturer's warranty covers the first two years. This contract might cost $60 for one year, or $5 per month.

Although buying a service contract might provide peace of mind, it is usually unwise financially because it makes little economic sense to insure against risks that can, if necessary, be paid for out of current income or savings. More than 80 percent of all service contracts are never used, and total payouts to consumers to make repairs amount to less than 10 percent of all money spent on the contracts.

Service contracts have become increasingly prevalent in the vehicle, appliance, and electronics markets because of the high profits involved and the persuasiveness of salespersons. Thus, they are "sold" to consumers. Automobile manufacturers and dealers offer service contract plans; in addition, a number of independent companies offer service contracts for new vehicles. Often, a deductible of about $100 must be paid with each use of the contract. Repairs are usually covered and may include preventive maintenance for covered components. The cost for such a contract on a vehicle can exceed $700, and, if offered by the manufacturer or dealer, it can be added to the purchase price of the vehicle and financed with the purchase loan. If $700 is charged for the plan, $400 or more of this amount may be dealer profit, with $250 going to the salesperson. A seller can afford to be more generous on a deal if he or she knows that most of the money will be made back on the service contract.

Negotiate and Decide On the Best Deal

4 Negotiate effectively and make informed decisions when buying vehicles and other expensive products.

Negotiating and decision making follow comparison shopping in the buying process. If you move through these steps too quickly, you may pay too much even when you have done a great job with your preshopping research and comparison shopping. Always remember that sellers of such products sell every day, and they are highly skilled; in contrast, consumers are amateurs when it comes to buying big-ticket items.

Successful Negotiators Are Armed with Information

Negotiating (or **haggling**) is the process of discussing the actual terms of an agreement with a seller. Consumers skip this step when making day-to-day purchases because prices in most stores are firm. With high-priced items—especially appliances, furniture, fine jewelry, and vehicles—there is an opportunity, and often an expectation, that offers and counteroffers will be made before arriving at the final price.

Negotiating is especially difficult for consumers when buying vehicles because so many variables must be considered, including the price of the vehicle, the trade-in value (if any), the possibility of a rebate, the prices of options, the interest rate, and possibly a service contract. The dealer can appear to be cooperative on one aspect and make up the difference elsewhere. The key to successful negotiation is to be armed with accurate information on all of these variables.

The complexity and uncertainty involved in negotiating the price of a new vehicle have inspired the development of several services intended to assist buyers. A **new-vehicle buying service** is a no-fee organization that arranges discount purchases for buyers of new cars who are referred to nearby participating automobile dealers who have agreed to charge specific discount prices. After you sign up, a local dealer will call you to offer a no-haggle price, which is often within 4 percent of the invoice price. The buying service earns its income by collecting a finder's fee from the dealer. **Professional shoppers,** in exchange for a fee (perhaps $150 to $450) based on the sticker price, will find the best available price from a nearby dealer and finalize the sale. Alternatively, for a lower fee (perhaps $100–$200), they will obtain price quotes so you can finalize the deal yourself. Visit www.autobytel.com, www.carpoint.msn.com, www.carsdirect.com, www.autoweb.com, www.autoadvisor.com [(800) 326-1976], www.carbargains.com [(800) 475-7283], or www.carsource1.com [(800) 517-2277] to obtain more information about these services.

The key when negotiating a vehicle purchase is to obtain a firm price from a dealer for the vehicle and optional equipment desired before discussing *any other* aspects of the deal. Do not mention financing or a trade-in until you have pinned the salesperson down to a price. You should know from your preshopping research and comparison shopping what a good price for the vehicle in question would be. Always start your bargaining from this low price rather than the asking price or sticker price on the vehicle. If possible, you should obtain prices from three or more dealers and then let each know that you have done so and whether their price is low compared with the others. The dealer will then have the chance to reduce the asking price to meet the competition. This strategy pressures the dealer to meet your needs rather than the other way around.

According to CNW Marketing/Research, the average reductions off the sticker prices on vehicles are as follows: budget, 15 percent; mid-size, 13 percent; luxury, 13 percent; sport, 19 percent; full-size pickup, 8 percent; compact SUV, 10 percent; and full-size SUV, 8 percent. Many consumers have caught on to the fiction of new car sticker prices and now focus on the **invoice price** or **seller's cost,** which reflects the price the dealer paid for the vehicle. Sometimes, however, manufacturers offer a **dealer holdback** (or **dealer rebate**) to dealers. A dealer holdback is a percentage of the invoice price that the dealer can hold back from (instead of paying to) the manufacturer, thereby providing the dealer with additional profit on the vehicle. Because of holdback incentives, dealers can advertise a car at $1 over invoice and still make a good profit. For this reason, you should not hesitate to negotiate for a price that is below the invoice price.

Consider the case of Gary Joseph, a production manager from Northville, Michigan. Gary had narrowed his choice of cars down to one model and two dealerships. He presented his list of desired options to the first dealer and was shown a suitable car on the lot. He had arranged for financing on his own and, therefore, was interested in only two issues: price and the dealer's willingness to offer an even lower APR. When Gary inquired about price, the salesperson asked what monthly payment Gary could afford. Gary countered by saying that his budget was not important and that he wanted to know the price. When the salesperson responded that it was the dealership's policy to get the affordable payment amount before answering any questions, Gary walked out of the dealership with the salesperson in hot pursuit seeking to continue the sale. The next day the salesperson called Gary at home, saying that he would lose his job if he quoted a price before getting an affordable monthly payment amount. By then, however, Gary had already bought his car at the other dealership. Had he responded to the questions, the salesperson could have tailored the price to Gary's figure, which likely would not have been the lowest price that the dealership would have accepted. A key to all negotiations is to be prepared to say "no" and go elsewhere if the terms are not satisfactory.

Make the Decision

Most people make buying decisions for expensive purchases inside a retail store or showroom. In fact, these locations are not the best places to decide because of pressures to buy that may be applied by the seller and/or by a customer's desire to complete the process. It is better to wait until you get home to make the final decision. There, you can rationally retrace your steps through the buying process, making sure that the decision is based on the proper facts and logic. After making your decision, you can return to the dealer's showroom and close the sale.

Some people use a decision-making grid that allows them to visually and mathematically weigh the decision they are about to make. Such a grid is illustrated in Table 8.2 for someone who might be deciding among three different washing machines. The first task in developing such a grid is to determine the various criteria for making the decision. In Table 8.2, these factors include price, durability, and styling. Each criterion is assigned a weight that reflects the importance each has in the mind of the purchaser. Each brand and model under consideration is then given a score (from 1 to 10 in this case) that indicates how well it performs on that criterion. The score (*S*) is multiplied by the weight (*W*) to obtain a weighted score. The total of the weighted scores for each brand/model can then be compared with the totals for the other choices to determine which one "wins." In Table 8.2, Appliance C, which has a total score of 8.0, would be chosen. Note that each purchaser will arrive at different scores because the weights

Table 8.2 Decision-Making Grid (Illustrated for a Washing Machine)		Appliance A		Appliance B		Appliance C	
Criteria	Decision Weight (*W*)	Score (*S*)*	*W* × *S*	Score (*S*)*	*W* × *S*	Score (*S*)*	*W* × *S*
Price	30%	9	2.7	7	2.1	5	1.5
Durability	25%	6	1.5	8	2.0	10	2.5
Features	20%	6	1.2	8	1.6	10	2.0
Warranty	15%	6	0.9	10	1.5	8	2.0
Styling	10%	10	1.0	6	0.6	8	0.8
TOTAL	**100%**		**7.3**		**7.8**		**8.0**

* Using a 10-point scale where 10 is the highest score.

Advice from an Expert

How to Buy a Used Vehicle

Most consumer-buying experts recommend purchasing late-model used cars to get the most from your car-buying dollar. You need to be careful when buying a used vehicle, however. Following some basic steps can help you avoid getting a lemon.

1. **Decide how much you can afford to spend.** You can purchase a used vehicle for as little as $500 or as much as $20,000 or $30,000. Decide in advance how much you can afford, and then search for vehicles in your price range.
2. **Decide which features and options you want.** Most people have specific desires for features such as power steering, air conditioning, or antilock brakes. If you want a specific option, you can usually obtain it without spending too much more simply by choosing an older model.
3. **Select several reliable makes and models in your price range.** The National Automobile Dealers Association (www.nadaguides.com) publishes weekly reports on the average retail and wholesale prices of various makes and models of used vehicles. The Internet is an excellent source of used-car pricing information. In addition, you should consult the most recent April issue of *Consumer Reports* for its lists of recommended used vehicles in various price ranges. The same issue lists frequency-of-repair histories for most makes and models as reported by the magazine's readers. You can also use the *Consumer Reports* Used Car Price Service to obtain this information for specific types of vehicles [www.consumerreports.org or call (800) 258-1169; each report is about $10]. Because *Consumer Reports* accepts no advertising in its publication, it is a source of unbiased information for consumers.

4. **Start your search.** Armed with the list of reliable makes and models in your price range, you are ready to look for specific vehicles for sale. Start with the classified advertisements in your local newspaper and used-vehicle advertising publications distributed at supermarkets and convenience stores. Some websites will search local dealership offerings for specific makes and models. You may purchase a used vehicle from a new car dealership, a used car dealership, a rental car company, a private individual, or a repossession auction. New car dealerships tend to offer the nicer, more reliable, and more expensive vehicles. Used car dealerships, on the other hand, tend to have the widest range of quality. Private individuals deserve your attention because they usually own the vehicle personally and know its history. Used cars sold by rental agencies such as Hertz and Avis can be good choices because the cars have been regularly maintained.

Regardless of the source, immediately rule out any vehicle that seems to have a problem or raises a ques-

assigned and the scores awarded will differ according to individual tastes and preferences. Someone who weighted "price" very high might purchase Appliance A, as it has the highest rating on that criterion. Similarly, each person would differ in how he or she scores an appliance's "styling" even if everyone weighted that criterion in the same way. Nonetheless, a grid of this type helps bring objectivity to the decision-making process and can be of benefit, especially when buying big-ticket items.

Be wary of a sales technique called **lowballing,** which involves an attempt to raise an orally negotiated price when it comes time to finalize the written contract. For example, after agreeing on the price of a vehicle with a buyer, the salesperson might write up the sale on the appropriate forms. Just before it is time to sign, the salesperson states that, as a formality, the approval of a manager is necessary. While the buyer is dreaming of driving home in the new car, the salesperson and the manager are talking about how much more they can get for the vehicle. When the salesperson returns, he or she indicates that some problem or mistake has occurred, and that the price has to be "*x* amount" higher. Perhaps the trade-in value is too high, or the sticker price can't be discounted by

tion in your mind. Do the same for sellers who do not seem cooperative. Too many vehicles are available to waste your time considering poor-quality vehicles or wrestling with uncooperative sellers.

Some of the most aggressive marketers of used cars are dealers that advertise that they cater to those with poor or limited credit histories. Using terms such as "credit rebuilders" or "buy here/pay here," they give the impression that they are willing to lend to all buyers quickly and easily. While their standards are certainly lower, they also charge very high interest rates and offer contract terms that are very unforgiving of late or missed payments. Always seek out lenders with high standards. They charge the lowest interest rates because they lend to the most reliable borrowers.

5. **Check your selections carefully.** By now you should have narrowed your choice to two or three specific vehicles. Inspect them inside and out. Take along a friend who is knowledgeable about cars if you are not car-savvy. Test-drive the vehicle and try out all of its functions. Ask for maintenance records if the seller is an individual or a rental company. Ask the dealer for the name, address, and phone number of the previous owner and give that person a telephone call. Before you agree to buy any vehicle, ask your mechanic to examine it. Although the examination may cost

$50 to $75, it could help you avoid purchasing a vehicle with problems and save hundreds of dollars in repairs later.

You can track your vehicle's history (including mileage) to determine whether the vehicle has been wrecked, salvaged, damaged, or bought back under a lemon law. To do so, go to www.carfax.com. It charges a nominal fee for this service.

6. **Negotiate and decide.** Never pay the asking price for a used vehicle. Sellers expect to negotiate and consequently set a price higher than required to give room for bargaining. Get all verbal promises and guarantees in writing. If a seller will not put his or her words in writing, shop elsewhere. Finally, return to the quiet of your home to consider your alternatives and to make your final decision. If necessary, put down a small deposit to hold the vehicle for a day or two while you make your decision.

7. **Arrange financing.** Financing the car should be a separate decision. Sometimes your credit union or bank will offer you the best deal. Dealers usually add a percentage point or two to the interest rates that they help you obtain through other lenders. Check interest rates yourself because it can pay to shop around.

Aimee D. Prawitz
Northern Illinois University

quite as much as planned, or the price of a certain option has increased. In reality, of course, lowballing is simply a ruse to allow the dealer to get more money. Sign only a **buyer's order** that names a specific vehicle and all charges. And do so only after the salesperson and sales manager have signed *first*. If you ever encounter lowballing, leave quickly without signing anything. Do not look back, and do not apologize. And don't be surprised if the salesperson calls you back and asks you to agree to the original terms.

Evaluate Your Decision

The planned buying process comes full circle when you evaluate your decision. The purpose of this step is to determine where things went well and where they went less smoothly. The lessons learned will prove useful when you need to make a similar purchase in the future.

5 Evaluate your purchase decisions and, if necessary, effectively seek redress.

Sometimes the process was so successful that you may want to compliment the seller. In other cases, you may want to complain about the product or service so as to obtain **redress**—that is, to right the wrong. This process should always start with the actual seller, as indicated in Table 8.3. Seeking redress through the first three channels in the complaint procedures as shown in the table can rectify almost all consumer complaints.

Sometimes your best efforts at redress may not prove successful. As a result, you might consider taking legal action in **small claims court.** In this state court, civil matters are often resolved without the assistance of attorneys (in some states, attorneys are actually prohibited from representing clients in small claims courts). Small claims courts usually place restrictions on the maximum amount under dispute, typically ranging from $500 to $2500, for which a claim may be made in those courts. To file a small claims court action, go to your local county courthouse and ask which court hears small claims.

Alternative dispute resolution programs are industry- or government-sponsored programs that provide an avenue to resolve disputes outside the formal court system. All vehicle manufacturers utilize these programs as part of their warranty procedures. **Mediation** is a procedure in which a neutral third party works with the parties involved in the dispute to arrive at a mutually agreeable solution. In **arbitration,** a neutral third party hears (or reads) the claims made and the positions taken by the parties to the dispute and then issues a ruling that is binding on one or both parties.

All states have enacted new-vehicle **lemon laws** that provide guidelines for arbitrators to use to order a dealer's buyback of a "lemon." A common definition of a lemon is a vehicle that was in the shop for repairs four times for the same problem in the first year after purchase. (For state-specific definitions, visit www.carlemon.com.) To enforce a lemon law, the buyer must go through the prescribed warranty process specified in the owner's manual. Eventually, if the problem is not resolved, an arbitration hearing will be held through which the owner can request a buyback. Some states have also enacted used-vehicle lemon laws.

Table 8.3 Complaint Procedure (Levels and Channels of Complaining)

Levels to Bring Your Complaint	Channels for Complaint
1. Local business	Salesperson → supervisor → manager/owner
2. Manufacturer	Consumer affairs department → president/chief executive officer
3. Self-regulatory organizations	Better Business Bureau → county medical societies → consumer action panels
4. Consumer-action agencies	Private consumer-action groups → media action lines → government agencies
5. Small claims or civil court	Small claims court → civil court

Summary

1. You can save money by following the basic rules of planned buying: control buying on impulse, pay cash when possible, buy at the right time, avoid paying extra for a "name," and avoid the high price of convenience.

2. The planned buying process includes three steps that occur prior to interacting with sellers: prioritizing wants, obtaining information during preshopping research (especially on-line), and fitting the planned purchase into the budget. These steps represent the homework needed when preparing to buy.

3. To interact effectively with sellers, you should comparison shop to find the best buy. When purchasing vehicles and other high-priced items, this shopping process includes comparing prices, financing arrangements, leasing options, warranties, and service contracts.

4. The next step after comparison shopping is negotiating with the seller, especially with items such as automobiles where haggling on price is generally expected. The final decision should be made at home, however.

5. The final step in planned buying, which occurs after the purchase is made, entails evaluating the decision and seeking redress, if needed.

Key Terms

arbitration, 224
as is, 218
best buy, 214
closed-end (walkaway) lease, 216
comparison shopping, 214
full warranty, 218
gross capitalized (gross cap) cost, 216
implied warranty, 218
invoice price (seller's cost), 220
limited warranty, 219
lowballing, 222
negotiating (haggling), 220
planned buying, 204
preshopping research, 208
rebate, 211
redress, 224
residual value, 216
small claims court, 224
sticker price, 208
upside-down, 210
want, 206

Chapter Review Questions

1. What is planned buying?

2. List the steps in the planned buying process.

3. Distinguish between *needs* and *wants,* and explain why it may be better to act as if no needs exist.

4. Describe the three steps in the buying process that involve direct interaction with sellers.

5. Explain why lease payments for a new vehicle are lower than loan payments for the same vehicle.

6. Describe the relationships among capital cost, capital cost reductions, and residual value in a lease.

7. Explain the difference between an implied warranty and an express warranty. How do they relate to the term "as is"?

8. What is the purpose of a service contract? What is a disadvantage of such a contract?

9. Describe three keys to success in negotiating the price of a new vehicle.

10. Define *redress* and explain the complaint procedure that a consumer could follow to obtain redress.

Group Discussion Issues

1. Do you or a family member tend to buy name-brand versions of certain products? Which ones? Why or why not?

2. Are all of the steps in the planned buying process used when buying simple everyday products (such as a loaf of bread or a half-gallon of milk) or are they used only when buying big-ticket items?

3. What benefits do you see in leasing a vehicle? What negatives exist when leasing?

4. What is the worst purchase decision that you ever made? What step(s) in the planned buying process could you have done better in that situation?

5. When was the last time your were seriously dissatisfied with a purchase? Did you complain? Why or why not? If you complained, what was the outcome?

Decision-Making Cases

▶ **Case 1**
Purchase of a New Refrigerator

Tracy Sullivan, a financial consultant from Spokane, Washington, is remodeling her kitchen. Tracy, who lives alone, has decided to replace her refrigerator with a new model that offers more conveniences. She has narrowed her choices to models that are about 19 cubic feet in size and have a top freezer. Quality models in this size cost about $750. Tracy has drawn up a list of possible convenience options and their prices: automatic defrost, $125; ice maker, $50; textured enamel surface, $75; glass shelving, $30; and ice-water port, $95. Tracy's credit union will loan her the necessary funds for one year at a 12 percent APR on the installment plan. Following is her budget, which includes $2140 in monthly take-home pay.

Food	$300
Entertainment	120
Clothing	60
Gifts	70
Charities	75
Car payment	330
Personal care	60
Automobile expenses	120
Savings	130
Housing	825
Miscellaneous	50
Total	**$2140**

(a) What preshopping research should Tracy do to select the best brand of refrigerator?

(b) Advise Tracy on which convenience options you think she should regard as high priority and which she should consider as low priority.

(c) Using the information in Table 7.3 on page 186 or the *Garman/Forgue* website, determine Tracy's monthly payment for (1) the basic model, (2) the basic model with high-priority options, and (3) the basic model with both high- and low-priority options.

(d) Fit each of the three monthly payments into Tracy's budget.

(e) Advise Tracy to help her make her decision.

▶ **Case 2**
A Dispute over New-Car Repairs

David Hardison, a high school football coach from Oklahoma City, Oklahoma, purchased a new SUV for $28,000. He used the vehicle often; in fact, in less than nine months he had put 14,000 miles on it. A 24,000-mile, two-year warranty was still in effect for the power-train equipment, although David had to pay the first $100 of each repair cost.

After 16,500 miles and in month 11 of driving, the car experienced some severe problems with the transmission. David took the vehicle to the dealer for repairs. A week later he picked the car up, but some transmission problems remained. When David took the car back to the dealer, the dealer said that no further problems could be identified. David was sure that the problem was still there, and he was amazed that the dealer would not correct it. The dealer told him he would take no other action.

(a) Was David within his rights to take the car back for repairs? Explain why or why not.

(b) What logical steps would David follow if he continues to be dissatisfied with the dealer's unwillingness or inability to repair the car?

(c) Should David seek any help from the court system? If so, describe what he could do without spending money on attorney's fees.

Financial Math Questions

1. Diana Forsythe of Destin, Florida, must decide whether to buy or lease a car she has selected. She has negotiated a purchase price of $24,700 and could borrow the money to buy from her credit union by putting $3000 down and paying $515 per month for 48 months at 6.5% APR. Alternatively, she could lease the car for 48 months at $260 per month by paying a $3000 capital cost reduction and a $350 disposition fee on the car, which is projected to have a residual value of $8100 at the end of the lease. Use the Decision-Making Worksheet on page 217 to advise about Diana whether she should buy or lease the car.

2. Tom Parker of Fayetteville, Arkansas, has been shopping for a new car for several weeks. So far, he has negotiated a price of $27,000 on a model that carries a choice of a $2500 rebate or dealer financing at 2 percent APR. The dealer loan would require a $1000 down payment and a monthly payment of $542 for 48 months. Tom has also arranged for a loan from his bank with a 7 percent APR. Use the Decision-Making Worksheet on page 212 to advise Tom about whether he should use the dealer financing or take the rebate and use the financing from the bank.

Money Matters Continuing Cases

Victor and Maria Hernandez Buy a Third Car

The Hernandezes' older son, Hector, has reached the age at which it is time to consider purchasing a car for him. Victor and Maria have decided to give Maria's old car to Hector and buy a later-model used car for Maria.

1. What sources of information can Victor and Maria use to access price and reliability information on various makes and models of used cars?

2. What sources of used cars might be available to Victor and Maria, and what differences might exist among them?

3. How might Victor and Maria check out the cars in which he is most interested?

4. What strategies might Victor and Maria employ when they negotiate the price for the car they select?

The Johnsons Decide to Buy a Car

The Johnsons have decided to move out of their apartment and into some form of owned housing. Although they have not decided what type of housing they will buy, they know that Belinda will no longer be able to ride the bus to work. Recognizing this fact, they are in the market for another car. They have decided not to buy a new car, but think they have some room in their budget for a used car, given the raises each has received this year (see Table 3.3 on page 73). Harry and Belinda estimate that they could afford to spend about $3200 on a used car by making a down payment of $600 and financing the remainder over 24 months at $120 per month.

1. Make suggestions about how the $120 might be integrated into the Johnsons' budget (Table 3.3) without changing the amount left over at the end of each month. Harry and Belinda want to retain that extra money to help defray some of the added expenses of home ownership.

2. Which sources of used cars should they consider? Why?

3. Assume that the Johnsons have narrowed their choices to two cars. Both have air conditioning, AM-FM radio, and automatic transmission. The first car is an eight-year-old Chevrolet Lumina with 102,000 miles; it is being sold for $3400 by a private individual. The hatchback-style car has a six-cylinder engine, and the seller has kept records of all repairs, tune-ups, and oil changes. The car will need new tires in about six months. The second car is a nine-year-old, two-door Ford Taurus with 116,000 miles, being sold by a used-car dealership. It has a four-cylinder engine. Harry contacted the previous owner and found that the car was given in trade on a new car about three months ago. The previous owner cited no major mechanical problems but simply wanted a bigger car. The dealer is offering a written 30-day warranty on parts only. The asking price is $3200. Which car would you advise the Johnsons to buy? Why?

What Would You Recommend Now?

Now that you have read the chapter on automobiles and other major purchases, what would you recommend to George and Emily Cosgrove in the case at the beginning of the chapter regarding:

1. How to search for two vehicles to replace those destroyed?

2. Whether to replace Emily's vehicle with a new or used vehicle?

3. Whether to lease or buy a vehicle?

4. How to decide between a rebate and a special low-APR financing opportunity? Should they decide to purchase a new vehicle for Emily?

5. How to negotiate with the sellers of the vehicles?

Exploring the World Wide Web

To complete these exercises, go to the *Garman/Forgue* website at college.hmco.com/business/students. Under General Business, select the title of this text. Click on the Internet Exercises link for this chapter, and answer the questions that appear on the Web page.

1. Visit the website of the Consumer Information Center in Pueblo, Colorado, where you will find an on-line copy of the *Consumer Action Handbook*. Download or order the handbook. How might having the handbook help you obtain redress in the marketplace?

2. Visit the website of Intellichoice, where you will find a series of auto reports. Select a Face-Off Report on four new automobile makes and models that interest you. View the results of the on-line comparisons of these vehicles. What value do you see in such comparisons?

3. Visit the website of the Federal Reserve Board, where you will find a Web page entitled "Keys to Vehicle Leasing" that expands upon the information in this book. Use this information to generate a list of pros and cons of leasing versus purchasing a vehicle. By clicking on "sample leasing form" on this Web page, you can view and print a copy of the required vehicle leasing disclosure form.

4. Visit the website of *Consumer Reports* magazine and click on the "Autos" tab. You will be sent to a page containing tips on buying used cars. In what ways are the strategies similar and in what ways do they differ from the tips offered in this book for buying a new car?

5. Visit the *Consumer Reports* website. At the bottom of the page, click on "About Us." Review the information describing how the magazine staff goes about testing products to be rated. What steps are particularly important for ensuring that the ratings are as unbiased as possible?

6. Visit the website for the Bank Rate Monitor, where you will find information on vehicle loan interest rates around the United States. View the information for the lenders in a large city near your home. How do the rates in the city you selected compare with average national rates? Use the links provided for one or two vehicle manufacturer sites to compare bank lending rates with manufacturer financing offers. Why are the bank rates and the manufacturer rates not directly comparable? How should you calculate comparable rates?

7. Visit the website for the Kelly Blue Book. For a used vehicle you currently own or one you would like to own, determine its "used car retail value," "trade-in value," and "private party value." Why do the three values differ?

Visit the Garman/Forgue website . . .

@college.hmco.com/business/students

Under General Business, select *Personal Finance 8e.* There, among other valuable resources, you will find a complete glossary, ACE questions, links to help you complete the chapter exercises, and links to other personal finance sites.

Chapter 9

The Housing Expenditure

LEARNING OBJECTIVES

After reading this chapter, you should be able to:

1 **Decide** whether rented or owned housing is better both financially and personally.

2 **List** the key steps in the home-buying process.

3 **Describe** conventional and alternative ways to finance a home.

4 **Define** the major initial and continuing costs of buying a home.

5 **Identify** the most important aspects in the process of selling a home.

Libby Clark has worked for a major consumer electronics retailer for 12 years since graduating from college. Although she has worked in several different stores, she has been based in the Atlanta area and had begun thinking about buying a home there rather than renting. Then last month, Libby was offered and accepted a promotion to a deputy regional management position in the Denver area. In 45 days she assumes the new position, which represents a step toward her becoming a regional manager (although this possibility lies four or five years in the future). Libby's company has operations in four geographic regions, based in Atlanta, Denver, Minneapolis, and Boston. Regional managers may or may not be promoted from within their current region.

What would you recommend to Libby on the subject of the housing expenditure regarding:

1. Buying or renting housing in the Denver area?
2. Steps she should take prior to actively looking at homes?
3. Finding a home and negotiating the purchase?
4. The closing process in home buying?
5. Things to consider regarding the sale of her home—should she ultimately be promoted to a position in another of the four regions?

I f you are like most people, the bulk of your monthly expenditures will be spent on four major areas: housing, food, transportation, and insurance. Of these four outlays, housing will consume as much as 30 or 40 percent of your disposable income. As a result, your housing expenses represent one of the most important components of your personal financial planning.

This chapter begins with a discussion of the question of renting versus buying housing. It next describes a series of steps you should take when you buy housing. For most people, this purchase entails the use of a **mortgage loan**—that is, a loan to purchase real estate in which the property itself serves as collateral. Details about the various types of mortgage loans follow. The next section explains how to estimate total home-buying costs, including real estate taxes and insurance. The chapter concludes with a look at the process of selling a home. The important topic of real estate as an investment is covered in Chapter 17, Real Estate and Speculative Investments.

1 Decide whether rented or owned housing is better both financially and personally.

Deciding Whether to Rent or Buy Your Home

A wide variety of rented and owned housing is available in most areas of the United States. Whether to rent or buy depends on your preferences and what you can afford. In the short run, renting is usually less expensive than buying. In the long run, the opposite is true. Nearly 90 percent of all households headed by persons younger than age 25 are rental households, compared with slightly less than 20 percent of those headed by persons aged 55 to 64.

Golden Rules of

The Housing Expenditure

Financial success comes from learning the Golden Rules of personal finance and then putting what you have learned into practice. Make the following your money habits in the housing expenditure:

1. Buy a home as soon as it fits your budget and lifestyle so you can take advantage of special income tax deductions and the likelihood of substantial price appreciation over time.
2. Save the funds for a down payment to buy a home in a tax-sheltered Roth IRA account.
3. Get your finances in order before shopping for a new home by reducing debt, budgeting better, and clearing up anything that keeps you from having a high credit score.
4. Thoroughly explore mortgage loan sources and options to determine which one fits your needs best. If interest rates decline in the future, consider refinancing.
5. If you make a down payment of less than 20 percent on a home, cancel private mortgage insurance as soon as the equity in your home pushes the loan-to-value ratio to 80 percent.
6. Read your leases and all other real estate contracts before signing.

Rented Housing

There are several reasons people may choose to rent housing. For instance, they may not have the funds for the down payment and high monthly loan payments associated with buying a home. Also, they may prefer the easy mobility of renting or want to avoid many of the responsibilities associated with buying. Prospective renters need to consider the monthly rental fee and related expenses, the lease agreement and restrictions, and tenant rights.

Rent, Deposit, and Related Expenses.   **Rent** is the cost charged for using an apartment or other housing space. It is usually due on a specific day each month, with a late penalty being assessed if the tenant is tardy in making the payment. Other fees could be assessed for features such as use of a clubhouse and pool, exercise facilities, cable television, and space for storage and for parking.

   A **security deposit** is an amount given in advance to a landlord to pay for repairing the unit beyond the damage expected from normal wear and tear. It is often charged before the tenant moves in, along with prepayment of the first and last months' rent. Thus, an apartment with a monthly rent of $800 might require prepayment of the first and last months' rent ($1600 total), plus a security deposit (perhaps another $800).

Lease Agreement and Restrictions.   A **lease** is a contract specifying the legal responsibilities of both the tenant and the landlord. It identifies the amount of rent and security deposit, the length of the lease (typically one year), payment responsibility for utilities and repairs, penalties for late payment of rent, eviction procedures for nonpayment of rent, and procedures to follow when the lease ends. You may have few legal protections if you rent a unit without signing a lease. Leases often state whether the security deposit accumulates interest, how soon the unit must be inspected for cleanliness after the tenant vacates the premises, and when the security deposit (or the balance) will be forwarded to the tenant. Local laws may also address these issues.

Two types of leases exist. The first type provides for **periodic tenancy** (for example, week-to-week or month-to-month residency), where the agreement can be terminated by either of the parties if they give proper notice in advance (for example, one week or one month). Without such notice, the agreement stays in effect. This arrangement also typically applies in situations where no written lease is established. The second type of lease provides for **tenancy for a specific time** (for example, one year). When this period expires, the agreement terminates unless notice is given by both parties that the agreement will be renewed.

Lease agreements may contain a variety of restrictions that are legally binding on tenants. For example, pets may or may not be permitted; when they are permitted, a larger security deposit is often required. Excessive noise from home entertainment systems or parties may be prohibited as well. To protect other renters from overcrowding, a clause may limit the number of overnight guests. An important restriction applies to **subleasing** (leasing the property from the original tenant to another tenant). A tenant who moves before the lease expires may need to obtain the landlord's permission before someone else can take over the rental unit. The new tenant may even have to be approved, and the original tenant may retain some financial liability until the term of the original lease expires.

Tenant Rights.   Tenants have a number of legal rights under laws in most states and many local communities. Some important rights are as follows (page 233):

How to . . .

Make Sure Your Security Deposit Is Returned

If you leave a rental unit clean and undamaged, you have a legal right to a refund of your security deposit when you move out. Several steps will help ensure that you receive a full refund.

- Make a list of all damages and defects when you first move into the unit. Have the landlord sign this list.
- Maintain the unit and keep it clean.
- Notify the landlord promptly (in writing, if necessary) of any maintenance problems and malfunctions.
- Give proper written notice of your intention to move out at least 30 days in advance of the lease expiration.
- Make a written list of all damages and defects after moving out but prior to turning over the keys. Have the landlord sign this second list.
- Use certified mail (with a return receipt) to request the return of your security deposit and to inform the landlord of your new address.
- Use small claims court (see Chapter 8), if necessary, to obtain a court-ordered refund.

- Prohibitions against harassment (rent increases, eviction, or utility shut-off) for reporting building-code violations or otherwise exercising the tenant's legal rights.
- Assurances of some legally prescribed minimum standard of habitability for items such as running water, heat, and a working stove and the safety of access areas such as stairways.
- The right to make minor repairs and deduct the cost from the tenant's next rent payment. This right is subject to certain restrictions, such as giving sufficient prior written notification to the landlord.
- Prompt return of security deposits, with limits placed on the kinds of deductions that can be made. Landlords must explain specific reasons for deductions. In some states, laws require that interest be paid on security deposits.
- The right to file a lawsuit against a landlord for nonperformance. All states give this right to tenants. Such suits can be brought in a small claims court.

Owned Housing

Americans have historically favored single-family dwellings to satisfy their owned-housing needs. However, less expensive alternatives such as condominiums, cooperatives, manufactured housing, and mobile homes have increased in popularity.

Single-Family Dwellings.   A housing unit that is detached from other units constitutes a **single-family dwelling.** Buyers have many choices available for both new and existing homes with varying floor plans and home features. Some people prefer the modern kitchens and other features found in newer homes; others prefer the larger rooms, higher ceilings, and completed landscaping of older homes.

Condominiums and Cooperatives.   The terms *condominium* and *cooperative* describe forms of ownership rather than types of buildings. Such "owned apartments" are located in multi-unit structures, as well as in townhouses and rowhouses. These forms of ownership usually cost less than single-family dwellings, offer recreation facilities, and have reduced maintenance obligations.

With a **condominium** (or **condo**), the owner holds legal title to a specific housing unit within a multi-unit building or project and owns a proportionate share in the common grounds and facilities. The entire complex is run by the owners through a **homeowner's association.** Use of the property must be in accordance with the association's bylaws. Besides making monthly loan payments, the condominium owner must pay a monthly **homeowner's fee** that is established by the homeowner's association. This fee covers expenses related to the management of the common grounds and facilities and insurance on the building. Insurance on the owner's personal property and contents is the responsibility of the condominium unit owner. Some areas of concern for the potential buyer include potential increases in homeowner's fees and limited resale appeal of the unit.

With a **cooperative** (or **co-op**), the owner holds a share of the corporation that owns and manages a group of housing units. The value of this share is equivalent to the value of the owner's particular unit. The owner also holds a proportional interest in all common areas. A monthly fee for the cooperative covers the same types of items as does a condominium fee, but also includes an amount to cover the professional management of the complex and payments on the cooperative's mortgage debt. (The pro rata share for interest and property taxes is deductible on each shareholder's income tax return.)

Manufactured Housing and Mobile Homes.

Manufactured housing consists of fully or partially factory-built housing units designed to be transported (often in portions) to the home site. Final assembly and readying of the housing for occupancy occurs at the home site. **Mobile homes,** in contrast, are fully factory-assembled housing units that are designed to be towed on a frame with a trailer hitch. Mobile homes rarely appreciate in value like other forms of housing; in fact, they usually depreciate.

Who Pays More—Renters or Owners?

According to conventional wisdom, homeowners enjoy a financial advantage over renters when total housing costs are calculated over many years. Renters generally pay out less money in terms of annual cash flow, but owners usually see an increase in the value of their homes over time and receive some income tax advantages that eventually can sharply improve their financial situation.

Based on Cash Flow, Renters Appear to Win.

The Decision-Making Worksheet, "Should You Buy or Rent?", illustrates a comparison between a small condominium and an apartment with similar space and amenities. For the apartment, rent would total $800 per month. Assume you could buy the condominium for $120,000 by using $24,000 in savings as a down payment and borrowing the remaining $96,000 for 25 years at 8 percent interest. As the worksheet shows, renting would have a cash-flow cost of $8910 after a reduction for the interest that could be earned on your savings. Buying requires several expenses beyond the monthly mortgage payment, including a $480 annual homeowner's fee. In this case, the cash-flow cost of buying is $12,216, or $3306 more than renting.

After Taxes and Appreciation, Owners Usually Win.

To make the comparison more accurate, we need to consider the tax and appreciation aspects of the two options. Both mortgage interest and real estate property taxes qualify as income tax deductions. If you buy the condominium, $1251 of the $8891 in annual mortgage loan payments during the first year will go toward the principal of the debt and the remainder, $7640 ($8891 − $1251), will go toward interest. If you are in the 25 percent marginal tax bracket, your taxes would be reduced by $1910 ($7640 × 0.25) as a result of deducting the mortgage interest and by $500 ($2000 × 0.25) as a result of deducting the real estate tax. Condominiums also have a likelihood of appreciation, or increase, in the home's value. A conservative assumption would be that the condominium will increase in value by 2.5 percent per year. A home valued at $120,000 would, therefore, be worth $123,000 ($120,000 × 1.025) after one year, a gain of $3000. If you rent, however, you would pay $240 ($960 × 0.25) in income taxes on the interest on the amount in your savings account ($24,000) not used for your down payment. In this case, buying is financially better than renting by approximately $3595 ($9150 − $5555).

2 List the key steps in the home-buying process.

The Steps of Home Buying

The steps in the home-buying process closely resemble the planned buying steps outlined in Chapter 8. It may take several weeks or months to find a home that represents

Decision-Making Worksheet

Should You Buy or Rent?

This worksheet can be used to estimate whether you would be better off renting housing or buying. If you are renting an apartment and planning to buy a house, qualitative differences will enter into your decision. This worksheet will put the financial picture into focus. A similar worksheet can be found on the Ginnie Mae website at www.ginniemae.gov.YPTH/rent_vs_buy/rent_vs_buy_calc.

	Example Amounts		Your Figures	
	Rent	Buy	Rent	Buy
Annual cash-flow considerations				
Annual rent ($800/month) or				
mortgage payments ($740.95/month)*	$9,600	$ 8,891	_____	_____
Property and liability insurance	270	525	_____	_____
Private mortgage insurance	N/A	0	N/A	_____
Real estate taxes	0	2,000	_____	_____
Maintenance	0	320	_____	_____
Other housing fees	0	480	_____	_____
Less interest earned on funds				
not used for down payment (at 4%)	960	N/A	_____	N/A
Cash-Flow Cost for the Year	**$8,910**	**$12,216**	_____	_____
Tax and appreciation considerations				
Less principal† repaid on the mortgage loan	N/A	1,251	N/A	_____
Plus tax on interest earned on funds not used	240	N/A	_____	N/A
for down payment (25% marginal tax bracket)				
Less tax savings due to deductibility of	N/A	1,910	N/A	_____
mortgage interest‡ (25% marginal tax bracket)				
Less tax savings due to deductibility of real estate	N/A	500	N/A	_____
property taxes (25% marginal tax bracket)				
Less appreciation on the dwelling				
(2.5% annual rate)	N/A	3,000	N/A	_____
Net Cost for the Year	**$9,150**	**$ 5,555**	_____	_____

*Calculated from Table 9.3.
†Calculated according to the method illustrated in Table 9.1
‡Mortgage interest tax savings equal total mortgage payments minus principal repaid multiplied by the marginal tax rate.

a good value and offers potential for price appreciation. Special attention will also need to be paid to five steps:

1. Getting your own finances in order

2. Prequalifying for a mortgage

3. Negotiating a purchase

4. Applying for a mortgage loan

5. Signing your name on closing day

Tax Considerations and Consequences

Buying Housing

Home ownership makes you eligible for three big tax breaks.

1. **Mortgage interest and real estate taxes are tax-deductible on federal (and most state) income tax returns.** These amounts usually exceed the IRS's standard deduction (see Chapter 4). You can then take advantage of even more deduction opportunities that are available to taxpayers who itemize.

2. **The profits made by selling a home can be tax-free.** If you sell a home for more than you originally paid, you have a *capital gain.* Gains are ordinarily taxable but homeowners can avoid paying taxes on gains of up to $500,000 if married and filing jointly, and up to $250,000 if single. To qualify, the home must have been owned and used as the principal residence for two of the last five years prior to the date of the sale. In the first few years of home ownership, any appreciation likely will be offset by the anticipated sales commission. This explains the advice that you should not buy a home unless you know you will live in it for three years.

3. **You can save the funds to buy a home in a tax-sheltered account.** Individuals can use Roth IRAs (see Chapter 18) to save for retirement. Once the account is five years old, as much as $10,000 may be withdrawn tax- and penalty-free, provided that a qualifying, first-time home buyer uses the funds for home-buying costs. This mechanism even allows parents or grandparents to make withdrawals from their Roth IRAs to help young family members buy their first home.

Getting Your Finances in Order

You will need to be financially ready when the time comes to buy your first (or any other) home. Most people know they need to prepare to make a down payment of as much as 20 percent. In addition, they must be ready to pay costs associated with obtaining financing, moving costs, purchasing new furnishings, and, possibly, painting and remodeling. Making three additional preparations can smooth out the process considerably: accurately estimating monthly housing costs, fitting housing costs into your budget, and doing a credit check-up.

Accurately Estimate Your Monthly Housing Costs. It is very important to have an accurate estimate of what you will have to pay on a monthly basis for your new home. Fortunately, that task is made much easier by accessing the resources available on the Internet.

1. Start by choosing the type of home you would like to own and the neighborhood in which you would like to live.

2. Go to the www.realtor.com website to search for housing that matches your interests. You will be able to estimate the selling price of similar housing and, by subtracting your likely down payment, estimate the amount you will need to borrow.

3. Go to the www.bankrate.com website to estimate the current interest rates on mortgage loans in your market.

4. Use the calculator at www.bankrate.com to estimate the monthly payment for a loan of the amount you need at the prevailing interest rates.

5. Add an additional 30 percent to the monthly payment on the loan for such things as homeowner's insurance, property taxes, maintenance, and upkeep.

Fit the Housing Costs into Your Budget. Once you have an estimate of the monthly costs associated with buying a home, you will need to see how these costs will fit into your budget. You may need to revise your goals by downsizing the type of home you desire or choosing housing in another neighborhood. If so, adjust the estimate of your monthly housing costs and fit these new costs into your budget.

Do a Credit Check-up. Your credit history can make or break your chances of buying the house of your dreams. Definitely obtain copies of your credit report and your credit scores from all three major credit reporting agencies (lenders use all three) about six months in advance of buying housing; you can then clear up any errors before the loan application process begins. See pages 162–163 for the steps to take to correct errors in your credit report. Most people can improve their credit scores by correcting history errors and rearranging credit accounts. See www.myFICIO.com for suggestions.

Prequalifying for a Mortgage

At this stage, you should start looking into whether you would qualify for a mortgage loan given the price range of homes that you desire and your intended down payment.

Did You Know? . . .

The Income Needed to Qualify for a Mortgage

The table below will give you a quick idea of how much income you need to buy a home at a certain price using a front-end ratio of 28 percent. The illustration is for a 30-year loan with a 20 percent down payment. For each home price, the top figure in each row shows the monthly payment for principal, interest, real estate taxes, and homeowner's insurance for the interest rates; the bottom figure shows the required gross annual income to qualify for the loan. For example, a 7 percent loan on a $180,000 home requires a monthly payment of $1,107 plus an income of $47,442 to qualify. Taxes and insurance are assumed to be 1 percent of the purchase price (divided by 12 months). Visit the *Garman/Forgue* website to perform these calculations for a variety of home prices and interest rates.

Interest Rate	Price of Home					
	$120,000	$150,000	$180,000	$210,000	$240,000	$270,000
5.0	615	769	924	1,076	1,230	1,386
	26,357	32,946	39,600	46,124	52,714	59,400
6.0	676	845	1,014	1,183	1,452	1,521
	28,971	36,214	43,458	50,699	51,834	65,187
7.0	739	924	1,107	1,293	1,478	1,660
	31,671	39,589	47,442	55,424	63,342	71,163
8.0	804	1,005	1,206	1,407	1,608	1,809
	34,457	43,071	51,687	60,300	68,914	77,530
9.0	872	1,090	1,308	1,526	1,744	1,962
	37,371	46,714	56,058	65,399	74,742	84,087
10.0	942	1,178	1,413	1,648	1,884	2,120
	40,371	50,464	60,558	70,649	80,742	90,837

You will also need to make a preliminary decision about the time period of the loan and the choice between a fixed or variable interest rate (topics covered later in this chapter). One goal is to find the lowest APR for loans available to you. A good place to start is with the financial institutions where you have your checking and savings accounts. In addition, you can search for low-rate loans at www.bankrate.com. Other helpful information can be found at the websites for the U.S. Department of Housing and Urban Development (www.hud.gov/buying/) and the Federal National Mortgage Association (www.homepath.com).

Once you have an idea of the interest rate you probably will pay, you can consult a variety of lenders to determine whether you would qualify for a mortgage in the amount you would like. Lenders use two rules of thumb to estimate the maximum affordability of housing expenses: the front-end ratio and the back-end ratio.

- The **front-end ratio** compares the total annual expenditures for housing (the principal and interest on the mortgage plus the real estate taxes and insurance) with the loan applicant's gross annual income. Generally, the total annual expenditures should not exceed 25 to 29 percent of gross annual income. Applying a 28 percent front-end ratio, a young couple with a combined gross annual income of $66,000 could qualify for a mortgage requiring total annual expenditures of less than $18,480 (0.28 × $66,000), or $1540 per month.

- The **back-end ratio** compares the total of all monthly debt payments (for the mortgage, real estate taxes, and insurance, plus auto loans and other debts) with gross monthly income. Generally, lenders require that monthly debt payments do not exceed 33 to 41 percent of gross monthly income. Applying a back-end ratio of 36 percent, the same couple could qualify for any loan that does not result in total monthly debt repayments exceeding $1980 (their monthly income of $5500 × 0.36).

Dual-earner couples should be cautious about applying these ratios. Many young couples base their housing affordability on their combined incomes. This locks them into a full-time, dual-income lifestyle once they have purchased a home. Family obligations may later disrupt their ability or willingness to continue that lifestyle. They might be better off gauging their housing affordability on just one income or on part-time work for the second income.

Did You Know? . . .

The Impact of Your Existing Debt on Your Ability to Qualify for a Mortgage

Lenders use both front-end and back-end ratios when setting limits on how much a home buyer can borrow. Using a front-end ratio, a couple earning a combined $66,000 per year could probably afford a modest starter home. However, to qualify based on the back-end ratio, they could owe only an additional $440 ($1980 − $1540) on all their other debts. Student loan debts, car loans, and credit card payments could easily exceed this amount.

Not surprisingly, qualifying based on the mortgage debt alone (the front-end ratio) is easier for many young couples. At the same time, the back-end ratio provides a higher hurdle because of the other debts many young people carry today. If you plan on buying a house someday, you need to be very careful about how much debt you take on while in school.

Negotiating a Purchase

Once you have your finances in order and have received assurances that you can qualify for a mortgage, you can start looking for a home in earnest. Sellers generally put a price on the property that is 5 to 15 percent higher than the amount that they actually expect to receive. Therefore, you probably should make an offer to buy that is somewhat lower than the asking price. Perhaps $10,000 to $30,000 is at stake here.

Make an Offer to Buy.   The written offer to purchase real estate is called a **purchase offer** (or an **offer to purchase**). Of course, you will specify a price, but other aspects of the sale may be included in your offer as well. Examples of conditions you might want to list include the following: seller-paid termite and radon inspections; certification of the plumbing, heating, cooling, and electrical systems; inclusion of the living room drapes and kitchen appliances; ability to obtain suitable financing. When you make an offer, you need to give the seller some **earnest money** as a deposit; one or two percent should be sufficient to show your good faith when making an offer to purchase the seller's property. This money is returned if the seller rejects the offer.

Respond to a Counteroffer.   Most home sellers do not accept the first offer from a buyer. Instead, they usually make a **counteroffer,** which is a legal offer to sell (or buy) a home at a different price and perhaps with different conditions from those outlined in the original offer. You can assume that a seller who is willing to make a counteroffer may also be willing to sell at a slightly lower price. Thus, if you make a counteroffer falling between the two prices, a sale will usually result. Of course, if you push the seller too far, you risk having the seller back out of the negotiations altogether. Plus, while you are negotiating, the seller could be receiving offers from other prospective buyers. In some hot real estate markets, buyers compete with each other by offering sellers "more" than the asking price. In such a scenario, the highest bidder wins.

Sign a Purchase Contract.   A **purchase contract** (or **sales contract**) is the formal legal document that outlines the actual agreement that results from the real estate negotiations. It includes the final negotiated price and a list of conditions that the seller has agreed to accept. It is wise to use preprinted forms available from real estate professionals and attorneys for the purchase contract because they often include protective clauses (for example, contingency clauses, as discussed below). When the purchase contract is signed, the seller keeps the earnest money as a deposit. In many cases, the seller keeps the home on the market to be open to additional offers. However, the home must be sold to the person whose offer was accepted unless the potential buyer fails to meet conditions agreed to in the contract. The most commonly seen failure on the buyer's part is being unable to secure appropriate financing. Thus, the home is not genuinely "off the market" until all details of the sale are completed. At that point, the earnest money given to the seller will be applied to the purchase of the home.

You will want to make sure that your earnest money is protected by a **contingency clause** in the purchase offer. Such a provision stipulates that the seller must refund the earnest money if the buyer cannot obtain satisfactory financing within a specified time period, usually 30 days. This clause protects you in case you cannot obtain a loan on the property. Another contingency clause should allow the buyer to opt out of the deal if the home fails to pass inspection. Buyers considering a previously owned home should order a professional inspection of the property for termite infestation, wood rot, and radon gas, as well as a general inspection of all aspects of its condition. Of course, if you simply change your mind about buying at this point, you will forfeit your earnest money and may be sued for damages.

Did You Know? . . .

The Role of Real Estate Agents

A **real estate broker** (**agent**) is a person licensed by a state to provide advice and assistance, for a fee, to buyers or sellers of real estate. Real estate brokers who are members of the National Association of Realtors often use the registered trademark of **Realtor®** to describe themselves. Brokers typically earn a commission of 5 to 7 percent on the sale price of a home. The seller—not the buyer—usually pays this commission. **Flat-fee** brokers, who charge a flat fee for their services rather than a percentage-based commission, are also available in most real estate markets.

Almost any agent can show you housing that is **listed** (under contract with the seller and the broker) by the realty firm. In addition, many communities have a **multiple-listing** (or **open-listing**) **service**, which is an information and referral network among real estate brokers allowing properties listed with a particular broker to be shown by all other brokers.

Buyers should understand that a real estate agent can play three possible roles. The **listing agent** is the party with whom the seller signs the listing agreement. The listing agent advertises the property, shows it to prospective buyers, and assists the seller in negotiations. He or she receives a commission when the home is sold and owes the seller undivided loyalty. A **selling agent** is any real estate agent that seeks out buyers for a home. Obviously, listing agents play this role, but any real estate agent can search for buyers for a property.

Most home buyers use a real estate agent in their search for a home. They should understand, however, that the agent's legal obligation is to the party who will pay his or her fee or commission (generally the seller). Buyers should be wary of this potential conflict of interest, and hire their own broker if they need such services. That is, home buyers who want an agent to represent their interests should obtain the services of a **buyer's agent.** This person will serve as the buyer's representative in the real estate negotiations and transaction.

Why is the distinction among the three types of agents important? Consider the example of a buyer who has asked a selling agent to help him find a house. During negotiations, the potential buyer decides to offer $175,000 for a house with an asking price of $189,000 but tells the selling agent that he would be willing to go as high as $180,000. The selling agent would then be legally obligated to tell the seller about this $180,000 figure.

Applying for a Mortgage Loan

Only after you sign a purchase contract do you formally apply for a mortgage loan on the specific home you have selected. The financial institution usually approves or turns down this request within a few days. About one-half of all mortgage loans today are arranged through a mortgage broker. A **mortgage broker** is an individual or company that acts as an intermediary between borrowers and lenders. In other words, it helps lenders find borrowers and borrowers find lenders. The broker might also negotiate with lenders to obtain the best possible financing deal for the borrower. The fee charged by the broker may be paid by either the lender or the borrower. If this fee is paid by the lender, the broker legally represents the lender. If it is paid by the borrower, the broker legally represents the borrower. Thus, if you want the broker to work to find you the lowest possible rate, you should be prepared to pay for the service.

When you apply for a mortgage, the lender must give you a **good-faith estimate** of all the costs associated with the loan, including the annual percentage rate, application and processing fees, and any other charges that must be paid when the deal is legally consummated. In addition, the loan applicant must receive a settlement information booklet that explains these details. You do not want to be surprised at the last minute with an unexpected fee of $1000 or $5000. More information on these disclosures can be found by going to www.hud.gov and searching for the keyword "RESPA".

Did You Know? . . .

Your Credit Score Affects the Mortgage Rate You Will Pay

Mortgage lenders charge interest rates based on your credit score. Here are illustrative credit scores and the corresponding mortgage loan interest rates.

Credit Score	APR
720–850	5.7%
700–719	5.9%
675–699	6.4%
620–674	7.6%
560–619	8.5%
500–559	9.3%

Loan applicants whose scores are lower than desired will be turned down or, more commonly, referred to a lender in the **sub-prime market,** which serves higher-risk applicants. Many individuals who are placed in this market are happy to have obtained a loan. However, they may fail to realize that they would have qualified for loans at standard rates if they had searched more extensively and taken steps to improve their credit scores.

Your exact interest rate may be the current rate at the time of application or the rate in force at the time of closing. If you expect rates to rise between the time you apply for the loan and the actual closing, you may wish to pay a small fee to obtain a **mortgage lock-in.** This agreement includes a lender's promise to hold a certain interest rate for a specified period of time, such as 60 days. It may be part of, but is not the same as, a **loan commitment** (or **loan preapproval**), which is a lender's promise to grant a loan.

Signing Your Name on Closing Day

To complete the sale, the buyer, the seller, and their chosen representatives generally gather in the lender's office for a meeting called the **closing.** At the closing, all required documents are signed and payments are made. A key document is the **uniform settlement statement,** which lists all of the costs and fees to be paid at the closing. You have the right to see this statement one business day before the closing so that you can avoid surprises and can compare the fees with the good-faith estimate provided earlier. Challenge any discrepancies. Illustrative closing costs are explained in detail later in this chapter.

Financing a Home

3 Describe conventional and alternative ways to finance a home.

People often must rent housing for five years or more before they are able to save enough to make a down payment to purchase a home. Some couples postpone having children, while other people cut back on entertainment and vacations and put off making major purchases. You sometimes can prepare financially for home ownership by renting a home with an option to purchase it. Ultimately, however, you must become knowledgeable about mortgage loans and learn how they are used to purchase a home.

Mortgage Loans

Mortgage loans are available from depository institutions (described in Chapters 5 and 7) and mortgage finance companies. In exchange for the loan, the lender (*mortgagee*) has a **lien** on the real estate—that is, the legal right to take and hold property or to sell it in the event the borrower (*mortgagor*) defaults on the loan. **Foreclosure** is a process in which the lender sues the borrower to prove default and asks the court to order the sale of the property to pay the debt.

The term *mortgage* receives its name from the concept of **amortization,** which is the process of gradually paying off a loan through a series of periodic payments to a lender. Each payment is allocated in two ways. First, a portion goes to pay the simple interest on the debt based on a monthly interest rate applied to the outstanding debt. The remainder goes to repay the **principal,** which is the debt remaining from the original amount borrowed. As the principal is paid down, increasingly smaller portions of the payments will be required to pay interest while payments devoted to the principal grow larger. These changes in the allocation of the payment are illustrated in Figure 9.1.

Note the slow decline in the amount of each monthly payment going toward interest. Most of each monthly payment during the early years of a mortgage loan is allocated to interest because the debt outstanding remains very high. Table 9.1 shows the interest and principal payment amounts for the first three months of a $100,000, 30-year, 8 percent mortgage loan. For the first month, $666.67 goes for interest costs, and only $67.09 goes toward retirement of the principal of the loan. Table 9.2 provides a partial **amortization schedule** for the same loan. When you take out a mortgage loan, you will receive a full amortization schedule for each month of the loan listing all the monthly payments, the portions that will go toward interest and principal, and the debt remaining after each payment is made.

Many years must typically pass before the monthly payment significantly reduces the outstanding balance of the loan. At any point, the amount that has been paid off (including the down payment) plus any appreciation in the value of the home represents the homeowner's **equity** (the dollar value of the home in excess of the amount owed on it). Figure 9.2 (page 244) illustrates the build-up of equity in a home resulting from reductions in the amount owed and the growth in the home's value. Note that the

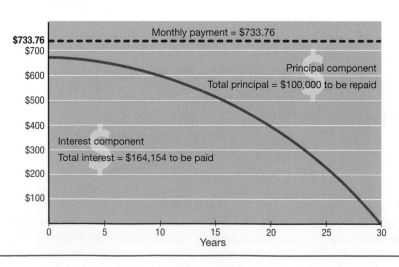

Figure 9.1

Change in Principal and Interest Components of the Monthly Payment on a $100,000 Mortgage Loan at an 8 Percent Interest Rate for 30 Years

Table 9.1 Amortization Effects of Monthly Payment of $733.76 on a $100,000, 30-Year Mortgage Loan at 8 Percent

First Month

$100,000 × 8% × $\frac{1}{12}$	=	$666.67	Interest payment
$733.76 − 666.67	=	67.09	Principal repayment
$100,000 − 67.09	=	$99,932.91	Balance due

Second Month

$99,932.91 × 8% × $\frac{1}{12}$	=	$666.21	Interest payment
$733.76 − 666.21	=	67.55	Principal repayment
$99,932.91 − 67.55	=	$99,865.36	Balance due

Third Month

$99,865.36 × 8% × $\frac{1}{12}$	=	$665.76	Interest payment
$733.76 − 665.76	=	68.00	Principal repayment
$99,865.36 − 68.00	=	$99,797.36	Balance due

Table 9.2 Partial Amortization Schedule for a $100,000, 30-Year (360-Payment) Mortgage Loan at 8 Percent

Payment Number (Month)	Monthly Payment Amount	Portion to Principal Repayment	Portion to Interest	Total of Payments to Date	Outstanding Loan Balance
1	$733.76	$67.09	$666.67	$ 733.76	$99,932.91
2	733.76	67.55	666.21	1,467.52	99,865.36
3	733.76	68.00	665.76	2,201.28	99,797.36
12	733.76	72.19	661.57	8,805.12	99,164.63
24	733.76	78.18	655.58	17,610.24	98,259.94
60	733.76	99.30	634.46	44,025.60	95,069.85
120	733.76	147.95	585.81	88,051.20	87,724.70
180	733.76	220.42	513.34	132,076.80	76,781.55
240	733.76	328.38	405.38	176,102.40	60,477.95
300	733.76	489.25	244.51	220,128.00	36,188.09
360	733.76	728.90	4.86	264,153.60	0

bulk of the increase in equity is due to increases in the market value of the home. Additional payments can be directed toward the principal at any time to reduce the amount owed, increase equity, and reduce the eventual total amount of interest paid on the loan.

Factors Affecting the Monthly Payment on a Mortgage

Three factors affect the monthly payment on a mortgage loan: the amount borrowed, the interest rate charged, and the length of maturity of the loan.

The Amount Borrowed.   The payment schedule illustrated in Table 9.3 (page 245) gives the monthly payment required for each $1000 of a mortgage loan at various interest rates. Using this table, you can calculate the monthly payment for mortgage loans of different amounts. For example, the $100,000 mortgage loan described earlier (8 percent

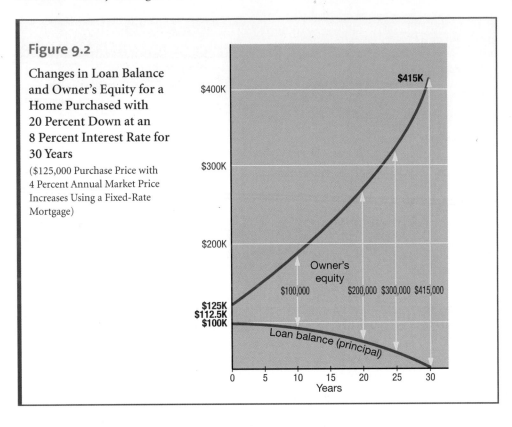

Figure 9.2

Changes in Loan Balance and Owner's Equity for a Home Purchased with 20 Percent Down at an 8 Percent Interest Rate for 30 Years

($125,000 Purchase Price with 4 Percent Annual Market Price Increases Using a Fixed-Rate Mortgage)

for 30 years) costs $7.3376 per $1000 per month. Thus, 100 × $7.3376 equals $733.76. If the loan amount was $120,000, then the monthly payment would be $880.40 (120 × $7.3376).

The amount borrowed is determined by the lender's desired **loan-to-value ratio,** which is calculated by dividing the maximum amount the lender will loan on a piece of property by the property's purchase price. The standard loan-to-value ratio is 80 percent—that is, a 20 percent down payment is required. Thus, a home with a value of $125,000 for which a lender desires the standard loan-to-value ratio of 0.80 will have a maximum loan of $100,000 (0.80 × 125,000) and the lender would require a down payment of $25,000. Making a down payment that is larger than required lowers the borrower's monthly payments. For example, a down payment of 30 percent, or $37,500, would lower the monthly payment on the loan to $642.04 [$7.3376 × ($125,000 − $37,500) ÷ 1000]. A smaller loan also carries lower total interest costs and may qualify for an interest rate that is perhaps 0.5 percentage point lower. In that case, the payment for the same loan would amount to only $611.81 [$6.9921 × ($125,000 ÷ $37,500) ÷ 1000].

Low-and moderate-income families often find it difficult to save the 20 percent down payment required by lenders. FHA and VA loans (discussed later in this chapter) provide some opportunity for low down payments but are not available to all borrowers or on all homes. Other programs have been developed for lower-income buyers and people buying homes for the first time. Lenders in your area can provide you with information about programs that target these special-needs groups. Through such programs, it may be possible to buy a home with a low (or no) down payment and at a low, government-subsidized interest rate.

Table 9.3 Estimating Mortgage Loan Payments for Principal and Interest (Monthly Payment per $1000 Borrowed)				
Interest Rate (%)	**Payment Period (Years)**			
	15	**20**	**25**	**30**
4.5	$ 7.6499	$6.3265	$5.5583	$5.0669
5.0	7.9079	6.5996	5.8459	5.3682
5.5	8.1708	6.8789	6.1409	5.6779
6.0	8.4386	7.1643	6.4430	5.9955
6.5	8.7111	7.4557	6.7521	6.3207
7.0	8.9883	7.7530	7.0678	6.6530
7.5	9.2701	8.0559	7.3899	6.9921
8.0	9.5565	8.3644	7.7182	7.3376
8.5	9.8474	8.6782	8.0523	7.6891
9.0	10.1427	8.9973	8.3920	8.0462
9.5	10.4422	9.3213	8.7370	8.4085
10.0	10.7461	9.6502	9.0870	8.7757

Note: To use this table to figure a monthly mortgage payment, divide the amount borrowed by 1000 and multiply by the appropriate figure in the table for the interest rate and time period of the loan. For example, an $80,000 loan for 20 years at 9 percent would require a payment of $719.78 [($80,000 ÷ 1000) × 8.9973]; over 30 years, it would require a payment of $643.70 [($80,000 ÷ 1000) × 8.0462]. For calculations for different interest rates, visit the *Garman/Forgue* website.

The Interest Rate.   The higher the interest rate, the higher the monthly payment on a mortgage loan (see Table 9.3). For example, a $733.76 monthly payment is required for a $100,000 mortgage loan taken out for 30 years at 8 percent. If the interest rate were 9.5 percent, the monthly mortgage payment would be $840.85 (100 × $8.4085), an increase of more than $100. The effects are even greater when you consider the total payback and the total interest paid over the life of the loan. The 8 percent loan will have total payments of $264,153.60 (360 × $733.76) with total interest of $164,153.60 ($264,153.60 − $100,000.00). For the 9.5 percent loan, total payments are $302,706.00 (360 × $840.85) and total interest is $202,706.00 ($302,706.00 − $100,000.00). Thus, the added cost for the 30-year loan at 9.5 percent is $38,552.40 over the life of the loan.

Some homeowners may find it advantageous to refinance a mortgage when interest rates decline. In **mortgage refinancing,** a new mortgage is obtained to pay off and replace an existing mortgage. Most often it is undertaken to lower the monthly payment on the home by taking out a loan with a lower interest rate. It may also be possible to borrow more than the current balance on the existing loan, thereby utilizing some of the equity built up in the home. Homeowners sometimes use part of this equity to pay off credit card debts and vehicle loans. As a result they lower their overall interest rate and can deduct the resulting interest. But the downside is that they have traded short-term debt for long-term debt. They will want to pay this debt off as soon as possible. Borrowers refinancing for more than the amount owed should understand that rebuilding the equity to its previous level may take many years.

Length of Maturity of the Loan.   Table 9.4 (page 247) illustrates the relationships among maturity length, monthly payment, and interest cost for a $100,000 loan at various interest rates. On the one hand, for loans with the same interest rate, a longer term of repayment results in a smaller payment. On the other hand, more total interest is paid over the longer repayment time period despite the lower monthly payment. For

Decision-Making Worksheet

Should You Refinance Your Mortgage?

The example here illustrates how to determine whether refinancing your mortgage is a wise choice. The original mortgage for $89,000 was obtained ten years ago at an 11 percent interest rate for 30 years. The monthly payment is $847.57. After ten years the principal owed has declined to $82,113.67. If interest rates for new mortgages have declined to 9 percent, the owner could take out a new mortgage at the lower rate. Borrowing $82,113.67 for 20 years at 9 percent saves approximately $109 per month ($847.57 − $738.80). Note, however, that refinancing brings up-front costs, including a possible prepayment penalty on the old mortgage and closing costs for the new mortgage. The question then becomes, Will these costs more than offset the monthly savings gained with a lower payment?

The following worksheet provides a means for estimating whether refinancing offers an advantage. It compares the future value of the reduced monthly payments (line 5) with the future value of the money used to pay the up-front costs of refinancing (line 8). The homeowner would need to estimate the number of months he or she expects to own the home after refinancing. Given an estimate of four years in this example, the net savings would be $743 (subtracting line 8 from line 5), and refinancing would benefit the owner. A similar worksheet can be found at cgi.money.cnn.com/tools/cutmortgage/cutmortgage.html.

Decision Factor	Example	Your Figures
1. Current monthly payment	$ 848	_____
2. New monthly payment	739	_____
3. Annual saving (line 1 − line 2 x 12)	1,308	_____
4. Additional years you expect to live in the house	4	_____
5. Future value of an account balance after 4 years if the annual savings were invested at 3% after taxes (using Appendix Table A.3)	5,472	_____
6. Prepayment penalty on current loan (if any)	1,000	_____
7. Points and fees for new loan	3,200	_____
8. Future value of an account balance after 4 years if the prepayment penalty and closing costs ($4200) had been invested instead at 3% after taxes (using Appendix Table A.1)	4,729	_____
9. Net saving after 49 months (line 5 − line 8)	$ 743	_____

example, the monthly payment on an 8 percent loan is $836 for 20 years but only $734 for 30 years. When the loan is paid back in 20 years, the total interest costs are much lower ($100,600 rather than $164,200, for a savings of $63,600).

Some borrowers opt for a mortgage loan with a comparatively short 15-year maturity. Its advantages include a faster build-up of equity, lower total interest, and a quicker payoff of the loan. These advantages can also be gained with a 20- or 30-year mortgage by simply paying additional amounts toward the principal during the time period of the loan. It is generally wise to take a longer repayment period even if you plan to pay off the loan in 15 (or fewer) years. With that strategy, the faster payoff is optional rather than mandatory.

Table 9.4 Monthly Payment and Total Interest to Repay a $100,000 Loan				
Length of Loan	**Interest Rate (%)**			
	6	**7**	**8**	**9**
30 years	$ 600	$ 665	$ 734	$ 805
	116,000	139,400	164,200	189,800
25 years	644	707	772	839
	93,200	112,100	131,600	151,700
20 years	716	775	836	900
	71,800	86,000	100,600	116,000
15 years	844	899	955	1,014
	51,900	61,800	71,900	82,500

Note: Figures are rounded. The top figure in each pair is the monthly payment, and the bottom figure is the total interest paid to the nearest $100.

The Conventional Mortgage Loan

A **conventional mortgage** is a fixed-rate, fixed-term, fixed-payment mortgage loan. The conventional mortgage has been the standard mortgage used in the United States for more than 65 years. Borrowers like conventional mortgages because they are so predictable. For example, a $100,000 loan could be granted at an 8 percent annual interest rate over a period of 30 years with a fixed monthly payment of $733.76.

The Adjustable-Rate Mortgage Loan

With an **adjustable-rate mortgage (ARM)**—sometimes called a **variable-rate mortgage**—the borrower's interest rate fluctuates according to some index of interest rates based on the rising or falling cost of credit in the economy. As a consequence, the monthly payment could increase or decrease, usually on an annual basis, but sometimes monthly. Borrowers with ARMs should always determine the "worst case" scenario for interest rate increases under their loan contract and calculate the monthly payment that would result. With an ARM, the risk of interest rate changes is assumed by the borrower, not the lender. As a result, published ARM rates are usually 1 to 3 percentage points below conventional mortgage rates. Lenders sometimes offer a **teaser rate** to encourage people to borrow using an ARM. Such a loan will carry an interest rate for the first year or so that may be 1 to 3 percentage points below the regular ARM loan rates, a substantial savings over a conventional mortgage. Borrowers using an ARM with a teaser rate must be prepared for the higher monthly payments that will occur when interest rates rise in the future.

Most ARMs have **interest-rate caps** that limit the amount by which the interest rate can increase (perhaps no more than 2 percent per year and no more than 5 percent over the life of the loan). **Payment caps,** in contrast, limit the amount by which the payment can vary on an ARM. Having a loan with a payment cap but without an equivalent interest-rate cap is an invitation to **negative amortization,** which occurs when monthly payments are actually smaller than necessary to pay the interest. This practice will result in a principal loan balance that rises, rather than falls.

Five variations of ARMs exist.

1. The *convertible adjustable-rate mortgage* allows conversion of an ARM to a fixed-rate mortgage, usually during years 2 through 5 of the ARM.

2. The *reduction-option loan* begins as a fixed-rate loan that allows a one-time optional adjustment in the interest rate to current rates, perhaps during years 2 through 6 of the original loan. If rates drop, you can take the option and reduce your payments. If rates do not drop, you simply choose not to exercise your option.

3. With the *price-level-adjusted mortgage,* the initial rate is extremely low, perhaps 4 percent, and amortization occurs. The interest rate and monthly payment are subsequently adjusted according to the inflation rate over the years. Over a 20-year period, for example, the monthly payment might double. In such a case, the borrower would hope that his or her income keeps pace with inflation, maintaining the affordability of the loan payments.

4. With the *two-step mortgage,* the interest is adjusted just once, usually at the end of the seventh year. Thus, in the first step, the mortgage has the original interest rate; the second step applies the current rate available in the market at the end of the seventh year. This option offers the benefit of a fixed monthly payment in the early years of loan repayment.

5. With a *hybrid loan,* the borrower pays a fixed interest rate for perhaps five or seven years; the rate becomes adjustable after this period. These loans carry interest rates that are between the current conventional mortgage and ARM rates. Borrowers who know that they will be moving out of the home during the fixed-rate years of the loan find hybrid loans attractive because of their low rates with no risk of rising payments.

Alternative Mortgage Loans

A number of new mortgage options have emerged in response to interest rate fluctuations and increasing costs for housing. In general, most alternative lending approaches aim to keep the monthly payment as low as possible, especially in the early years of the loan for first-time and lower-income buyers. The lower payments also permit borrowers to purchase larger, more expensive homes than they could afford with a traditional loan.

Graduated-Payment Mortgage.   With a **graduated-payment mortgage,** smaller-than-normal payments are required in the early years but gradually increase to larger-than-normal payments in later years. The interest rate is fixed, but payments early in the life of the mortgage may be lower than necessary to pay even the interest, resulting in possible negative amortization. Graduated-payment mortgages are attractive to buyers who expect substantial increases in their income in the future.

Lender Buy-Down Mortgage.   With a **lender buy-down mortgage,** a base interest rate is set for the loan that is perhaps 0.5 percentage point higher than the interest rate for a conventional mortgage. For the first year, the borrower pays a rate 2 percentage points below the base rate. In the second year, the rate is 1 point below the base rate. In the third and future years, the base rate would be charged. These changes are known in advance and are contractual. First-time home buyers often use buy-down mortgages to take advantage of lower monthly payments in early years of the loan.

Rollover (Renegotiable-Rate) Mortgage.   A **rollover mortgage** consists of a series of short-term loans for two- to five-year time periods, but with total amortization spread over the usual 25 to 30 years. The loan is renewed for each time period at the market interest rates that prevail at the time of the renewal.

Shared-Appreciation Mortgage.   With a **shared-appreciation mortgage,** the lender offers an interest rate about one-third less than the market rate. In exchange, the lender gains the right to receive perhaps one-third of any appreciation in the home's value when the home is sold or ten years after the time of the loan.

Growing-Equity Mortgage.   The **growing-equity mortgage (GEM)** is meant for people who design their loan in advance to reduce interest costs by paying off the mortgage loan early. One form of GEM is the **biweekly mortgage,** which calls for payments to be made every two weeks that represent half of the normal monthly payment. The borrower, therefore, makes 26 payments per year. For example, a $100,000, 8 percent, 30-year loan requires a $733.76 monthly payment for a total of $8805.12 (12 × $733.76) paid in one year. On a biweekly basis with payments of $366.88 ($733.76 ÷ 2), the total amount paid each year would be $9538.88 ($366.88 × 26). The difference of $733.76 ($9538.88 − $8805.12) is equivalent to one extra monthly payment per year and is applied to the principal of the loan. Under the biweekly repayment plan, a loan may be repaid in approximately 20 years, rather than the 30 years dictated by the monthly payment plan. Almost all mortgage lenders permit payment of additional amounts toward principal at any time. For example, paying an additional $50 per month on the preceding loan would cause the loan to be paid off in 23 years and would save about $39,000 in interest costs.

Assumable Mortgage.   With an **assumable mortgage,** the buyer pays the seller a down payment generally equal to the seller's equity in the home and takes responsibility for the mortgage loan payments for the remaining term of the seller's existing mortgage loan. The buyer's goal is to obtain the loan at the original interest rate, which should be below current market rates. This approach will work only if the original mortgage loan agreement does not include a **due-on-sale clause.** Such a clause requires that the mortgage loan be fully paid off if the home is sold. It can impose a burden on the seller because it prohibits a buyer from assuming the mortgage loan.

The down payment for an assumable mortgage may be large because the home will have increased in value and the principal of the loan will have been reduced over the years. To assume an existing mortgage, the buyer sometimes must obtain a **second mortgage** to cover a portion of the down payment. A second mortgage is an additional loan on a residence besides the original mortgage. In case of default, the amount owed on the original mortgage must be paid first. Because of this additional risk, the interest rate on a second mortgage is often 2 to 5 percentage points higher than current market rates for first mortgages.

As an example, suppose Robert and Louise Webster, a dual-earner family from Van Nuys, California, wish to buy a $350,000 home from the Roget family. The Websters want to assume the Rogets' remaining mortgage of $270,000, but they have only $50,000 available to pay the Rogets for their equity of $80,000 ($350,000 − $270,000). A lender (perhaps the Rogets?) that thinks the Websters can afford to make two mortgage payments might give them a second mortgage loan of $30,000 to make up the difference. Second mortgages often run from three to ten years in length, so the Websters can look forward to having only one mortgage payment at some point. Of course, they may face considerable budget stress while paying on both mortgages at the same time.

Seller Financing.

Seller financing occurs whenever the seller of a home agrees to accept all or a portion of the purchase price in installments rather than as a lump sum. The Webster family in the preceding example could have used seller financing if the Rogets agreed to accept installment payments on the $30,000 that the Websters lacked for the equity. Such a case would be labeled a "seller-financed second mortgage." Other variations also exist. For example, a seller may be willing to finance the entire purchase price for 20 or 30 years with a 10 or 20 percent down payment, thereby acting much like a mortgage lending institution. Usually seller financing is a short-term arrangement, however, with payments based on amortization occurring over perhaps 20 years and a balloon payment due after perhaps five years. That is, all principal not paid after five years would be due at once. This extremely large sum would typically require refinancing via a mortgage from a financial institution. Such a loan should not be difficult to obtain, assuming that equity has built up in the property.

In most seller financing, the buyer obtains the title to the property when the deal is closed and the contract is signed. A **land contract** (or **contract for deed**), in contrast, brings greater risk for the buyer because all terms in the contract (including payment of the debt) must be satisfied before transfer of title will occur. As a result, if you move before paying off the contract in full, you forfeit all money paid in installments to the seller and any appreciation in the home's value. You build no equity until the contract is completed.

Reverse Mortgage.

A **reverse mortgage,** also known as a **home-equity conversion loan,** allows a homeowner older than age 61 to borrow against the equity in a home

Did You Know? . . .

About Second Mortgage Loans

Home values have increased significantly in recent years, allowing many people to see higher than expected increases in their home equity. You can use a second mortgage to borrow based on this home equity, with the property serving as collateral for both the first and second mortgage loans. The first mortgage lender has first claim on the property if the home is sold or if either loan goes into foreclosure. Reflecting this risk, the interest rate on a second mortgage is usually 1.5 to 2.0 percentage points higher than the prevailing first-mortgage rates in the market.

Historically, people have used second mortgages to pay for major remodeling projects, finance college costs for children, pay off medical bills, or start a business. Today, some people use these funds for everyday living expenses, an unwise practice dubbed "eating one's house."

Two types of second mortgages exist:

■ The *home-equity installment loan,* where a specific amount of money is borrowed for a fixed time period with fixed monthly payments.

■ The *home-equity line of credit,* where a maximum loan amount is established and the loan operates as open-ended credit, much like a credit card account.

These line-of-credit loans often have variable interest rates and flexible repayment schedules. The credit limit on a second mortgage loan is usually set at 80 percent (but can go as high as 125 percent)* of the home's appraised value minus the amount owed on the first mortgage. For example, a person with a home appraised at $200,000 with a balance owed of $100,000 on a first mortgage might be allowed to take out a $60,000 second mortgage [($200,000 × 0.80) − $100,000]. Under the law, you have three days to cancel any loan that uses your already mortgaged home as collateral.

*Only the interest on borrowings up to 100 percent of the home's market value can be used as a deduction when filing state and federal income taxes.

that is fully paid for and to receive the proceeds in a series of monthly payments, often over a period of 5 to 15 years or for life. The contract allows the person to continue living in the home. Essentially, the borrower trades his or her equity in the home in return for either a fixed monthly income or a line of credit that can be drawn upon at the option of the homeowner. The most likely prospects for such loans are elderly persons who have paid off their mortgages but are strapped for income. The mortgage does not have to be paid back until the last surviving owner sells the house, moves out permanently, or dies.

What Does It Cost to Buy a Home?

 4 Define the major initial and continuing costs of buying a home.

Some prospective home buyers look at homes that are too expensive but end up buying them anyway. Such buyers will have nice homes but could be called "house poor" because they will spend such a large proportion of their income on housing costs that very little money will be left over for other items like furnishings. Another surprise to many people is the amount of **closing costs.** These costs must be paid at the closing and include fees and charges other than the down payment. Closing costs may vary from 2 to 10 percent of the mortgage loan amount.

To avoid becoming house poor, the wise financial planner carefully estimates all initial and subsequent costs of housing and thus makes more knowledgeable decisions. In the discussion that follows, we assume that the prospective homeowner has $15,000 to use as a down payment on a small $115,000 vacation home. All other costs are described in the following sections, and Table 9.5 (page 252) shows a summary of estimated costs.

Principal and Interest

A mortgage loan requires repayment of both principal (P) and interest (I), which are the first two letters of the acronym **PITI,** which real estate agents and lenders often use to indicate a mortgage payment that includes principal, interest, real estate taxes, and insurance. Figure 9.1 on page 242 and Tables 9.1 and 9.2 on page 243 illustrate the principal and interest components of a mortgage payment.

Taxes and Insurance

Taxes (T) and insurance (I) represent the last two letters of PITI. Real estate property taxes must be paid to local governments. The amount varies by community, but usually ranges from 1 to 4 percent of the value of the home. The total property tax ($1500 in our example) is due once each year when the government sends out its tax bill. When an escrow account is used, lenders require that the borrower deposit in advance a pro rata share (one-twelfth) of the estimated real estate taxes each month ($125 in our example). An **escrow account** is a special reserve account at a financial institution (in this case, the lender) where funds are held until they are paid to a third party (in this case, the taxing agency and the insurance company). If a buyer takes possession at the midpoint of the tax year, the seller, who owes those taxes, should make one-half ($750 here) of the taxes due available out of the escrow account to the buyer on the day of the closing.

Table 9.5   Estimated Buying and Closing Costs
(Purchase Price of a Vacation Home, $115,000 with $15,000 Down; Closing on July 1)

Home Buying Costs	At Closing	Monthly
Down payment	$15,000	—
Points (2)	2,000	—
Loan application fee	100	—
Principal and interest (from Table 9.3 for a $100,000 loan for 30 years at 8%)	—	$733.76
Property taxes (for first half-year, then monthly)	750*	125.00
Homeowner's insurance (for first half-year, then monthly)	480†	40.00
Mortgage insurance	—	41.67
Loan origination fee	500	—
Title search	100	—
Title insurance (to protect lender)	200	—
Title insurance (to protect buyer)	200	—
Attorney's fee	300	—
Credit reports	25	—
Recording fees	20	—
Appraisal fee	150	—
Termite and radon inspection fee	130	—
Survey fee	100	—
Notary fee	50	—
Subtotal	**$20,105**	**$940.43**
Less amount owed by seller	−750*	—
Subtotal	**$19,355**	
Warranty insurance (optional)	240	20.00
Total	**$19,595**	**$960.43**

*Would be received from seller, who legally owes these taxes, and then deposited in escrow account.
†Would be paid to escrow account.

Real estate property taxes are based on the value of buildings and land. To calculate these taxes, first local government officials establish a **fair market value** for the owner's home and land. Next, the **assessed value** of the property is calculated. A home with a fair market value of $100,000, for example, might have an assessed value of $60,000. Although you can do little to influence the tax rate on real estate property, you can claim that the assessed valuation of your home is too high. If your appeal is successful, your tax bill will be lowered accordingly. On a national basis, about one-half of all appeals succeed.

Lenders always require homeowners to insure the home itself in case of fire or other calamity. In contrast, insurance on the contents of the home is the responsibility of the homeowner. Both the home and its contents can be covered in a typical homeowner's insurance policy. (Chapter 10 covers this information in detail.) The annual premium for such insurance must be paid each year in advance. Lenders require prepayment of a pro rata share (one-twelfth) each month ($40 here) of the next year's estimated insurance premium. In addition, on the closing day, the purchaser must be prepared to pay one year's premium ($480 here) in advance.

Mortgage Insurance

First-time buyers often have minimal funds available to make a down payment on a home. Fortunately, a number of programs are open to these buyers that allow for down payments as low as 1 percent of the purchase price of the home. When a buyer makes a down payment that is less than 20 percent of the home's purchase price, the lender almost always requires that the borrower obtain mortgage insurance. **Mortgage insurance** insures the difference between the amount of down payment required by an 80 percent loan-to-value ratio and the actual, lower down payment.

Figure 9.2 on page 244 illustrates a situation in which the borrower would need to obtain mortgage insurance. In this example, a 90 percent loan-to-value ratio would result in a loan of $112,500 rather than the $100,000 standard down payment (80 percent loan-to-value ratio). The mortgage insurance company would insure the gap between the two amounts. In this way, the lender would be assured of payment of the loan balance if the home were later repossessed for default and sold for less than the amount owed. Mortgage insurance may be obtained from several sources.

Private Mortgage Insurance. **Private mortgage insurance (PMI)** is obtained from a private company rather than a government agency. The largest private mortgage insurer is the Mortgage Guaranty Insurance Corporation (MGIC, pronounced "magic"). The cost of PMI varies from 0.25 to 2.0 percent of the debt, depending on how much less than 20 percent the down payment is. In this example, assume an annual premium charge totaling 1.0 percent of the mortgage loan, or $1125 (0.01 × $112,500), to be paid in monthly installments ($93.75) to the lender, which in turn forwards it to the mortgage insurance company.

Instead of making monthly payments for PMI, it may be possible to obtain lender-paid mortgage insurance. In such a case, the lender pays the mortgage insurance premium and in return charges a higher interest rate on the loan of perhaps an additional ¼ to ¾ of a percentage point. The mortgage insurance premium is tax-deductible because it represents part of the interest payments, but the insurance cannot be dropped without completely refinancing the loan.

FHA Mortgage Insurance. To encourage lending, the **Federal Housing Administration (FHA)** of the U.S. Department of Housing and Urban Development (HUD) insures loans that meet its standards. To obtain such mortgage insurance, the borrower must be creditworthy and the home must meet the FHA's minimum-quality standards. (For information on HUD mortgage programs, visit www.hud.gov/buying/mortprog.cfm.)

An FHA mortgage is granted by a mortgage lender such as a bank, which is insured against borrower default by the federal government. Like private mortgage insurers, the FHA charges the borrower a mortgage insurance premium. This premium may be paid as a single up-front, lump-sum payment, or it may be financed and paid in monthly amounts in the same way as private mortgage insurance.

Usually, only a very small down payment (approximately 3 percent, including closing costs) is required on an FHA-insured mortgage because the loan is backed by the federal government. Such mortgage loans cannot exceed FHA lending limits, which change frequently and vary across the country according to local housing market prices. Terms can be up to 30 years, and it often takes 60 to 90 days to process an application.

VA Mortgage Insurance. The federal Department of Veterans Affairs (VA) promotes home ownership among military veterans (active-duty, reserve, and National

▶Case 3
Jeremy Decides to Sell His Home Himself

Jeremy Jorgensen of St. Paul, Minnesota, is concerned about the costs involved in selling his home, so he has decided to sell his house himself rather than pay a broker to do it.

(a) What challenges will Jeremy encounter, if any, when selling his own home?

(b) How would you advise Jeremy if he asked you whether he should sell the house himself or list with a broker? Explain your answer.

(c) Would Jeremy really save money by selling his home himself if he considers his time as part of his costs? Why or why not?

(d) Can you suggest any ways that Jeremy might reduce his selling costs without doing the selling himself? Explain.

Financial Math Questions

1. Walt and Mary Jensen of Atlanta, Georgia, both of whom are in their late twenties, currently are renting an unfurnished two-bedroom apartment for $880 per month, plus an additional $130 for utilities and $34 for insurance. They have found a condominium they can buy for $160,000 with a 15 percent down payment and a 30-year, 7 percent mortgage. Principal and interest payments are estimated at $851 per month, with property taxes amounting to $110 per year and a homeowner's insurance premium of $450 per year. Private mortgage insurance will cost the couple about $60 per month. Closing costs are estimated at $3200. The monthly homeowner's association fee is $275, and utility costs are estimated at $160 per month. The Jensens have a combined income of $57,000 per year, with take-home pay of $4100 per month. They are in the 25 percent tax bracket, pay $225 per month on an installment loan (ten payments left), and have $39,000 in savings and investments.

   (a) Can the Jensens afford to buy the condo? Use the results from the *Garman/Forgue* website or the information on pages 234–235 to support your answer. Also, consider the effect of the purchase on their savings and monthly budget.

   (b) Walt and Mary think that their monthly housing costs would be lower the first year if they bought the condo. Do you agree? Support your answer.

   (c) If they buy, how much will Walt and Mary have left in savings to pay for moving expenses?

   (d) Available financial information suggests that mortgage rates might drop over the next few months. If the Jensens wait until the rates drop to 6.0 percent, how much will they save on their monthly mortgage payment? Use the information in Table 9.3 or the *Garman/Forgue* website to calculate the payment.

2. Steve and Marcie Moore of Holyoke, Massachusetts, have an annual income of $120,000 and want to buy a home. Currently, mortgage rates are 7 percent. The Moores want to take out a mortgage for 30 years. Real estate taxes are estimated to be $4800 per year for homes similar to what they would like to buy, and homeowner's insurance would be about $720 per year.

   (a) Using a 28 percent front-end ratio, what are the total annual and monthly expenditures for which they would qualify?

   (b) Using a 36 percent back-end ratio, what monthly mortgage payment (including taxes and insurance) could they afford given that they have an automobile loan payment of $470, a student loan payment of $350, and credit card payments of $250? (Hint: Subtract these amounts from the total monthly affordable payments for their income to determine the amount left over to spend on a mortgage.)

   (c) If mortgage interest rates are around 7 percent and the Moores want a 30-year mortgage, use Table 9.3 to estimate how much they could borrow given your answer to part b. (Hint: Subtract the monthly real estate taxes and homeowner's insurance from your part b answer first.)

3. Phillip Guadet of Monroe, Louisiana, has been renting a small, two-bedroom house for several years. He pays $950 per month in rent for the home and $300 per year in property and liability insurance. The owner of the house wants to sell it, and Phillip is considering making an offer. The owner wants $130,000 for the property, but Phillip thinks he could get the house for $120,000 and use his $25,000 in 5 percent certificates of deposit that are ready to mature for the down payment. Phillip has talked to his banker and could get a 7 percent mortgage loan for 25 years to finance the remainder of the purchase price. The banker advised Phillip that he would reduce his debt principal by $1850 during the first year of the loan. Property taxes on the house are $1800 per year. Phillip estimates that he would need to upgrade his property and liability insurance to $500 per year and would incur about $1000 in costs the first year for maintenance. Property values are increasing at about 3.5 percent per year in the neighborhood. Phillip is in the 25 percent marginal tax bracket.

   (a) Use Table 9.3 to calculate the monthly mortgage payment for the mortgage loan that Phillip would need.

   (b) How much interest would Phillip pay during the first year of the loan?

(c) Use the Decision-Making Worksheet, "Should You Buy or Rent?", on page 235 to determine whether Phillip would be better off buying or renting based on his cash flow.

4. Kevin Raymond of Rochester Hills, Michigan, has owned his home for 15 years and expects to live in it for five more years. He originally borrowed $105,000 at 8 percent interest for 30 years to buy the home. He still owes $85,750 on the loan. Interest rates have since fallen to 6.5 percent, and Kevin is considering refinancing the loan for 15 years. He would have to pay 2 points on the new loan with no prepayment penalty on the current loan.

(a) What is Kevin's current monthly payment?

(b) Calculate the monthly payment on the new loan.

(c) Advise Kevin on whether he should refinance his mortgage using the Decision-Making Worksheet, "Should You Refinance Your Mortgage?", on page 246.

Money Matters Continuing Cases

Victor and Maria Hernandez Learn About Real Estate Agents

Victor and Maria have been thinking about selling their home and buying a house with more yard space so that they can indulge their passion for gardening. Before they make such a decision, they want to explore the market to see what might be available and in what price ranges. They will then list their house with a real estate agent and begin searching in earnest for a new home.

1. What services could a real estate agent provide for the couple, and what types of agents would represent them as they sell their current home?

2. A friend has advised them that they really need a buyer's agent for the purchase of a new home. Explain to the Hernandezes the difference between buyer's and seller's agents.

The Johnsons Decide to Buy a Condominium

Belinda Johnson's parents and maternal grandmother have combined their finances and presented Harry and Belinda with $25,000 with which to purchase a condominium. The Johnsons have shopped and found one that they like very much. They could either borrow from the condominium developer or obtain a loan from one of three other mortgage lenders. The financial alternatives are presented below, and data for the condo are summarized in the accompanying table on page 262.

1. Which plan has the lowest total up-front costs? The highest?

2. What would be the full monthly payment for PITI and PMI for each of the options?

3. If the Johnsons had enough spare cash to make the 20 percent down payment, would you recommend lender 1 or lender 2? Why?

4. Assuming that the Johnsons will need about $3000 for moving costs (in addition to closing costs), which financing option would you recommend? Why?

5. Assume that after five years the interest for the Johnsons' ARM has jumped to the maximum of 9.5 percent with a remaining balance of $122,500 for 25 years. Use the information in Table 9.3 or on the *Garman/Forgue* website to calculate their monthly payment.

Financing Details on a Condominium Available to the Johnsons

Price: $140,000. Developer A will finance the purchase with a 10 percent down payment and a 30-year, 6.5 percent ARM loan with 2 interest points. The initial monthly payment for principal and interest is $796.41 ($126,000 loan after the down payment is made; 126 × $6.3207). After one year, the rate rises to 8 percent, with a principal plus interest payment of $921.91. At that point, the rate can go up or down as much as 2 percent per year, depending on the cost of an index of mortgage funds. There is an interest-rate cap of 5 percent over the life of the loan. Taxes are estimated to be about $1500, and the homeowner's insurance premium should be about $600 annually. A mortgage insurance premium of $78 per month must be paid monthly on the two 10-percent down options.

Condo: Price, $140,000; Taxes, $1500; Insurance, $600

	Developer A	**Lender 1**	**Lender 2**	**Lender 3**
Loan term and type	30-year ARM*	30-year CON†	15-year CON	20-year REN‡
Interest rate	6.5%	7.5%	8%	7.5%
Down payment	$ 14,000	$ 28,000	$ 28,000	$ 14,000
Loan amount	126,000	112,000	112,000	126,000
Points	2,520	1,120	0	3,780
Principal and interest payment	796.41	783.12	1,204.12	1,015.04
PMI	78	0	0	78

*Adjustable-rate mortgage.
†Conventional.
‡Renegotiable every five years.

What Would You Recommend Now?

Now that you have read the chapter on housing expenditures, what would you recommend to Libby Clark in the case at the beginning of the chapter regarding:

1. Buying or renting housing in the Denver area?

2. Steps she should take prior to actively looking at homes?

3. Finding a home and negotiating the purchase?

4. The closing process in home buying?

5. Things to consider regarding the sale of her home should she ultimately be promoted to a position in another of the four regions?

Exploring the World Wide Web

To complete these exercises, go to the *Garman/Forgue* website at college.hmco.com/business/students. Under General Business, select the title of this text. Click on the Internet Exercises link for this chapter, and answer the questions that appear on the Web page.

1. Visit the website for Interest.com, where you will find a calculator that determines the monthly payment for any mortgage loan given a time period, interest rate, and loan amount. Assume you wish to borrow $100,000 to buy a home. Vary the time period and interest rate of the loan to see how these variations affect your monthly payment.

2. Visit the website for the Bank Rate Monitor, where you will find information on mortgage interest rates around the United States. View the information for the lenders in a large city near your home. How does the information compare with the interest rates on your own credit card account(s)? How do the rates in the city you selected compare with other rates found in the United States?

3. Visit the website for FinanCenter, where you will find a calculator to compare the benefits of prepaying a portion of your mortgage or investing the funds elsewhere.

   (a) Assume that you had the choice of putting $1000 into an investment earning 8 percent or using the $1000 to pay extra on a mortgage. (Use the interest rate on your current mortgage or the rate found as your answer to Exercise 1.) Which would be the better option?

   (b) Would your answer differ if you invested the $1000 in a tax-sheltered investment, such as a Roth IRA?

4. Visit the website for CalcBuilder, where you will find a calculator that helps you determine the amount you can afford for the purchase of a home given your income and funds available for a down payment, closing costs, and other home-buying expenses. Enter the data requested for your current situation. What does the calculator tell you about your housing affordability? Change the entered data for some point in the future when you project a better financial situation for yourself. How do the results change?

5. Visit the website for CalcBuilder, where you will find a calculator that allows you to generate an amortization schedule for a mortgage loan. Enter a loan amount, interest rate, time period, and other data to generate a schedule for a hypothetical or real loan.

6. Visit the website for *Kiplinger's Personal Finance Magazine,* where you can compare two loans with varying interest rates, time periods, closing costs, points, and other variables. Compare two hypothetical loan situations.

7. Visit the website for the National Association of Realtors, where you can search for owned housing in various locales around the United States. Look for housing in your local area of a type that would interest you and in your price range. Were you able to find housing that meets your criteria? Also search for similar housing in the San Diego, California (high-cost area), and Syracuse, New York (low-cost area), metropolitan areas. Compare these cost results to the housing found in your area.

Visit the Garman/Forgue website . . .

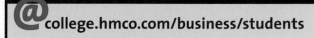

@college.hmco.com/business/students

Under General Business, select *Personal Finance 8e.* There, among other valuable resources, you will find a complete glossary, ACE questions, links to help you complete the chapter exercises, and links to other personal finance sites.

Part Three

Income and
Asset Protection

CHAPTER 10   Risk Management and Property/Liability
              Insurance

CHAPTER 11   Health Care Planning

CHAPTER 12   Life Insurance Planning

Chapter 10

Risk Management and Property Liability/Insurance

LEARNING OBJECTIVES

After reading this chapter, you should be able to:

1 **Apply** the risk-management process to address the risks to your property and income.

2 **Explain** basic insurance terms and the relationship between risk and insurance.

3 **Design** a homeowner's or renter's insurance program to meet your needs.

4 **Design** an automobile insurance program to meet your needs.

5 **Describe** other types of property and liability insurance.

6 **Outline** how to make an insurance claim.

George and Emily Cosgrove of Manhattan, Kansas, recently had a fire in their garage that destroyed two of their vehicles and did considerable damage to the garage and to the outside of their home. After receiving their reimbursements from their homeowner's and automobile insurance policies, the Cosgroves realized that they were severely underinsured. One vehicle was not insured for fire, and the insurance on their dwelling amounted to only 60 percent of its current replacement value.

What would you recommend to George and Emily on homeowner's and automobile insurance regarding:

1. The risk-management steps they should take to update their insurance coverages?

2. The relationship between severity and frequency of loss when deciding whether to buy insurance?

3. Adequately insuring their home?

4. The use of deductibles and policy limits to keep their automobile insurance premiums at a manageable level while still maintaining vital coverage?

Up to this point, we have focused on ways to manage your money and strategies for using financial resources to achieve your personal goals. Importantly, you also need to protect your resources and assets from the possibility of financial loss. You can achieve some of this protection by locking doors, minimizing fire hazards, and driving safely. Nevertheless, you need additional protection from the risk of financial loss associated with owning an automobile and home, providing for health care, financially supporting yourself and dependents, and many other aspects of life. Chapter 10 and the next two chapters focus on ways you can manage risk and protect your assets and income through insurance.

This chapter begins by discussing the topic of risk management, of which insurance represents just one component. Next, we examine the concept of insurance by considering its definition and its associated terminology. Central to this discussion is an understanding of the relationship between risk and insurance. We then discuss two major forms of property and liability insurance—homeowner's insurance and automobile insurance—before turning to several specialized types of policies. The final section of this chapter examines the process of making a claim to an insurance company when a property or liability loss occurs.

Risk and Risk Management

1 Apply the risk-management process to address the risks to your property and income.

Risk is uncertainty about the outcome of a situation or event. It arises out of the possibility that the outcome will differ from what is expected. In the area of potential financial losses, risk consists of uncertainty about whether the financial loss will occur and how large it might be.

Golden Rules of

Risk Management and Property/Liability Insurance

Financial success comes from learning the Golden Rules of personal finance and then putting what you have learned into practice. Make the following your money habits in risk management and property/liability insurance.

1. Once each year employ the risk-management process to reassess what types of and how much insurance coverage you need.
2. Never drive or ride in a vehicle or live in a home that is uninsured.
3. Purchase insurance policies with very high liability limits to protect against the possibility of catastrophic losses, and consider purchasing an umbrella liability insurance policy.
4. Never let a large potential loss go uncovered by insurance just to save a few dollars in premiums.
5. Verify that your auto insurance policy covers rental car losses so you can wisely ignore sales pressure to purchase such overpriced coverage.
6. Because prices for the same insurance coverage vary 50 to 100 percent, or more, always comparison shop for insurance locally as well as on-line.

The Nature of Risk

Two types of risk exist. **Speculative risk** is present when a situation offers a potential for gain as well as for loss. Investments, such as in those made in the stock market, involve speculative risk. **Pure risk** exists when there is no potential for gain, only the possibility of loss. Fires, automobile accidents, illness, and theft are examples of events involving pure risk. Insurance addresses pure risk.

Many people think of odds or games of chance when they hear the word "risk." In fact, risk and chance are different concepts. The difference between the two is subtle but very important. An event with a 95 percent chance of occurring is highly likely to occur. Thus, both uncertainty and risk are low. An event with a 0.000001 percent chance of occurring is highly likely not to occur. Thus, both uncertainty and risk are low. When an event has a moderate chance of occurring—5 percent, for example—the uncertainty and risk are relatively high, because it is difficult to predict the one person in 20 who will experience the event. In such cases, insurance often represents a wise choice for reducing risk.

The Risk-Management Process

Risk management is the process of identifying and evaluating situations involving pure risk to determine and implement the appropriate means for its management. The goal is to minimize any risk or potential for risk through advanced awareness and planning. Risk management entails making the most efficient arrangements before a loss occurs so as to minimize any after-loss effects on your financial status. It is an important part of overall personal financial management, in that it preserves the results of your other financial planning efforts. Insurance is merely one of many possible ways of handling risk, and it is not always the best choice.

The risk-management process involves five steps; Table 10.1 outlines these steps in the risk-management process.

1. Gather information to identify risk exposures and potential losses.

2. Evaluate the potential losses.

3. Decide on the best ways to handle risk and losses.

4. Administer the risk-management program.

5. Periodically evaluate and adjust the program.

Step 1: Gather Information to Identify Risk Exposures.

Sources of risk, called **exposures,** are the items you own and the activities in which you engage that expose you to potential financial loss. Owning an automobile is a very common exposure. In risk management, you should take an inventory of what you own and what you do to identify your exposures to loss.

You face the possibility of loss in one of four ways. First, you may suffer a loss to your property, such as can happen during a house fire. **Property insurance** protects you from financial losses resulting from the damage to or destruction of your property or possessions. Second, you could be held legally responsible for losses suffered by others, which might occur if you caused an automobile accident, for example. **Liability insurance** protects you from financial losses suffered when you are held liable for the losses of others. Third, you may become ill or be uninsured and have losses associated

Table 10.1 The Risk-Management Process

	Possession	Activity	Accompanying Peril
Step 1 *Gather information to identify your exposures to risks.* Determine the source of risk.	Vehicle House Jewelry	Driving Smoking Traveling	Accident Fire Theft
Step 2 *Evaluate risk and potential losses.*	(a) Determine the likely frequency of losses associated with each exposure. (b) Determine the potential severity and magnitude of losses associated with each exposure.		
Step 3 *Choose among mechanisms for handling the risk exposures and losses.*	(a) Avoid risk. (b) Retain risk. (c) Control losses. (d) Transfer risk. (e) Reduce risk.		
Step 4 *Implement and administer your overall risk-management plan.*	(a) Refrain from certain activities. (b) Take extra precautions. (c) Buy insurance		
Step 5 *Periodically evaluate the risk-management plan and adjust if necessary.*			

What Would You Recommend Now?

Now that you have read the chapter on risk management and property liability insurance, what would you recommend to George and Emily in the case at the beginning of the chapter regarding:

1. The risk-management steps they should take to update their insurance coverages?

2. The relationship between severity and frequency of loss when deciding whether to buy insurance?

3. Adequately insuring their home?

4. The use of deductibles and policy limits to keep their automobile insurance premiums at a manageable level while still maintaining vital coverage?

Exploring the World Wide Web

To complete these exercises, go to the *Garman/Forgue* website at college.hmco.com/business/students. Under General Business, select the title of this text. Click on the Internet Exercises link for this chapter, and answer the questions that appear on the Web page.

1. Visit the website for the National Association of Insurance Commissioners, where you will find a map of the United States through which you can link to your state insurance regulator's website. If available, obtain an insurance buyer's guide for automobile and homeowner's insurance that describes policy provisions and compares insurance rates. Use these rate comparisons to select two automobile insurance companies that would be appropriate for your needs. Write or telephone the companies to obtain specific premium quotations for the desired insurance protection. Do the same for single-family dwelling, condominium, or renter's insurance, depending on your circumstances.

2. Visit the website for insure.com. Check the minimum automobile liability insurance requirements for your state.

3. Visit the website for A. M. Best, Inc. For your automobile and homeowner's insurance providers (and perhaps one or two others that you have seen advertised), determine the current rating for each company on the basis of its financial strength. When you have found the rating for the first company, click "ratings category" to see an explanation of the ratings given by A. M. Best.

4. Visit the website for the Highway Loss Data Institute. For your own vehicle and one or two you would like to own, check how the vehicles stack up against the competition in terms of injury and collision and theft losses.

5. Visit the website for A. M. Best, Inc., where you will find an explanation of the coverages provided by flood insurance. Discuss if such insurance would be appropriate for you.

Visit the Garman/Forgue website . . .

college.hmco.com/business/students

Under General Business, select *Personal Finance 8e*. There, among other valuable resources, you will find a complete glossary, ACE questions, links to help you complete the chapter exercises, and links to other personal finance sites.

Chapter 11

Health Care Planning

LEARNING OBJECTIVES

After reading this chapter, you should be able to:

1 **Distinguish** among the three major sources of health care protection.

2 **Describe** the general benefits of health care plans and key payment and coverage limitations.

3 **Describe** the types of medical costs that may be covered by a health care plan.

4 **Present** an overview of long-term care insurance.

5 **Describe** how disability income insurance and Social Security disability income insurance can replace a portion of an eligible disabled person's income.

Monica DiMartino is a 43-year-old single mother with two children, ages 10 and 14. Her 10-year-old daughter has a history of ear infections that require doctor's office visits four or five times per year. Monica's 71-year-old mother lives with the family for financial reasons; she has hereditary high blood pressure and cholesterol as well as diabetes. Monica's mother has enrolled in Medicare Parts A and B and qualifies as Monica's dependent.

Monica's employer sponsors a health care plan to cover the company's workers, their spouses, and their dependents. The employer pays for the worker's coverage under the lowest-cost plan (an HMO); the employee must then pay an additional amount to have family members be covered under the plan or to select one of the higher-cost plan options. Monica must choose among three options: (1) an HMO managed by a local university medical school/hospital at an additional cost to Monica of $122 per month, (2) a health insurance plan with a PPO at that same medical center at an additional cost to Monica of $245 per month, and (3) a traditional health insurance plan that provides access to virtually all medical care providers in her community at an additional cost to Monica of $455 per month.

What would you recommend to Monica DiMartino on the subject of health care planning regarding:

1. Choosing among the three alternatives available to her?

2. Monica's concerns about providing for her mother's health care needs?

3. Monica's need for her own disability and long-term care insurance?

Few things in life are more important than having good health. Unfortunately, illness and injuries do occur from time to time, so it is also important to have access to a reliable health care plan. A **health care plan** is a generic name for any program that pays for or provides reimbursement for direct health care expenditures. Approximately 85 percent of all adults in the United States are covered by a health care plan. The current health care system in America has generated considerable controversy, partly because health-related costs continue to skyrocket and because employees are being asked to pay an ever increasing share of those costs. This chapter is designed to help you realize the full value of your health care plan.

We begin by distinguishing among the three major sources of health care protection: health maintenance organizations, traditional health insurance, and government health care plans. All health care plans can be complicated, with many limitations being placed on the protections offered, such as deductibles and coinsurance. These issues are explained in conjunction with a summary of the general benefits of health care plans and key payment and coverage limitations. People also need to understand exactly which medical costs are and are not covered by their health care plans. The chapter closes with an overview of long-term care insurance and a description of how disability income insurance and Social Security disability income insurance can replace a portion of an eligible disabled person's income.

Golden Rules of

Health Care Planning

Financial success comes from learning the Golden Rules of personal finance and then putting what you have learned into practice. Make the following your money habits in health care planning.

1. Take advantage of access to group health care plans when available.
2. Either work for an employer that provides health care benefits or purchase a high-deductible health plan and contribute to a tax-sheltered health savings account.
3. Working people should sign up for an employer sponsored–premium conversion plan and a flexible spending account for health care spending, when available, to save money on taxes.
4. Choose health care employee benefits based on your likely medical care needs, not just cost.
5. If you are a frequent user of health care, reduce spending on deductibles and coinsurance by choosing an HMO or PPO.
6. Take advantage of employer-sponsored long-term disability income insurance or consider purchasing protection individually.
7. Extend the benefit period of long-term care insurance by selecting a longer waiting period.
8. When changing employers, consider continuing your health care plan coverage using rights established through the COBRA law.

Sources of Health Care Benefits

1 Distinguish among the three major sources of health care protection.

Three types of losses are associated with injury or illness. The most obvious is the expense for direct medical care itself. In contrast, the other two losses are often overlooked: losses resulting from the need for recuperative care and income lost while the patient is unable to work. Table 11.1 (page 304) outlines these three types of losses and the types of protection available to address them. When thinking about health care planning, keep all three types of losses in mind. To cover them, there are three major sources of health care benefits: health maintenance organizations, traditional health insurance, and government health care.

You can obtain health care benefits as an individual or as a member of a group. A **group health care plan** is sold collectively to an entire group of persons rather than to individuals. Group health care plans generally have an **open enrollment period** each year that lasts for about one month; during this time, you can begin or make changes in coverage or switch among alternative plans. Open enrollment period requirements are generally waived for such family changes as births, adoptions, and marriage.

Participating in a group plan may be more desirable than obtaining health care benefits individually for three reasons. First, a participant may be able to obtain group coverage at a lower cost. Second, employers often provide group coverage as an employee benefit for their workers. Third, persons who have existing health problems may find it easier to obtain group coverage because the underwriting is based on the needs of the entire group rather than the individual's particular situation.

Table 11.1 Types of Protection from Health-Related Losses

Type of Loss	Medical Care		Recuperative Care	Lost Income
Provider	Health maintenance organizations (HMOs).	Traditional health insurance.	Long-term care insurance.	Disability income insurance.
Services	Provide hospital, surgical, and medical services directly or under contract with providers.	Reimburses or pays for hospital, surgical, medical, and other health care costs.	Reimburses for costs associated with custodial care (not health care).	Provides a monthly income to replace that lost when the insured is unable to work due to accident or injury.
Payment mode	Charge a monthly fee on a prepaid basis. Purchased by individuals or by employers as an employee benefit.	Charges monthly premiums for the insurance coverage. Purchased by individuals or by employers as an employee benefit.	Charges monthly or annual premiums. Purchased by individuals.	Charges a monthly premium. Purchased by individuals or by employers as an employee benefit.

When a health care plan is available as an employee benefit, the employer typically pays most of the cost for the worker (possibly including other members of his or her immediate family) for the lowest-cost option (usually the health maintenance organization). Employees can choose a higher-priced option or add family members to the coverage by paying an additional charge. New employees generally must make a choice among the available plans within the first few days of being hired and must stick with that decision until the next open enrollment period.

How to . . .

Avoid Duplication of Employee Health Care Benefits

Dual-income households often have overlapping health care benefits. For example, both Harry and Belinda Johnson's employers provide partially subsidized family health insurance plans as employee benefits. The Johnsons chose to be covered under Belinda's policy because it provides more protection and is less expensive. Belinda's coverage is fully paid for and she can add Harry to the plan for $125 per month.

Harry's employer offers a flexible approach toward providing employee benefits. Employees are provided with $600 per month to be used for any of the employee benefits available from a "menu" of benefits offered by the employer. If Harry chose his employer's health care plan, he would need to pay $375 of the $600 for this benefit. He could use the remaining $225 for life insurance, dental insurance, and membership in a health club. Harry has decided to forgo his health insurance and will pay the extra $125 to be covered under Belinda's plan. As a result, he has $250 ($600 − $225 − $125) available for other options. Harry decided to receive tuition support for his master's degree and sign up for disability insurance.

Health Maintenance Organizations

Health maintenance organizations (HMOs) provide a broad range of health care services to members for a set monthly fee on a prepaid basis. For the specific monthly fee, HMO members receive a wide array of health care services, including hospital, surgical, and preventive medical care. Some HMO plans require a small copayment of $5 to $20 for each office visit or prescription. A goal of HMOs is to catch problems early, thereby reducing the probability of subsequent high-cost medical treatment. HMO services are available to both groups and individuals.

The monthly fee charged by an HMO is based on the medical services that the average plan member would tend to use. HMOs do not put dollar limits on how much health care can be used. Instead, they are one of several types of **managed care plans.** Such plans seek to control the conditions under which health care can be obtained. Examples of controls can range from preapproval of hospital admissions to restrictions on which hospital or doctor can be used to mandates regarding the type of procedures that will be employed to treat a specific medical problem.

HMO subscribers are assigned a **primary-care physician** by the HMO. The primary-care physician usually must order or approve referrals to specialized health care providers (for example, a cardiologist) within or outside the HMO. If the HMO itself does not provide certain types of care, it contracts with a local hospital or clinic for those services. Typically, HMOs operate out of one building or a cluster of buildings housing physicians' offices, operating rooms, laboratories, and so forth.

One HMO variation is the **individual practice organization (IPO),** a structure in which the HMO contracts with—rather than hires—groups of physicians. These physicians maintain their own offices in various locations around town and serve as the primary-care physicians and specialists for the HMO. Another variation is a **point-of-service (POS) plan,** through which the covered party chooses a primary-care physician from an approved list. The POS primary-care physician either provides treatment or refers the patient to other approved providers. Unlike HMOs, POS plans allow the patient to choose another provider in return for paying much higher deductibles and co-payments (as discussed later).

It would certainly pay to investigate the HMO alternative if it is available to you either through a group or as an individual. Although the monthly HMO fee may be slightly higher than the group or individual health insurance premiums, the avoidance of deductibles and coinsurance costs can more than offset the extra monthly cost, especially for people who are frequent users of basic medical services. When considering an HMO, ask questions about turnover rates among the physicians (high is bad, low is good), the level of satisfaction among current members, reimbursement policies for medical expenses incurred when you are out of town, and the waiting time for a non-emergency appointment (10 to 14 days should be the maximum). The National Committee for Quality Assurance maintains a website that provides its ratings of HMOs (www.healthchoices.org).

Traditional Health Insurance

Health insurance provides protection against financial losses resulting from illness, injury, and disability. It may cover hospital, surgical, dental, and other medical expenditures. Unlike the case with HMOs, where you are buying health care in advance, health insurance is based on the concept of reimbursement for losses—in this, case medical costs. For this reason, health insurance plans are often referred to as **indemnity plans.**

Health insurance companies tend to be less restrictive about the type of and source of health care than HMOs. The type of care to be administered is chosen by the provider and the patient. Note that health insurers do place dollar limits on the coverage provided, usually on an individual, family, annual, and lifetime basis. In addition, they typically have deductibles and coinsurance requirements that result in out-of-pocket costs for the insured. Managed care does exist in health insurance, however. Two examples are described next.

Preferred Provider Organizations.   A **preferred provider organization (PPO)** is a group of medical care providers (doctors, hospitals, and other health care providers) who contract with a health insurance company to provide services at a discount. This discount is then passed along to the policyholders in the form of reductions or elimination of deductibles and coinsurance requirements if they choose the PPO providers for their medical care. The discounts do not apply if the policyholders receive health care from non-PPO members. Should the fee charged by a nonmember provider exceed the amount that the insurer considers reasonable, the policyholder must pay the excess.

Consider the case of Dru Cameron, who works for a large marketing firm in Charlotte, North Carolina. Her firm's health insurance plan has contracted with a PPO representing a local university's teaching hospital and its affiliated physicians. Because Dru chose the university hospital for treatment of a broken ankle, she saved $150 on the $250 deductible and did not have to pay the usual 20 percent coinsurance share of office visit charges. Of course, she gave up the right to go to her family doctor, who is not a PPO member, although she could still see that physician for other health care needs in the future.

Provider Sponsored Networks.   In a **provider sponsored network** (**PSN,** also called a **provider sponsored association**), a group of cooperating physicians and hospitals band together to cover health insurance contracts. Such networks operate primarily in rural areas, where access to HMOs may be limited. As a group, the members of the PSN coordinate and deliver health care services and manage the insurance plan financially. They contract with outside providers for medical services not available through members of the group. Contracts are marketed to firms wishing to provide health care plans to their employees, to individuals, and as options for those persons covered by government health care plans.

Government Health Care Plans

The government operates two major health care programs: Medicare and Medicaid. **Medicare*** is a program administered by the Social Security Administration that pays for hospital and medical expenses of persons aged 65 and older and some others. **Medicaid** is a health care program for the poor that is jointly administered and funded by the federal and state governments.

Medicare.   Medicare is funded by means of the Medicare payroll tax. This tax is paid by both workers and employers, much like the Social Security tax. Its beneficiaries include persons aged 65 and older who are eligible for Social Security retirement benefits, federal civilian employees aged 65 and older who retired after 1982, persons who are

---

***Medicare supplement insurance** (sometimes called **Medigap insurance**) is available in the private insurance market to broaden and add to the protection provided by the government's Medicare program.

eligible for Social Security disability benefits, and individuals with kidney disorders that require kidney dialysis treatments. Medicare is divided into two parts. **Medicare Part A** is the hospitalization portion of the program; it requires no premium. **Medicare Part B** is the supplementary medical expense insurance portion for outpatient care, doctor office visits, or certain other services of the Medicare program; it requires payment of a monthly premium.

Medicaid.   Eligibility for Medicaid is based on household income and net worth. The health services provided through this program vary from state to state but generally include hospital, surgical, and medical care. In some states, dental care for children may be covered as well. A key feature of Medicaid is its coverage of custodial long-term and nursing home care. Elderly who have "spent down" their assets on long-term care may be eligible to receive Medicaid reimbursement.

Making Sense of Your Health Plan Benefits

2 Describe the general benefits of health care plans and key payment and coverage limitations.

This section overviews the general benefits offered by health care plans and key payment and coverage limitations governing those plans. If you have group health insurance, you will receive a **certificate of insurance** that outlines benefit and policy provisions. If you are in an HMO, either as an individual or as a group member, the HMO (or your employer, if the plan is considered an employee benefit) can provide you with a description of benefits, costs, and procedures for obtaining care.

General Terms and Provisions

It is important to understand the definitions of terms used in a plan, identify who is covered by the plan, and recognize the time period of the protection.

Definitions.   The definitions of the terms used in the plan are of vital importance. For example, a plan may promise to pay $100 for each day of a hospital stay. But what is considered a hospital? Would such a plan cover nursing home care? Probably not. Would it cover a stay in an osteopathic hospital? Maybe.

Two critical definitions contained in a health insurance policy are those for injury and illness. Expenses resulting from an injury may be covered to a greater or lesser degree than those resulting from an illness.

Who Is Covered.   Health care plans can be written to cover an individual, a family, or a group. Few misunderstandings arise when an individual is the focus of the coverage, but family policies can be more complex. Generally, a family consists of a parent or parents and dependent children. Are children who are born while the plan is in effect automatically covered from the moment of birth? What about stepchildren? At what age are children no longer covered? These questions must be answered to ensure that all family members receive adequate protection.

The question of who is covered under a group plan is also very important. All group members are usually covered, but new members may have to endure a waiting period before receiving protection. If the group includes the employees of a business, different

Tax Considerations and Consequences

Health Care Planning

The Internal Revenue Code allows four principal avenues for reducing income taxes when you have expenses related to health care plan premiums and medical care expenses.

1. Health care expenditures (including a portion of certain long-term care insurance premiums) can be used as **itemized deductions** on one's income tax return. However, only the amount that exceeds 7.5 percent of the adjusted gross income is deductible. Self-employed people may deduct (as a business expense, not an itemized deduction) the cost of medical expense premiums for themselves and their dependents.
2. Many employees may save on taxes when they use **premium conversion plans** to pay the their health care insurance premiums. With premium conversion the employee's share of the premiums are paid with pretax dollars; those amounts are not included when the employer reports the employee's income to the IRS.
3. Many employers offer **flexible spending accounts** (see Chapter 1), allowing employees to place a portion of their salary into an account that is used to pay

some of their health care expenditures, including employee-paid health plan premiums. Recall, however, that flexible spending accounts are a "use it or lose it" proposition. Thus, you should set aside only an amount that you are sure you will use.

4. Individuals can establish a **health savings account (HSA)** in which they may make tax-sheltered deposits into an investment account earmarked for future payment of health care expenses. Health savings accounts are available to persons who have no health care plan through their work or if their employer-provided plan is a high-deductible plan. A high-deductible health plan has a higher annual deductible than typical health plans ($1000 individual and $2000 family deductibles) and places a maximum limit on the sum of the deductible and the annual out-of-pocket medical expenses that must paid by the saver for covered expenses ($5000 individual and $10,000 family maximums). Such high-deductible plans have lower premiums because a large portion of a health care bill is paid by workers out of their HSAs.

protection may be offered for full-time and part-time employees. The family of the group member may be covered but, once again, the definition of "family" must be understood.

The Time Period. Individual and group health care plans are usually written on an annual basis. An annual plan beginning on January 1 will start at 12:00 A.M. that day and end at 11:59 P.M. on December 31. Any illness that begins during the year will be covered. But will coverage continue if the plan expires while you are in the hospital? The answer is usually yes. Similarly, a surgical procedure performed after a plan expires but for an illness or injury for which treatment was sought during the plan period may be covered.

Payment Limitations

Health care plans contain provisions that specify the level of payments for covered expenses. These provisions include deductibles, copayment and coinsurance requirements, policy limits, and coordination-of-benefits requirements. For most plans, mental health care has lower policy limits and higher deductibles, copayments, and coinsurance requirements.

Deductibles and Copayments.   **Deductibles** are clauses in health care plans that require you to pay an initial portion of losses before receiving reimbursement. They are generally stated on an annual basis. Having an annual deductible of $200 per year on a policy, for example, would mean that the first $200 of the medical costs for the year is paid by the patient.

Family plans warrant special attention. Generally, they include a deductible for each family member (again, perhaps $200 per year) with a maximum family deductible (perhaps $500 per year). Once the deductible payments for individual family members reach the maximum family deductible ($500 in this example), further individual deductibles will be waived.

A **copayment,** which is a variation of a deductible, requires you to pay a specific dollar amount each time you have a specific covered expense item. A copayment is often required for doctor's office visits and prescription drugs. For example, you might have to pay $25 for each prescription, with the insurer paying the remainder. A copayment differs from a deductible in that it might require that you pay the first $35 of each office visit even after the deductible is met.

Coinsurance.   A **coinsurance clause** requires you to pay a proportion of any loss suffered. The typical share is 80/20, with the insurer paying the larger percentage. Usually, a coinsurance cap limits the annual out-of-pocket payments made by the patient when meeting the coinsurance. The following example illustrates how a deductible of $250 and an 80/20 coinsurance provision with a $1000 coinsurance cap work together to affect the coverage for an $8760 health care bill. Because the deductible is the responsibility of the insured party, the patient pays the first $250. The coinsurance ratio is applied to the remaining $8510 ($8760 − $250) until the portion paid by the patient reaches the coinsurance cap. Thus, $1000 is covered by the insured and $4000 by the insurer. The additional expenses of $3510 ($8510 − $1000 − $4000) are covered 100 percent by the insurance company up to the overall limits of coverage (perhaps $100,000). In this example, the insured party will pay $1250 ($250 deductible + $1000 coinsurance) and the insurer will pay $7510 ($4000 coinsurance + $3510 remaining charges).

Policy Limits.   Policy limits specify the maximum dollar amounts that a health insurance plan will pay to reimburse a covered loss. HMO plans generally do not have maximum policy limits specified in dollars. Instead, they limit the health care services they will provide for a specified diagnosis. To illustrate policy limits for a health insurance plan, we will consider the case of Karl Gruenfeld, an unmarried electrician from Las Vegas, New Mexico, who has a major medical insurance policy.

- **Item limits** specify the maximum reimbursement for a particular health care expense. Karl's policy contains a $75 maximum per X ray. Karl suffered a heart attack and had X-ray expenses of $840 (seven sets of X rays at $120 each). The policy will pay $525 (7 × $75) of this expense, and Karl must pay the remaining $315.
- **Episode limits** specify the maximum payment for health care expenses arising from a single episode of illness or injury, with each episode being considered separately. Karl's policy contains an episode limit of $25,000 for all covered expenses. After his heart attack, Karl was hospitalized for two weeks and incurred $31,223 in medical charges (including the covered portion of the X rays). His policy will pay $25,000 of these charges. One month later, Karl suffered burns in a cooking accident at his home and was hospitalized for two days, incurring hospital care costs of $1310. His policy will pay these expenses in full because the second hospitalization is considered a separate episode.

- **Time period limits** specify the maximum payment for covered expenses occurring within a specified time period, usually one year. Consider Karl's heart attack and burn hospitalizations. If his policy had contained a $50,000 annual time period limit, Karl would have used $26,310 ($25,000 + $1310) of this amount and would have only $23,690 ($50,000 − $26,310) remaining for the year.
- **Aggregate limits** place an overall maximum on the total amount of reimbursement available under a policy. If Karl's policy has an aggregate limit of $100,000, no more than $100,000 will be reimbursed for all medical expenses that Karl incurs during the life of the policy.

Aggregate dollar limits are always higher than time period limits, which are in turn higher than episode limits. A policy with high aggregate limits may seem attractive, but it may not be a good buy if the episode limits are too low. Analyze each limit separately to determine whether it provides sufficient protection.

Coordination of Benefits.   A **coordination-of-benefits clause** prevents you from collecting insurance benefits that exceed the loss suffered. Such a clause designates the order in which plans will pay benefits if multiple plans apply to a loss. The primary plan is the first applied to any loss when more than one plan provides coverage. If it fails to reimburse 100 percent of the loss, then any secondary (or excess) plans will be applied in order until the loss is fully paid or until benefits are exhausted, whichever occurs first.

Coverage Limitations

In addition to limits on the dollar amounts reimbursed, health care plans may contain provisions that limit the types of expenses covered by the plan. Three categories of coverage limitations exist: (1) limitations based on timing of the loss, (2) general exclusions, and (3) maternity benefits.

Limitations Based on Timing of the Loss.   Health plans usually contain provisions that prohibit coverage for **preexisting conditions,** which are medical conditions or symptoms that were known to the participant or diagnosed within a certain time period, usually one or two years, before the effective date of the plan. Imagine that you develop a serious ulcer and are told by your doctor that surgery will be needed. You might be tempted to buy a health care plan before having the surgery if you were not already covered. Because the surgery is a preexisting condition, however, the new policy would not cover its expense. Group plans exclude fewer preexisting conditions than individual plans.

Disputes sometimes arise over whether a medical loss actually results from a preexisting condition. To clarify matters and to prevent such disputes, insurance plans may dictate waiting periods for specific types of expenses. For example, a one-year waiting period is often required for maternity benefits to be covered under a new health care plan. Disputes may also center on whether a recurrence of an illness represents a separate episode. If the recurrence is considered a separate episode, the deductible must be paid, but reimbursement will be available up to the full episode limits. If the recurrence is considered a continuation of the original episode, the second deductible will not apply, but the loss may exceed the episode limit. A **recurring clause** clarifies conditions under which a recurrence of an illness is considered a continuation of the first episode or a separate episode.

Advice from an Expert

Maintain Your Health Care Plan Between Jobs

What happens when you no longer work (you voluntarily resign or retire, or you are terminated for any reason other than gross misconduct) for an employer that offers a group health care plan and you want to continue the coverage? You can assert your **COBRA rights** (Consolidated Omnibus Budget Reconciliation Act of 1985). These rules allow you to remain a member of a group health plan for as long as 18 months if you worked for an employer with more than 20 workers. They apply to you and to any of your dependents who had been covered under the employer's plan. COBRA rights apply to your dependents for 36 months. These rights must be exercised within 60 days after the termination of employment, and you must pay the full premiums (including both the employee's and the employer's portions) plus a 2 percent administrative fee.

Eventually, eligibility to remain under the group plan will run out. Federal law also mandates a **portability option** that allows you to convert your group coverage to individual coverage within 180 days before COBRA ends, if that is part of the employer's plan originally or as amended. Your individual policy premiums will be higher but the waiting period and preexisting condition provisions will not apply.

Martin Carrigan, Esq.
The University of Findlay, Ohio

Limitations on General Exclusions. **Exclusions** narrow the focus of and eliminate specific coverage provided in a plan. Losses resulting from war, riot, and civil disturbance may be excluded from health care plans, for example. Most policies exclude expenses for voluntary cosmetic surgery, and many deny coverage if the illness or injury occurs outside the United States. Expenses resulting from self-inflicted wounds are commonly excluded during the first two years of the policy as well.

Maternity Benefits. Maternity benefits are often considered separately from other benefits in a health care plan, and specific limits and exclusions may apply in case of pregnancy. The best coverage treats maternity care in the same way as any other health care episode.

What Medical Costs Are Covered by Health Care Plans?

3 Describe the types of medical costs that may be covered by a health care plan.

The purchaser of a health care plan faces a situation not unlike that of a diner who must choose from an à la carte menu. That is, he or she must select among various plans to find the one that provides the appropriate coverage for medical expenses, recuperative care, and rehabilitative care. This section discusses the health benefits "menu" from the perspective of traditional health insurance. HMOs and government health care plans follow a very similar pattern of benefits, except that the covered individual never sees a bill for an insurer to pay.

Hospital Coverage

Hospital (or **hospitalization**) **coverage** protects you from the costs arising out of a stay in a hospital, including room and board charges, routine laboratory expenses, general nursing services, basic supplies, and drugs. Approximately 80 percent of all Americans have some form of hospital coverage, although many have inadequate protection.

Traditional health insurance plans address hospital coverage in one of three ways: (1) hospital expense insurance, (2) hospital-service-incurred plans, and (3) hospital indemnity insurance. **Hospital expense insurance** provides cash reimbursement for specific hospital expense items incurred during a hospital stay. These expenses include the per-day hospital room charges and miscellaneous hospital expenses (for example, drugs and supplies). A **hospital-service-incurred** (or **fee-for-service**) **plan** pays the hospital directly for the covered services, rather than providing a cash reimbursement to the insured for hospital expenses. **Hospital indemnity insurance** provides a cash payment of a specific amount per day of hospitalization. No attempt is made to match the payment to a specific item of expense. Such a plan might pay up to $200 per day of hospitalization, up to a maximum number of days.

Surgical Coverage

Surgical coverage protects you from the expenses related to surgical procedures. A **surgical-service-incurred** (or **fee-for-service**) **plan** pays the surgical service providers—the surgeon, anesthesiologist, hospital, and others—directly for their services. A surgical-service-incurred plan typically pays the **usual, customary, and reasonable (ucr)** charge, based on what most service providers charge for similar services within your specific geographic area. If your surgeon charges more than the plan's allowable charge, you may be liable for the difference, especially if you choose a care provider who is not approved under your plan. Surgical plans may have deductible and coinsurance requirements.

Medical Expense Coverage

Medical expense coverage provides reimbursement for physician and medical services other than those directly connected with surgery. For example, it may pay for nonsur-

Did You Know? . . .

Who Pays if You Are Hurt on the Job

If you are injured on the job or become ill as a direct result of your employment, state law requires your employer to pay any resulting medical costs. **Workers' compensation insurance** covers employers for liability losses for injury or disease suffered by employees that result from employment-related causes. The benefits to the employee include health care, recuperative care, replacement of lost income, and, if necessary, rehabilitation. Thus, workers' compensation insurance covers the full range of health-related losses. Because only those losses resulting from work-related accidents are covered and benefits are limited, workers' compensation can only supplement your total health insurance plan.

gical outpatient procedures, X rays, doctor's visits, prescription drugs, and other bills. Such plans usually include a dollar maximum per year as well as coinsurance and deductible clauses. The deductible clause is often written on an item basis rather than in terms of an annual dollar amount.

Major Medical Expense Insurance

The three types of health care coverage discussed thus far are sometimes referred to as providing "first dollar" protection. In other words, they will pay the first dollar (or nearly so) of a covered health care expense. HMOs cover all three areas regardless of the dollar amount of the expense, whereas insurance plans specify dollar limits in these areas. If you rely solely on hospital, surgical, and medical expense *insurance* coverage, you may be reimbursed for small losses but could be wiped out by a serious illness whose costs exceed the limits of your protection.

Major medical expense insurance provides reimbursement for a broad range of related expenses, including hospital, surgical, and medical expenses. This insurance may have policy limits as high as $1 million and annual deductibles as high as $1000. It is often used as a supplement to hospital, surgical, and medical expense coverage. Thus, major medical insurance will cover expenses beyond those covered by the more basic plans, but only after its deductible has been met.

Most major medical policies include a coinsurance clause, which requires you to pay a percentage (usually 20 percent) of health care expenses (up to some limit) once the deductible is met.

Comprehensive Health Insurance

A **comprehensive health insurance** plan combines the protection provided by hospital insurance, surgical insurance, medical expense insurance, and major medical expense insurance into a single policy. Such a package of protections provides both the coverage of the basic plans and the broad, high-limit coverage of major medical insurance. Comprehensive health insurance plans usually include a $100 or $200 annual deductible and a 20 percent coinsurance requirement for all expenses up to the coinsurance cap. Policy limits of $1 million or more are common. One advantage of a comprehensive policy is that you do not need to determine which policy applies to a given expense. Comprehensive health insurance plans are primarily available on a group basis, and many employers that wish to provide a full line of health insurance coverage to workers take the approach of offering one comprehensive policy.

Dental Expense and Vision Care Insurance

Dental expense insurance provides reimbursement for dental care expenses. It is similar to other forms of health insurance in that it includes deductibles, coinsurance requirements, maximum payments for specific procedures, and overall policy limits. Oral surgery is often excluded from such policies but may be covered under surgical expense insurance. Orthodontics and procedures such as crowns and caps are also typically excluded or else have maximum payouts that fall far short of the typical charges. Typically, dental expense insurance is written on a group basis as an employment benefit.

Vision care insurance provides reimbursement for the expenses related to the purchase of glasses and contact lenses. Such a policy would cover eye examinations, refraction tests, fitting of the lenses, and the cost of the lenses and frames. Most vision care insurance is written on a group basis as an employment benefit. For an individual, vision care insurance is probably not a good buy because the highest expenses for eye care arise out of diseases and injuries to the eyes, which would be covered under general health insurance plans.

Accident and Dread Disease Health Insurance

Accident and dread disease health insurance is often purchased by people who have no other health care plan or fear that their health care plan will fall short of their needs. **Accident insurance** pays a specific amount per day—for example, $100 for a hospital stay arising out of an accident—or a specific amount for the loss of certain limbs or body parts—for example, $2000 for the loss of a finger or an arm. **Dread disease insurance** provides reimbursement for medical expenses arising out of the occurrence of a specific disease, most commonly cancer. These plans are designed to provide reimburse-

Advice from an Expert

Shop Carefully for a Private and Individual Health Care Plan

Shopping for an individual health care plan (a plan that is not provided through a group) requires a comparison of the many options available. You should focus your attention on three areas: (1) the cost, (2) the company, and (3) the plan itself.

The Cost

A sound health insurance plan, when purchased outside of a group, can easily cost more than $600 per month for a typical family of four. Obviously, comparison shopping is essential. When you apply for an individual health care plan, the company's decision whether to accept you is based on a number of underwriting factors, including your age, gender, occupation, family and personal health history, and physical condition. Each of these factors has a bearing on the likelihood of health-related expenditures and, therefore, the cost.

Medical information bureaus (similar to credit bureaus) maintain files on insurance applicants.* Both medical and nonmedical information are maintained in these files. If you are charged more or turned down for credit or insurance because of information in such a file, you should know your consumer rights. If you were denied coverage or charged extra, you have the right to be told that the information came from a medical information bureau. You can then request a copy of the report to verify the accuracy of the information.

The Company

It is important to choose a financially sound health care company. Wise financial planners always ask about the percentage of premiums collected by an insurance company that is subsequently paid out to reimburse the losses of the participants. The **claims ratio (payout ratio)** formula is

ment in addition to that provided by the standard plans. Most of these plans are over-priced and are less generous than implied in sales promotions. Typically, you are covered for a narrow range of services and are reimbursed for only a small portion of the expenses supposedly "covered." Purchasers often remain unaware of these limitations until they request reimbursement. It is much wiser to put the funds toward the purchase of a major medical policy with high limits, which is available through most employers.

Long-Term Health Care Insurance

Many health care episodes include a period of time when the patient no longer needs skilled medical care but does need assistance to a degree that requires confinement in a nursing home or special help at home. This need is especially prevalent with the extremely elderly and patients with certain conditions such as Alzheimer's disease. Such costs are not covered by HMOs, health insurance, or Medicare because the care is usually considered "not medically necessary" by these providers.

Long-term care insurance provides reimbursement for costs associated with intermediate-term and custodial care in a nursing facility or at home. The cost of such

4 Present an overview of long-term care insurance.

$$\text{Claims ratio} = \frac{\text{losses paid}}{\text{premiums collected}} \qquad (11.1)$$

Top companies typically have claims ratios that exceed 90 percent. At the other extreme are companies (especially those that sell hospital indemnity and dread disease insurance by mail, over the phone, or through newspaper inserts) that have claims ratios of less than 25 percent. The lower the claims ratio, the lower the return (the actual benefits) to the policyholder on the premium dollar paid.

The Plan

The most effective way to compare health care plans is to set some criteria for judging whether a policy provides the needed coverage. The plans that do provide the needed coverage (and have high claims ratios) can then be compared on a price basis. To make such a comparison, you might wish to complete Exercise 3 in the Exploring the World Wide Web exercises at the end of this chapter.

No plan should be purchased "sight unseen." If an agent or company will not allow you to study a plan for a few days, buy your policy elsewhere.

Holly Hunts
Montana State University

*To obtain a copy of your report ($8 or free within 30 days of an adverse report), write the Medical Information Bureau at P.O. Box 105, Essex Station, Boston, MA 02112; call (617) 426-3660 for an application; or visit www.mib.com.

care can amount to $40,000 per year or more. Key features to assess when considering such a policy include the following:

1. **The degree of impairment required for benefits to begin.** Insurance companies use the inability to perform a certain number of "activities of daily living" (ADLs) as a criterion for deciding when the insured becomes eligible for long-term care benefits. Typically, a policy pays benefits when a person cannot perform two or three ADLs without assistance. The ADLs most commonly used in this type of decision making are bathing, bladder control, dressing oneself, eating without assistance, toileting (moving on and off the toilet), and transferring (getting in and out of bed). Because bathing is often one of the first ADLs that is lost, a policy that does not list bathing as a criterion makes it more difficult to reach the threshold at which benefits become available.

2. **The level of care covered.** The levels of nursing home care are usually categorized three ways. *Skilled nursing care* is intended for persons who need intensive care, meaning 24-hours-a-day supervision and treatment by a registered nurse, under the direction of a doctor. *Intermediate care* is appropriate for persons who do not require around-the-clock nursing, but who are not able to live alone. *Custodial care* is suitable for many persons who do not need skilled nursing care, but who nevertheless require supervision (for example, help with eating or personal hygiene). Insurance companies' definitions of these levels of care may differ and must be considered when policies are evaluated. Although the largest expenses related to long-term care result from a stay in a nursing home, many people are able to remain in their homes with the assistance of visiting nurses, therapists, and even housekeepers. Long-term care policies can be written to cover such in-home care.

3. **The person's age.** The younger the person when the policy is purchased, the lower the premium. This difference arises because premiums can be collected for many years before long-term care is needed at an advanced age. The trade-off lies between buying young and paying premiums for many years versus waiting to purchase a policy, at which time it may be difficult to afford coverage because of preexisting conditions and consequently high policy costs.

4. **The benefit amount.** Long-term care plans are generally written to provide a specific dollar benefit per day of care. If the cost per day for nursing homes in your geographic area is typically $140, you might buy a policy for $110 per day, thereby coinsuring for a portion of the expenses.

5. **The benefit period.** Although it is possible to buy a policy with lifetime benefits, this option can be very expensive. The average nursing home stay is about two and one-half years. A policy with a three-year limit might cost one-third less than a policy with a lifetime benefit period.

6. **The waiting period.** Policies can pay benefits from the first day of nursing home care or they can include a waiting period. Selecting a 30-day or 90-day waiting period can significantly reduce premiums.

7. **Inflation protection.** If a policy is purchased prior to age 60, the buyer faces a significant risk in that inflation may render the daily benefit woefully inadequate when care is ultimately needed. Some policies increase the daily benefit by 4 or 5 percent per year to adjust for inflation, but this protection adds considerably to the premium. The younger your age when a policy is purchased, the more you might need inflation protection.

Disability Income Insurance

5 Describe how disability income insurance and Social Security disability income insurance can replace a portion of an eligible disabled person's income.

A number of resources are available for income protection during a period of disability. Many U.S. workers have sick pay benefits that can help ease the burden of a short period of disability. Some employers offer group disability income insurance, although typically the coverage lasts for only a short term (less than two years). In addition, many pension plans provide benefits to workers who become disabled while still employed. Such benefits plans, however, often fall far short of fully meeting the needs of young and middle-aged workers, who may have accumulated only a small amount of retirement funds.

Disability income insurance replaces a portion of the income lost when you cannot work because of illness or injury. Although probably the most overlooked type of insurance, it is vitally important for all workers. For example, a 22-year-old without dependents would probably need no life insurance but would likely need disability insurance to support himself or herself during a period of disability. Furthermore, at age 22, a person's chances of becoming disabled for at least three months are seven times greater than his or her chances of dying. (The probability of death for a man aged 22 is 18.9 per 10,000; the likelihood of disability is 142.8 per 10,000.)

Social Security disability income insurance is designed to help replace a portion of the lost income of eligible disabled workers. It provides these workers and their dependents with income during a period of disability expected to last at least 12 full months or until the worker's death. Benefits begin after a five-month waiting period, and the disability must be total. That is, the recipient must not be able to engage in any substantial, gainful activity. Social Security disability income protection may provide more than $20,000 annually in tax-free income to the family of a fully insured disabled worker. See Appendix B at the end of the book or on the *Garman/Forgue* website for an illustration of how to estimate these benefits, or visit www.ssa.gov/top10.html.

Level of Need

The first question to ask when contemplating disability income insurance is, "How much protection do I need?" The dollar limits on disability income policies are written either in increments of $100 per month or as a percentage of monthly income. Most companies will not write policies for more than 60 to 80 percent of the insured's after-tax earnings.

Determining the amount of protection needed may be difficult because some sources of help may not actually be available for all disabilities. For example, recall the five-month waiting period and total disability requirements (for which 70 percent of all applicants are rejected) under Social Security. A less severe disability that does not qualify for Social Security disability income insurance may create a need for more disability insurance than a more severe disability that does qualify for Social Security.

In addition, some disability benefits may cover short-term, but not long-term, disability. Nevertheless, it would be wise to complete the calculations in the Decision-Making Worksheet, "Determining Disability Income Insurance Needs" (page 318). You can use the figure obtained in the worksheet as a starting point when shopping for disability income insurance protection.

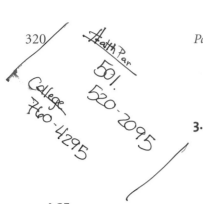

which prevents the lapse of a policy if a payment is late. The policy remains fully in force during the grace period, but only if the insured pays the premium before the end of the grace period.

3. **Noncancellable policies** must be continued in force without premium changes up to age 65 as long as the participant pays the required premium. Noncancellable policies are recommended when buying disability income insurance.

Summary

ACE
Self-tests

1. Health-related losses include the cost of direct medical care, the cost of recuperative care, and the lost income when one is ill or injured. HMOs, traditional health insurance, and the government-sponsored Medicare and Medicaid programs address the need for direct medical care. Long-term care insurance and disability income insurance focus on recuperative care costs and lost income, respectively. All of these plans can be obtained on an individual or group basis.

2. Health care policies contain language that outlines coverage in general and, more importantly, describes the limitations and conditions that determine the level of protection afforded under the plan. Some of the more important plan provisions include definitions of terms used in the plan, identification of who is covered under the plan, and the time period for the coverage. Important limitations include deductibles and copayments, coinsurance requirements, and restrictions on the types of losses covered.

3. The major benefits provided by health care plans are hospital, surgical, medical expense, major medical expense, comprehensive coverage, dental expense benefits, and vision care benefits.

4. Long-term care insurance provides a per-day dollar reimbursement when the insured person must stay in a nursing home or other long-term care facility. It is not designed to provide medical care protection, as that coverage is available through other plans such as an HMO, private insurance, or Medicare/Medicaid.

5. Disability income insurance replaces a portion of the income lost when you cannot work as a result of illness or injury. The amount you need is equal to your monthly after-tax income less any benefits to which you are entitled (for example, Social Security). By selecting among various policy provisions, you can tailor a policy that fills any gaps in your existing disability protection.

Key Terms

aggregate limits, 310
benefit period, 318
COBRA rights, 311
coinsurance clause, 309
copayment, 309
deductibles, 309
disability income insurance, 317
group health care plan, 303
guaranteed renewable policy, 319
health care plan, 302
health insurance, 305
health maintenance organization (HMO), 305
long-term care insurance, 315
Medicare, 306
open enrollment period, 303
preexisting conditions, 310
preferred provider organization (PPO), 306
primary-care physician, 305
Social Security disability income insurance, 317
waiting (elimination) period, 318

Chapter Review Questions

1. Categorize the losses that can result from an injury or illness, and list the providers that address each type of loss.

2. Identify one positive aspect of group health care plans.

3. Distinguish between HMOs and traditional health insurance.

4. Distinguish between PPOs and HMOs.

5. What are COBRA rights, and how do they relate to the portability of group health care protection to individual health care protection?

6. Distinguish among item limits, episode limits, time period limits, and aggregate limits as used in health insurance policies.

7. What are the differences between a deductible and a copayment?

8. Define long-term care insurance, and describe four considerations you must keep in mind when selecting this type of insurance.

9. Identify the major policy provisions to consider when purchasing disability income insurance, and explain how you determine your level of need for such insurance.

10. Explain the various renewability options typically used in health care plans.

Group Discussion Issues

1. Are you covered by a health care plan? If so, what do you see as the largest potential for losses should you become ill or injured? How well do you understand the plan?

2. HMO plans and health insurance plans take different approaches to health care. What are the major differences between the two types of plans? Which plan would you prefer for your own health care protection?

3. Are you covered by a long-term care insurance plan? What would happen if you became so incapacitated that such care was necessary? What could you do?

4. Are you covered by disability income insurance? What would happen if you were unable to work for two or three years due to illness or injury?

Decision-Making Cases

Case 1
A New Employee Ponders Disability Insurance

Jim Napier of Bethlehem, Pennsylvania, recently took a new job as a manufacturer's representative for an aluminum castings company. While looking over his employee benefits materials, he discovered that his employer would provide 10 sick days per year. Jim can accumulate a maximum of 60 sick days if any go unused in a given year. In addition, his employer provides a $1000-per-month, short-term, one-year total disability policy. When he called the employee benefits office, Jim found that he might qualify for $400 per month in Social Security disability benefits if he became unable to work. Jim also knew that he could cease paying $50 per month in life insurance premiums if he became disabled under a waiver-of-premium option in his life insurance policy. Jim earns a base salary of $1500 per month and expects

to earn about that same amount in commissions, for an average after-tax income of $2100 per month. After considering this information, Jim became understandably concerned that a disability might destroy his financial future.

(a) What is the level of Jim's short-term, one-year disability insurance needs?

(b) What is the level of Jim's long-term disability insurance needs?

(c) Help Jim select from among the important disability insurance policy provisions to design a disability insurance program tailored to his needs.

Case 2
A CPA Selects a Health Insurance Plan

Your friend Taliesha Jackson of Tulsa, Oklahoma, recently started a new job as a CPA in a moderate-size accounting firm. Knowing that you were taking a personal finance course, she asked your advice about selecting the best health insurance plan. Her employer offered four options:

- **Option A:** A package of hospital, surgical, and medical expense insurance plus a major medical policy. The "first-dollar" coverages provide for 45 days of hospitalization per year and will pay the usual, customary, and reasonable charges for almost any event, including maternity. The major medical policy has a $500 annual deductible and an 80 percent/20 percent coinsurance clause with a $20,000 coinsurance cap. The major medical policy has a $100,000 aggregate limit.

- **Option B:** A comprehensive health insurance policy with a $250 annual deductible, an 80 percent/20 percent coinsurance clause with a $10,000 coinsurance cap, and a $250,000 aggregate limit.

- **Option C:** Same as option B except that a PPO is associated with the plan. If Taliesha agrees to have services provided by the PPO, her annual deductible drops to $100 and the coinsurance clause is waived. As an incentive to get employees to select option C, Taliesha's employer will provide dental expense insurance worth about $20 per month.

- **Option D:** Membership in an HMO. Taliesha will have to contribute $25 extra each month if she chooses this option.

(a) To help her make a decision, Taliesha has asked you to list three positive points and three negative points about each plan. Prepare such a list.

(b) Why might Taliesha's employer provide an incentive of dental insurance if she chooses option C?

Financial Math Questions

1. Bernard Haley of Rockford, Illinois, aged 61, recently suffered a severe stroke. He was in intensive care for 12 days and was hospitalized for 18 more days. After being discharged from the hospital, he spent 45 days in a nursing home for medically necessary nursing and rehabilitative care. Bernard had hospital, surgical, and medical expense insurance through his employer. He had also purchased major medical insurance through a group plan with a $1000 deductible, a $50,000 episode limit, and a $250,000 aggregate limit. The major medical policy had an 80/20 coinsurance clause with a $2000 coinsurance cap. All of Bernard's policies covered medically necessary services performed in a nursing home setting. His total medical bill was $125,765, and his insurance from his employer covered $42,814 of these charges.

   (a) Of the remainder, how much did the major medical policy pay?

   (b) How much did Bernard pay?

2. Michael Howitt of Berkley, Michigan, recently had his gallbladder removed. His total bill for this event, which was his only health care expense for the year, came to $13,890. His health insurance plan has a $500 annual deductible and a 75/25 coinsurance provision. The cap on Michael's coinsurance share is $2000.

   (a) How much of the bill will Michael pay?

   (b) How much of the bill will be paid by Michael's insurance?

3. Marjorie Woffstead, a mortgage broker in Tucson, Arizona, had heart bypass surgery last year. Marjorie was covered by both Parts A and B of Medicare with the following information applicable at that time.

Part A annual deductible:	$876
Part B annual deductible:	$100
Part A coinsurance:	
For each day hospitalized over 60 and up to 90 days	$219/day
For days 21–100 for skilled nursing home care	$110/day
For nonskilled approved home health care	20%
For approved durable medical equipment	20%
Part B coinsurance:	
For Medicare-approved services	20%

   Given this information and the additional billing information for Marjorie's surgery and recovery, calculate her share of each component.

   (a) The hospital bill:

7 days in intensive care at $700 per day	$ 4,900
14 days in a regular room at $350 per day	4,900

Operating room, X rays, tests	5,000
Total	$14,800

   (b) The physician's bills:

Cardiologist for surgery and follow-up	$ 3,000
Anesthesiologist	1,000
Primary-care physician for hospital visits	1,320
Total	$5,320

   (c) Recovery expense bills after the hospital stay:

Skilled nursing home care for 30 days at $300 per day	$9,000
Nonskilled home health care for 14 days at $100 per day	1,400
Total	$10,400

   (d) What was the total amount paid by Marjorie?

Money Matters Continuing Cases

The Hernandezes Face the Possibility of Long-Term Care

Victor Hernandez recently learned that his uncle has Alzheimer's disease. While discussing this tragedy with Maria, he realized that two of his grandparents probably had the disease, although no formal diagnosis was ever made. As a result, Victor and Maria have become interested in how they might protect themselves from the financial effects of long-term health care.

1. What factors should the Hernandezes consider as they shop for long-term care protection?

2. Victor is still in his forties. How does his age affect their decisions related to long-term care protection?

The Johnsons Consider Buying Disability Insurance

Although Belinda's employer offers a generous employee benefit program, it does not provide disability income protection other than 8 sick days per year, which may accumulate to 20 days if Belinda does not use them. Harry also has no disability income insurance. Although both have worked long enough to qualify for Social Security disability benefits, Belinda has estimated that Harry would receive about $640 and she would receive about $800 per month if they qualified for Social Security. Harry and Belinda realize that they could not maintain their current living standards on only one salary. Thus, the need for disability income insurance has become evident even though they probably cannot afford such protection at this time. In fact, they chose not to purchase the disability waiver of premium option when they purchased their life insurance. Advise them on the following points:

1. Use the Decision-Making Worksheet on page 318 to determine how much disability insurance Harry and Belinda each need. Use the December salary figures from Table 3.3 on page 73. To determine the amount of taxes and Social Security paid by each, assume that Harry, whose salary represents approximately 42 percent of their total income, paid a comparable percentage of the taxes.

2. Use the information on pages 317–320 to advise the Johnsons about their selections related to the following major policy provisions:

   (a) Elimination period

   (b) Benefit period

   (c) Residual clause

   (d) Social Security rider

   (e) Cost-of-living adjustments

What Would You Recommend Now?

Now that you have read the chapter on health care planning, what would you recommend to Monica DiMartino in the case at the beginning of the chapter regarding:

1. Choosing among the three alternatives available to her?

2. Monica's concerns about providing for her mother's health care needs?

3. Monica's need for disability and long-term care insurance?

Exploring the World Wide Web

To complete these exercises, go to the *Garman/Forgue* website at college.hmco.com/business/students. Under General Business, select the title of this text. Click on the Internet Exercises link for this chapter, and answer the questions that appear on the Web page.

1. Visit the website for the National Committee on Quality Assurance, where you will find information assessing the quality of and accreditation status of health care plans. If you are covered by a health care plan, search for information on your plan. If you are not covered or if data are not available on your plan, select a major city and obtain the report on a plan in that city. What information, criteria, and other data in the report might assist you in assessing the quality of any plan? Also, print a copy of NCQA's consumer brochure.

2. On the *Garman/Forgue* website, you will find the Decision-Making Worksheet on page 318 that you can use to calculate your disability income insurance needs. Visit the website for InsQuote.com, InsWeb.com, or QuoteSmith.com to obtain policy information and premium quotations on policies that would fit your needs.

3. Visit the website for *Money* magazine where you will find tips for buying health insurance and selecting among the various types of plans based on your particular health care needs. What plans and plan features are best for you?

4. Visit the website for the Social Security Administration and use its "BEST" on-line screening tool to determine whether you are currently eligible to receive Social Security Disability Income benefits should you become disabled.

5. Visit the website for A. M. Best, Inc. and read its discussion of how to choose a long-term care insurance policy. How might such protection fit into your risk-management program or that of your family?

Visit the Garman/Forgue website . . .

@ **college.hmco.com/business/students**

Under General Business, select *Personal Finance 8e*. There, among other valuable resources, you will find a complete glossary, ACE questions, links to help you complete the chapter exercises, and links to other personal finance sites.

Chapter 12

Life Insurance Planning

After reading this chapter, you should be able to:

1 **Explain** the financial planning needs that are met through life insurance.

2 **Calculate** your need for life insurance.

3 **Distinguish** among the types of life insurance.

4 **Explain** the purposes of the major provisions of a life insurance policy.

5 **Summarize** the strategies for selecting and purchasing life insurance to meet your needs.

Karen Bridgeman, age 28, and her husband Bobby, age 30, are planning to start a family in the next year. Both have small cash-value life insurance policies ($25,000 and $50,000, respectively) that their parents purchased when they were children. Karen is a real estate attorney and earns $90,000 per year. She plans to continue working after having a child. Her employer provides a life insurance policy equal to her salary as an employee benefit. Karen's employer also offers a 401(k) plan into which she can contribute a maximum of 6 percent of her salary each year matched by her employer one-half of 1 percent for each 1 percent that Karen contributes. To date, she has been contributing 4 percent. Bobby is a high-school teacher and track coach and makes $39,000 per year. His employer provides the full cost of his teacher retirement pension plan. An optional supplemental retirement plan is available into which Bobby can contribute 5 percent of his salary. He has not done so as yet. Bobby has an employer-provided life insurance policy equal to twice his salary.

What would you recommend to Karen and Bobby on the subject of life insurance planning regarding:

1. Their changing need for life insurance once they have a child?

2. What type of life insurance they should consider and whether they should use multiple policies?

3. Coordinating their retirement and other investments with their life insurance program?

4. Shopping for life insurance?

Death is certain. Its timing is not. With this uncertainty comes the risk of financial losses. **Life insurance** is insurance that protects against financial losses resulting from death. This chapter examines the role of life insurance in your overall personal risk-management plan. Topics covered include reasons for buying life insurance, ways to determine your insurance needs, the many types of life insurance available, the life insurance policy and its major provisions, and strategies for buying life insurance.

1 Explain the financial planning needs that are met through life insurance.

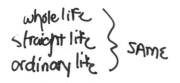

Why Do People Need Life Insurance?

It might appear to you that the term "life insurance" is a misnomer. After all, the person on whose life an insurance policy is issued will not be protected from death. In another sense, however, life insurance is appropriately named. The primary reason for buying life insurance is to allow the survivors and heirs of the deceased to continue with their lives free from the financial burdens that death can bring. Home ownership can be safeguarded. A surviving spouse and children can continue to live a similar lifestyle. College or other educational plans can remain intact. Retirement income can be made available for the surviving spouse. In essence, life insurance is for your loved ones, not for yourself. And, although most people will live to at least retirement age, approximately one-quarter of today's adults will die during their working years.

In addition to feeling grief over the personal loss involved in the death of a loved one, survivors may experience severe financial losses. These losses can include the lost income of the deceased and expenditures for final expenses, a readjustment period, debt repayment, and education for children. Existing life insurance, financial assets, and Social Security may partially offset such losses.

Existing Insurance and Assets Reduce the Level of Need

Employers often provide life insurance to their employees as an employee benefit. In addition, many people have existing life insurance that was purchased for them as children or that they purchased previously. These coverages can reduce the need for additional life insurance purchases.

As time passes, individuals and families usually acquire at least a minimal amount of savings and investments. The funds held in savings accounts, certificates of deposit, stocks, bonds, and mutual funds often are specifically earmarked for some special goal, such as retirement, travel, or college for children. In the event of a premature death, they could be used to pay final and readjustment expenses as well as to replace lost income, even though it might be wiser to retain these funds for their originally intended purpose. Pension funds and retirement plans of the deceased, such as 401(k) and 403(b) plans and IRAs (discussed in Chapter 18), are also sometimes viewed as resources. Younger families should be wary of using retirement money for living expenses after the death of an income provider, however, as this strategy may jeopardize the surviving spouse's retirement. As a general rule, life insurance needs decrease and assets increase over the course of one's life. At some point, savings and investments should exceed potential losses and eliminate the need for life insurance—especially after age 60, when retirement is imminent or has arrived.

2 Calculate your need for life insurance.

Calculating Your Need for Life Insurance

Determining the magnitude of the possible losses resulting from a premature death can be complicated. One calculation method involves an attempt to put a dollar value on the life to be insured based on some notion of the psychological loss that would be felt. This approach is particularly inadequate and hazardous because it has no connection to the actual financial loss that will be suffered.

The Multiple-of-Earnings Approach Is an Inaccurate Method

Some people use a **multiple-of-earnings approach** to estimate the amount of life insurance needed. This simple method multiplies one's income by some factor to derive a rough estimate of the level of need. For example, one rule-of-thumb, multiple-of-earnings approach is to have life insurance five or six times one's annual income. One could also use the interest factors from Appendix Table A.4 for a given after-tax, after-inflation interest rate and a given number of years of need. For example, someone who wishes to replace income of $36,000 for 20 years at an interest rate of 4 percent would need to have $489,240 of life insurance protection. Note that the multiple-of-earnings approach addresses only one of the factors affecting life insurance needs—income-replacement needs. It does not take into consideration such factors as age, family situation, and losses other than income that can occur when someone dies. Thus, it is an imprecise (although relatively easy-to-use) method for determining life insurance needs.

The Needs Approach Is a Better Method

The **needs approach** to estimating life insurance needs considers all of the factors that might potentially affect the level of need. It improves upon the calculations of the multiple-of-earnings approach by including a more accurate assessment of income-replacement needs and incorporates factors that add to and reduce the level of need. The Decision-Making Worksheet, "The Needs Approach to Life Insurance" (page 330), illustrates calculations made via the needs approach. You would be wise to calculate your current needs for life insurance and then to revisit those calculations every three years and when your family situation or health status changes.

Calculating Life Insurance Needs for a Couple with Small Children.   Consider the example of Zoel Raymond, a 35-year-old factory foreman from Holyoke, Massachusetts, who has a spouse (aged 30) and three sons (aged eight, seven, and three years). Zoel earns $48,000 annually and desires to replace his income for 30 years, at which time his spouse would no longer need to support their children financially. The "Example" column of the Decision-Making Worksheet expands on the situation faced by Zoel.

1. **Income-replacement needs.** Zoel's income of $48,000 is multiplied by 0.75 and the interest factor of 17.292. This factor was used because Zoel decided that it would be best to replace his lost income for 30 years or until Mary, his wife, reached age 60 and passed through the Social Security blackout period. Zoel and Mary are moderate-risk investors and believe that she could earn a 4 percent after-tax, after-inflation rate of return on life insurance proceeds. Income-replacement needs based on these conditions amount to $622,512.

2. **Final-expense needs.** Zoel estimates his final expenses for funeral, burial, and other expenses at $10,000.

3. **Readjustment-period needs.** Mary has a career as a columnist for a local newspaper, which earns her an annual income of $38,000. Allocating $19,000 for readjustment-period needs would allow her to take a six-month leave of absence from her job or meet other readjustment needs.

4. **Debt-repayment needs.** Zoel and Mary owe $10,000 on various credit cards and an auto loan. They also owe about $128,000 on their home mortgage. Mary would like to pay off all debts except the mortgage debt should Zoel die. The mortgage debt would be affordable if Zoel's income was adequately replaced.

5. **College-expense needs.** Zoel estimates that it would currently cost $25,000 for each of his sons to attend the local campus of a public university. Should he die, $25,000 of the life insurance proceeds could be invested for each son. If invested appropriately, the funds would grow at a rate sufficient to keep up with increasing costs of a college education.

6. **Other special needs.** Zoel and Mary do not have any unusual needs related to life insurance planning, so they entered zero for this factor.

7. **Subtotal.** The Raymonds total items 1 through 6 on the worksheet and determine that the family's financial needs arising out of Zoel's death would amount to $736,512. Although this sum seems large to them, they have access to two resources that can reduce this figure, as indicated in items 8 and 9.

Decision-Making Worksheet

The Needs Approach to Life Insurance

This worksheet provides a mechanism for estimating life insurance needs using the needs approach. The amounts needed for income replacement, final expenses, readjustment needs, debt repayment, college expenses, and other special needs are calculated and then reduced by funds available from government benefits and any current insurance or assets that could cover the need. This worksheet is also available on the *Garman/Forgue* website.

Factors Affecting Need	Example	Your Figures
1. Income-replacement needs Multiply 75 percent of annual income* by the interest factor from Appendix Table A.4 that corresponds to the number of years that the income is to be replaced and the assumed after-tax, after-inflation rate of return. ($36,000 × 17.292 for 30 years at a 4% rate of return)	$ 622,512	$_____
2. Final-expense needs Includes funeral, burial, travel, and other items of expense just prior to and after death.	+ 10,000	+_____
3. Readjustment-period needs To cover employment interruptions and possible education expenses for surviving spouse and dependents.	+ 19,000	+_____
4. Debt-repayment needs Provides repayment of short-term and installment debt, including credit cards and personal loans.	+ 10,000	+_____
5. College-expense needs To provide a fund to help meet college expenses of dependents.	+ 75,000	+_____
6. Other special needs	+ 0	+_____
7. Subtotal (combined effects of items 1–6)	+ $736,512	+_____
8. Government benefits Present value of Social Security survivor's benefits and other benefits. Multiply monthly benefit estimate by 12 and use Table A.4 for the number of years that benefits will be received and the same interest rate that was used in item 1. ($2725 × 12 × 11.118 for 15 years of benefits and a 4% rate of return)	− 363,558	−_____
9. Current insurance assets	− 98,000	−_____
10. Life insurance needed	$ 274,954	$_____

*Seventy-five percent is used because about 25 percent of income is used for personal needs.

8. Government benefits. Zoel estimates that his family would qualify for monthly Social Security survivor's benefits of $2725.* These benefits would be paid for 15 years, until his youngest son turns 18. The present value of this stream of benefits is $363,558 (from Appendix Table A.4), assuming a 4 percent return for 15 years.

*Social Security benefits can be estimated by requesting a Personal Earnings and Benefits Estimate (PEBES) from the Social Security Administration (www.ssa.gov).

9. **Current insurance and assets.** Zoel has a $50,000 life insurance policy purchased five years ago. His employer also pays for a group policy equal to his $48,000 gross annual income. Zoel's major assets include his home and his retirement plan. Because he does not want Mary to have to liquidate these assets if he dies, he includes only the $98,000 insurance coverage in item 9.

10. **Life insurance needed.** After subtracting worksheet items 8 and 9 from the subtotal, Zoel estimates that he needs an additional $274,954 in life insurance. This amount may seem like a large sum of insurance, but Zoel can meet this need through term life insurance for as little as $30 per month.

Because Mary earns an income about 80 percent of Zoel's, her life insurance needs may be about 20 percent lower; to determine the specific amount, however, the couple must complete a worksheet for her as well. Next, the Raymonds will need to decide what type of life insurance is best and from whom to buy additional life insurance. These topics are covered later in this chapter.

Calculating Life Insurance Needs for a Young Professional.

Irene Leech of Napa, California, recently graduated with a degree in tourism management and has accepted a position paying $33,000 per year. Irene is single and lives with her sister. She owes $9500 on a car loan and $11,800 in education loans. She has about $4000 in the bank. Among her employee benefits is an employer-paid term insurance policy equal to her annual salary.

Irene has been approached by a life insurance agent who used the multiple-of-earnings approach to suggest that she needs $165,000 in life insurance, or about five times her income. Does she? If you apply the needs approach to Irene's situation, you will see the following:

■ Because Irene has no dependents, she needs no insurance for income-replacement needs, readjustment-period needs, college-expense needs, or other special needs. Items 1, 3, 5, and 6 in the needs approach worksheet on page 330 are, therefore, zero.

■ Irene's survivors will not qualify for any government benefits, so item 8 will also be zero.

■ Irene estimates her burial costs at $6000, which she entered for item 2.

■ Irene would like to see her $9500 automobile loan and $11,800 education loans repaid in the event of her death. She feels better knowing that her younger sister could inherit her car free and clear. She entered $19,300 for item 4.

■ Irene has combined life insurance and assets of $37,000, so she entered that amount for item 8.

The resulting calculations show that Irene needs *no* additional life insurance ($6000 + $21,300 − $37,000 = −$9700). The lesson here is that you should not buy life insurance simply to lock in low rates unless you have a personal or family-based medical history that might interfere with the purchase of life insurance when needed later. The agent suggested that Irene buy now while she is young and rates are low. In fact, that would be like buying car insurance before you own a car. When her circumstances change, Irene should reappraise her life insurance needs accordingly.

The Two Basic Types of Life Insurance

Although many people are confused by the variety of life insurance policies available, in reality only two types of life insurance exist: term life insurance and cash-value life insurance. **Term life insurance** is often described as "pure protection" because it pays benefits only if the insured person dies within the time period (term) covered by the policy. The policy must be renewed if coverage is desired for another time period. **Cash-value life insurance** pays benefits at death and includes a savings/investment element that can provide benefits to the policyholder prior to the death of the insured person. Thus, it includes a **cash value** representing the value of the investment element in the life insurance policy. Due to its investment aspect, many people automatically believe it is the better option. Cash-value life insurance costs more than term insurance, however, and it is usually not a good investment technique.

Term Life Insurance

Term life insurance contracts are most often written for time periods of 1, 5, or 10 years. If the insured survives the specified time period, the beneficiary receives no monetary benefits. Term insurance can be purchased in contracts with face amounts in multiples of $1000, usually with a minimum face amount of $50,000. The **face amount** is the dollar value of protection as listed in the policy and used to calculate the premium.

Unless otherwise stipulated by the original contract, you must apply for a new contract and may be required to undergo a medical examination to renew the policy. The premium will increase with each renewal, reflecting your increasing age and greater likelihood of dying while the new policy remains in force. If you have a health problem, you may be denied a new policy or be asked to pay even higher premiums. For example, a $100,000 five-year renewable term policy for a man aged 25 might have an annual premium of $100; at age 35, the policy might cost $135; and at age 45, it might cost $220. Term policies are less expensive than cash-value policies because they do not include a savings/investment element.

Guaranteed Renewable Term Insurance.   Proving insurability at renewal may be difficult should you develop a health problem during the period of a term policy. Term life insurance policies, however, are usually written as **guaranteed renewable term insurance.** The guarantee protects you against the possibility of becoming uninsurable. The number of renewals you can make without proving insurability may be limited, and a maximum age may be specified for these renewals (usually 65 or 70 years). Unless you are positive that you will not need a renewal, guaranteed renewable term insurance is recommended.

Level-Premium Term Insurance.   You can partially avoid term insurance premium increases as you grow older by buying **level-premium** (or **guaranteed level-premium**) **term insurance,** which is a term policy with a long time period (perhaps 5, 10, or 20 years). Under such a policy, the premiums remain constant, possibly throughout the entire life of the policy. Premiums charged in early years are higher than necessary to balance out the lower-than-necessary premiums in later years covered by the policy. Premiums on policies written for 10 or more years usually remain constant for a 5-year interval, then might increase to a new constant rate for another 5- or 10-year interval. Such level-premium policies may include a **re-enter provision,** requiring proof of good health at the beginning of each 5-year interval. If his or her health status changes, the insured must re-enter the policy at a higher rate than originally anticipated. Be wary of policies with such a provision, especially if you anticipate needing coverage beyond the initial level-premium interval.

Decreasing Term Insurance.

With **decreasing term insurance,** the face amount of coverage declines annually, while the premiums remain constant. The owner chooses an initial face amount and a contract period, after which the face amount of the policy gradually declines (usually each year) to some minimum (such as $50,000) in the last year of the contract. For example, a woman aged 35 might buy a 30-year $200,000 decreasing term policy that declines by $5000 each year. The major benefit of decreasing term policies is that they more closely fit changing insurance needs, which typically decline as a person ages.

Convertible Term Insurance.

Convertible term insurance offers the policyholder the option of exchanging a term policy for a cash-value policy without evidence of insurability. Usually, this conversion is available only in the early years of the term policy. Some policies provide for an automatic conversion from term to cash-value insurance after a specific number of years.

There are two ways to convert a term policy to a cash-value policy. First, you can simply request the conversion and begin paying the higher premiums required for the cash-value policy. The savings/investment element of the cash-value policy will begin accumulating as of the date of the conversion. Second, you can pay the company the cash value that would have built up had the policy originally been written on a cash-value basis. Although this lump sum may be a considerable amount, it does represent an asset for the policyholder. Furthermore, the new premiums will be based on your age at the time that you bought the original term policy, which may result in lower premiums.

Group Term Life Insurance.

Group term life insurance is issued to people as members of a group rather than as individuals. Most such policies are written for a large number of employees, with premiums being paid in full or in part by the employer. Group life insurance premiums are average rates based on the characteristics of the group as a whole. Unlike with health insurance, however, group life insurance rates are not consistently lower than individual rates. If you are a good risk, you usually can do better buying life insurance on your own. If you are insured under a group plan, you need not prove your insurability, and you can usually convert the policy to an individual basis without proof of insurability if you leave the group. Such convertibility represents a major benefit for persons whose health status makes individual life insurance unaffordable or unattainable.

Credit Term Life Insurance.

Credit term life insurance will pay the remaining balance of a loan if the insured dies before repaying the debt. In essence, it is a decreasing term insurance policy with the creditor named as beneficiary. This product is usually grossly overpriced, and the only people who should consider its purchase are those who are uninsurable because of a serious health condition. Most people are insurable and can obtain term life coverage for a minimal cost, so they do not need credit term life insurance.

Advice from an Expert

Buy Term and Invest the Rest

The principle behind the strategy "buy term and invest the rest" is simple: If you invest the money difference between the cost of premiums for a term life insurance policy and the cost of premiums for a far more expensive cash-value policy, you will *always* come out ahead financially. To see why, consider the buildup of protection shown in the accompanying table for Seth Cameron, a 30-year-old who is considering life insurance policies. Seth could pay an $870 annual premium to buy a $100,000 whole life policy. Alternatively, he could spend $130 for the first-year premium of a $100,000 five-year renewable term policy and invest the $740 difference ($870 − $130) in a mutual fund account and earn a 5 percent after-tax rate of return.

If Seth dies tomorrow, the policy's beneficiary would receive both the $100,000 in insurance proceeds and the $740 in savings. After five years (age 35), Seth's annual $710 in savings would have grown to $4293; should he die at that time, the total death benefit would be $104,293. If Seth dies years into the future, the estate is even further ahead because of the growing principal in the account. By age 60, Seth's mutual fund investment would have grown to $58,052. If the fund earned higher than 5 percent annually, the amount would be much greater.

By the time Seth reached age 60, the term insurance

premiums would exceed the premiums for the cash-value policy. However, his need for life insurance would presumably be greatly reduced at that point. If Seth's children were self-supporting by then, he could probably drop the term insurance policy altogether. Nevertheless, his mutual fund account would remain to provide a financial nest egg of $58,052 or more to his heirs.

With the "buy term and invest the rest" strategy, Seth would have been insured over 30 years at total premium cost of just $7350. By contrast, the cash-value policy would have required total premiums of $26,100 ($870 × 30) and the policy's cash value at year 30 would be around $44,000.

For "buy term and invest the rest" to work, however, the difference between the term and cash-value policy premiums must, in fact, be invested on a regular basis. Many people say that they will invest this money but then fail to follow through on that promise. You can succeed with a little discipline. The easiest way to ensure that your money is actually invested is to set up an **automatic investment program** (AIP) in which a mutual fund is authorized to withdraw money from your checking account, perhaps monthly, to buy mutual fund shares. When you agree to invest the "difference" automatically, the strategy will work well for you. (See Chapters 13 and 15.)

Estate Buildup If a Term Life Insurance Buyer Invests the Difference

Age	Premium for Five-Year Renewable Term	Difference (Not Spent on Whole Life)	Total Investment and Earnings* at 5 Percent	Total Estate
30	$ 130	$ 740	$ 740	$100,740
35	150	720	4,293	104,293
40	180	690	9,657	109,657
45	210	660	16,328	116,328
50	240	630	24,668	124,668
55	590	290	35,139	135,139
60			58,052	58,052

*This illustration makes the following assumptions: The whole life policy premium for the same $100,000 in coverage is fixed at $870 every year; the buyer pays the five-year renewable term premium at the beginning of each year; and the difference is invested. Those amounts stay in the investments account all year, as does the previous year's ending balance. Investments earn a compounded 5 percent after-tax annual rate of return. Upon the insured's death, the beneficiary would receive the $100,000 face amount of the term life insurance policy plus the amount built up in the investments account earning 5 percent.

Jordan E. Goodman, "America's Money Answers Man" (www.MoneyAnswers.com)
Author of Everyone's Money Book *and* Everyone's Money Book Series

has the potential to support himself or herself if the other partner were to die. The arrival of children, however, triggers a sharp increase in life insurance needs. Children often require as many as 25 years of parental support, during which time they usually have little ability to provide for themselves. As children grow older, however, the number of years of their remaining dependency declines, reducing the need for life insurance. Most parents eventually see a diminished need for life insurance once their children become independent, in part because parental responsibility for children declines and in part because the parent's investment program may have grown large enough to be used for income when needed. Retirement and the likelihood of another period of singlehood reduce the need for life insurance or may even eliminate it altogether.

Figure 12.3 depicts a life insurance and investment plan recommended over an individual's life cycle. This plan is built on two cornerstones: (1) the purchase of term insurance for the bulk of life insurance needs (because term insurance is more flexible than cash-value insurance and provides more protection for each premium dollar) and (2) a systematic, regular investment program. At the age of 20, the average person needs little or no life insurance. If desired, a small term or cash-value policy with guaranteed insurability is usually sufficient. Over time, however, an individual's responsibilities for the financial well-being of others may increase. These responsibilities will, in turn, increase the need for financial-support protection through life insurance. Because the early years of an investment program likely will not yield enough protection, life insurance should be purchased to cover the financial-support shortage. The amount you will

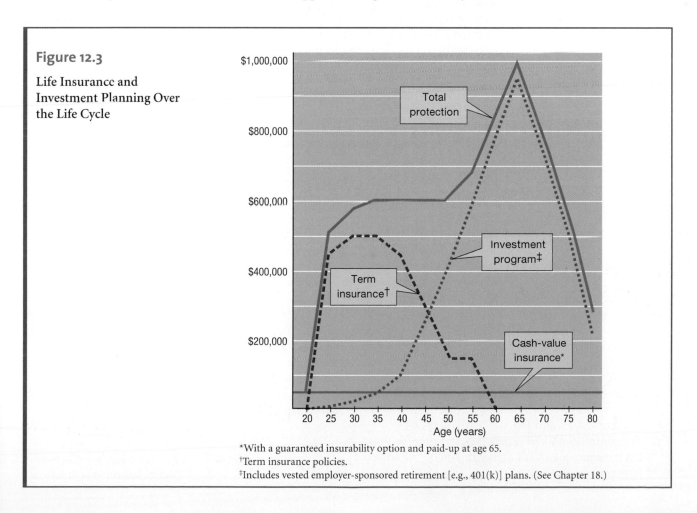

Figure 12.3

Life Insurance and Investment Planning Over the Life Cycle

*With a guaranteed insurability option and paid-up at age 65.
†Term insurance policies.
‡Includes vested employer-sponsored retirement [e.g., 401(k)] plans. (See Chapter 18.)

need to purchase will depend on your family's financial circumstances; Figure 12.3 shows a typical pattern.

At about age 50, the probable losses from a premature death typically begin to diminish because the investment program (started at age 23 in Figure 12.3) should have grown sufficiently to offer some protection from a premature death. In addition, children may begin to go out on their own and no longer need substantial financial support. Reflecting this new reality, life insurance needs will level off or decrease around the same time that term insurance premiums become more expensive. By the age of 65, your life insurance needs should be greatly reduced or eliminated, and your investment program should have grown sufficiently to provide for you and your family during your older years.

Of course, this scenario requires that you implement an investment program. Chapters 13 through 17 cover investments in detail to provide you with the necessary tools to construct this program.

Choose a Financially Strong Company

The most important feature of any life insurance company is its ability to pay its obligations. The company must have the stability and financial strength to survive for the many years your policy will remain in force. Banks that sell life insurance do so through subsidiary companies that are not federally insured. Thus, these subsidiary insurance companies should be just as financially strong as traditional insurance companies. Ratings of the financial strengths of insurance companies are available from A. M. Best Company (www.ambest.com). You can also find information about companies through your state's insurance regulatory agency (www.naic.org/1regulator/usamap.htm).

Tax Considerations and Consequences

Life Insurance Planning

Many people consider cash-value life insurance to be a tax-advantaged way to invest for retirement. Life insurance does have some tax-sheltering aspects because the cash value built up in the policy is not subject to income taxes. For a number of other reasons, however, cash-value life insurance does not compare favorably with qualified retirement plans available through your employer or with IRAs (discussed in Chapter 18):

1. The rate of return on cash-value life insurance has historically lagged well behind what can be achieved by a diversified portfolio of stock and bond mutual funds. Mutual funds can be purchased through various tax-sheltered retirement accounts (discussed in Chapters 14, 15, and 18).
2. The commissions and expense charges on cash-value life insurance are much higher than those associated

with many no-load mutual funds. This is especially true for index mutual funds. (See Chapter 15.)
3. The premiums paid on life insurance policies cannot be used to reduce taxable income. Individual retirement accounts and 401(k) plans do offer this significant advantage.

You should be contributing the maximum amount possible into available tax-sheltered retirement plans before you consider the purchase of cash-value life insurance as a retirement savings vehicle. Warning bells should go off in your mind if you discover that a purchase of cash-value life insurance gets in the way of fully participating in your retirement plan at work.

Life insurance companies, like all insurance companies, make money in two ways. First, they make **underwriting profits,** which result when the premiums collected exceed the expenses of providing coverage plus the losses paid by the company. Second, insurance companies do not simply hold the premiums that they collect until the funds are used to pay for the losses of their customers, but rather invest this money. These investments provide **investment profits,** which result from the return on the investments made with premiums collected from the insureds. Insurers need not make an underwriting profit to be profitable.

Choose an Agent

The most obvious source of information about the cost of life insurance is the agent selling the policy. An **insurance agent** is a representative of an insurance company authorized to sell, modify, service, and terminate insurance contracts. In the United States, life insurance is typically sold through exclusive agents who represent only one company, although some independent agents represent more than one company. Some life insurance companies also sell policies directly through the mail or on the Web.

The life insurance agent must be qualified to design a program tailored to your specific needs and should understand the dynamics of family relationships, which influence all life insurance needs. The agent should have earned a professional designation, such as chartered life underwriter (CLU). To earn the CLU, an agent must have three years of experience and pass a ten-course program in life insurance counseling. Some agents also may have earned the certified financial planner (CFP) or chartered financial consultant (ChFC) designation (see page 50).

Your agent should be willing to take the time to provide personal service and to answer all of your questions about the policy both before and after you purchase it. Always ask an agent about the first-year commission on any policies you are considering. In addition, you should check your agent's reputation with your state's insurance regulatory agency. Although this agency will not tell you about consumer complaints or pending disciplinary action, it will notify you of formal disciplinary actions that may have already been taken. Because many life insurance agents sell variable life insurance, they must have securities dealer licenses, so you can also contact your state's securities regulatory department for information.

Compare Costs Among Policies

The price people pay for life insurance depends on their age, health, and lifestyle. Age is important, of course, because the probability of dying increases with age. A person who has a health problem such as heart disease or diabetes may pay considerably higher rates for life insurance or may not be able to obtain coverage at any price. People with hazardous occupations (police officers) or dangerous hobbies (skydivers) are sometimes required to pay higher life insurance premiums as well. Life insurance companies typically offer their lowest prices to "preferred" applicants whose health status and lifestyle (for example, nonsmokers) suggest longevity. "Standard" and "impaired" applicants would pay more. Because companies differ on how they assign these labels to applicants, you should shop around for the best treatment. Some companies even specialize in insurance for persons with certain types of medical conditions, such as diabetes.

Popular magazines such as *Kiplinger's Personal Finance Magazine, Consumer Reports,* and *Money* regularly publish articles that give average or typical premiums for different types of policies. In addition, your state department of insurance may publish life insurance buyer's guides containing price guidelines that may prove useful in selecting companies with the lowest prices. You can shop for life insurance on the Web by using quote services that offer computer-generated comparisons among the 20 to 80 companies they represent to help you select the least expensive life insurance policies and companies. Such services can be found at www.quotesmith.com, www.quotescout .com, and www.Accuquote.com. These websites also offer on-line life insurance needs calculators and a wealth of information on life insurance from an unbiased perspective.

Comparing Term Insurance Policies.

You may save a substantial amount on term life insurance premiums by using a **premium quote service.** These independent life insurance agents or groups of agents concentrate on marketing term life insurance at the lowest possible rates. Life insurance premiums are usually quoted in dollars per $1000 of coverage. Generally, the higher the face amount of the policy, the lower the rate per $1000. For example, a company might sell term life insurance for $1 per $1000 per year when purchased in face amounts of $100,000 or more and for $1.25 per $1000 per year for policies of less than $100,000. In fact, policies with face amounts of $1 million can cost less than $0.50 per $1000 per year for people younger than age 35.

Of course, it is easy to pay too much for term life insurance, especially if you do not comparison-shop. The rates shown in Table 12.4 represent good values for term insurance. Note that smokers pay much higher premiums than nonsmokers because as a group smokers die ten years earlier than nonsmokers. Men pay more than women because they typically die three years earlier.

Comparing Cash-Value Policies.

The cost of insurance measured in dollars per $1000 is not an appropriate decision criterion when comparing term and cash-value insurance or when examining various types of cash-value insurance. Table 12.5 lists annual premiums that are near the average required for various types of insurance policies. Three methods are used to compare insurance premium costs:

Table 12.4 Fair Prices for Term Life Insurance*
(Authors' estimates based on Internet shopping on the major quote services.)

Age	Nonsmokers		Smokers	
	Male	Female	Male	Female
18–30	$0.70	$0.67	$1.00	$0.95
35	$0.83	$0.74	$1.25	$1.15
40	$1.08	$1.00	$1.95	$1.60
45	$1.67	$1.60	$2.80	$2.40
50	$2.30	$2.20	$4.00	$3.25

*Multiply the rate by each $1000 of coverage and add $60 for estimated administrative fees. For example, a fair annual premium for a $50,000 policy for a 36-year-old male nonsmoker might be $101.50 ($0.83 × 50 = $41.50 + $60).

Table 12.5 Typical Premiums for Various Types of Life Insurance (Face Amount $100,000)								
	Policy Year							
Policy Type	**1**	**2**	**3**	**5**	**10**	**11**	**20**	**Age 65**
Annual renewable term (guaranteed renewability to age 70)	$80	$81	$82	$83	$ 90	$ 92	$110	$2400
Decreasing term (over 20 years)	160	160	160	160	160	160	160	0
Convertible term (within 5 years)	170	170	170	170	940	940	940	940
Whole life	870	870	870	870	870	870	870	870
Universal life	590	590	590	590	680	730	760	790
Limited-pay life (paid at age 65)	920	920	920	920	920	920	920	0

*Premiums quoted are for a 21-year-old male nonsmoker.

1. **Net cost method.** The **net cost** of a life insurance policy equals the total of all premiums to be paid minus any accumulated cash value and accrued dividends. It is calculated for a specific point in time during the life of the policy—for example, at the end of the tenth or twentieth year. The net cost is often a negative figure, giving a false impression that the policy will pay for itself. You should ignore net cost calculations provided by a life insurance agent.

2. **Interest-adjusted cost index method.** A **cost index** is a numerical method used to compare the costs of similar plans of life insurance. The **interest-adjusted cost index** (**IACI**) measures the cost of life insurance, taking into account the interest that would have been earned had the premiums been invested rather than used to buy insurance. The lower the IACI, the lower the cost of the policy. The IACI is calculated for a specific point in time—usually the twentieth year—during the life of the policy. Reputable agents should have IACI information on hand. In fact, agents in most states are required to disclose the information (usually an IACI for the twentieth year) if asked. Ask for 5-, 10-, and 30-year IACI values as well, because companies have been known to manipulate their dividend and cash-value accumulations to look especially good at the 20-year point. You should insist on being told the index before you agree to buy a policy, and you should shop elsewhere if the agent refuses, resists, or tries to imply that the index has little value. Unfortunately, the IACI does not provide an accurate means of comparing types of policies that differ widely. It is totally inappropriate, for example, when comparing term insurance and cash-value insurance.

3. **Interest-adjusted net payment index method.** The IACI assumes that the policy will be cashed in and surrendered at the end of a certain period (usually 20 years) rather than remaining in force until the death of the insured. If the policy will remain in force until death, you can use the **interest-adjusted net payment index** (**IANPI**) to more effectively measure the cost of cash-value insurance. The lower the IANPI, the lower the cost of the policy.

Summary

1. Life insurance is designed to provide protection from the financial losses that result from death. The reasons to purchase life insurance change over the life cycle. The need for this type of protection is very small or even nonexistent for children and single adults. Factors affecting life insurance needs include the need to replace income, final-expense needs, readjustment-period needs, debt-repayment needs, college-expense needs, availability of government programs, and ownership of other life insurance and assets.

2. Two methods to calculate life insurance needs are the multiple-of-earnings approach and the needs approach. The needs approach is the more accurate of the two, and calculations based on this approach should be revisited every three years or whenever your family situation changes.

3. Two basic types of life insurance exist: term life insurance and cash-value life insurance. Variations on term life insurance include decreasing term insurance, guaranteed renewable term insurance, convertible term insurance, and credit life insurance. Variations on cash-value insurance include whole life insurance, limited-pay life insurance, and universal and variable life insurance.

4. A life insurance policy is a written contract between the insurance purchaser and the insurance company, spelling out in detail the terms of the agreement. When buying life insurance, you should pay special attention to the policy's general terms and conditions, the special features of cash-value life insurance, and settlement options.

5. Life insurance should be purchased to address the dying-too-soon problem. Your investments should manage the living-too-long problem. Addressing these two problems appropriately requires a small amount of cash-value life insurance, high amounts of term insurance while you are raising children, and a sound investment program to prepare for your retirement years. You should not purchase any life insurance until you have determined the actual dollar amount and type of policy you need and analyzed comparative premiums using various life insurance cost indices.

Key Terms

automatic premium loan, 345
beneficiary, 340
cash surrender value, 344
death benefit, 342
face amount, 332
guaranteed insurability option, 346
guaranteed renewable term insurance, 332
insurance dividends, 342
interest-adjusted net payment index (IANPI), 353
life insurance, 325
limited-pay whole life insurance, 336
needs approach, 329
nonforfeiture values, 344
owner (policyholder), 340
policy illustration, 344
settlement options, 343
Social Security survivor's benefits, 327
term life insurance, 332
variable-universal life insurance, 339
whole life insurance (straight life; ordinary life), 336

Chapter Review Questions

1. Describe five factors affecting the need for life insurance.

2. How do term life insurance and cash-value life insurance differ?

3. What is meant by "layering" term insurance policies?

4. Explain why the amount of "insurance" declines over time under a cash-value life insurance policy.

5. Distinguish between the owner, the insured, the beneficiary, and the contingent beneficiary of a life insurance policy.

6. How do guaranteed renewable term insurance and the guaranteed insurability option on cash-value insurance protect insured people who may develop serious health conditions?

7. What is meant by the term "settlement options," and what options are available to life insurance beneficiaries?

8. What might you gain by "buying term and investing the rest"?

9. What weaknesses does cash-value life insurance have as a retirement savings vehicle?

10. How does the pattern of life insurance needs vary from young adulthood through one's retirement years?

Group Discussion Issues

1. What were your feelings about life insurance before you read this chapter? What are they now?

2. Are you covered by life insurance? If so, how much? Do you feel that you are over- or underinsured?

3. Why do you think people persist in buying cash value life insurance when, in most cases, they would be better off buying term insurance and investing the money saved into a tax-sheltered retirement account?

4. In many married-couple families one of the spouses is the primary breadwinner and the other focuses more on homemaking duties. In your view, how does such an arrangement affect the approach that should be taken for each spouse in terms of life insurance?

5. Many young people today choose to cohabitate rather than marry (at least for some time period). Should this affect their thinking about life insurance?

Decision-Making Cases

▶Case 1
Life Insurance for a Newly Married Couple

Just-married couples sometimes overindulge in the type and amount of life insurance that they buy. Bryson and Nancy Greenwood of Gunnison, Colorado, took a different approach. Both were working and had a small amount of life insurance provided through their respective employee benefit programs: Bryson, $40,000, and Nancy, $50,000. During their discussion of life insurance needs and related costs, they decided that if Nancy completed her master's degree in industrial psychology, she would have better employment opportunities. Consequently, they decided to use money they had available for additional life insurance to pay for Nancy's education. They both feel, however, that they do not want to have inadequate life insurance.

(a) In what way does Nancy's return to school alter the Greenwoods' life insurance needs?

(b) Would you agree that the amount of life insurance provided by the Greenwoods' respective employers is adequate while Nancy is in school? Explain your response.

(c) Summarize how the Greenwoods' life insurance needs might change over their life cycle.

▶Case 2
Fraternity Members Contemplate Permanent Life Insurance

Lee Chen is a college student from Santa Ana, California. Soon to graduate, Lee was approached recently by a life insurance agent, who set up a group meeting for several members of his fraternity. During the meeting, the agent presented six life insurance plans and was very persuasive about the benefits of a universal life insurance plan that his company calls Affordable Life II. Under the plan, the prospective graduate can buy $100,000 of permanent life insurance for a very low premium during the first five years and then pay a higher premium later when income presumably will have increased. Lee was confused after the meeting, as were his friends. Armed with your knowledge from this personal finance book, you have been asked to respond to some of their questions.

(a) Do you think universal life insurance is a good deal for these people? Why or why not?

(b) How can the individual fraternity members decide how much life insurance they need?

(c) Life insurance cannot be as confusing as the agent made it seem. What clearer explanation would you give to the fraternity members?

(d) What type of life insurance, if any, would you advise for the fraternity brothers?

(e) How would they know if a life insurance policy is offered at a fair price?

Financial Math Questions

1. Glenda Crabcrow of Portland, Maine, has a $100,000 participating cash-value policy written on her life. The policy has accumulated $4700 in cash value; Glenda has borrowed $3000 of this value. The policy also has accumulated unpaid dividends of $1666. Yesterday Glenda paid her premium of $1200 for the coming year. What is the current death benefit from this policy?

2. Wanda and Desmond Hensley of Savannah, Georgia, are a married couple in their mid-thirties. They have two children, ages five and three, and Wanda is pregnant with their third child. Wanda is a book indexer who earned $15,000 after taxes last year. Because she performs much of her work at home, it is unlikely that she will need to curtail her work after the baby is born. Desmond is a family therapist with a thriving practice; he earned $48,000 last year after taxes. Because both are self-employed, Wanda and Desmond do not have access to group life insurance. They are each covered by $50,000 universal life policies they purchased three years ago. In addition, Desmond is covered by a $50,000, five-year guaranteed renewable term policy, which will expire next year. The Hensleys are currently reassessing their life insurance program. As a preliminary step in their analysis, they have determined that Wanda's account with Social Security would yield the family about $1094 per month, or an annual benefit of $13,128, if she were to die. For Desmond, the figure would be $2072 per month, or an annual benefit of $24,864. Both agree that they would like to support each of their children to age 22 but to date they have been unable to start a college savings fund. The couple estimates that it would cost $30,000 to put each child through college as measured in today's dollars. They expect that burial expenses for each spouse would total about $6000, and they would like to have a lump sum of life insurance clearly marked for paying off their $70,000 home mortgage. They also feel that each spouse would want to take a six-month leave from work if the other were to die.

(a) Calculate the amount of life insurance that Wanda needs based on the information given. Use the Decision-Making Worksheet on page 330 or the *Garman/Forgue* website. Assume a 3 percent rate of return after taxes and inflation and an income need for 22 years, because the unborn child will need financial support for that many years.

(b) Calculate the amount of life insurance that Desmond needs based on the information given. Use the Decision-Making Worksheet on page 330 or the *Garman/Forgue* website. Assume a 3 percent rate of return after taxes and inflation and an income need for 22 years, because the unborn child will need financial support for that many years.

(c) If Wanda and Desmond purchased term insurance to cover their additional needs, how much more would each need to spend on life insurance?

Money Matters Continuing Cases

Victor and Maria Hernandez Contemplate Switching Life Insurance Policies

Victor and Maria Hernandez have a total of $200,000 in life insurance. Victor has a $50,000 cash-value policy purchased more than 20 years ago when the couple was first married and a $100,000 group term policy through his employer. Maria has a $50,000 group term insurance policy through her employer. The couple has been approached by a life insurance agent who thinks that they need to change their policy mix because, he says, they are inadequately insured. Specifically, the agent has suggested that Victor cash in his

cash-value policy and buy a new variable-universal life insurance policy.

1. If Victor cashes in his policy, what options would he have when receiving the cash value?

2. Determine what the $16,000 in cash value in Victor's life insurance policy would be worth in 20 years if that sum were invested somewhere else and earned an 8 percent annual return. (Hint: Use the *Garman/Forgue* website.)

3. Would cashing in the policy be a wise decision? Why or why not?

4. As the Hernandezes' children are now grown and out on their own, and both Victor and Maria are employed full-time, give general reasons why Victor may need more or less insurance.

5. Explain why it would be a bad idea for Victor to buy a variable-universal life insurance policy.

The Johnsons Change Their Life Insurance Coverage

Harry and Belinda Johnson spend $9 per month on life insurance in the form of a premium on a $10,000, paid-at-65 cash-value policy on Harry. Belinda has a group term insurance policy from her employer with a face amount of $59,400 (1.5 times her annual salary). By choosing a group life insurance plan from his "menu" of employee benefits, Harry now has $30,900 (his annual salary) of group term life insurance. Harry and Belinda have decided that, because they have no children, they could reduce their life insurance needs by protecting one another's income for only four years, assuming the survivor would be able to fend for himself or herself after that time. They also realize that their savings fund is so low that it would have no bearing on their life insurance needs. Harry and Belinda are basing their calculations on a projected 4 percent rate of return after taxes and inflation. They also estimate the following expenses: $8000 for final expenses, $4000 for readjustment expenses, and $5000 for repayment of short-term debts.

1. Should the $3000 interest earnings from Harry's trust fund be included in his annual income for the purposes of calculating the likely dollar loss if he were to die? (See the discussions about the Johnsons at the end of Chapter 2.) Explain your response.

2. Based on your response to the previous question, how much more life insurance does Harry need? Use the Decision-Making Worksheet on page 330 to arrive at your answer.

3. Repeat the calculations to arrive at the additional life insurance needed on Belinda's life.

4. How might the Johnsons most economically meet any additional life insurance needs you have determined they may have?

5. In addition to their life insurance planning, how might the Johnsons begin to prepare for their retirement years?

What Would You Recommend Now?

Now that you have read the chapter on life insurance planning, what would you recommend to Karen and Bobby Bridgeman in the case at the beginning of the chapter regarding:

1. Their changing need for life insurance once they have a child?

2. What type of life insurance they should consider and whether they should use multiple policies?

3. Coordinating their retirement and other investments with their life insurance program?

4. Shopping for life insurance?

Exploring the World Wide Web

To complete these exercises, go to the *Garman/Forgue* website at college.hmco.com/business/students. Under General Business, select the title of this text. Click on the Internet Exercises link for this chapter, and answer the questions that appear on the Web page.

1. Use the Decision-Making Worksheet on page 330 of the text or on-line at the *Garman/Forgue* website to calculate your life insurance needs. Are you underinsured, overinsured, or appropriately insured? Also, visit the website for life-line.org, which provides a life insurance needs calculator. Follow the directions to calculate your life insurance needs. Why do the *Personal Finance* text worksheet and the life-line.org calculator yield differing results? (Hint: Note how the two versions handle income replacement.)

2. Visit the website for QuoteSmith to obtain a quote for the annual premium on a $100,000 guaranteed renewable, ten-year term policy for you. Then call a life insurance agent in your community to obtain a quote on the same term insurance coverage. How do the term rates quoted by your local agent compare with the rates found over the Internet? Also, ask for the quote on a $100,000 universal life policy with guaranteed insurability and waiver-of-premium options. Ask the agent to explain why the

quotes for the two types of policies differ. Analyze his or her response based on what you learned in this chapter.

3. Visit the website for the Social Security Administration and use its "BEST" on-line screening tool to determine your eligibility status, which indicates whether your family could receive Social Security survivor's benefits should you die.

4. Visit the website for A. M. Best Company and check the ratings for the insurance company recommended by the agent in Exercise 2 as well as the lowest-cost company for term insurance that you found on the Web. What do the ratings tell you about the relative strengths of those companies?

5. Call a local life insurance office and talk to one of the agents about the potential for someone interested in a career in life insurance. As part of the discussion, ask his or her advice about what professional certifications are most valuable. Also, visit the website for the American College to read up on the requirements for the professional designation of chartered life underwriter (CLU) mentioned in the text.

6. Visit the website for the National Association of Insurance Commissioners and use its map of the states to bring up the site of the insurance regulatory agency in your home state. Explore the information that your state provides to assist consumers in the purchase of life insurance. Then visit the insurance regulatory agency for California, New York, or Florida. How does the information provided by your state compare with that provided by one of those states?

7. Visit the website for the Social Security Administration to order a copy of your Personal Earnings and Benefits Estimate Statement. The PEBES will provide you with baseline information on your eligibility for Social Security benefits, including survivor's benefits. The statement will be sent to you by U.S. mail, although eventually this information will be made available on-line.

Visit the Garman/Forgue website . . .

@college.hmco.com/business/students

Under General Business, select *Personal Finance 8e*. There, among other valuable resources, you will find a complete glossary, ACE questions, links to help you complete the chapter exercises, and links to other personal finance sites.

Part Four

Investments

CHAPTER 13   Investment Fundamentals

CHAPTER 14   Investing in Stocks and Bonds

CHAPTER 15   Investing Through Mutual Funds

CHAPTER 16   Buying and Selling Securities

CHAPTER 17   Real Estate and Speculative Investments

Chapter 13

Investment Fundamentals

LEARNING OBJECTIVES

After reading this chapter, you should be able to:

1 **Explain** why you should establish an investment program and how to get started.

2 **Discover** your own investment philosophy.

3 **Identify** the kinds of investments you want to make.

4 **Describe** the major factors that affect the rate of return on investments.

5 **Explain** the five strategies of long-term investors.

6 **Summarize** the steps to take for effective long-term investing.

What Would You Recommend?

Jennifer and Julia are 29-year-old twins, but they handle their finances very differently. Jennifer drives a leased BMW convertible, and she makes about $42,000, including tips, as a part-time bartender at two different restaurants. Although she has no employee benefits, she enjoys having flexible work hours so that she can go to the beach and the local casinos. Currently, Jennifer has $10,000 in credit card debt. She has $1500 in a bank savings account, and two years ago she opened an individual retirement account (IRA) with a $1000 investment in a mutual fund. Her sister Julia drives a paid-for Geo, pays her credit card purchases in full each month, and sacrifices some of her salary by putting $100 per month into her employer's company stock through her 401(k) retirement account. Over the past seven years, the stock price, which was once about $40, has risen to almost $70, and Julia's 401(k) plan is now worth about $16,000. Julia also has invested about $14,000 in aggressive-growth mutual funds, and she plans on using that money for a down payment on a home purchase. She earns $58,000 as a manager of a restaurant, plus she receives an annual bonus ranging from $2000 to $4000 every January that she uses for a spring vacation in Mexico. Julia has lots of employee benefits where she works.

What would you recommend to Jennifer and Julia on the subject of investment fundamentals regarding:

1. Getting more money to save and invest?
2. Prerequisites to investing for Jennifer?
3. Dollar-cost averaging for Jennifer?
4. Portfolio diversification for Julia?
5. Investment alternatives for Julia?

At many points in this book, we have encouraged you to set aside funds for the future, especially by accumulating funds through regular savings. This approach is a wise course of action, but building real wealth requires an additional consideration—earning a good rate of return on your money. The difference in the rate of return is a major distinction between mere savings and investing. Many successful investors ultimately become able to live off the earnings on their accumulated wealth, often without spending the wealth itself.

The most common ways that people invest are by putting money into assets such as stocks, bonds, and mutual funds (collectively called **securities**), particularly through their employer-sponsored retirement accounts, and by buying real estate. Stocks are shares of ownership in a corporation, and bonds represent loans to companies and governments. All of your investment assets make up your **portfolio,** the collection of investments assembled to meet your investment goals. Your investments can increase your income and help maximize your enjoyment of life.

Of course, to achieve this higher level of living in the future, you cannot spend every dollar that you earn today. Instead, you must set aside some of your income and invest it to help secure that future lifestyle. To be financially successful you should start investing early in your life, invest regularly, and stay invested. Why? Because, for every five years you delay investing, you will have to double your monthly investment amount to achieve the same goals. Remember this: You—and no one else—are responsible for your own financial success.

This chapter begins by examining why and how people start to invest. It then provides some tools to help you identify your personal investment philosophy. The next section provides an overview of the many investment possibilities—whether you as an investor want to lend or own, whether you prefer to be a short- or long-term investor, and which types of investments are best for you given your investment goals. Also examined are the major factors that affect an investment's rate of return, such as inflation, market volatility, and taxes. Rather than trying to time the market, the wise investor uses the investment strategies of buy-and-hold, portfolio diversification, asset allocation, modern portfolio theory, and dollar-cost averaging. A well-diversified portfolio of investments has an excellent chance of earning a total return high enough to outpace inflation over the long term. Finally, this chapter lists several steps that will help you attain your long-term investment goals.

1 Explain why you should establish an investment program and how to get started.

Why You Should Establish an Investment Program and How to Get Started

Before creating an investment plan, you need to know the reasons why people invest. In addition, some prerequisites for investing must be satisfied. You should also know the sources of investment returns and ways to obtain money to invest. And most important, you need to understand the wisdom of starting to invest early in life. This point is emphasized throughout this book, and a good illustration is shown in Table 13.1.

Why People Invest

People invest for four general reasons:

1. To achieve financial goals, such as the purchase of a new car, a down payment on a home, or paying for a child's education

Golden Rules of

Investment Fundamentals

Financial success comes from learning the Golden Rules of personal finance and then putting what you have learned into practice. Make the following your money habits in investments:

1. Spend less than you earn and sacrifice some of your income to invest for your future needs and lifestyle.
2. Use stocks, bonds, mutual funds, and real estate to build your investment portfolio, not life insurance or annuities.
3. Start early in life to invest in a diversified portfolio of assets consistent with your investment philosophy in order to obtain a high average return at a level of risk you are willing to accept.
4. Use an asset allocation strategy and invest regularly using dollar-cost averaging through your employer's retirement plan.
5. Follow the buy-and-hold long-term approach to investing through both good and bad economic times, and keep your investments well diversified.
6. Never allow your ownership in your employer's stock to amount to more than 15 percent of your portfolio.

2. To increase current income

3. To gain wealth and a feeling of financial security

4. To have funds available during retirement years

Prerequisites to Investing

Before you embark on an investment program, make sure you have taken the following steps:

1. **Balance your budget.** If you find yourself constantly running short of cash toward the end of the month or if you make only minimum payments on your credit card balances, you need to institute budget controls, so you can live within your means.

2. **Continue a savings program.** A good financial manager forgoes some spending to save regularly to build an emergency fund, acquire goods and services, and achieve other goals.

3. **Establish sufficient credit card maximum limits.** In addition to paying credit card bills in full each month, you need to have a maximum credit limit high enough to help you meet personal financial emergencies without having to resort to selling investments. This also reduces the need to keep large amounts of savings readily available.

4. **Carry adequate insurance to protect against major catastrophes.** Liability insurance can protect your assets and lifestyle in the event you are sued, and health insurance can defray your expenses if you become ill. Term life insurance can protect the lifestyle of dependents in the event of the investor's death. Insurance provides a safety net in that it enables you to gain some measure of control over the unexpected.

5. **Establish investment goals.** When you have specific reasons to invest, such as to buy a home or retirement, you will be more likely to consider "investments" as a high-priority category in your budget. As soon as you can, you should participate in and invest the maximum contributions possible to your 401(k) retirement plan.

Table 13.1 The Wisdom of Starting to Invest Early in Life

| Age | Cumulative Investments | | Account Value | |
	Early Investor*	Late Investor†	Early Investor*	Late Investor†
30	$ 2,000	$ 0	$ 2,180	$ 0
35	10,000	0	13,047	0
40	20,000	2,000	33,121	2,180
45	0	10,000	50,960	13,047
50	0	20,000	78,408	33,121
55	0	30,000	120,641	64,007
60	0	40,000	185,621	111,529
65	0	50,000	285,601	184,648

Conclusion: $20,000 gets the early investor $285,601; $50,000 gets the late investor only $184,648.

*The early investor invested $2,000 at the beginning of every year from ages 30 to 39 (10 years of cumulative investing totaling $20,000), and the funds compounded at 9 percent annually.

†The late investor invested $2,000 at the beginning of every year from ages 40 to 64 (25 years of cumulative investing totaling $50,000), and the funds compounded at 9 percent annually.

An Investment Plan

To get an investment plan started, think about your reasons for investing. For example, you may have as a goal to save and invest $10,000 per year for five years with the expectation of earning an 8 percent annual return and using the proceeds (ideally close to $60,000) for a down payment on a new home. Another of your goals may be to save and invest $4000 annually for 30 years earning 9 percent annually to create a $545,000 retirement fund. An **investment plan** is an explanation of how your funds will be invested for the purpose of reaching a specific goal. It is best to write down the details of your investment plan, even if the plan is only one or two pages in length. You will select from the investment alternatives described in the following four chapters. The best investment plan begins with a good savings plan.

Investment Returns

All investments involve taking risks. Figure 13.1 shows the long-term rates of return on some popular investments. A key to understanding the world of investments is under-

How to . . .

Get Money to Save and Invest

Many people delay beginning an investment program because they feel they lack the funds or discipline to do so. Here are some tips for getting started.

- **Pay yourself first through forced saving and investment plans.** You should "pay yourself" every time you receive income—that is, you should treat investing as a fixed expense in your budget.
- **Make investing automatic.** Arrange to have funds automatically transferred from your bank to an investment account. You can save and invest every payday in your employer's 401(k) retirement plan. After taking these steps, you have to take action *not* to save, making it easier to continue saving and investing.
- **Save—don't spend—extra funds.** When unexpected money arrives, you will be able to add substantially to your investment balance. Examples of extra money might include a year-end bonus from an employer, a commission check, the after-tax amount of a raise above your previous salary, money gifts, and income tax refunds. In addition, when budgeted costs do not exceed income for a given time period, you should invest part of the surplus.
- **Make installment payments to yourself.** If you make installment repayments on a debt, you have an unusual opportunity to invest after making the last repayment on the debt. Simply continue to make the payments—but to your investment account.
- **Break a habit.** Put aside the amount you would have spent.
- **Scrimp one month each year.** If you make a concerted effort to scrimp on all expenses one month each year, you can accumulate a sizable amount of money to invest. To accomplish this goal, cut back on some planned expenditures and question every possible expense. Knowing that this level of frugality will end after 30 days will help motivate you toward success.

standing how investment returns are achieved. When people invest their money, they take a **financial risk** (also called **business risk**)—namely, the possibility that the investment will fail to pay a return to the investor. For example, a company could have a very good year, earning a considerable profit, or it could go bankrupt, causing investors to lose all of their money. Investors hope, of course, that the investment will earn them a positive **return,** which is the income an investment generates from current income and capital gains (also called the **total return**). **Current income** is money received while you own an investment. It is usually received on a regular basis in the form of interest, rent, or dividends. **Interest** is earned when you are owed money by others, such as occurs when you invest in bonds. **Rent** is payment received in return for allowing someone to use your real estate property, such as land or a building. A **dividend** is a portion of a company's earnings that the firm pays out to its shareholders. For example, Nina Diaz from Oneonta, New York, purchased 100 shares of H&M stock at $45 per share ($4500) last year. The company paid dividends of $3 per share during the year, so Nina received $300 in cash dividends as current income.

A **capital gain** occurs only when you actually sell the investment; it results from an increase in the value of the initial investment. It is calculated by subtracting the total amount paid for the investment (including purchase transaction costs) from the higher price at which it is sold (minus any sales transaction costs). For example, if the price of H&M company stock rose to $52 during the year, Nina could sell it for a capital gain. If Nina paid a transaction cost of $1 per share at both purchase and sale of sale, her capital gain would be $500 [($5200 − $100) − ($4500 + $100)].

Of course, *capital losses* can occur as well. For most investments, a trade-off exists between capital gains and current income. Investments with high capital gains potential often pay little current income, and investments that pay substantial current income generally have little or no potential for capital gains. Long-term investors are usually willing to forgo much current income in favor of possibly earning substantial future capital gains.

The **rate of return,** or **yield,** is the total return on an investment expressed as a percentage of its price. It is usually stated on an annualized basis. For example, if Nina sells the H&M stock for $52 per share after one year, she will have a total return of $800 ($300 in dividends plus $500 in capital gains). Her yield would be 17.78 percent ($800 ÷ $4500). In contrast, if the market price of H&M stock had declined during the year, Nina could have potentially had a negative rate of return. This possibility demonstrates the risk associated with investing in stocks.

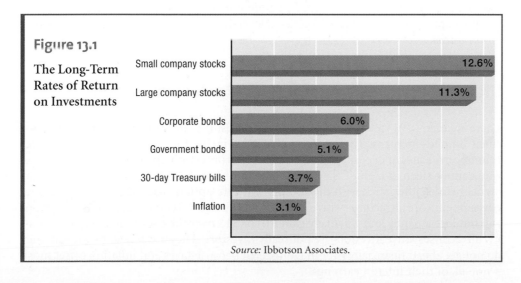

Figure 13.1

The Long-Term Rates of Return on Investments

Small company stocks	12.6%
Large company stocks	11.3%
Corporate bonds	6.0%
Government bonds	5.1%
30-day Treasury bills	3.7%
Inflation	3.1%

Source: Ibbotson Associates.

Discover Your Own Approach to Investing

Many individual investors are inept at investing. Independent research often shows that individuals earn much less than the averages in the stock markets. Why? Because they make emotional errors. They fail to stay within the bounds of their personal investment philosophy. Greed leads to bad decisions, such as chasing the latest investment fad. Impatience leads to jumping in and out of investments. Investors who buy what they do not understand often wind up with a mishmash of investments. This unhappy result arises when people forget to match their financial decisions with their disposition toward risk.

How Do You Handle Investment Risk?

The investor needs the promise of a high return to warrant placing his or her money at risk in an investment. If you wanted a completely safe investment, you could invest your money by buying U.S. Treasury bills (T-bills, discussed in Chapter 14), which are backed by the full faith and credit of the U.S. government. With this sort of investment, you loan your money to the federal government for a few months and it is later returned with interest. Although T-bills are risk-free investments, today they pay only about 2 or 3 percent interest—far too low a return for most people.

If you invest only in Treasury bills, you will miss out on the significantly higher returns that can be earned with other investments such as stocks and stock mutual funds. When buying these securities, investors demand a **risk premium** for their willingness to make investments for which there is no guarantee of future success. This risk premium constitutes the difference between the riskier investment's return and the totally safe return on the T-bill. One investor may demand a risk premium of 5 percent, whereas another may require 10 percent or more. A variety of investment alternatives are available to fit each investor's requirements.

Investment risk—and your ability to handle it—greatly influences your personal investment philosophy. **Investment risk** represents the uncertainty that the yield on an investment will deviate from what is expected. For most investments, the greater the risk, the higher the potential return. This potential for gain is what motivates people to accept increasingly greater levels of risk. Nevertheless, many people remain seriously averse to risk.

Ultraconservative "Investors" Are Really Just "Savers"

There are many ways to save that offer no risk of losing your principal and respectable—albeit limited—returns. These financial vehicles include federally insured savings accounts, certificates of deposit, and EE bonds. Ultraconservative investors, especially those who cannot sleep at night if they think their money is at risk, do not consider investments because they stick with the 100 percent safe options backed by the U.S. federal government. An ultraconservative investor who places $1000 in one of these options will not lose a penny and will likely gain $10 or $15 over the course of a year. In actuality, ultraconservative investors are not really investors. They are savers. As a result, they do not get ahead financially over the long term because taxes and inflation offset most, if not all, of their interest earnings.

What Is Your Investment Philosophy?

Smart investors select investments based on their **investment philosophy,** which is nothing more than their general approach to investment risk, whether it be conservative, moderate, or aggressive. The more risk you take, within reason, the more you can expect to earn and accumulate over the long term. Smart investors succeed by following their philosophy without wavering; they do not change course unless their basic objectives change.

Is It Conservative?   If you have a **conservative investment philosophy,** you accept very little risk and are generally rewarded with relatively low rates of return for seeking the twin goals of a moderate amount of current income and preservation of capital. **Preservation of capital** means that you do not want to lose any of the money you have invested. In short, you could be characterized as a "risk averter."

Conservative investors focus on protecting themselves. They do so by carefully avoiding losses and trying to stay with investments that demonstrate gains, often for long time periods (perhaps for five or ten years). Tactically, they rarely sell their investments. Most investors who are approaching retirement or who are planning to withdraw money from their investments in the near future adhere to a conservative investment philosophy.

Conservative investors typically consider investing in obligations issued by the government. Examples include Treasury bills, notes, and bonds (insured as to timely payment of principal and interest by the U.S. government), municipal bonds, high-quality (blue-chip) corporate bonds and stocks, balanced mutual funds (which own both stocks and bonds), certificates of deposit, and annuities. A **bond** is essentially a loan that the investor makes to a government or a corporation. Thus, a bond is a debt of the issuer. Bond investors also tend to spread their funds among a large number of investment alternatives. A conservative investor with $1000 might lose $30 over the course of a year or gain $50 to $60 during the same period.

Is It Moderate?   People with a **moderate investment philosophy** seek capital gains through slow and steady growth in the value of their investments and some current income. They invite only a fair amount of risk of capital loss. Most have no immediate need for the funds but instead focus on laying the investment foundation for later years or building on such a base. Moderate investors are fairly comfortable during rising and falling market conditions. They remain secure in the knowledge that they are investing for the long term. Their tactics might include spreading investment funds among several choices and trading some assets no more than once a year.

People seeking moderate returns consider investing in dividend-paying common stocks, growth and income mutual funds, high-quality corporate bonds, government bonds, and real estate. A moderate investor with $1000 might lose $150 over the course of a year or gain $80 to $100.

Is It Aggressive?   If you choose to strive for a very high return by accepting a high level of risk, you have an **aggressive investment philosophy.** As such, you could be characterized as a "risk seeker." Aggressive investors primarily seek capital gains. Many such investors take a short-term approach, remaining confident that they can profit substantially during major upswings in market prices.

People seeking exceptionally high returns consider investing in common stocks of new or fast-growing companies, high-yielding junk bonds, and aggressive-growth mutual funds. Such investors put their money into limited real estate partnerships, undeveloped land, precious metals, gems, commodity futures, stock-index futures, and collectibles. Devotees of this investment philosophy sometimes do not spread their funds among many alternatives. Also, they may adopt short-term tactics to increase capital gains. For example, an aggressive investor might place most of his or her investment funds in a single stock in the hope that it will rise 10 percent over 90 days, giving an annual yield of more than 40 percent. Those shares can then be sold and the money invested elsewhere.

Investment tactics for aggressive investors are discussed further in Chapter 17. Note that aggressive investors must be emotionally and financially able to weather substantial short-term losses—for example, a downward swing in a stock's price of 30 or 40 percent. They have the expectation that an even stronger upswing in price will occur in the future. An aggressive investor with $1000 might lose $300 during a year or gain $150 to $300 over the same time frame.

Should You Take an Active or Passive Investing Approach?

Another aspect of your personal investment philosophy is your level of involvement in investing. That is, do you want to be an active or passive investor? An **active investor** carefully studies the economy, market trends, and investment alternatives; regularly monitors these factors; and makes decisions to buy and sell, perhaps several times a year, with or without the advice of a professional. In addition, because the prices of many investments vary with certain news events, world happenings, and economic and political variables, investors need to stay alert. Knowing what is going on in the larger world helps active investors understand when to buy or to sell stocks quickly so as to reap profits or reduce losses.

* higher in long run *

A **passive investor** does not actively engage in trading of securities or spend large amounts of time in monitoring his or her investments. Such an individual is often a long-term investor who makes regular investments in securities, such as mutual funds (described in Chapter 15), and his or her assets are rarely sold for short-term profits. Instead, passive investors simply aim to match the returns of the entire market. They ignore "hot" tips and investments touted in the financial press. They keep their emotions in check, and they earn higher returns than active investors over the long term.

Once you have clarified your investment philosophy, you will be able to make future decisions about investing with confidence and conviction. You will be able to show patience by following your long-term views rather than making emotional and wrong decisions—in other words, mistakes—about your money. As a result, you will realize investment returns that match your philosophy and objectives.

3 Identify the kinds of investments you want to make.

Identify the Types of Investments You Want to Make

You have three key decisions to make when choosing investments:

1. Do you want to lend your money or own an asset?

2. Do you want to invest for the short term or the long term?

3. Which types of investments are best given your investment goals?

Do You Want to Lend or Own?

You can invest money in two ways, by lending or by owning. When you lend your money, you receive some form of IOU and the promise of repayment plus interest. The interest is a form of current income while you hold the investment. Lending investments rarely result in capital gains.

You can lend by depositing money in banks, credit unions, and savings and loan associations (via savings accounts and certificates of deposit) or by lending money to governments (via Treasury notes and bonds as well as state and local bonds), businesses (corporate bonds), mortgage-backed bonds (such as Ginnie Maes), and life insurance companies (annuities). Such lending investments, or **debts,** generally offer both a fixed maturity and a fixed income. With a **fixed maturity,** the borrower agrees to repay the principal to the investor on a specific date. With a **fixed income,** the borrower agrees to pay the investor a specific rate of return for use of the principal. Such investments allow lenders to be fairly confident that they will receive a certain amount of interest income for a specified period of time and that the borrowed funds will eventually be returned. Thus, the return is somewhat assured. No matter how much profit the borrower makes with your funds, however, the investing lender receives only the fixed return promised at the time of the initial investment.

Alternatively, you may invest money through ownership of an asset. When you buy an investment asset, you typically either own the asset outright or purchase it on credit. Ownership investments have the potential for providing both current income and capital gains.

Ownership investments are often called **equities.** You can buy common or preferred corporate stock (to obtain part-ownership in a corporation) in publicly owned companies, purchase shares in a mutual fund company (which invests your funds in corporate stocks and bonds), put money into your own business, purchase real estate, buy commodity futures (pork bellies or oranges), or buy investment-quality collectibles (such as rare antiques or stamps). Investment owners have the potential to obtain a substantial return because they typically share all the profits.

Do You Want to Make Short-Term or Long-Term Investments?

If you are investing for the short term, perhaps up to five years, you probably want to be confident that you preserve the value of what you have. After all, you don't want to lose money in an investment when you need to use that money for a near-term goal or need to redeem investments in an emergency. People with a short time horizon require investments that offer some predictability and stability. As a result, short-term investors are usually more interested in current income than capital gains. If you are investing to achieve long-term goals, by contrast, you want your money to grow and, therefore, you are likely to keep your money in the same investments for 10 or 15 years. Long-term investors are usually more interested in capital gains than current income.

Regardless of the length of the investment period, you should periodically reexamine your investments to verify that they are working toward your goals. There are trade-offs between investing for the short term or for the long term, and Table 13.2 (page 370) provides an overview of possible investments that match specific investment time horizons.

| Table 13.2 | Match the Investment Alternatives to the Time Horizon of Your Goals | | |

Time	Investment Goals	Trade-offs	Possible Investments
Less than 2 years	Easy access to funds Moderate yields Low volatility Steady income Stable prices	Low returns Vulnerable to inflation	NOW checking account Savings account Money market account Certificates of deposit Treasury issues and corporate bonds maturing within 2 years
2 to 5 years	Moderately high yields Steady income Narrow price movements	Less safety than for shorter-term investments Subject to market swings Lower returns than for longer-term investments Some vulnerability to inflation	Corporate bonds maturing within 5 years Ginnie Mae bonds Stocks paying high dividends Balanced mutual funds
6 to 10 years	Moderately high yields Predictable price movements	Less safety than for shorter-term investments Lower returns than for longer-term investments	Stocks paying high dividends Ginnie Mae bonds Short-term bonds Long-term bonds Long-term certificates of deposit (CDs) Growth and income mutual funds Real estate
More than 10 years	High long-term yields Potential for appreciation Returns that outpace inflation	Price volatility May have limited liquidity and marketability Patience required	Growth stocks Long-term bonds Precious metals Aggressive-growth mutual funds Real estate

Which Types of Investments Are Best Given Your Investment Goals?

This chapter provides the background information and tools of analysis that will permit you to decide which types of investments work best for you. It also gives guidelines for deciding when investments should be sold. The next four chapters examine the details of the various types of investments. Chapter 14 focuses on investing in individual stocks and bonds. Next, Chapter 15 examines investing in mutual funds—the most popular of all investments owned by individuals and families. Chapter 16 looks at the complexities of buying and selling of investments. Finally, Chapter 17 examines real estate (when viewed as an investment rather than as property for personal use) and speculative investments, such as collectibles and options contracts. After reading these chapters, you should have learned enough about investments to make informed decisions on your own.

Factors That Affect the Rate of Return on Different Investments

4 Describe the major factors that affect the rate of return on investments.

To be a successful investor, you must understand the major factors that affect the rate of return on different investments. You can then take the risks that are appropriate for reaching your goals. Your **risk tolerance** is your ability to weather changes in the values of your investments. In addition to the risk that an investment could totally fail, other factors influence investment returns.

Investment Risk

Pure risk, which concerns the uncertainty that events might occur with no potential for gain, was discussed in Chapter 10. Investments, in contrast, are subject to **speculative risk,** which involves the potential for either gain or loss. For example, common stock may rise or fall in value; which event will occur is an unknown. Because of the uncertainty that surrounds investments, many people follow a conservative course in an effort to keep their risk low—but they may risk not reaching their goals. As a result, to obtain high yields, they must accept greater unknowns and higher risk.

Figure 13.2 graphically presents the risk pyramid, which illustrates the trade-offs between risk and return for a number of investments. All four investments guaranteed by the U.S. government (savings bonds, certificates of deposit, insured bank accounts, and Treasury securities) offer a virtually "risk-free return." In exchange for this certainty, however, they offer a relatively low return.

Figure 13.2

The Risk Pyramid Reveals the Trade-offs Between Investment Risk and Return

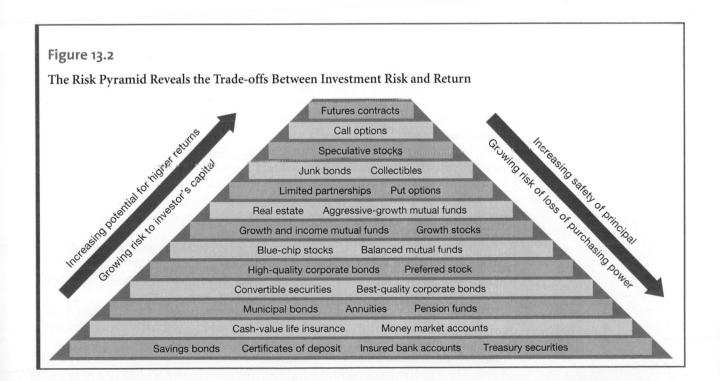

Types of Investment Risk.   A number of risks affect the likelihood that a particular investment will not provide an appropriate return to the investor:

- **Inflation risk.** Inflation risk may be the most important concern for the long-term investor. **Inflation risk,** or **purchasing power risk,** is the danger that your money will not grow as fast as inflation or be worth as much in the future as it is today. In this case, the concern is that your investment returns may be diminished or reversed by the cumulative effects of inflation. Inflation risk is present for all types of investments.

- **Deflation risk.** Houses, real estate, and other ownership investments are subject to **deflation risk.** This risk encompasses the chance that the general price level in the economy might drop, thereby reducing the investment's value. Such events have occurred recently in certain regional real estate markets in the United States.

- **Business-cycle risk.** Economic growth usually does not occur in a smooth and steady manner. Instead, periods of expansion lasting three or four years are often followed by contractions in the economy, called recessions, that often last a year or longer. The profits of most industries follow the business cycle. Some businesses, however, continue to earn profits during economic downturns, such as gasoline retailers, supermarkets, and utility companies.

- **Time risk.** Whether you buy or sell or own or lend, the role of time affects all investments. The sooner your invested money is supposed to be returned to you—the **time horizon** of an investment—the less the likelihood that something could go wrong. The more time your money is invested, the more it is at risk. For taking long-term risks, investors expect and normally receive higher returns.

- **Market-volatility risk.** All investments are subject to occasional sharp changes in price due to events affecting a particular company or the overall market for similar investments. For example, the value of a single stock, such as that of a technology company like Microsoft, might change from 10 to 30 percent in a single day. Also, all technology stocks could decline 2 or perhaps 4 percent if two or three competitors announce poor earnings projections. In addition, the price of a typical stock fluctuates up and down by about 50 percent in an average year; thus, the price of a stock selling for $30 per share in January might range from $15 to $45 before the end of the following December.

- **Liquidity risk. Liquidity** is the speed and ease with which an asset can be converted to cash. You can convert your savings into cash instantly. You can sell your stocks and bonds in one day but it may take four more days to have the proceeds available in cash.

- **Marketability risk.** When you have to sell a certain asset quickly, you may be forced to take a lower price. This possibility is referred to as **marketability risk.** Selling real estate in a hurry, for example, may require the seller to make price concessions because few potential buyers may want the property. An investment with marketability risk is also considered to be illiquid because the asset cannot be quickly converted to cash.

- **Reinvestment risk.** Cash distributions in the form of interest payments from bonds and cash dividends from stocks and mutual funds typically need to be reinvested. Your long-term return will suffer if you cannot reinvest these funds at the same rate earned by your original investment.

- **Interest-rate risk. Interest-rate risk** stems from the possibility that interest rates will rise and, as a result, the value of certain investments will fall. This type of risk affects fixed-interest-rate obligations such as bonds and preferred stocks, which have an almost guaranteed rate of return. For example, suppose that you buy a 20-year, $1000 government bond at 6 percent. The government is obligated to pay you $60 per year ($1000 × 0.06) and to repay the $1000 principal 20 years from now. If interest rates in the economy rise substantially, perhaps to 8 percent, the market value of the 6 percent bond will decline. Because investors could buy a new bond for $1000 that pays 8 percent, they might offer to buy your 6 percent bond for $750, which would raise their effective yield to 8 percent ($60 ÷ $750). Note that your capital loss would be realized only if you actually sold your bond.

■ **Political risk.** The political environment can dramatically influence the value of investments. For example, the imposition of wage and price controls, government efforts to settle labor strikes, and the election of officials who change defense spending, tariff policies, and income tax rates can all affect investments negatively or positively.

Table 13.3 (pages 374–375) summarizes the degree of each kind of risk associated with each type of investment. You may want to return to this table, as well as to Table 13.2, as you study these types of investments in more depth in the following chapters.

Random and Market Risk.   **Random risk** (also called **unsystematic risk**) is the risk associated with owning only one investment of a particular type (such as stock in one company) that, by chance, may do very poorly in the future due to uncontrollable or random factors, such as labor unrest, lawsuits, and product recalls. If you invest in only one stock, its value might rise or fall. If you invest in two or three stocks, however, the odds are lessened that all of their prices will fall. Such **diversification**—the process of reducing risk by spreading investment money among several investment opportunities—provides one effective method of managing random risk. It results in a potential rate of return on all of the investments that is generally lower than the potential return on a single alternative, but the return is more predictable and the risk of loss is lower.

Research suggests that you can cut random risk in half by diversifying into as few as five stocks or bonds; you can eliminate random risk by holding 15 or more stocks or bonds. If you were very confident that interest rates would decline in future years, for example, you might choose to put $10,000 into one company's high-yielding corporate bonds (perhaps paying 9 percent) before the interest rates slipped further. If you were wrong and interest rates increased, pulling these bond rates upward as well, the value of your bonds would temporarily decline sharply. The tenth column in Table 13.3 shows that bonds carry a high risk related to interest rates and that real estate is associated with a low risk from inflation (real estate prices generally rise during inflationary times). By making several investments in other companies' bonds, you can reduce your random risk. Rational investors diversify so as to reduce random risk.

Diversification among stocks or bonds cannot eliminate all risks, however. Some risk would exist even if you owned all of the stocks in a market, because stock (and bond) prices in general move up and down over time. This movement results in **market risk** (or **systematic risk**). In this case, the value of an investment may drop due to influences and events that affect all similar investments. Examples include a change in economic, social, political or general market conditions; fluctuations in investor preferences; or other broad market-moving factors (such as terrorist attacks).

Market risk is unaffected by diversification across investments in the same market such as stocks or bonds. It is the risk that remains after an investor's portfolio has been fully diversified within a particular market. Over the years, market risk has averaged about 8 percent. As a consequence of this risk, the return on any single securities investment, through no fault of its own, might vary up and down about 8 percent annually. The total risk in an investment consists of the sum of the random risk and the market risk.

Table 13.3 Types of Investments and Degrees of Risk

| Type of Investment | Type of Risk | | | | |
	Financial	Inflation	Deflation	Business Cycle	Time
Insurance (cash value)	Low	Medium	Low	Low	Low
Insurance annuities	Low	High	Low	High	Low
Bonds (best quality)	Low	High	Low	High	High
Bonds (high quality)	Medium	High	Low	High	High
Common stocks	Medium	Medium	Medium	High	Medium
Mutual funds	Medium	Medium	Medium	High	Medium
Real estate	Low	Low	Low	Medium	Low
Precious metals, options, and commodities	High	Low	Low	Low	Medium

To address market risk, an investor should diversify among stocks and bonds while maintaining some funds in cash equivalents (savings), as illustrated in Figure 13.3. Note that the total return on the diversified portfolio (9.6 percent) shown in the figure is less than the highest available return, which is achieved with the equities portion of the portfolio (12 percent). Note also that the risk of loss is reduced. Most investors in equities put their money into stocks and stock mutual funds, which are the primary focus of Chapters 14 and 15.

Leverage

Another factor that can affect return on investment is **leverage.** In the leveraging process, borrowed funds are used to make an investment with the goal of earning a rate of return in excess of the after-tax costs of borrowing. Investing in real estate for its rental income provides an illustration of leverage, as shown in Table 13.4. Assume that

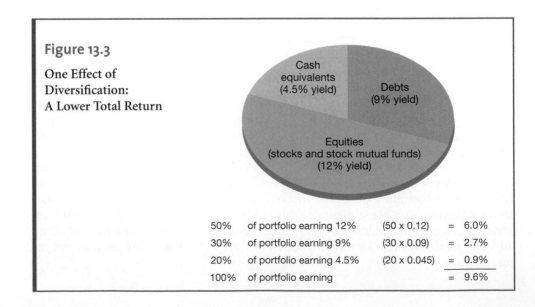

Figure 13.3

One Effect of Diversification: A Lower Total Return

Cash equivalents (4.5% yield)

Debts (9% yield)

Equities (stocks and stock mutual funds) (12% yield)

50%	of portfolio earning 12%	(50 x 0.12)	= 6.0%
30%	of portfolio earning 9%	(30 x 0.09)	= 2.7%
20%	of portfolio earning 4.5%	(20 x 0.045)	= 0.9%
100%	of portfolio earning		= 9.6%

| Type of Risk | | | | | |
Market Volatility	Liquidity	Market-ability	Reinvestment	Interest Rate	Political
Low	Low	Low	Low	Low	Low
Low	Low	Low	Low	Low	Low
Medium	Low	Low	High	High	Low
Medium	Low	Low	High	High	Low
High	Low	Low	Medium	Medium	High
High	Low	Low	Medium	Medium	High
Low	High	High	Low	Medium	High
High	Low	High	Low	Low	High

a person can buy a small office building either by making a $30,000 down payment and borrowing $270,000 or by paying $300,000 cash. If the rental income is $30,000 annually ($2500 per month) and the person pays income taxes at a 25 percent rate, it would be better to use credit to buy the building because the yield would be 31.38 percent versus a 7.5 percent yield when paying cash.

Leverage can prove particularly beneficial when substantial capital gains occur, as this strategy sharply boosts the return on the investment. Assume that at the end of one year, the value of the building described in the previous example has appreciated 7 percent and you could sell it for $321,000 (excluding commission costs). If you had purchased the property for $300,000 cash and then sold it for $321,000, the capital gain on the sale would be 7 percent (the $21,000 return divided by the $300,000 originally invested). If you had bought it using credit, however, the capital gain would be 70 percent (the $21,000 return divided by the $30,000 originally invested, ignoring transaction costs, taxes, and inflation).

Of course, leverage has a potentially negative side as well. In the preceding example, if you used credit to purchase the property, you would need a minimum rental income of $20,479 (from Table 9.3 on page 244, 6½ percent interest on a 30-year loan) to make the mortgage loan payments. A few months of vacancy or expensive repairs to the building could result in a losing situation. Furthermore, any decline in value would be

Table 13.4 Illustration of Leverage: Buying Real Estate Using Credit

	Pay Cash	Use Credit
Purchase price of office building	$300,000	$300,000
Amount borrowed	0	− 270,000
Amount invested	300,000	30,000
Rental income ($2500 per month)	30,000	30,000
Minus tax-deductible interest		
(6.5%, 30-year loan on $270,000)	− 0	− 17,450
Net earnings before taxes	30,000	12,550
Minus income tax liability (25% bracket)	− 7,500	− 3,137
Rental earnings after taxes	$22,500	$9,413
	÷ 300,000	÷ 30,000
Percentage return on amount invested	7.5%	31.38%

magnified when you use leverage. You can become financially overextended by using leverage for investments, a factor that you should not ignore.

Income Taxes

When comparing similar investments, your objective should be to earn the best **after-tax return.** This return is the net amount earned on an investment after payment of income taxes. Increasing the after-tax return on your investments requires an understanding of your marginal tax rate and the concept of taxable versus tax-free income.

Marginal Tax Rate.   The **marginal tax rate** is the tax rate on your last dollar of earnings. It gives you three pieces of information: (1) the amount that you pay the government, (2) the amount that you keep after paying income taxes, and (3) the tax savings benefit of a tax-deductible expense. If you earn an extra $100 and pay taxes at the 25 percent marginal tax rate, for example, you pay the government $25, you keep $75, and, for every dollar you can come up with as a tax deduction, you save 25 cents. The concept of the marginal tax rate is discussed in more detail in Chapters 1 and 4.

Taxable Versus Tax-Free Income.   Investors should use a taxable investment's after-tax yield when making comparisons with tax-free alternatives. For example, Ibrahim Sallah, a member of a two-income family in Logan, Utah, is comparing a $1000 corporate bond paying a 7.6 percent return with a municipal bond paying a 5.9 percent return. Because he is in the 25 percent marginal tax bracket, $19 of the $76 interest earned annually on the corporate bond would go to income taxes ($76 × 0.25). Thus, Ibrahim would be left with an after-tax return of 5.70 percent ($76 − $19 = $57 ÷ $1000). The municipal bond's annual interest of $59 would be exempt from federal income taxes. Ibrahim should choose the municipal bond because it is the better deal. The after-tax return of 5.9 percent ($59 ÷ $1000) is 0.2 percentage point higher than the after-tax return on the corporate bond (5.9 percent − 5.7 percent).

Your decision to invest in tax-free opportunities should depend on the yields available and your marginal tax rate. Equation (4.1) on page 118 demonstrates how to determine the after-tax equivalent yield on any type of investment. In addition, Chapter 14 provides more information on tax-free investments.

Commissions and Transaction Costs

Buying and selling investments may result in a number of transaction costs. Examples include "fix-up costs" when preparing a home for sale, appraisals for collectibles, and storage costs for precious metals. The largest transaction cost in investments, however, usually comprises **commissions.** These fees or percentages of sales are paid to salespersons, agents, and companies for their services—that is, to buy or sell an investment. The commission charged to buy an investment (one commission) and then later sell it (a second commission) is partially based on the value of the transaction. Typical ranges for commissions are as follows: stocks, 1.5–2.5 percent (although trades can be made on the Internet for less than $20); bonds, 0–2.0 percent; mutual funds, 0–8.5 percent; real estate, 5.0–7.0 percent; options and futures contracts, 4.0–6.0 percent; limited partnerships, 10.0–15.0 percent; and collectibles, 15.0–30.0 percent. You can increase your return by holding down commission expenses. (Additional details on these types of investments are provided in later chapters.)

Inflation

Inflation is an extremely important factor when considering an investment because it can significantly affect the "real" return on the investment. Consider Shirley Robinson, a manufacturing worker from Dover, Delaware, who thought she had hedged against inflation by purchasing a certificate of deposit (CD) paying 3 percent interest. Her account earned $30 interest during the year; unfortunately, the inflation rate for the year was 4 percent. To beat inflation, Shirley must invest her money so that it earns a higher return than the inflation rate.

Over the long term, increases in inflation have averaged approximately 3.1 percent per year. During periods of high inflation, the real values of most assets decline. Historically, the values of common stocks and real estate have tended to rise with inflation over several years. Conversely, bonds generally lose value during inflationary times because they are fixed-dollar investments that offer the return of a certain number of dollars—dollars that are losing their original purchasing power.

The Strategies of Long-Term Investors

5 Explain the five strategies of long-term investors.

Most long-term investors seek genuine growth in the value of their investment that exceeds the rate of inflation. In other words, they want their investments to provide a positive **real rate of return** (the return after subtracting the effects of both inflation and income taxes). A long-term investor generally wants to hold an investment as long as it provides a return commensurate with its risk, usually for 10 or 15 years. Knowledgeable amateurs can obtain excellent long-term investment results. To do so, however, you must exercise discipline and make a concerted effort to manage your investments according to your investment philosophy.

How to . . .

Calculate the Real Rate of Return (After Taxes and Inflation) on Investments

1. **Identify the rate of return before income taxes.** Perhaps you think that a stock will offer a return of 10 percent in one year, including current income and capital gains.
2. **Subtract the effects of your marginal tax rate on the rate of return to obtain the after-tax return.** If you are in the 25 percent federal income tax bracket, the calculation is $(1 - 0.25) \times 0.10 = 0.075 = 7.5$ percent.
3. **Subtract the effects of inflation from the after-tax return to obtain the real rate of return on the investment after taxes and inflation.** If you estimate an annual inflation of 4 percent, the calculation gives 3.5 percent (7.5 percent − 4.0 percent). Thus, your before-tax rate of return of 10 percent provides a real rate of return of 3.5 percent after taxes and inflation.

Investors Understand Market Movements

In addition to understanding the overall economic picture (see Chapter 1), long-term investors should understand how the **securities markets** (places where stocks and bonds are traded) are performing as a whole. That is, are the markets moving up, moving down, or remaining stagnant? A securities market in which prices have declined in value by 20 percent or more from previous highs, often over the course of several weeks or months, is called a **bear market.** Since 1926, several bear markets have occurred, and the most recent bear market lasted from 2000 to 2002. In contrast, a **bull market** results when securities prices have risen 20 percent or more over time. Historically, the more than 20 bull markets have seen an average gain of 110 percent. The bull market of the 1990s saw prices rise more than 300 percent! A **bull** in the market is a person who expects securities prices to go up; a **bear** expects the general market to decline. The origin of these terms is unknown, but some suggest that they refer to the ways that the animals attack: Bears thrust their claws downward, and bulls move their horns upward. Bear markets last, on average, about 9 months; bull markets average 29 months in length.

Wise investors will simply choose appropriate long-term strategies and—very importantly—remain invested in the market. This persistence provides the opportunity to earn the historic average returns of the equities markets (11.4 percent annually).

Long-term investors should not follow or react emotionally to the day-to-day changes that occur in the market. Because most people are sensitive to short-term losses, daily monitoring might motivate them to change their investment policy and make short-sighted buying and selling decisions. The secret to success is benign neglect. The tough part is learning to stay the course during normal market downturns. Long-term investors need to relax with the confidence and knowledge that investing regularly every month, and not trading frequently, will create a substantial portfolio over time.

Investors Understand That Trying to Time the Market Is Too Difficult to Accomplish

All long-term investors must be able to withstand some market volatility, the likelihood of large price swings in their chosen securities. However, some investors can best be described as **market timers.** Market timing entails shifting your money into cash or bonds when you think stocks and stock mutual funds are overpriced and then later reinvesting your money in stocks and stock mutual funds when you think they have gotten cheap. Market timers pull out of stocks or bonds in anticipation of a market decline or hold back from investing until the market "settles down." In this scenario, investors try to "time" their investments, hoping to capture most of the upside of rising stock prices while avoiding most of the downside.

To succeed in timing the market, you need to know just the right time to buy and just the right time to sell. Research shows that most of the market's gains are realized in a few trading days that occur every now and then. If market timers are out of the market on those days, they lose. In times of rising markets, it is very easy for market timers to sell "too early" and as a result miss out on much larger profits as the bull market continues to push prices up even more. Those who sell after a sudden drop in investment value, a "down market," actually lock in their losses.

Very few market timers succeed in simultaneously lowering their risk and raising their returns. In fact, most of these investors earn returns far worse than the averages, in part because they pay too many transaction fees. The reality is that market timing increases market risk. Short-term buying and selling is more like gambling than investing. What contributes the most to successful investing is not timing, but time.

Most investors realize that they cannot time the market with any consistency. Long-term investors wisely ignore the ups and downs of the stock market and the business cycle, and simply buy and hold their investments using the investment strategies of diversification, asset allocation, modern portfolio theory, and dollar-cost-averaging.

Strategy: Buy-and-Hold Anticipates Long-Term Economic Growth

Most investors use the **buy-and-hold** (also called **buy-to-hold**) approach to investing. That is, they buy a widely diversified mix of stocks and/or mutual funds, reinvest the dividends by buying more stocks and mutual funds, and hold on to those investments almost indefinitely. With this approach, the investor expects that the values of the assets will increase over the long run in tandem with the growth of the U.S. and world economies. The investment may pay current income as well. The investor's emphasis is on holding the assets through both good and bad economic times with the confidence that their values will go up over time. This is a wise strategy.

Of course, investors should not blindly hold on to an investment for years. Instead, they should review all holdings at least once a year to make sure that each remains a good investment. Ask the question, "Does this asset still fit my investment plan?" The buy-and-hold strategy works well in combination with portfolio diversification, asset allocation, modern portfolio theory, and dollar-cost averaging, all of which are examined in the following sections.

Strategy: Portfolio Diversification Reduces Portfolio Volatility

Diversification is the single most important rule in investing. **Portfolio diversification** is the practice of selecting a collection of different asset classes of investments (such as stocks, bonds, mutual funds, and real estate) that are selected not only for their potential returns but also for their dissimilar risk-return characteristics. The goal of portfolio diversification is to create a collection of investments that will provide an acceptable level of return and an acceptable exposure to risk. This outcome can be achieved because asset classes typically react differently to economic and marketplace changes. The major benefit of having a diversified portfolio is that when one asset class performs poorly, there is a good chance that another will perform well, and vice versa. Portfolio diversification successfully addresses both random risk and market risk. Over the long term, it reduces the volatility of the portfolio without substantially cutting the return. Diversification lowers the odds that you will lose money investing and increases the odds that you will make money.

Owning too much of any one investment creates too great a financial risk. Experts advise that you should never keep more than 15 percent of your assets in one stock, including your employer's stock. Many employees who did not diversify properly have seen their retirement funds disappear or be drastically reduced in value when their employers' stocks plunged in price.

Strategy: Asset Allocation Keeps You in the Right Investment Categories at the Right Time

Asset allocation, a form of diversification, simply involves deciding the proportions of your investment portfolio that will be devoted to various categories of assets. To achieve an appropriate mix of growth, income, and stability in your portfolio, you should have a combination of stocks and/or stock mutual funds (equities), bonds (generically called debt), and cash or cash equivalents. Once you decide how much to invest in each allocation category, stick with your plan. Asset allocation helps preserve capital by selecting assets so as to protect the entire portfolio from negative events while remaining in a position to gain from positive events. This strategy helps control your exposure to risk.

Asset allocation requires that you keep your equities, debt, and cash equivalents at a fixed ratio for long time periods, occasionally rebalancing the allocations—perhaps annually—so as to continue to meet your investment objectives. This may mean selling some investments in an asset class if it has grown too large as a proportion of the overall portfolio (perhaps 5 percent greater than originally allocated) and buying more of the asset classes that have gotten smaller. When rebalancing, you will be selling high and buying low—the goal of all investors.

Your allocation proportions and investment choices should reflect your age, income, family responsibilities, financial resources, risk tolerance, goals, retirement plans, and investment time horizon. You need not change your proportions until your broad investment goals change—possibly not for another 5 or 10 years. When your investment objectives do change, perhaps because of marriage, birth of a child, child graduating

Figure 13.4

Illustrative Diversified Investment Portfolios

Conservative Investment Philosophy (aiming for a 5 or 6% annual return, accepts little risk, aims to preserve capital, needs current income to live on, appropriate for divorced mothers/retirees)

Blue-chip stock funds 15%	Balanced mutual funds 10%	Growth stock funds 10%	Long-term bond funds 15%	CDs and short-term bond funds 30%	Money market funds 20%

Moderate Investment Philosophy (aiming for an annual return of 8–10%, average risk tolerance, seeks steady growth, use funds for future goals, appropriate for anyone under 60 years of age)

Aggressive-growth stocks 10%	Stock mutual funds 25%	Blue-chip stock funds 10%	Foreign mutual funds 10%	Long-term bond funds 25%	CDs and short-term bond funds 10%	Money market funds 10%

Aggressive Investment Philosophy (aiming for a 15% or higher annual return, risk seeker, aiming for maximum capital gains, use funds for future goals, appropriate for anyone under 40

Aggressive-growth stocks or stock mutual funds 30%	Growth mutual funds 10%	Foreign growth mutual funds 20%	Small-cap stocks 15%	Long-term bond funds 15%	Money market funds 10%

from college, loss of employment, divorce, or death of a spouse, you will need to change your asset allocation as well.

Figure 13.4 illustrates how several investors diversified their assets by allocating them across various types of investments. A young, risk-tolerant investor with an aggressive investment philosophy might have a portfolio with 90 percent in equities, because equities offer the highest return over the long term, and the remainder in cash (money market funds). Younger investors also have ample time to ride out market fluctuations and make up any major losses. Middle-aged investors might decide to pursue a more balanced portfolio (a moderate approach), because stocks can be volatile over any given five-year period; as a consequence, such investors may not want to keep all of their money there. An investor nearing retirement might choose to reduce the proportion of equity holdings to 30 or 35 percent to reflect a conservative investment philosophy.

According to financial experts, overwhelming evidence shows that more than 90 percent of returns earned by long-term investors result from having one's assets allocated in a diversified portfolio. For investors who do little trading, most of the return comes not from specific security selections but rather is derived from owning the right asset categories at the right time. Through diversification and asset allocation, you can successfully manage investment risks under a variety of economic and market conditions and achieve your investment goals.

Strategy: Modern Portfolio Theory Evolves from Asset Allocation

A sophistical application of asset allocation can be accomplished using **modern portfolio theory.** Here, the goal is to identify the investor's acceptable level of risk tolerance and then find an optimal portfolio of assets that will have the highest expected returns for that level of risk. **Monte Carlo** is an analytical technique for solving a problem by performing a large number of trial runs, called simulations, and inferring a solution from the collective results of the trial runs. Given the specific investments chosen by a particular investor, Monte Carlo simulation mathematically calculates hundreds or even thousands of possible investment combinations to determine the probability that a particular selection of investments will reach the investor's established goal, such as a specific retirement income at a certain point in the future. See the green and yellow portions in Figure 13.5 (page 382).

Many software programs can be used to assist investors in creating an efficient portfolio. Products are available from Financial Engines, Morningstar, and Vanguard; access and use fees range from $150 to $300 annually. For an interactive Monte Carlo graph showing how your expected returns and expected fluctuations may affect the likely outcomes of your investments, see *www.moneychimp.com/articles/risk/riskintro.htm.* Monte Carlo simulations are frequently used in retirement planning, which is discussed in Chapter 18.

Strategy: Dollar-Cost Averaging Buys at "Below-Average" Costs

Dollar-cost averaging is a systematic program of investing equal sums of money at regular intervals regardless of the price of the investment. In this approach, the same fixed dollar amount is invested in the same stock or mutual fund at regular intervals over a long time. The "averaging" means that you purchase more shares when the price

Figure 13.5

Monte Carlo Simulation from Financial Engines

(The analysis and recommendations pictured are hypothetical and are provided for ilustrative purposes only. This illustration should not be relied on for investment advice.)

How we create your Forecast

Overview

How much you'll have in the future depends on how your investments perform over time. To give you our best estimate, we explore thousands of possible economic scenarios using a technique known as "Monte Carlo" simulation. The animation below is a visual representation of this process.

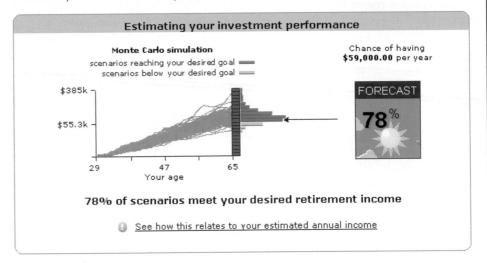

Each economic scenario we explore makes different, realistic assumptions about inflation, interest rates, and returns on asset classes (stocks, bonds, and so forth) for each year of possible growth.

To make sense out of the thousands of estimated portfolio values, we carefully sort and count them. Then we show you three very important numbers. Your median estimate is the most likely of the three, but you should be prepared for the downside just in case:

- **Upside:** if your investments perform well, you may end up with a portfolio in the best 5% of the scenarios.
- **Median:** if your investments perform average, you may end up with a portfolio near the middle of the scenarios.
- **Downside:** if your investments perform poorly, you may end up with a portfolio in the worst 5% of the scenarios.

Source: Copyright © Financial Engines. Used with permission.

is down and fewer shares when the price is high. Most of the shares are, therefore, purchased at below-average costs. This strategy avoids the risks and responsibilities of investment timing because the stock purchases are made regularly (usually every month) regardless of the price. It also ignores all outside events and short-term gyrations of the market, providing the investor with a disciplined buying strategy. It is important to note that the dollar-cost averaging method assumes that the investor has done basic research on the quality of the investment and selected an asset with good future prospects. A well-diversified stock mutual fund would be an excellent example of this type of investment. Chapters 14 through 17 are designed to improve your ability to identify such quality investments.

Table 13.5 shows the results of dollar-cost averaging for a stock under varying market conditions. (Commissions are excluded.) As an example, assume that you invest $300 into a stock every three months. Notice that dollar-cost averaging is successful in all three scenarios illustrated.

Table 13.5 Dollar-Cost Averaging for a Stock or Mutual Fund Investment

Fluctuating Market			Declining Market			Rising Market		
Regular Investment	Share Price	Shares Acquired	Regular Investment	Share Price	Shares Acquired	Regular Investment	Share Price	Shares Acquired
$ 300	$15	20	$ 300	$15	20	$ 300	$ 6	50
300	10	30	300	10	30	300	10	30
300	15	20	300	10	30	300	12	25
300	10	30	300	6	50	300	15	20
300	15	20	300	5	60	300	20	15
Totals $1,500	$65	120	$1,500	$46	190	$1,500	$63	140

Average share price: $13.00
($65 ÷ 5)*

Average share cost: $12.50
($1500 ÷ 120)†

Average share price: $9.20
($46 ÷ 5)*

Average share cost: $7.89
($1500 ÷ 190)†

Average share price: $12.60
($63 ÷ 5)*

Average share cost: $10.71
($1500 ÷ 140)†

*Sum of share price total ÷ number of investment periods.
†Total amount invested ÷ total shares purchased.

Dollar-Cost Averaging in a Fluctuating Market.   To illustrate the effects of dollar-cost averaging, assume that you first invested funds during the "fluctuating market" shown in Table 13.5. Because the initial price is $15 per share, you receive 20 shares for your investment of $300. Then the market drops—an extreme but easy-to-follow example—and the price falls to $10 per share. When you buy $300 worth of the stock now, you receive 30 shares. Three months later, the market price rebounds to $15 and you invest another $300, receiving 20 shares. The price then drops and rises again.

You now own 120 shares, thanks to your total investment of $1500. The **average share price** is calculated by averaging the amounts paid for the investment: Simply divide the share price total by the number of investment periods. In this example, the average share price is $13.00 ($65 ÷ 5). The **average share cost,** a more meaningful figure, is the actual cost basis of the investment used for income tax purposes. It is calculated by dividing the total amount invested by the total shares purchased. In this example, it is $12.50 ($1500 ÷ 120). Based on the recent price of $15 per share, each of your 120 shares is worth on average $2.50 ($15 − $12.50) more than you paid for it. Thus, your gain is $300 (120 × $2.50; or $15 × 120 = $1800, $1800 − $1500 = $300).

Dollar-Cost Averaging in a Declining Market.   Markets may also decline over a time period. The "declining market" columns in Table 13.5 (representing a prolonged bear market of 15 months) show purchases of 190 shares for increasingly lower prices that eventually reach $5 per share at the bottom of the business cycle. In a declining market, if you keep investing using dollar-cost averaging, you will purchase a large volume of shares. If you sell when the market is down substantially, you will not profit. In this example, you have purchased 190 shares at an average cost of $7.89, and they now have a depressed price of $5. Selling at this point would result in a substantial loss of $550 [$1500 − (190 × $5)]. Dollar-cost averaging requires that you continue to invest if the longer-term prospects suggest an eventual increase in price.

Dollar-Cost Averaging in a Rising Market.   During the "rising market" in Table 13.5, you continue to invest but buy fewer shares. The $1500 investment during the bull market bought only 140 shares for an average cost of $10.71. In this rising market, you profit because your 140 shares have a recent market price of $20 per share, for a total value of $2800 (140 × $20).

Almost anyone can profit in a rising market. If you use dollar-cost averaging over the long term, however, you will continue to buy in rising, falling, and fluctuating markets. The overall result will be that you buy more shares when the cost is down, thereby lowering the average share cost to below-average prices. The totals in Table 13.5, for example, reveal an overall investment of $4500 ($1500 + $1500 + $1500) used to purchase 450 shares (120 + 190 + 140) for an average cost of $10 per share ($4500 ÷ 450). With the recent market price at $20, you will realize a long-term gain of $4500 ($20 current market price × 450 shares = $9000; $9000 − $4500 invested = $4500 gain). Note that the dollar-cost averaging method would remain valid if the time interval for investing were monthly, quarterly, or even semiannually; benefits are derived from the regularity of investing.

Dollar-cost averaging offers two advantages. First, it reduces the average cost of shares of stock purchased over a relatively long period. Profits occur when prices for an investment fluctuate and eventually go up. Although this approach does not eliminate the possibility of loss, it does limit losses during times of declining prices. The most important factor is that profits accelerate during rising prices. Second, dollar-cost averaging dictates investor discipline. This strategy of investing is not particularly glamorous, but it is the only approach that is almost guaranteed to make a profit for the investor. It takes neither brilliance nor luck, just discipline. People who invest through individual retirement accounts (IRAs), employee stock ownership programs, and 401(k) retirement plans (all discussed in Chapter 18) similarly enjoy the benefits of dollar-cost averaging when they invest regularly.

6 Summarize the steps to take for effective long-term investing.

Steps to Take for Effective Long-Term Investing

Follow these steps in investing to attain your long-term investment goals:

1. **Identify your personal investment philosophy.** Before you make any investment, you must decide whether you follow a conservative, moderate, or aggressive philosophy.

2. **Keep an eye on local situations.** According to Peter Lynch, the highly successful former manager of the Fidelity Magellan Fund, amateur investors have an advantage over the large investors. Three to five years before analysts really start to follow such developments, local people can be among the first to see the industry in which they work start to turn around. They may also see nearby businesses with bright futures.

3. **Set a time horizon for investing objectives.** Are you building up an amount for a down payment on a home, creating a college fund for a child, or putting money away for retirement? Keep in mind why you are investing and proceed accordingly.

4. **Choose investments for their components of total return.** Your task is to select a portfolio of investments that will provide the necessary potential total return through income and price appreciation in the proportions that you desire. One stock might provide an anticipated cash dividend of 1.5 percent and an expected annual price appreciation of 10 percent, for a total anticipated return of 11.5 percent. Another choice offering the same projected total return might be a stock with expected annual cash dividends of 4.5 percent and capital gains of 7 percent.

Advice from an Expert

Buy Shares of Stock Directly Using a Dividend-Reinvestment Plan

More than 1000 well-known companies allow investors to purchase shares of stock directly from them without the assistance of a stockbroker and then to continue to invest on a regular basis without paying brokerage commissions. Such a program is known as a **dividend-reinvestment plan (DRIP).** You simply sign up with the company, agreeing to buy a certain number of shares and to reinvest cash dividends into more shares of stock for little or no transaction fee. Investors' accounts are credited with fractional shares, too.

Wal-Mart is illustrative. It requires a minimum investment of $250, and continuing investments of $50 thereafter. The enrollment fee is $20 plus $0.10 per share. Most companies will buy back shares for a transaction fee of only $10. Companies offering DRIPs include Ameritech, ExxonMobil, Home Depot, Tenneco, Wal-Mart, McDonalds, and Sears, Roebuck and Company. For a list of companies offering direct purchases, see the Securities Transfer Association at www.netstockdirect.com or the Direct Stock Purchase Plan Clearinghouse at www.dripinvestor.com/clearinghouse/home.asp.

Buying shares regularly through a DRIP is a great example of dollar-cost averaging. It allows you to take advantage of fluctuating stock prices by purchasing on a regular basis at below-average costs.

Linda Gorham
Berklee College of Music, Boston, Massachusetts

5. **Choose your preferred investment medium.** Study carefully and decide which type of investment that you prefer to earn the desired total return. Some people love stocks and hate bonds; others prefer real estate to either type of security; and many others seek to earn good yields using mutual funds. Take your time because you do not have to make a particular investment today, this week, or even this year. Carefully research the industry and the competition.

6. **Invest in companies and industries that will outearn their competitors.** Consider only those investments that will likely be industry leaders—not necessarily the largest firms and fastest-growing industries, but the pacesetters in terms of profitability. You should invest because you have good reasons related to profitability, such as a new division that is turning around, competitors that are losing ground, product research that looks promising, or an industry that "will be" the future driver of profits in the economy.

7. **Develop a plan for investing and stick with it.** Investors often do best by setting target prices and making a list of probable strategies and actions. For example, you might decide to buy a certain stock currently selling at $37 when its price slips to $35 and then hold it for five years or a little longer. In addition, you may decide that if the price appreciates more than 30 percent during any given year after you have held the stock for two years, you will consider selling to take your profits. Alternatively, if the issue loses more than 20 percent of its value over any 12-month time period, you will consider selling and investing the proceeds elsewhere.

Advice from an Expert

When to Sell an Investment

It is time to sell an investment when one of the following conditions has been met:

- Something significant about the company's business or its earnings has changed dramatically for the worse since you bought it.
- The stock is doing so well that it is overvalued, and the share price is much higher than what you believe the company is worth.
- The investment is performing poorly and causing you undue anxiety. The great financier Bernard Baruch advised, "Sell down to the level where you are sleeping well."
- You need cash for a worthwhile purpose, and this investment appears the most fully priced.
- The investment no longer fits your situation or goals, and you have a more promising place to invest your money.

Reynolds Griffith
Stephen F. Austin State University

8. **Maintain a diversified portfolio.** It is critical that you do not put all of your investment "eggs" in one basket. For example, you might buy a number of mutual funds, perhaps including a balanced fund, an asset-allocation fund, a life-cycle fund, and an aggressive-growth fund. Similarly, you could invest in three or four stocks within an industry group instead of just one.

9. **Invest regularly, reinvest your earnings, and relax.** Successful investing requires making investments over a long time period. Reinvesting will boost your return. Keep investing with the confident knowledge that your portfolio will increase in value, along with the U.S. economy and the world's stock markets.

Summary

1. Investing requires understanding why people invest, what they should accomplish before beginning to invest, how to obtain the initial funds for investing, and what types of investment returns are possible. Investor returns come from dividends, interest, rent, and capital gains.

2. Your personal tolerance for risk is a critical factor in discovering your own investment philosophy—that is, whether it is conservative, moderate, or aggressive, as well

as whether you want to be an active or passive investor. Ultraconservative "investors" are not investors at all.

3. You have three key decisions to make when choosing investments. First, do you want to lend your money or own an asset? Second, do you want to invest for the short term or the long term? Third, which types of investment are best for you given your investment goals?

4. The major factors that affect the rate of return on investments include several types of investment risk (such as market-volatility risk, marketability risk, and interest-rate risk) as well as leverage, income taxes, and commissions and other selling costs.

5. Rather than trying to time the market, long-term investors follow five basic strategies to investing: buy-and-hold, portfolio diversification, asset allocation, modern portfolio theory, and dollar-cost averaging. Investors need to earn returns in excess of inflation and income taxes.

6. Investors should follow several steps to attain their long-term objectives, including identifying their investment philosophy, keeping an eye on local conditions, choosing investments for their components of total return, and investing in companies and industries that will outearn their competitors.

Key Terms

active investor, 368
aggressive investment philosophy, 367
asset allocation, 380
average share price, 383
bear market, 378
capital gain, 365
current income, 365
diversification, 373
dividend-reinvestment plan (DRIP), 385
dollar-cost averaging, 381
financial (business) risk, 365
interest-rate risk, 372
leverage, 374
liquidity risk, 372
market (systematic) risk, 373
market timers, 378
market-volatility risk, 372
passive investor, 368
rate of return (yield), 365
real rate of return, 377
risk tolerance, 371

Chapter Review Questions

1. Describe three ways to get money to save and invest.

2. Distinguish between current income and capital gains as the sources of returns on investments.

3. What are the key differences among the three types of investment philosophies?

4. Distinguish between active and passive investing.

5. Describe the trade-offs between risk and return as illustrated in the risk pyramid.

6. Summarize why it is so difficult for investors to time the market.

7. Comment on the wisdom of the buy-and-hold strategy of investing for the long term.

8. Explain how portfolio diversification works to resolve both random and market risk, and give an example of this strategy.

9. Describe the logic of asset allocation.

10. What two goals does dollar-cost averaging accomplish, and how does it work?

Group Discussion Issues

1. Why should people invest? Give three reasons each for college students, young twenty-something college graduates, couples with young children, and people in their fifties.

2. The text offers five prerequisites to investing. For each item, make a list of likely dates when you think you will have accomplished that prerequisite (perhaps in one or two years). Give some reasons for those dates.

3. What is your tolerance for risk in investing? Is it the same as for other members of your group? List two reasons why or why not.

4. Is your investment philosophy conservative, moderate, or aggressive? Give three reasons to support your adoption of this philosophy. Compare your view to the philosophies of other members of your group.

5. The text discusses five strategies for long-term investors. Which one appeals to you most? Give two reasons why you find this strategy attractive.

6. Assume that you have graduated and have a good-paying job. If you had to commit to investing right now, how much money would you put away every month? Give three reasons why.

Decision-Making Cases

▶Case 1
A Veteran Invests to Buy a Condominium

Ron Witherspoon, a paraplegic disabled veteran of the U.S. Navy and self-employed "computer nerd" from Omaha,

Nebraska, hopes to continue his savings and investment program for three more years before making a down payment on a condominium. The home that he wants to purchase is currently priced at $190,000.

(a) If inflation is 4 percent for each of the next three years, how much will the condominium probably cost? See Appendix Table A.1 or use the *Garman/Forgue* website to make your calculation. (See the section on the time value of money in Chapter 1 beginning on page 16.)

(b) If Ron wants to make a 20 percent down payment, how much money will he need in the future given the projected value of the condominium?

(c) Should Ron invest his money during the next three years by lending or owning? Why?

▶ Case 2
Investing a Gift of Cash

Shelly Marsh, a recently married dentist from Houston, Texas, is thinking about investing a $20,000 gift that her uncle gave her. You can help Shelley by answering some questions about return on investment.

(a) How much will Shelly's real return be (after taxes and inflation) if she earns a 6 percent total return on a stock investment this year, assuming that inflation is 4 percent and she and her husband are in the 25 percent marginal tax bracket? Use the information on page 377 or the *Garman/Forgue* website.

(b) How much will Shelly's real return be if she earns an 8 percent total return on the investment? Use the information on page 377 or the *Garman/Forgue* website.

(c) If Shelly invests the money in a mutual fund that earns a 10 percent return for the next 20 years, how much will the account be worth at that time (assume that no income taxes must be paid and all dividends are reinvested)? Use Appendix Table A.1 or the *Garman/Forgue* website.

(d) How much will the account be worth in 30 years if its interest continues to compound at 12 percent annually? Use Appendix Table A.1 or the *Garman/Forgue* website.

Financial Math Questions

1. George and Carolyn Clumson have decided to establish a college fund for their newborn daughter. They estimate that they will need $100,000 in 18 years. Assuming that the Clumsons could obtain a return of 6 percent, how much would they need to invest annually to reach their goal? Use Appendix Table A.3 or the *Garman/Forgue* website.

2. George's mother wants to help pay for her grandchild's education. How many years will it take to reach her goal

of $30,000 if she invests $1000 per year, earning 6 percent? Use Appendix Table A.3 or the *Garman/Forgue* website.

3. If one year of college currently costs $15,000, how much will it cost Joshua's new daughter, Serena, in 18 years, assuming a 5 percent annual rate of inflation? Use Appendix Table A.1 or the *Garman/Forgue* website.

4. Louis and Charles, who are twins, took different approaches to investing. Louis saved $2000 per year for ten years starting at age 22 and never added any more money to the account. Charles saved $2000 per year for 20 years starting at age 35. Assuming that the brothers earned an 8 percent return, who had accumulated the most by the time they reached age 65? Use Appendix Table A.3, Appendix Table A.1, or the *Garman/Forgue* website.

5. Martha Robinson has a choice of two investments: a $1000 tax-free municipal bond that pays 4.3 percent interest or a $1000 taxable corporate bond that pays 6.3 percent interest. Both bonds will mature in five years. If Martha is in the 25 percent tax bracket, which bond should she choose? Use the information on page 118 or the *Garman/Forgue* website.

Money Matters Continuing Cases

Victor and Maria Hernandez Try to Catch Up on Their Investments

The expenses associated with sending two children through college prevented Victor and Maria Hernandez from adding substantially to their investment program. Now that their younger son John has completed school and is working full-time, they would like to build up their investments quickly. Victor is 47 years old and wants to retire early, perhaps by age 60. In addition to the retirement program at his place of employment, Victor believes that their investment portfolio, currently valued at $70,000, will need to triple to $210,000 by retirement time. He and Maria realize that they will have to sacrifice a lot of current spending to save and invest for retirement.

1. What rate of return is needed on the $70,000 portfolio to reach their goal of $210,000? Use the *Garman/Forgue* website or Appendix Table A.3.

2. Victor and Maria think they will need a total of $400,000 for a retirement financial nest egg. Therefore, they will need to create an additional sum of $190,000 through new investments. Assuming an annual return of 8 percent, how much do the Hernandezes need to invest each year to reach their goal of $190,000? Use Appendix Table A.3 or visit the *Garman/Forgue* website.

3. If they assume a 6 percent annual return, how much do the Hernandezes need to invest each year to reach their goal of $190,000? Use Appendix Table A.3 or the *Garman/Forgue* website.

The Johnsons Start an Investment Program

Harry and Belinda's finances have improved in recent months, even though they have incurred new debts for an automobile loan and a condominium. The improvement has occurred because they cut back in their spending on discretionary items (clothing, food, and entertainment) and because Harry recently received a sizable increase in salary after changing employers. His new job as an assistant designer at Medical Facilities, Inc., pays $6000 more than his other job. The new job is also a mile closer to home, reducing Harry's commuting time. The Johnsons have decided to forgo some current spending to concentrate on getting a solid investment program under way while they have two incomes available. They are willing to accept a moderate amount of risk and expect to invest between $200 and $400 per month over the next five years. Assuming that they have an adequate savings program, respond to the following questions:

1. In what types of investments (choose only two) might the Johnsons place the first $2000? (Review Tables 13.2 and 13.3 for ideas and available options, and consider the types of investment risks inherent in each choice.) Give reasons for your selections.

2. In what types of investments might they place the next $4000? Why?

3. What types of investments should they choose for the next $10,000? Why?

4. If inflation is 4 percent, what would their earnings for the year be if they earn 8 percent on a $400 monthly investment? Calculate the projected earnings using the *Garman/Forgue* website.

What Would You Recommend Now?

Now that you have read the chapter on investment fundamentals, what would you recommend to Jennifer and Julia in the case at the beginning of the chapter regarding:

1. Getting more money to save and invest?

2. Prerequisites to investing for Jennifer?

3. Dollar-cost averaging for Jennifer?

4. Portfolio diversification for Julia?

5. Investment alternatives for Julia?

Exploring the World Wide Web

To complete these exercises, go to the *Garman/Forgue* website at college.hmco.com/business/students. Under General Business, select the title of this text. Click on the Internet Exercises link for this chapter, and answer the questions that appear on the Web page.

1. Visit the website for the National Association of Investors (click on "Frequently Asked Questions") for an overview of its investment principles. Also, ask several people for their personal guidelines on how they would select investments. Compare the results from your discussions with the principles found on the Web and with what you have read in this chapter.

2. Visit the website for Vanguard's Investor Questionnaire. What do the results of the quiz tell you about your tolerance for risk? Also, survey a number of people to ascertain their investment philosophy—conservative, moderate, or aggressive. Probe further by asking them questions similar to those found on the risk quiz. Are their perceptions of their risk tolerance congruent with the results they might find from taking the risk quiz?

3. Visit the website for Yahoo! Finance. Read its discussion of risk versus return and answer the following questions:

(a) What likely rate of return should you expect as an investor with a moderate investment philosophy?

(b) What types of investments are recommended for persons with such a philosophy?

4. Visit the website for Stockfirst.com. Read the lesson on dollar-cost averaging and answer the following questions:

(a) What are the principal benefits of using the dollar-cost averaging approach?

(b) What investment philosophies are most congruent with dollar-cost averaging?

5. Visit the website for CNN Money for an overview of asset allocation. Describe how an investor's goals, time horizon, risk tolerance, and financial resources affect his or her asset-allocation decisions.

6. Visit the website for *The Wall Street Journal*. From its free on-line stock quote service, determine the closing stock price for one of the following companies for each year of the past decade: Coca-Cola, IBM, General Electric, or General Motors. Assume that you had invested $10,000 at the end of each year using dollar-cost averaging to purchase shares of that company. Calculate the number of shares you would have purchased, the average share price, the average share cost, and the total value of those shares today (you will also have to look up the stock's current market price).

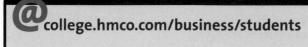

Visit the Garman/Forgue website...

@college.hmco.com/business/students

Under General Business, select *Personal Finance 8e.* There, among other valuable resources, you will find a complete glossary, ACE questions, links to help you complete the chapter exercises, and links to other personal finance sites.

Chapter 14

Investing in Stocks and Bonds

LEARNING OBJECTIVES

After reading this chapter, you should be able to:

1 **Describe** how stocks and bonds are used in the world of investments.

2 **List** key numeric measures of stock performance that influence investment decisions.

3 **Distinguish** among the classifications of stocks.

4 **Identify** the major characteristics of bonds, and differentiate among corporate, U.S. government, and municipal bonds.

5 **Evaluate** bond prices and returns, and summarize the decisions that bond investors must make.

Carlena Diaz, age 42, is a senior Web designer for a communications company in Los Angeles. She earns $92,000 annually. From her salary, Carlena contributes $200 per month to her 401(k) retirement account, through which she invests in the company's stock. Carlena is divorced and has custody of her three children, twins aged 10 and a 12-year-old. Her ex-husband pays $1500 per month in child support. Carlena and her former spouse contribute $3000 each annually to a college fund for their children. Over the last 15 years, Carlena has built a $300,000 stock portfolio after starting by investing the proceeds of a $50,000 life insurance policy following the death of her first husband. Currently, her portfolio is allocated 40 percent into preferred stocks (paying 4½ percent), 30 percent into cyclical, blue-chip common stocks (P/E ratio of 18), 10 percent into Treasury bonds (paying 3.2 percent), 10 percent into municipal bonds (paying 2.7 percent), and 10 percent into AAA corporate bonds (paying 4.5 percent). Today's comparable corporate bonds pay 5 percent. Carlena's total return in recent years has been about 4 percent annually. Her investment goals are to have sufficient cash to pay for her children's education and to retire in about 18 years.

What would you recommend to Carlena on the subject of stocks and bonds regarding:

1. Investing for retirement in 18 years?

2. Owning blue-chip common stocks and preferred stocks rather than other common stocks given Carlena's investment horizon?

3. The wisdom of owning municipal bonds rather than corporate bonds?

4. The likely selling price of her corporate bonds, if sold today?

5. Investments that might be appropriate to fund her children's education?

If you keep all of your extra money in ultraconservative cash equivalents, such as certificates of deposit, you likely will be frustrated by the low returns. Indeed, they will be barely adequate to cover inflation and taxes on the interest earned. To do better, you must begin to think about increasing your level of risk to increase your potential yield. When you invest in stock, bond, and mutual funds carefully, you can increase returns significantly while simultaneously increasing risk only slightly. These investments belong in everyone's investment portfolio, including yours, because they provide opportunities for conservative, moderate, and aggressive investors alike. Most investors prefer to own common stocks (or stock mutual funds), rather than preferred stocks or bonds, because the returns on common stocks have historically been about twice as high as the returns on bonds. Mutual funds are examined in Chapter 15, and this chapter focuses on stocks and bonds.

We begin by describing stocks and bonds and illustrating how corporations and investors use them in the world of investments. This section is followed by a discussion of several key numeric measures of stock performance that influence investment decisions. You need to understand these measures to select the best stock investments for meeting your goals. Next, we describe the basic classifications of stocks (such as income and growth stocks). The chapter then reviews the major characteristics of bonds as investments. It also distinguishes between corporate and government bonds and explains how to evaluate bond prices and returns. Finally, the chapter identifies the four decisions that every bond investor must make.

Golden Rules of

Investing in Stocks and Bonds

Financial success comes from learning the Golden Rules of personal finance and then putting what you have learned into practice. Make the following your money habits when investing in stocks and bonds.

1. Definitely include stocks and/or stock mutual funds in your diversified investment portfolio.
2. Use fundamental analysis to determine a company's basic value before investing in a stock for the long-term.
3. Consider investing the conservative part of your portfolio in TIPS (Treasury Inflation-Protected Securities) to beat inflation.
4. Instead of investing in individual corporate bonds, minimize financial and interest-rate risks by investing in bond mutual funds.
5. Consider zero-coupon bonds to help fund a child's education and/or your retirement.

Stocks and Bonds and How They Are Used

1 Describe how stocks and bonds are used in the world of investments.

The corporate form of business ownership is very popular in the United States. The main reason is that corporations can raise large sums of investment capital by selling stock, which can then be used to expand their business. A **corporation** is a state-chartered legal entity that can conduct business operations in its own name. Its ability to sell shares of ownership to investors offers a corporation the opportunity to develop into a firm of considerable size. Such a company may have a large number of investors and can continue to exist even as ownership of its shares changes hands.

A corporation's financial needs may vary over time. To begin its operations, a new corporation needs **startup capital** (funds initially invested in a business enterprise). During its life, a corporation may need additional money to grow. To raise capital and finance its goals, it may issue three types of **securities** (negotiable instruments of ownership or debt): common stock, preferred stock, and bonds.

Common Stock

Stocks are shares of ownership in the assets and earnings of a business corporation. **Common stock** is the most basic form of ownership of a corporation. The owner of a stock—called a **shareholder** or **stockholder**—has a claim on the firm's assets and earnings. A corporation may have a single owner/shareholder or it may issue millions of shares that are owned by numerous owners/shareholders. Each shareholder has a proportionate interest in the ownership (a very small slice) and, therefore, in the assets and income of the corporation. In particular, common stockholders have a residual claim after any claims made by bondholders and preferred stockholders have been satisfied.

Each common stockholder may vote to elect the company's board of directors. This group of individuals sets policy and names the principal officers of the company who run the firm's day-to-day operations. The number of votes cast by each shareholder depends on the number of shares he or she owns. If the corporation becomes bankrupt, the common stockholder's ownership value consists of the amount left per share after the claims of all creditors are satisfied first. At the same time, the shareholder's liability for business losses is limited to the amount invested in the shares of stock owned. This risk of financial loss is balanced by the potential to share in substantial profits when the corporation performs well.

Stocks represent potential income for investors because stockholders own a piece of the future profits of the company. People who own stocks typically have two expectations: (1) the corporation will be profitable enough that income will exceed expenses, thereby allowing the firm to pay **cash dividends** (a share of profits distributed in cash), and (2) the **market price** of a share of stock, which is the current price that a buyer is willing to pay a willing seller, will increase. Stocks call for a low minimum investment. A share of stock could sell for as little as $5 or $10, although it is rare to purchase one share at a time.

Stocks are a topic of considerable interest today in part because many employers give stock options to attract and retain employees. An **employee stock option (ESO)** is a gift, like a bonus, from an employer to an employee that allows employees to benefit from the appreciation of their employer's stock without putting any money down. The company gives the employee the right and opportunity to "exercise" the option by buying the stock sometime in the future at an "exercise" or "striking" price established when the option was given. If the company prospers, when the employee eventually decides to exercise the options, the current share price may be much higher than the exercise price, allowing the employee to buy the shares at a considerable discount.

Preferred Stock

Preferred stock is a type of fixed-income ownership security in a corporation. Owners of a preferred stock receive a fixed dividend per share that the corporation must distribute before any dividends are paid out to common stockholders. These regular dividend payments appeal to retired investors and others who desire a reliable stream of income. Preferred stockholders typically have no voting privileges. They receive no extra income from the stock than their fixed dividend, even when the firm is highly profitable.

The market price of shares of preferred stock is primarily based on prevailing interest rates in the economy. When interest rates rise, the market price of a preferred stock will drop so that the real yield remains competitive with similar-risk investments. For example, suppose you own a preferred stock that costs $100 and pays an annual cash dividend of $6; this stock would, therefore, provide a 6 percent return. If returns on other investments of similar risk climbed to 8 percent, the market price that others would be willing to pay for your preferred stock would drop to reflect the differences in the rates of return. After all, who would pay $100 for a preferred stock with a dividend of $6 when they could put their money into a similar investment (such as a corporate bond) and receive $8? With a cash dividend of only $6, the market price of the preferred stock would have to drop to approximately $75 to increase the yield to 8 percent ($6 ÷ 0.08 = $75).

Sometimes a corporation decides not to pay dividends to preferred stockholders. It may do so because it lacks profits or simply because it wants to retain and reinvest all of its earnings. With **cumulative preferred stock,** when the board of directors votes to skip (**pass**) making a cash dividend to preferred stockholders, that dividend must be paid to these stockholders before any future dividends are distributed to the common stockholders. For example, assume that a company passes on the first two quarterly dividends of $2.25 each to preferred stockholders, who expect to receive $9 each year ($2.25 × 4 quarters). If the company prospers and wants to give a cash dividend to its common stockholders in the third quarter, it must first pay the passed $4.50 to the cumulative preferred stockholders. Furthermore, the usual third-quarter cash dividend of $2.25 must be made to the preferred stockholders before the common stockholders can receive any dividends. In the case of **noncumulative preferred stock,** the preferred stockholders would have no claim to previously skipped dividends. If a company goes bankrupt, the claims of bondholders supersede those of preferred stockholders.

Bonds

A **bond** is an interest-bearing negotiable certificate of long-term debt issued by a corporation, a municipality (such as a city or state), or the U.S. federal government. Bonds are basically IOUs. The initial purchaser of the bond lends the issuer a certain amount of money—the **principal**—and, in return, the issuer makes two promises: (1) to pay interest over the life of the bond, and (2) to repay the investor's principal at some point in the future—the **maturity date.** Corporations and governments often use the proceeds from bonds to finance expensive construction projects and to purchase costly equipment. As with preferred stock, the regular pattern of dividends appeals to retired investors and others who desire a reliable stream of income.

Once bonds are initially issued (typically in $1000 units) and purchased by investors, most can be readily bought and sold many times by subsequent investors in a **secondary market** prior to maturity. This market is also called an **aftermarket,** because existing securities that have already been sold to the public are bought and sold there. A stock and bond exchange, such as the New York Stock Exchange, is an example of such an aftermarket.

Investment-grade bond investments offer a reasonable certainty of regularly receiving the periodic income (interest) and retrieving the amount originally invested. For taking this relatively small financial risk, an investor typically earns a low to moderate return, an appropriate yield when compared with the higher total returns earned on riskier stocks and stock mutual fund investments. Fewer than 800 of the 23,000 large U.S. companies that issue bonds meet the highest investment grade rating standards. Good-quality bonds also represent attractive investments, however, because those held to maturity carry little financial risk relative to investments in common stocks or real estate. The total annual after-tax return on bonds (and bond mutual funds, which are examined in Chapter 15) is historically well above the returns on savings accounts, but only about one-half the returns on stocks and stock mutual funds.

The only type of bond that pays a high interest rate is a junk bond. **Junk bonds** are long-term, high-risk, high-interest-rate corporate (or municipal) IOUs issued by companies (or municipalities) with poor or no credit ratings. Also called "high-yield" bonds, these bonds carry ratings that are below traditional investment grade and carry a higher default risk. The default rate on high-quality bonds is less than 1 percent, whereas the default rate on junk bonds ranges from 2 to 31 percent. Wise investors avoid buying individual junk bonds because of the substantial financial risk involved with owning too few investments. Instead, they minimize risk by diversifying their investments through a "high-yield income" bond mutual fund that owns junk bonds.

An Illustration: Running Paws Cat Food Company

To better understand how a corporation finances its goals by issuing common and preferred stock while paying returns for stockholders, consider the example of Running Paws Cat Food Company. This small family business was started in New Jersey by Linda Webtek. She developed a wonderful recipe for cat food and sold the product through a local grocery store. As her sales increased, Linda decided to incorporate the business, expand its operations, and share ownership of the company with the public by asking people to invest in the company's future. Running Paws issued 10,000 shares of common stock at $10 per share. Three friends each bought 2500 shares, and Linda signed over the cat food recipe and equipment to the corporation itself in exchange for the remaining 2500 shares. At that point, Running Paws had $75,000 in working capital (7500 shares sold at $10 each), equipment, a great recipe, and a four-person board of directors. Each of the directors worked for the firm, although they paid themselves very low salaries.

The sales revenues of a corporation like Running Paws are used to pay (1) expenses, (2) interest to bondholders, (3) taxes, (4) cash dividends to preferred stockholders, and (5) cash dividends to common stockholders, in that order. If money is left over after items 1 and 2 are paid, the corporation has earned a profit. If funds are available after item 3 is paid, the company has a net (after-tax) profit. The average corporation pays out 40 to 60 percent of its after-tax profit in cash dividends to stockholders. The remainder, called **retained earnings,** is left to accumulate and finance the company's goals—often expansion and growth. In its early years, Running Paws retained all of its profits and distributed no dividends.

Common stockholders, like the stockholders of Running Paws Cat Food Company, are not guaranteed dividends. However, most profitable companies do pay common stockholders a small dividend on a quarterly basis until increased earnings justify paying out a higher amount. Given that Running Paws retained all its earnings, you might wonder why people would invest in such a company. Two reasons explain the attraction. First, as a company becomes more efficient and profitable, cash dividends to common stockholders may not only begin but also rise—sometimes sharply. Second, the market price of the stock may increase as more investors become interested in the future profitability of a growing company. Common stock constitutes a share of ownership; as the company grows, the price of its common stock follows suit. Also remember that the retained earnings are owned by the common stockholders.

At Running Paws Cat Food Company, increasing sales meant more production. Soon more orders were coming in from New York City than the firm could handle. After three years, the owners of Running Paws decided to expand once again. They wanted to borrow an additional $100,000, but their business was so new and its future so uncertain that lenders demanded an extremely high interest rate. To raise the needed funds, the owners decided to issue 5000 shares of preferred stock at $20 per share, promising to pay a cash dividend of $1.20 per share annually. When the owners of Running Paws found that no one wanted to buy preferred shares with that yield ($1.20 ÷ $20 = 6 percent), they voted to increase the dividend to $1.80 annually, providing a 9 percent yield to investors. The preferred stock was then sold to outside investors, but the original investors retained control of the company through their common stock. Recall that preferred stockholders may not vote for the board of directors.

Following its pattern of expanding into new markets, Running Paws soon developed additional lines of cat food, which sold well. With the proceeds from the sale of preferred stock, and after a new plant in Los Angeles opened, the income of the four-year-old business finally exceeded expenses, and it had a profit of $13,000. The board of directors declared the promised preferred stock dividend of $9000 (5000 preferred shares $\times$ $1.80), but no dividend for common stockholders. In the following year, net profits after taxes amounted to $28,000. Once again the board paid the $9000 dividend to preferred stockholders but retained the remainder of the profits to finance continued expansion and improved efficiency.

Then one of the original partners wanted to exit the business and needed to sell her 2500 shares of stock, for which she had originally paid $25,000. Because Running Paws was beginning to show some profits, two other private investors recommended by a local stockbroker made offers to purchase her shares. The shares were sold at $16 per share, with 1500 shares going to one investor and 1000 shares to another investor. Thus, this original investor gained $15,000 in price appreciation ($16 $\times$ 2500 = $40,000; $40,000 − $25,000 = $15,000) when she sold out. (Note that the corporation did not profit from this transaction.) Now five owners of the common stock, including the two new ones, voted for the board of directors, with each share having one vote.

During the sixth year, the company's sales again increased and its earnings totaled $39,000. This time the board voted $9000 for the preferred stockholders and $5000 ($0.50 per share) for the common stockholders but retained the remaining $25,000. With the $5000 distribution, the common stockholders finally began to receive cash dividends.

Even with its success, Running Paws faced another difficult decision. To distribute its products nationally would mean another $400,000 to $500,000 in expansion costs. After much discussion, the board voted to sell additional shares of stock and issue some bonds. Specifically, the company sold 10,000 shares of common stock at $25 per share. This action diluted the owners' proportion of ownership by half (although they could buy some of the shares themselves to maintain their proportionate interest), but the potential for profit was considered to be much higher because of the increased production capacity. It took several months to sell all of the new common stock, because so few people knew that the company had stock available for sale. Various local stockbrokers took selling commissions totaling $16,000, leaving $234,000 available for the company to use for expansion.

Running Paws also issued $200,000 in bonds with a coupon rate of 8 percent, a high-yield bond rate made necessary because the company was largely unknown. After brokerage expenses, the company netted more than $190,000 to help finance the expansion. If Running Paws continues to prosper, its board of directors might work toward having its stock listed on a regional stock exchange (see Chapter 16) to facilitate trading of shares and to further enhance the company's image.

Numeric Measures of Stock Performance That Influence Investment Decisions

2 List key numeric measures of stock performance that influence investment decisions.

When you invest in the stock market, you buy shares in companies and become one of their owners. Therefore, you should invest only in the stocks of companies that you believe will make money over the next five to ten years. To make good choices, you need to understand some important numbers that are key measures of stock performance.

Cash Dividends

Most stocks pay dividends. Cash dividends are distributions made in cash to holders of stock. They are the current income that you receive while you own the shares in the company. The firm's board of directors usually declares a dividend on a quarterly basis (four times per corporate year), typically at the end of March, June, September, and December. Dividends are ordinarily paid out of current earnings, but, in the event of unprofitable times (low earnings or none), the money might come from cash reserves held by the company. Occasionally, a company will borrow to pay the dividend so as to maintain its reputation of consistently paying dividends. Of course, later profits must be used to repay any funds borrowed for this purpose.

Dividend Payout Ratio

The **dividend payout ratio** is the dividends per share divided by earnings per share. It helps you judge the likelihood of dividends. For example, imagine that Running Paws Cat Food Company earned $32,000 (after paying preferred stockholders), paid out a cash dividend of $8000 to company stockholders, and retained the remaining $24,000 to facilitate growth of the company. In this case, the dividend payout ratio equals 0.25 ($8000 ÷ $32,000). For that year, Running Paws paid a dividend equal to 25 percent of earnings. Newer companies usually retain most, if not all, of their profits to facilitate growth. An investor interested in growth would, therefore, seek a company with a low payout ratio. The lower the payout ratio, the greater the likelihood that the company will grow, resulting in capital gains for investors.

Dividends per Share

The **dividends per share** measure translates the total cash dividends paid out by a company to common stockholders into a per-share figure. For example, Running Paws might elect to declare a total cash dividend of $8000 for the year to common stockholders. In that case, cash dividends per share would amount to $0.40 ($8000 ÷ 20,000 shares).

Dividend Yield

The **dividend yield**—the cash dividend return to an investor expressed as a percentage of the current market price of a security—also can be determined. For example, the $0.40 cash dividend of Running Paws divided by the current $25 market price for its stock reveals a dividend yield of 1.6 percent ($0.40 ÷ $25). Growth and speculative companies typically pay little or no cash dividends, so they have limited dividend yields. Such companies are attractive to investors who are most interested in capital gains.

Book Value

Book value (also known as **shareholder's equity**) is the net worth of a company, which is determined by subtracting the company's total liabilities from its assets. It theoretically indicates a company's worth if its assets were sold, its debts were paid off, and the net proceeds were distributed to the investors who own the outstanding shares of common stock.

Did You Know? . . .

How Stock Dividends and Stock Splits Work

A **stock dividend** is a dividend paid in the form of securities instead of cash. For example, a company's board of directors might declare a 10 percent stock dividend to stockholders who currently own shares. In this case, if you owned 100 shares, the company would send you 10 more shares. A stock dividend has no effect on price because the owners retain their same proportional ownership in the company.

A **stock split** occurs when the shares of stock owned by existing shareholders are divided into a larger number of shares. A reverse stock split results in a smaller number of shares. For example, a two-for-one split—

say, from $80 to $40 per share—will reduce the value of each share by 50 percent. Thus, twice as many shares are available but each is worth only half as much as before. The company typically cuts the dividend by 50 percent as well. Boards of directors split shares to change the stock price, often lowering it in an effort to open up trading to a greater number of investors. In general, investors are more attracted to a stock that is selling at $40 rather than at $80 or $120. Stock splits are seen by many as an indicator that the company expects better profits in the years ahead.

Book Value per Share

The **book value per share** reflects the book value of a company divided by the number of shares of common stock outstanding. Running Paws has a net worth of $230,000, which, when divided by 20,000 shares, gives a book value per share of $11.50.

Often little relationship exists between the book value of a company and its earnings or the market price of its stock. In fact, the market price for a company's common stock usually exceeds its book value per share. The reason for this discrepancy is that stockholders anticipate earnings and dividends in the future and expect the market price to rise. When the book value per share exceeds the price per share, the stock may truly be underpriced.

Price-to-Book Ratio

The **price-to-book ratio** (**P/B ratio,** also called the **market-to-book ratio**) identifies firms that are asset-rich, such as many banks, brokerage firms, and insurance companies. The P/B ratio is the current stock price divided by the per-share net value of the company's plant, equipment, and other assets (book value). It tells you the premium that you are paying for the net assets of the company.

In the Running Paws example, the book value per share of $11.50 would be divided into the most recent price at which the stock was sold ($25 in this case); thus, the P/B ratio for Running Paws is 2.17. The current P/B ratio for most stocks lies between 2.1 and 1.0. The lower the ratio, the less highly a company's assets have been valued, indicating that the stock may be currently underpriced. If the ratio is less than 1, the assets may be utilized ineffectively. In such cases, an underperforming and undervalued company may become a target of a corporate takeover.

Earnings per Share

The **earnings per share (EPS)** is the amount of profit of the company divided by the number of outstanding shares. It indicates the income that a company has available, on a per-share basis, to pay dividends and reinvest as retained earnings. The EPS is a measure of the firm's profitability on a common-stock-per-share basis, and it is helpful because investors can use it to compare financial conditions of many companies. The EPS is reported in the business section of many newspapers.

In our example, assume that, next year after payment of $9,000 in dividends to preferred stockholders, Running Paws had a net profit of $32,000. With 20,000 shares of stock, the company's EPS would be $1.60 ($32,000 ÷ 20,000).

Price/Earning Ratio

The **price/earnings ratio (P/E ratio)** is the current market price of a stock divided by earnings per share over the past four quarters. This ratio is the primary means of valuing a stock. It demonstrates how expensive the stock is versus the company's recently reported earnings, by revealing how much you are paying for each $1 of earnings. The P/E ratio is sometimes referred to as a stock's "multiple." For example, if the market price of a share of Running Paws stock is currently $25 and the company's EPS is $1.70, the P/E ratio will be 16 ($25 ÷ $1.60 = 15.6, which rounds to 16). This value could also be called a 16-to-1 ratio or a P/E ratio of 16. The P/E ratios of many corporations are widely reported as financial news (for example, in newspapers and on the Internet). In general, stocks with low P/E ratios tend to have higher dividend yields, less risk, lower prices, and slower earnings growth.

To assess a company's financial status, you could compare that firm's P/E ratio with the P/E ratios for other stocks within the same industry. The P/E ratios for most corporations typically range from 5 to 25. Financially successful companies that have been paying good dividends through the years might have a P/E ratio ranging from 7 to 10. Rapidly growing companies would most likely have a much higher P/E ratio—15 to 25. Speculative companies might have P/E ratios of 40 or 50, because they have low earnings now but anticipate much higher earnings in the future. Firms that are expected to have strong earnings growth generally have a high stock price and a correspondingly high P/E ratio.

The standard P/E ratio is, in fact, a "trailing" measure because it is calculated using recently reported earnings, usually from the previous four quarters. Intelligent investors focus on future prospects when analyzing the value of a stock. A "forward price/earnings ratio" divides price by projected earnings over the coming four quarters, an estimate available via most on-line stock quote providers. The **earnings yield,** which is the inverse of the P/E ratio (Running Paws's earnings yield is 6.4% [$1.60 ÷ $25]), helps investors think more clearly about expectations for investments.

Price-to-Sales Ratio

The **price-to-sales ratio (PSR)** can be used to identify companies with a solid financial future but currently have depressed profit margins. The PSR is obtained by dividing a company's total market capitalization by its sales for the past four quarters. For example, if Running Paws Cat Food Company's common stock currently sells for $25 per share and 20,000 shares of the company's stock are outstanding, its total capitalization is $500,000. If company revenues (sales of cat food) were $750,000 over the past year, the stock's PSR would be 0.67 ($500,000 ÷ $750,000). The PSR tells you how much you are paying for $1 of revenue. The lower the PSR ratio, the better the marketability of the stock. Market analysts generally suggest that investors avoid companies with a PSR greater than 1.5 and favor those having a PSR of less than 0.75.

Beta

The **beta** value (or **beta coefficient**) is a measure of an investment's volatility compared with a broad market index for similar investments. It reports the relative history of an investment's up-and-down price changes. For large-company stocks, the S&P Stock Index often serves as a benchmark. The average for all stocks in the market has arbitrarily been assigned a beta of +1.0, and a beta greater than 1.0 indicates higher-than-market volatility.

Most individual stocks have positive betas between +0.5 and +2.0. A beta of zero suggests that the price of the stock is independent of the market, much like that of a risk-free U.S. Treasury security. A beta of less than 1.0 (0.0 to 0.9) means that the stock price is less sensitive to the market because it moves in the same direction as the general market, but not to the same degree. A beta of more than +1.0 to +2.0 (or higher) indicates that the price of the security is more sensitive to the market because its price moves in the same direction as the market but by a greater percentage. Higher betas mean greater risk relative to the market. A stock with a negative beta is called a **countercyclical stock** because it exhibits price changes that are contrary to movements in the business cycle (such as cigarette and utility company stocks). Thus, the prices of such stocks remain steady or go up during an economic recession. You may look up betas for stocks at www.investor.reuters.com/stockEntry.aspx?target-/stocks and www.finance.yahoo.com/?u.

The Classifications of Stocks

3 Distinguish among the classifications of stocks.

Investors group stocks according to specific classifications. These designations can then be used to match an investor's preferences with certain stocks. There are three basic classifications of corporate stock: (1) income stocks, (2) growth stocks, and (3) speculative stocks. Other terms are also used to meaningfully characterize stocks.

Income Stocks

A company whose stock is classified as an **income stock** characteristically may not grow too quickly, but it pays a cash dividend higher than that offered by most companies year after year. It does so because the firm has fairly high earnings and chooses to retain only a small portion of the earnings. To declare high cash dividends regularly, a company must have a steady stream of income. Stocks issued by telephone, electric, and gas utility companies fit this profile and are normally labeled income stocks. Investors in these companies usually are not very concerned with the P/E ratio or the growth potential of the price of the stock. The betas of such stocks are often less than 1.0. People in or near retirement who rely on dividends to supplement their income are often attracted to income stocks.

Did You Know? . . .

Shareholders Have Voting and Preemptive Rights

Owners of common stock normally have **voting rights.** This right is the proportionate authority to express an opinion or choice in matters affecting the company. Each share of common stock gives the holder one vote. At the annual meeting of the company, the board of directors is elected (or reelected), and stockholders vote on matters of special interest. Each stockholder may participate in these activities by either attending an annual meeting or voting by **proxy.** A proxy is written authorization given by a shareholder to someone else to represent him or her and to vote his or her shares at a stockholder's meeting.

When Running Paws Cat Food Company from this chapter's ongoing example issued additional shares of its stock to finance growth in its fifth year, current stockholders were concerned that they would lose their proportionate interest in the company. Common stockholders usually have a **preemptive right** to purchase additional shares, frequently at a discount from the market price before new shares are offered to the public. Exercising this right enables them to maintain their proportionate ownership.

Growth Stocks

The term **growth stock** describes a company that offers the promise of much higher profits tomorrow and has a consistent record of relatively rapid growth in earnings in all economic conditions. The return to investors from growth stocks comes primarily from increases in share prices. Such stocks typically pay low or no dividends because most of their earnings are retained to maintain company growth.

Stocks of companies that are leaders in their fields, that dominate their markets, and that have several consecutive years of above-industry-average earnings are considered **well-known growth stocks**. Investor awareness of such corporations is widespread, and expectations for continued growth are high. The P/E ratio is high, too. Many growth stocks have a glamorous reputation that improves or declines sharply in conjunction with the overall market and, therefore, have betas of 1.5 or more. Investors generally seem to prefer well-known growth stocks, because they typically pay some dividends and offer a good opportunity for price appreciation. In the past, well-known growth stocks have included those offered by Microsoft, Oracle, eBay, Coca-Cola, Intel, Nike, and Wal-Mart.

Because some **lesser-known growth stocks** are not as popular with investors, the P/E ratios for such firms are generally lower (although still high) than those of the more glamorous growth stocks. Often such firms represent regional businesses with strong earnings or companies that may be the third- or fourth-leading firm in an industry. In recent years, lesser-known growth stocks have included Gibson Greetings, Long's Drug Stores, and Healthdyne. Their betas are usually 1.5 or more.

Speculative Stocks

The term **speculative stock** describes a company that has a potential for substantial earnings at some time in the future. These stocks are considered speculative because those earnings may never be realized. Companies offering speculative stocks often have

Did You Know? . . .

How Most Investors Pick Stocks

The premise underlying **fundamental analysis** is that each stock has an intrinsic (or true) value based on its expected stream of future earnings. Most stock investors take this approach to investing. It suggests that you can identify some stocks that will outperform other stocks. The fundamental approach presumes that current and future earnings trends, expected levels of interest rates, industry outlook, and management's expertise determine a stock's price movement. Furthermore, because knowledge about companies' futures is not perfect, some stocks are underpriced and some stocks are overpriced. The investor studies certain fundamental factors, such as the company's sales, assets, earnings, products or services, markets, and management, to determine a company's basic value. He or she then estimates the value of a company by comparing its history and expected future profitability with those of competing firms. The aim is to seek out sound stocks—perhaps even unfashionable ones—that are priced below the market's multiples of earnings.

An opposing and minority view on valuing common stocks is advocated by proponents of **technical analysis.** Here an investor (or more often a newsletter author) focuses on a stock's supply and demand and uses charts, graphs, mathematics, and software programs to identify and predict trends that reflect financial, economic, and perhaps psychological factors that could affect prices. Technical analysis has proved to be of little value, although some novice investors may find technical analysts' logic appealing.

a spotty earnings record or are so new that no earnings pattern has emerged. Investors in these types of firms incur some risk because of the companies' recent history of earnings and dividends. They rank the safety of their principal as a secondary factor when selecting a stock. Such investors hope that the company will make a new discovery, invent a new product, or generate valuable information that later may push up the price of the stock. That would create substantial capital gains.

Examples of speculative companies include computer graphics and video game companies, Internet applications firms, small oil businesses, genetic engineering firms, and some pharmaceutical manufacturers. For these firms, the P/E ratio fluctuates widely in tandem with the company's fortunes, and beta values exceeding 2.0 are common. For every speculative company that succeeds, many others do poorly or fail altogether.

Other Characterizations for Common Stocks

A variety of other terms are used to describe particular stocks within the three basic classifications in greater detail. These terms include blue-chip, value, cyclical, and countercyclical stocks, as well as terms based on capitalization size.

Blue-Chip Stocks. The term **blue-chip stock** suggests a company that has been around for a long time, has a well-regarded reputation, dominates its industry (often with annual revenues of $1 billion or more), and is known for being a solid, relatively safe investment. Typically, it has a history of both good earnings and consistent cash dividends, and it grows at approximately the same rate as the overall economy. Blue-chip stock shares are widely held by individual investors, mutual funds, and pension plans. The earnings of blue-chip companies (which are usually considered income stocks or well-known growth stocks) are expected to increase at a consistent but unspectacular rate because these highly stable firms are the leaders in their industries.

Examples of such stocks include Dow Chemical, ExxonMobil, Johnson & Johnson, General Electric, and Boeing. Investing in such companies is considered much less risky than investing in other types of firms.

Value Stocks.   A **value stock** is one that may sell for less than the true worth of its assets today. These are companies that are temporarily out of favor with investors. The market price of such a stock is low given its historical earnings record and the current value of its assets. These stocks are favored by investors willing to buy "a dollar for 50 cents." Such a stock is said to be underappreciated by most investors; thus, its current price makes it look like an investment bargain. Value stocks often operate within industries that benefit from a growing economy. Although their stock prices may have changed, some past examples of value stocks have included DuPont, Eastman, IBM, Lockheed, Time Warner, and Westinghouse Electric.

Cyclical Stocks.   The term **cyclical stock** describes a company whose profits are greatly influenced by changes in the economic business cycle. Typically, such companies operate in the major consumer-dependent industries, such as automobiles, housing, airlines, and publishing. The market prices of cyclical stocks mirror the general state of the economy and reflect the various phases of the business cycle. During times of prosperity and economic expansion, corporate earnings rise, profits grow, and stock prices climb; during a recession, these measures decline sharply. In addition to companies in the basic industries (such as retailing, steel, tires, and heavy machinery), many firms characterized as blue-chip, income, growth, value, or speculative stocks can be described as cyclical stocks. Most cyclical stocks have a beta of about 1.0.

Countercyclical Stocks.   Even when economic activity suffers a general decline, some companies maintain substantial earnings because their products are always in demand. These firms are considered **countercyclical (or defensive) stocks** because they perform well even in an environment characterized by weak economic activity and sliding interest rates. Most cigarette smokers, for example, do not quit during a recession, and people usually continue to go to movies, consume soft drinks, purchase kitty litter, buy electric utility service, have their clothes dry-cleaned and their cars washed, and buy groceries during downturns. For this reason, for example, utility companies generally continue to have good earnings during periods of economic decline. During rising markets, the prices of these recession-resistant stocks tend to rise less quickly than the prices of cyclical stocks, and they still may drop somewhat in a declining market. Countercyclical stocks, by definition, have a beta that is less than 1.0 or even negative. Investors interested in receiving regular cash dividends sometimes choose these stocks.

Capitalization Size.   A company's size in the stock market is based on its market capital, which is determined by multiplying the price of the stock by the number of shares outstanding. **Large-cap stocks** are those of firms that have issued $3 to $4 billion (or more) of stocks. Most are considered blue-chip companies, too. Examples include Texaco, Microsoft, AT&T, and IBM. Even though they are the dominant companies in the stock market, large-cap stocks are often outperformed by midsize and smaller firms.

   Mid-cap stocks are the stocks of those remaining companies that are quite substantial in terms of capitalization—perhaps $750 million to $3 billion in size—but not among the very largest firms. Examples include Wendy's and Starbucks. A **small-cap stock** is a company that has a capitalization of less than $750 million. **Micro-caps** are firms with less than $100 million in capitalization, and perhaps as little as $10 million. When the smaller firms achieve substantial increases in sales and earnings, their stock prices typically jump quite sharply.

How to ...

Use the Internet to Help You Invest in Stocks and Bonds

Stock selection takes time because the stocks of more than 7000 public companies are available. Most public corporations maintain websites that provide the company executives' perspectives on the firm's future prospects and the latest financial data. When visiting these sites, look for links to "investor relations," "financial information," or "annual reports."

Search engines, like those operated by Yahoo and Google (google.com), can direct you to an enormous amount of financial and industry information in chart, table, and graph formats. Historical financial data are provided as well as up-to-date details and reports on individual companies. The search engines also typically contain a **stock screener** feature that allows the investor to select and compare companies that meet the investor's own criteria for screening stocks. These measures might include price-earnings ratio, return on equity, and dividend payout. Similar information is available, often for free, through a variety of other financial information providers, such as Yahoo (screen.yahoo.com/stocks.html), Morningstar (screen.morningstar.com/stockselector.html?hsection-toolcenterstsel), and MSNMoney (moneycentral.msn.com/investor/finder/customstocksdl.asp). Also see Moody's (moodys.com), Standard & Poor's (standardpoor.com), and the Securities Industry Association (sia.com). Information from message boards and chat rooms should never be trusted, however. Information is also available from individual companies on their debt issues and bonds. Investors can check out bond details at independent websites like www.bondpickers.com, moodys.com, standardandpoors.com, and fitchratings.com.

Characteristics of Bonds

> **4** Identify the major characteristics of bonds, and differentiate between corporate, U.S. government, and municipal bonds.

A bond is a certificate that represents a debt obligation of the bond issuer (a corporation or government) to the bondholder-investor. Investors lend their money with the expectation that it will be paid back along with interest. Investors are primarily interested in receiving regular interest payments at a fixed rate of return for many years and, of course, they want their principal eventually returned. Having bonds in your portfolio offers several advantages, including that they reduce risk through diversification, they produce a steady income, and they can be a safe investment if held to maturity.

Bonds have certain characteristics that distinguish them from other investment alternatives. For instance, bonds are usually issued at a **par value** (also known as **face value**) of $1000; this amount is specified on the certificate. The bond's **coupon rate** (also known as the **coupon, coupon yield,** or **stated interest rate**) is the interest rate printed on the certificate when the bond is issued. It reflects the total annual fixed rate of interest that will be paid. For example, Bonny Llewellyn, a retired teacher from Salt Lake City, bought a 20-year, $1000 Running Paws Cat Food Company bond last week with a coupon rate of 7 percent that promises to pay her $70 in interest annually (normally, bonds pay interest in two semiannual installments—$35 in this instance). A disadvantage of bonds is that the investment does not provide the automatic benefit of compounding of interest. Investors must find other alternatives into which to invest the interest payments.

The coupon rate of a bond remains the same until the maturity date, when the face amount is due and the debt must be paid off (or **retired**). Most corporate bonds mature in 20 to 30 years. Occasionally, bonds are retired serially; that is, each bond is numbered consecutively and matures according to a pre-numbered schedule at stated intervals. These investments are known as **serial bonds.** Many bonds include a **sinking fund** through which money is set aside with a trustee each year for repayment of the principal portion of the debt. The details about each bond issue are contained in its **indenture.** This written, legal agreement between a group of bondholders (representing each bondholder) and the debtor describes the terms of the debt by setting forth the maturity date, interest rate, and other factors.

Bonds Are Either Secured or Unsecured

Bonds are issued as either secured or unsecured. A corporation issuing a **secured bond** pledges specific assets as collateral in the indenture or has the principal and interest guaranteed by another corporation or a government agency. In the event of default, the trustee could take legal action to seize and sell such assets. In the event of bankruptcy, the claims of secured creditors are paid first.

An **unsecured bond** (or **debenture**) does not name collateral as security for the debt and is backed only by the good faith and reputation of the issuing agency. Although secured bonds might appear safer than unsecured bonds at first glance, this assumption may not be true. All government bonds are unsecured, for example, and the "full faith, credit, and taxing power of the U.S. government" guarantees the timely payment of principal and interest. In addition, the strong financial reputations of many large corporations enable them to offer unsecured bonds that are safer than the secured bonds of many other companies.

Bonds Are Registered and Issued in Book-Entry Form

By law, all bonds issued in recent years have been **registered bonds.** This approach provides for the recording of the bondholder's name so that checks or electronic funds transfers for payment of interest and principal can be safely forwarded when due. The Internal Revenue Service is notified of the payments as well. A registered bond can be transferred only when it is endorsed by the registered owner.

All bonds today are issued in **book-entry form,** which means that certificates are not issued. Instead, an account is set up in the name of the issuing organization or the brokerage firm that sold the bond, and interest is paid into this account when due. In the past, all corporations issued **bearer bonds** (also called **coupon bonds** because owners redeemed the coupons for interest). Some of these older bonds are still traded today.

Bonds Are Callable

Bonds and preferred stocks are **callable.** If the issuer desires, it can buy back the security from the investor before the maturity date according to dates and terms detailed in the indenture. In such a case, the issuer repurchases the bond at par value or by paying a premium, usually one year's worth of interest.

An issuer might desire to exercise a call option when interest rates drop substantially. For example, assume that a company issues bonds paying a $90 annual dividend (9 percent coupon rate). When interest rates drop to 7 percent or perhaps 6 percent, the 9 percent bonds may represent a high cost for money for the corporation. Therefore, if the bonds have a callable feature, the issuer might seek to redeem the bonds early. Approximately 80 percent of long-term bonds and preferred stocks are classified as callable.

Corporate, U.S. Government, and Municipal Bonds

Three general types of bonds are available: (1) corporate bonds, (2) U.S. government securities, and (3) municipal government bonds. Of these, corporate bonds pay the highest interest rates. The default risk among corporations varies, however. U.S. government securities, such as Treasury bills, notes, and bonds are backed by the full faith of the federal government. Municipal government bonds, known as "munies" and "tax-exempt bonds," pay lower nominal yields but the investor's returns are not subject to federal income taxes.

Corporate Bonds.   **Corporate bonds** are interest-bearing certificates of long-term debt of a company. They represent an important source of funds for corporations. In today's business world, the dollar value of newly issued bonds is three times the dollar value of newly issued stocks. Because of tax regulations, corporations often finance major projects by issuing long-term bonds instead of selling stocks. One reason why is that payments of dividends to common and preferred stockholders are not tax-deductible for corporations, unlike interest paid to bondholders.

State laws require corporations to make bond interest payments on time. Therefore, companies in financial difficulty must pay bondholders before paying any short-term creditors.

It is important for investors to compare the risks and potential rewards of bond investments. To help you in appraising such risks, independent advisory services, such as Moody's Investors Service and Standard & Poor's, grade bonds for credit risk. These firms publish unbiased ratings of the financial conditions of corporations and municipalities that issue bonds. A **bond rating** represents the opinion of an outsider on the quality—or creditworthiness—of the issuing organization. It reflects the likelihood that the issuing organization will be able to repay its debt. Thus, investors have access to measures of the **default risk** (or **credit risk**), which is the uncertainty associated with not receiving the promised periodic interest payments and the principal amount when it becomes due at maturity. Bond rating directories are available in most large libraries; they are also available on-line. Ratings for each bond issue are continually reevaluated, and they often change after the original security has been sold to the public.

Table 14.1 (page 408) shows the rating scales used by Moody's and Standard & Poor's. The higher the rating, the greater the probable safety of the bond and the lower the default risk. In contrast, the lower the rating of the bond, the higher the stated interest rate or the effective interest rate when such bonds are reduced in price from their face amount, as more risk is involved. Higher ratings denote confidence that the issuer will not default and, if necessary, that the bond can readily be sold before its maturity date in a secondary market. Investment-grade corporate bonds may provide returns as much as 1.5 percentage points higher than the returns available on comparable U.S. government securities. Why? Because corporate bonds are not 100 percent guaranteed safe by the federal government.

U.S. Government Bills, Notes, and Bonds.   U.S. Treasury securities offer the highest degree of creditworthiness available in the world. U.S. government securities are classified into two general groups: (1) Treasury bills, notes, and bonds and (2) federal

Table 14.1 Summary of Municipal and Corporate Bond Ratings

Ratings		Interpretation of Ratings
Moody's	**Standard & Poor's**	
Aaa Aa A	AAA AA A	High investment quality suggests ability to repay principal and interest on time. Aaa and AAA bonds are generally referred to as "gilt-edged" because issuers have demonstrated profitability over the years and have paid their bondholders their interest without interruption; thus, they carry the smallest risk.
Baa Ba	BBB BB B	Medium-quality investments that adequately provide security to principal and interest. They are neither highly protected nor poorly secured; thus, they may have some speculative characteristics.
B Caa Ca	CCC CC C	Lack characteristics of a desirable investment and investors have decreasing assurance of repayment as the rating declines. Elements of danger may be present regarding repayment of principal and interest.
C	DDD DD D	In default with little prospect of regaining any investment standing.

Note: Bonds rated Baa and higher by Moody's and BBB and higher by S&P are investment-grade quality; Ba, BB, and lower-rated bonds are junk bonds.

agency issue notes, bonds, and certificates. Treasury bills, notes, and bonds are collectively knowns as **Treasury securities,** or "Treasuries." The federal government uses these debt instruments to finance the public national debt. Treasury securities have excellent liquidity and are simple to acquire and sell.

The interest rates on federal government securities are lower than those on corporate bonds because they are virtually risk-free. The possibility of default is near zero. Conservative investors are often attracted to the certainty offered by U.S. government securities. Investors can purchase Treasury securities through their bank or broker or directly from the Treasury. Investors buy Treasury issues to protect some of their assets and to diversify their portfolios. The Treasury no longer sells fixed-principal bonds, but they may be purchased on the secondary market. Although interest income is subject to federal income taxes, interest earned on Treasury securities is exempt from state and local income taxes.

Treasure Bills, Notes, and Bonds. **Treasury bills,** or **T-bills,** are short-term U.S. Government securities issued with maturities of a year or less. They are sold at a discount from their face value (par). The difference between the original purchase price and what the Treasury pays you at maturity, the gain or "par," is interest This interest is exempt from state and local income taxes but must be reported as interest income on your federal tax return in the year the Treasury bill matures. Stated as an interest rate, the return on such investments is called a **discount yield.** For example, if you buy a $10,000 26-week Treasury bill for $9,925 and hold it until maturity, your interest will be $75.

While the one-year T-bill is no longer available, the Treasury Department does publish a proxy figure for T-bills, the "constant money rate," so that investors can gain a feel for the yield on a totally safe short-term, one-year investment. An investor can hold a bill until maturity or sell before it is due, at the current market rate. When a bill matures, the proceeds can be reinvested into another bill or redeemed and the principal will be deposited into the investor's checking or savings account.

A **Treasury note** is a fixed-principal, fixed-interest rate government security issued for an intermediate term of 2, 3, 5, or 10 years. Notes exist only as electronic entries in accounts. The interest rate is slightly higher than the rates for T-bills, since the lending period is longer. Owners of Treasury notes receive interest payments every six months, which must be reported as interest income on their federal tax return in the year received. When the note matures, the investor is repaid the principal. Investors can hold a note until maturity or sell it. If you hold a fixed-principal note until maturity, you can reinvest its principal into another note; if you don't reinvest, the principal will be deposited into your checking or savings account. To buy a Treasury note or T-bill, you may place a bid in a competitive auction (and you may or may not be awarded the security). Alternatively, if you place a noncompetitive bid, you will receive the security and the interest rate will be determined at the auction.

I Bonds are savings bonds backed by the U.S. Government that pay an earnings rate that is a combination of two rates: a fixed interest rate that is set when the investor buys the bond and a semiannual variable interest rate tied to inflation that protects the investor's purchasing power. I Bonds are available in electronic, paperless form. I Bonds are sold at face value, such as $50 for a $50 bond, and interest stops accruing 30 years after issue. The maximum purchase allowed in one calendar year is $30,000. All earnings on savings bonds are exempt from both state and local income taxes, while federal taxes can be deferred until the bonds are either redeemed or reach final maturity. Thus, I Bonds are a logical choice to help diversify a taxable investment account because you can choose to pay no taxes until the bonds are redeemed. If you redeem I Bonds within the first five years, you'll forfeit the three most recent months' interest; after five years, you will not be penalized.

Treasury Inflation-Protected Securities (TIPS) are marketable Treasury securities whose value increases as inflation occurs. These inflation-indexed bonds are the only investment that guarantees that the investor's return will outpace inflation. TIPS bonds are sold in terms of 5, 10, and 20 years and interest is paid to TIPS owners every six months until they mature. The interest rate is set when the security is purchased, and the rate never changes. The principal is adjusted every six months according to the rise and fall of the consumer price index (CPI); if inflation occurs and the CPI rises, the principal increases.

The fixed interest rate on TIPS is applied to the inflation-adjusted principal; so, if inflation occurs throughout the life of a TIPS security, every interest payment will be greater than the one before it. The amount of each interest payment is determined by multiplying the inflation-adjusted principal by one-half the interest rate. The inflation-adjusted amount added to the principal on a TIPS bond every six months is taxable,

Did You Know? . . .

You Can Buy New Treasury Securities Only from the Government

New Treasury securities can be purchased only by using the Treasury Direct Plan. To open a **Treasury Direct account,** download the form at www.publicdebt.treas.gov. You must provide the government with both your Social Security number and your bank account number. Purchases are recorded electronically, with all interest, principal, and other payments being deposited with your local financial institution. In addition, a written statement of the transactions is forwarded to the investor. No commissions, charges, or fees are due when buying and redeeming Treasury securities directly with the government. In contrast, when a bank or stock brokerage firm handles such transactions, fees of $50 to $60 per transaction are charged. Fixed-principal old bonds are traded on stock and bond exchanges.

even though the investor does not receive the money until the bond matures. Thus, TIPS bonds pay "phantom taxable interest income," like zero-coupon bonds (described on page 411), so the investor must pay taxes on the interest earned anyway. As a result, the investor must use other funds to pay the taxes on that income.

When TIPS mature, the federal government pays the inflation-adjusted principal (or the original principal if it is greater). Investors can hold a TIPS bond until it matures or sell it before it matures.

If desired, owners of Treasuries may notify the Internal Revenue Service that they are choosing to switch from annual reporting of interest income to deferred reporting of interest. A tax-saving option is to buy savings bonds in a child's name. If the child's interest is reported annually, taxes can be eliminated on interest earnings during years when the child's income is low. Investors also can avoid paying income taxes on that interest by electing to defer the tax until it reaches maturity or by keeping the bond in a tax-deferred retirement account (discussed in Chapter 18). Note that the Treasury's Education Savings Bond Program allows the interest on TIPS bonds to be excluded—completely or partially—from federal income tax when the bond owner pays tuition and fees for higher education the year the bonds are redeemed.

Federal Agency Debt Issues.   More than 100 different bonds, notes, and certificates of debt are issued by various federal agencies that are government-sponsored but stockholder-owned. Examples of these agencies include Government National Mortgage Association (Ginnie Mae), Federal National Mortgage Association (Fannie Mae), Federal Home Loan Mortgage Corporation (Freddie Mac), and Student Loan Marketing Association (Sallie Mae). Ginnie Mae and Fannie Mae buy mortgage loans from lenders, thereby supplying them with more cash to make loans. These **agency issues** are backed by the assets and resources of the issuing agency. Although the federal government does not guarantee the debt issued by such agencies, investors nevertheless believe it would step in if they faced default. Each security represents interest in a pool of mortgages that are sold to institutions and investors in units of $25,000 (they can also be purchased in smaller units through a mutual fund). When homeowners make their monthly mortgage payments to Ginnie Mae, part of the principal and interest is passed to investors. Agency issues are not as widely publicized as Treasury securities, yet they often pay a yield that is three-quarters of a percentage point higher than the yield for comparable-term Treasury securities because of their somewhat higher degree of risk.

Municipal Government Bonds.   **Municipal government bonds** (also called **munies**) are long-term debts issued by local governments (cities, states, and various districts and political subdivisions) and their agencies. Their proceeds are used to finance public improvement projects, such as roads, bridges, and parks, or to pay ongoing expenses. Moody's Bond Record rates some 20,000 munies, and twice as many unrated securities exist. Bonds range in quality from AAA-rated state highway bonds to unrated securities issued by local governmental parking authorities.

The U.S. Constitution requires that municipal bond interest be exempt from federal income tax. Because the interest income is tax-free, municipal bonds are also known as **tax-free bonds** or **tax-exempt bonds**. In addition, interest income on munies is exempt from state and local income taxes if the investor lives in the state that issued the bond. Capital gains on the sale of munies are taxable, however. Such gains may be realized when bonds are bought at a discount and then sold at a higher price or redeemed for full value at maturity. In addition, bonds bought in the secondary market at a premium may appreciate to produce a gain.

Municipal bonds almost always offer a lower stated return than other bonds. If your

Advice from an Expert

Zero-Coupon Bonds Pay Phantom Interest

Zero-coupon bonds (also called **zeros** or **deep discount bonds**) are municipal, corporate, and Treasury bonds that pay no annual interest. They are sold to investors at sharp discounts from their face value and may be redeemed at full value upon maturity. For example, a 7 percent, $1000 zero-coupon bond to be redeemed in the year 2025 might sell today for $258. Zeros pay no current income to investors, so investors do not have to worry about reinvesting any interest payments. The interest, which is usually compounded semiannually, accumulates within the bond itself, and the return to the investor comes from redeeming the bond at its stated face value at the maturity date. In this manner, zeros operate much like Series EE savings bonds and T-bills. The maturity date for a zero could range from a few months to as long as 30 years.

Parents often invest in zero-coupon bonds to help pay for their children's college education, and they wisely establish ownership of the zeros in the child's name. The phantom income "paid" to the child is generally so small that little, if any, income taxes are due.

Treasury zeros, unlike most other zeros, are not callable. People planning for retirement buy zeros because they know exactly how much will be received at maturity. Because zeros pay "phantom interest," the investor owes income taxes every year on the interest that accumulates within the bond, even though the investor receives no interest money until maturity. Many investors avoid income taxes altogether by buying zeros with funds in a qualified tax-sheltered retirement plan account.

Elizabeth Dolan
University of New Hampshire

---

marginal tax rate is higher than 25 percent, it generally makes economic sense to invest in municipal bonds. To compare the after-tax return of investments, see page 118.

Evaluate Bond Prices and Returns

5 Evaluate bond prices and returns, and summarize the decisions bond investors must make.

A number of key factors affect bond prices and returns to the investor: interest rates, premiums and discounts, current yield, and yield to maturity. These factors help you evaluate in which bonds you should invest.

Interest-Rate Risk Results in Variable Value

A bond's price, or its value on any given day, is affected by a whole host of factors. These include its type, coupon rate, availability in the marketplace, demand for the bond, prices for similar bonds, the underlying credit quality of the issuer, and the number of years that must elapse before its maturity. The price also varies because of fluctuations in current market interest rates in the general economy. The state of the economy and the supply and demand for credit affect **market interest rates.** These are the current long- and short-term interest rates paid on various types of corporate and government debts that carry similar levels of risk. Long-term rates are largely set by investors in the bond market, primarily based on their expectations of future inflation. Short-term interest rates are manipulated by the Federal Reserve Board, which is popularly known as the **Fed.** When the economy slows, the Fed often lowers the interest rates on short-term Treasury issues in an attempt to stimulate economic activity by making borrowing cheaper. When inflation rises, the Fed often raises interest rates.

Interest-rate risk is the risk that interest rates will rise and bond prices will fall, thereby lowering the value of your bond investments. This decline in value ensures that the existing bond and the new bond will offer potential investors approximately the same yield. As a result, bonds generally have a **fixed yield** (the interest income payment remains the same) but a **variable value.** For example, assume that you buy a 20-year, $1000 bond with a stated annual interest rate of 8 percent, or an annual return of $80 ($1000 × 0.08). If interest rates in the general economy jump to 10 percent after one year, no one will want to buy your bond for $1000 because it pays only $80 per year. Should you want to sell it at that time, the price of the bond will have to be lowered, probably to $800 [Equation (14.1), the **bond-selling price formula,** shows the calculation involved].

$$\text{Bond selling price} = \frac{\text{annual interest income in dollars}}{\text{current market interest rate}} \qquad \textbf{(14.1)}$$

Conversely, if interest rates on newly issued bonds slip to 6 percent after one year, the price of your bond will increase sharply (probably to $1333). This occurs because investors will be willing to pay a **premium** (a sum of money paid in addition to a regular price) to own your bond paying 8 percent when other rates are only 6 percent. It is important to remember that bond yields and prices move in opposite directions—as one goes up, the other goes down.

Bond prices are most volatile in the following circumstances: (1) when bonds are sold at less than face value when first issued, (2) when the stated rate is low, and (3) when the bond maturity time is long. The investor who holds a bond to maturity might ignore such information, but the person considering selling before maturity might be shocked to see price swings of 20 percent or more, as illustrated on page 413. A person with a moderate or aggressive investment philosophy might regard such rapid price changes as opportunities.

Premiums and Discounts

When a bond is first issued, it is sold in one of three ways: (1) at its face value (the value of the bond as stated on the certificate), which is also the amount the investor will receive when the bond matures, (2) at a discount below its face value, or (3) at a premium above its face value. Later, because the stated interest rate on the bond remains fixed, the market price changes to provide a competitive effective rate of return.

As an example, assume that Running Paws Cat Food Company decided to issue 20-year bonds at 8.8 percent. While the bonds were being printed and prepared for sale, the market interest rate on comparable bonds rose to 9 percent. In this instance, Running Paws will sell the bonds at a slight discount to provide a competitive return. Discounts and premiums on bonds reflect changing interest rates in the economy and the number of years to maturity.

Current Yield

The **current yield** equals the bond's fixed annual interest payment divided by its bond price. It is a measure of the current annual income (the total of both semiannual interest payments in dollars) expressed as a percentage when divided by the bond's current market price. When you buy a bond at par, its current yield equals its coupon yield. For example, a bond with a 5.5 percent coupon yield purchased at par for $1000 has a current yield of 5.5 percent. As bond prices fluctuate because of interest rate changes and other factors, the current yield also changes. For example, if Bonnie Llewellyn paid $940 for a $1000 bond paying $55 per year, the bond's current yield is 5.85 percent, as shown by the *current yield formula* on page 414.

Did You Know? . . .

How Far Bond Prices Will Move When Interest Rates Change

On any given day, the major determinant of bond prices is the prevailing level of interest rates in the economy. Figure 14.1 illustrates the price changes for bonds when interest rates rise or fall. In general, rising interest rates reduce bond prices, and falling rates increase bond prices. In addition, the longer the time until maturity of a bond, the more sensitive the price to changes in interest rates. Thus, prices for long-term bonds fluctuate much more dramatically than those for short-term securities.

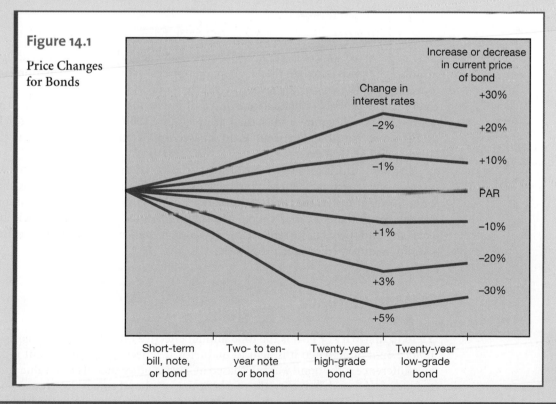

Figure 14.1

Price Changes for Bonds

How to . . .

Estimate the Selling Price of a Bond After Interest Rates Have Changed

Bond prices are influenced partially by supply and demand, but mostly by the cost of money. If you paid $1000 for a 20-year, 7 percent bond and then were forced to sell it after interest rates on comparable bonds had increased to 9 percent, you would lose more than $200. You can estimate the selling price of an existing bond (assuming it is more than a few years from maturity) after interest rates change by using the bond-selling price formula, given in Equation (14.1) on page 412.

Using Equation (14.1), the selling price equals $777.78 ($70 ÷ 0.09) for the preceding example. If you bought the bond for $1000, you will lose $222.22 if you sell it for $777.78. If interest rates drop to 5.5 percent instead of increasing, however, you could sell your 7 percent bond at a profit of $272.72 ($70 ÷ 0.055 = $1272.72 − $1000). Of course, if you keep the bond until maturity, the issuer is obligated to retire it for $1000.

Exact calculations of selling prices can be performed by a brokerage firm. The formula in Equation (14.1) is duplicated on the *Garman/Forgue* website.

$$\text{Current yield} = \frac{\text{current annual income}}{\text{current market price}} \qquad (14.2)$$

$$= \frac{\$\ 55}{\$940}$$

$$= 5.85\%$$

Financial sections of larger newspapers usually publish the current yields for a great number of bonds based on that day's market prices. While this information is useful, it does not tell an investor the current yield that a previously purchased bond earns because it was probably obtained at a price different than the current market price (at a premium or discount) rather than at precisely $1000 (as was the case for Bonnie). Realize, too, that a bond's current yield is based on the purchase price, not on the prices at which it later trades.

The total return on a bond investment consists of the same components as the return on any investment: current income and capital gains. In Bonnie's case, she will receive $1000 at the maturity date (20 years from now) even though she paid only $940 for the bond; therefore, her anticipated total return (or effective yield) will be higher than the 5.85 percent current yield. How much higher is accurately revealed by the yield to maturity (discussed below).

Yield to Maturity

Yield to maturity (YTM) is the total annual effective rate of return earned by a bondholder on a bond when it is held to maturity. It reflects both the current income and any difference if the bond was purchased at a price other than its face value spread over the life of the bond. In reality, the market price of a bond equals the present value of its future interest payments and the present value of its face value when the bond matures. Three generalizations can be made about the yield to maturity:

1. If a bond is purchased for exactly its face value, the YTM is the same as the coupon rate printed on the certificate.

2. If a bond is purchased at a premium, the YTM will be lower than the coupon rate.

3. If a bond is purchased at a discount, the YTM will be higher than the coupon rate.

For example, because Bonnie Llewellyn bought her 20-year bond with a coupon rate of 5.5 percent at a discount for $940, her yield to maturity must be greater than the coupon rate because she will receive $60 more than she paid for the bond when she receives the $1000 at maturity. Exactly how much greater can be determined by calculating an approximate yield to maturity when contemplating a bond purchase, because bonds that seem comparable may have different YTMs. The **yield to maturity (YTM) formula,** which is duplicated on the *Garman/Forgue* website, factors in the approximate appreciation when a bond is bought at a discount or at a premium:

$$\text{YTM} = \frac{I + [(FV - CV)/N]}{(FV + CV)/2} \tag{14.3}$$

where

$I = Interest$ paid annually in dollars
$FV = Face\ Value$
$CV = Current\ Value$ (price)
$N = Number$ of years until maturity

For example, if Bonnie Llewellyn paid $940 for a 20-year bond with a 5.5 percent coupon rate, the YTM is calculated as follows:

$$\text{YTM} = \frac{\$55 + [(\$1000 - \$940)/20]}{(\$1000 + \$940)/2}$$

$$= \frac{\$\ 58}{\$970}$$

$$= 5.98\%$$

If you plan to buy and hold a bond until its maturity, you should compare YTMs instead of current yields when considering a purchase because YTMs fairly represent all factors. The current yield on a bond is not an effective measure of the total annual return to the investor; in fact, the fewer years until maturity, the worse an indicator it becomes. As calculated above, Bonnie Llewellyn's 20-year bond with a coupon rate of 5.5 percent and a current yield of 5.85 percent has a YTM of 5.98 percent. If the same bond had been purchased with only 10 years until maturity, the YTM would be 6.29 percent; with 5 years until maturity, the YTM would be 6.90 percent; and with 2 years until maturity, the YTM would be 8.76 percent. Exact YTMs are listed in detailed bond tables available at large libraries, at brokers' offices, and on-line.

Decisions Bond Investors Must Make

Bond investors must make four decisions:

1. **Decide on risk level.** The level of financial risk is related to the likely rate of return; the safest bonds offer the lowest yields. Securities of the U.S. government offer virtually no risk. For slightly more risk, consider the highest-rated corporate and municipal bonds. Lower-rated bonds, such as Baa or B bonds, offer higher yields but carry substantial risk.

Tax Considerations and Consequences

Bonds

People generally invest in bonds with the intention of receiving current income in the form of interest (usually paid semiannually). Interest income is taxed at one's regular tax rate. While earnings from Treasury bills, notes, and bonds are subject to federal income taxes, they are exempt from state and local income taxes. Interest from municipal bonds is exempt from federal income taxes and from state and local taxes when the investor lives in the state that issued the bonds. Zero-coupon bonds and TIPS bonds pay "phantom" interest, and even though no annual interest is actually received with such bonds, you must nevertheless pay income taxes on the interest earned every year (unless the bonds are held in a qualified tax-sheltered retirement plan account). Capital gains on the sale of bonds are taxable.

2. **Decide on maturity.** Consider the time schedule of your financial needs. Bonds with a short maturity generally have a lower current yield but greater price stability.

3. **Determine the after-tax return.** Assuming equivalent risk, choose the bond (taxable or tax-exempt) that provides the better after-tax return. To compare the after-tax return of investments, see page 118. Tax-exempt securities sometimes offer a higher after-tax return than taxable alternatives.

4. **Select the highest yield to maturity.** Given similar bond securities with comparable risk, maturity, and tax equivalency, investors should choose the one that offers the highest yield to maturity, as calculated by Equation (14.3).

Furthermore, bond investors should recognize that in some situations it might be wise to sell a bond before it matures. When interest rates have dropped, you can sell an existing bond at a profit because rate decreases will push up the value of your bond. Also, if the bond rating has seriously slipped, it could mean greater risk and possible default. Finally, you can profit when you expect definite shifts in interest rates depending on the types of bonds you hold and the direction of the shift.

ACE

Self-tests

Summary

1. To raise capital and finance its goals, a corporation may issue three types of securities (negotiable instruments of ownership or debt): common stock, preferred stock, and bonds. Stocks are shares of ownership in the assets and earnings of a business corporation. They represent potential income for investors because stockholders own a stake in the future direction and profits of the company. Bonds are interest-bearing, negotiable certificates of long-term debt issued by a corporation, a municipality (such as a city or state), or the federal government. Bond investors expect to receive periodic income every six months in the form of interest; in addition, they anticipate receiving the amount originally invested when the bond matures.

2. When you invest in the stock market, you are buying companies—not lottery tickets. Therefore, you should invest only in the stocks of companies that you believe will make money over the next 5 to 10 years. To make good choices, you need to understand some important numbers that are key numeric measures of stock performance. These include book value per share, earnings per share, price/earning ratio, and beta.

3. Stocks may be categorized as income, growth, or speculative stocks. Other terms used to characterize stocks in-

clude blue-chip, value, cyclical, and countercyclical stocks. Stocks are described according to their capitalization size as well, such as large-cap and mid-cap stocks.

4. A bond is a certificate that represents a debt obligation of the bond issuer (a corporation or government) to the bondholder-investor. You lend your money to the bond issuer, and it is paid back with interest. Bonds have certain characteristics that distinguish them from other investments, including being secured or unsecured, registered, in book-entry form, and callable. The three general types of bonds are corporate, U.S. government securities, and municipal government bonds.

5. A number of key factors affect bond prices and returns to investors: interest rates, premiums and discounts, current yield, and yield to maturity. These factors help investors decide in which bonds they will choose to invest. The bond investor must make four decisions: decide on risk, decide on maturity, determine the after-tax return, and select the highest yield to maturity.

3. What does the price/earnings ratio mean, and how would you interpret a P/E ratio of 8:1?

4. Explain why a particular growth stock could also be called a cyclical stock.

5. Summarize how most investors pick stocks.

6. Distinguish among the following types of stocks: blue-chip, value, and countercyclical.

7. Describe a situation in which a bond issuer would exercise a bond's callable feature.

8. Compare and contrast the three types of bonds: corporate, U.S. government, and municipal government.

9. Describe how the principal on a Treasury inflation-protected security can increase over the life of the bond, and explain why it is important to the investor.

10. Explain how zero-coupon bonds work, and describe which types of investors might be attracted to them.

Key Terms

beta (beta coefficient), 401
blue-chip stock, 403
bond rating, 407
book value per share, 399
callable, 406
cash dividends, 397
common stock, 393
countercyclical (defensive) stock, 404
coupon rate (coupon, coupon yield, stated interest rate), 405
earnings per share (EPS), 400
employee stock option (ESO), 394
fundamental analysis, 403
growth stock, 402
large-cap stock, 404
price/earnings ratio (P/E ratio), 400
Treasury bills (T-bills), 408
Treasury inflation-protected securities (TIPS), 409
value stock, 404
yield to maturity (YTM), 414
zero-coupon bonds (zeros, deep discount bonds), 411

Group Discussion Issues

1. Make a list of 10 products and services that you buy on a weekly or monthly basis and the companies that sell them. Offer your initial views on whether each company would be a good place to invest money.

2. The text introduced a variety of ways to measure stock performance. Name two of those measures that you probably would use in your own decision making. Offer three reasons for selecting those measures.

3. You have just heard that Microsoft's stock price dropped $20. If you had the money, would you buy 100 shares? Give three reasons why or why not.

4. Review the three basic classifications of common stock and the other descriptive terms. Based on your personal comfort level for risk, which type of stock would be of most interest to you? Give three reasons why.

5. Assume you graduated from college a few years ago, have a good job paying $55,000 annually, and want to invest $200 per month in common stocks. Which combination of stocks would you invest in and why?

Chapter Review Questions

1. Explain how common stocks represent ownership to the investor.

2. What are junk bonds, and why do people invest in them?

Decision-Making Cases

▶Case 1
Two Brothers' Attitudes Toward Investments

Kyle Broffoski, an English instructor in Syracuse, New York, has purchased several corporate and government bonds over the years, and his total bond investment now exceeds $40,000. He prefers a variable-value investment with some inflation protection. His brother Ike, a highly paid physician, has more than $150,000 invested in various blue-chip income stocks in a variety of industries.

(a) Justify Kyle's attitude toward bond investments.

(b) Justify Ike's attitude toward stock investments.

(c) Explain why both brothers might be very happy by investing in TIPS bonds.

▶Case 2
A College Student Ponders Investing in the Stock Market

Richard Ford of Athens, Georgia, has $5000 that he wants to invest in the stock market. Richard is in college on a scholarship and does not plan on using the $5000 or any dividend income for another five years, when he plans to buy a new automobile. He is currently considering a stock selling for $25 per share with an EPS of $1.25. Last year, the company earned $900,000, of which $250,000 was paid out in dividends.

(a) What classification of common stock would you recommend to Richard? Why?

(b) Calculate the price/earnings ratio and the dividend payout ratio for this stock. Given this information and your recommendation, would this stock be an appropriate purchase for Richard? Why or why not? 25 / 1.25 = 20 rapidly growing co.

(c) Identify the components of the total return Richard might expect, and estimate how much he might expect annually from each component.

▶Case 3
An Aggressive Investor Seeks Rewards in the Bond Market

Karen Varcoe, who is single, works as a drug manufacturer's representative based in Riverside, California. She is an aggressive investor who believes that interest rates will drop over the next year or two because of an economic slowdown. Karen, who is in the 25 percent marginal tax rate, wants to profit in the bond market by buying and selling during the next several months. She has asked your advice on how to invest her $15,000.

(a) If Karen buys corporate or municipal bonds, what rating should her selections have? Why?

(b) Karen has a choice between two $1000 bonds: a corporate bond with a coupon rate of 8.4 percent, and a municipal bond with a coupon rate of 5.8 percent. Which bond provides the better after-tax return? [Hint: See Equation (4.1) on page 118.]

(c) If Karen buys fifteen 30-year, $1000 corporate bonds with an 8.4 percent coupon rate for $960 each, what is her current yield? [Hint: Use Equation (14.2).]

(d) If market interest rates for comparable corporate bonds drop 2 percent over the next 12 months (from 8.4 percent to 6.4 percent), what will be the approximate market price of Karen's corporate bonds in (c)? [Hint: Use Equation (14.1).]

(e) Assuming market interest rates drop 2 percent in 12 months, how much is Karen's capital gain on the $15,000 investment if she sells? How much was her current return for the two semiannual interest payments? How much was her total return, both in dollars and as an annual yield? (Ignore transaction costs.)

(f) If Karen is wrong in her projections and interest rates go up 1 percent over the year, what would be the probable market price of her corporate bonds? [Hint: Use Equation (14.1).] Explain why you would advise her to sell or not to sell.

Financial Math Questions

1. A stock sells at $15 per share.

   (a) What is the EPS for the company if it has a P/E ratio of 20?

   (b) If the company's dividend yield is 5 percent, what is its dividend per share?

   (c) What is the book value of the company if the price-to-book ratio is 1.5 and it has 100,000 shares of stock outstanding?

2. What is the market price of a $1000, 20-year, 8.8 percent bond if comparable market interest rates drop to 7.0 percent?

3. What is the market price of a $1000, 20-year, 8.3 percent bond if comparable market interest rates drop to 7.0 percent?

4. What is the market price of a $1000, 20-year, 8.8 percent bond if comparable market interest rates rise to 9.6 percent?

5. What is the market price of a $1000, 20-year, 8.3 percent bond if comparable market interest rates rise to 9.6 percent?

6. For a municipal bond paying 5.4 percent for a taxpayer in the 25 percent tax bracket, what is the equivalent taxable yield? (Hint: See the footnote on page 118.)

7. For a municipal bond paying 5.7 percent for a taxpayer in the 33 percent tax bracket, what is the equivalent taxable yield? (Hint: See the footnote on page 118.)

8. For a corporate bond paying 8.7 percent for a taxpayer in the 25 percent tax bracket, what is the equivalent after-tax yield? [Hint: See Equation (4.1).]

9. A corporate bond maturing in 20 years with a coupon rate of 8.9 percent was purchased for $980.

(a) What is its current yield?

(b) What will its selling price be if comparable market interest rates drop 2 percent in two years?

(c) Calculate the bond's YTM using Equation (14.3) or the *Garman/Forgue* website.

10. A corporate bond maturing in 18 years with a coupon rate of 8.2 percent was purchased for $1100.

(a) What is its current yield?

(b) Calculate the bond's YTM using Equation (14.3) or the *Garman/Forgue* website.

(c) What will the bond's selling price be if comparable market interest rates rise 1.5 percent in two years?

Money Matters Continuing Cases

Victor and Maria Hernandez Wonder About Investing

Victor and Maria are considering making investments in stocks and bonds. They plan to invest between $8000 and $9000 every year for the next 13 years.

1. Why should Victor and Maria consider buying common stock as an investment?

2. If Victor and Maria bought a stock with a market price of $50 and a beta value of 1.8, what would be the likely price of an $8000 investment after one year if the general market for stocks rose 20 percent?

3. What would the same investment be worth if the general market for stocks dropped 20 percent?

4. Assume that Victor and Maria bought $8000 in 13-year bonds with a coupon rate of 8 percent and that interest rates dropped to 7 percent after one year. What is the approximate current price of their bonds if they were to sell? [Hint: Use Equation (14.1) or visit the *Garman/Forgue* website.]

5. If inflation averages 3 percent for the next 13 years and their $8000 bond is redeemed by the issuer, how much buying power will the Hernandez family have with their $8000?

The Johnsons Want Greater Yields on Investments

Harry and Belinda Johnson have saved $6000 toward a down payment on a luxury automobile they hope to purchase in the next three to five years. Because they are not receiving a very high rate of return on their money market account, they are seeking greater yields with bond investments. Examine the table below, which identifies eight investment alternatives, and then respond to the questions that follow. The coupon rates vary because the issue dates range widely, and market prices are above par because older bonds paid higher interest than today's issues.

1. What is the current yield of each investment alternative? Use Equation (14.2) or visit the *Garman/Forgue* website. (Write your responses in the proper column in the table.)

2. What is the yield to maturity for each investment alternative? (Write your responses in the proper column in the table.) You may calculate the YTMs by using Equation (14.3) or by visiting the *Garman/Forgue* website.

Name of Issue	Bond Denomination	Coupon Rate Percent	Years until Maturity	Moody's Rating	Market Price	Current Yield	YTM
Corporate ABC	$1000	7.0	4	Aa	$1400		
Corporate DEF	1000	7.5	20	Aa	1550		
Corporate GHI	1000	5.9	12	Baa	1250		
Corporate JKL	1000	7.8	5	Aaa	1500		
Corporate MNO	1000	6.1	15	B	1260		
Corporate PQR	1000	5.8	11	B	1200		
Treasury note	1000	7.9	3	—	1600		
Municipal bond	1000	4.1	20	Aa	1200		

3. Knowing that the Johnsons follow a moderate investment philosophy, which one of the six corporate bonds would you recommend? Why?

4. Given that the Johnsons are in the 25 percent federal marginal tax rate, what is the equivalent taxable yield for the municipal bond choice? Should they invest in your recommendation in Question 3 or in the municipal bond? Why? You may calculate the equivalent taxable yield using the footnote on page 118.

5. Which three of the eight alternatives would you recommend as a group so that the Johnsons would have some diversification protection for their $6000? Why do you suggest that combination?

6. Assume that the Johnsons bought all three of your recommendations in Question 5. If market interest rates drop by 2 percent in two years because of a severe economic slowdown (for example, from 5.1 percent to 3.1 percent), what are your recommendations for buying or selling each alternative? Why? Support your answer by calculating the selling price for each bond using Equation (14.1) or by visiting the *Garman/Forgue* website.

What Would You Recommend Now?

Now that you have read the chapter on stocks and bonds, what would you recommend to Carlena Diaz in the case at the beginning of the chapter regarding:

1. Investing for retirement in 18 years?

2. Owning blue-chip common stocks and preferred stocks rather than other common stocks given Carlena's investment horizon?

3. The wisdom of owning municipal bonds rather than corporate bonds?

4. The likely selling price of her corporate bonds, if sold today?

5. Investments that might be appropriate to fund her children's education?

Exploring the World Wide Web

To complete these exercises, go to the *Garman/Forgue* website at college.hmco.com/business/students. Under General Business, select the title of this text. Click on the Internet Exercises link for this chapter, and answer the questions that appear on the Web page.

1. Visit Yahoo! Money Stock Screener Web page. Search among the S&P 500 stocks for companies with a $50 minimum share price. How many companies meet this criterion? Select again using a P/E ratio from 0 to 20. How many companies meet this new criterion? Why is this list longer? Do you recognize any of the companies on either list?

2. Visit the stock research page at kiplinger.com. Type in the symbols for the following companies: Coca-Cola (KO), General Motors (GM), Microsoft (MSFT), and Disney (DIS), and click on "full report." Evaluate these four firms on the basis of earnings per share, dividend yield, and price/earnings ratio. What do these data suggest to you about the relative attractiveness of these companies for investors?

3. Visit the website for Money.com. Under "Get a Quote," type in the symbol for each of the companies from Exercise 2. Use the "time frame" dropdown menu to determine which of the four has seen the greatest stock price appreciation over the past year and over the past four years.

4. Visit the website for the Bureau of Public Debt of the U.S. Treasury Department, where you will find the results of recent auctions for Treasury notes and bonds. What do the results of the auctions over the past year tell you about market expectations for movement of interest rates in the future? (Hint: Compare auction rates for bonds and notes with similar maturity periods.)

5. Visit the website for *Kiplinger's Personal Finance Magazine.* Browse through the financial news articles for investors. Identify one or two investment opportunities with potential for positive growth and one or two areas that investors might want to avoid.

6. Visit the Money 101 website for CNN/Money. Compare the information provided in the "Top Things to Know" with the information in this chapter. Develop your own list of a baker's dozen (13) key points every beginning investor in stocks and bonds should know.

Visit the Garman/Forgue website . . .

@**college.hmco.com/business/students**

Under General Business, select *Personal Finance 8e.* There, among other valuable resources, you will find a complete glossary, ACE questions, links to help you complete the chapter exercises, and links to other personal finance sites.

Chapter 15

Investing Through Mutual Funds

LEARNING OBJECTIVES

After reading this chapter, you should be able to:

1 **Summarize** the two types of investment returns that investors expect from mutual funds.

2 **Classify** mutual funds by investment objectives.

3 **Describe** the unique features of mutual funds that make them an attractive investment.

4 **Distinguish** between load and no-load mutual funds and explain how to avoid some of their numerous charges and fees.

5 **Explain** how to evaluate mutual funds in which to invest.

Doug and Cheryl Circarelli, a couple in their early thirties, have a two-year-old child, and they enjoy living in a moderately priced downtown apartment. Doug, a librarian section manager, earns $44,000 annually. Cheryl earns $59,000 as a merchandise buyer for a specialty store. They are big savers: Together they have been putting $1000 to $2000 per month into certificates of deposit, and the couple now has a portfolio balance worth $120,000 paying about 4 percent annually. The Circarellis are conservative investors and want to retire in about 20 years.

What would you recommend to Doug and Cheryl on the subject of investing through mutual funds regarding:

1. Buying mutual funds through their employers' 401(k) retirement accounts?

2. The disadvantage of paying income taxes on interest earned on certificates of deposit?

3. Redeeming their certificates of deposit and investing in mutual funds rather than saving through certificates of deposit?

4. Buying no-load rather than load mutual funds?

5. Buying balanced mutual funds instead of aggressive-growth funds?

An **investment company** is a corporation, trust, or partnership in which investors with similar financial goals pool their funds so as to utilize professional management and to diversify their investments in securities and other investments. A **mutual fund** is an investment company that combines the funds of investors who have purchased shares of ownership in the investment company and then invests that money in a diversified portfolio of stocks and bonds issued by other corporations or governments. This approach might seem appealing to you, because investing in a mutual fund reduces the risk you face when selecting individual stock and bond investments. Indeed, millions of other investors share this desire to reduce risk. Mutual funds also make it easy and convenient for investors to open an account and continue investing. As a consequence, mutual funds are currently the most common form of investment in the United States. Figure 15.1 graphically illustrates the concept underlying mutual funds.

This chapter examines mutual funds as an investment. It shows you in a step-by-step process how to select mutual funds that meet your investment objectives, including planning for a child's education and for your own retirement. The chapter begins by discussing the returns investors expect from mutual funds: current income (from dividends) and capital gains (from price appreciation). We then distinguish among the four investment objectives of mutual funds. Different funds achieve their objectives in different ways, albeit primarily through selecting certain investments for their portfolios. Millions of people are attracted to investing in mutual funds (rather than stocks, bonds, or real estate) because these funds offer so many unique investor-friendly features. Finally, no discussion of mutual funds is complete without a review of mutual fund fees, some of which can be avoided. The chapter closes by providing details on how to evaluate mutual funds for your investments.

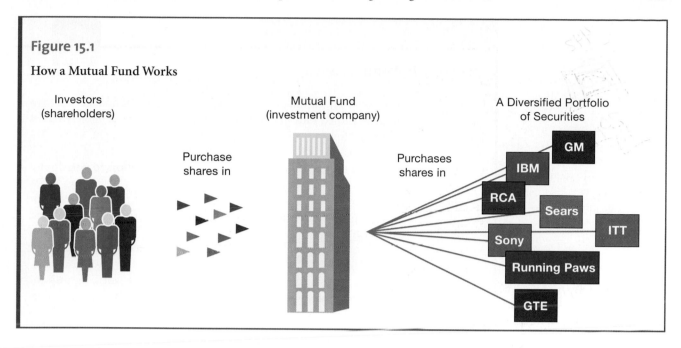

Figure 15.1

How a Mutual Fund Works

What Investors Expect from Mutual Funds

1 Summarize the two types of investment returns that investors expect from mutual funds.

Most investors prefer to avoid purchasing individual stocks and bonds because of the high financial risk associated with owning too few investments. The average investor usually cannot accumulate a portfolio diversified enough to minimize the risk linked to the failure of a single holding. To avoid that risk, individuals invest in the stock and bond markets through mutual funds, which typically buy hundreds of stocks and bonds.

Approximately half of all working adults in the United States currently invest through mutual funds—the highest proportion in history. The growth in mutual fund investing has been spurred by several factors: Newer and more attractive types of funds have been created; many funds carry few or no sales charges; and some have performed much better than the average common stock. The major driving force behind the growth of these investments, however, is the fact that mutual funds are the best option available to people saving for retirement through 401(k) plans and IRAs (topics examined in Chapter 18). Selecting a mutual fund is much easier than selecting specific stocks or bonds (topics discussed in Chapter 14). Mutual funds clearly state their investment objectives, allowing investors to readily choose those funds that match their own objectives.

Experts agree that mutual funds represent appropriate investment choices for both beginning and sophisticated investors. Investors in mutual funds incur minimal financial risk because the fund diversifies the investments in a variety of stocks and/or bonds of many companies and governments. Mutual funds offer investors a convenient means of investing relatively small amounts of money while using the services of a team of professional managers. The investor in mutual funds, using common sense and a little knowledge of the world of investments, can obtain very good returns.

One type of mutual fund is a **closed-end investment company**, which issues a limited and fixed number of shares and does not buy them back. After the original issue is

Golden Rules of

Investing in Mutual Funds

Financial success comes from learning the Golden Rules of personal finance and then putting what you have learned into practice. Make the following your money habits when investing in mutual funds:

1. Invest only in no-load mutual funds that have a low expense ratio and also do not assess a 12b-1 fee.
2. When choosing mutual funds, always match your investment philosophy and financial goals to a mutual fund's objectives by gathering information about fund volatility and performance.
3. When investing for long-term goals, definitely sign up for automatic reinvestment of your mutual fund dividends.
4. If you have a defined contribution retirement plan available at work, sign up for payroll withholding to automatically forward a portion of each paycheck to a mutual fund.
5. Invest most of your "serious" money—such as that to pay for your child's education and your retirement—in one or more low-fee diversified index funds.
6. Don't jump in and out of the mutual fund market; instead, keep it simple by investing in a few funds and leave your money alone. That's all.

sold, the price of a share depends on the performance of the investment company in particular and on market conditions in general. Closed-end shares are traded much like the common stock or bonds of a corporation.

A second type of mutual fund, accounting for more than 90 percent of all funds, is an **open-end mutual fund.** These companies are so named because they are always ready to sell new shares of ownership and to buy back previously sold shares at the fund's current share price. Today, open-end mutual funds (more than 8100) outnumber companies listed on the New York Stock Exchange (approximately 2800 companies). Open-end shares can be purchased through the mutual fund itself or through a financial planner, a bank, or a brokerage firm. When desired, shares can always be sold back to the fund. No trading occurs among individual investors. This chapter focuses on open-end mutual funds.

All open-end mutual fund companies operate in a similar manner. That is, they pool funds obtained by selling shares to investors and then make investments to achieve the financial goal of income or growth (or sometimes both). Most mutual funds invest in stocks and bonds. *Stocks* are shares of ownership in the assets and earnings of a business corporation, such as General Motors, IBM, Sears, or Running Paws Cat Food Company (our example from Chapter 14). *Bonds* are interest-paying negotiable certificates of long-term debt (often with maturities of 10 to 30 years) issued by a corporation, municipality (such as a city or state), or the federal government. You can best understand mutual funds if you keep in mind that the mutual fund company owns the investments it makes. The mutual fund investors own the mutual fund company.

A mutual fund's investment decisions are made by its professional managers. The managers choose a mutual fund **portfolio** consisting of a collection of securities (stocks and bonds) and other investment alternatives. Investors pay a fee for this management service. Mutual funds must distribute virtually all of their income annually to avoid paying income tax on the earnings.

Investors Expect Mutual Fund Dividend Income

The first type of return expected by the investor in mutual funds comprises **mutual fund dividends**—that is, income paid to investors out of profits earned by the mutual fund from the investments it has made. Mutual funds dividends represent current income to mutual fund shareholders because the dividends are received while the investor owns the mutual funds shares. An investor in a profitable mutual fund receives a mutual fund dividend check that represents both ordinary income dividend distributions and capital gains distributions.

Ordinary Income Dividend Distributions.   **Ordinary income dividend distributions** occur when the fund pays out dividend income and interest it has received from securities it owns. These distributions to the fund shareholders may be made on a monthly, quarterly, or annual basis. Unless the fund is held within a qualified tax-sheltered retirement account, income taxes must be paid on these distributions. Income taxes can also be avoided when the earnings represent interest from tax-exempt municipal bonds.

Capital Gains Distributions.   **Capital gains distributions** represent the net gains (capital gains minus capital losses) that a fund realizes when it sells securities that were held in the fund's portfolio. Mutual fund investors must pay personal income taxes on capital gains distributions even if those funds are automatically reinvested. However, taxes on these earnings can be deferred if the mutual fund shares are owned through an IRS-qualified tax-sheltered retirement account (as discussed in Chapters 1, 4, and 18).

Investors Expect Capital Gains Through Price Appreciation

Mutual fund investors also expect to profit when they sell their shares. If a mutual fund investor sells shares at a net asset value higher than that paid when they purchased the shares (after transaction costs), he or she will have a capital gain. The **net asset value (NAV)** is the per-share value of the mutual fund. It is calculated by summing the values of all the securities in the fund's portfolio, subtracting liabilities, and then dividing by the total number of shares outstanding. It is the price one must pay (excluding any transaction cost) to buy a share of a mutual fund.

The NAV rises or falls to reflect changes in the market value of the investments held by the mutual fund company. If the managers hold securities that have risen in price, the NAV will go up. This value is typically calculated at the end of each trading day, though a few funds calculate the NAV at more frequent intervals and then process buy or sell orders at those values. The business sections of most newspapers publish the NAVs for hundreds of mutual funds every day.

For example, if your mutual fund owns IBM and General Electric common stocks and the market values of those two companies increase, the rising stock prices will push up the net worth of the mutual fund. The increased value of the underlying securities is directly reflected in the NAV of fund shares. Technically, such increases in the NAV represent **unrealized capital gains** because at this point they are merely "paper profits" on the accounts of the mutual fund. (When such gains are "realized" by the mutual fund company, they are paid to fund investors as capital gains distributions.) Logically, the mutual fund company desires to remain invested in a number of quality stocks and bonds whose values will continue to grow. These unrealized capital gains, when not distributed (although they are still taxable income to investors), will continue to increase the mutual fund's NAV. The individual mutual funds investor expects to profit from the gains in the NAV by selling his or her shares after the NAV has risen. When realized, such gains are considered taxable income to individual investors (unless the money is kept in an IRS-qualified tax-sheltered retirement account, as discussed in Chapter 18).

2 Classify mutual funds by investment objectives.

Mutual Funds Have Different Investment Objectives

The thousands of different mutual funds available mean that some fund will fit almost every investor's needs. Each mutual fund tries to achieve its investment objectives by selecting securities from a wide range of investment opportunities. A mutual fund's investment objectives must be stated in its **prospectus.** This document is a legally prescribed written disclosure to the Securities and Exchange Commission (SEC) and to current and prospective investors that details pertinent operational and financial facts about a mutual fund. It describes the experience of its management, its financial status, any anticipated legal matters that could affect the company, and potential risks. The prospectus also identifies one of four major objectives for the fund: (1) income, (2) balanced, (3) growth, or (4) growth and income. Individual investors can easily review a number of mutual funds and select some that match the investor's particular investment objectives, time horizon, and tolerance for risk.

Funds with an Income Objective

A mutual fund that has an income objective as its primary focus aims almost exclusively to earn a high level of current interest and dividends from the investments in its portfolio. Long-term capital gains represent a secondary consideration. For example, a bond fund might seek to achieve an annual return of 6 percent. Such a mutual fund would purchase investment-quality corporate bonds, preferred stocks, and blue-chip income stocks.

A **bond fund** is the most popular example of a fund with an income objective. In this case, the aim is to earn current income without incurring undue risk and to pay ordinary income dividend distributions. The term "bond fund" is actually a misnomer because these funds usually hold a portfolio of bonds and other investments, such as preferred stocks and common stocks that pay high dividends.

Bond funds are categorized according to the maturities of their portfolio holdings. Short-term bond funds invest in securities maturing in 1 to 5 years, intermediate funds invest in securities with 5- to 10-year maturities, and long-term funds specialize in investments maturing in 10 to 30 years. When you sell a bond fund, the price you receive reflects the current bond market prices. As a result, short-term bond funds feature little fluctuation in NAV and a moderate return.

Intermediate- to long-term bond funds provide more income accompanied by moderate to severe fluctuations in NAV. This difference arises because, unlike a bond, a bond fund never matures. As a consequence, it is always subject to interest rate risk. Also, some bond funds specialize in investing in riskier, high-yielding bonds that are popularly known as *junk bonds* (see Chapter 14). Examples of bond funds include Pacific Horizon Capital Income, Concord Income Convertible, Vanguard Convertible Securities, and American Capital Harbor A.

Another type of income fund is a **municipal bond (tax-exempt) fund.** Such a fund attempts to earn current tax-exempt income by investing solely in municipal bonds issued by cities, states, and various districts and political subdivisions. The interest income earned on these bonds is exempt from federal personal income taxes. Popular municipal bond funds include General Municipal Bond and Financial Tax-Free Inc. Shares. A **mortgage fund** invests in mortgage-backed securities, such as Ginnie Mae issues. Examples of mortgage funds include Alliance Mortgage Securities Income and American Capital Federal Mortgage.

Funds with a Balanced Objective

Mutual funds with a balanced objective seek to preserve the investors' capital (the money initially invested), provide current income, and provide moderate long-term growth of NAV. **Balanced funds** invest in a mixture of bonds, preferred stocks, and blue-chip common stocks. A balanced fund might seek to achieve an annual return of 8 percent. Its investment policy calls for the fund to preserve capital by maintaining a balance of holdings and varying them according to economic conditions. Balanced funds include Twentieth Century Balanced, Pasadena Balanced Return, Equitable Balance B, and Kemper Investment Portfolio Total Return.

Funds with a Growth Objective

Many diversified mutual funds include only common stocks in their portfolios, with their primary objective being to increase the NAV over the long term through price appreciation. Growth funds own a variety of investment assets and seek a return ranging from perhaps 8 to 15 percent.

The typical **growth fund** seeks long-term capital appreciation by investing in the common stocks of companies whose values are expected to grow faster than usual. Such a fund buys and holds the common stocks of growing companies whose earnings are expected to increase at a better-than-average rate under most economic conditions. These firms (such as Wal-Mart, Microsoft, and Coca-Cola) tend not to declare cash dividends but instead reinvest most of their earnings to facilitate future growth. The prices of these companies' stocks generally increase over long periods of time, which consequently pushes up the mutual fund's NAV. Funds with a growth objective strive to provide a very good total return, perhaps 10 percent, for the investor who is willing to accept some risk, although substantial fluctuations in NAV are expected. Popular growth funds include Janus Twenty, Berger 100, Twentieth Century Growth, and Fidelity Magellan.

Another popular type of growth fund is a **value fund.** It specializes in growth stocks whose prices appear to be low (as measured by their price-to-book or price-to-earnings ratio), based on the logic that such stocks are currently out of favor and underpriced. The underappreciated common stocks in a value fund are expected to benefit from a growing economy, especially during the early stages of an economic recovery. According to some experts, the term "value fund," rather than describing a type of fund, actually refers to a manager's style of investing—that is, the fund manager purposefully seeks out underpriced stocks. A value fund might seek to achieve an annual return of 10 percent. Mutual funds that are currently described as value funds include Quest for Value Small Capitalization Fund, Royce Premier Fund, Founders Discovery Fund, and Legg Mason Special Investment Trust.

An **aggressive-growth fund,** also known as a **maximum capital gains fund,** differs from a growth fund. It seeks the greatest long-term capital appreciation and incurs the greatest fluctuation in the price of its shares. It does not emphasize income dividends, but rather relies primarily on NAV appreciation to produce a return. Holdings could involve small companies with high P/E ratios whose share prices are more volatile than the norm, such as rapidly growing companies, firms developing new technologies, and other emerging businesses with good long-term profit potential, located both in the United States and abroad. Such funds often employ high-risk investment techniques, such as borrowing money for leverage, short selling, hedging, and options. An aggressive-growth fund might seek to achieve an annual return of 12 percent. Popular funds classified under this moniker include Kaufmann, Enterprise Capital Appreciation, Thomson Opportunity B, and AIM Constellation.

A **small-cap fund** (also called a **small-capitalization fund**) specializes in investing in lesser-known mid-sized companies with a market capitalization of less than $1 billion that are expected to grow rapidly. Such stocks pay little, if any, cash dividends but offer strong potential for growth. A small-cap fund might seek to achieve an annual return of 12 percent. Examples of popular small-cap funds include Twentieth Century Ultra Investors, Alger Small Capital Union, Hartwell Emerging Growth, and Robertson Stephens Emerging Growth. Other descriptors in the same vein are "micro-cap" funds (investing in companies with a market capitalization of less than $300 million) and "mid-cap" funds (investing in companies with a market capitalization of less than $5 billion).

A **sector fund** heavily invests in common stocks from one industry or one portion of the economy that are expected to grow, perhaps very rapidly. Investing in a single sector increases risk as well as the potential return—even in a diversified portfolio. A sector fund might seek to achieve an annual return of 12 percent. Popular sector funds include Vanguard Special Health Portfolio, Fidelity Select Biotechnology, and Fidelity Technology.

Precious metals and gold funds seek long-term capital appreciation by investing in securities associated with gold, silver, and other precious metals. Popular precious metal funds include Enterprise Precious Metals, Vanguard Specialized Gold, and Keystone Precious Metals.

A **global fund** invests primarily in growth stocks of companies listed on foreign exchanges. Popular global funds include Harbor International, Vanguard World-International Growth, and GT Japan Growth. **International funds** hold only foreign stocks, and some such funds focus on a single country or geographic region, such as Asia or Europe. Examples of diversified international funds include Van Eck Work Income, MFS Worldwide Governments, and Merrill Lynch Global B. **Emerging market funds** seek out stocks in countries whose economies are small but growing. These funds are volatile because these countries tend to be less stable politically. Global, international, and emerging market funds might seek to achieve an annual return of 12 percent.

Funds with a Growth and Income Objective

A **growth and income fund** whose objective is a combination of growth and income invests in companies expected to show average or better growth and to pay steady or rising dividends. Such funds might seek to achieve an annual return of 9 percent—not as low as the return offered by funds with an income or balanced objective, but not as high as that offered by funds with a growth objective. They invest in common stocks that pay reasonable dividends as well as stocks from lesser-known firms with strong growth potential. Growth and income funds should entail less risk than aggressive-growth funds and are more conservative than growth funds. Not surprisingly, such funds are very popular among investors, particularly those saving and investing for retirement. The return will consist of mutual fund income dividends and sizable long-term price appreciation in the fund's NAV. Examples of growth and income funds include AIM Charter, Cigna Value, SteinRoe Prime Equities, and Vanguard Quantitative.

Life-cycle funds work in a similar fashion, creating a diversified, all-in-one portfolio for those individuals who do not wish to actively manage their own investments. **Socially conscious funds** usually invest in firms with respectable employee relations, strong records of community involvement, excellence on environmental issues, respect for human rights, and safe products (see www.socialinvest.org for examples). **Mutual fund funds,** such as Vanguard Star, Rightime Fund, and Fund Trust Aggressive Growth, earn a return by investing in other mutual funds, thereby providing extensive diversification.

Unique Features of Mutual Funds

3 Describe the unique features of mutual funds that make them an attractive investment.

Mutual funds clearly have a number of advantages for investors: diversification, small minimum investment required, professional management, minimal transaction costs, liquidity, thousands of choices, and no difficulty selecting funds that match your investment objectives. Mutual funds also have a number of unique features, several of which are discussed here: easy purchase and sale, check writing, automatic investment, automatic reinvestment, switching privileges, recordkeeping, beneficiary designation, easy establishment of retirement plans, and withdrawal plans.

Easy Purchase and Sale

Shares in an open-end mutual fund can be bought and sold by communicating with the company via telephone, wire, facsimile, the Internet, or mail. Each share is redeemed at the closing price—that is, the NAV—at the end of the trading day.

After you have opened an account with a mutual fund company, you can easily buy and sell shares. To open an account, you fill out a brief application form and forward the initial investment, which generally must be a minimum amount of $250 to $2000. To order the mutual fund company to electronically transfer funds from one account to another or to and from another financial institution, you may use a PIN number on the fund's website or call a toll-free number—where operators record your verbal instructions. Because mutual fund investors can buy and sell shares so quickly, these investments have excellent liquidity.

Did You Know? . . .

The Total Long-Term Returns for Various Types of Stock Mutual Funds Are Roughly the Same

Data from the Investment Company Institute reveal that the type of stock mutual fund in which you invest over the long term makes very little difference. Over time (for example, ten years), the average annual returns for different types of diversified stock funds (growth, domestic equity, growth and income, equity income, and balanced) converge around 11 percent (11.2 percent, according to Ibbotson Associates). The only secret to obtaining such a good return is to remain patient and keep investing. Returns over one, three, and five years vary widely, but over the long term the returns of major categories of diversified mutual funds are roughly the same.

Advice from an Expert

Managed Funds or Index Funds?

Most mutual funds are **managed funds,** meaning that professional managers are constantly evaluating and choosing securities using a specific investment approach. On a daily basis, "active managers" select the stocks and bonds in which to invest and sell them when they deem appropriate. The managers earn a fee for their services, and ultimately their choices are responsible for the performance of the fund. Oftentimes, however, investing in a managed mutual fund is not the best choice for investors.

An **index fund** is a mutual fund that simply buys and holds the stocks or bonds that constitute a market index. Thus, by definition, it is a diversified investment. The objective of this type of mutual fund is to track a stock or bond index as closely as possible. Therefore, an index fund invests in the securities that make up a particular index. For example, the stocks in an S&P 500 fund would effectively mirror the companies in the index, which are primarily large-cap U.S. stocks, by owning common stock in all 500 companies. The Russell 2000 Index Fund invests in the 2000 small-cap stocks in the index. The Wilshire 5000 Index tracks almost all of the more than 6500 U.S. stocks. The NASDAQ 100 Index tracks the largest domestic and international nonfinancial companies.

Index funds are called **unmanaged funds** because their managers do not evaluate and select individual securities. Rather, they simply buy and hold all—or a representative selection of—the stocks in a particular index. As a consequence, index funds' annual management fees are extremely low, perhaps only 0.30 to 0.50 percent. For example, Vanguard's S&P 500 fund charges 0.18 percent. By comparison, the average annual fee for managed funds is more than 1.50 percent. The constant buying and selling of securities increases the transaction costs of managed funds compared to the buy-and-hold approach of index funds.

The returns achieved by actively traded stock funds typically trail the stock market averages by about 1.5 percentage points per year. It is hard to beat the averages, particularly over many years. John Bogle, founder of the no-load giant the Vanguard Group, argues that indexing eliminates many of the risks associated with picking individual stocks, portfolio managers, and investment styles, such as growth or income. Over the past 20 years, the Vanguard S&P 500 Index fund has beaten the returns of 4 out of 5 domestic stock funds.

Many experts invest their "serious money" in index funds. This is money that you do not want to lose by placing it in a high-risk investment, including money invested for your retirement or for a child's education. Because index funds rarely realize capital gains, they are highly tax-efficient, which is another reason investors should invest most of their money in these funds.

An investment product that is similar to an index fund is an **exchange-traded fund (ETF).** An ETF is a basket of passively managed securities (like an index fund) that trade on an exchange like a stock. ETFs, such as Vanguard Total Stock Market VIPERs, are listed on securities market exchanges and can be traded throughout the day just like stocks. The more than 100 ETFs currently in existence include SPDRs (S&P 500), Diamonds (the Dow), iShares (foreign and domestic index and individual sectors), IJH (S&P 400 mid-cap stocks), QQQ (the NASDAQ 100 index), and EFA (Asian and Australian stocks). The annual management expenses for these funds are extremely low, perhaps 0.35 percent or even 0.10 percent, so they are suitable choices for long-term investors. However, unlike no-load mutual funds, ETFs must be purchased and sold through brokers, so commissions are charged.

Index funds and ETFs are excellent ways to invest for retirement and an intelligent choice for employees who are investing through their employers' 401(k) retirement plans. Investors who put their money in these funds can relax, knowing that their money will grow as the U.S. and world economies continue to grow over the years.

Jean M. Lown
Utah State University, Logan, Utah

Check Writing and Wiring of Funds

Most mutual funds offer one or more interest-earning money market funds where investors can accumulate their cash, accept dividends, or simply hold their money while making decisions about investing. Conveniently, investors can write checks from money market funds, usually for a minimum of $250. A money market fund invests exclusively in cash and cash equivalents. Investors also can choose to have their money wired from the mutual fund to a bank account.

[handwritten margin note: check in?]

Automatic Investment

Most funds allow investors to make periodic monthly or quarterly payments using money automatically transferred from their bank account to the mutual fund company. You can invest as little as $50 per month. Note that this process results in dollar-cost averaging.

Automatic Reinvestment

Unlike most other investment alternatives, mutual funds permit **automatic reinvestment.** This provision allows for the automatic use of ordinary income dividend distributions, capital gains distributions, and interest to buy additional shares of the fund without paying any commissions. Fractional shares are purchased as needed. More than three-fourths of mutual fund shareholders have their income reinvested, which greatly compounds share ownership. Figure 15.2 (page 432) illustrates the positive results obtained by reinvesting dividends. The initial $10,000 investment in Vanguard's S&P 500 Index Fund grew to $110,897 over 20 years, instead of $66,931, because of the reinvestment of dividends. According to Standard & Poor's Dave Guarino, "Automatic reinvestment of dividends is one of the most overlooked ways of accumulating wealth. In addition to the benefits of compounding, it also provides a mechanism to dollar-cost average investments."

Switching Privileges Within a Mutual Fund Family

A **switching privilege** (also called an **exchange privilege**) permits mutual fund shareholders to easily swap shares (via a letter, fax, Internet, or telephone order) on a dollar-for-dollar basis for shares in another mutual fund within a mutual fund family. Transfer from one fund to another can be accomplished at no cost or for only a small charge, typically $5 or $10 per transaction, called an **exchange fee. A mutual fund family** exists when the same management company operates a variety of mutual funds, each with its own investment objectives. Fidelity Investments, for example, offers more than 175 funds, ranging from an aggressive-growth fund to a technology sector fund to a municipal bond fund to a money market fund. The variety of mutual fund families and the many specific funds available within them make it fairly easy to choose a fund that matches your investment objectives. Popular mutual fund families include those managed by Fidelity, Charles Schwab, T. Rowe Price, and Vanguard Group.

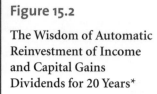

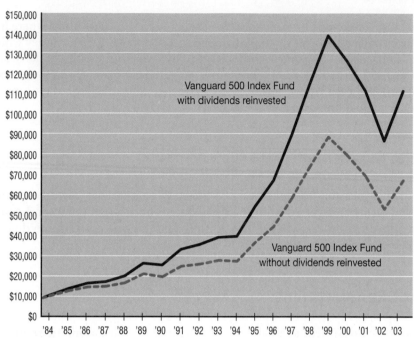

Figure 15.2

The Wisdom of Automatic Reinvestment of Income and Capital Gains Dividends for 20 Years*

An initial investment of $10,000 in the Vanguard 500 Index Fund grew to $66,931 in 20 years because the value of the underlying securities pushed up the net asset value. By comparison, with automatic reinvestment of dividends, the investment grew to $110,897.

*The Vanguard 500 Index Fund is a mutual fund that invests in all 500 of the stocks tracked by the S&P 500 Index (a registered trademark of the Standard & Poor's Corporation), which is an unmanaged index of common stock prices. Reprinted with permission.
Source: The Vanguard Group, Inc.

Recordkeeping and Help with Taxes

Mutual fund companies must send shareholders periodic reports and annual tax statements. This information helps keep the investor apprised of the fund's performance. **Confirmation statements,** which indicate the number of shares owned and the value of the holdings, must also be forwarded to the mutual fund shareholder every time a transaction occurs in the account. These statements provide evidence of ownership as well. Investors in a mutual fund family receive **consolidated statements** that report all of their holdings and transactions in the mutual fund family. Recordkeeping is a vital part of mutual fund investments, because taxable gains and losses must be carefully calculated for income tax purposes (unless such investments are made within an IRS-qualified tax-sheltered retirement account, as discussed in Chapter 18).

Beneficiary Designation

When opening a mutual fund account, the investor is given the opportunity to complete a form to designate a beneficiary in case of the investor's death. A **beneficiary des-**

ignation enables the shareholder to name one or more beneficiaries so that the proceeds go to them without going through probate. The delays and expenses of probate are discussed in Chapter 19.

Easy Establishment of Retirement Plans

Most mutual funds provide programs that "qualify" under IRS regulations as tax-deferred ways to invest money for retirement. Depending on the eligibility qualifications, you can put thousands of dollars into a mutual fund each year and deduct the amount from your taxable income. Then you can watch value of the fund increase over the years, paying no income taxes on any of its profits until you withdraw your funds during your retirement. Such qualified programs include individual retirement accounts (IRAs), 403(b), 401(k), 457, Salary Reduction Simplified Employee Pension Plans, and Keogh retirement programs. Chapter 18 discusses the role of these programs in retirement planning. Employers who offer retirement plans usually offer payroll transfer plans, which permit investors to automatically forward a specified portion of each paycheck to a mutual fund so as to buy shares.

Withdrawal Plans

All mutual funds make various types of **withdrawal plans** (also called **systematic withdrawal plans**) available to shareholders who want a periodic income from their mutual fund investments. Each withdrawal usually must be at least $50. The fund forwards the amounts to you (or to anyone you designate) at regular intervals (monthly or quarterly). You can take your funds out of a mutual fund using one of four methods:

- By taking a set dollar amount each month
- By cashing in a set number of shares each month
- By taking the current income as cash
- By taking a portion of the asset growth

Mutual Fund Fees

4 Distinguish between load and no-load mutual funds and explain how to avoid some of their numerous charges and fees.

The costs and fees associated with investing in mutual funds are many and they can be confusing. Some fees can be avoided. There are transaction fees that may be assessed when shares are bought and sold and special fees that may be levied annually while you own the fund shares.

Mutual Fund Transaction Fees

As with many types of investments, you may be required to pay a transaction fee when you purchase and sell your mutual fund shares.

Load Funds Always Charge Transaction Fees.   Mutual funds are classified according to whether they assess a **sales charge** or **commission** at the time of purchase of initial and subsequent shares, also called a **load.** Mutual funds that levy such sales charges are called **load funds.** Load funds are generally *sold* by stock brokerage firms, banks, and financial planners rather than marketed directly by the mutual fund company. Basically, the load represents the commission paid to the salesperson.

This commission, also called a **front-end load,** typically amounts to 4 to 8.5 percent of the amount invested. For example, assume that you have discussed the investment potential of the Conglomerate Cat and Dog Food Mutual Fund with a salesperson. After examining the prospectus, you decide to invest $10,000. Because this load fund charges a commission of 8.5 percent (the maximum permitted by the Securities and Exchange Commission), the salesperson receives $850 ($10,000 $\times$ 0.085). As a result, only $9150 is actually available to purchase shares. This commission is much higher than stock transaction costs, which are usually 1/2 to 2 percent of the security's purchase price.

The sales charge may be shown either as the stated commission or as a percentage of the amount invested. The stated commission (8.5 percent in our example) is always somewhat misleading. In contrast, the percentage of the amount invested is a more accurate figure because it is based on the actual money invested and working. A stated commission of 8.5 percent actually amounts to 9.3 percent of the amount invested: $10,000 $-$ $9150 = $850; $850 $\div$ $9150 = 9.3%. If you want to invest a full $10,000 in this load fund, you will need to pay out $10,930 [$10,930 $-$ ($10,930 $\times$ 8.5%) = $10,000].

Investments of $10,000 or more often receive a discount on the load. So-called **low-load funds** may carry a sales charge of perhaps 1 to 3 percent. These funds may also be sold by brokers, but are sometimes sold via mail and through retailers in shopping centers. About half of all mutual funds levy a load. "If you pick your own funds, sales charges [and loads] are a total waste of money," observes Fred W. Frailey, editor of *Kiplinger's Personal Finance Magazine.*

No-Load Funds Sometimes Charge Transaction Fees.

A mutual fund that does not assess a sales charge at the time of the investment purchase is called a **no-load fund.** These mutual fund companies let people purchase shares directly from the mutual fund company without the services of a broker, banker, or financial planner. Interested investors simply seek out advertisements for these funds in financial newspapers and magazines and make contact through toll-free telephone numbers, Internet or by mail. No-load mutual funds sell their shares at the net asset value without the addition of sales charges. Note, however, that the SEC allows funds to be called "no-load" even if they assess a "service fee" of 0.25 percent or less when shares are purchased. Many no-load funds are described and analyzed in popular publications such as *Business Week, Consumer Reports, Forbes, Fortune, Kiplinger's Personal Finance Magazine,* and *Money.*

Deferred Load and Redemption Charges.

Approximately 60 percent of all no-load mutual funds and many load funds assess additional fees for transactions, including deferred load and redemption charges. These charges and commissions often are not readily apparent to the mutual fund investor, but they do reduce the investor's anticipated total return, as illustrated in Table 15.1.

A **deferred load,** also known as a **back-end load,** is a sales commission that is imposed only when shares are sold. Deferred loads are often on a sliding scale. Typically, the fee declines one percentage point for each year the investor owns the fund. For example, a fund might charge a 6 percent fee if an investor redeems the shares within one year of purchase, and then steadily decline on an annual basis, until it reaches zero after six years.

A **redemption charge** (or **exit fee**) is similar to a deferred load, although often it is much less and is used to reduce excessive trading of fund shares. It typically disappears

				5.5% Front-	5% Back-
		3% Front-	8.5% Front-	end Load	end Load with
Years	No-Load*	end Load	end Load	with 0.25% 12b-1	1% 12b-1†
1	$10,890	$10,560	$ 9,960	$10,260	$10,280
3	12,900	12,500	11,800	12,150	12,230
5	15,320	14,860	14,020	14,380	14,460
7	18,170	17,620	16,620	18,000	16,930
10	23,470	22,770	21,480	22,800	21,200

Table 15.1 The Effect of Loads and Fees on Mutual Fund Returns
(Estimated figures based on a $10,000 investment and assuming a 10 percent gain each year.)

*1 percent annual management fee.
† A declining redemption fee of 5 percent the first year that goes to zero after the fifth year.

after the investment has been held for six months or a year. The fee is usually 1 percent of the value of the shares redeemed. Long-term investors should not shy away from funds with redemption fees that disappear after a year.

Mutual Fund Expense Charges

You can avoid mutual fund transaction fees by purchasing no-load funds and holding your shares long enough to avoid deferred load and redemption fees. You can avoid some but not all other expenses that are charged while you hold your mutual fund shares.

Management Fees.   All mutual funds charge a **management fee,** which is an annual assessment to pay the advisors who operate the mutual fund. The fee is calculated as an annual percentage of the average net assets of the mutual fund and it typically ranges from 0.10 to 2.3 percent of the fund's assets.

12b-1 Fees.   A common expense assessed to mutual fund shareholders is a **12b-1 fee** (named for the SEC rule that permits the charge), which is an annual charge deducted by the fund company from a fund's assets to pay for advertising, marketing, distribution, and promotional costs. The 12b-1 fees are also known as **distribution fees.** These charges also pay for **trailing commissions,** which is compensation paid to salespersons for months or years in the future. Although the funds do not call 12b-1 fees "loads" because they are not charged up front, they have the same effect as loads—that is, they reduce the annual and total return to investors.

Many call this a "hidden load" because it decreases a shareholder's earning power each year without being described as a sales commission. A 12b-1 fee is actually a "perpetual sales load" because it is assessed on the initial investment as well as on reinvested dividends, every year, forever. If you pay 1 percent per year in 12b-1 fees for a mutual fund in which you invest for ten years, you will be giving up nearly 10 percent of your investment amount in trailing commissions. You would be well advised to invest in a load fund rather than pay 12b-1 assessments if you plan to own the fund for more than five years. The SEC caps 12b-1 fees at 0.75 percent, although it permits a 0.25 percent "service fee," which brings the total cap to 1 percent. Some funds stop assessing 12b-1 fees after four to eight years. Many funds do not have a 12b-1 fee, which increases the return to investors.

Did You Know? . . .

Commissions on Load Funds Depend on Share Class

A single mutual fund company may offer more than one "class" of load shares to investors: Class A, B, or C. Although the amount of your initial investment made to each load fund may be the same, each class has important differences in fees and expenses. The distinct classes give you, as an investor in load funds, a choice about how much you will pay in expenses and how much the broker will be paid to sell you the fund. Average costs—

which reduce your fund's returns—are noted in the table.

After a certain amount of time, typically six to eight years, many load funds automatically convert B shares to A shares, which carry 12b-1 fees. To determine which class of load funds suits your needs, use the Mutual Fund Cost Calculator at www.sec.gov or the Cost Analyzer at www.morningstar.com.

	Class A Shares	Class B Shares	Class C Shares
Front-end load	High, 3.0–8.5%	None	None or low, perhaps 1% annually
Deferred back-end load	None	Yes, high	None or low
12b–1 fee	Low, perhaps 1/2% annually	High, perhaps 3/4% annually	Very high, perhaps 1% annually
Annual management expenses	Moderate, perhaps 1.25%	High moderate, perhaps 2.0%	Very high, more than 2%

Disclosure of Fees

To assist the investing public, the SEC requires that a mutual fund's prospectus include a **standardized expense table** within its first three pages that describes and illustrates in an identical manner the effects of all of its fees and other expenses projected over five years. This description must estimate the hypothetical total costs that a mutual fund investor would pay on a $1000 investment that earns 5 percent annually and is withdrawn after ten years. All figures must be adjusted to reflect the effects of loads and fees. Funds are required to provide both before- and after-tax performance information.

You will also want to look for the fund's **expense ratio,** which is the combined percentage charged annually for expense charges including management fees, 12b-1 fees, and other expenses of the mutual fund company. According to Lipper, expense ratios average 1.45 percent for diversified stock funds and 0.40 percent for index funds.

What's Best: Load or No-Load? Low-Fee or High-Fee?

The sales commissions charged by load funds indisputably reduce total returns. When investment results are adjusted to account for the effects of sales charges, no-load mutual funds have an initial advantage because the investor has more money at work. In general, the shorter the time period you own the shares, the greater the negative impact of loads on the total return for the mutual fund investor. Up-front load charges are costly to the investor in the short run (less than five years), whereas annual 12b-1 charges are very costly over the long run. Individuals who investigate and purchase mutual funds on their own, rather than buying such investments through a stockbroker or financial planner, usually invest in no-load funds.

Independent research by numerous organizations, including a recent study by Financial Research Group, has found that over five-year periods lower-cost funds always deliver returns better than those offered by higher-cost funds. Even a small difference in fees can seriously affect long-term returns. For example, a $50,000 portfolio earning an 8 percent annual return would grow to $176,182 in 20 years with a 1.5 percent management fee. By comparison, over the same time span it would grow to $193,484 with a 1.0 percent fee and to $212,393 with a 0.5 fee. Over 30 years the returns with these fee rates would be $330,718, $380,613, and $437,748, respectively. As you see, the negative effects of high fees on long-term returns are enormous. Thus, the investor would be wise to invest in no-load fee mutual funds that have low management fees.

How to Evaluate Mutual Funds in Which to Invest

5 Explain how to evaluate mutual funds in which to invest.

Evaluating and selecting a mutual fund requires gathering information and comparing the performance of various funds. Fortunately, a tremendous amount of objective information is available to help in your decision making.

Match Your Investment Philosophy and Financial Goals to a Mutual Fund's Objectives

Your first task is to match your interpretation of a mutual fund's objectives with your own investment philosophy (conservative, moderate, or aggressive) and financial goals (for example, retirement, college fund). The investor must balance risk and return on the various types of mutual funds given that they have different objectives (Figure 15.3, page 438). Mutual funds that offer the potential for high returns inevitably involve more risk. In selecting mutual funds, investors need to balance their expectations for capital gains or income with their need to preserve capital.

Read Prospectuses and Annual Reports

Both annual reports and prospectuses (described earlier) detail a mutual fund's operations and finances. An **annual report** is a published summary of the financial activities of a mutual fund company (or any other corporation) for the year. The SEC requires mutual fund prospectuses to be updated annually and to present yields, expenses, and returns in a standardized format. In addition, funds must compare their short- and long-term performance, after expenses, with the performance of a standard market index, such as Standard & Poor's 500-stock index. The SEC prohibits the dissemination of false and misleading investment literature.

The ultimate authority on a fund's track record is its current prospectus. Most investors neglect to read the prospectus, instead seeking information about mutual funds from other sources.

Figure 15.3

Balancing Risk and Returns on Mutual Funds

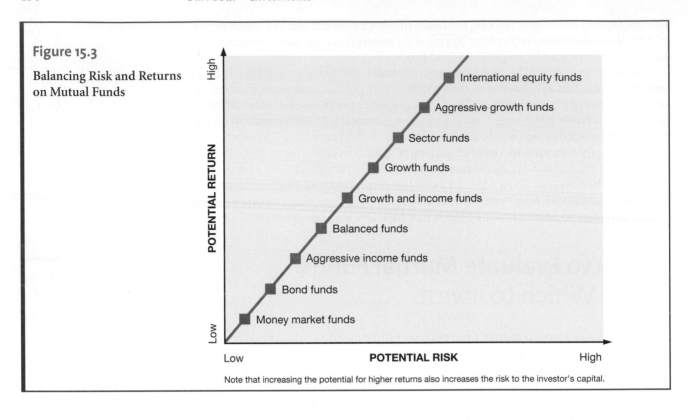

Note that increasing the potential for higher returns also increases the risk to the investor's capital.

Locate Sources of Comparative Performance Data

Current information about mutual funds is available from a large number of useful sources. When comparing the track records of mutual funds, investors should focus on three factors: expenses, volatility, and past performance. To compare funds on a consistent basis, you might want to use data from only one of the investment publications mentioned below.

The Financial Press.   The most useful news publications are *The Wall Street Journal, Barron's, Investor's Business Daily,* and the business sections of newspapers, such as *The New York Times* and *USA Today.* In addition, a number of on-line news and quote services are priced for the small investor, including Compu-Serve, Dow Jones News/Retrieval-Private Investor Edition, Farcast, Personal Journal, Quotecom, and Reuters Money Network.

Specialized Mutual Fund Investment Publications.   A number of specialized publications examine mutual funds in considerable detail; these resources are often available in large libraries. Among the best for ranking funds by total return over long periods of time are *Morningstar Mutual Funds, Morningstar No-Load Funds, Mutual Funds Update, Investment Companies Yearbook, IBC/Donoghue's Mutual Funds Almanac, Standard & Poor's, Lipper Mutual Fund Profiles,* and *The Value Line Mutual Fund Survey.* Moody's Investment Service now rates mutual funds as well. Data from specialized mutual fund investment publications are very informative for the potential investor. Dozens of newsletters that specialize in mutual funds are available, too.

Magazines That Rate Mutual Funds.   Magazines that are extremely helpful in comparing performance over time include *Business Week, Consumer Reports, Forbes, Fortune, Kiplinger's Personal Finance Magazine, Money,* and *Worth.* The late August issue of *Forbes,* the October issue of *Money,* the late February issue of *Business Week,* and the September issue of *Kiplinger's Personal Finance Magazine* all feature comprehensive examinations of the performance of numerous mutual funds.

Internet Sources on Mutual Funds.   The Internet is a useful source of up-to-date comparative data on mutual funds. One of the best websites is run by Morningstar (www.morningstar.com). The Investment Company Institute (www.ici.org) provides information on more than 12,000 mutual funds. The popular personal finance magazines, especially *Money* (www.money.com) and *Kiplinger's Personal Finance Magazine* (www.kiplinger.com), are excellent sources of information.

Interpret Comparative Performance Information over Time

Publications that offer comparative performance information about mutual funds generally rank each fund based on its one-, three-, five-, and ten-year performance.

Consider a Fund's Volatility.   **Volatility** characterizes a security's or mutual fund's tendency to rise or fall in price over a period of time. A popular measure of volatility is the **standard deviation,** which gauges the degree to which a security's historical return rises above or falls below its long-term average return—and therefore may be likely to do so again in the future. Of course, a standard deviation is a probability indicator, not an economic forecast. The bigger an investment's standard deviation, the more volatile its price will probably be in the future. High volatility suggests greater long-term rewards but a greater-than-normal risk of short-term losses during economic downturns. You can find standard deviations and beta coefficients for mutual funds in profiles maintained by financial analysis firms such as Morningstar or Lipper Analytical Services. Conservative investors can use standard deviations to avoid the most volatile stock funds, while aggressive investors might seek them out.

For example, *Kiplinger's Personal Finance Magazine* provides a volatility ranking for mutual funds. Its system measures the volatility of a fund's results on a scale ranging from 1 (least volatile) to 10 (most volatile), indicating how much the fund's NAV could decline in a falling market or increase in a rising market relative to other mutual funds. Morningstar publishes a "downside risk" score for each fund based on how its record compares with the average for its peers. *U.S. News & World Report* uses "OPI (overall performance index)" as a measure of investment returns and volatility compared to similar funds.

Tax Considerations and Consequences

Mutual Funds

Mutual funds distribute dividends each quarter to their shareholders. These distributions to regular accounts are taxable, no matter whether you take them in cash or reinvest them to buy more shares. Mutual fund investments within a tax-sheltered retirement plan, such as a 401(k) or an individual retirement account (IRA), are not subject to income taxes on ordinary income dividends or capital gains distributions until the funds are actually withdrawn, however. Withdrawal of funds generally involves selling shares, whether the fund holding is through a qualified retirement plan or not.

To save on taxes, you will want to take the time to review exactly which shares might be the best ones to sell. Fortunately, the mutual fund companies keep detailed records for shareholders. You might choose to sell only those shares that result in the lowest tax liability. For example, you might want to sell losers and take those capital losses against other funds sold for a profit. If you do not want to determine the prices paid for those exact shares, you may use the **average-cost basis method** to determine your capital gain or loss. With this method, the investor uses the average price paid for all of his or her shares.

Be careful when considering investing in a mutual fund toward the end of the calendar year. Check with the mutual fund company about any planned year-end capital gains distributions. If the fund expects to make a significant payout, consider waiting until just after the distribution, known as the record date, before making your investment. On the **record date,** investors who own shares receive the capital gains distribution. If you invest before this date, you may owe income taxes on the capital distribution even though it is just a paper gain.

Consider a Fund's Long- and Short-Term Performance.   A complication in comparing performance arises when distinctions are drawn between long- and short-term performance. Some funds have operated for less than a decade, whereas some older funds may have changed managers, grown substantially, and modified their investment styles. Long-term investors usually focus on a fund's long-term performance.

Consider the Size of the Fund.   The size of the mutual fund is important because smaller funds (those that have less than $100 million in assets to invest) have greater flexibility than more stable, larger funds. For example, Fidelity Investments' enormous, $100 billion Magellan Fund owns 1 million or more shares in dozens of major corporations; consequently, its buying and selling decisions can seriously affect overall trading in those stocks and may inhibit Magellan from making decisive moves.

Consider Fund Performance in Up and Down Markets.   While long-term investors may seek out funds that have performed well over the past several years, it is also useful to compare the performance of mutual funds in both up (rising) and down (declining) markets. A down market or an up market (when prices of securities are generally falling or rising) usually lasts six months to one year—but sometimes longer. Table 15.2 contains recent performance data for a number of growth and maximum-growth mutual funds from *Kiplinger's Personal Finance Magazine.*

Table 15.2 Mutual Fund Performance

Fund Name	1 Yr Return	3 Yr Return	5 Yr Return	Universe	Category	Style	Decile Rank Within Style 2003	2002	2001	2000	1999	Down Mkt	Volatility Rank	Turnover	Assets (mil.)	Manager Since	Min. Invest.	Max. Load	Exp. Ratio
Calvert Social Investment A (CSIEX)	18.0%	0.9%	5.3%	Stock	Growth	LarVal	2	1	3	3	—	−12.3%	5	29.00%	$660.3	1998	$1,000	4.75%	1.29%
First Eagle Fund of America (FEAFX)	24.3%	6.8%	5.4%	Stock	Growth	MidBlnd	1	3	3	10	—	6.9%	2	47.9%	$609.4	1987	$2,500	—	1.50%
Fidelity Contrafund II (FDSVX)	17.2%	−2.9%	1.4%	Stock	Growth	LarGro	1	5	5	2	—	−30.7%	3	367.00%	$582.2	2000	$2,500	—	0.97%
Fidelity Mid Cap Stock (FMCSX)	26.0%	−3.9%	7.2%	Stock	Growth	MidGro	8	7	3	5	—	−11.0%	9	120.00%	$8,522.7	2001	$2,500	—	0.66%
AARP Capital Growth (ACGFX)	19.6%	−7.9%	−3.8%	Stock	Growth	LarGro	8	9	7	2	—	−33.8%	7	22.00%	$988.8	2002	$1,000	—	0.97%
Vanguard Growth Index (VIGRX)	19.0%	−2.4%	−4.7%	Stock	Growth	LarGro	2	4	9	4	—	−43.7%	5	44.00%	$7,721.0	1992	$3,000	—	0.23%
Boyar Value (BOYAX)	19.5%	6.3%	7.0%	Stock	Growth	AllCap	1	2	3	9	—	1.5%	2	19.00%	$30.1	1998	$5,000	5.00%	1.75%
Gabelli Growth (GABGX)	23.8%	−9.6%	−5.4%	Stock	Growth	LarGro	10	10	9	1	—	−39.0%	9	42.00%	$1,739.3	1995	$1,000	—	1.47%
Neuberger Berman Partners (NBSRX)	22.9%	3.7%	2.6%	Stock	Growth	LarVal	1	2	3	8	—	−10.9%	5	62.00%	$214.7	2001	$1,000	—	1.07%

Note: The above examples were chosen to meet the requirements of the end-of-chapter questions on pages 444–445.
Source: Kiplinger.com, May 12, 2004. Standard & Poor's.

Advice from an Expert

Invest Only Fun Money Aggressively

Many people with a moderate or conservative investment philosophy have the occasional urge to invest aggressively in a speculative stock or mutual fund. Once the investor has his or her financial plans in place, taking on more risk is acceptable—but *only* within the limits of the individual's "fun money." **Fun money** is a sum of investment money that you can afford to lose, without doing serious damage to your total portfolio.

Resolve to trade with a specific sum, such as $5000, or perhaps no more than 2 or 3 percent of your portfolio. Decide mentally that if and when the money is gone, it has been spent on an activity that you enjoyed trying, but accept that the money lost is lost forever. In particular, avoid the temptation to "throw good money after bad" in trying to recover your losses. Very speculative investing is not much different from gambling but, if you are armed with appropriate information, you can avoid investments where you might lose 100 percent of your fun money. One of the biggest dangers of fun money investing is that you might be successful. Success can give you the confidence—albeit perhaps false confidence—that you are a great investor. While you might be the next Warren Buffet, such success is likely to tempt you to aggressively invest even more of the assets in your total portfolio. That approach can result in disaster.

Investing in speculative stocks and aggressive-growth mutual funds for some individuals might be a lot of fun, particularly when the amount of money at stake is small. Over time, however, you will be best served by pursuing a disciplined investing plan with a focus on diversification. As financial columnist Jane Bryant Quinn observes, "The money you really need for life is better off in broadly diversified mutual funds, where a mistake is not forever."

Robert O. Weagley
University of Missouri–Columbia

Summary

1. More people are investing through mutual funds than ever before because many funds carry low or no sales charges and because some funds have performed much better than the average common stock. Investors in mutual funds expect both current dividend income while they own the fund's shares and capital gains when they sell their shares.

2. Mutual funds have one of four different investment objectives: income, balanced, growth, and growth and income. A fund must identify its objective in its prospectus. The thousands of mutual funds available mean that some fund will fit almost every investor's needs.

3. Mutual funds offer a number of advantages for investors: diversification, small minimum investment required, professional management, minimal transaction costs, liquidity, and thousands of choices to match your investment objectives. They also have a number of unique features: easy purchase and sale, check writing, automatic investment, automatic reinvestment, switching privileges, recordkeeping, beneficiary designation, and easy establishment of retirement plans.

4. The costs of investing in mutual funds can be confusing because they charge investors a variety of fees, some of which can be avoided. Examples of such charges include transaction fees such as front-end loads and deferred loads, as well as expenses such as management fees and 12b-1 fees. All fees must be disclosed to investors.

5. Evaluating and selecting a mutual fund requires gathering information and comparing the performance of various funds. Fortunately, a tremendous amount of objective information is available to help in your decision making, including fund prospectuses, annual reports, and comparative performance data published by a number of independent sources.

Key Terms

aggressive-growth (maximum capital gains) fund, 427
automatic reinvestment, 431
balanced funds, 427
capital gains distributions, 425
deferred (back-end) load, 434
exchange-traded fund (ETF), 430
expense ratio, 436
front-end load, 434
growth and income fund, 428
index fund, 430
life-cycle funds, 429
management fee, 435
mutual fund family, 431
net asset value (NAV), 425
no-load fund, 434
redemption charge (exit fee), 434
small-cap (small-capitalization) fund, 428
standardized expense table, 436
switching (exchange) privilege, 431
12b-1 (distribution) fee, 435

Chapter Review Questions

1. Summarize price appreciation, explaining how the net asset value (NAV) of a mutual fund can increase.

2. Compare and contrast a mutual fund with an income objective to one with a growth and income objective.

3. Distinguish between an aggressive-growth fund and a sector fund.

4. Explain why so many investors put most of their money into an index fund rather than a managed fund.

5. Describe how mutual funds can be easily purchased and sold.

6. Explain the value of automatically reinvesting dividends and capital gains in mutual funds.

7. Explain what having a switching privilege means.

8. Why do mutual funds charge management fees, and what are typical fee amounts?

9. What is a 12b-1 fee, and why do many investors avoid buying funds that charge such fees?

10. What is volatility, and how can a mutual fund investor make use of that information?

Group Discussion Issues

1. Review the four major objectives of mutual funds and the several portfolio classifications. Based on your risk tolerance, which type of fund would be of most interest to you? Give three reasons why.

2. Assume you graduated from college a few years ago, had a good job paying $55,000 annually, and wanted to invest

$200 per month in mutual funds. Which combination of mutual funds would you think appropriate? Give reasons for each of your selections.

3. Assume that you have $50,000 to invest solely in mutual funds. Based on your point in the life cycle and your personal comfort level for risk, which type of investment allocation would be appropriate for you?

4. Identify the types of mutual funds that would be good choices to meet the following investment objectives: emergency fund, house down payment, college fund for two-year-old child, and retirement fund for a 25-year-old. Give two reasons why each of your recommendations would be appropriate.

5. Which is a better choice for you, load or no-load mutual funds? Give some reasons for your opinion.

Decision-Making Cases

▶Case 1
Matching Mutual Fund Investments to Economic Projections

Glenn Sandler, a veterinarian for the past ten years in Ames, Iowa, is married and has one child. He is interested in investing in mutual funds. Glenn wants to put half of his $20,000 of accumulated savings into a stock mutual fund and then continue to invest $200 monthly for the foreseeable future, perhaps using the money for retirement starting in about 25 years. Glenn has limited his choices to the mutual funds listed in Table 15.2.

(a) Glenn wants to invest the full $10,000 now and diversify his holdings into two mutual funds. His personal economic projections for the next few years include low interest rates, moderate inflation, and medium-to-high economic growth. Given those assumptions, which two funds listed in Table 15.2 do you recommend as investments for his $10,000? Why? (You may want to review the section on making economic projections in Chapter 1 before responding.)

(b) If Glenn's short-term economic forecast had projected high interest rates, moderate-to-high inflation, and sluggish economic growth (perhaps even with a recession), would you recommend that he put the $10,000 into mutual funds right now? If yes, explain why and suggest a fund from Table 15.2. If no, explain why not and suggest an alternative investment option for the $10,000.

(c) Glenn also wants to invest $200 per month into one mutual fund over the next 25 years. Assuming favorable long-term economic projections, which of the funds listed in Table 15.2 would you recommend? Why?

▶Case 2
Selection of a Mutual Fund as Part of a Retirement Plan

Etta Mae Westbrook, a single mother of a six-year-old child, works in a marketing firm in Knoxville, Tennessee, and is willing to invest $2000 to $3000 per year in a mutual fund. She wants the investment income to supplement her retirement pension starting in approximately 20 years and she has a moderate investment philosophy. Advise Etta Mae by responding to the following questions:

(a) Should Etta Mae invest in a mutual fund with a growth objective or one with a growth and income objective? Why?

(b) Etta Mae wants to invest in a mutual fund that focuses on common stocks. Which two stock funds in Table 15.2 would you recommend that she avoid? Why?

(c) Explain your reasons for having Etta Mae invest in a load fund or a no-load fund.

(d) Assume that after 20 years Etta Mae's investments have done very well. In fact, she's considering a plan for periodically withdrawing income. Advise her on the advantages and disadvantages of this plan given her long-term investment objective.

Financial Math Questions

1. Last January Mike invested $1000 by buying 100 shares of the Can't Lose Mutual Fund, an aggressive-growth no-load mutual fund. Mike reinvested his dividends all year. So far, the NAV for Mike's investment has risen from $10 per share to $13.25.

(a) What is the percentage increase in the value of Mike's mutual fund?

(b) If Mike redeemed his mutual fund investment for $13.25 per share, how much profit would he realize?

(c) Assuming Mike pays income taxes at the 25 percent rate, how much income tax will he have to pay if he sells his shares?

(d) Assuming Mike pays income taxes at the 25 percent rate, how much income tax will he have to pay if he chooses not to sell his shares but to remain invested?

2. Two years ago Jane invested $1000 by buying 125 shares ($8 per share NAV) in the Can't Lose Mutual Fund, an aggressive-growth no-load mutual fund. Last year she made two additional investments of $500 each (50 shares at $10 and 40 shares at $12.50). Jane reinvested all of her dividends. So far, the NAV for her investment has risen from $8 per share to $13.25. Late in the year, she sold 60 shares at $13.25.

(a) What were the proceeds from Jane's sale of the 60 shares?

(b) To use the Internal Revenue Service's average-cost basis method of determining the average price paid for one share, begin by calculating the average price paid for the shares. In this instance, the $2000 is divided by 215 shares (125 shares + 50 shares + 40 shares). What was the average price paid by Jane?

(c) To finally determine the average-cost basis of shares sold, you multiply the average price per share times the number of shares sold—in this case, 60. What is the total cost basis for Jane's 60 shares?

(d) Assuming that Jane must pay income taxes on the difference between the sales price for the 60 shares and their cost, how much is this difference?

(e) If Jane's mutual fund transactions were conducted within an IRS-qualified tax-sheltered retirement account, what would her income tax liability be if she were paying income taxes at the 25 percent rate?

Money Matters Continuing Cases

Victor and Maria Invest for Retirement

Victor and Maria Hernandez plan to retire in less than 15 years. Their current investment portfolio is distributed as follows: 40 percent in growth mutual funds, 40 percent in corporate bonds and bond mutual funds, and 20 percent in cash equivalents. They have decided to increase the amount of risk in their portfolio by taking 10 percent from their cash equivalent investments and investing in some mutual funds with strong growth possibilities.

1. Of the mutual funds listed in Table 15.2, which two would you recommend to meet the Hernandezes' goals? Why?

2. If those two investments perform over the next decade as well as they did in the past five years, would you recommend that the Hernandezes remain invested in those two funds during their retirement years? Why or why not?

The Johnsons Decide to Invest Through Mutual Funds

After learning about mutual funds, the Johnsons are convinced that they are a good way to invest, especially because of the diversification and professional management such funds offer. The couple has a financial nest egg of $9500 to invest through mutual funds. In addition, they want to invest another $300 per month on a regular basis.

Although not yet completely firm, Harry and Belinda's goals at this point are as follows:

- They want to continue to build for retirement income.

- They will need about $10,000 in six to eight years to use as supplemental income if Belinda has a baby and does not work for six months.

- They might buy a super-expensive luxury automobile requiring a $10,000 down payment if they decide not to have a child.

Knowing that the Johnsons have a moderate investment philosophy, that they live on a reasonable budget, and that they have a well-established cash-management plan, advise them on their mutual fund investments by responding to the following questions:

1. After looking at Figure 15.3, which two types of funds would you recommend to meet the Johnson's goals? Why?

2. How would you divide the $9500 between the two types of funds? Why?

3. How much of the $300 monthly investment amount would you allocate to each type of fund? Why?

4. Some comparable mutual fund performance data on stock funds are shown in Table 15.2. Using only that information and assuming that you are recommending some funds for the Johnsons' retirement needs, which three funds would you recommend? Why?

5. Assume that all three funds perform above average for the next ten years. A bear market then occurs, causing the NAVs to drop 25 percent from the previous year. What conditions must exist before you would recommend that the Johnsons sell their accumulated shares in the funds?

6. Determine the value of their $9500 investment in ten years, assuming that the three funds' NAVs increase 13 percent annually for the next ten years. (Use the *Garman/Forgue* website.)

What Would You Recommend Now?

Now that you have read the chapter on mutual funds, what would you recommend to Doug and Cheryl Circarelli in the case at the beginning of the chapter regarding:

1. Buying mutual funds through their employers' 401(k) retirement accounts?

2. The disadvantage of paying income taxes on interest earned on certificates of deposit?

3. Redeeming their certificates of deposit and investing in mutual funds rather than saving through certificates of deposit?

4. Buying no-load rather than load mutual funds?

5. Buying balanced mutual funds instead of aggressive-growth funds?

Exploring the World Wide Web

To complete these exercises, go to the *Garman/Forgue* website at college.hmco.com/business/students. Under General Business, select the title of this text. Click on the Internet Exercises link for this chapter, and answer the questions that appear on the Web page.

1. Visit the website for T. Rowe Price and its Investment Insights section. Access its "Insights Reports Library." Compare the information provided in the "Investing with Mutual Funds" article with the information in this text chapter. Develop a list of ten key points that every beginning investor in mutual funds should know. Also list four advantages that investing in stock mutual funds provide as opposed to direct purchase of stock.

2. Visit Morningstar's Mutual Funds OnDemand website. Use its "fund screening" feature to search for "five star" mutual funds that meet your criteria (do not enter a ticker symbol). Complete the requested criteria information on fund return, objective, and so on, and then initiate your search. From the search results, select one fund to research further. Type the ticker symbol for that fund in the "advice search" box at the top of the page to obtain research information on that fund. How would the information provided be of assistance to the mutual fund investor? (Hint: You may need to use trial and error to obtain a list of funds and find one that has been researched.) For one of the funds on your search list, try to find the website for that fund company to gather additional information.

3. Visit the websites for three of the more prominent mutual fund families: Vanguard, Fidelity, and American Cen-

tury. What types of information do these sites provide to entice investors to buy fund shares through their families of funds? What types of informational and educational resources do these sites provide to investors, regardless of where they decide to invest? For one or two of the funds, request that it send you (a) an application to open an account and (b) recent performance information.

4. Visit the website for the Vanguard family of mutual funds. Take its quiz focusing on your knowledge of mutual funds. When you receive your quiz results, review the lessons for the questions for which you had the incorrect answer.

5. Visit the website for Brill's Mutual Fund Interactive. Click on "Profiles" and read three or four of the profiles of mutual fund managers. What common themes do you see in their professional training and background?

6. Visit the website for Kiplinger's Personal Finance to find information on mutual funds. Click on "Basics" and read the articles on mutual fund expenses. How might you minimize the effects of expenses on your mutual fund choices?

7. Visit the website for CNN/Money. On its "Mutual Fund" page, access its "Winners and Losers" section to review the best and worst performing funds over the past three months, past one year, and past five years. What differences do you detect in the lists? What might this information tell you about the approach that might be taken by investors with longer time horizons?

Chapter 16

Buying and Selling Securities

LEARNING OBJECTIVES

After reading this chapter, you should be able to:

1 **Describe** how stocks are bought and sold and how to select a brokerage firm.

2 **Explain** how to order securities transactions and read newspaper price quotations for stocks, bonds, and mutual funds.

3 **Understand** how to obtain and use investment information.

4 **Determine** whether one's required rate of return is exceeded by its potential return.

5 **Recognize** the risks associated with the trading techniques of margin buying and selling short.

Bob Class, a 29-year-old, works for a national beer manufacturer and earns $90,000 annually. He was just transferred to a new city, where he purchased a condominium downtown. Bob drives a new Maxima and enjoys the world of investments. For almost ten years, he has been investing every month in both company stock and various aggressive-growth mutual funds through his 401(k) retirement account at work. His 401(k) has grown to $110,000 with annual rates of returns ranging from minus 6 to a positive 19 percent. In addition, Bob actively trades securities in a separate brokerage account at Merrill Lynch, where his best friend, Mike, works as a broker. That account has grown from $10,000 to a balance of $60,000. Bob uses market orders to trade between $5000 and $10,000 at least once a month, trying to profit on the ups and downs of high-tech and biotechnology stocks in the market. His trading so far this year has resulted in about $3000 in profits and $7000 in losses, primarily because of some trades he has executed using the technique of selling short.

What would you recommend to Bob on the subject of buying and selling securities regarding:

1. Retaining his account with his long-time broker or opening an account at a general brokerage firm, opening an account at a discount brokerage firm, or doing both?

2. Using a limit order rather than a market order when buying and selling stocks?

3. Deciding whether to purchase mutual funds outside of his 401(k) retirement program?

4. Using beta values to help estimate the required rate of return on an investment given its risk?

5. Reporting his gains and losses in securities transactions on his income taxes?

6. Using selling short as a trading technique?

The actual process of buying and selling securities is rather simple. It takes only a quick telephone call to a brokerage firm or a mutual fund company. Most transactions can be carried out via telephone, Internet, or mail. A **brokerage firm** specializes in facilitating the purchase and sale of negotiable securities, such as stocks, bonds, and mutual fund shares. Although you must become familiar with a lot of technical information, new terms, and symbols to participate in this market, the buying and selling process itself is quite straightforward. Unfortunately, the information available about buying and selling investments can prove overwhelming, confusing, and sometimes contradictory, but you will soon learn enough to be able to identify the most credible sources. In addition, you will learn how to estimate the potential rate of return on an investment. This step is important because you have little incentive to make an investment if you do not have some confidence (i.e., numbers) indicating that it is a smart move to go forward and invest your money.

This chapter opens with an examination of how the securities markets operate. It includes lots of investing terms heard everyday on television, like "Dow Jones" and "S&P 500." Next come suggestions on choosing a brokerage firm (or two) to execute your buying and selling transactions. The various ways in which trades can be executed are discussed as well—an important consideration because some techniques can help you avoid a loss as well as lock in your profits. This discussion is followed by an overview of how to read newspaper quotations for stocks, bonds, and mutual funds. We then turn to the very heart of investing: obtaining and using investment information so that you can make the best investments for yourself. You will learn how to determine whether an investment has a sufficient potential rate of return, which will allow you to invest your money in what you think is the best option given your investment philosophy and personal circumstances. The chapter closes with an overview of the trading techniques of buying on margin and selling short.

Golden Rules of

Buying and Selling Securities

Financial success comes from learning the Golden Rules of personal finance and then putting what you have learned into practice. Make the following your money habits in buying and selling securities:

1. Use a discount broker to pay the lowest brokerage fees on securities transactions.
2. When trading stocks, use limit and stop orders to protect your profits and reduce your losses.
3. Stay abreast of general economic conditions and financial news so you can use that information to your advantage when buying and selling securities.
4. Use on-line investment screening software and portfolio tracking services to help make good buying and selling decisions.
5. Before putting money in an investment, always calculate your required rate of return given its risk as well as the investment's potential rate of return.
6. Do not engage in the risky practices of day trading, short selling, and margin buying with any portion of your portfolio unless you have an aggressive investment philosophy.

Securities Markets and Brokerage Firms

1 Describe how stocks are bought and sold and how to select a brokerage firm.

Securities markets exist for businesses to raise capital and arrange for investors the buying and selling of stocks and bonds. Individual securities are bought and sold in primary and secondary markets. A **primary market** exists anywhere issuers and buyers of new offerings of stocks and bonds are brought together. For example, when Linda Webtek sold the original shares in Running Paws Cat Food Company to her three friends, the primary market was her living room. A **secondary market** (also called an **aftermarket**) is where the trading of previously purchased securities takes place. Aftermarkets include organized stock exchanges and over-the-counter markets as discussed below. The activities of securities markets are regulated by various government agencies and self-regulated by the securities industry itself.

Primary Markets

In the primary markets, companies that need capital to begin or expand their operations sell new issues of stocks, bonds, or both to the investing public. New issues of stock are referred to as **initial public offerings (IPOs).** A firm's later capital needs may be financed by reinvesting corporate profits or by selling additional new stock issues or bonds. **Investment banking firms** serve as intermediaries between companies issuing new stocks and bonds and the investing public in the primary markets.

For example, assume that Running Paws, now a successful small corporation, wants to sell its products nationally. The owners have calculated that they will need about $5 million to fund this expansion. After careful analysis, they estimate that the per-share market value of their new 100,000 shares of stock will be approximately $25. (The remainder of the needed funds will be raised by issuing long-term bonds and by taking money out of profits.) The investment banker negotiates a purchase price—perhaps

$24 per share—after assessing the likely marketability of the stock and the expenses anticipated in selling it. The $1 difference between the purchase price and the expected resale price represents the potential profit for both the investment banker and the brokerage firm that eventually sells the stock to the investing public. When negotiations are complete, the investment banker publicly announces the availability of the stock as of a certain date. The investment banker sells blocks of shares to brokerage firms, which in this example will pay $24.50 per share, thus earning $0.50 per share for the investment banker. When the shares are sold to the investing public for $25, the other $0.50 represents the brokerage firms' per-share profit. Brokerage firms charge investors no sales commissions on the sale of new securities. Figure 16.1 illustrates this flow of stocks and bonds in the primary markets.

Secondary Markets

You can buy or sell securities through a stockbroker who works for a brokerage firm that has access to the securities markets. A **stockbroker** (also known as an **account executive**) is licensed to buy and sell securities on behalf of the brokerage firm's clients. Put succinctly, stockbrokers arrange the transactions between buyers and sellers, for which they generally collect a commission on each purchase or sale of securities. In addition, they provide investors with investment advice and information. As a matter of convenience and to facilitate resale, most investors prefer to leave securities certificates in the name of their brokerage firm rather than to take physical possession themselves. Securities certificates kept in the brokerage firm's name instead of the name of the individual investor are known as the security's **street name.**

Brokers have a duty to assess each client's suitability for particular investments. They must also disclose when they are selling securities owned by the firm for which they work. Figure 16.2 shows the flow of stocks, bonds, and other securities in secondary markets. Note that the issuing corporations are no longer involved in any of the transactions.

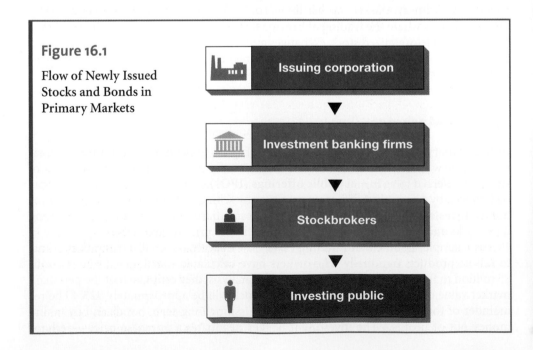

Figure 16.1

Flow of Newly Issued Stocks and Bonds in Primary Markets

Issuing corporation

Investment banking firms

Stockbrokers

Investing public

Figure 16.2

Flow of Previously
Issued Securities in
Secondary Markets

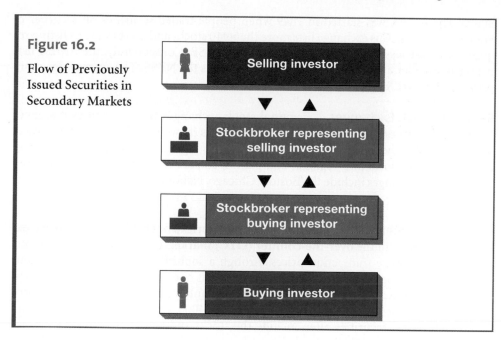

Organized Stock Exchanges

An **organized stock exchange** (or **stock market**) is a market where agents of buyers
and sellers bring together supply and demand for securities. Each exchange trades only
listed securities. Securities with this designation have been approved by the exchange
for sale on its trading floor. The issuing companies must have met various criteria regarding number of stockholders, numbers of shares owned by the public (outstanding
shares), market value of each share, and corporate earnings and assets. These minimum
requirements provide some assurance to investors that the stocks traded have been issued by reputable companies. Companies may be delisted if they fail to meet the minimum requirements at a later date. Note that the same stocks can be sold on more than
one exchange.

Only brokerage firms that are members of each stock exchange can trade securities
on the trading floor of the exchange. These **member firms** have purchased a seat on the
exchange, which gives them the legal right to buy and sell securities on the exchange.
The New York Stock Exchange contains 1366 seats (a fixed number), and large brokerage firms own multiple seats on the exchange.

New York Stock Exchange.   Founded in 1792, the New York Stock Exchange (NYSE),
also known as the "Big Board," is by far the largest exchange in the world and has the
most stringent requirements for listing a security. Corporations must have minimum
earnings of $2.5 million before taxes, net assets of at least $16 million, a minimum of
1.2 million shares publicly held, a market value of outstanding stocks of no less than
$18 million, and a minimum of 2000 shareholders owning at least 100 shares each to be
listed. The more than 3250 stocks offered by the approximately 2750 companies on the
NYSE account for about three-quarters of the market value of all listed stocks on the
various exchanges. The average price per share on the NYSE is $33.

American Stock Exchange.   The American Stock Exchange, popularly referred to
as Amex and also located in New York City, is the second-largest exchange in the United

States. The AMEX was started in 1849 when people traded securities on a corner of Wall Street. Today, this exchange lists more than 940 stocks and 260 bonds. Its listing requirements are less stringent than those of the NYSE. Consequently, the AMEX lists primarily smaller and younger companies than does the NYSE. The average per-share price on the AMEX is $24.

Regional Stock Exchanges.

Regional stock exchanges trade securities mainly of interest to investors living in certain geographic areas (as well as other securities). Many stocks listed on the NYSE are also listed on some regional exchanges to encourage more trading of local and regional companies; smaller firms are listed as well. Regional stock exchanges include the Boston, Chicago, National, Pacific, and Philadelphia stock exchanges.

Over-the-Counter Market.

Publicly traded securities not sold on an organized exchange are traded in the **over-the-counter (OTC) market.** In the OTC market, buyers and sellers negotiate transaction prices through a sophisticated telecommunications network connecting brokerage firms. This network is operated by the National Association of Securities Dealers (NASD). Its **NASDAQ** automated quotations system provides prices on securities offered by more than 4000 small domestic and foreign companies. These securities often include the stocks and bonds of firms that do not have many shares outstanding and do not have much trading interest. A number of large companies are also listed in the OTC market, however. No central exchange floor for the OTC transactions exists; instead, trades are accomplished via computer. The OTC market has few listing requirements, and the price per share for a typical OTC stock is $11.

In an OTC sale, a stockbroker at a brokerage firm representing a buyer communicates with another brokerage firm that has the desired securities. The second brokerage firm is more accurately known as a **broker/dealer** because, in addition to offering the usual brokerage services, it can "make a market" for one or more securities. That is, broker/dealers both buy and sell securities. **Market making** occurs when a broker/dealer attempts to provide a continuous market by maintaining an inventory of specific securities to sell to other brokerage firms and stands ready to buy reasonable quantities of the same securities at market prices. To avoid potential conflicts of interest with a client, when a stockbroker sells securities in which the brokerage firm has made a market, the buying investor must be informed of that fact.

The transaction price is negotiated because two prices are involved. The **bid price** is the highest price anyone has declared that he or she wants to pay for a security. Thus, it represents the amount a brokerage firm is willing to pay for a particular security. The **asked price** is the lowest price anyone will accept at that time for a particular security. Thus, it represents the amount for which another brokerage firm is willing to sell a particular security. The **spread** represents the difference between the bid price, at which a broker/dealer will buy shares, and the higher asked price, at which the broker/dealer will sell shares. The spread can be as little as 5 cents per share, but it can range from 10 to 20 cents for OTC stocks. In addition to paying the asked price, the investor typically pays a nominal sales commission to his or her own stockbroker for executing the transaction.

Electronic Communications Networks.

Today, the traditional organized stock markets are being challenged by competition from **electronic communications networks (ECNs).** The ECNs eliminate the need for most middlemen from transactions. Their computers simply look for matching buy and sell orders and execute the trades. Popular ECNs include Island and Instinet. They act much like an eBay for stocks.

Did You Know? . . .

About Securities Markets Regulation

Public trust is vital to the success of the securities industry; without it, consumers will not invest. Securities markets regulation aims to provide investors with accurate and reliable information about securities, maintain ethical standards, and prevent fraud against investors. This regulation occurs at four levels.

First, individual brokerage firms have established standards of conduct for brokers that govern how they deal with investors.

Second, the New York Stock Exchange, the National Association of Securities Dealers, and other self-regulatory organizations enforce standards of conduct for their members and their member organizations. They dictate rules for listing and for trading securities.

Third, the Securities and Exchange Commission (SEC), a federal government agency, focuses on ensuring disclosure of information about securities to the investing public and on approving the rules and regulations employed by the organized securities exchanges. The SEC requires registration of listed securities with appropriate and updated information. It also prohibits manipulative practices, such as using insider information for illegal personal gain or causing the price of a security to rise or fall for false reasons. In addition, all states require registration of securities sold within their states. Note that state governments also regulate the securities industry.

Fourth, the U.S. Congress decides when investors need more laws or regulatory organizations. For example, Congress created a limited insurance program to protect the investing public. Although investment losses are not covered, the Security Investors Protection Corporation (SIPC) protects investors when an SEC-registered brokerage firm goes bankrupt. Each of an investor's accounts at a brokerage firm is protected against financial loss as a result of unreturned securities and cash up to a total of $500,000, but no more than $100,000 in cash.

How to Select a Brokerage Firm

To trade securities, you will need a brokerage firm to act as your agent. You can open an account at a full-service general brokerage firm or a discount brokerage firm. Each charges a commission for any trading it conducts on your behalf. You should make clear to the brokerage firm, in writing, your investment objectives and your desired level of risk. You can open an account rather easily at any brokerage firm. A **cash account** requires an initial deposit (perhaps as little as $100) and specifies that full settlement is due to the brokerage firm within three business days after a buy or sell order has been given. After each transaction occurs, your account is debited or credited and written confirmation is immediately forwarded to you.

Full-Service General Brokerage Firms.   A traditional **general brokerage firm** typically offers a full range of services to customers. It generally provides a company investment newsletter that discusses general economic trends and offers investment recommendations and periodic reports that cover particular market trends and industries. In addition, a general brokerage firm offers short, succinct research analyses on hundreds of individual companies (available to customers just for the asking) and the personal advice and attention of one of the thousands of stockbrokers working for the firm.

The philosophy of general brokerage firms, such as Merrill Lynch or Smith Barney, is to provide personal investment advice. These firms maintain up-to-the-minute contact with the investment world through electronic equipment, including a **quotation**

board. This electronic display reports all security transactions on the major exchanges as they occur. General brokerage firms also subscribe to valuable news wire services that can keep them and their customers apprised of world news affecting particular investments. The interested investor may obtain price quotations on securities over the telephone or via the Internet. Investors receive monthly statements summarizing all of the transactions in their account and commissions, dividends, and interest.

Broker's Commissions and Fees.   Brokerage firms receive a commission on each securities transaction to cover the direct expenses of executing the transaction and other overhead expenses. Most firms have established fee schedules that they use when dealing with any except the largest investors. These fees reflect a commission rate that declines as the total value of the transaction increases. For example, in lieu of a minimum commission charge of $25, a brokerage firm might charge 2.8 percent on a transaction amounting to less than $800, 1.8 percent on transactions between $800 and $2500, 1.6 percent on amounts between $2500 and $5000, and 1.2 percent on amounts exceeding $5000.

Transaction costs are based on sales of **round lots,** which are standard units of trading of 100 shares of stock and $1000 or $5000 par value for bonds. **Odd lots** comprise transactions of any number of shares that is less than its normal trading unit. When brokerage firms buy or sell shares in odd lots, they may charge a fee of 12.5 cents (called an **eighth**) per share on the odd-lot portion of the transaction, which is called the **differential.**

The payment of commissions can quickly reduce the return on any investment. A purchase commission of 2 percent added to a sales commission of another 2 percent, for example, means that the investor must earn a 4 percent yield just to pay the transaction costs. Broker's commissions typically range from $10 to 3 percent of the value of the transaction. The easiest way to hold down investing costs is to find a brokerage firm that charges low commissions.

Discount Brokers.   Many investors use **discount brokers** because they charge commissions to execute trades that are about 40 to 60 percent less than the fees charged by full-service brokers. These brokers feature low commissions because they provide limited services to customers. That is, they focus on a single function: efficiently executing orders to buy and sell securities and mutual funds. Discount brokerage firms do not typically conduct research or provide specific investment advice to customers. Transactions can be completed on-line as well as via a toll-free telephone number, where the investor can also obtain price quotes, check the status of his or her accounts, and transfer funds. Discounters include Quick & Reilly, Ameritrade, Scottrade, E*Trade, Share-Builder, and BUYandHOLD.

Day Trading.   The advent of on-line discount brokers, especially those with on-line accounts, has reduced the cost of executing trades to perhaps $10 for many transactions. **Day trading** occurs when an investor buys and sells stocks quickly throughout the day with the hope that the price will move enough to cover transaction costs and earn some profits. It is a risky practice, however. Some day traders sell stocks short by borrowing shares from brokers with the hope that prices will decline so they can buy them back to give to the broker. Day trading is not a wise choice for long-term investors. As one of billionaire Warren Buffett's commandments for getting ahead in business and in life states, "You will lose money if you trade stocks actively."

Advice from an Expert

Check Your Stockbroker's Background

You can check the background of a stockbroker or a brokerage firm by filling out an information request form provided by the National Association of Securities Dealers (www.nasdr.com). The NASD will then inform you whether a securities firm or any of its employees have been subject to disciplinary proceedings.

   Every year some investors neglect to investigate a stockbroker and lose money as a result. Sometimes the broker absconds with the investor's funds; at other times the investor receives really poor advice. Don't let it happen to you!

Allen Martin
California State University–Northridge

Ordering Securities Transactions and Reading Newspaper Price Quotations

2 Explain how to order securities transactions and read newspaper price quotations for stocks, bonds, and mutual funds.

Hundreds of millions of shares of stocks, bonds, and mutual funds may be traded daily on the stock markets in the United States. Every trade brings together a buyer and a seller to complete the transaction at a given price. In the actual transaction to buy or sell securities, brokers match or negotiate the final price. Sellers of stocks can place a market order, a limit order, or a stop order, and time limits for making a deal can be established to help the investor reduce losses and protect gains in securities transactions. Corporate bonds and mutual funds may be purchased or sold through a brokerage firm, although most investors buy and sell no-load mutual funds directly from the fund companies.

The Process of Trading Stocks

To illustrate the process of trading stocks, assume you instruct brokerage firm A to purchase a certain number of shares at a specific price. The firm relays the buy order to its representative, who coordinates trading. Because the brokerage firm has a seat on the exchange, the buy order is then given to the brokerage firm's contact person at the exchange—a **floor broker.** This broker contacts a **specialist,** a person on the floor of the exchange who handles trades of that particular stock in an effort to maintain a fair and orderly market. The buy order is then filled, either by taking shares from the specialist's own inventory or by matching it with another investor's sell order.

Matching or Negotiating Stock Prices

On the organized exchanges, a match must occur between the stock buyer's price and the seller's price for a sale to take place. Therefore, a specialist could hold a specific order for a few minutes, a few hours, or even a week before making a match. With actively traded issues, a transaction normally is completed in just a few minutes. A slower-selling security can be traded more quickly if an investor is willing to accept the current market price (as discussed below).

In the over-the-counter market, the bid and asked prices represent negotiation of a stock's final price. If a buyer does not want to pay the asking price, he or she instructs the stockbroker to offer a lower bid price, which may or may not be accepted. If it is refused, the buyer might cancel the first order and raise the bid slightly in a second order in the hope that the owner will sell the shares at that price. Otherwise, the buyer may have to pay the full, asked price to complete the deal. Generally, OTC trades occur at prices somewhere between the bid and asked figures.

Types of Stock Orders

Basically, only two types of orders exist—buy and sell. The stockbroker will buy or sell securities according to prescribed instructions in a process called executing an order. Those instructions can place constraints on the prices at which those orders are carried out.

Market Order.   A **market order** instructs the stockbroker to execute an order at the prevailing market price—that is, the current selling price of the stock. A stockbroker can generally conduct the desired transaction within a few minutes. In reality, the floor broker tries to match the instructions from many investors with the narrow range of prices available from the specialist. Traders on the floor of the stock market typically shout and signal back and forth as part of this effort to match buyers and sellers. Most trades are market orders.

Limit Order.   A **limit order** instructs the stockbroker to buy or sell a stock at a specific price. It may include instructions to buy at the best possible price but not above a specified limit, or to sell at the best possible price but not below a specified limit. A limit order provides some protection against buying a security at a price higher than desired or selling at a price deemed too low. The stockbroker transmits the limit order to the specialist. The order is executed if and when the specified price (or better) is reached and all other previously received orders on the specialist's book have been considered.

A disadvantage for a buyer who places a limit order is that the investor might miss an excellent opportunity. For example, assume that you place a limit order with your stockbroker to buy 100 shares of Running Paws common stock at $60.50 or lower. You have read in the newspaper that the stock has recently been selling at $61 and $61.25, and you hope to save $0.50 to $1.00 on each share. On that same day, the company announces publicly that it plans to expand into the dog food area for the first time. Investor confidence in the new sales effort pushes the price up to 70. If you had given your stockbroker a market order instead, you would have purchased 100 shares of Running Paws at perhaps $61.50, which would have given you an immediate profit of $850 ($70 − $61.50 = $8.50; $8.50 × 100 shares = $850) on an initial investment of $6150 ($61.50 × 100).

A disadvantage for a seller placing a limit order is that it could result in no sale if the price drops because of negative news. Assume that you bought stock at 50 that is currently selling at 58 and that you have placed a limit order to sell at a price of no less than 60 so as to take your profit. The price could creep up to 59 and then fall back to 48, however. In this event, you did not sell the securities because the limit order was priced too high, and they are now worth less than what you originally paid for them. A limit order is best used when you expect great fluctuations in the price of a stock and when you buy or sell infrequently traded securities on the over-the-counter market. Limit orders account for about 35 percent of all trades.

Stop Order.   A **stop order** instructs a stockbroker to sell your shares of stock at the market price if a stock declines to or goes below a specified price. It is often called a **stop-loss order** because the investor uses it to protect against a sharp drop in price and thus to stop a loss. The specialist executes the order as soon as the stop-order price is reached and a buyer is matched at the next market price.

As an example of how to stop a loss, assume that you bought 100 shares of Running Paws stock at $70. You are nervous about the company's entry into the competitive dog food business, however, and you fear that it might lose money. As a consequence, you place a stop order to sell your shares if the price drops to $56, thereby limiting your potential loss to 20 percent ($70 − $56 = $14; $14 ÷ $70 = 0.20). Some months later, you read in the financial section of your newspaper that even after six months Running Paws still has less than 1 percent of the dog food market. You call your stockbroker, who informs you that the price of Running Paws stock dropped drastically in response to the article, which was published in the previous day's *Wall Street Journal*. The broker reports that all of your shares were sold at $55, that the current price is $49, and that the sales transaction notice is already in the mail to your home. The stop order cut your losses to slightly more than 20 percent ($70 − $55 = $15; $15 ÷ $70 = 21.4 percent) and saved an additional loss of $6 ($55 − $49) per share. Thus, the stop order reduced your loss to $1500 [(100 × $70 = $7000) − (100 × $55 = $5500)] instead of $2100 [(100 × $70 = $7000) − (100 × $49 = $4900)].

You can use a stop order to protect your profits, too. Assume that you bought 100 shares of Alpo Dog Food Company at $60 per share, which now has a current selling price of $75. Your paper profit is $1500 ($75 − $60 = $15; $15 × 100 shares = $1500), less commissions. To protect part of that profit, you place a stop order with your stockbroker to sell at $65 if the price drops that low. If your stock is sold, you will realize a real profit of $500 ($65 − $60 = $5; $5 × 100 shares = $500). If Alpo Dog Food stock climbs in price instead, perhaps in response to the bad news about Running Paws, the stop order would have cost you nothing. If the price does climb, you might replace the stop order with one having a higher price to lock in an even greater amount of profit.

Time Limits.   Investors have several ways to place time limits on their orders to buy or sell stocks. A **fill-or-kill order** instructs the stockbroker to buy or sell the stock at the market price immediately or else cancel the order. A **day order** is valid only for the remainder of the trading day during which it was given to the brokerage firm. Unless otherwise indicated, any order received by a stockbroker is assumed to be a day order. A **week order** remains valid until the close of trading on Friday of the current week. A **month order** is effective until the close of trading on the last business day of the current month. An **open order,** also called a **good-til-canceled (GTC) order,** remains valid until executed by the stockbroker or canceled by the investor. If you give an order longer than a week in duration, you must carefully monitor events and then alter the order if the situation changes substantially.

Buying and Selling Mutual Funds

You can purchase shares in a mutual fund by ordering them via telephone, mail, online, or electronic funds transfer and then paying for them. People generally invest in no-load shares by buying them directly from a mutual fund company; they invest in load shares by purchasing them through a brokerage firm or financial planner. No-load funds typically do not assess any transaction costs, whereas purchases made through a financial planner or a brokerage firm are likely to include a sales commission (a load). The firm mails out a written confirmation for each transaction after receipt of an invested amount. On the statement, ownership of fractional shares is measured to three decimal points.

Many of the millions of Americans who own mutual funds purchase them through their retirement plans, such as individual retirement accounts (IRAs) and 401(k) plans. It is very easy to open and set up a tax-deferred retirement account through a mutual fund company.

Reading Newspaper Price Quotations

The millions of daily buying and selling transactions involving stocks, bonds, and mutual funds on secondary markets are summarized in *The Wall Street Journal,* the most widely read financial newspaper in the United States. Also, many daily newspapers publish abbreviated information. Most security prices are quoted and traded to two decimal points. Illustrative newspaper quotations are shown next for stocks, bonds, and mutual funds.

Stock Quotations.   Figure 16.3 shows price quotations for stocks being traded on the New York Stock Exchange. Examine the listing for Wal-Mart, a retailer.

Column 1: YTD % Change. The numbers in this column report the "year to date (YTD) as a percentage" change in the price (+8.6%) of Wal-Mart stock since January 1 of the present calendar year.

Columns 2 and 3: 52 Weeks, High and Low. This column shows that Wal-Mart stock traded at a high price of $63.08 and a low price of $41.50 during the previous 52 weeks, not including the previous trading day.

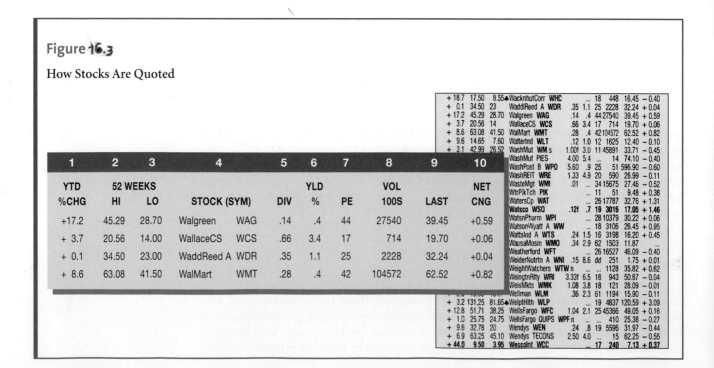

Figure 16.3

How Stocks Are Quoted

1	2	3	4		5	6	7	8	9	10
YTD	52 WEEKS					YLD		VOL		NET
%CHG	HI	LO	STOCK (SYM)		DIV	%	PE	100S	LAST	CNG
+17.2	45.29	28.70	Walgreen	WAG	.14	.4	44	27540	39.45	+0.59
+ 3.7	20.56	14.00	WallaceCS	WCS	.66	3.4	17	714	19.70	+0.06
+ 0.1	34.50	23.00	WaddReed A	WDR	.35	1.1	25	2228	32.24	+0.04
+ 8.6	63.08	41.50	WalMart	WMT	.28	.4	42	104572	62.52	+0.82

Column 4: Stock and Sym. This column gives the name of the stock (Wal-Mart in this example) and its abbreviated trading symbol (WMT).

Column 5: Div. The dividend amount is based on the last quarterly declaration by the company. For example, Wal-Mart last paid a quarterly dividend that, when converted to an annual basis, amounts to an estimated $0.28 annual dividend.

Column 6: Yld %. The figure in this column represents the yield as a percentage of a dividend income, calculated by dividing the current price of the stock into the most recent estimated dividend. The yield of the Wal-Mart stock is 0.04 percent.

Column 7: PE. This figure provides the price/earnings ratio based on the current price. The earnings figure used to calculate the price is not published in the newspaper but is the latest available. When Wal-Mart's "last" or closing price of $62.52 is divided by earnings, it gives a P/E ratio of 42.

Column 8: Vol 100s. This figure indicates the total volume of trading activity for the stock measured in hundreds of shares. Thus, 10,457,200 shares of Wal-Mart were traded on that day.

Column 9: Last. The price of the last trade of the day before the market closed for Wal-Mart was $62.52.

Column 10: Net Chg. The net change, +$0.82, represents the difference between the closing price (last) on this day and the closing price of the previous trading day. Today's Wal-Mart closing (last) price of $62.52 was up $0.82 from the previous closing price, which must have been $61.70.

Bond Quotations.   Unlike stocks and mutual funds, which are priced in decimals or dollars and cents, most bonds follow the traditional pricing scheme and are quoted in fractions of sixteenths, where each sixteenth represents 6.25 cents. The first line in Figure 16.4 shows corporate bond quotations for one issue of a bond (a bond that matures in 2024 and has a coupon rate of 8⅛, which is $8.125 when converted to decimals) by the AT&T Corporation for a particular week. The current yield is 8.2 percent and $86,000 worth of bonds traded that week. The last trade before the market closed on the previous trading day was at $99⅝ ($99.625), representing a net change of minus 1, or down $1.00 from the previous closing price, which must have been $100⅝, or $100.625.

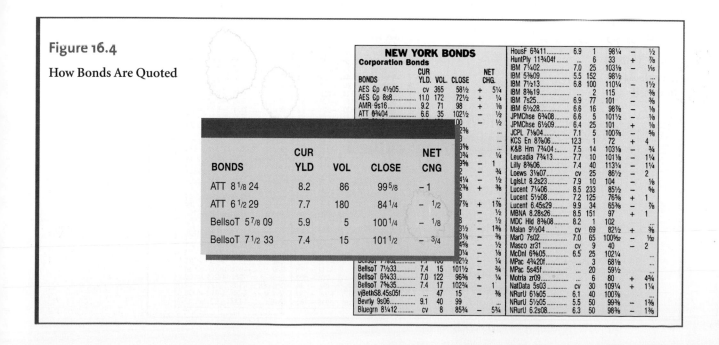

Figure 16.4

How Bonds Are Quoted

Mutual Fund Quotations.   Newspapers' quotations for no-load mutual funds list the name of the fund (see Figure 16.5) followed by columns for its net asset value, net change from the previous day, and year-to-date percentage return. For example, within the group listing for Fidelity Investments mutual funds, the Balanced Fund (abbreviated as Balanc) has a net asset value (NAV) of $15.14, had a change in the net asset value (NET CHG) of −$0.20 from the closing price of the previous trading day, and has a year-to-date percentage return (YTD %RET) of 1.1 percent. In mutual funds, the NAV is also known as the **mutual fund bid price.** Shareholders receive this amount per share when they cash in (**redeem**) their shares—that is, the company is willing to pay this amount to buy the shares back. Also, the NAV is the amount per share an investor will pay to purchase a fund, assuming it is a no-load fund. A no-load fund is indicated as such by the alphabetic letter "n" at the end of the fund's name.

The **mutual fund asked price** (or **offer price**) is the price at which a mutual fund's share can be purchased by investors. It equals the current NAV per share plus sales charges, if any. If you wanted to buy or sell shares of Fidelity Balanced Fund, a no-load (note the superscript "n" in Figure 16.5) mutual fund, the price would be $15.14 per share. The funds listed without "n" are load funds. The SEC requires that appropriate footnotes appear in newspaper listings of mutual funds to indicate other expenses and charges.

---

3 Understand how to obtain and use investment information.

Obtaining and Using Investment Information

To reduce investment risks and increase returns, the wise investor seeks out and utilizes information on securities market indexes, general economic conditions reported in the financial news, facts about industry trends, and specific details about individual companies and funds. The vast amounts of information available on-line can seem overwhelming. Nevertheless, by following up your own ideas with good research, you can

---

Figure 16.5

How Mutual Funds Are Quoted

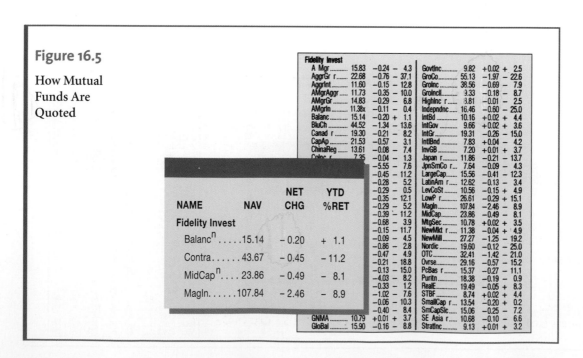

succeed in building a portfolio of common stocks, bonds, mutual funds, and other investments that is superior to a portfolio created by simply relying on suggestions and tips from stockbrokers, friends, and family members. Indeed, individual investors often enjoy an edge over the more than 20,000 professional analysts working for large institutions, such as mutual funds and pension funds. Individual investors can change the mix in their portfolios very quickly, and they have more choices than professionals who trade big blocks of securities.

If you like the idea of getting together with other small investors by forming an investment club, contact the National Association of Investors Corporation (www.better investing.org) to find a club located nearby.

Securities Market Indexes

Securities market indexes measure the average value of a number of securities chosen as a sample to reflect the behavior of a more general market. Investors use such indexes to determine trends that might guide them in investment decisions because short-run price movements may or may not be important compared with longer-term situations. Ideally, for example, an investor would buy low and sell high. The most popular indexes are described in the following paragraphs.

Dow Jones Averages.   The Dow Jones Industrial Average (DJIA) is the most widely reported of all indexes, having been used continuously since 1884. In determining the DJIA, the prices of only 30 actively traded blue-chip stocks are followed. These stocks include well-known companies such as American Express, AT&T, Caterpillar, Citigroup, Coca-Cola, General Motors, Hewlett-Packard, Home Depot, Wal-Mart, and Walt Disney. When an evening newscast reports that "the Dow rose 110 points today in heavy trading," you should realize that these "points" are changes in the index, not actual dollar changes in the value of the stocks. The average is calculated by adding the closing prices of the 30 stocks and dividing by a number adjusted for splits, spin-offs, and dividends. The index has long served as a popular barometer of the national economic trend and the daily activity of securities traded on the New York Stock Exchange, even though it is not truly representative of the overall broader market. Dow Jones also publishes a number of other indexes (for example, transportation, utilities, and composite indexes).

Standard & Poor's Indexes.   The popular Standard & Poor's (S&P) 500 index reports price movements of 500 stocks of large, established, publicly traded firms It includes stocks of 400 industrial firms, 40 financial institutions, 40 public utilities, and 20 transportation companies. Although not as widely reported as the DJIA, the S&P 500 more accurately reflects daily transactions of the investing public thanks to its greater breadth of representation. Companies with the highest market values influence the index the most. Standard and Poor's also publishes a number of other indexes (for example, financial, public utility, mid-cap, and small-cap indexes).

New York Stock Exchange Composite.   This index includes all stocks traded on the NYSE. Consequently, it provides a comprehensive measure of the price movements and value changes of those stocks.

NASDAQ Composite Index.   The NASDAQ Composite Index takes into account virtually all U.S. stocks (about 8000) traded in the over-the-counter market in the automated quotations system operated by the National Association of Securities Dealers.

As a consequence, it provides a measure of companies not as popular or as large in size as those traded on the NYSE. The index assesses the price behavior of many smaller, more speculative companies, although some big companies (such as Cisco Systems, Intel, and Microsoft) are listed as well. The NASDAQ is technology and biomedical oriented.

Wilshire 5000 Index.   The Wilshire 5000 index represents the total market value (trillions of dollars) of the more than 6500 most actively traded stocks.

Nikkei Dow.   Japan's best-known barometer of stock prices represents the activity of 300 stocks. Because this market is open at night in the United States, U.S. investors often check the Nikkei Dow in the morning to gain a hint of what might happen that day in the U.S. stock market. Other major stock exchanges exist in many other countries (for example, Canada, Germany, and the United Kingdom).

General Economic Conditions and Financial News

A little reading on a regular basis will keep you abreast of general economic conditions. You can then use that information to your advantage when buying and selling securities. You need to know the stage of the business cycle (recession or prosperity), identify the current interest and inflation rates, and possess an understanding of how economic conditions are likely to change over the next 12 to 18 months. (These topics were examined in Chapters 1 and 13.)

You can stay abreast of economic conditions by checking the Bloomberg, Investorama, Kiplinger, Morningstar, NewsHub, and Quicken websites. Also, check the "business" and "economics" sections of some major search engines (for example, Yahoo!, Google, Momma, QueryServerMetaGopher) and investment-oriented sites (for example, those associated with the publications *Business Week, Money,* and *Worth*).

Also consider checking the websites of *USA Today,* a national newspaper, or a big-city newspaper like the *Los Angeles Times, New York Times,* or *Washington Post.* You can also obtain economic news from *The Wall Street Journal, Barron's,* or *Investor's Business Daily (IBD),* three popular financial newspapers, as well as *Business Week, Fortune, Forbes, Financial World, U.S. News & World Report, Money,* and *Kiplinger's Personal Finance Magazine.* You may subscribe to the on-line editions, which are priced lower than standard subscriptions.

Facts About Industry Trends

The current prices of individual companies' securities are often affected by the performance of their industry as a whole. Economic events can significantly influence entire industries, such as aerospace, apparel, automobiles, beverages, chemicals, construction, electronics, finance, foods, machinery, metals, and pharmaceuticals; they may even depress the stock of a very profitable company. "For example," says Phil Edwards from Standard & Poor's, "if you believe that JCPenney is a fundamentally strong company whose stock price is negatively affected by a short-term trend in retail sales, then that should create a buying opportunity for the investor." Table 16.1 illustrates profitability data for selected industries.

Studying industries of interest to you will help you make intelligent buying and selling decisions. Excellent reference sources often found in large libraries include *Business*

Table 16.1 10 Best-Performing and 10 Worst-Performing Industries
(From multiple industry sources.)

10 Best-Performing Industries

Industry Name	Percent Change
Consumer Electronics	+383
Home Construction	+208
Coal	+172
Marine Transport	+131
Water Utilities	+116
Casinos (US)	+115
Advance Medical Supplies	+115
Oil Companies, Secondary	+104
Factory Equipment	+91
Savings & Loans	+75

10 Worst-Performing Industries

Industry Name	Percent Change
Tires	−77
Fixed-Line Communications	67
Auto Parts & Tires	−67
Telecommunications	−65
Airlines	−56
Communications Technology	−54
Electric Components & Equipment	−52
Gas Utilities	−52
Automobile Manufacturers	−51
Office Equipment	−47

Note: The time period selected in September 2004 was for the previous five years.

Week, Value Line Investment Survey (Volume 1), *Standard & Poor's Industry Surveys, Moody's Industry Review,* and the *Wall Street Journal.*

Trade Associations.   A **trade association** is an organization representing the interests of companies in the same industry. For example, the American Council of Life Insurance includes representatives of life insurance companies, and the American Bankers Association represents the interests of the banking industry. In addition to lobbying elected officials to present the views of their members, trade associations gather a tremendous amount of detailed information on the history, current activities, and future prospects of the industry. Although their projections for the future often appear overly optimistic, it is useful to know how an industry views its own prospects.

To contact the trade associations of interest to you, look up their names and addresses in the *Encyclopedia of Associations* (published by Gale Research Company) and *National Trade and Professional Associations* (published by the U.S. Department of Commerce). Both references are available in larger libraries. Look on-line, too.

Industry-Oriented Investment Publications.   Industry information is reported in such publications as *Business Week* and *Forbes* (one issue of *Forbes* analyzes the performance of all major industries each year). You can also spend money subscribing to investment publications and advisory services. Some examples include *Industry*

Surveys and *The Outlook* (published by Standard & Poor's), *Value Line Investment Survey* (Value Line Publishing), *Monthly Economic Letter* (Citibank), and *Industrial Manual* (Moody's). These publications can be found in large libraries (especially at colleges) and in brokerage firms' offices.

Information About Specific Companies and Funds

Investment guru Peter Lynch wisely says that investors should buy only when they have a clear, simple understanding of why the value of their investment is likely to rise. Therefore, before purchasing any securities, you should learn about the company that offers them. You can obtain this information from a number of sources, including the key ones described in this section. In your analysis, focus on the quality of management, the firm's financial stability, the company's earnings stream, and its competitive position. A large number of sources provide on-line price quotes and background reports on stocks and mutual funds, including *Money* magazine, *Kiplinger's Personal Finance Magazine,* and Morningstar.

Annual Reports.   Companies issue an annual report once a year (hence the name). The **annual report** summarizes the firm's financial activities for the year. It includes information on sales, earnings, profit, and legal problems, and it forecasts the company's future. Most annual reports offer analysis on the current economic situation, provide an overview of trends affecting the firm's industry as a whole, and explain the details about any special situations affecting the company in particular. Investors use these reports to compare the company's financial results from recent years and to find out about management's views of the immediate future. Annual reports often speak with an optimistic voice, because the company wants investors to think highly of its prospects. Some especially interesting information—sometimes negative—is often found in the footnotes. To receive an annual report, ask a brokerage firm for this document or obtain it via the Internet.

In addition to an annual report, publicly traded companies are required to publish their financial performance data, such as sales volume and current and projected profits, four times per year.

Prospectuses.   When a company issues any new security, it must file a **prospectus** with the Securities and Exchange Commission. This disclosure describes the experience of the corporation's management, its financial status, any anticipated legal matters that could affect the company, and potential risks of investing in the firm. The language is legalistic and full of technical jargon, but the interested investor can still sift through the details.

Profile Prospectuses.   A **profile prospectus** supplements the lengthier prospectuses required by the SEC that are provided to mutual fund investors. It offers a two- to four-page summary presentation of information contained in a legal prospectus that specifically answers 11 key investor questions (including details about the fund's ten-year performance record). It is written in lay language.

10-K Reports.   Every company registered with the SEC must report many financial particulars by filing a **10-K report** once each year to ensure public availability of accurate, current information about the firm. This comprehensive document contains much of the same type of information as a prospectus or annual report plus updated financial details on corporate activities. You can obtain 10-K reports from the SEC (also available on-line at www.sec.gov) or find them in many college libraries.

Stock, Bond, and Mutual Fund Advisory Services.   You can read about a specific public corporation in the United States in a number of investment ratings publications. Some of the best stock, bond, and mutual fund advisory services are offered by Moody's, Standards & Poor's, and Value Line. These organizations rank and rate the projected future earnings and profitability of corporations in concise reports. For example, a stock report for a corporation typically contains a brief summary description and current outlook, important developments, comparisons with competitors, and tables with financial data going back ten years. Morningstar is an authoritative source for stocks, bond, and mutual funds.

You can find such publications in larger public libraries, college libraries, and the offices of brokerage firms. They are also available on the Internet (see finance.yahoo.com, www.finance.lycos.com, and www.money.cnn.com).

Research Reports.   Basic investment research tries to separate companies that are on the way up financially from those that are heading down. Most brokerage houses have on-staff analysts who write research reports on companies and industries. Although these reports usually recommend that investors buy certain stocks, they rarely suggest selling. Hence, the prudent approach for the individual investor is to interpret research reports' "hold" recommendations as a clear signal to sell. Although the quality of advice is uneven, ranging from brilliant to pedestrian (analysts have a tendency to run with the herd and make similar recommendations), collectively this research is the best conducted on securities investments. Ask your stockbroker which reports can be made available to you.

Extensive Investment Information Is Available On-line

The Internet is a seemingly endless source of up-to-the minute, high-quality information on investments.

Basic Investment Information.   An excellent website for basic investing information is *The Motley Fool* (fool.com). Also see the websites of *Kiplinger's Personal Finance Magazine*, *Money* magazine, and CNNMoney (money.cnn.com). Top sources for stock, bond, and/or mutual fund information include Morningstar (morningstar.com) and Bloomberg (bloomberg.com). Corporate and mutual fund filings that are required by the SEC are available on the Internet from the Electronic Data Gathering and Retrieval (Edgar) project (www.edgar-online.com). You may also use or subscribe to professional advisory services, such as Standard & Poor's Financial Information Services (www.standardandpoors.com) and Value Line (www.valueline.com).

Keeping track of several stock, bond, and mutual fund investments requires careful recordkeeping, particularly for income tax purposes. These tasks can be performed easily using a computer software program available on disk, CD-ROM, or on-line.

On-line Investment Screening.   You can conduct in-depth research on stocks, bonds, and mutual funds by using screening tools available on the Internet. Numerous websites offer dozens of pages of financial data on individual companies—an overwhelming amount of information, in fact. Screening enables you to quickly sift through hundreds of companies to find those that best suit your investment objectives.

Case 2
A Florist Considers Margin and Short Selling

Becky Stiehl, a florist from St. Paul, Minnesota, has a house with a small mortgage, a good life insurance plan for herself and her two children, and several thousand dollars in secure savings accounts. An annuity guarantees her a monthly income of $3800 until her death. Becky recently inherited $190,000 in cash from a relative; the money came from the sale of the deceased's home. Becky has neither a conservative or aggressive investment philosophy. A friend of Becky's, a stockbroker, has recommended that she think about taking on more risk when investing the $190,000.

(a) Approximately what beta would be appropriate for Becky if she invested the $190,000 in the stock market?

(b) Should Becky consider buying stocks on margin? Why or why not?

(c) Becky was puzzled because a friend was elated that the price of a stock had fallen in a short-selling deal. She thought a good deal required that the stock price rise. Explain to her how short selling works.

Financial Math Questions

1. Michael Margolis is a single parent and a motivational training consultant from Kansas City, Missouri. He is wondering about potential returns on investments given certain amounts of risk. Michael recently invested a total of $6000 in three stocks ($2000 in each) with different betas: stock A with a beta of 0.8, stock B with a beta of 1.7, and stock C with a beta of 2.5.

(a) If the stock market rises 12 percent over the next year, what is the likely value of each investment?

(b) If the stock market rises 19 percent over the next year, what is the likely value of each investment?

(c) If the stock market declines 8 percent over the next year, what is the likely value of each investment?

(d) Compare the value of the total portfolio in parts (a) and (c). Would Michael have obtained better results if he owned any one stock? (That is, would a $6000 investment in one stock leave him better off if the market went up or down the next year?)

2. Mary Porterfield, a married mother of three and part-time Mary Kay Cosmetics sales representative from DeKalb, Illinois, is trying to explain to her friend Elizabeth Shrader how to read the newspaper financial data on mutual funds. Mary turned to the financial section of the newspaper and located the data for mutual funds. Using Figure 16.5, help Mary and Elizabeth by responding to the following questions about the Fidelity Investments group of mutual funds:

(a) Assuming that Fidelity Magellan (Magln) has a load of 3 percent, how much would it cost to buy 100 shares?

(b) What would the commission charged be in terms of dollars and as a percentage of the amount invested?

(c) If Elizabeth already owned 100 shares of Magellan, how much would she receive per share if she redeemed them?

(d) If Mary wanted to invest in Fidelity Mid-Cap, a no-load fund, how much would it cost to buy 100 shares?

3. Xiao and Shiao Jing-jian, newlyweds from Kingston, Rhode Island, have decided to begin investing for the future. Xiao is a 7-Eleven store manager, and Shiao is a high school math teacher. The couple intends to take $3000 out of their savings for investment purposes and then continue to invest an additional $200 to $400 per month. Both have a moderate investment philosophy and seek some cash dividends as well as price appreciation.

(a) Calculate the five-year return on the investment choices in the table on page 477. Put your calculations in tabular form like that shown in Table 16.2. (Hint: At the end of the first year, the EPS for Running Paws will be $2.40 with a dividend of $0.66, and the EPS for Eagle Packaging will be $2.76 with a projected dividend of $0.86.)

(b) Using the appropriate P/E ratios, what are the estimated market prices of the Running Paws and Eagle Packaging stocks after five years?

(c) Show your calculations in determining the projected price appreciations for the two stocks over the five years.

(d) Add the projected price appreciation of each stock to its projected cash dividends, and show the total five-year percentage returns for the two stocks.

(e) Determine the average annual dividend for each stock, and use these figures in calculating the approximate compound yields for each.

(f) Assume that the beta is 2.5 for Running Paws and 2.8 for Eagle Packaging. If the market went up 20 percent during the year, what would be the likely stock prices for Running Paws and Eagle Packaging?

(g) Assume that inflation is approximately 4 percent and the return on high-quality, long-term corporate bonds is 8 percent. Given the Jing-jians' investment philosophy, explain why you would recommend (1) Running Paws, (2) Eagle Packaging, or (3) a high-quality, long-term corporate bond as a growth investment. Support your answer by calculating the potential rate of return using the information on page 469 or by using the *Garman/Forgue* website. The Jing-jians are in the 25 percent marginal tax bracket.

	Running Paws	Eagle Packaging
Currrent price	$30.00	$48.00
Current earnings per share (EPS)	$2.00	$2.30
Current quarterly cash dividend	$0.15	$0.18
Current P/E ratio	15	21
Projected earnings annual growth rate	20%	20%
Projected cash divided growth rate	10%	10%

4. Bill Deck, an assistant golf professional from Athens, West Virginia, wants to buy 100 shares of DEF Company stock on margin. Assume that the margin requirement is 50 percent, DEF stock sells for $40 per share, and commissions are ignored.

   (a) How much can Bill borrow?

   (b) If the interest rate is 10 percent per year compounded annually, how much interest will Bill pay if he keeps the position open for one year?

   (c) If Bill sells the stock at the end of the year for $30 per share, how much money will he lose, expressed both in dollars and as a percentage of the amount he invested?

   (d) If Bill sells the stock for $50 per share at the end of one year, what is the amount of his gain, expressed both in dollars and as a percentage of the amount he invested?

5. Celia Alvarez, a physical therapist from Miami, Florida, wants to sell 100 shares of XYZ Company stock short because she believes that its market price will decline during the next month. The XYZ stock currently sells at $30 per share. Assume that the margin rate is 50 percent and ignore commissions.

   (a) How much will the brokerage firm hold in the short sale account?

   (b) If Celia closes the position in one month with the stock priced at $40 per share, how much will she lose, expressed both in dollars and as a percentage of the amount she invested?

   (c) If Celia's forecast is right and the price drops to $25 per share, how much will she gain, expressed both in dollars and as a percentage of the amount she invested?

Money Matters Continuing Cases

The Hernandez Family Has Some Investment Questions

In recent years, the Hernandezes have been saving with an eye toward retirement. Victor and Maria currently plan to retire in eight years. Through payroll deductions, Victor now has $25,000 saved at his credit union. Maria has put away $10,000 from her part-time employment. These amounts are in addition to Victor's investments through the retirement plan offered by his employer. Thinking that the past performance of various industries might be a fairly good predictor of earnings in the future, the couple has sought your advice on where they might invest their funds. The Hernandezes expect to sell some of the investments immediately after their retirement begins to have money for living expenses.

1. Suggest to the Hernandezes three industries that have enjoyed successful earnings in recent years (see Table 16.1).

2. Give your opinion on why those industries might be successful in the future decade.

3. Briefly tell the Hernandezes how and when to obtain information about those industries and particular companies.

4. If their $35,000 investment earns an annual return of 8 percent, what will be the future value of the investment after eight years? (Hint: Use Appendix Table A.1 or the *Garman/Forgue* website.)

5. Assume that the $35,000 initial investment grows to $70,000 by the time that Victor and Maria retire and that it will continue to earn a return of 8 percent annually. If they plan on living an additional 20 years, how much can they withdraw each year so that the fund will be liquidated only after 20 years? (Hint: Use Appendix Table A.4 or the *Garman/Forgue* website.)

The Johnsons Want to Invest in Stock

After reviewing several types of investments, Harry and Belinda Johnson have decided to invest $1200 now and then $200 to $400 per month for the next two years. All income from their investments will be automatically reinvested, but they expect some price appreciation as well. Harry and Belinda are busy learning about different investments and generally are "following the market."

1. Harry has been watching Walgreen stock, and Belinda is interested in Wal-Mart. Which stock had the greatest volume of trading? Which stock reported the greatest net change in price? (See Figure 16.3.)

2. Based on only the P/E ratios for the two stocks, which is the better value?

3. If the Johnsons had a "windfall" and purchased 100 shares of Walgreen stock, how much in commissions would they pay? How much in commissions would they pay on 100 shares of Wal-Mart stock? Assume the purchases were made at the highest price of the day.

4. Briefly discuss the factors the Johnsons should consider in choosing a stock brokerage firm, particularly given that they plan to invest and trade regularly.

What Would You Recommend Now?

Now that you have read the chapter on buying and selling securities, what would you recommend to Bob Class in the case at the beginning of the chapter regarding:

1. Retaining his account with his long-time broker or opening an account at a general brokerage firm, opening an account at a discount brokerage firm, or doing both?

2. Using a limit order rather than a market order when buying and selling stocks?

3. Deciding whether to purchase mutual funds outside of his 401(k) retirement program?

4. Using beta values to help estimate the required rate of return on an investment given its risk?

5. Reporting his gains and losses in securities transactions on his income taxes?

6. Using selling short as a trading technique?

Exploring the World Wide Web

To complete these exercises, go to the *Garman/Forgue* website at college.hmco.com/business/students. Under General Business, select the title of this text. Click on the Internet Exercises link for this chapter, and answer the questions that appear on the Web page.

1. Visit the website for the General Motors Corporation annual report. Then visit the Securities and Exchange Commission website for the most recent 10-K report for General Motors (in the search box, type "general plus motors plus 10-K"). How do the tone and feel of the two reports differ?

2. Visit the website for the New York Stock Exchange. Click on "regulation" and then on "arbitration." Describe this mechanism, which is used by consumers who have disputes within the securities industry.

3. Visit the website of the National Association of Securities Dealers. There you will find a description of the Office of Ombudsman. What is the role of this office, and how might investors use it to their advantage?

4. Visit the websites for E-Trade and Charles Schwab (click on "newly reduced trade pricing"). Review their fee structures and compare them to information in this chapter about typical full-service brokerage fees. How do the services provided compare and contrast with those provided by traditional full-service brokers? How might the advent of Web trading services affect traditional investment houses?

5. Visit the website for CNNMoney. There you will find a glossary defining various stop and limit orders to protect your stock investments from market swings. What are the advantages of using these techniques?

6. Visit the websites for the Securities and Exchange Commission and the New York Stock Exchange. Compare the SEC's efforts at industry regulation to the NYSE's self-regulation efforts.

7. Visit the website for Vanguard Securities. There you will find information on using a margin account. What are the current margin rates for the following types of investments: equities (stocks), municipal bonds, corporate bonds, and short sales?

Visit the Garman/Forgue website . . .

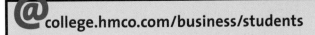

@college.hmco.com/business/students

Under General Business, select *Personal Finance 8e*. There, among other valuable resources, you will find a complete glossary, ACE questions, links to help you complete the chapter exercises, and links to other personal finance sites.

Chapter 17

Real Estate and Speculative Investments

After reading this chapter, you should be able to:

1 **Distinguish** between direct and indirect real estate investments and realize that timeshares are not investments.

2 **Estimate** the proper price to pay for a potential real estate investment using the discounted cash-flow method.

3 **Assess** both the non-economic and economic advantages and disadvantages of investing in real estate.

4 **Consider** the challenges associated with investing in collectibles and precious metals and stones.

5 **Be aware** of the potential rewards and very high risks associated with trading options and futures.

Kim Day, a 34-year-old marketing manager for a large corporation, earns $110,000 per year. She saves about $1800 each month beyond her contributions to her employer's 401(k) retirement plan. To date, Kim has been investing her 401(k) plan money primarily in stock mutual funds and the remainder in her employer's company stock. She has found excellent success investing in the mutual funds within the plan, and her investments have grown at a healthy pace through the years. Her total 401(k) holdings are worth $260,000.

Ever since her grandfather gave her some stocks as a child, Kim has loved investing—and she has enjoyed a good track record with her efforts. She invests through accounts maintained with a full-service and a discount stockbroker. Kim is an active trader, often trading every three or four weeks, primarily in the oil, electricity, and prescription drug industries. Every year, of course, she has some losses as well as gains. Her private portfolio is currently worth $160,000. Kim has never bought or sold options or traded in futures contracts, but her stockbroker recently suggested that she try investing in them. Kim also has a friend who owns several residential rental properties who has asked her to consider investing as her partner in her next real estate venture.

What would you recommend to Kim on the subject of real estate and speculative investments regarding:

1. Investing in real estate?

2. Putting some of her money in a speculative investment, like collectibles?

3. Buying and selling options and futures contracts?

Your choices as an investor are not limited to buying and selling stocks, bonds, and mutual funds. Certainly you realize that your home is an investment and accomplishes more than just putting a roof over your head. Your home is also an investment because it will probably increase in value over the long term. This likelihood may lead you to consider real estate as an investment option. Later, as you gain more sophistication as an investor, you might consider the possibility of owning certain tangible assets, such as collectibles, precious metals, and gems for their investment potential. Or perhaps you may be attracted to options and futures contracts. These investment alternatives are referred to as **speculative** (or **high-risk**) **investments** because they have the potential for significant fluctuations in return over very short time periods; perhaps only days or weeks. Because options and futures are much riskier than the traditional securities investments, they are suitable only for investors with an aggressive investment philosophy. In order to be successful in higher risk investments, like real estate, collectibles, or options, you need to know the market very well and be realistic about the possible outcomes. You also need to ask experts for advice.

This chapter begins by discussing direct and indirect ownership of real estate investments. We then consider how to determine the value—that is, the proper price that might be paid—for a particular piece of property. This coverage is followed by a discussion of the non-economic and economic advantages and disadvantages of investing in real estate. The chapter continues with an overview of investments in tangible assets such as collectibles and precious metals and stones. We also examine the potential rewards and high risks associated with trading in options and futures. Keep in mind that investors think of assets like something that they would like to own for the long term. Speculators buy now in the hope that someone else will pay more for it in the not-to-distant future.

Golden Rules of

Real Estate and Speculative Investments

Financial success comes from learning the Golden Rules of personal finance and then putting what you have learned into practice. Make the following your money habits in real estate and speculative investments:

1. Do not get into a real estate investment until you have carefully considered both the non-economic and economic advantages and disadvantages of ownership.
2. Never consider a timeshare an investment; instead recognize it as a vacation opportunity.
3. If you want real estate as part of your investment portfolio, consider both direct and indirect ownership opportunities.
4. Before investing in any income-producing real estate, carefully calculate property valuations using the discounted cash-flow method.
5. Avoid investing in collectibles and precious metals and stones; they are not good investments.
6. Avoid trading in options and futures because the profits typically go to the experts and not the amateurs.

Direct and Indirect Ownership Investments in Real Estate

1 Distinguish between direct and indirect real estate investments and realize that timeshares are not investments.

Real estate is property consisting of land, all structures permanently attached to that land, and accompanying rights and privileges, such as crops and mineral rights. A real estate investment is termed **direct ownership** when an investor holds actual legal title to the property. For example, you can invest directly as an individual or jointly with other investors to buy an apartment building. Indirect ownership is also possible. In an **indirect investment** in real estate, a trustee, not the investors, hold actual legal title to the property. Examples of such investments include real estate syndicates and real estate investment trusts. Investors can obtain information on these alternatives from brokerage firms.

Direct Ownership Investments in Real Estate

Two general types of direct ownership investments in real estate exist: (1) residential property units and commercial properties, and (2) raw land and residential lots.

Residential Units and Commercial Properties.   **Residential units** are properties designed for residential living. Examples include houses, duplexes, apartments, mobile homes, and condominiums that offer a potential to produce investment profits. **Commercial properties** are properties designed for business uses. Examples include office buildings, medical centers, gasoline stations, and motels that carry a potential to produce a profit. Realizing a good investment income from these properties normally requires that you take an active role in their management.

Residential units are probably the least complex real estate investments with which to begin, the easiest to sell, and the least profitable. In particular, condominium prices typically rise very slowly in contrast to the comparatively faster price increases that typify single-family dwellings. One popular way to start in real estate investment is to purchase **sweat equity property.** With this approach, you would seek a property that needs repairs but has good underlying value. You buy it at a favorable price and "sweat" by spending many hours cleaning, painting, and repairing it to sell at a profit or to rent to tenants.

Commercial properties carry more risk of remaining unrented than do residential units. In addition, business tenants usually expect more extensive and costly services, and the buildings have a greater likelihood of obsolescence. Accordingly, you can charge higher rents on commercial properties to offset the higher risk involved.

When choosing either type of income-producing rental property, you need to consider several criteria, including location (good or poor), dependability of income, current value of the property, and condition of the property. Also important are likely effects of future competition of similar real estate, availability of reasonable financing, moderately priced utilities, stable real estate property taxes, and, of course, return on investment after taxes. Although they are not sufficient by themselves, "location, location, and location" are regarded as the first three rules of successful real estate investing.

Raw Land and Residential Lots.   Investing in raw land or residential lots on which you do not intend to build is a risky venture. **Raw land** is undeveloped acreage, typically far from established communities, with no utilities and no improvements except perhaps a substandard access road. A **residential lot** consists of subdivided acreage with utilities—typically water, electricity, and sewerage—located within or adjacent to established communities. Many developers buy raw land and residential lots to sell to people who "think" they will build in the future.

Buying raw land is often an investment that provides no revenue, no income, no return, and sometimes no enjoyment. If you are tempted, you should not buy any acreage unless you firmly believe the following: (1) the price paid today is substantially less than what it might be in the future; (2) comparable acreage will not be available in the future when needed by buyers; or (3) you will later build on the property yourself. Never buy land in some distant new city, retirement village, or resort. A potential investor should always see the land, hire an attorney to review the deal, and read the **property report** (a document legally required under the federal Interstate Land Sales Act for properties offered for sale across state lines). Investors also should pay for a private property appraisal.

Timesharing Is Not an Investment.   **Timesharing** is the joint ownership or lease of vacation property through which the principals occupy the property individually for set periods of time. Timesharing is not an investment, although it is often promoted as a way to simultaneously invest and obtain vacation housing. For $5000 to $20,000, buyers can purchase one or more weeks' use of luxury vacation housing furnished right down to the salt and pepper shakers. Each timeshare vacationer also pays an annual maintenance fee for each week of ownership, perhaps amounting to $100 to $200 per week.

With **deeded timesharing,** the buyer obtains a legal title or deed to limited time periods of use of real estate. Purchasers thus become secured creditors who are guaranteed continued use of the property throughout any bankruptcy proceedings. They also really own their week of the property.

Most timeshares, however, are sold without a deed. **Nondeeded timesharing** is legally a right-to-use purchase of a limited, preplanned timesharing period of use of a vacation property that actually is only a license, club membership, or lease. It does not grant legal real estate ownership interest to the purchaser. Instead, it provides a long-term lease permitting use of a hotel suite, condominium, or other accommodation. As in some other situations that involve leasing, should the true owner of the property— the developer—go bankrupt, problems abound. The timeshare purchasers (actually tenants) can be locked out of the premises by the creditors. Also, these leases commonly expire in 20 to 25 years.

It is very difficult to sell a timeshare. A survey from the Resort Property Owners Association estimates that the average timeshare unit languishes on the market for 4.4 years before being sold. At any point in time, 60 percent of all timeshares are up for sale. Timeshare sellers rarely receive more than 50 percent of their original investment in the sale. If you are interested in such property for vacation purposes, buy a deeded timeshare.

Vacationers should realize that sales commissions on timeshares sales amount to 25 percent of the price. For this reason, the salespersons will do almost anything to make a sale, including offering valuable gifts. From the developer's perspective, timeshares are a terrific moneymaker. It may cost only $75,000 to build an apartment unit that is timeshared. When sold for 50 weeks at $6000 per week, the timeshare brings the developer revenues of $300,000 (50 × $6000). That's a 400 percent return! From the consumer's perspective, timesharing is a prepaid vacation expense.

Indirect Ownership Investments in Real Estate

Two popular indirect ownership investments in real estate are real estate syndicates and real estate investment trusts. A **real estate syndicate** is an indirect form of real property investment, often organized as a temporary limited partnership. Here a number of shares are sold to investors for as little as $5000 or $10,000 per share to raise capital for real estate projects. The parties own and develop the property, with the main profit coming from the sale of the property. Syndicates finance the building of many office buildings, shopping centers, factories, apartment houses, supermarkets, and motels. The **limited partnership** form of real estate syndicate involves two classes of partners: the general partner and the limited partners. The **general partner** (usually the organizer and initial investor) operates the syndicate and has unlimited financial liability. The **limited partners** (the outside investors) receive part of the profits and the tax-shelter benefits but remain inactive in the management of the business and have no personal liability for the operations of the partnership beyond their initial investment.

A **real estate investment trust (REIT)** is a trust or corporation that serves as a conduit for the real estate investments of its shareholders. It raises money by selling shares to 100 or more investors. It owns property and/or provides mortgage lending to developers. REITs typically specialize in a segment of the real estate market, such as shopping centers, apartment buildings, or medical offices. About 300 REITs trade on stock exchanges or over the counter, and share prices are volatile since such illiquid issues are usually not actively traded.

[handwritten margin notes:] Syndicate: buy shares → lump sum build condos → sell → get principal & interest (part of profit)

2 Estimate the proper price to pay for a potential real estate investment using the discounted cash-flow method.

What Should You Pay for a Real Estate Investment?

A sure way to go wrong in a real estate investment is to pay too much for the property. The **discounted cash-flow method** is an effective way to estimate the value or asking price of a real estate investment. It emphasizes after-tax cash flow and the return on the invested dollars discounted over time to reflect a discounted yield. Computer software programs are available to help calculate the discounted cash flows. You also can use Appendix Table A.2, as illustrated in Table 17.1.

To illustrate how this method works, assume that you require an after-rate of return of 10 percent on a condominium advertised for sale at $200,000. You estimate that rents can be increased each year for five years. After all expenses are paid, you expect to have after-tax cash flows of $4000, $4200, $4400, $4600, and $4800 for the five years. Assuming some price appreciation, you anticipate selling the property for $265,000 after all expenses are incurred. How much should you pay now to buy the property?

Table 17.1 explains how to answer this question. Multiply the estimated after-tax cash flows and the expected proceeds of $265,000 to be realized on the sale of the property by the present value of a dollar at 10 percent (the required rate of return). Add the present values together to obtain the total present value of the property—in this case, $181,097. Thus, the asking price of $200,000 is too high for you to earn an after-tax return of 10 percent. Your choices are to negotiate the price down, accept a return of less than 10 percent, hope that the sale price of the property will be higher than $265,000 five years from now, or consider another investment. The discounted cash-flow method provides an effective way to estimate real estate values because it takes into account the selling price of the property, the effect of income taxes, and the time value of money.

Table 17.1 Discounted Cash-Flow Method Illustration

	After-Tax Cash Flow	Present Value of $1 at 10 Percent*	Present Value of After-Tax Cash Flow
1 year	$ 4,000	0.909	$ 3,636
2 years	4,200	0.826	3,469
3 years	4,400	0.751	3,304
4 years	4,600	0.683	3,142
5 years	4,800	0.621	2,981
Sell property	$265,000	0.621	164,565
Present value of property			$181,097

*From Appendix Table A.2.

3 Assess both the non-economic and economic advantages and disadvantages of investing in real estate.

Advantages and Disadvantages of Real Estate Investments

The ultimate goal of investing in real estate is economic—the maximization of positive after-tax returns. The best returns in real estate often come from commercial properties, although many people do well with residential properties. They often invest in used or new residential properties located near good schools, supermarkets, and public transportation. Residential real estate prices typically rise every year by a little more than the rate of inflation. Although this growth is less than the long-term returns possible in the securities markets, returns from real estate may be quite substantial. In some local markets around the country, home prices are rising by 10 percent (or more) per year. No one knows how long such increases will continue. In other communities, property values have actually declined over the past five years. For this reason, you should be cautious about investing in real estate as an alternative to investing in securities, and carefully consider the advantages and disadvantages. Some non-economic reasons for investing in real estate are that most such investors like being closely involved with their investments and enjoy the feelings of pride and emotional satisfaction associated with owning property. A good way to learn about investing in real estate is by contacting the National Real Estate Investors Association (www.nationalreia.com), which has chapters in most major cities.

Advantages of Real Estate Investments

Real estate investments provide four economic advantages: (1) the possibility of a positive cash flow, (2) the potential for capital gains through price appreciation, (3) the availability of leverage, and (4) a number of beneficial tax treatments.

Positive Cash Flow.   Recall that all sorts of investors can benefit from both current income and capital gains. In real estate investing, current income takes the form of positive cash flow. For an income-producing real estate investment, you pay operating expenses out of rental income. If the property has a mortgage (a common occurrence), payments toward the mortgage principal and interest also must be made out of rental income. The amount of rental income you have left after paying all operating expenses (including repairs) and mortgage expenses is called **cash flow.** The amount of cash flow—obtained by subtracting any cash outlays from the cash income—depends on the amount of rent received, the amount of expenses paid, and the amount necessary to repay the mortgage debt. Investors usually prefer a positive cash flow to a negative cash flow because any shortages represent out-of-pocket expenses for the investor. Most real estate investments will not generate a positive cash flow, even though they may offer the likelihood of high potential returns. Many investors, however, can manage a negative cash flow for a few years while waiting for capital gains to materialize. They aim to eventually sell the property at a higher price to profit from their investment.

Price Appreciation: A Hedge Against Inflation.   **Price appreciation** comprises the amount above ownership costs for which an investment is sold; it is similar to the capital gains realized on a stock investment. In real estate, ownership costs include the original purchase price as well as expenditures for any capital improvements made to a property prior to sale. **Capital improvements** are costs incurred in making changes in real property that add to its value. Paneling a living room, adding a new roof, and putting up a fence represent capital improvements. In contrast, **repairs** are expenses (usually tax-deductible against an investor's cash-flow income) necessary to maintain the value of the property. Repainting, mending roof leaks, and fixing plumbing are examples of repairs.

As an example, assume that Ryland Webb, an unmarried schoolteacher from Daytona, Florida, bought a small rental house as an investment five years ago for $120,000 in cash that he received as an inheritance. He fixed some roof leaks (repairs) for $1000 and then added a new shed and some kitchen cabinets (capital improvements) at a cost of $10,000 before selling the property this year for $160,000. As a result, Ryland happily realized a net price appreciation of $30,000 ($160,000 minus $120,000 purchase price minus $10,000 capital improvements).

Leverage.   An investor's return can be increased by taking advantage of **leverage.** This practice involves using borrowed funds to make an investment with the goal of earning a rate of return in excess of the after-tax costs of borrowing. Lenders normally permit real estate investors to borrow from 75 to 95 percent of the price of an investment property.

Suppose that Ryland, instead of paying cash for the house, had made a down payment of $25,000 and borrowed the remainder. What effect would this borrowing have on his return? In the first instance, Ryland paid $120,000 cash for the property and thus earned a 25 percent return on his investment ($30,000 ÷ $120,000) over the five-year period, or roughly 5 percent per year. In the second situation, using leverage, he would have an apparent return of 120 percent ($30,000 ÷ $25,000), or roughly 24 percent per year. The true return would be lower because of mortgage payments, interest expenses, property taxes, and repairs, but would still be a double-digit return.

The **loan-to-value ratio** measures the amount of leverage in a real estate investment project. It is calculated by dividing the amount of debt by the value of the total original investment. For example, because his down payment was $25,000 on the $120,000 property ($95,000 ÷ $120,000), Ryland had a loan-to-value ratio of 79 percent, or 79 percent leverage.

Beneficial Tax Treatments.   The U.S. Congress, through provisions in the Internal Revenue Code, encourages real estate investments by giving investors five special tax treatments. These provisions relate to capital gains, depreciation, interest deductions, tax-free exchanges, and rental income tax regulations.

1. Capital Gains.   Capital gains on real estate are realized through price appreciation. For most taxpayers, long-term capital gains are taxed at a rate of 15 percent, and taxpayers in the 10 to 15 percent tax brackets pay a long-term capital gains tax of 5 percent. (See Chapters 4 and 16 for more information.)

2. Depreciation Deduction.   Investors in real estate become successful by understanding the "numbers" of real estate investing. For example, assume that Marilyn Furry, a lawyer from University Park, Pennsylvania, invested $200,000 in a residential building ($170,000) and land ($30,000). She rents the property to a tenant for $24,000 per year. You might think that Marilyn must pay income taxes on the entire $24,000 in rental income. In reality, IRS regulations allow taxpayers to deduct depreciation from rental income. **Depreciation** represents the decline in value of an asset over time due to normal wear and tear and obsolescence. A proportionate amount of a capital asset representing depreciation may be deducted against income each year over the asset's estimated life. Land cannot be depreciated.

Marilyn can deduct an equal part of the building's cost over the estimated life of the property. According to the IRS guidelines, residential properties may be depreciated over 27.5 years and 39 years for nonresidential property. Thus, Marilyn calculates (from Table 17.2) the amount she can annually deduct from income to be $6182 ($170,000 ÷ 27.5). Table 17.2 shows the effects of depreciation on her income taxes, assuming Marilyn pays income taxes at a combined federal and state rate of 36 percent. In this example, the depreciation deduction lowers taxable income on the property from $24,000 to $17,818 ($24,000 − $6182) and increases the return on the investment to 9.29 percent.

3. Interest Deduction.   Real estate investors incur several general business expenses in attempting to earn a profit: interest on a mortgage, real estate taxes, insur-

Table 17.2 Effect of Depreciation on Income Taxes and Return

				Without Depreciation	With Depreciation
Total amount invested	$200,000	Gross rental income		$24,000	$24,000
Cost of land	− 30,000	Less annual depreciation expense		0	6,182
Cost of rental building	$170,000	Taxable income		24,000	17,818
Depreciation for 27.5 years	$6,182	Income taxes			
		(36 percent combined federal and			
		state tax rate)		8,640	6,414
		After-tax return		$15,360	$17,586
		After-tax yield			
		(divide return by $200,000)		7.68%	8.79%

ance, utilities, capital improvements, and repairs. The largest of these costs often is the interest expense, as most properties are purchased with a mortgage loan. Table 17.3 illustrates the effect of interest expenses on income taxes. Assume Marilyn borrowed $175,000 to purchase her $200,000 property. After deducting annual depreciation of $6182 and interest expenses of $13,050, her taxable income is reduced to $4768. Because her income tax liability is only $1716, Marilyn's after-tax return of $9234 yields 36.94 percent on her leveraged investment.

Tax laws permit investors to deduct interest expenses, with the amount allowed depending on the investor's marginal tax bracket. Marilyn's interest deduction gives her a cash flow after paying mortgage interest of $10,950 ($24,000 − $13,050). In essence, the $13,050 in interest is paid with $4698 ($13,050 × 36 percent combined federal and state income tax rate) of the money that was not sent to the federal and state governments and $8352 ($13,050 − $4698) of Marilyn's money. Essentially, a major advantage of using borrowed money to invest is that a substantial part of the cost of financing real estate shifts from the taxpayer to the government. While this example illustrates the impact of mortgage interest paid on a real estate investment, Table 17.1 provides a more accurate analysis (page 484).

4. Tax-Free Exchanges. Another special tax treatment results when a real estate investor trades equity in one property for equity in a similar property. If none of the

Table 17.3 Additional Effect of Interest Paid on Income Taxes on Return

Gross rental income	$24,000
Less annual depreciation deduction	− 6,182
Subtotal	$17,818
Less interest expense for the year	
(7.5 percent mortgage loan)	−13,050
Taxable income	$ 4,768
Cash flow after paying interest	
($24,000 − $13,050)	10,950
Less income tax liability (0.36 × $4,768)	− 1,716
After-tax return ($10,950 − $1,716)	$ 9,234
After-tax yield	
[$9,234 ÷ ($200,000 − $175,000)]	36.94%

people involved in the trade receives any other form of property or money, the transaction is considered a **tax-free exchange.** If one person receives some money or other property, only that person must report the extra proceeds as a taxable gain. For example, assume that you bought a residential rental property five years ago for $220,000 and today it is worth much more money. You trade it with your friend by giving $10,000 in cash for your friend's $280,000 single-family rental home. Your friend needs to report only the $10,000 as income this year. In contrast, you do not need to report your long-term gain, $50,000 ($280,000 − $10,000 − $220,000), until you actually sell the new property.

5. Rental Income Tax Regulations on Vacation Homes.   If you rent out your vacation property for 14 or fewer days during the year, you can pocket the income tax-free, regardless of how much you charge. The IRS does not want to hear about this gain. The home is considered a personal residence, so you can deduct mortgage interest and property taxes just as you would for your principal residence.

Renting a vacation home for more than 14 days turns the endeavor into a business, and you must report all rental income. You can also deduct rental expenses up to the level of rental income you report. When your adjusted gross income (AGI) is less than $100,000, a maximum of $25,000 of rental-related losses may be deducted each year to offset income from *any* source, including your salary. The $25,000 limit is gradually phased out as your AGI moves between $100,000 and $150,000. Thus, this ability to shelter income from taxes represents a terrific benefit for most people who invest in real estate on a small scale.

Disadvantages of Real Estate Investments

Investing in real estate also has some economic and non-economic disadvantages.

- **Financial Risk.** It is quite possible to lose money in real estate investments. Sometimes property values fall, and so do rents. Rents will not keep up with costs in communities where industries and jobs are moving elsewhere or in deteriorating neighborhoods.
- **Complexity.** Real estate investments require more study and careful investigation than do most other investments. Zoning changes can slash housing values.
- **Large Initial Investment.** Investment in real estate generally requires many thousands of dollars, often with an initial outlay of $15,000 to $30,000 or more.
- **Lack of Diversification.** So much capital is required in most real estate that spreading risk is difficult to achieve.
- **Dealing with Tenants.** Someone has to screen rental applicants for their credit histories, criminal records, work references, and experience with previous landlords. Some state laws make it impossible to evict a deadbeat tenant for several months. Picking the wrong tenants can quickly turn a real estate property into a financial loss.
- **Time-Consuming Management Demands.** Managing a real estate investment requires time for collecting overdue rents, conducting regular inspections of the property, dealing with insurance companies, and making repairs.
- **Low Current Income.** Sometimes expenses may reduce cash-flow return to less than 2 percent or even generate a loss.
- **Unpredictable Costs.** Estimating costs presents many difficulties. For example, while the tenants may pay for heat and electricity, the investor's water bill can skyrocket if a property is full of "visiting relatives."

- **Legal Fees.** The services of a real estate attorney will be needed to help handle the real estate purchase, sale, building inspections, zoning issues, tenant problems, insurance disputes, other problem bearers, and any liability issues.
- **Illiquidity.** Real estate is expensive and the market for investment property is much smaller than the securities market. As a result, it is common to experience difficulty in selling. It may take months or even years to find a buyer, arrange the financing, and close the sale of a real estate investment.
- **High Transfer Costs.** Substantial transfer costs, often representing 6 to 7 percent of the property's sale price, may be incurred when real estate is bought or sold.

Collectibles and Precious Metals and Stones

4 Consider the challenges associated with investing in collectibles and precious metals and stones.

Investing in collectibles and precious metals and stones is a challenging and speculative venture. In these types of investments, the investor owns illiquid real assets, not intangible items represented by pieces of paper. **Collectibles** are cultural artifacts that have value because of their beauty, age, scarcity, or popularity. Buying collectibles can be a relaxing hobby that you pursue for fun. Some collectibles gain value as well as give pleasure. The only return on collectibles—baseball cards, posters, sports jerseys, photographs, comic books, watches, lunchboxes, matchbooks, glassware, spoons, stamps, rare coins, art, antiques—occurs through price appreciation, and you must sell to realize a profit. Although buying collectibles can be fun and easy, turning a profit on your investment can prove difficult. Items that are almost certain to lose value include those that are mass-produced and marketed as collectibles or limited editions. The risks include the wholesale-to-retail price spread. Prices on collectibles vary greatly from item to item and year to year. Markets are fickle.

The collectibles industry is rife with forgeries, scams, and frauds, particularly with regard to sports items. While the Internet provides access to a wide selection of goods, many rip-offs have been known to occur. One key to success in finding collectibles that will increase in value is quality. The higher, the better. As noted earlier, the collector has to sell to realize a profit, but that can be hard to do when you collect items that give you pleasure, that you enjoyed buying, and that you love.

Similarly, precious metals (for example, gold, gold bullion coins, silver, platinum, palladium, rhodium) and precious stones (for example, diamonds, sapphires, rubies, emeralds) are high-risk investments. Investors typically purchase investment-grade gems as "loose stones" rather than as pieces of jewelry. The best-quality precious gems and metals are sold by wholesale firms, not jewelers. Unless they are lucky, novice investors often buy at retail and then wind up trying to sell at retail. This approach is the opposite of smart investing—that is, buying low and selling high. Sales commissions on precious metals and stones are high, too.

Many people around the world invest in precious metals and stones to preserve capital in difficult economic times, reasoning that if their national economies crash they will be able to trade gold even if their paper currency is devalued. The prices of precious metals and stones tend to increase in times of economic and political turmoil, especially when inflation is high.

The values of collectibles and precious metals and stones rely solely upon the authority of "experts" who purport to determine their worth, and such blind trust invites risk to potential investors. When an asset does not generate a readily quantifiable return (such as rent, interest, or dividends), its value is determined by supply and demand—

Tax Considerations and Consequences

An Income-Producing Real Estate Investment

When you are considering a real estate investment, you use the investment amount (purchase price or down payment) to begin the process of estimating the likely rate of return. This calculation may then be compared with other investment alternatives. Because some of the many assumptions in real estate calculations could be incorrect, however, caution is warranted in real estate analyses.

The following table shows five-year estimates for a hypothetical residential property with a purchase price of $200,000. The building will be purchased with a $150,000 mortgage loan, so the buyer has to make a $50,000 down payment plus pay $8000 in closing costs. The gross rental income of $18,000 annually is projected to rise at an annual rate of 5 percent, vacancies and un-

paid rent at 10 percent, real estate taxes at 7 percent, insurance at 8 percent, and maintenance at 10 percent. Virtually the entire payment for the 30-year, $150,000, 8 percent, fixed-rate mortgage loan is assumed to be interest during these early years. For income tax purposes, the land is valued at $20,000, and the building is depreciated over 27.5 years. Thus, the amount of annual straight-line depreciation is calculated to be $6546 ($200,000 − $20,000 = $180,000; $180,000 ÷ 27.5).

Note (in line D) how difficult it is to earn current income from rental properties. During the first year, the total cash-flow loss is projected to be $2808. However, because the income tax laws permit depreciation (line E, $6546) to be recorded as a real estate investment expense,

Estimates for a Successful Real Estate Investment

	Year				
	1	2	3	4	5
A. Gross rental income	$ 18,000	$ 18,900	$ 19,845	$ 20,837	$ 21,879
Less vacancies and unpaid rent	1,800	1,890	1,985	2,084	2,188
B. Projected gross income	$ 16,200	$ 17,010	$ 17,860	$ 18,753	$ 19,691
C. Less operating expenses					
Principal and Interest $(P + I)$	$ 13,208	$ 13,208	$ 13,208	$ 13,208	$ 13,208
Real estate taxes (T)	2,600	2,782	2,977	3,185	3,408
Insurance (I)	800	864	933	1,008	1,089
Maintenance	2,400	2,640	2,904	3,194	3,513
Total operating expenses	$ 19,008	$ 19,494	$ 20,022	$ 20,595	$ 21,218
D. Total cash flow (negative)	$ (2,808)	$ (2,484)	$ (2,162)	$ (1,842)	$ (1,527)
E. Less depreciation expense	6,546	6,546	6,546	6,546	6,546
F. Taxable income (or loss) $(D − E)$	$ (9,354)	$ (9,030)	$ (8,708)	$ (8,388)	$ (8,073)
G. Annual tax savings (30 percent marginal rate)	2,806	2,709	2,612	2,516	2,422
H. Net cash-flow gain (or loss) after taxes $(G − D)$	$ (2)	$ 225	$ 450	$ 674	$ 895

and rumors. Scams and frauds abound with these investments, as "professional liars" tell tales about skyrocketing prices and high profit potentials to encourage their purchase. Some people are persuaded by telemarketers to buy precious metals and stones. As noted earlier, these investments do not pay current income, and some even require that the investor pay fees for safe storage of the objects.

even though it is not an out-of-pocket cost, the total taxable loss (line F) is projected to be $9354. This loss can be deducted on the investor's income tax returns. Because the investor pays a 30 percent combined federal and state income tax rate, the loss results in a first-year annual tax savings of $2806. Therefore, instead of sending the $2806 to the government in taxes, the investor can use that amount to help pay the operating expenses of the investment. Consequently, the net cash-flow income (line D) of $2808 is reduced by tax savings (line G) of $2806 to result in a net cash-flow gain after taxes of $2 ($2808 − $2806).

Assume that the property appreciates in value at an annual rate of 6 percent and will be worth $267,645 (line K) in five years ($200,000 × 1.06 × 1.06 × 1.06 × 1.06 × 1.06). If it is sold at this price, a 6 percent real estate sales commission of $16,059 ($267,645 × 0.06) would reduce the net proceeds to $251,586 ($267,645 − $16,059).

Now we can calculate the **crude annual rate of return** on the property, as shown in the second table. A crude rate of return is a rough measure of the yield on amounts invested that assumes that equal portions of the gain are earned each year. The total return in this example was substantial. The investor made out-of-pocket cash investments of $25,000 for the down payment and $8000 in closing costs, and we subtract the accumulated net cash flow (line N) of $2242 (adding all the numbers across line H, because the investor already has received that money) for a total investment (line O) of $35,750. The investor has a capital gain (line M) of $76,316. After dividing to determine the before-tax total return (line R) to obtain 214 percent, the crude annual rate of return (line S) is 42.6 percent annually over the five years (214 percent ÷ 5 years).

Crude Rate of Return on a Successful Real Estate Investment

I.	**Taxable cost**	
	Purchase price	$200,000
	($50,000 down payment;	
	$150,000 loan)	
	Closing costs	8,000
	Subtotal	208,000
J.	Less accumulated depreciation	32,730
	Taxable cost (adjusted basis)	$175,270
	Proceeds (after paying off mortgage)	
K.	Sale price	$267,645
	Less sales commission	16,059
	Net proceeds	$251,586
L.	Less taxable cost (J)	175,270
M.	Taxable proceeds (capital gain)	$ 76,316
	Amount invested	
	Down payment	$ 50,000
	Closing costs	8,000
N.	Less accumulated net cash-flow gains	(2,242)
O.	Total invested	$ 55,758
	Crude annual rate of return	
P	Total invested	$ 55,758
Q.	Taxable proceeds (capital gain from M)	$ 76,316
R.	Before-tax total return ($ 76,316 ÷ $55,758)	137%
S.	Crude before-tax annual rate of return (137 percent ÷ 5 years)	27.4%

Other investment alternatives—stocks, bonds, and mutual funds—can easily be converted to cash, unlike illiquid collectibles and precious metals and stones. While worldwide demand for precious metals and stones certainly exists, professional traders are the ones who make the profits on these investments. Ninety-nine percent of consumers do not need to put money into collectibles and other tangible investments. Such alternatives are not wise choices for the casual investor.

Options and Futures Contracts

To succeed in investing in options and futures contracts, you need to develop a thorough knowledge of unfamiliar and complicated investment terminology and use formulas and mechanisms appropriate only under certain circumstances. You need to stay constantly alert to developments affecting your investments and become quite familiar with the intricacies of trading. Investors often must act decisively and quickly to ensure their profits and cut their losses. People who pursue options and futures investments need even temperaments and strong stomachs. They should recognize that the funds used for such investments should be only those that they can afford to lose, because the money invested may never be seen again. Because of the likelihood of loss, those who try to profit in speculative investments should limit their exposure to a relatively small portion of their portfolio, perhaps 10 percent or less.

Options Allow You to Buy or Sell an Asset at a Predetermined Price

An **option** is a contract to buy or sell an asset at some point in the future at a specified price. The most common type of option is a **stock option.** This security gives the holder the right to buy or sell a specific number of shares (normally 100) of a certain stock at a specified price (the **striking price**) before a specified date (the **expiration date,** typically three, six, or nine months). Stock options are high-risk investments, although conservative investors may use options—in a different way—to profit as well.[*]

Options Are Created by an Option Writer.   An **option writer** signs an option contract through a brokerage firm and promises either to buy or to sell a specified asset for a fixed striking price. In return, the option writer receives an **option premium** (the price of the option itself) for standing ready to buy or sell the asset at the wishes of the option purchaser. Once written and sold, an option may change hands many times before its expiration. The **option holder** is the person who actually owns the option contract. The original option writer always remains responsible for buying or selling the asset if requested by the holder of the option contract.

Two types of option contracts exist: calls and puts. A **call option** gives the option holder the right to *buy* the optioned asset from the option writer at the striking price. A **put option** gives the option holder the right to *sell* the optioned asset to the option writer at the striking price. "How to Make Sense of Option Contracts" explains the relationships between option writers and option holders for both puts and calls.

Most option contracts expire without being exercised by the option holder, and the option writer is the only person to earn a profit. The profit results from the premium charged when the option was originally sold. Buying and selling options are techniques used by both conservative and aggressive investors.

Conservative Writers Profit by Selling Covered Calls.   Conservative option writers own the underlying asset (the stock). When they sell a call, for example, it is described as a **covered option** because the writer has an ownership position. (If the writer

---

[*]Recall from Chapter 14 that some employers give stock options as a way to attract and retain employees. If the price of the underlying stock increases sufficiently, the employee can profit by exercising the option to buy the shares at the predetermined price and then selling the shares at today's higher price.

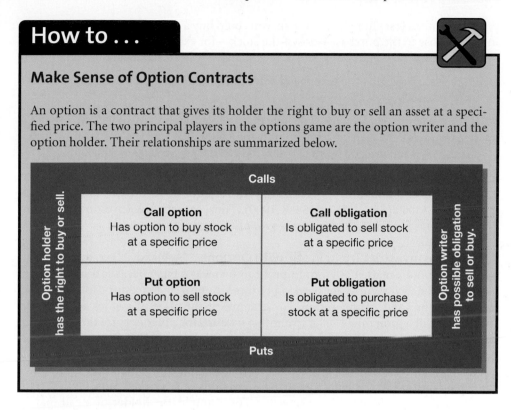

How to . . .

Make Sense of Option Contracts

An option is a contract that gives its holder the right to buy or sell an asset at a specified price. The two principal players in the options game are the option writer and the option holder. Their relationships are summarized below.

Calls

Option holder has the right to buy or sell.

Call option	Call obligation
Has option to buy stock at a specific price	Is obligated to sell stock at a specific price
Put option	**Put obligation**
Has option to sell stock at a specific price	Is obligated to purchase stock at a specific price

Option writer has possible obligation to sell or buy.

Puts

does not own the asset, it is a **naked option,** or speculative position.) When used effectively by conservative option writers, calls can potentially pick up an extra return of perhaps 1 to 2 percent every three months.

As a conservative investor, you can profit by selling a call on stock already owned, giving the buyer the right to purchase your shares at a fixed strike price for a time period. Assume that you have 1000 shares of ABC stock originally bought for $56 (total investment of $56,000) and you write a call to sell the shares at a strike price of $60. The option price is $2, so you gain an instant premium of $2000 (omitting commissions). Three scenarios are possible:

1. If the stock price does not change in three months, the call expires. As the covered call writer, you profit from the $2000 premium.

2. If the stock price rises to $65, the holder exercises the call and buys the stock at $60. Your profit is $6000 ($4000 from appreciation in the stock price from $56 to $60, plus the $2000 premium). You missed out on potentially greater profits, however, because you sold the stocks at the striking price of $60. Without the option, you could have sold the stock at $65 per share.

3. If the stock price drops to $50, the buyer of the call will not exercise it because the market price is less than the striking price. You keep the $2000 premium, which cuts your loss from $6000 to $4000 ($56 − $50 = 6 × 1000).

Conservative Investors Reduce Risks by Purchasing Covered Puts.   Conservative investors who own the asset may also use puts to set up a "collar" to safeguard their profits. Puts allow the holder of the contract to sell an asset at a specific striking price for a certain time period, commonly three months. For example, if you own 1000 shares of ABC stock originally purchased at $56 per share (total investment of $56,000), you hope that the market price of the stock will go up. If it goes down instead, you may suffer a loss. To reduce this risk, you could buy a put for 1000 shares at a striking price close to the purchase price of the stock—for example, $52. The total price of the option contract might be $2000 ($2 per share). Three scenarios are possible:

1. If the stock price does not change in three months, the put expires, and you are out only the $2000.

2. If the stock price rises to $65, you allow the put to expire because it is greater than the striking price, and again you are out only the $2000. Alternatively, you could sell your shares at $65 and realize a profit of $7000 ($65 × 1000 = $65,000 − $56,000 − $2000).

3. If the stock price drops to $50, you would exercise the put and sell your stock at the striking price of $52, thereby hedging your loss from $6000 ($56 − $50 = $6 × 1000) to $4000 ($56 − $52 = $4 × 1000). Thus, conservative investors might buy put options for protection against severe price declines.

Speculative Investors Try to Profit with Options.
Aggressive investors speculating in the options market attempt to profit in two ways. First, because a market typically exists for each security for a period of three months, the investor can hope for an increase in the value of the option. For example, if the price of a stock is rising, the holder of a call option might sell it to another investor for a higher price than that originally paid. Second, the investor can exercise the option at the striking price, take ownership of the underlying securities, and sell them at a profit.

Aggressive investors take a particularly speculative position when they do not own the underlying asset, as when they buy naked options or sell naked puts. Option traders can suffer considerable losses, however. For example, the holder of a call may be forced to take a loss when the market price of the optioned asset rises above the striking price instead of declining. The investor would then be forced to buy the asset at its current higher price and sell it at the lower striking price. Conversely, the writer of a put may incur a loss when the market price of an optioned asset drops below the striking price. The writer would be forced to buy the asset from the option holder at a price higher than the market price. Clearly, writing naked options is a highly speculative activity.

Speculative Investors Buy Calls to Create Tremendous Leverage.
The lure of a call is that the option holder can control a relatively large asset with a small amount of capital for a specified period of time. If the market price of the asset rises to exceed the striking price plus the premium, the holder could make a substantial profit. For example, Al Dietrich, a technology expert from New Bedford, Massachusetts, bought a stock option call on Xerox in March, when the stock was selling for $55 per share. The striking price is $60, the expiration date is the third Friday in March, and the price (premium) of the call is $2 per share. Thus, the option contract cost $200 ($2 × 100 shares under his control). Al hopes that the per-share price for Xerox will rise. He prefers not to buy the stock outright because 100 shares of Xerox would cost him a great deal more—$5500 ($55 × 100).

For Al to break even on the call option deal, the price of Xerox shares must rise to $62 before the call expires, as shown in Equation (17.2). If Al exercises the call option, he can buy the stock at $60 from the option writer and sell it on the market for the current market price of $62 (ignoring commissions). In this instance, he earns $2 per share ($62 − $60), which offsets the $2 per share purchase price of the option. If the price of Xerox stock rises to $65, Al would make a $3 profit per share, for a total profit of $300. Based on his $200 investment, this gain amounts to a 150 percent return ($300 ÷ $200) earned over a short period. Of course, if the Xerox stock price fails to reach $60

Advice from an Expert

How to Calculate Break-Even Prices for Option Contracts

Investors need to know the **break-even price** for option contracts. At this price, the cost of a contract is negated by a profit (or the cost is reduced by hedging a loss). The break-even prices for two types of option contracts—puts and calls—are calculated using Equations (17.1) and (17.2), respectively. (Both formulas appear on the *Garman/Forgue* website.) If the striking price on a put option contract was $52 and the option contract cost $2000 and provided for the control of 1000 shares of stock, then the break-even price of a share of the stock would be $50, as the calculation shows. If the striking price on a call was $60 and the option contract cost $200 and provided for the control of 100 shares of stock, then the break-even price of a share of the stock would be $62.

$$\text{Break-even price on puts} = \text{striking price} - \frac{\text{contract cost}}{\begin{array}{c}\text{number of shares}\\ \text{under control}\end{array}} \qquad \textbf{(17.1)}$$

$$= \$52 - \frac{\$2000}{1000}$$

$$= \$50$$

$$\text{Break-even price on calls} = \text{striking price} - \frac{\text{contract cost}}{\begin{array}{c}\text{number of shares}\\ \text{under control}\end{array}} \qquad \textbf{(17.2)}$$

$$= \$60 + \frac{\$200}{100}$$

$$= \$62$$

When calculating the break-even prices for both puts and calls, it is important to include all transaction costs in the contract cost. These costs include the option premium and perhaps sizable commissions paid to brokers. Commissions will be paid on the option contract itself, and subsequent commissions may be paid related to execution or sale of the option contract. In the preceding put example, a price below $50 triggers the sale of 1000 shares that will come at an additional, and perhaps unanticipated, commission cost. This possibility leads to some sage advice: When planning always consider the full and subsequent costs of the deal.

Jonathan Fox
Ohio State University

by late March, Al's $200 in calls will expire with no value at all and he will lose his entire investment.

Selling Options.   You would want to sell a put or a call when its market price has risen sufficiently due to changes in the market price of the underlying asset to ensure a profit. Alternatively, you might sell an option if its market price is dropping to prevent further losses.

Futures Contracts Focus on Market Price Changes in Certain Types of Commodities

A **futures contract** is very similar to an option in that it is a type of forward contract that is standardized (usually in terms of size of contract, quality of product to be delivered, and delivery date) and traded on an organized exchange. The difference is that futures contracts require the holder to buy the asset on the date specified. If the holder does not want to buy the asset, he or she must sell the contract to some other investor or to someone who wants to actually use the asset.

Futures contracts usually focus on certain agricultural, commercial, and mining products. Organized commodities markets include the Chicago Mercantile Exchange (trading commodities such as pigs, pork bellies, eggs, potatoes, and cattle); the Chicago Board of Trade (corn, wheat, soybeans, soybean oil, oats, silver, and plywood); the New York Coffee and Sugar Exchange; the New York Cocoa Exchange; the International Monetary Market, which is part of the Chicago Mercantile Exchange (foreign currencies and U.S. Treasury bills); the New York Commodity Exchange (gold and silver); and the New York Mercantile Exchange (platinum). Stock futures are also traded on the New York Futures Exchange; in this case, the "commodity" is the S&P 500 or the index of another exchange.

Economic Need Creates Futures Markets.   A farmer planting a 10,000-bushel soybean crop might want to sell part of it now to ensure the receipt of a certain price when the crop is actually harvested. Similarly, a food-processing company might want to purchase corn or wheat now to protect itself against sharp price increases in the future. An orange juice manufacturer might want to lock in a supply of oranges at a definite price now rather than run the risk that a winter freeze might push up prices. These economic needs create futures markets.

Speculators May Trade in Futures Markets.   The speculative investor who buys (or sells) a commodity contract is hoping that the market price of the commodity will rise (or fall) before the contract matures, usually 3 to 18 months after it is written. Futures offer the potential for extremely high profits. Depending on the commodity, the volatility of the market, and the brokerage house requirements, an investor can put up as little as 5 to 15 percent of the total value of the contract. Some contracts require a deposit of only $300. Commissions average about $20 for each purchase and sale.

To illustrate the use of leverage in buying futures contracts, assume that Benoit Sorhaindo, a scuba-diving instructor from the U.S. Virgin Islands, purchases a wheat contract for 5000 bushels at $3.80 per bushel in July. The contract value is $19,000 ($3.80 × 5000), but Benoit puts up only $2500. Each $0.01 increase in the price of wheat represents a total of $50 profit to him ($0.01 × 5000). If the price rises $0.50 to reach $4.30 by late July, Benoit will make $2500 ($0.50 × 5000 bushels) and double his investment. In essence, he could buy the wheat for $3.80 per bushel (as stipulated in the contract) rather than the market price of $4.30 in late July. Of course, as a speculator, Benoit does not actually want the wheat—but he could certainly find a flour mill to buy his futures contract.

The potential for loss exists, too. If the price drops $0.50 to reach $3.30, Benoit would lose $2500. If the price declines, the broker will make a margin call and ask Benoit to provide more money to back up the contract. If Benoit does not have these additional funds, the broker can legally sell Benoit's contract and "close out" the position, which results in a true cash loss for Benoit. Because of the risks involved, most brokerage houses require their futures customers to have a minimum net worth of $50,000 to $75,000, exclusive of home and life insurance.

In each commodity transaction, a winner and a loser will emerge. A buyer of a futures contract benefits if the price of the commodity increases, but the seller suffers. When prices decline, the reverse is true. An estimated 90 percent of investors in the futures market lose money; 5 percent (mostly the professionals) make good profits from the losers; and the remaining 5 percent break even.

Futures Are a Zero-Sum Game.   Investors should be aware that they are dealing in very sophisticated markets when they trade in options or futures. This last speculative investing technique introduced in this chapter, futures, is a **zero-sum game** in which the wealth of all investors remains the same; the trading simply redistributes the wealth among those traders. Each profit must be offset by an equivalent loss. Thus, the average rate of return for all investors in futures is zero. The return actually becomes negative if transaction costs are included. In the world of speculative investments, losers outnumber winners.

Summary

1. Real estate is property consisting of land, all structures permanently attached to that land, and accompanying rights and privileges, such as crops and mineral rights. A real estate investment is known as direct ownership when an investor holds actual legal title to the property. Types of direct ownership investment in real estate include residential units, commercial properties, raw land, and residential lots. Indirect ownership is also possible. Examples of indirect ownership include real estate investment trusts (REITs) and limited partnerships. Timesharing is not an investment.

2. The discounted cash-flow method is an effective way to estimate the proper price to pay for a real estate investment. It emphasizes after-tax cash flow and the return on the invested dollars discounted over time to reflect a discounted yield.

3. People invest in real estate to maximize their after-tax returns and to realize the four advantages of real estate investing: the possibility of a positive cash flow, the potential for price appreciation, the availability of leverage, and special tax treatments that can enhance profits. Disadvantages of real estate investing include the large initial investment, time-consuming management demands, illiquidity, and high transfer costs.

4. Speculative investments offer the potential for high profits along with a clear danger of losing some or all of the invested funds. Although buying collectibles and precious metals and stones can be fun and easy, turning a profit on this type of investment is challenging. Such investments do not pay current income, and the owner has to sell to realize a profit.

5. The fluctuations in prices of certain securities—both up and down—provide high-risk profit opportunities for investors. Stock options can be used to buy or sell shares at a specified price in the future. Futures contracts specify a future price to be paid to buy or sell certain agricultural commodities and other marketable assets.

Key Terms

break-even price, 495
call option, 492
cash flow, 485
covered option, 492
crude annual rate of return, 491
depreciation, 486
discounted cash-flow method, 484
futures contracts, 496
leverage, 486
option premium, 492
real estate investment trust (REIT), 483
repairs, 485
residential units, 481
speculative (high-risk) investments, 480
stock option, 492
striking price, 492
sweat equity property, 482
tax-free exchange, 488
timesharing, 482
zero-sum game, 497

Chapter Review Questions

1. Contrast direct and indirect ownership investments in real estate.

2. Distinguish between a deeded and nondeeded purchase of vacation timesharing property.

3. Describe the elements that make the discounted cash-flow method of estimating the value of a real estate property effective.

4. Explain the difference between capital improvements and repairs, and give examples of each.

5. Explain how leverage can benefit a real estate investor.

6. Summarize how depreciation and interest costs can benefit the real estate investor.

7. Explain why a real estate investment can be successful despite having a negative cash flow.

8. What are some of the negative aspects of investing in collectibles?

9. Why is investing in futures contracts a zero-sum game?

10. Why do speculative securities trading techniques appeal to some investors?

Group Discussion Issues

1. Assume you have $30,000 in cash. Give three reasons why you might be persuaded to invest that money in a real estate investment. Offer two reasons why other members of your class might not be willing to invest in real estate.

2. The text describes several disadvantages of real estate investments. Identify two that might stop you from investing in real estate. Identify ways to circumvent those two obstacles.

3. Explain why timeshares should never be considered an investment. What are some reasons why people buy timeshares?

4. What percentage of your portfolio do you think should be invested in high-risk investments? And should this be an area where people should begin to learn about investing? Explain.

5. The text identified the high-risk investments of options and futures. Identify one that seems like an unwise idea, and explain why it is unappealing.

Decision-Making Cases

▶Case 1
Real Estate or Stocks?

Linda Stayer, a senior research analyst in Austin, Texas, has bought and sold high-technology stocks profitably for years. Lately, however, some of her stock investments have done poorly, including one company that went bankrupt. May, a long-time friend at work, has suggested that the two of them invest in real estate together, because property values of the area have been rising rapidly. May has looked at three small office buildings and some residential duplexes as possible investments.

(a) Contrast the wisdom of investing in commercial office buildings versus the attraction of investing in residential properties.

(b) List three of the advantages associated with real estate investments.

(c) List three things that can go wrong for real estate investors.

▶Case 2
From Real Estate to Options and Futures

Billy and Mark Wilkes, long-time partners in San Jose, California, have bought and sold real estate properties for almost 10 years. They have profited on every transaction and now have a portfolio of real estate worth about $4.7 million, on which they owe only $2.9 million. Mark has read about investing in options and futures contracts, and last week he talked with a stockbroker about the possibilities.

(a) Offer some reasons why Mark might gain by investing $100,000 or $200,000 in options and futures contracts.

(b) List some of the risks of options trading for Billy and Mark.

(c) From an investor's point of view, contrast trading in futures contracts with buying highly leveraged real estate.

Financial Math Questions

1. Dave Bixler, an electrician from Indianapolis, Indiana, is interested in the numbers of real estate investments. He has reviewed the figures in Table 17.3 and is impressed with the potential 36.9 percent return after taxes. Dave is in the 25 percent marginal tax bracket. Answer the following questions to help guide his investment decisions:

   (a) Substitute Dave's 25 percent marginal tax bracket in Table 17.3, and calculate the taxable income and return after taxes.

(b) Why does real estate appear to be a favorable investment for Dave?

(c) What one factor might be changed in Table 17.3 to increase Dave's return?

(d) Calculate the after-tax return for Dave, assuming that he bought the property and financed it with a 7 percent, $170,000 mortgage with annual interest costs of $11,175.

2. Donna Beall, a caterer from Lewisburg, West Virginia, is considering buying a vacation condominium apartment for $265,000 in Park City, Utah. Donna hopes to rent the condo to others to keep her costs down. Answer the following questions to help Donna with her decisions:

(a) Donna's $210,000 30-year mortgage loan costs $16,766 annually (from Table 9.2 on page 244). She figures that $1020 of her $1397 monthly mortgage payment will go for interest. On top of that are monthly expenses for property taxes ($140), homeowner's insurance ($80), and homeowner's association fee ($100). These amounts total $1717 a month. Which of these costs will be tax-deductible?

(b) If Donna is in the 30 percent combined federal and state marginal tax bracket, how much less in taxes will she pay if she buys this condo?

(c) Given that should would like to personally use the condo for vacations totaling 10 to 12 days per year, how many days will Donna have to rent it out before she would become eligible to deduct rental losses from her taxes?

(d) Because Park City is primarily a winter ski resort, few condo renters can be found in the off-season; therefore, Donna is concerned about qualifying to deduct rental losses. Assuming she could rent the condo for $400 per day, summarize the IRS-approved rental alternative she could use to generate some tax-free income. Calculate the maximum amount of money Donna could obtain using that plan.

(e) Figure Donna's annual net out-of-pocket cost to buy the condominium and rent it out minimally for tax-free income. List the costs and total on an annualized basis. Next, deduct the savings on income taxes as well as the presumed rental for the number of IRS-allowed days.

(f) Using the figure derived in part (e), what would Donna's out-of-pocket cost per day be to use the condo herself if she stayed there ten days each year? Fifteen days each year?

Money Matters Continuing Cases

Victor and Maria Consider Hedging an Investment with Puts

Victor and Maria Hernandez recently invested in 200 shares of Pharmacia Corporation common stock at $93 per share. They purchased the stock because the company is testing a new drug that may represent a significant medical breakthrough. The stock's value has already risen $8 in three months, in anticipation of the U.S. Food and Drug Administration's approval of the new drug. Many observers believe that the price of the stock could reach $120 if the drug is successful. If it does not prove to be the breakthrough anticipated, however, the price of the stock could drop back to the $85 range, or even lower. The Hernandezes are optimistic but feel that they should hedge their position a bit. As a result, they have decided to purchase two nine-month Pharmacia 100-share puts for $3 per share at a striking price of $93 per share. Ignore commissions when answering the following questions.

1. What price would the Pharmacia stock need to reach for the Hernandezes to break even on their investment?

2. How much would the Hernandezes gain if they sold the stock for $102 six months from now?

3. How much would the return be as a percentage on an annualized basis?

4. If the price of the stock dropped to $85 in six months, how much would the Hernandezes lose?

The Johnsons Consider a Real Estate Investment

Harry and Belinda Johnson are considering purchasing a residential income property as an investment. The Johnsons want to achieve an after-tax total return of 10 percent. They are considering a property with an asking price of $190,000 that should produce $27,000 in gross rental income and $15,000 in net operating income.

1. Calculate the present value of after-tax cash flow for the property, assuming that the after-tax cash-flow numbers are $8000 for the first year, $8400 for the second year, $8800 for the third year, $9200 for the fourth year, and $9600 for the fifth year, and that the selling price of the property will be $220,000 in five years. Prepare your information in a format similar to Tables 17.2 and 17.3, using Appendix Table A.2 or the *Garman/Forgue* website to discount the future after-tax cash flows to their present values.

2. Give the Johnsons your advice on whether they should invest in the property at its current price of $190,000.

What Would You Recommend Now?

Now that you have read the chapter on real estate and speculative investments, what would you recommend to Kim Day in the case at the beginning of the chapter regarding:

1. Investing in real estate?

2. Putting some of her money in a speculative investment, like collectibles?

3. Buying and selling options and futures contracts?

Exploring the World Wide Web

To complete these exercises, go to the *Garman/Forgue* website at college.hmco.com/business/students. Under General Business, select the title of this text. Click on the Internet Exercises link for this chapter, and answer the questions that appear on the Web page.

1. Visit the website for the Chicago Board of Trade (CBOT). Use its Education section and glossary to answer the following questions:

   (a) What is a futures contract?

   (b) What is the difference between a stock market and a futures exchange?

   (c) Browse the site further to determine what commodities are traded on the CBOT.

2. Visit the website for the National Association of Real Estate Investment Trusts (NAREIT). Select the "Answers to Frequently Asked Questions" section in the "About REITs" area to answer the following questions.

   (a) Why were REITs created?

   (b) How are REITs managed?

   (c) What makes a REIT attractive to investors?

   (d) How are the REITs of today different than those of 25 years ago?

   (e) How many REITs are currently available in the United States?

3. Visit the website for Investopedia.com. There you will find information on the basics of option investing, buying a put, and buying a call. When might an investor want to use options in his or her investment portfolio? Identify several exchanges on which options are traded.

4. Visit the website for About.com. Read its information on real estate as an investment. How is real estate investing different from investing in securities?

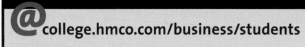

Visit the Garman/Forgue website . . .

@ college.hmco.com/business/students

Under General Business, select *Personal Finance 8e.* There, among other valuable resources, you will find a complete glossary, ACE questions, links to help you complete the chapter exercises, and links to other personal finance sites.

Part Five

Retirement and Estate Planning

CHAPTER 18   Retirement Planning

CHAPTER 19   Estate Planning

Chapter 18

Retirement Planning

LEARNING OBJECTIVES

After reading this chapter, you should be able to:

1 **Recognize** that you are solely responsible for funding your retirement and must sacrifice some current spending and invest for your future lifestyle.

2 **Estimate** your Social Security retirement income benefit.

3 **Calculate** your estimated retirement savings needs in today's dollars.

4 **Understand** why you should save for retirement within tax-sheltered retirement accounts.

5 **Distinguish** among the types of employer-sponsored retirement plans.

6 **Explain** the various types of personally established tax-sheltered retirement accounts.

7 **Understand** ways to be a "do-it-yourself" retirement investor using long-term investment techniques and Monte Carlo simulations.

8 **List** the negative impacts of withdrawing money early from a tax-sheltered retirement account.

9 **Identify** techniques for living in retirement without running out of money.

Maryanne Johnson, age 32, worked for a previous employer for eight years. When she left that job, Maryanne left her retirement money (now worth $90,000) in that employer's defined-contribution plan. After getting divorced and remarried four years ago, she has been working as an assistant food services manager for a large convention center, earning $80,000 per year. Maryanne contributes $267 each month (4 percent of her salary) to her account in her employer's 401(k) retirement plan. Her employer provides a 100 percent match for the first 4 percent of Maryanne's salary contributions and a 50 percent match for the next 2 percent. Today, Maryanne's 401(k) account balance is $21,000. Her investments are equally divided among three mutual funds: a growth fund, a value fund, and an S&P index fund.

Maryanne's husband, Bob, is permanently disabled, and most of his medical expenses are paid for through Maryanne's health benefits at work. Bob receives $1000 per month in disability insurance benefits, and he earns about $5000 per year as a freelance cartoonist. Maryanne is hoping that she and Bob can retire when she is age 55.

What would you recommend to Maryanne and Bob on the subject of retirement and estate planning regarding:

1. The major steps in the process to determine the amount of Maryanne's and Bob's retirement savings goal?

2. How Bob's net income could be invested in a personal tax-sheltered retirement account?

3. The kinds of investment accounts into which they should be putting additional money over the next 23 years if they determined they needed $1 million to meet their retirement savings goal?

4. The investment strategies that Maryanne and Bob should follow for accumulating their retirement funds?

Today's Americans are healthier, are better educated, will live longer, and have higher expectations than their counterparts from earlier generations. For example, your expectations probably include retiring to a comfortable and happy life with little stress and lots of leisure. Enjoying financial security during your retirement years is not a matter of luck, however—it takes planning. You must accumulate sufficient assets during your pre-retirement years to provide for your spend-down retirement years. This means you must sacrifice some current spending and invest for your future lifestyle. As this chapter illustrates, the ability to execute such plans for asset accumulation is entirely within reach of those who understand and utilize the available opportunities. By starting early and contributing regularly, you can turn small monthly investments into hundreds, then thousands, and eventually millions of dollars over the years.

This chapter is designed to help you successfully develop and execute a plan to prepare for a financially successful retirement.[*] Because motivation is key to your success, the first section of the chapter explains why you—and you alone—are responsible for planning and funding your retirement. To begin your planning, you will first learn how to make a realistic estimate of your Social Security retirement benefits. This calculation is followed by a complete illustration of how to estimate your retirement needs in today's dollars. This amount will be a large number, perhaps $500,000 or even $1 million or more. While compiling this seemingly enormous sum may seem like a scary proposition today, it can be done.

Fortunately, a variety of tax-sheltered opportunities are available to help you voluntarily save and invest in ways that are specifically designed for building retirement assets. **Tax-sheltering** means that the tax laws allow certain income to remain exempt

[*]All figures in this chapter pertain to the year 2004, unless otherwise noted.

from income taxes in the current year or permit an adjustment, reduction, deferral, or elimination of income tax liability. You will become familiar with employer-sponsored retirement plans as well as personal retirement accounts that you can set up outside of an employer's plan.

Next we discuss how you, as a "do-it-yourself" retirement investor, should invest your retirement funds. This coverage includes Monte Carlo simulations to help you estimate the odds of your investment portfolio hitting the retirement savings goal you have set. Then we review the negative impacts of withdrawing money from a tax-sheltered retirement account. The chapter closes with suggestions on how to live in retirement without running out of money.

1   Recognize that you are solely responsible for funding your retirement and must sacrifice some current spending and invest for your future lifestyle.

Retirement Planning Is Your Responsibility

For millions of years, humans worked until they died. In recent times, however, new medicines and healthier lifestyles have significantly lengthened life expectancies. One hundred years ago the average lifespan in the United States was 40 years. Today's actuarial tables indicate that among those individuals who survive to age 65, men will live another 15.0 years and women will live 18.2 more years. Furthermore, a 65-year-old male has a 25 percent chance of living to age 92; if a couple is married and reach age 65,

Golden Rules of

Retirement Planning

Financial success comes from learning the Golden Rules of personal finance and then putting what you have learned into practice. Make the following your money habits in retirement planning:

1. Take charge of your own retirement planning by beginning early in life to invest in mutual funds through tax-sheltered retirement accounts and continuing to invest as much as possible every year.
2. Use long-term investment strategies, being certain to take enough risk to increase the likelihood that you will have enough money in retirement.
3. Always save within an employer-sponsored retirement plan at least the amount required to obtain the largest matching contribution from your employer.
4. Every two years re-estimate your retirement expenses and income, including Social Security retirement benefits, and your retirement savings goal in today's dollars.
5. Contribute to Roth IRA and traditional IRA accounts, if necessary, to supplement your employer-sponsored plans and during years when you are not eligible for an employer-sponsored plan.
6. Leave your retirement money where it belongs during your working life—in your retirement accounts. Do not borrow it. Do not withdraw it. When changing employers, roll over the funds into the new employer's plan or a rollover-IRA.
7. To guarantee a portion of your retirement income for life, consider using some of your retirement funds to buy a low-cost annuity when you near retirement age.

there is a similar chance that one or both spouses will live to age 97. Thus, both you and your children will likely live into your nineties, and you may need to support yourself in retirement for 25 years or longer.

This extended longevity requires that you think about your personal finances differently than your parents and grandparents did. Your retirement planning will be complicated by the effects of inflation, the likelihood of post-retirement employment, the effect of income taxes on retirement income, the role of government programs like Social Security and Medicare, and a need to pay out perhaps 20 percent of your retirement income for health care costs.

Retirement is the time in life when the source of most of one's income changes from earned income (such as salary or wages) to employer-based retirement benefits, private savings and investments, and perhaps income from Social Security and part-time employment. (See Figure 18.1, page 506.) Planning for retirement has changed dramatically in recent years. Yesterday's employer-provided pensions were commonly a reward for 30-plus years of working for one employer, but they are no longer widely available. Instead, most of today's employers offer "voluntary" retirement plans to which employees may or may not choose to contribute. As a result, both the responsibility of investing for retirement and the risk of making poor investments have been shifted from the employer to the employee. You must accept the fact that you—and only you—are solely responsible for meeting your retirement needs. And your expenses may very well include all of your health care costs.

On the day when your regular full-time paycheck stops, you are considered to be **retired.** If you have not saved enough money to enjoy the lifestyle you prefer, you will have to lower your level of living, continue working part-time, or do both. Many of today's retirees continue to work part-time because they need to supplement their retirement income, they enjoy working, and want an employer's subsidized health benefits. Others continue working simply because they must do so to survive. You may choose to save and invest for your retirement or you can work forever.

Most financial planners say that people need 80 to 100 percent of their pre-retirement gross income to meet their expenses in retirement and maintain their current lifestyle. This amount includes what you have to pay in income taxes. You can use the "rule of 72" (see page 18) to estimate how fast your retirement living expenses will double. If, for example, 60-year-old John Jolly estimates his annual retirement living expenses in 2005 to be $40,000 and he assumes a 3 percent inflation rate, his expenses will double to $80,000 in 24 years ($72 \div 3 = 24$) in 2029 when John will be 84 years of age. At a 5 percent inflation rate, the doubling occurs in just over 14 years ($72 \div 5$).

To prepare for a financially successful retirement, you must build a sufficient amount of savings and investments to supplement other sources of income in retirement, such as checks from the Social Security Administration (SSA). To succeed in this endeavor, during your 30 or 40 years in the workforce you must select among the various retirement plans and accounts that are available to you and adequately fund them through regular and consistent savings. In addition, you must make sound investment decisions regarding your retirement assets. You are advised to start early to save and invest for retirement and to continue this effort throughout your lifetime. You can let the magical powers of compounding fully fund your needs and wants during the latter third of your life.

Workers who are in their twenties who contribute regularly to their retirement accounts may very well accumulate sufficient funds (along with Social Security benefits) to replace 80 to 100 percent of their pre-retirement income. Of course, achieving this goal will be a big challenge, but it is one you can meet successfully. As the American Savings Education Council reminds you, "You have the power to choose today how you will spend your retirement tomorrow."

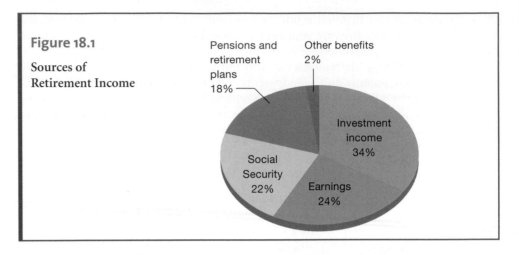

Figure 18.1

Sources of
Retirement Income

Pensions and retirement plans 18%

Other benefits 2%

Investment income 34%

Social Security 22%

Earnings 24%

2 Estimate your Social Security retirement income benefit.

Understanding Your Social Security Retirement Income Benefits

One of the great social and economic successes of the twentieth century was the effort to enact meaningful social insurance legislation. In the 1930s, being old all too often meant being poor. Many men and women at that time faced what was termed "the stark terror of penniless, helpless old age." Today, thanks largely to Social Security, most people know that they will have a dependable foundation of income when they retire. In addition to providing retirement income, the Social Security program includes survivor's benefits, disability benefits, health care benefits, and automatic cost-of-living adjustments.* The Social Security program has become the most successful, most popular domestic government program in U.S. history. More than 50 million checks are mailed out to program recipients by the SSA each month.

Funding for Social Security benefits comes from a compulsory payroll tax whose payment is split equally between employee and employer. Social Security taxes with-

Did You Know? . . .

?

About Women and Retirement Planning

Women are less likely to get retirement benefits from their employers (32 percent of women receive such benefits as compared with 55 percent of men). This occurs, in part, because women are more likely to work for employers who do not offer a retirement plan. Furthermore, due to their lower average incomes, women receive less income than men from Social Security (about $700 per month compared to $875). Women also live longer than men. Thus, women often need to save more money for retirement than men do.

*Estimated average monthly Social Security benefits are currently $922 for all retired workers, $1523 to an aged couple with both spouses receiving benefits, $1904 to a widowed mother with two children, $888 to an aged widow(er) who lives alone, and $1442 to a disabled worker with a spouse and one or more children.

held from wages are called **FICA taxes** (named for the Federal Insurance Contributions Act). The amounts withheld are put into the Social Security trust fund accounts from which benefits are paid to current program recipients. Currently, the taxes collected from workers exceed the benefits paid to retirees. By 2030, however, the ability of the Social Security trust fund to meet Americans' retirement needs will probably exceed the taxes being collected. This prospect continues to generate concern among many people. Although Social Security retirement benefits will likely remain an important contributor to the retirement income of today's workers, these benefits will represent a smaller percentage of their overall income. This trend further emphasizes the need for you to take specific actions to fund the remaining need.

Your Contributions to Social Security

Wage earners pay both FICA and Medicare taxes to the SSA. The FICA tax is paid on wage income up to the **maximum taxable yearly earnings (MTYE),** which comprises the maximum amount to which the FICA tax is applied. The MTYE figure—currently $87,900—is adjusted annually for inflation. In recent years, the total FICA tax rate has been 12.4 percent, consisting of 6.2 percent paid by employees and 6.2 percent paid by employers. Self-employed workers pay a FICA tax rate of 12.4 percent, twice that of wage earners, because they are their own employers. Thus, a self-employed person earning $87,900 per year would have $10,900 ($87,900 × 0.062 × 2) in FICA taxes paid on that income.

Wage earners also pay a 1.45 percent Medicare tax on all earnings matched by their employer. Note that the MTYE limit does not apply to the Medicare tax. Thus, the typical worker sends 7.65 (6.2 + 1.45) percent of his or her earnings to the SSA. For example, a person earning $25,000 pays a combined FICA and Medicare tax of $1912.50 ($25,000 × 0.0765) and a person earning $95,000 pays $5449.80 ($87,900 × 0.062) plus $1377.50 ($95,000 × 0.0145), or a total of $6827.30.

How You Can Become Qualified for Social Security Benefits

The Social Security program covers nine out of every ten U.S. employees. Some federal, state, and local government employees are exempt because their employers have instituted other plans. You must be insured under the Social Security program before retirement, survivor's, or disability insurance benefits can be paid to you or your family.

To qualify for benefits, a worker accumulates credits for employment in any work subject to the FICA taxes, including part-time and temporary employment. The periods of employment in which you earn credits need not be consecutive. Military service also provides credits. You earn **Social Security credits** for a certain amount of work covered under Social Security during a calendar year. For example, workers receive one credit if they earned $900 during any one of the four 90-day periods during the year and the annual maximum of four credits if they earned $3600 (4 × $900). The dollar figure required for each credit earned is raised annually to keep pace with inflation.

The number of credits determines your eligibility for benefits. During your working years, your wages are posted to your SSA record, and you receive earnings credits based on those wages. Social Security uses these credits to determine your eligibility for retirement benefits and for disability or survivor's benefits if you should become disabled or die. The SSA recognizes four statuses of eligibility:

Fully insured. Fully insured status requires 40 credits and provides the worker and his or her family with benefits under the retirement, survivor's, and disability programs. Once obtained, this status cannot be lost even if the person never works again. Although it is required to receive retirement benefits, "fully insured" status does not imply that the worker will receive the maximum benefits allowable. Instead, the actual dollar amount of benefits is based on the average of the highest 35 years of earnings during the working years.

Currently insured. To achieve **currently insured** status, six credits must be earned in the most recent three years. This status provides for some survivor's or disability benefits but no retirement benefits. To remain eligible for these benefits, a worker must continue to earn at least six credits every three years or meet a minimum number of covered years of work established by the SSA.

Transitionally insured. Transitionally insured status applies only to retired workers who reach the age of 72 without accumulating 40 credits (ten years). These people are eligible for limited retirement benefits.

Not insured. Workers younger than age 72 who have fewer than six credits of work experience are **not insured.**

Table 18.1 shows the length-of-work requirements to receive Social Security benefits.

How to Estimate Your Social Security Retirement Benefits

Social Security retirement benefits are based on earnings averaged over most of a worker's lifetime. Your actual earnings are first adjusted, or **indexed,** to account for changes in average wages since the year the earnings were received. The SSA then calculates your average monthly indexed earnings during the 35 years in which you earned the most. The agency applies a formula to these earnings to arrive at your **basic retirement benefit** (or **primary insurance amount**). This is the amount you would receive at your **full-benefit retirement age**—historically age 65. However, for persons born in 1938 or later (those reaching age 65 in 2003 or later), the full-benefit retirement age will be gradually increased, until it reaches 67 for those born in 1960 or later.

You can compute your own retirement benefit estimate using a program that you can download to your computer from www.ssa.gov/OACT/ANYPIA/. You will have three choices concerning when you want to begin receiving Social Security retirement benefits.

Begin Receiving Benefits at Your Full-Benefit Age.
Once you have reached your full-benefit retirement age, you are eligible to receive your basic retirement benefit. You can begin collecting these benefits even if you continue working full- or part-time. Your level of employment income will not affect your level of benefits, though it may affect the income taxes that you pay on your Social Security benefits (as discussed later in this chapter).

Begin Receiving Reduced Benefits at a Younger Age.
You can choose to start receiving retirement benefits as early as age 62, regardless of your full-benefit retirement age. If you do so, however, your basic retirement benefit will be permanently reduced. The check will be reduced 30 percent for people born after 1960. If you choose to take early Social Security retirement benefits, you will be ahead financially if you do not survive to age 80. Today, 60 percent of retirees elect to take their Social Security benefits early.

Table 18.1 Length-of-Work Requirements for Social Security Benefits

Types of Benefits	Payable to	Minimum Years of Work Under Social Security
Retirement	You, your spouse, child, dependent spouse 62 or older	10 years (fully insured status).
Survivors* Full	Widow(er) 60 or older, disabled widow(er) 50–59, widow(er) if caring for child 18 years or younger, dependent children, dependent widow(er) 62 or older, disabled dependent widow(er) 50–61, dependent parent at 62	10 years (fully insured status)
Current	Widow(er) caring for child 18 years or younger, dependent children	1½ years of last 3 years before death (currently insured status).
Disability	You and your dependents	If younger than age 24, you need 1½ years of work in the 3 years prior to disablement; if between ages 24 and 31, you need to work half the time between when you turned 21 and your date of disablement; if age 31 or older, you must have 5 years of credit during the 10 years prior to disablement.
Medicare Hospitalization (Part A: automatic benefits)	Anyone 65 or older plus some others, such as the disabled	Anyone qualified for the Social Security retirement program is qualified for Medicare Part A at age 65; others may qualify by paying a monthly premium for Part A.
Medical expense (Part B: voluntary benefits)	Anyone eligible for Part A and anyone else 65 or older (payment of monthly premiums required)	No prior work under Social Security is required

*A lump-sum death benefit no greater than $255 is also granted to dependents of those either fully or currently insured.

Source: U.S. Department of Health and Human Services.

People considering early Social Security retirement benefits need to be aware that their checks will be reduced if they have earned income above the annual limit ($11,640 this year). Those who earn more than the annual limit have their Social Security benefits reduced $1 for every $2 in earnings. A person entitled to $750 per month ($9000 per year) in early retirement benefits who has an earned income of $30,000 or more should not apply for Social Security benefits because he or she makes too much money to be eligible for any benefit.

Begin Receiving Larger Benefits at a Later Age. You can delay taking benefits beyond your full-benefit retirement age. In such a case, your benefit would be permanently increased by as much as 8 percent per year. You can continue to work even after you begin taking these delayed benefits. Again, your level of employment income will not affect your level of benefits, but it may affect the income taxes that you pay on your Social Security benefits.

Check the Accuracy of Your Social Security Statement

The **Social Security statement** is a document that the SSA periodically sends to all workers. It includes a record of your earnings history, a record of how much you and your various employers paid in Social Security taxes, and an estimate of the benefits that you and your family might be eligible for now and in the future. You can also request a Social Security statement at any time at www.ssa.gov/statement/ or by telephone at (800) 772-1213. When reviewing this statement, make sure that the SSA's records are up-to-date and accurate. Workers have three years to correct any errors.

Advice from an Expert

How to Collect Retirement Benefits and Social Security from a Divorced Spouse

Federal law allows courts to split retirement money between husbands and wives at their divorce. To receive a share of a private-sector defined-benefit or defined-contribution retirement plan, a former spouse needs her (or his) attorney to prepare a **qualified domestic-relations order (QDRO).** Upon approval by the court, a QDRO establishes the rights of an alternate payee to receive all or a portion of a participant's retirement plan benefits upon divorce or as soon as the participant leaves a job or reaches retirement age. In the case of public-sector pensions, a **domestic-relations order** (or court order acceptable for processing) must be filed instead of a QDRO.

Rules on receiving benefits from other pension plans vary depending on the state laws where the divorce occurred, the specific rules in the plan, and the competence of your legal representation. Be sure to ask your lawyer to explain your rights under various scenarios, including the death or disability of your ex-spouse or your own remarriage. Annuities and individual retirement accounts also may be divided as part of a divorce agreement.

To qualify for Social Security retirement benefits based on your former spouse's earnings, your marriage must have lasted at least ten years, you must be unmarried and have been divorced for at least two years, and both you and your ex-spouse must be at least 62 years old. Your benefits will not be affected if the ex-spouse remarries. On the other hand, you will lose the right to benefits based on your former spouse's earnings if you remarry, unless your second marriage also ended in divorce. Your benefit amount consists of 50 percent of a living divorced spouse's benefit or 100 percent of a deceased ex-spouse's benefit. Social Security is the only plan that provides automatic benefits to a divorced spouse.

Sue Alexander Greninger
University of Texas at Austin

How to Calculate Your Estimated Retirement Needs in Today's Dollars

To plan for a financially successful retirement, you first need to set a goal. Otherwise, as one of the most quoted figures in sports, Yogi Berra, says, "If you don't know where you are going, you will end up somewhere else." Your **retirement savings goal,** or **retirement nest egg,** is the total amount of accumulated savings and investments needed to support your desired retirement lifestyle.

Setting a personally meaningful retirement goal will help motivate you take the necessary saving and investing actions. Also, if you begin to save and invest for retirement early in life, the compounding effect on money over time will make it fairly easy for you to reach your retirement savings goal. Conversely, if you delay too long in setting and striving to achieve a retirement savings goal, you may become too old to be able to do much about the situation.

Projecting Your Annual Retirement Expenses and Income

Projecting your annual retirement expenses in current dollars and being knowledgeable about the sources of income that might support these expenditures lead logically to a key question that may be asked in several ways: "How much money must be set aside to provide that support?", "What is my retirement savings goal?", or "How large a financial nest egg do I need for retirement?" You can use the Decision-Making Worksheet, "Estimating Your Retirement Savings Goal in Today's Dollars" (page 512), to calculate this amount. In the following example, you will see how to use this worksheet to arrive at the amount that you would need to save each year to realize your desired, financially comfortable retirement lifestyle. Couples can use the same worksheet by simply combining their dollar amounts where appropriate. You do not have to remain clueless about how much money you will need when you retire. Simply do the math.

A Retirement Needs Illustration

Consider the case of Erik McKartmann, aged 35 and single, the manager of a weight-loss business in West Park, Colorado. Erik currently earns $50,000 per year and has worked for his employer since age 27. He has been saving $160 per month ($1920 annually) by contributing it to his account within his employer's 401(k) plan. Erik plans to retire at age 62.

1. Erik has chosen not to develop a retirement budget at this time. Instead, he multiplied his current salary by 70 percent to arrive at an annual income (in current dollars) needed in retirement of $35,000 ($50,000 $\times$ 0.70). This amount was entered on line 1 of the worksheet. If Erik wants to increase the amount of dollars to support a higher retirement lifestyle, he can simply increase the percentage in the calculation.

2. Erik checked the SSA website to estimate his benefits. At age 62 he could expect a monthly benefit of $1100 (in current dollars). Multiplying by 12 gave an expected annual Social Security benefit of $13,200 (in current dollars), which Erik entered on line 2 of the worksheet.

Decision-Making Worksheet

Estimating Your Retirement Savings Goal in Today's Dollars

This worksheet will help you calculate the amount you need to set aside each year in today's dollars so that you will have adequate funds for your retirement. The example here assumes that a single person is now 35 years old, will retire at age 62, has a current income of $50,000, currently saves and invests about $2000 per year, contributes zero to an employer-sponsored retirement plan, anticipates needing a retirement income of $35,0000 per year assuming a spending lifestyle at 70 percent of current income ($50,000 × .70), and will live an additional

20 years beyond retirement. Investment returns are assumed to be 3 percent after inflation—a fair estimate for a typical portfolio. The financial needs would differ if the growth rate of the investments is less than 3 percent. This approach simplifies the calculations and puts the numbers to estimate retirement needs into today's dollars. The amount saved must be higher if substantial inflation occurs.

	Example	**Your Numbers**
1. Annual income needed at retirement in today's dollars (Use carefully estimated numbers or a certain percentage, such as 70% or 80%.)	$ 35,000	_____
2. Estimated Social Security retirement benefit in today's dollars	$ 13,200	_____
3. Estimated employer pension benefit in today's dollars (Ask your retirement benefit advisor to make an estimate of your future pension, assuming that you remain in the same job at the same salary, or make your own conservative estimate.)	$ 5,800	_____
4. Total estimated retirement income from Social Security and employer pension in today's dollars (line 2 + line 3)	$ 19,000	_____
5. Additional income needed at retirement in today's dollars (line 1 − line 4)	$ 16,000	_____
6. Amount you must have at retirement in today's dollars to receive additional annual income in retirement (line 5) for 20 years (from Appendix Table A.4, assuming a 3% return over 20 years, or 14.8775 × $16,000)	$238,040	_____
7. Amount already available as savings and investments in today's dollars (add lines 7-A through 7-D, and record the total on line 7-E)		
A Employer savings plans, such as a 401(k), SEP-IRA, or profit-sharing plan	0	
B IRAs and Keoghs	$ 24,000	
C Other investments, such as mutual funds, stocks, bonds, real estate, and other assets available for retirement	$ 13,000	
D If you wish to include a portion of the equity in your home as savings, enter its present value minus the cost of another home in retirement	0	
E Total retirement savings (add lines A through D)	$ 37,000	_____
8. Future value of current savings/investments at time of retirement (using Appendix Table A.1 and a growth rate of 3% over 27 years, the factor is 2.2213; thus, 2.2213 × $37,000)	$ 82,188	_____
9. Additional retirement savings and investments needed at time of retirement (line 6 − line 8)	$155,852	_____
10. Annual savings needed (to reach amount in line 9) before retirement (using Appendix Table A.3 and a growth rate of 3% over 27 years, the factor is 40.7096; thus, $155,852 ÷ 40.7096)	$ 3,828	_____
11. Current annual contribution to savings and investment plans	$ 2,000	_____
12. Additional amount of annual savings that you need to set aside in today's dollars to achieve retirement goal (in line 1) (line 10 − line 11)	$ 1,828	_____

3. Line 3 of the worksheet, which calls for Erik's expected pension benefit, is appropriate for defined-benefit plans. After discussing his expected employer pension with the benefits counselor at work, Erik found that the company retirement plan had recently changed from a defined-benefit plan to a defined-contribution plan. His anticipated benefit under the old plan would amount to approximately $5800 annually, assuming that he remained with the company until his retirement, so he entered that figure on line 3.

4. Erik adds lines 2 and 3 to determine his total estimated retirement income from Social Security and his employer pension. The amount on line 4 would be $19,000 ($13,200 + $5800).

5. Subtracting line 4 from line 1 reveals that Erik would need an additional income of $16,000 ($35,000 − $19,000) in today's dollars from savings and investments to meet his annual retirement income needs.

6. At this point, Erik has considered only his annual needs and benefits. Because he plans to retire at age 62, Erik will need income for 20 years based on his life expectancy. (Of course, Erik could live well into his eighties, which would mean that he would need the inflation-adjusted equivalent of his annual retirement expenditures for more than 20 years.) Using Appendix Table A.4 and assuming a return that is 3 percent above the inflation rate, Erik finds the multiplier 14.8775 where 3 percent and 20 years intersect. He then calculates that he needs an additional amount of $238,040 (14.8775 × $16,000) at retirement. That's a big number! And it is in current dollars. The number does not dissuade Erik from saving, however, because he knows he has time and the magic of compounding on his side.

7. Erik's current savings and investments can be used to offset the $238,040 he will need for retirement. Erik has zero savings in his employer's 401(k) account. However, he does have some money invested in an IRA ($24,000), plus some other investments ($13,000). These amounts are totaled ($37,000) and recorded on line 7E.

8. If left untouched, the $37,000 that Erik has built up will continue to earn interest and dividends until he retires. Because he has 27 more years until retirement, Erik can use Appendix Table A.1 and, assuming a growth rate of 3 percent over 27 years, find the factor 2.2213 and multiply it by the total amount in line 7. Erik's $37,000 should have a future value of $82,188 at his retirement, so he puts this amount on line 8.

9. Subtracting line 8 from line 6 reveals that Erik's financial nest egg will need an additional $155,852 at the time of retirement.

10. Using Appendix Table A.3 and a growth rate of 3 percent over 27 years, Erik finds a factor of 40.7096. When divided into $155,852, it reveals that he needs savings and investments of $3828 per year until retirement.

11. Erik records his current savings and investments of $2000 per year on line 11.

12. Erik subtracts line 11 from line 10 to determine the additional amount of annual savings that he should set aside in today's dollars to achieve his retirement goal. His shortfall totals $1828 per year. By saving an extra $153 each month ($1828 ÷ 12), he can reach his retirement goal established in step 1. Thus, Erik needs to continue what he is doing—saving and investing—plus save a little more so he can enjoy his lifestyle when his full-time career ends. Erik should discuss with his benefits counselor how much he can save and invest via the company's new 401(k) program.

Erik needs to save more for retirement by contributing an additional $1828 per year into his account within his employer's 401(k) plan—that is, about 3.7 percent of his salary. To create an extra margin of safety, and if the rules of his employer's retirement plan permit it, he could save even more of his salary. His employer might also make a matching contribution (discussed below) of some of Erik's 401(k) contributions.

The additional $1828 in current dollars assumes that the growth of his investments will be 3 percent higher than the inflation rate, a reasonable assumption. If his income goes up sharply, Erik should increase his savings because he will have a much larger amount of income to replace at retirement. If something happens to severely depress the stock markets, such as acts of terrorism, he can modify his retirement planning by postponing retirement, cutting back on planned expenditures, and/or balancing his budget with part-time work income. In any event, redoing the calculations every year or two will help keep Erik informed and on track for a financially successful retirement.*

4 Understand why you should save for retirement within tax-sheltered retirement accounts.

Invest Your Retirement Money in Tax-Sheltered Retirement Accounts

The funds you put into personal taxable investment accounts represent **after-tax money.** Assume, for example, that a person in the 25 percent tax bracket earns an extra $1000 and is considering investing those funds. He or she will pay $250 in income taxes on the extra income, which leaves only $750 in after-tax money available to invest. Furthermore, all profits from the invested funds are also subject to income taxes.

Matters are much different when you invest in tax-sheltered retirement accounts. The tax laws give special treatment to voluntary contributions to qualified tax-sheltered accounts. As a consequence, most workers who save for retirement do so by voluntarily contributing money into one or more IRS-qualified tax-sheltered retirement accounts. This section describes reasons why you should contribute to qualified accounts.

Contributions May Be Tax-Deductible

Contributions up to the annual maximum IRS dollar amount (explained later in this chapter as well as in Chapter 4) may be "deductible" from your taxable income in the year the contributions are made. In this situation, you pay zero taxes on the contributed amount of income in the current year. This means that you are investing **pretax money,** and the salary amount you defer, or contribute, to a qualified tax-sheltered retirement account comes out of your earnings before income taxes are calculated. Here the taxpayer gains an immediate reduction in income tax liability for the current year.

Earnings Are Tax-Deferred

Income earned on funds in qualified tax-sheltered accounts accumulates **tax-deferred.** In other words, the individual does not have to pay income taxes on the earnings (interest, dividends, and capital gains) reinvested within the retirement account. Taxes may or may not be due in the future when withdrawals occur. **Withdrawals** mean removing assets from an account.

---

*If you want to spend only five minutes to get a basic idea of the savings you will need when you retire, see the American Savings Education Council's *Ballpark Estimate* (www.asec.org/ballpark) for an easy-to-use, one-page worksheet.

Withdrawals Might Be Tax-Free

IRS regulations permit tax-free withdrawals from one type of retirement account, the Roth IRA, which is discussed later. "Tax-free" means that withdrawals are never taxed.

Much More Money Can Be Accumulated

You will have much more money when it is time to retire if you use tax-sheltered accounts, instead of personal taxable accounts, for your investing. The following examples assume that a person who pays combined federal and state income taxes at a 25 percent rate invests $3000 per year for 20 years in a diversified portfolio of stock, bonds, and mutual funds that earns 8 percent annually. Calculations are from Appendix Table A.4.

Example 1—$110,357: Make Annual After-Tax Investments That Are Not Tax-Sheltered.   The sum of $3000 in after-tax money is invested in a personal taxable account every year for 20 years. Because the 8 percent return is subject to annual income taxes, the return rate is effectively reduced to 6 percent [8 percent × (1 − 0.25)]. A $3000 annual investment for 20 years that earns 6 percent annually will grow to $110,357. The person has invested $60,000.

Example 2—$137,286: Make Annual After-Tax Investments That Are Tax-Sheltered.   The sum of $3000 in after-tax money is invested in a tax-sheltered account every year for 20 years. Because no income taxes are assessed on the interest, dividends, and capital gains while they accumulate, the return rate is 8 percent. A $3000 annual investment for 20 years that earns 8 percent annually will grow to $137,286. The person has invested $60,000.

Example 3—$137,286: Make Annual Pretax Investments That Are Tax-Sheltered Using Some of the IRS's Money.   The $3000 in pretax money is invested in a tax-sheltered account every year for 20 years. Pretax contributions to qualified accounts reduce the current year's income tax liability, so the investor saves $750 ($3000 × 0.25) in income taxes. Instead of the $750 going to the government, those dollars are used to reduce the amount the person had to invest. A $3000 annual investment for 20 years that earns 8 percent annually will grow to $137,286. However, of the $60,000 invested, the person put in only $45,000 because $15,000 was money that would have otherwise gone to the IRS.

Example 4—$171,608: Make Annual Investments That Tax-Shelter Growth and Invest the Money That Would Have Gone to the IRS in Taxes.   The $3000 in pretax money is invested in a tax-sheltered account every year for 20 years. Pretax contributions to qualified accounts reduce the current year's income tax liability, so the investor saves $750 ($3000 × 0.25) in income taxes. This time, however, the investor uses that $750 to help fund a larger contribution—$3750 instead of $3000. A $3750 annual investment for 20 years ($75,000 invested, although only $60,000 was the investor's money and $15,000 was money that would have otherwise gone to the IRS) that earns 8 percent annually will grow to $171,608.

You Have Greater Flexibility

Some qualified tax-sheltered retirement accounts are sponsored by employers, such as a 401(k) plan. Other tax-sheltered retirement accounts, such as IRAs, may be established by individuals. The worker makes the decisions about which types of accounts to use and, very importantly, where to invest the funds in the accounts. Options include trust accounts at financial institutions, such as a bank, federally insured credit union, savings and loan association, brokerage firm, mutual fund company, or life insurance company. Individuals who contribute to tax-sheltered retirement accounts usually invest their money in stocks and mutual funds, particularly index funds. You can change investments whenever desired. In addition, you may choose to contribute once to a tax-sheltered retirement account and then never do so again, or you can contribute regularly for many years.

You Have Ownership and Portability

Assets held in tax-sheltered retirement accounts are always owned by the person who opened the account. When you open a retirement account, you must sign a **beneficiary designation form.** This document contractually determines who will inherit the funds in that retirement account in case you die before the funds are distributed. This designation generally overrides any provisions in a will, and it keeps those assets out of one's estate, as discussed in Chapter 19.

    Portability means that upon termination of employment, an employee can keep his or her savings in a tax-sheltered account by transferring the retirement funds from the employer's account to another account without penalty.

The Three Major Types of Employer-Sponsored Retirement Plans

5 Distinguish among the types of employer-sponsored retirement plans.

Employers usually offer retirement plans to their employees because the promise of a secure retirement represents an effective way to recruit and retain valuable workers. An **employer-sponsored retirement (or qualified plan)** is an IRS-approved plan supported by an employer. Approximately one-third of all workers at small firms voluntarily participate in an employer-sponsored retirement plan, compared with four-fifths of workers in medium-sized to large firms. Participating in such a plan can serve as the cornerstone of your retirement planning. If you do not have access to an employer plan, you should make alternative preparations for retirement. Useful suggestions on funding your own personal retirement accounts are offered later in this chapter.

    The **Employee Retirement Income Security Act (ERISA)** does not require companies to offer retirement plans, but it does regulate those plans that are provided. Among other things, ERISA calls for proper plan reporting and disclosure to participants. For example, it mandates that the plan include a spousal consent requirement that protects the interests of surviving spouses. Three types of employer-sponsored retirement plans are available: defined-contribution, defined-benefit, and cash-balance.

Did You Know? . . .

Retirement Plan Contribution Tax Credit for Low-Income and Moderate-Income Savers

Singles with adjusted gross incomes of less than $25,000 and joint filers earning less than $50,000 can claim a nonrefundable **retirement plan contribution credit** (also known as a **saver's tax credit**). This credit ranges from 10 to 50 percent of every dollar they contribute to an IRA or employer-sponsored retirement plan up to $2000. Married couples filing jointly qualify for a 50 percent credit if their AGI is $30,000 or less, for a 20 percent credit

if their AGI is between $30,001 and $32,500, and for a 10 percent credit if their AGI is between $32,501 and $50,000. For singles, the income limits are $15,000 or less for the 50 percent credit, $15,001 to $16,250 for the 20 percent credit, and $16,251 to $25,000 for the 10 percent credit. Some employed college students can qualify for this tax credit.

Defined-Contribution Retirement Plan—Today's Standard

A **defined-contribution retirement plan** is distinguished by its "contributions"—that is, the amount of money put into each participating employee's individual account. The eventual retirement benefit in such an employer-sponsored plan consists solely of assets (including investment returns) that have accumulated in the various individual accounts. In a **noncontributory plan,** money to fund the retirement plan is contributed only by the employer. In a **contributory plan,** money to fund the plan is provided by both the employer and the participant or solely by the employee. Most plans are contributory.

When you elect to participate and contribute to such a retirement plan, you take a portion of your salary and postpone receiving it. That money goes into your account. Because it goes there before you receive it, those funds are not subject to income taxes. Defined-contribution retirement plans are sometimes known as **salary-reduction plans** because the contributed income is not included in an employee's salary. The tax-free contributions are designated as such on the employee's W-2 form. In effect, says financial expert Steve Lansing, a defined-contribution plan can be viewed as an interest-free loan from the government, via the income taxes saved, to help finance a retirement plan.

Each employee's contributions are deposited with a **trustee** (usually a financial institution, bank, or trust company that has fiduciary responsibility for holding certain assets), which invests the money in various securities, including mutual funds, and sometimes the stocks and bonds of the employer. Each employee's funds are managed in a separate account, out of reach of corporate creditors should the employer go bankrupt.

Such retirement plans are also called **self-directed,** because the employee makes all of the important decisions. The employee controls the assets in his or her account, meaning that individual selects how to invest, how much risk to take, how much to invest, and how often contributions are made to the account.

The balance amassed in such an account consists of the employer's and employee's contributions plus any investment income and gains, minus expenses and losses. The money contributions devoted to the account are clearly specified, but the amount of the money in the account remains unknown until retirement, when the money begins to be withdrawn or distributed. This uncertainty occurs because the sum available to the retiree depends greatly on the success of the investments made.

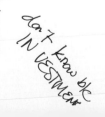

Advice from an Expert

Think Smart About Retirement Savings

The large retirement savings goal dollar amount scares some people. To allay such concerns, the following novel approach to thinking about retirement saving has been suggested: You should look at your retirement as something you "buy." The "retail price" is the financial nest egg itself. From that amount, you can subtract "discounts" for Social Security, employer-sponsored retirement accounts, personal retirement accounts, and any other funds you have already accumulated. Then you identify the difference—the shortfall indicated on line 9 of the Decision-Making Worksheet—and buy it on a "layaway plan." The additional amounts you periodically save and invest are, therefore, the "layaway payments" with which you "buy" your retirement.

This is smart thinking! Think smart and take charge of your future now by doing the math to calculate the retirement savings goal you need to hit—and take actions to save and invest to succeed.

Dennis R. Ackley
Ackley & Associates, Kansas City, Missouri

Investment Decisions.   In defined-contribution retirement plans, the worker—not the employer—bears the risk of investment losses and the rewards of investment profits. Each person takes on the responsibility to learn about investing and to create and maintain a properly diversified portfolio. The employee is also responsible for following applicable IRS rules.

Matching Contributions.   Most employers offer a full or partial **matching contribution** (up to a certain limit) to the employee's account in proportion to each dollar of contributions made by the participant. The match may be a full, 100 percent contribution or a partial match, such as 50 percent on a designated portion of income, such as 6 percent. Because your employer makes a contribution to your account every time you do, in effect you obtain an "instant return" on your retirement savings.

For example, Daryl Jackson, a computer programmer from Memphis, Tennessee, earns $70,000 per year and is allowed to contribute as much as 4 percent of his salary to a tax-sheltered plan, or $2800 in this instance ($70,000 × 0.04). His employer offers all employees a 50 percent match on the first 4 percent of employee contributions. For Daryl, that means his employer will contribute a 50 percent match of $1400 ($70,000 × 0.04 × 0.50) but only if Daryl contributes 4 percent of his salary to the retirement plan. Thus, Daryl's contribution this year will be $2800 and his employer will put $1400 into his retirement account. In effect, Daryl receives a fantastic 50 percent "instant return" on the first $1400 he saves for retirement ($1400 ÷ $2800).

Over time, these contributions can grow to substantial sums. After 30 years earning a 10 percent return, Daryl's single contribution of $2800 will grow to $48,858 (17.4494 × $2800 from Appendix Table A.1). With his employer's match of $1400, the account will total $73,287 (17.4494 × [$2800 + $1400] from Appendix Table A.1). That's $73,287 with zero additional contributions. In an employee-sponsored retirement plan, you should definitely make contributions to your account at least up to the amount where you will obtain the largest matching contribution from your employer. After all, the matching contribution is "free money" from your employer, and the government subsidizes every dollar you save.

Limits on Contributions.   There are limits on the maximum amount of income that an employee may contribute to an employer-sponsored plan. The maximum contribution limit to 401(k), 403(b), and 457 plans (described later in this chapter) is $14,000 in 2005 ($15,000 in 2006). For SIMPLE IRA plans, the limit is $10,000 in 2005 (this limit is indexed to inflation starting in 2006). The Center on Budget and Policy Priorities notes that fewer than 5 percent of 401(k) participants contribute amounts up to the maximum limit.

Catch-up Provisions.   A **catch-up provision** permits workers age 50 or older to contribute an additional $4000 ($5000 in 2006) to most employer-sponsored plans. Thus, millions of people who got a late start on saving—including women who have gone back to work after raising children—can put more money away for retirement.

Types of Employer-Sponsored Plans.   Several types of employer-sponsored defined-contribution plans exist. The most common are the 401(k), 403(b), and 457 plans (named after sections of the IRS tax code) and the SIMPLE IRA. Each plan is restricted to a specific group of workers. You may contribute to these plans only if your employer offers them.

The **401(k) plan** is the best-known defined-contribution plan. It is designed for employees of private corporations. Eligible employees of nonprofit organizations (colleges, hospitals, religious organizations, and some other not-for-profit institutions) may contribute to a **403(b) plan** that has the same contribution limits. Employees of state and local governments and nonprofit organizations may contribute to **457 plans.** When the employing organization has 100 or fewer employees, it may set up a **Savings Incentive Match Plan for Employees IRA (SIMPLE IRA).** This salary-reduction retirement plan requires little administrative paperwork and incurs low costs to set up and operate. Regulations vary somewhat regarding each type of plan.

Vesting Gives You Rights to Your Benefits.   Most employers require a waiting period of one year before allowing new employees to participate in the company's retirement plan. To be eligible for any retirement benefits, an employee must first participate in the employer-sponsored retirement plan. Then, to gain access to the *employer's* contribution and the investment growth resulting from those contributions, he or she must be vested. All previous time worked for the employer since the worker was aged 18 must count toward vesting.

Vesting ensures that a retirement plan participant has the right to take full possession of all employer contributions and earnings if the employee is dismissed, resigns, or retires. Once vested, the worker has a legal right to the entire amount of money in his or her account in a defined-contribution plan. If an employee has not worked long enough for the employer to be vested before leaving his or her job, the employer's contributions will be forfeited back to the employer's plan, and the employee will have no future rights to those benefits. No matter when you leave an employer, you always have a vested right to the money that you personally contributed to your account in a retirement plan at work.

Employees may be vested as soon as an employer desires, but no later than specified by one of the following three options:

- **Immediate vesting.** The employee owns the money just as soon as the employer deposits funds into his or her account.
- **Graduated vesting.** By law, the longest graded vesting schedule a plan can have is six years. Employees must be at least 20 percent vested after two years of service

and gain an additional 20 percent for each subsequent year until, at the end of year six, the account is fully vested.

- **Cliff vesting.** The employee is fully vested within three years of employment with no graduations.

Defined-Benefit Retirement Plan—Yesterday's Standard

The second type of employer-sponsored retirement plan, a **defined-benefit retirement plan,** is commonly called a "pension" or a "final-average plan." A **pension** is a sum of money paid regularly as a retirement benefit. Pensions are paid to retirees, and sometimes their survivors, by the Social Security Administration, various government agencies, and some employers.

Defined-benefit plans pay benefits based on a formula based on the years of service at the employer, average pay in the last few working years, and a percentage. For example, an employee might have a defined annual retirement benefit of 2 percent multiplied by the number of years of service and multiplied by the average annual income during the last five years of employment. In this example, a worker with 20 years' service and an average income of $48,000 over the last five years of work would have an annual benefit of $19,200 (20 × 0.02 × $48,000), or $1600 per month. In another example, an employee with 30 years of service might qualify for 60 percent of the average income over the last five years of work. With a $48,000 average salary over those five years, this worker might receive $28,800 annually, or $2400 per month.

Defined-benefit plans were the "standard" a generation ago, but are offered today by fewer than one-fourth of employers, primarily because the other retirement plan alternatives are less costly. Some employers offer both defined-benefit and defined-contribution plans to their employees. Vesting requirements and participant rights are the same for all retirement plans.

Normal or Early Retirement?   The earlier you retire, the smaller your monthly retirement pension from a defined-benefit plan will be, because you are expected to receive income for more years as a retired person. To illustrate, assume you are eligible for a full retirement pension of $24,000 per year at age 65. Your benefit may be reduced 5 percent per year if you retire at age 58 or reduced 3 percent annually if you retire at age 62. Smaller monthly pension payments are paid to the early retiree in a defined-benefit plan so that he or she will receive, in theory, the same present value amount of benefits as the person who retires later.

The financial advantage of taking early retirement depends in part on the person's life expectancy and the rate at which benefits are reduced. People who expect to live for a shorter period than the average expectancy may achieve a better financial position by retiring early. Most employees are allowed to work for as long as they choose, but companies generally do not increase benefits for employees who postpone retirement beyond age 65.

Disability and Survivor's Benefits.   The prospect of financial security during retirement is heartening, but survivor and disability benefits also represent concerns for workers who have spouses or children. A person's full retirement pension forms the basis for any benefits paid to survivors and, when part of a retirement plan, for disability benefits as well. **Disability benefits** can be paid to employees who become disabled prior to retirement. People receiving either survivor's or disability benefits are generally entitled to an amount that is substantially less than the full retirement amount. For example, if you were entitled to a retirement benefit of $2000 per month, your disability benefit might be only $1100 per month.

If a survivor is entitled to benefits, that pension amount must be paid over two people's lives instead of a single person's life; consequently, the monthly payment is different. Using the benefit described in the preceding example, if your surviving spouse is five years older than you, he or she might be entitled to $1300 per month. In contrast, if your spouse is five years younger, he or she might be entitled to only $1000 per month.

A qualified **joint and survivor benefit** (or **survivor's benefit**) is an annuity whose payments continue to the surviving spouse after the participant's death, equal to at least 50 percent of the participant's benefit. This requirement can be waived if desired, but only after marriage—not in a prenuptial agreement. Federal law dictates that a spouse or ex-spouse who qualifies for benefits under the plan of a spouse or former spouse must agree in writing to a waiver of the spousal benefit. This **spousal consent** requirement protects the interests of surviving spouses. If the spouse does waive his or her survivor's benefits, the worker's retirement benefit will increase. Of course, upon the worker's death, the spouse will not receive any survivor's benefits when a waiver has been signed. Unless a spouse has his or her own retirement benefits, it is usually wise to keep the spousal benefit.

Retirement Plan Insurance.   ERISA established the Pension Benefit Guarantee Corporation (PBGC; www.pbgc.gov). This insurance program guarantees certain benefits to eligible workers whose employers' defined-benefit plans are not financially sound enough to pay their obligations. PBGC insurance never insures defined-contribution plans, but it does insure some cash-balance plans.

Cash-Balance Plan—The Newest Retirement Deal

The third type of qualified employer-sponsored retirement plan has emerged only recently. An increasing number of employers have established or amended their existing retirement plans to create hybrid forms of the defined-contribution and defined-benefit plans. A **cash-balance plan** is a defined-benefit plan that gives each participant an interest-earning account credited with a percentage of pay on a monthly basis. It is distinguished by the "balance of money" in an employee's account at any point in time. The employer contributes 100 percent of the funds and the employees contribute nothing, so the employer assumes all the investment risk. For most employees participating in such a plan, the employer contributes a straight percentage of perhaps 5 percent of the employee's salary every payday to his or her individual cash-balance account. Interest on cash-balance accounts is credited at a rate (perhaps 5 percent) guaranteed by the employer. As a result, the amount in the account grows at a regular rate. Thus, an employee can look ahead 5 or 25 years and calculate how much money will be in his or her account.

Vesting requirements for cash-balance plans are the same as those for other employer-sponsored retirement plans. At separation from employment or retirement, the vested employee has the right to all money in the account.

Cash-Balance Plans Are Growing in Popularity.   Many large employers are shifting to cash-balance retirement plans in part because they are often much less costly to administer. Cash-balance plans are controversial, however, because when substituted for a defined-benefit plan they typically give older workers smaller benefits. Recognizing this concern, many cash-balance plans now provide a higher contribution, sometimes as large as 10 percent, for those employees age 55 and older. Younger workers who are more inclined to move from job to job may appreciate a benefit that can move with them, rather than one that offers a substantial payout only after decades of job loyalty.

Summing Up.   Only the traditional defined-benefit retirement pension program brings a guaranteed monthly pension benefit, early retirement supplements, survivor annuities, and disability benefits. Cash-balance and 401(k) plans do not. Participants in the latter plans will need to tap into their retirement accounts to pay for disability and survivor needs, if necessary.

Additional Employer-Sponsored Plans

In addition to providing employees with one or more retirement plans, some employers offer supplemental savings plans to employees.

ESOP.   An **employee stock-ownership plan (ESOP)** is a benefit plan through which the employer makes tax-deductible contributions of company stock into a trust, which are then allocated into accounts for individual employees. When employees leave the company, they get their shares of stock and can sell them. In effect, the retirement fund consists of stock in the company. If the company prospers over time, the employees will own some valuable stock. Of course, the opposite can occur as well. (Note that "ESOP" does not stand for "employee stock *option* plan" [see Chapter 14]; ESOPs and stock options are entirely different.)

Profit-Sharing Plan.   A **profit-sharing plan** is an employer-sponsored plan that shares some of the profits with employees in the form of end-of-year cash or common stock contributions to employees' 401(k) accounts. The level of contributions made to the plan may reflect each person's performance as well as the level of profits achieved by the employer. Contributions might be fixed (perhaps at 10 percent of profits) or be discretionary. They can vary from year to year. Some companies offer a voluntary profit-sharing plan through which employees can regularly purchase shares of stock in the company at discounted prices. To be properly diversified, experts recommend that employees have no more than 15 percent of their retirement assets invested in their employer's company stock.

Money-Purchase Plan.   A **money-purchase plan** permits an employer to contribute a set amount or percentage of the employee's salary every year to a retirement plan. Once established, the employer must continue making contributions every year.

Thrift and Savings Plan.   A **thrift and savings plan** is an employer benefit that allows employees to make excess salary-reduction contributions to an account, up to a ceiling of 15 percent of annual income; the funds then accumulate tax-free. Although the employees pay current-year income taxes on their contributions, the investment earnings are not taxed. Many employers will fully or partially match the money contributed by an employee. This mechanism offers substantial benefits for two groups of people: (1) those approaching retirement who realize that they have set aside too little and need to catch up, and (2) those who want to contribute more to a salary-reduction program but have already reached the maximum allowed under an employer-sponsored plan.

Deferred-Compensation Plan.   With a **deferred-compensation plan,** an employee and employer agree to postpone large payments for services rendered to a later date, perhaps when the employee enters a lower marginal tax bracket. Highly paid athletes and executives, for example, often prefer such arrangements and frequently request that some of their compensation be paid during their retirement years. Deferred income is not income until it is paid, so it is not taxed until received by the employee.

Did You Know? . . .

What Questions to Ask About Your Employer's Retirement Plan

As you think about retirement, find out as much as you can about your employer-sponsored retirement plan by asking the questions indicated by an "X" for each plan.

	Defined-Contribution Plan	Defined-Benefit Plan	Cash-Balance Plan
1. When is an employee eligible to participate in the plan?	X	X	X
2. How much money can the employer and/or employee contribute?	X		X
3. Is the plan optional or required?	X	X	X
4. How are benefits calculated?		X	X
5. Is the plan insured by the Pension Benefit Guaranty Corporation?		X	
6. When does vesting begin?	X	X	X
7. Can the plan be discontinued or changed by the employer and, if so, how?	X	X	X
8. What is the maximum amount that an employee can contribute?	X		X
9. How much of a matching contribution does the employer make?	X		X
10. What investment options are available, and under what rules may the employee switch among investment options?	X		X
11. Are the employer's contributions in the form of company stock?	X		X
12. Are participants required to purchase stock in the company with their retirement savings?	X		X
13. What is the formula used to define the full retirement benefit?		X	X
14. What is the normal retirement age?		X	X
15. What is the amount of the retirement benefit?		X	X
16. What is the amount of survivor's benefits, if any?		X	X
17. What is the earliest retirement age?	X	X	X
18. Is the retirement benefit integrated with Social Security benefits and, if so, how?		X	
19. What is the reduction in benefits for early retirement?		X	X
20. Are the retirement benefits guaranteed for life once a person retires?		X	X
21. What are the disability benefits?		X	X
22. At separation from employment or retirement, does the employee have the right to the vested lump-sum amount in the account rather than a monthly pension?	X	X	X
23. Are the retirement benefits portable, meaning upon termination of employment, an employee can transfer retirement funds from one employer's account to another retirement account without penalty?	X	X	X
24. What are the procedures for applying for benefits?	X	X	X
25. Are financial planning services and education provided to assist employees when making retirement and other financial decisions?	X	X	X

6 Explain the various types of personally established tax-sheltered retirement accounts.

You Can Also Contribute to Personal Retirement Accounts

IRS regulations allow you to take advantage of other personally established tax-sheltered retirement accounts. These self-directed accounts include the traditional IRA (individual retirement account), Roth IRA, Keogh (pronounced "key-oh"), and SEP-IRA (simplified employee pension–individual retirement accounts).

Individual Retirement Accounts

An **individual retirement account (IRA)** is a personal retirement account in which a person can make annual contributions. These accounts are created and funded at the discretion of the individual who sets them up. An IRA is much like any other account opened at a bank, credit union, brokerage firm, or mutual fund company. It is not an investment, but rather an account in which to hold investments, such as stocks and mutual funds. You can invest IRA money almost any way you desire, including collectibles like art, gems, stamps, antiques, rugs, metals, guns, and certain coins and metals. In addition, you may open as many accounts as you want and change investments whenever you please. You can obtain information about opening a new IRA quickly over the telephone or on-line. To fund the account, you may make a new contribution and/or transfer a lump-sum distribution received from another employer plan or another IRA account to your IRA account(s).

Even if you participate in a 401(k) or another employer-sponsored tax-advantaged savings plan, you should consider investing in an IRA to augment your retirement savings. IRAs are similar to 401(k) plans in that you do not pay taxes each year on capital gains, dividends, and other distributions from securities held within the account. The maximum contribution you may make to an IRA is $4000 per year ($5000 in 2008). An additional contribution of $500 ($1000 in 2006) may be made by people age 50 and older. You may not borrow from an IRA, however.

Traditional IRAs. A **traditional** (or **regular**) **IRA** offers tax-deferred growth. Also, if you qualify, your contributions may be tax-deductible, which means that you can use all or part of your contributions to reduce your taxable income. Qualifying depends on how much your earnings are (restrictions exist to prevent some high-income earners from getting the deduction) and whether you and your spouse are eligible to participate in an employer-sponsored retirement plan. To see if you qualify for a tax-deductible IRA, use the following guidelines:

1. If you have no retirement plan at work, you can invest in a traditional IRA and deduct the entire amount from your taxes.

2. If you are married and you are not an active participant in an employer retirement plan, but your spouse is an active participant, you may deduct all of your contribution to a traditional IRA.

3. If you have a retirement plan at work, you may fully or partially deduct your IRA contribution only if your adjusted gross income qualifies. Also, if either spouse participates in an employer-sponsored retirement plan, the allowable contribution depends on the couple's income. The amount begins to be reduced for single taxpayers

IRA:
☆ any way want

Cap't gains not taxes

earning about $50,000 ($60,000 in 2006) and about $70,000 ($100,000 in 2007) for joint returns.

4. If you have a nonworking spouse, that person may contribute to a **spousal IRA.** Each partner may invest up to the limit and deduct the full amount if the combined compensation of both spouses is at least equal to the contributed amount.

In the past, people who were ineligible to make tax-deductible IRA contributions often made non-deductible contributions to a traditional IRA. However, since Congress created the Roth IRA (discussed next), it is smarter strategy for those people to contribute to Roth IRAs. Generally, you are better off in a Roth IRA if you expect to be in a higher tax bracket when you retire. Anyone who qualifies for a full IRA deduction also may want to consider making non-deductible contributions to a Roth IRA.

Roth IRAs.   A **Roth IRA** is a non-deductible, after-tax IRA that offers significant tax and retirement planning advantages for taxpayers earning less than approximately $100,000. Although contributions to Roth IRAs are not tax-deductible, funds in the account grow tax-free. As a consequence, you will owe zero tax when you make withdrawals in retirement. In addition, tax-free and penalty-free withdrawals of earnings may be made after a five-year waiting period if you are older than age 59½, you are disabled, or you use the funds for qualifying first-time homebuyer expenses or educational expenses. If desired, a traditional IRA may be converted to a Roth IRA.

A *single* $2000 contribution made at age 25, for example, growing at a 10 percent annual rate would amount to $67,275 in 20 years (6.7175 from Appendix Table A.1)—and be completely tax-free forever. That's *$65,275 of tax-free growth!* If you are already saving the maximum allowed in your employer's 401(k) plan, consider taking any additional cash on hand and placing it in a Roth IRA.

Distributions from IRAs.   Distributions from traditional IRAs may be fully or partially taxable, depending on whether your account includes non-deductible contributions. If the account is funded solely by tax-deductible contributions, any distributions are fully taxable when received. If you also made non-deductible contributions, logically some amount should not be taxed at withdrawal as it has already been taxed earlier. You should maintain adequate records of all IRA contributions—even for 40 years or more—to avoid paying too much in taxes. That means saving all annual reports of account activities. The IRS requires that withdrawals from traditional IRAs begin no later than starting at age 70½.

Distributions from Roth IRAs are tax-free. There is no mandatory withdrawal schedule for Roth IRAs, and money in the account can pass to an heir free of estate taxes (see Chapter 19).

Keoghs and SEP-IRAs

A **Keogh** is a tax-deferred retirement account designed for self-employed and small business owners. Depending on the type of Keogh established (profit-sharing or money-purchase), a person can save as much as 25 percent of self-employment earned income, with most plan contributions capped at $41,000 per participant. If the income comes from self-employment, contributions can still be made after age 70½. Money in Keoghs may be invested in real estate. In addition, an individual can convert his or her Keogh to a SEP-IRA.

Did You Know? . . .

Congress Is Considering Establishing Some New Retirement Accounts

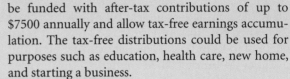

RSA - replace IRAs

- **Retirement Savings Account (RSA).** This proposed account would replace traditional IRAs and Roth IRAs and allow after-tax contributions of $7500 annually, tax-free earnings accumulation, and tax-free distributions.
- **Employer Retirement Savings Account (ERSA).** This proposed account would replace 401(k) and similar plans. The ERSA would allow pretax contributions of $15,000 annually and tax-free earnings accumulation. Distributions from the plan would be taxed.
- **Lifetime Savings Account (LSA).** This proposed special savings account (not retirement account) would

be funded with after-tax contributions of up to $7500 annually and allow tax-free earnings accumulation. The tax-free distributions could be used for purposes such as education, health care, new home, and starting a business.

- **Personal Retirement Account (PRA).** Under the proposal to privatize Social Security, workers who pay Social Security taxes could redirect perhaps one-third of their payroll taxes into individually owned Personal Retirement Accounts, where the worker could invest the funds in the stock market.

A **simplified employee pension–individual retirement account (SEP-IRA)** is intended for taxpayers with self-employment income and owners of small businesses. A SEP-IRA is easier to set up and maintain than a Keogh. The maximum contribution limit to a SEP-IRA is the same as a Keogh. People with income from a sideline business can contribute substantial amounts to a SEP-IRA account.

7 Understand ways to be a do-it-yourself retirement investor using long-term investment techniques and Monte Carlo simulations.

Suggestions for the "Do-It-Yourself" Retirement Investor, Including Monte Carlo Simulations

This section begins with an overview of the retirement planning mistakes that you will want to avoid. It also examines the things that you simply must do right when investing within your retirement accounts, such as starting to save early in your career. Retirement planning is not rocket science. Anyone can follow the suggestions that follow, including using Monte Carlo simulations to estimate the odds of your investment portfolio hitting the retirement savings goal you have set. When you take the appropriate retirement planning action steps, including a moderate amount of risk when investing, you will be able to relax with the confidence that you are making wise decisions about your investment assets and the knowledge that your money will grow and will be there to fund your lifestyle during the last third of your life.

All of the advice on retirement planning presented here is geared toward the "do-it-yourself" investor. If you prefer a "someone-to-do-it-for-you" approach, you can hire a financial expert to make the decisions. Many large financial firms, such as Fidelity and Vanguard, offer account management services. For an annual fee, you can have the firm pick the mutual funds (or stocks) and periodically rebalance your portfolio.

Avoid the Big Mistakes in Retirement Planning

Many people make serious mistakes in their retirement planning. These errors must be avoided because they can dramatically reduce your chances of achieving a financially successful retirement:

1. Underestimating your retirement savings goal. To avoid this problem, perform the necessary calculations on-line or use the worksheet provided in this chapter. Having too much saved at retirement is a pleasant problem. Having too little is painful.

2. Starting too late to save and invest, and being overly optimistic about your retirement age. The road to retirement security is a long one, not a difficult one. It is time that builds wealth. The time to start preparing for your retirement is now.

3. Not contributing enough of your own money to maximize your employer's matching contribution. Employers' contributions are free money and are tax-deferred. Why miss out on such a golden opportunity?

4. Avoiding risk by investing too conservatively. This allows inflation to eat away at your investment return. Putting 75 percent of your retirement money in a total bond index fund and 25 percent in a total stock index fund will create a retirement fund. But reversing those percentages will outperform most individual and professional investors and your financial nest egg is likely to be much larger.

5. Buying and selling assets more often than annually. Frequent movement of funds from one investment option to another is very risky. A "buy-and-hold-and-watch" approach using asset allocation (see pages 380–382) is the best way to go.

6. Taking cash distributions or account loans before retirement. Retirement money should be reserved for retirement, and the large financial nest egg needed requires regular contributions and consistent compounding. Many people cash out their retirement accounts when they change employers; instead, they should roll the money over into an IRA or the plan of a new employer.

7. Underestimating how long you will live. You should plan on being retired for 25 years or longer.

8. Overestimating how much you can withdraw from your portfolio without depleting it. Your rate of withdrawal must fit with your life expectancy. Many retirees take the money out too fast and run out of money.

What if No Employer-Sponsored Retirement Plan Is Available?

When no employer-sponsored retirement plan is offered, you should contribute to either a traditional IRA or a Roth IRA. Recall that you get a tax reduction with the traditional IRA and that the dollars contributed to such an account are taxed upon withdrawal. While contributions to a Roth IRA are not tax-deductible, the money coming out avoids income taxes. Roth IRAs are usually an excellent investment for people in their twenties and thirties because they have many years of tax-free compounding available.

Most mutual fund websites provide worksheets to help you decide (in 5 minutes) whether a traditional IRA or a Roth IRA is best for you. (For examples of such worksheets, see www.troweprice.com, www.kiplinger.com, or www.fidelity.com.) These calculations will be based on your present age, current marginal tax rate, expected annual yield, years to retirement, years in retirement, and marginal income tax rate during the distribution years.

How Much Should You Save?

People who start saving and investing for retirement during their twenties should aim to reserve 12 to 15 percent of their pretax income every year, *including* employer contributions, for this purpose. Those who have delayed planning for retirement until their late thirties or forties should begin investing 20 to 25 percent annually in an effort to catch up; they also may have to be more aggressive in their investment choices.

Start to Save Early in Your Career and Save as Much as You Can

If you cannot save the amounts suggested in the preceding section, do not despair. You still need to save something! Every payday, place a little money into a retirement account so you put time on your side. Recall from Table 1.3 on page 24 and Table 13.1 on page 363 that successful compounding of investment returns is highly dependent on using the return from earlier years to build greater asset balances. Indeed, the bulk of the growth in the latter years of saving for retirement comes from the earnings off of earnings rather than from new deposits into the account.

The future dollar amounts suggested in retirement needs calculations may seem too difficult to accumulate, but that is not an excuse for postponing getting started. Later in life when you earn more money you can increase the amount of your contributions for retirement.

Use Long-Term Investment Strategies

The challenge facing long-term investors—those who are saving and investing for retirement—is to earn a return that beats inflation.

Chapters 13 through 17 of this book provide sound advice about how to succeed as a long-term investor. The strategies presented in those chapters include buy-and-hold, portfolio diversification, asset allocation (including Monte Carlo simulation), and dollar-cost averaging. Recall that the value of a well-diversified portfolio is that it has the best chance (in contrast to a portfolio of mostly equities or mostly bonds) of earning a total return large enough to substantially outpace inflation and, therefore, provides an opportunity for your retirement savings to grow, reach your retirement financial goal, and last throughout your retirement. It also was observed that many experts invest their "serious money" in index funds. These funds include money that you certainly do not want to place in a high-risk investment and lose, such as money invested to pay for a child's education and to fund your retirement. The primary reason for following this path of investing in index funds is that it is difficult for individual investors to select a portfolio of stocks that earns a total return more than the averages, particularly over many years.

Advice from an Expert

Apply Sound Principles for Managing Your Retirement Accounts

The following principles can help you successfully manage your retirement accounts.

1. Start with a plan.
2. Invest for the long term.
3. Diversify your investments.
4. Use reasonable assumptions.
5. Stay with your plan.
6. Rebalance at least annually.
7. Keep your money invested for as long as possible.
8. Understand the emotions of investing.
9. When you are 50, make a new plan.

David Wray
Profit Sharing/401(k) Council of America

Source: Wray, David, *Apply Sound Principles for Managing Your Retirement Accounts*, by Profit Sharing/401(k), Council of America. Reprinted with Permission.

Use Monte Carlo Simulations to Help Guide Your Retirement Investment Decisions

Wouldn't it be nice if good answers were readily available to you for the questions "Where should I invest for retirement?", "How long will my money last?", and "What happens to my investments if the economy changes?" In fact, these answers are available, thanks to the evolution of the long-term investment strategy of asset allocation into modern portfolio theory, as noted in Chapter 13 (see pages 380–382).

A **Monte Carlo simulation,** named for the famous casino site, can be used to simulate the performance of hundreds or even thousands of individual mutual funds and stocks through thousands of fluctuating securities markets; in this way, it allows you to estimate the probability of reaching your financial goals. The mathematical simulations are based on long-term historical risk and return characteristics for various mixes of stock, bond, and short-term investment asset classes. Each simulation estimates how much you need to save if your investments performed better or worse than expected, and it gives the odds that your assets will last throughout the retirement time period after you choose a given set of investments and establish a withdrawal amount. Note that these calculations are probabilities, not certainties.

By using Monte Carlo simulations, investors can get a more realistic view of how much their current investments may yield in retirement. Sometimes investors will learn that they are playing it too safe by investing too conservatively. This may prevent them from reaching their goals. By evaluating the trade-offs among various combinations of retirement plan contribution levels, diverse investment mixes, overall portfolio risk, projected retirement age, and retirement income goals, Monte Carlo simulations let you understand how certain changes in these factors will affect the chance that you will have enough money in retirement. Some investors may have to learn to be comfortable with increased risk while others may have to save more or work longer. See Figure 18.2 for illustrative Monte Carlo calculations.

Monte Carlo simulations can be performed with any of the top-rated retirement planning computer software programs: Financial Engines (www.financialengines.com), Morningstar (www.morningstar.com) Vanguard (www.vanguard.com), Fidelity (www.fidelity.com), Quicken (www.Intuit.com), PricewaterhouseCooper's (www.PricewaterhouseCoopers.com), and T. Rowe Price (www.troweprice.com). Many employers provide free access to these software programs as part of the educational efforts associated with a 401(k) plan. These services include retirement forecasts, portfolio monitoring, newsletters, and information on finances and investing. To try out interactive Monte Carlo simulations, see www.moneychimp.com/articles/risk/riskintro. htm.

Did You Know? . . .

How to Avoid Rollover Penalties When Changing Employers or Retiring

When changing employers or retiring, you may have four choices:

1. Leave the money invested in your account at your former employer until you wish to begin taking withdrawals.
2. Transfer the money to a retirement account at a new employer.
3. Transfer the money to an IRA.
4. Take the money in cash and pay income taxes and penalties.

Options 2, 3, and 4 result in a **lump-sum distribution** because all the funds are removed from a retirement account at one time. Such a transfer must be executed correctly according to the IRS's "rollover regulations" or the taxpayer will be subject to a substantial tax bill, a penalty, and perhaps a need to borrow money to pay the IRS. A **rollover** is the action of moving assets from one tax-sheltered account to another tax-sheltered account or to an IRA within 60 days of a distribution. This procedure preserves the benefits of having funds in a tax-sheltered account.

The IRS's **20 percent withholding rule** applies if the participant takes direct possession of the funds (choice 4 above). This rule requires that an employer collect a 20 percent tax from any lump-sum distribution that is paid directly to a former employee. This amount is forwarded to the IRS to prepay some of the income taxes that will be owed on the withdrawn funds. To avoid the 20 percent withholding rule, a **trustee-to-trustee rollover** must occur. In this procedure (choices 2 and 3 above), the funds go directly from the previous employer's trustee to the trustee of the new account, with no payment to the employee occurring.

For example, a $300,000 lump-sum distribution made directly to an employee would result in that person receiving $240,000 and the employer withholding $60,000 for the IRS. Government regulations further require that the employee put the entire $300,000 into an account at another employer or a **rollover IRA** (an IRA opened to accept rollover funds) within 60 days—even though only $240,000 was actually received by the employee. The investor must supply the difference ($60,000 in this instance) on his or her own. Substantial penalties are assessed for noncompliance. The 20 percent amount that was withheld may be retrieved the following tax year by filing an income tax return to claim a refund. The IRS wants taxpayers to transfer retirement funds in such a way that the previously untaxed money remains accountable and, eventually, taxable.

Figure 18.2

Monte Carlo Simulation from Financial Engines

(The analysis and recommendations pictured are hypothetical and are provided for illustrative purposes only. This illustration should not be relied on for investment advice.)

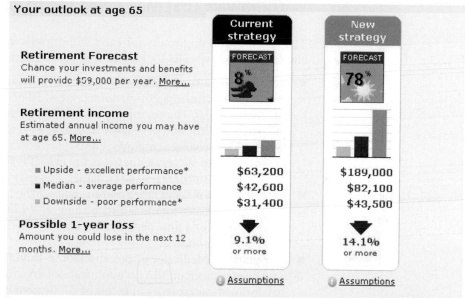

You're on track!

The Forecast for your new strategy looks good! Click the **Next** button to receive your Advice Action Kit.

Your decisions

	Current	New
Your contribution	$3,400/year	$6,100/year
Employer contribution	$1,300/year	$1,300/year
Your investments	Current	Advice
Your risk level	Mod. conserv.(0.82)	Mod. aggr.(1.25)
Retirement age	65	67
Desired income	$59,000	$59,000
Minimum income	$42,000	$42,000

Your outlook at age 65

	Current strategy	New strategy
Retirement Forecast Chance your investments and benefits will provide $59,000 per year. More...	FORECAST 8%	FORECAST 78%

Retirement income
Estimated annual income you may have at age 65. More...

	Current strategy	New strategy
■ Upside - excellent performance*	$63,200	$189,000
■ Median - average performance	$42,600	$82,100
■ Downside - poor performance*	$31,400	$43,500

Possible 1-year loss
Amount you could lose in the next 12 months. More...

	Current strategy	New strategy
	9.1% or more	14.1% or more
	Assumptions	Assumptions

*Note: There is a 5% chance you'll have less than the downside amount and a 5% chance you'll have more than the upside amount. Amounts shown are in pre-tax dollars and have been adjusted for inflation.

Your personalized investment advice is based on your decisions. How we created your investment advice.

Investment advice

	Current strategy	New strategy
401(k) Account		
Redwood Money Market	5%	0%
Platinum Growth	17%	10%
Cypress Balanced Fund	11%	0%
Maple Bond Market	13%	13%
Sequoia Small Cap	25%	0%
Granite S&P 500 Index	29%	30%
Silver Growth and Income	0%	23%
Chestnut Idx:500 Idx	0%	24%

Source: Copyright © Financial Engines. Used with permission.

8 List the negative impacts of withdrawing money early from a tax-sheltered retirement account.

Withdrawing Money Early from a Tax-Sheltered Retirement Account

You should only contribute money to a tax-sheltered retirement account that you will not need until retirement. Early withdrawals—typically defined as a premature distribution before age 59½—are taxed as ordinary income (probably at a 25 percent rate) and the IRS assesses a 10 percent (or perhaps 25 percent) penalty on the amount withdrawn. If you take an early withdrawal of $2000, for example, you must include that $2000 as part of your income on your income tax form and pay perhaps $700 to the IRS (a $200 penalty and, if you are in the 25 percent tax bracket, $500 in extra income taxes).

Withdrawals That May Avoid the 10 Percent IRS Penalty

The IRS imposes no penalty for early withdrawals in a few situations, although your employer may have rules for its plan that restrict withdrawals.

- **Account Loan.** You may borrow up to half of your accumulated assets in an employer-sponsored account, not to exceed 50 percent of the balance or $50,000, whichever is less. The borrower pays interest on the loan, which is then credited to the person's account. Loans must be repaid with after-tax money plus interest. If the employee changes employers, he or she must repay the full, unpaid balance of the loan within 30 days. Otherwise, the loan is reclassified as a withdrawal, which results in additional taxes and penalties. You may not borrow from IRA accounts.
- **Early Retirement.** You may avoid a penalty if you are disabled or retire early and you are willing to receive annual distributions according to an IRS approved annuity-type method for a time period of no less than five years. You must pay taxes on the withdrawn amount.
- **Expenses for Medical, College, and Home-Buying.** You can make penalty-free withdrawals from an IRA account (but not an employer-sponsored plan) if you pay for medical expenses in excess of 7.5 percent of your adjusted gross income, you pay medical insurance premiums after being on unemployment for at least 12 weeks, you pay qualified higher education expenses, or the distribution of less than $10,000 is used for qualifying expenses of first-time home-buyer expenses. You still have to pay income taxes on the amount withdrawn.

Withdrawals Cause Bad Things to Happen to Your Retirement Accounts

When money is withdrawn from a tax-sheltered retirement account before the rules permit—perhaps to buy a car, take a vacation, or pay off a credit card debt—three bad things happen to your retirement planning.

- **The Investment Does Not Grow.** Withdrawing money means that the cash is no longer in the investment. The lost time for compounding will substantially shrink your financial nest egg. For example, if William Wacky, a 35-year-old with $25,000 in a tax-sheltered retirement account, withdraws $8000 out of the account, the forgone return on that $8000 growing at 8 percent over the next 30 years is a whopping $80,502 (from Appendix Table A.1).

- **More Taxes Are Due to the Government.** Continuing the previous example, if William pays combined federal and state income taxes at the 30 percent rate, his $8000 withdrawal must be included as part of his taxable income. That will cost him an extra $2400 ($8000 × 0.30) in income taxes.
- **Penalties Are Assessed.** Because William withdrew $8000, he must also pay a penalty tax of $800 ($8000 × 0.10).

Summing up this example, William's early withdrawal of $8000 nets him only $4800 after taxes and penalties ($8000 − $2400 − $800), and he gave up a future value of more than $80,000 in his retirement account. Sixty percent of workers age 18 to 34 take all the money out of their employer's tax-sheltered retirement account when they change jobs. One consequence is a lower degree of comfort and financial stability during retirement. Clearly, the message here is to avoid making withdrawals from your retirement accounts until you are retired.

Some people borrow from their retirement accounts to buy Christmas gifts, purchase a vehicle, or remodel a home. Borrowing diverts the money from its intended purpose. Borrowers can never make up for the lost compound growth in their retirement accounts.

Living in Retirement Without Running Out of Money

9 Identify techniques for living in retirement without running out of money.

Once you have accumulated a substantial financial nest egg for retirement, you should congratulate yourself. For many years you sacrificed spending and invested instead. Now your task is to plan your finances so you—and perhaps a significant other—can live during retirement without the worry of running out of money. To do so you can carefully manage your retirement account withdrawals, consider purchasing an annuity with a portion of your retirement funds, and/or work part-time during your early retirement years.

Figure Out How Many Years Your Money Will Last in Retirement and Make Monthly Withdrawals Accordingly

"How long will my financial nest egg last during my retirement years?" The answer to this question depends on three factors: (1) the amount of money in the nest egg; (2) the rate of return earned on the funds; and (3) the amount of money withdrawn from the account each year.

Appendix Table A.4 provides factors that can be divided into the money in a retirement fund to determine the amount available for spending each year. Consider the example of Wayne and Susan Neu, 58-year-old retirees from Plano, Texas, who want their $250,000 financial nest egg to last 20 years, assuming that it will earn a 6 percent annual return in the future. The present value factor in the table in the "20 years" column and

Tax Considerations and Consequences

Retirement Planning

Withdrawals from tax-deferred retirement accounts, such as 401(k)s and traditional IRAs, receive no special tax breaks. This occurs because the money contributed to such accounts was excluded from income taxation some years earlier when the funds were originally put into the retirement accounts. Accordingly, the investor has delayed paying taxes on the amounts invested. When withdrawals occur, however, the funds are finally taxed. Distributions from those accounts are taxed at ordinary rates—15 percent and 25 percent for most retirees.

Another source of retirement income is personal taxable investments. The income in this case may be in the form of interest, dividends, and strategically planned sales of assets.

Interest. Interest is an amount received for the use of money that is to be repaid in full at a specified time or on demand. Interest income is taxed at ordinary income tax rates. An insurance dividend is not a true dividend, but rather a return of the premium. Dividends from a savings and loan association or credit union are interest, not dividends.

Dividends. Dividends are the stockholder's share of the profits of a corporation. Dividends from mutual funds and from real estate investment trusts are taxed at ordinary rates. Qualified dividend income from domestic and foreign corporations is taxed at 5 percent for taxpayers in the 10 and 15 percent brackets and at 15 percent for taxpayers in other income brackets.

Capital Gain. A capital gain is the net income received from the sale of an asset above the costs incurred to purchase and sell that asset. Net gains on assets held for less than one year are taxed at ordinary income tax rates. Long-term net capital gains are taxed at lower tax rates (5 percent for taxpayers in the 10 and 15 percent brackets) that max out at 15 percent.

the "6 percent" row in Appendix Table A.4 is 11.4699. Dividing $250,000 by 11.4699 reveals that Wayne and Susan could withdraw $21,796, or $1816 per month ($21,796 ÷ 12 months), for 20 years before the fund was depleted. But what if they live for 30 more years? The factor for 30 years is 13.7648, and the answer is $18,162, or $1513 per month.

A slightly higher rate of withdrawal can significantly decrease your years of retirement income. For example, a portfolio of $1 million with a 4 percent annual withdrawal rate could provide 20-plus years more retirement income than the same portfolio with a 5 percent annual withdrawal rate. People planning for retirement, generally speaking, should be cautious and withdraw at a rate, perhaps 3½ to 4 percent, that should not deplete their funds too rapidly. Then they can be more confident that their money will last the desired number of years.

Buy an Annuity and Receive Monthly Checks

Rather than continuing to manage their own investments during retirement and make planned withdrawals over the years, some people take a portion of their retirement financial nest egg (such as ⅓ or ½) to buy an annuity. An **annuity** is a contract made with an insurance company that provides for a series of payments to be received at stated intervals (usually monthly) for a fixed or variable time period. For retirees who buy an annuity, this means that an insurance company will manage a lump sum of their retirement financial nest egg and promise to send monthly distribution payments according to an agreed upon schedule, usually for the life of the person covered by the annuity (the **annuitant**).

This is best accomplished by purchasing an **immediate annuity** with a single payment during retirement. The income payments will then begin at the end of the first month after purchase. People who buy an immediate annuity typically do so with a lump sum of money rolled over from an individual retirement account, from an employer's de-fined-contribution retirement account, from the cash-value or death benefit of a life insurance policy, or from other savings and investments.

Annuities offer several options for drawing down the funds used to purchase the annuity. In the following examples of hypothetical income payments, assume that a seventy-year-old retiree has purchased an annuity for $100,000. A **straight annuity** might provide a lifetime income of perhaps $790 monthly for the rest of the life of the annuitant only. An **installment-certain annuity** might provide a payment of $680 monthly for the rest of the life of the annuitant with a guarantee that if the person dies before receiving a specific number of payments his or her beneficiary will receive a cer-tain number of payments for a particular time period (such as ten years in this exam-ple). A **joint-and-survivor annuity** might provide $640 monthly for as long as one of the two persons—usually a husband and wife —is alive.

The purchase of an annuity can involve a variety of high sales commissions and fees, and, as such, they can substantially reduce the amount of income paid out. Those considering buying an annuity should shop for the best product, perhaps by beginning with the low-fee, AAA-rated industry leader TIAA-CREF.

Another type of annuity is a **deferred annuity**. Here the person pays premiums during his or her life and income payments start at some future date, such as at retire-ment. A common type of deferred annuity sold by insurance salespersons is called a **variable annuity.** This is an annuity whose value rises and falls like mutual funds, and it pays a limited death benefit via an insurance contract. Variable annuities are sold very aggressively because sellers earn commissions of 5 percent or more, and they charge an-nual fees that often average 3 percent or more. An investor will have to wait 15 to 20 years before an annuity becomes as efficient an investment as a mutual fund. Variable annuities are not a practical investment for 99 percent of investors.

People should absolutely, positively not consider investing in an annuity until *all* other tax-sheltered vehicles to save and invest for retirement have been maximized. This means that people saving for retirement should first contribute the legally permit-ted maximum amounts to 401(k), traditional IRA, and Roth IRA accounts, perhaps to-taling $20,000 each year. The tax-sheltered benefits of these retirement accounts are far better than those offered by a salesperson promoting a deferred annuity. Annuities are replete with numerous restrictions, administrative charges, commissions, purchase fees, withdrawal charges, and penalties. If you need life insurance, buy term life insur-ance, not an annuity (see Chapter 12); if you need to save for retirement, invest in mu-tual funds through tax-sheltered retirement accounts.

Consider Working Part-Time

For a variety of reasons, including reducing the worry of outliving one's retirement in-come, instead of retiring completely, some people choose to work part-time for a while during their early retirement years. They either continue working for their last em-ployer or go to work part-time for a new employer. Reasons include wanting the extra income, enjoying being with co-workers and obtaining employer-provided health care benefits. Predictions are that most retirees will work part-time if for no other reason than to continue to feel active and be a contributing member of society.

Summary

1. In today's world of retirement planning, the employee is responsible for both the obligation to invest and the risk of making poor investments. Carrying out this responsibility successfully likely will require accumulating enough money to provide 80 to 100 percent of your pre-retirement gross income to pay for your living expenses in retirement. You are likely to live into your nineties, so plans must be made for maintaining your lifestyle for a long time.

2. Social Security retirement benefits are funded by worker- and employer-paid taxes. They will provide an important supplemental portion of the income you will need during retirement. You can calculate an estimate of your benefits on-line.

3. You can readily calculate an estimate of your retirement needs in today's dollars. The process begins with identifying your annual retirement expenses and income in current dollars, calculating any shortfall, and determining the additional dollar amount to be set aside each year for your future retirement.

4. The benefits of making voluntary contributions to tax-sheltered retirement accounts are tremendous. You can use pretax money for these funds. Because the contributions enjoy tax-deferred status, money invested in retirement accounts that accumulates tax-free can build up more quickly than similar funds placed into personal investment accounts. Your money avoids taxation until the funds are withdrawn some years in the future. You own your accounts, and they are portable.

5. An employer-sponsored retirement plan can serve as the cornerstone of your retirement planning. Today's standard is a defined-contribution retirement plan into which contributions are made by employees and sometimes employers. The most well known is the 401(k) plan. A defined-benefit retirement plan gives participants a pension upon their retirement. Few employers offer employees both defined-contribution and defined-benefit plans. Many, however, are amending their retirement programs to offer employees cash-balance retirement accounts.

6. Personal retirement accounts include the traditional individual retirement account (IRA), Roth IRA, Keogh, and SEP-IRA. They are appropriate vehicles for retirement investing for individuals who do not have access to a tax-sheltered employer-sponsored retirement plan. Anyone can contribute to a Roth IRA with after-tax money.

7. To invest wisely for retirement, follow long-term investment strategies, accept some reasonable risks, and keep a substantial part of your money in index mutual funds. Start to save early in your career and save as much as you can. Also, consider using Monte Carlo simulations to help guide your investment decisions.

8. You should only contribute money to a tax-sheltered retirement account that you will not need until retirement. Early withdrawals—typically defined as a premature distribution before age 59½—are taxed as ordinary income (probably at a 25 percent rate) and the IRS assesses a 10 percent penalty on the amount withdrawn. Some types of withdrawals are not penalized.

9. Realize that you can live in retirement without running out of money. You can manage your financial nest egg yourself or buy a low-cost annuity.

Key Terms

after-tax money, 514
beneficiary designation form, 516
cash-balance plan, 521
cliff vesting, 520
contributory plan, 517
currently insured, 508
401(k) plan, 519
full-benefit retirement age, 508
individual retirement account (IRA), 524
joint and survivor (survivor's) benefit, 521
matching contribution, 518
Monte Carlo simulation, 529
retirement savings goal (retirement nest egg), 511
rollover, 530
Roth IRA, 525
salary-reduction plan, 517
Social Security statement, 510
tax-sheltering, 503
transitionally insured, 508
vesting, 519

Chapter Review Questions

1. Summarize why people today basically have no choice but to make voluntary contributions to their own retirement accounts.

2. Explain how much workers typically pay in Social Security taxes, and summarize what they get for their money.

3. Explain the benefits of making voluntary contributions to tax-sheltered retirement accounts, and include in

your comments the terms *after-tax money* and *pretax money.*

4. Using different dollar amounts found in examples in this book, illustrate how contributing money to a qualified tax-sheltered retirement account can create larger returns than putting the same money into a traditional investment.

5. Distinguish between a defined-contribution retirement plan and a defined-benefit plan.

6. Summarize some key aspects of a defined-contribution retirement plan, and include in your comments the terms *salary reduction, matching contribution,* and *catch-up provision.*

7. Summarize the advice from expert suggestions on "How to think smart about retirement savings."

8. Explain vesting rights.

9. Compare and contrast a traditional IRA with a Roth IRA, being sure to comment on deductibility and withdrawals.

10. List three major mistakes that people make in retirement planning.

Group Discussion Issues

1. Do you know anyone who has estimated his or her retirement savings goal in today's dollars? Offer two reasons why many people do not perform those calculations. Offer two reasons why it would be smart for people to determine a financial target.

2. If you go to work for an employer that does not sponsor a retirement plan, which kind of personal retirement account would you probably establish? A traditional IRA or a Roth IRA? Give two reasons to support your response. How much money do you think could accumulate in the account?

3. What kinds of people do you think are likely to not plan ahead and save for retirement in a tax-sheltered account? What can be done to help those people prepare for retirement?

4. Of all the mistakes that people make when planning for retirement, which one might be most likely to negatively affect your retirement planning? Give two reasons why.

5. If you had $10,000 in your employer's 401(k) plan retirement account, explain how you would invest these funds. Tell why.

Decision-Making Cases

▶ **Case 1**
Estimating Early and Normal Retirement Benefits

Ben Dietrick of St. Louis, Missouri, age 35, is single and does not expect to marry. He is busily making plans for his retirement from employment in state government. He is anxious to maintain his current lifestyle without "scrimping," but still wants to actively save more for his retirement to take advantage of compounding. Currently, Ben earns $40,000 per year, with an adjusted gross income of $39,000 and an after-tax income of $29,000. He anticipates receiving $10,000 from Social Security annually, and $13,000 per year in a defined-benefit pension upon his retirement at age 65. If he retires at age 55, his pension benefits will be lowered to approximately $9000. To date, Ben has about $10,000 of investments.

(a) Using the Decision-Making Worksheet on page 512, calculate the additional amount of annual savings that Ben needs to set aside to reach his goal of retiring at age 55 with 70 percent of his current income.

(b) What amount of savings for retirement would Ben need if he decided to work to age 65? Use the same worksheet to solve for the answer.

(c) Would you recommend that Ben invest in a traditional IRA or a Roth IRA? Why or why not?

▶ **Case 2**
Calculation of Annual Savings Needed to Meet a Retirement Goal

Melinda Smith, age 40, single, and from San Diego, California, is trying to estimate the amount she needs to save annually to meet her retirement needs. Melinda currently earns $30,000 per year. She expects to need 80 percent of her current salary to live on at retirement. Melinda anticipates that she will receive $800 per month in Social Security benefits. Using the Decision-Making Worksheet on page 512, answer the following questions.

(a) What annual income would Melinda need for retirement?

(b) What would her annual expected Social Security benefit be?

(c) Melinda expects to receive $500 per month from her defined-benefit pension at work. What is her annual benefit?

(d) How much annual retirement income will she need from savings?

(e) How much will Melinda need to save by retirement in today's dollars if she plans to retire at age 65?

(f) Melinda currently has $5000 in a traditional IRA. Assuming a growth rate of 8 percent, what will be the value of her IRA when she retires?

(g) How much will she still need to save?

(h) What is the amount she needs to save each year to reach this goal?

Financial Math Questions

1. George Clum is considering the tax consequences of investing $2000 at the end of each year for 20 years, assuming that the investment earns 6 percent annually.

   (a) How much will the account total if the growth in the investment remains sheltered from taxes?

   (b) How much will the account total if the investments are not sheltered from taxes? See the examples in the Tax Considerations and Consequences feature on page 534 for guidance. (Hint: Use Appendix Table A.3 or the *Garman/Forgue* website.)

2. Over the years, Joe and Marie Paget have accumulated $200,000 and $220,000, respectively, in their employer-sponsored retirement plans. If the amounts in their two accounts earn a 6 percent rate of return over Joe and Marie's anticipated 20 years of retirement, how large an amount could be withdrawn from the two accounts each month? Use the *Garman/Forgue* website or Appendix Table A.4 to make your calculations.

3. Joe Paget from Question 2 is an aggressive investor *and* lucky. Assume that his $200,000 financial nest egg will earn 8 percent while his wife Marie's investments earn 6 percent. How large an amount could be withdrawn from the two funds each month over the next 20 years? Use the *Garman/Forgue* website or Appendix Table A.4 to make your calculations.

4. Becky and Sam Riley desire an annual retirement income of $40,000. They expect to live for 30 years past retirement. Assuming that the couple could earn a 3 percent after-tax and after-inflation rate of return on their investments, what amount of accumulated savings and investments would they need? Use Appendix Table A.4 or the *Garman/Forgue* website to solve for the answer.

5. Raul and Juanita Selenas hope to sell their large home for $280,000 and retire to a smaller residence valued at $150,000. After they sell the property, they plan to invest the $130,000 in equity ($280,000 − $150,000, omitting selling expenses) and earn a 4 percent after-tax return. Approximately how much annual income will be earned? Use Appendix Table A.4 or the *Garman/Forgue* website to solve for the answer.

6. Bea Ake plans to invest $3000 in a mutual fund for the next 25 years to accumulate savings for retirement. Her twin sister Linda plans to invest the same amount for the same length of time in the same mutual fund. Instead of investing with after-tax money, however, Linda will invest through an employer-sponsored retirement plan. If both mutual fund accounts provide a 9 percent rate of return, how much more will Linda have in her retirement account after 25 years? How much will Linda have if she also invests the amount saved in income taxes? Assume both women pay income taxes at a 25 percent rate. Use Appendix Table A.3 or the *Garman/Forgue* website to solve for the answer.

7. Patti Cowley is currently putting $9500 per year into her tax-sheltered employer-sponsored retirement plan at work. Patti's employer will match $0.50 for each $1 that each employee contributes to his or her retirement account on amounts up to 6 percent of the employee's salary—$4200 in Patti's case, as her annual salary is $70,000. How much will Patti accumulate after 18 years if her annual $9500 investments plus the employer's $2100 contributions grow at a 2 percent rate of return after taxes and inflation? (Patti assumes that her increases in salary will equal the value of inflation and income taxes, so her real income will not change.) Use Appendix Table A.3 or the *Garman/Forgue* website to solve for the answer.

8. Dave Jenkins wants to invest $4000 annually for his retirement 30 years from now. He has a conservative investment philosophy and expects to earn a return of 3 percent in a tax-sheltered account. If he took a more aggressive investment approach and earned a return of 5 percent, how much more would Dave accumulate? Use Appendix Table A.3 or the *Garman/Forgue* website to solve for the answer.

Money Matters Continuing Cases

Victor and Maria's Retirement Plans

Victor, now aged 61, and Maria, aged 59, are retiring at the end of the year. Since his retail management employer changed from a defined-benefit retirement plan to a defined-contribution plan ten years ago, Victor has been contributing the maximum amount of his salary to several different mutual funds offered through the plan, although his employer never matched any of his contributions. Victor's tax-sheltered account, which now has a balance of $144,000, has been growing at a rate of 9 percent through the years. Under the previous defined-benefit plan, Victor is entitled to a single-life pension of $360 per month or a joint and survivor option paying $240 per month. The value of Victor's investment of $20,000 in Pharmacia stock eight years ago has now grown to $56,000.

Maria's earlier career as a dental hygienist provided no retirement program, although she did save $10,000 through her credit union, which was later used to purchase zero-coupon bonds now worth $28,000. Maria's second career as a pharmaceutical representative for Pharmacia allowed her to contribute about $27,000 to her retirement account over the past nine years. Pharmacia matched a portion of her contributions, and that account is now worth $112,000; its growth rate has ranged from 6 to 10 percent annually. When Maria's mother died last year, Maria inherited her home, which is rented for $900 per month; the house has a market value of $170,000. The Hernandezes' personal residence is worth $180,000. They pay combined federal and state income taxes at a 30 percent rate.

1. Sum up the present values of the Hernandezes' assets, excluding their personal residence, and identify which assets derive from tax-sheltered accounts.

2. Assume that the Hernandezes sold their stocks, bonds, and rental property, realizing a gain of $238,000 after income taxes and commissions. If that sum earned a 7 percent rate of return over the Hernandezes' anticipated 20 years of retirement, how large an amount could be withdrawn each month? How large an amount could be withdrawn each month if they needed the money over 30 years? How large an amount could be withdrawn each month if the proceeds earned 6 percent for 20 years? For 30 years?

3. Victor's $144,000 and Maria's $112,000 in retirement funds have been sheltered from income taxes for many years. Explain the advantages the couple realized by leaving the money in the tax-sheltered accounts. Offer them a rationale to keep the money in the accounts as long as possible before making withdrawals.

The Johnsons Consider Retirement Planning

Harry Johnson's father, William, was recently forced into early retirement at age 63 because of poor health. In addition to the psychological drawbacks of the unanticipated retirement, William's financial situation is poor because he had not planned adequately for retirement. His situation has inspired Harry and Belinda to take a look at their own retirement planning. Together they now make about $66,000 per year and would like to have a similar level of living when they retire. Harry and Belinda are both 28 years old and, although their retirement is a long way off, they know that the sooner they start a retirement account, the larger their financial nest egg will be.

1. Belinda believes that the couple could maintain their current level of living if their retirement income represented 75 percent of their current annual income after adjusting for inflation. Assuming a 4 percent inflation rate, what would Harry and Belinda's annual income need to be when they retire at age 65? (Hint: Use Appendix Table A.1 or visit the *Garman/Forgue* website.)

2. Both Harry and Belinda are covered by defined-contribution plans at work. Harry's employer contributes $1000 per year, and Belinda's employer contributes $2000 per year. Assuming a 7 percent rate of return, what would their financial nest egg total at retirement 40 years from now? (Hint: Use Appendix Table A.3 or visit the *Garman/Forgue* website.)

3. For how many years would the financial nest egg provide the amount of income indicated in Question 1? Assume a 4 percent return after taxes and inflation. (Hint: Use Appendix Table A.4 or visit the *Garman/Forgue* website.)

4. One of Harry's dreams is to retire at age 55. What would the answers to Questions 1, 2, and 3 be if he and Belinda were to retire at that age?

5. How would early retirement at age 55 affect the couple's Social Security benefits?

6. What would you advise Harry and Belinda to do to meet their income needs for retirement?

What Would You Recommend Now?

Now that you have read the chapter on retirement and estate planning, what would you recommend to Maryanne and Bob Johnson in the case at the beginning of the chapter regarding:

1. The major steps in the process to determine the amount of Maryanne's and Bob's retirement savings goal?

2. How Bob's net income could be invested in a personal tax-sheltered retirement account?

3. The kinds of investment accounts into which they should be putting additional money over the next 23 years if they determined they needed $1 million to meet their retirement savings goal?

4. The investment strategies that Maryanne and Bob should follow for accumulating their retirement funds?

Exploring the World Wide Web

To complete these exercises, go to the *Garman/Forgue* website at college.hmco.com/business/students. Under General Business, select the title of this text. Click on the Internet Exercises link for this chapter, and answer the questions that appear on the Web page.

1. Use the Decision-Making Worksheet on page 512 of the text or on the *Garman/Forgue* website to estimate the additional amount you would need to save to reach your retirement goal. Then visit the T. Rowe Price website, where you will find a similar worksheet. Use it to estimate your retirement savings needs using similar assumptions. What explanation can you give for the differences?

2. Visit the website for the Social Security Administration. There you will find a quick benefits calculator that can be used to estimate your Social Security benefit in today's dollars. Use an income figure that approximates what you expect to earn in the first full year after graduating from college. When the calculator provides your answer, click on "break-even age" to see when you would be better off if you had waited until age 67 to begin taking benefits rather than age 62.

3. Visit the website of the American Association of Retired Persons (AARP). Investigate AARP's answers to the following questions: Is the Social Security system broke? Will Social Security be there for me when I retire? Wouldn't I do better investing my money on my own?

4. Visit the website for Kiplinger.com. Use its IRA calculator to determine whether you would be better off using a traditional IRA or a Roth IRA.

5. Visit the website for Valic. There you will find a list of 12 tips for attaining your dreams. Which of those tips have you already implemented, which can you implement in the near future, and which will you need to wait to address later?

6. Visit the website for the U.S. Department of Labor. There you will find an article on 401(k) fees and the effects they can have on retirement savings. Develop a list of four or five questions that employees with a 401(k) plan might ask their employers about the fees charged under their plans.

Visit the Garman/Forgue website . . .

college.hmco.com/business/students

Under General Business, select *Personal Finance 8e.* There, among other valuable resources, you will find a complete glossary, ACE questions, links to help you complete the chapter exercises, and links to other personal finance sites.

Chapter 19

Estate Planning

After reading this chapter, you should be able to:

1 **Distinguish** among the appropriate ways to transfer your estate to your heirs.

2 **Describe** how trusts can be used to transfer assets and perhaps to reduce estate taxes.

3 **Summarize** the reasons for and features of advance directive documents.

4 **Be** aware of the impact of estate and inheritance taxes on assets to be distributed to one's heirs.

Orlando Molina, age 34, the ballet master at a professional ballet company, recently remarried after being single for several years. He shares custody of his son with his first wife. Orlando married into a ready-made family: Giselle, his new wife, who divorced her husband two years ago, has two children, Jamie and Jon. Like most married couples, Orlando and Giselle, who is a modern dance choreographer, have a variety of financial assets. These include bank accounts, money market accounts, mutual fund accounts, 401(k) plans, Roth IRAs, and whole life insurance policies. The couple also plan on buying a larger home in the near future. Soon after they returned from their honeymoon, Orlando's father, who is only 56 years of age, had a serious stroke. Despite undergoing physical therapy, he is now in a nursing home and likely will reside there for the remainder of his life. The financial and emotional impacts of the elder Mr. Molina's illness have forced Orlando and Giselle to talk about some delicate financial circumstances in their own family.

What would you recommend to Orlando and Giselle on the subject of estate planning regarding:

1. Beneficiary designations for their financial assets?
2. Joint ownership of certain physical assets?
3. Making a will and establishing guardianship for the children?
4. Using advance directive documents to avoid a situation like that confronting Orlando's father?
5. Establishing trusts for their children?

You will work hard over the course of your life to build an **estate** consisting of your worldly possessions and financial wealth accumulated over time less any debts you owe. As this book amply illustrates, you can and should develop and execute plans for spending, for saving, for investing, for pre-retirement asset accumulation, for the protection of those assets, and for the spend-down years of retirement. Now is the time to think about donating your assets, and your final financial planning task is to plan the transfer of your estate to others. Most college-educated people now in their twenties will likely have an estate worth $2 million or more at retirement. They will want to avoid having these assets become depleted because of an extended end-of-life hospital stay, mental incapacitation, or a catastrophic health problem. Furthermore, they will want to have their estate transferred to the desired persons or organizations at death.

This book's closing chapter offers guidance in making these transfers through proper estate planning. **Estate planning** comprises the arrangements you make during your lifetime for the administration and transfer of your worldly possessions and assets after your death. Protecting and transferring your estate can be an emotional process, and it is both smart and practical to take the necessary steps while you are young. You can also seek ways to avoid having your estate become eroded by legal costs and "death taxes."

The chapter begins by discussing what happens when a person dies, with or without a will. It continues by reviewing three popular ways of transferring assets automatically at the end of life: designation by beneficiary, property ownership, and payable-at-death designation. The rights of spouses and former spouses to an estate are examined in the context of partnership marriage rights and common law. Next, transfers via trusts are summarized. The chapter then details the importance of preparing advance directive documents in case you become incapacitated. It concludes with an overview of estate and inheritance taxes.

Golden Rules of

Estate Planning

Financial success comes from learning the Golden Rules of personal finance and then putting what you have learned into practice. Make the following your money habits in estate planning:

1. Every three years or whenever your family situation changes, review the beneficiary and ownership designations in your life on insurance policies, retirement plans, bank accounts, and other assets to make certain they will transfer the property according to your wishes.
2. Always have both an up-to-date will and a letter of last instructions and revise them as major life events occur to be confident property will be transferred to the right heirs.
3. Prepare and regularly update advance directive documents so others can make the right decisions for you should you become incapacitated.
4. Once a year, discuss with your spouse or significant other your family's financial and estate plans.
5. Be positive that certain family members or friends know where you keep financial records, advance directives, your will, and other important documents.

Appropriate Ways to Transfer Your Estate

1 Distinguish among the appropriate ways to transfer your estate to your heirs.

The initial step in estate planning is to inventory everything you own and owe. You may already have created a balance sheet, as discussed in Chapter 2, that lists all of your obvious assets, such as bank accounts, mutual funds, stocks, residences, real estate, motor vehicles, and ownership interest in a family-owned business. Do not forget the assets within your retirement accounts. Also add to your list all valuable personal property, such as artwork, furniture, and family heirlooms. Then record reasonable estimates of each item's current value. Create a comprehensive list describing all essential assets, documents, and financial information and where they are located. Next, sit down with your spouse or significant other and discuss your wishes about who should get what and under what circumstances. Finally, review and decide which of the following estate planning tools are the most appropriate choices for your situation.

The deceased person cannot "walk away" from his or her debts when death occurs. Before any money is distributed to heirs, state law requires that the heirs notify all of the deceased's creditors of the death. One can telephone or write creditors, but sometimes state law requires posting a notice in a local newspaper. In this manner, creditors can collect what they are owed from the estate. Surviving relatives have no personal obligation to repay the decedent's creditors for debts that exceed the assets of the estate.

When planning for the disposal of your estate, you should understand that your surviving family members do not conduct the distribution of your assets after death. Instead, the distributions are either set up by you before your death or conducted by a **probate court**—a special court that is specifically charged to conduct the distribution of assets of persons who have died. **Probate** is a court-supervised process that allows creditors to present claims against an estate and ensures the transfer of a decedent's assets to the rightful beneficiaries according to a properly executed and valid will or, when no will exists, to the persons, agencies, or organizations required by state law.

The probate court will follow your directions if you have previously created a valid will. A **will** is a written document in which a person, the **testator,** tells the probate court how his or her remaining assets should be given away after death. If you die without a will, the probate court will follow state law to determine how your assets will be distributed. As you can see, a will is vitally important in estate planning. As discussed later in this chapter, the most effective estate plans recognize that you should avoid having most, or even all, of your assets go through the probate process. Avoiding this process is desirable in most cases because probating an estate in some states can take between 4 and 18 months and potentially cost several thousand dollars.

A simple will that is prepared by an attorney can cost $125 to $400. Minor changes in a will may be made with a **codicil,** instead of revoking the existing will and writing a completely new one, as you would when making major changes. Most people know exactly what they want to do with their property, so they can use software and online programs to prepare an uncomplicated will. Examples include BuildaWill.com, Kiplinger's WILLPower, Legalzoom, and Quicken WILLPower.* You should see an attorney if your estate will be subject to estate taxes and if you want to set up trusts, have a special-needs person in your life, or believe someone may contest your will.

Figure 19.1 illustrates the different ways that your property can be distributed after your death. **Non-probate property**, which does not go through probate, includes assets transferred to survivors by contract (such as naming a beneficiary for your retirement plan or with bank accounts owned with another person through joint tenancy with right of survivorship). Trusts (discussed in the next section) can also be used to transfer assets outside of probate.

The remaining **probate property** goes through the court-supervised probate process and is collectively known as the **probate estate.** Generally, a decedent's probate estate consists of property that the decedent owned individually and totally in his or her own name. Probate property also includes the value of assets jointly owned through tenancy in common; in such a case, the heirs will receive the deceased's share, but not the co-owner's share. In some states, the decedent's half of community property owned with a spouse is included in a person's estate. The proceeds of life insurance payable to the estate of the deceased—exactly the wrong thing to do—(instead of payable directly to beneficiaries) are included in one's estate as well.[†]

Having a Valid Will Is a Smart Way to Transfer Your Assets

You need a will unless all of your property is non-probate property. A will is one of the primary—and smartest—ways to transfer your assets upon your death.

Transfers with a Will Go to Your Proper Heirs.   If you die with a valid will, the probate court will transfer or distribute your property according to your wishes. A person who inherits or is entitled by law or by the terms of a will to inherit some asset is called an **heir.** A will that is properly drafted by an attorney, signed, and witnessed is unlikely to be successfully challenged by someone who is dissatisfied with the intended distribution of assets. Your will should name an **executor** (or **personal representative**).

---

*Visit www.courttv.com/people/wills to see some wills of famous people.

[†]While the beneficiary does not have to pay income taxes on the life insurance proceeds, they are still included in a person's estate for federal estate taxes purposes if the deceased, while alive, retained any ownership interest, such as the right to change beneficiaries or to borrow against any cash value of the policy. Assigning ownership of the policy to someone else, such as the beneficiary, prior to death solves this problem.

Figure 19.1

How Your Estate
Is Distributed

YOUR ENTIRE ESTATE	
Your non-probate property is transferred at your death before your estate goes through probate court. These transfers can be implemented:	Your probate property is transferred by the probate court in accordance with:
By contracts you set up before death, such as: ■ Beneficiary designations in life insurance and retirement plans ■ Assets owned by joint ownership with rights of survivorship ■ Payable-at-death clauses in bank accounts **By setting up trusts that designate who will receive the property at your death** ■ Living trusts established while you are still alive ■ Testamentary trusts designed to take effect at your death	**Your wishes as outlined in your will** **OR** **If you have no will, the intestate succession laws in your state**

This person should be good with paperwork because he or she is responsible for carrying out the provisions of a will and managing the assets until the estate is passed onto heirs. The executor identifies assets, collects any money due, pays off debts, liquidates assets, files final income tax and estate tax returns, and with the court's permission distributes the balance of any remaining money and property to the beneficiaries. Some people select a friend or relative to perform the executor's duties, whereas others name an accountant or attorney to play this role. The executor's fee for carrying out these complicated tasks ranges from 1 to 5 percent of the estate.

If you have minor children, you should appoint a legal **guardian** for each child in your will. This person is responsible for caring for and raising any child under the age of 18 and for managing the child's estate. The guardian should be someone who shares your values and views on childrearing. Financial columnist Michelle Singletary suggests that you might avoid as potential guardians those who are too old, too ill, or too tired from raising their own children, and those who don't really know the children. Consider naming an alternate candidate in case your first choice cannot take on this responsibility. If you have not taken steps to name a legal guardian, the court will appoint one.

Many people prepare a non-legal **letter of last instructions** along with their will that contains suggestions and recommendations regarding funeral and burial instructions, organ donation wishes, material to be included in the obituary, contact information for relatives and friends, and other information useful to the survivors, such as the location of important documents. Sometimes a letter of last instructions specifies that certain pieces of jewelry or art are to go to specific people. However, if it contains different instructions on these matters, the will prevails. Family members and others are not legally bound by details in a letter of last instructions.

Without a Will Your Property May Not Go to the Correct Heirs.   When a person dies without a valid will (or the court rejects a will), the deceased is assumed to have died **intestate.** In such a case, the probate court will divide all property according to a set formula and transfer assets to the legal heirs. If no surviving relatives exist (a rare situation), the estate will go to the state by right of **escheat.** Your friends and charities will get nothing. If you die without leaving a valid will, the intestate succession laws in the state where you lived prior to death then determine how your property will be divided. This legal determination may force your heirs to share money in ways you did not intend, and those provisions may exclude distribution of your assets to non-marital partners, stepchildren, friends, and charities. The probate court will also see that the debts, income taxes, and expenses of the deceased are paid. Dying intestate can cost much more in taxes and cause legal, bureaucratic, and emotional difficulties for survivors.

When one dies without a will, the manner in which the assets are divided varies enormously from state to state. For example, one state might make the following distributions of a $120,000 estate: If a person with no surviving kin except a spouse dies without a will, the spouse receives the entire estate of $120,000. If the deceased had children with that spouse, the spouse takes $60,000 and the balance is divided equally between the spouse and their children. If the couple were not married, the children would get 100 percent. If the deceased also had children from another marriage, one-half of the estate goes to the spouse and the balance is divided among all his children. If the decedent is survived by a spouse and a parent, the spouse receives $60,000 and one-half of the balance, with the remainder passing to the parent.

As you can see, state laws contain a number of complex provisions that govern who constitutes a legal heir and how much (if any) of an estate an heir may be entitled to receive. What may appear least fair in the intestate distributions just described is that, if the decedent has no children, his or her spouse may be required to share the assets with a distant relative. More than half of all adults and two-thirds of all parents with dependent children do not have wills.

Transfers That Avoid Probate

While your estate includes everything you own, only some of your assets may be subject to probate. Non-probate assets may be transferred without using a will. Such transfers occur prior to the probate process. For example, if two people own a joint bank account with rights of survivorship, upon the death of one owner the account is then owned by the other. Avoiding probate means that the court does not have to oversee the process of publicly administering an estate. Probate can be both costly and time-consuming, so this is a smart move.

Transfers by Beneficiary Designation.   Many individually owned assets are required to have a named beneficiary, such as IRAs, 401(k) plans, Keogh plans, bank and credit union accounts, life and disability income insurance policies, stock brokerage accounts, and mutual funds. A **beneficiary** is a person or organization designated to receive a benefit.* A **beneficiary designation** is a legal form signed by the owner of an asset providing that the property goes to a certain person or organization in the event of the owner's death. The form also contains a place to designate a **contingent** (or **secondary**) **beneficiary** in case the first-named beneficiary has died. If no one has been named as

---

*If you are the beneficiary of an IRA, 401(k), or other retirement account where the money in the account was tax-deferred, those funds will be made available to you. If the beneficiary chooses to take possession of the money, he or she will owe income taxes on the funds. A spouse beneficiary is not subject to the 10 percent early withdrawal penalty, however. Furthermore, a spouse beneficiary may use the rollover process to transfer the tax-free inherited funds into his or her own traditional IRA, where income taxes can continue to be avoided until withdrawals begin. A non-spouse beneficiary does not have this option. A non-spouse beneficiary may be required to make withdrawals over a five-year period or perhaps make equal withdrawals annually over his or her lifetime.

beneficiary for a particular asset or if that person and a named contingent beneficiary have died, the property will go to one's estate and probate court for distribution.

Assigning beneficiaries for their life insurance and retirement plan assets is one of the first things most people do when starting a new job for an employer that offers such benefits.

Keeping your beneficiary designations current is extremely important, particularly if you become a parent or get divorced or remarried. Otherwise, assets such as your life insurance death benefit, 401(k) balance, and pension benefits may be transferred to the wrong person. Note that divorce does not automatically terminate an ex-spouse's status as the beneficiary of a retirement plan or a life insurance policy. Retirement plan administrators are required by the Employee Retirement Income Security Act (ERISA) to pay benefits in the plan to the beneficiaries identified in the plan documents. If the employee dies without changing the beneficiary, an ex-spouse might inherit all of the plan assets, even if state law views the children as the rightful heirs. Some people inadvertently leave retirement savings to parents or siblings who die before they do and never update the forms. It is smart to review your beneficiary and ownership designations every three years or as your family situation changes.

Transfers by Property Ownership Designation.   **Joint tenancy with right of survivorship** (also called **joint tenancy;** see page 144) is the most common form of joint ownership, especially for husbands and wives. In this case, each person owns the whole of the asset, such as a bank account or home, and can dispose of it without the approval of the other owners. Assets owned in this way can include bank accounts, stocks, bonds, real estate, mutual funds, government bonds, and virtually any other type of asset. Upon the death of one owner, the surviving owners receive the property by operation of law rather than through the provisions of a will. Simply stated, the surviving owners owned all the asset before the death and own all of it after death.

Transfers by Payable-at-Death Designation.   It is often impractical, undesirable, or inappropriate to own certain types of property using joint tenancy. For example, two elderly unmarried siblings might want each other to have access to funds in individual savings accounts earmarked to pay for their funerals but not have those accounts be available to the other sibling during life. They could, of course, designate each other as heirs in their wills. However, the funds would then remain tied up until the probate process is complete. To solve this dilemma, each could name the other to receive the funds upon their death using a **payable-at-death** designation for the account. To access the funds, the surviving sibling would simply need to present the death certificate to the bank and show proper identification, and access to the account would be granted.

Use of Trusts to Transfer Assets and Reduce Estate Taxes

2 Describe how trusts can be used to transfer assets and perhaps to reduce estate taxes.

By creating one or more trusts, portions of an estate can be transferred to others in a way that avoids probate and may reduce or eliminate the federal estate tax. A **trust** is a legal arrangement between you as the **grantor** or creator of the trust and the **trustee**, the person designated to control and manage any assets in the trust. The agreement requires the trustee to faithfully and wisely manage and administer wealth for specific purposes to the benefit of the creator and others. Trusts can be established during the creator's life as well as upon his or her death.

People who should consider setting up a trust include those who have complex estates, hold relatively few liquid assets, desire privacy for their heirs, fear a battle over the provisions of a will, or live in a state with high probate costs or cumbersome probate procedures. Trusts may be created to safeguard the inheritances of survivors, reduce estate taxes, fund a child's education, provide the down payment on someone's home, provide financial assistance for minor children, manage property for young children or disabled elders, and provide income for future generations.

Some of the important terms associated with trusts are as follows:

- **Grantor:** The person who makes a grant of assets to establish a trust. Also called the **settler, donor,** or **trustor.**
- **Trustee:** The person or corporation to whom the property is entrusted to manage for the use and benefit of the beneficiary or beneficiaries.
- **Corpus:** The assets put into a trust. Also called the **trust estate** or **fund.**
- **Beneficiary:** The person for whose benefit a trust is created. Also called the **donee.**
- **Remainder beneficiaries:** The parties named in the trust who are to receive the corpus upon termination of the trust agreement.

Living Trusts

Trusts fall into two broad categories: (1) **living trusts** (established while the creator is alive) and (2) **testamentary trusts** (established upon death). For estate planning purposes, the greatest distinction between living trusts is their permanency. This section

---

Did You Know? . . .

Spouses Have Legal Rights to Each Other's Estates

The **partnership theory of marriage rights** presumes that wedded couples intend to share their fortunes equally. Thus, property acquired during the marriage and titled in the name of only one partner (other than property acquired by gift or inheritance) becomes the property of both spouses. A decedent who disinherits a surviving spouse or who leaves that person with less than a fair share of the estate is judged to have reneged on the partnership. A surviving spouse disinherited in this manner has some claim in probate court to a portion of the decedent's estate, if he or she chooses to elect that option. All states give a surviving spouse the right to claim one-fourth to one-half of the other spouse's estate, no matter what a will provides. The remaining portion may pass to other heirs.

Furthermore, in states with **community property laws,**[*] the law assumes that the surviving spouse owns half of everything that both partners earned during the marriage, no matter how much was actually contributed by either partner and even if only one spouse held legal title to the property. States with community property laws provide the same spousal rights for marriages that end in divorce.

Community property consists of property acquired during marriage, except for separable property. **Separable property** is a property wholly owned by one spouse. That is, separable property belonged to one spouse before marriage or was received by that person as a gift or an inheritance during the marriage.

You may not disinherit a spouse unless that person's right to inheritance was voluntarily given up in a signed agreement—and even that type of document may be challenged in court. States often limit the right to contest a will by providing that survivors have six months to challenge it and claim a legal share. Domestic partners usually have no legal claim on the estate of their deceased partners.

[*]Arizona, California, Idaho, Louisiana, Nevada, New Mexico, Puerto Rico, Texas, Washington, and Wisconsin.

examines the two forms of living trusts—revocable and irrevocable—and the following section examines testamentary trusts. Transfers to a trust made within three years of death may, however, be brought back into the decedent's estate for tax purposes.

Irrevocable Living Trusts.   An **irrevocable living trust** specifies who controls your assets while you are alive and what happens to them when you die. It cannot be changed or undone by the grantor during his or her lifetime. Thus the assets in the trust permanently bypass probate and estate taxes applied to the person who instituted the trust. The grantor gives up three key rights under an irrevocable living trust: (1) control of the property, (2) change of the beneficiaries, and (3) change of the trustees. Because irrevocable trusts are generally considered separate tax entities, the trust pays any income taxes due. To set up such a trust, a one-time fee ranging from $750 to $2500 is required.

Revocable Living Trusts.   A **revocable living trust** is used to protect and manage a person's assets. The person creating the trust maintains the right to change its terms or cancel the trust at any time, for any reason, during his or her lifetime. Thus, the grantor retains control over the assets for as long as he or she lives, and any taxable events must be reported by the person who established the trust. Most revocable living trusts also establish the grantor as the trustee.

A revocable living trust can provide for the orderly management and distribution of assets should the grantor become incapacitated or incompetent, as a new trustee can easily be named. Revocable trusts are commonly used to establish newly created trusts upon the death of the grantor (testamentary trusts, discussed in the next section) that are governed by the terms established in the revocable living trust. A revocable living trust operates much like a will and can prove more difficult to contest. Such trusts do not reduce gift and estate taxes, however. If a trust is revocable, its assets stay in the taxable estate of the grantor.

Testamentary Trusts

The second broad category of trusts used in connection with estate planning comprises **testamentary trusts.** A testamentary trust becomes effective upon the death of the grantor according to the terms of the grantor's will or a revocable living trust. Such trusts can be designed to provide money or asset management after the grantor's death, to provide income for a surviving spouse and children, and to give assets to grandchildren or great-grandchildren while providing income from the assets to the surviving spouse and children, among other things.

A generation-skipping trust can be utilized at the time of death. A federal generation-skipping transfer tax will be applied in addition to relevant estate and gift taxes, although a $1.5 million exemption, indexed for inflation, is allowed on transfers. This is a **bypass trust,** also known as a credit shelter trust, exemption trust, or family trust. It can transfer separately titled assets, including stocks and mutual funds held outside a retirement plan, to children or grandchildren. Then the income generated in a bypass trust can be used by your spouse and/or other family members during the spouse's lifetime. At the spouse's death, the remaining assets will pass to your children or other beneficiaries free of estate taxes.

In summary, properly drawn trusts can save you and your family time, trouble, and money. These laudable objectives can be achieved only with the assistance of an experienced attorney who specializes in carefully drafting, planning, and executing strategies and techniques in estate planning.

3 Summarize the reasons for and features of advance directive documents.

Prepare Advance Directive Documents in Case You Become Incapacitated

You can save your loved ones the burden of making some very difficult decisions by writing down what you want to happen should you become incapacitated. Many illnesses, such as Alzheimer's disease, strokes, and cancer, can result in a period of mental incompetence before death. An **advance directive** is any document that establishes who will make financial, medical, and/or other decisions for you should you become mentally incompetent and/or unable to communicate your wishes. It specifies in advance your desires related to those decisions.

A **living will** is a written statement created by a person, while well, declaring their desire to die a natural death. The person does not want extraordinary medical treatment to be used to keep them alive. This document may relieve family members of making a difficult, painful decision to allow a person's life to end. To be effective and to avoid varying interpretations, a living will must speak to specific circumstances. For example, a living will could dictate a "do not resuscitate order" designed to prohibit health care providers from attempting cardiopulmonary resuscitation (CPR) in case of cardiac or respiratory arrest. A federal law requires hospitals to inform patients of their rights to make such decisions about medical care. Living wills need to conform precisely to the statutes in the state where the person lives. A number of states have adopted a **medical power of attorney** that permits the signer to authorize the named individual to make health care decisions on his or her behalf if the signer becomes unable (incompetent) to make such decisions.

A **durable power of attorney** is a document that appoints someone to handle your financial affairs if you later become incapacitated. It remains valid and operative as long as you live, unless you explicitly revoke it. This document should detail the specific aspects of your affairs that it covers and should even mention specific institutions (banks or brokerage firms, for example) and account numbers. A durable power of at-

Tax Considerations and Consequences

Use of a Charitable Remainder Trust to Boost Current Income

Effective use of an irrevocable **charitable remainder trust (CRT)** is popular for people who want to leave a portion of their estate to charity because it can boost one's income during the grantor's lifetime. You set up the trust and irrevocably give it assets. The trust then pays you income from the assets in the trust for a set period, usually for life, and possibly your spouse's life as well. The charity eventually receives the corpus of the CRT when you (and your spouse, if so arranged) die. For example, Amy Louise, a widow from Hyattsville, Maryland, increased the after-tax income on her $60,000 investment portfolio from $1000 to $4800 per year by earmarking the assets for the National Wildlife Federation. According to her attorney, Matthew Paul,

the charitable trust that Amy created to hold the gift until her death first sold the assets without incurring any capital gains taxes and then reinvested the proceeds to obtain a higher return.

A bonus associated with a CRT is that the projected future value of the gift can be discounted to a present value. This amount can then be written off as a charitable contribution on Amy's current income tax return, saving her even more money. It is wise to give to a CRT because the donor can avoid capital gains taxes while still realizing the full benefit of the asset's current value. Thus a CRT works well for people who show wealth on paper because of appreciated assets.

torney gives the designated person virtually absolute power to manage your financial affairs, so choose a trusted individual who knows your wishes. A **limited power of attorney** is narrower in scope and could be restricted to a certain time period or to certain tasks. A **springing power of attorney** does not take effect until a specified event occurs, usually mental incapacitation.

A tender conversation held now with family members about retaining your dignity with advance directives can help avoid the need to make difficult decisions later. Give

Advice from an Expert

Ten Things Every Spouse Must Know About Financial, Estate, Tax, and Investment Planning

The following checklist lists items that spouses should know about financial, estate, tax, and investment planning. After all, it is never what we know that will get us in trouble, but rather what we don't know.

1. Understand your current financial situation—assets and liabilities, net worth, and family income and expenses.
2. Have a plan for all emergencies. Know exactly what financial resources would be needed if your spouse were to become disabled or unemployed. Make certain your auto, homeowner's, and medical insurance coverages are adequate for your situation.
3. Carry sufficient life insurance on yourself and your spouse. Determine whether sufficient resources are available to raise your family and provide for your children's education if you or your spouse were to die. Know what benefits your spouse's employer offers and what benefits have been selected.
4. Verify that your estate documents (wills, trusts, guardianships, durable powers of attorney, and so on) reflect your current wishes for your family.
5. Understand your income taxes and pursue aggressive, but legal, strategies for reducing your tax liabilities.
6. Create a written investment plan and follow it. Understand the rate of return that you must realize on your investments to achieve your goal. Monitor your results quarterly.
7. Know how to invest—when to buy and sell—so that you can consistently obtain a rate of return that will allow your family to achieve and maintain financial independence. Do not expect someone else to care more about your money than you do.
8. Have a plan for funding your children's education, home ownership, and your retirement.
9. Thoroughly understand your employer- and government-provided benefits. If they are not sufficient to achieve your goals, make a career change. There is no sense in riding a dead horse.
10. Communicate with your children and other members of your family to teach them about financial, estate, tax, and investment planning. Remember, the most expensive form of education is to learn through your own bad experiences.

Lorraine R. Decker
Decker & Associates, Inc., www.DeckerUSA.com

Source: Decker, Lorraine R., CLU, ChFC, MSFS, President, Decker & Associates, Inc., "Ten Things Every Spouse Must Know About Finance, Estate Tax, and Investment Planning." Copyright © 2004 by Decker & Associates, Inc. Reprinted with permission.

copies of these documents and your letter of last instructions in sealed envelopes to members of your family and other responsible persons in your life, and your wishes in these matters may be controlled as you desire. Your original will and trust documents should be kept in a safe place, such as a safe-deposit box or at an attorney's office. If desired, copies may be given to certain family members or friends.

4 Be aware of the impact of estate and inheritance taxes on assets to be distributed to one's heirs.

Estate and Inheritance Taxes

The **federal estate tax** is levied on the transfer of property at death and is a tax on the deceased's estate, not on the beneficiary who is to receive the property. While heirs do not directly pay any estate taxes, the amount of the tax can significantly reduce the amount of property available to transfer to heirs.

You are not likely to be subject to federal estate taxes, because they affect fewer than 2 percent of Americans each year. The first $1.5 million of a taxable estate is exempt from the federal estate tax. Referred to as the **exclusion amount,** it is the value of assets that may be transferred to heirs without incurring an estate tax. Estates valued at higher than the exclusion amount, however, are subject to a 47 percent tax. The federal estate tax exclusion amount rises to $2 million in 2006, $3.5 in 2009, and then the tax disappears for one year in 2010. Under current law, in 2011 estates valued at more than $1 million will be subject to a 50 percent estate tax.

Wealthy people use a number of different strategies to reduce or avoid estate taxes, including setting up complicated trusts and making gifts. In addition, the **marital deduction** allows an estate to pass on an unlimited amount of assets to a surviving spouse free of estate taxes. However, when the surviving spouse who inherited assets dies, his or her estate would be subject to any federal estate taxes in effect at that time.

Ohio and Oklahoma are the only states that have a state estate tax. Eight states[*] impose an **inheritance tax** assessed by the decedent's state of residence on *beneficiaries* who receive inherited property. This tax is based on how much the beneficiaries get and their right to receive it. In those states, transfers to spouses, children, and sometimes other close relatives are either exempt or subject to a lower state inheritance tax rate. The beneficiaries are responsible for paying inheritance taxes, although typically the estate pays the taxes before distributing any remaining assets to the heirs.

[handwritten margin note: Fed estate tax 1.5mil. State estate (only Ok & Ohio) 8 states - inheritance tax on BENEFICIARY]

Summary

ACE ✓ Self-tests

1. There are several ways to transfer your estate. Writing a valid will ensures that your wishes regarding the distribution of your worldly goods and wealth will be carried out. Three transfer techniques that avoid probate are designation of a beneficiary, property ownership, and payable-at-death designation. The partnership theory of marriage rights and community property laws assures

that the surviving spouse will receive a fair share of an estate regardless of the provisions in a will. If you do not have a will, the disposal of your estate may be determined by a probate court.

2. Trusts may be used to transfer assets and perhaps reduce taxes. A trust is a legal arrangement between you as the grantor or creator of the trust and the trustee, who is designated to control and manage any assets in the trust for the benefit of the ultimate recipient or beneficiary of the trust assets. The agreement requires the trustee to faithfully and wisely manage and administer wealth for specific purposes to the benefit of the creator and others.

[*]Connecticut, Indiana, Iowa, Kentucky, Maryland, Nebraska, New Jersey, and Pennsylvania.

Trusts can be established during the creator's life (a living trust) as well as upon his or her death (a testamentary trust).

3. Many illnesses, such as Alzheimer's disease, strokes, and cancer, can result in a period of mental incompetence before death. You can utilize advance directives to establish who will make financial, medical, and/or other decisions for you should you be mentally incompetent and/or unable to communicate your wishes before you die. Some key documents include a living will, medical power of attorney, and durable power of attorney.

4. The federal estate tax may be levied on a person's estate at death. Very few people will have to pay the federal estate tax, because it is imposed only on estates that exceed a certain threshold valuation, currently $1.5 million. However, eight states impose an inheritance tax on assets received by heirs to an estate.

4. Give examples of assets that can be transferred by beneficiary designation.

5. What rights do the partnership theory of marriage rights and common law do for a surviving spouse?

6. Why do many people prefer to avoid probate court?

7. Summarize how a charitable remainder trust can be used to boost current income.

8. Distinguish between a living will and a medical power of attorney.

9. What is the federal estate tax marital deduction and how is it used?

10. What proportion of estates are subject to estate taxes, and what is the dollar threshold under which zero estate taxes are payable?

Key Terms

advance directive, 550
beneficiary designation, 546
charitable remainder trust (CRT), 550
community property laws, 548
durable power of attorney, 550
escheat, 545
estate planning, 542
federal estate tax, 552
guardian, 545
intestate, 545
irrevocable living trust, 549
joint tenancy with right of survivorship (joint tenancy), 547
letter of last instructions, 545
marital deduction, 552
medical power of attorney, 550
probate, 543
probate court, 543
probate property, 544
testamentary trusts, 549
will, 544

Chapter Review Questions

1. Summarize the reasons why people should have a will.

2. What types of information do people put in their letter of last instructions?

3. If a person dies intestate, how might his or her assets be distributed?

Group Discussion Issues

1. Do college students really need a will at this point in their lives? Why or why not? What probably would happen to the typical college student's assets if he or she died without a will?

2. What are some criteria that you would use to select the executor for your estate or the guardian for your children if you and your spouse or significant other died at the same time?

3. Think about some famous people who have died. Should they have their wills publicized in probate court? Why or why not?

4. If you were thinking about signing a living will, what are some provisions that you might put into the document?

5. Identify topics that you would cover in your letter of last instructions.

6. Do you think it is appropriate for parents and grandparents to put conditions in a trust set up for their children or grandchildren that relate to the behavior of those assets?

Decision-Making Cases

▶Case 1
A Couple Considers the Ramifications of Dying Intestate

Louise Merryweather of Seattle, Washington, is a 34-year-old police detective earning $58,000 per year. She and her husband Chris have two children in elementary school. They own a modestly furnished home and two late-model cars. Louise also owns a snowmobile. Both spouses have 401(k) retirement accounts where they work, and their employers provide them with $50,000 group term life policies. Louise also has a $50,000 term life policy of her own. The couple has about $5000 in their joint checking account. Neither has a will.

(a) List four negative things that could happen if either Louise or Chris were to die without a will.

(b) What would be the most important negative consequence of not having a will if both Louise and Chris were to die together in an accident?

(c) Which assets could be jointly owned so that they will automatically transfer to the other spouse if either Louise or Chris should die?

(d) What qualities should Louise and Chris look for when naming the executors of their wills?

(e) Once they have completed and signed their wills, where should the Merryweathers keep the original documents and any copies?

▶Case 2
A Lottery Winner Practices Estate Planning

Your good friend and next-door neighbor, Robert, has just announced that he has the sole winning ticket in the $7 million lottery drawing of last week. Robert is 60 years old and divorced. He has two adult children (Mary and Kitty) and four grandchildren. Recognizing that you are not an attorney, and knowing that your friend needs personal finance advice, offer some estate planning suggestions regarding the following points:

(a) Assume that Robert's taxable estate now amounts to $7,200,000 and after the $1,500,000 exclusion, his remaining estate could be taxed at 47 percent. If he died tomorrow, how much would he owe? Give him that figure while offering him a single piece of general advice.

(b) Name two types of trusts that Robert might consider to reduce his eventual estate taxes and summarize what those trusts might help him accomplish.

(c) Offer some suggestions on how Robert might use life insurance to avoid estate taxes.

(d) Offer Robert some suggestions for things he might want to put into his letter of last instructions.

Financial Math Questions

1. Randy Marcos died recently without a valid will. His estate for federal estate purposes was $3.2 million. Randy's wife, Imelda, and three children were his only survivors. Answer the following questions, assuming that Randy's state of residence followed the typical guidelines of division (one-half for the spouse with the children equally splitting the remainder):

(a) What will be the proportional division of assets for the wife and children?

(b) What dollar amount will be inherited by Imelda?

(c) If Imelda now dies without a will, what will be the proportional division of assets, assuming that she has no other children?

(d) If Imelda has personal assets (beyond her inheritance from Randy) that have a fair market value of $400,000, when she dies, how much will her estate total?

(e) Assuming Imelda's estate paid $15,000 for her funeral expenses, $14,000 for probate costs, and $180,000 to pay off the remaining debts and mortgages, what was Imelda's taxable estate?

2. Laura Kim of Mount Pleasant, Michigan, lives with her elderly mother, Haejeong. Her mother owns two profitable auto parts stores that are worth millions. Because current law has the federal estate tax going to zero in 2010, the pair is wondering about how these taxes might affect Haejeong's estate. Laura hopes that her mother, who is in excellent health, lives at least another 20 years. If she doesn't, the federal estate tax will apply in all years except 2010. If Haejeong's estate is valued at $4 million, calculate the following (Hint: Subtract the exclusion before multiplying the rate.):

(a) The amount of the federal estate tax if she dies in 2005.

(b) The amount of the federal estate tax if she dies in 2007.

(c) The amount of the federal estate tax if she dies in 2010.

(d) The amount of the federal estate tax if she dies in 2011.

Money Matters Continuing Cases

Victor and Maria Update Their Estate Plans

Since retiring earlier this year, Victor and Maria have found that their assets amount to approximately $800,000, made up of the following: Victor's half-interest in their home ($90,000), his tax-sheltered pension plan ($144,000), his stock ($56,000), and personal property ($50,000); Maria's half-interest in their home ($90,000), the inherited home from her mother ($120,000), her tax-sheltered pension plan ($112,000), the present value (obtained from Victor's employer) of the survivor's benefits under her husband's defined-benefit pension plan ($60,000), personal property ($50,000), and her zero-coupon bonds ($28,000).

1. Offer the Hernandezes advice about how each might establish a durable power of attorney.

2. Should both Victor and Maria have living wills and medical powers of attorney? Why or why not?

3. Victor purchased his $100,000 term life insurance policy through his employer, and he has been paying on his privately purchased $50,000 whole life insurance policy for many years (which now has a cash value of $30,000). Maria is listed as the beneficiary on both policies. Assuming that Victor owns both policies, what advice can you offer regarding ownership of the two policies?

4. Offer Victor and Maria some suggestions on how to ease the transfer of assets to their adult children and grandchildren.

Belinda Johnson Helps Her Uncle Plan His Estate

Belinda Johnson has been approached by her uncle, David Lawrence, who seeks advice about planning his estate. She has been handling some of David's investments, and he trusts her judgment on financial matters. David has a net worth of $2,340,000. At age 54, he is concerned about preparing his finances so that as much as possible of his estate will go to his heirs according to his wishes. David has no will but has written down some of his ideas. He has no wife or children but wants to be able to provide for his mother, four nephews, Belinda, and a disabled sister.

1. What is the first action David should take in planning his estate?

2. Why might an irrevocable living trust be a good idea for David in providing for his mother and sister?

3. What other types of trusts might David use in his estate planning?

What Would You Recommend Now?

Now that you have read the chapter on estate planning, what would you recommend to Orlando and Giselle Molina in the case at the beginning of the chapter regarding:

1. Beneficiary designations for their financial assets?

2. Joint ownership of certain physical assets?

3. Making a will and establishing guardianship for the children?

4. Using advance directive documents to avoid a situation like that confronting Orlando's father?

5. Establishing trusts for their children?

Exploring the World Wide Web

To complete these exercises, go to the *Garman/Forgue* website at college.hmco.com/business/students. Under General Business, select the title of this text. Click on the Internet Exercises link for this chapter, and answer the questions that appear on the Web page.

1. Visit the website for TaxPlanet.com, where you can read about recent changes in the federal gift and estate taxes. How might these changes affect your family's estate tax situation?

2. Visit the website of TaxPlanet.com, where you can link to your state's tax department. Does your state assess an inheritance tax? What information does the department provide that is helpful to the typical family?

3. Upon death, a person's will may become a public document through the probate process. Visit the Court TV website, where the wills of some famous people have been posted. Select a person whose will interests you. Identify one of the estate planning techniques outlined in this chapter that were used by that person.

4. Visit the website for Partnership for Caring. There you will find an explanation of advance directives and can download forms and information on the laws in all states and the District of Columbia. Read and/or download the information and forms for your state. Is an advance di-

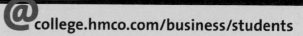

Visit the Garman/Forgue website . . .

@**college.hmco.com/business/students**

Under General Business, select *Personal Finance 8e*. There, among other valuable resources, you will find a complete glossary, ACE questions, links to help you complete the chapter exercises, and links to other personal finance sites.

Appendixes

APPENDIX A   **Present and Future Value Tables**

APPENDIX B   **Estimating Social Security Benefits**

Appendix A

Present and Future Value Tables

Many problems in personal finance involve decisions about money values at varying points in time. These values can be directly and fairly compared only when they are adjusted to a common point in time. Chapter 1 introduced the basic time value concepts. This appendix offers more details about the time value of money. In addition, it provides tables listing the future and present value of $1 with which to make calculations.

Four assumptions must be made to eliminate unnecessary complications:

1. Each planning period is one year long.

2. Only annual interest rates are considered.

3. Interest rates are the same during each of the annual periods.

4. Interest is compounded and continues earning a return in subsequent periods.

Tables of present and future values can be constructed to make these adjustments. **Future values** are derived from the principles of compounding the dollar values ahead in time. **Present values** are derived by discounting (which is the inverse of compounding) the dollar values and transferring them to an earlier point in time.

It is usually unnecessary to precisely identify whether the interest is paid/received at the *beginning* of a period or at the *end* of a period, or to know whether interest compounds daily or quarterly instead of annually. (These calculations require even more tables.) The following present and future value tables assume that money is accumulated, received, paid, compounded, or whatever at the *end* of a period. The tables can be used to compute the mathematics of personal finance with high certainty and to confirm (or reject as inaccurate) what people tell you about financial matters.

The most significant task is to find the correct table. Accordingly, each table is clearly described here, and illustrations of its use appear on the facing page where possible. In addition, the appropriate mathematical equation is shown and can be easily solved using a calculator.

Illustrations Using Table A.1:
Future Value of a Single Amount ($1)

To use Table A.1 on page A-5, locate the future value factor for the time period and the interest rate.

1. You invest $500 at a 15 percent rate of return for 12 years. How much will you have at the end of that 12-year period?

    The future value factor is 5.350; hence, the solution is $500 × 5.350, or $2675.

2. Property values in your neighborhood are increasing at a rate of 5 percent per year. If your home is presently worth $90,000, what will its worth be in 7 years?

    The future value factor is 1.407; hence, the solution is $90,000 × 1.407, or $126,630.

3. You need to amass $40,000 in the next 10 years to make a balloon payment on your home mortgage. You have $17,000 available to invest. What annual interest rate must be earned to realize the $40,000?

    $40,000 ÷ $17,000 = 2.353. Read down the periods (*n*) column to 10 years and across to 2.367 (close enough), which is found under the 9 percent column. Hence, the $17,000 invested at 9 percent for 10 years will grow to a future value of slightly more than $40,000.

4. An apartment building is currently valued at $160,000, and it has been appreciating at 8 percent per year. If this rate continues, in how many years will it be worth $300,000?

    $300,000 ÷ $160,000 = 1.875. Read down the 8 percent column until you reach 1.851 (close enough to 1.875). This number corresponds to a period of 8 years. Hence, the $160,000 property appreciating at 8 percent annually will grow to a future value of $300,000 in slightly more than 8 years.

5. You have the choice of receiving a down payment from someone who wants to purchase your rental property as $15,000 today or as a personal note for $25,000 payable in 6 years. If you could expect to earn 8 percent on such funds, which is the better choice?

    The future value factor is 1.587; hence, the future value of $15,000 at 8 percent is $15,000 × 1.587, or $23,805. Thus, it would be better to take the note for $25,000.

6. How much will an automobile now priced at $20,000 cost in 4 years, assuming an annual inflation rate of 5 percent?

    Read down the 5 percent column and across the row for 4 years to locate the future value factor of 1.216. Hence, the solution is $20,000 × 1.216, or $24,320.

7. How large a lump-sum investment do you need now to have $20,000 available in 5 years, assuming a 10 percent annual rate of return?

    The $20,000 future value is divided by 1.611 (10 percent at 5 years), resulting in a current lump-sum investment of $12,415.

8. You have $5000 now and need $10,000 in 9 years. What rate of return is needed to reach that goal?

    Divide the future value of $10,000 by the present value of the lump sum of $5000 to obtain a future value factor of 2.0. In the row for 9 years, locate the future value factor of 1.999 (very close to 2.0). Read up the column to find that an 8 percent return on investment is needed.

9. How many years will it take your lump-sum investment of $10,000 to grow to $16,000, given an annual rate of return of 7 percent?

Divide the future value of $16,000 by the present value of the $10,000 lump sum to compute a future value factor of 1.6; look down the 7 percent column to find 1.606 (close enough). Read across the row to find that an investment period of 7 years is needed.

An alternative approach is to use a calculator to determine the future value, *FV*, of a sum of money invested today, assuming that the amount remains in the investment for a specified number of time periods (usually years) and that it earns a certain rate of return each period. The equation is

$$FV = PV(1.0 + i)^n \tag{A.1}$$

where

$$
\begin{aligned}
FV &= \textit{Future Value} \\
PV &= \textit{Present Value} \text{ of the investment} \\
i &= \textit{Interest} \text{ rate per period} \\
n &= \textit{Number} \text{ of periods the PV is invested}
\end{aligned}
$$

Table A.1 Future Value of a Single Amount ($1 at the End of *n* Periods)
(Used to Compute the Compounded Future Value of a Known Lump Sum)

n	1%	2%	3%	4%	5%	6%	7%	8%	9%	10%	11%	12%	13%	14%	15%	16%	17%	18%	19%	20%
1	1.0100	1.0200	1.0300	1.0400	1.0500	1.0600	1.0700	1.0800	1.0900	1.1000	1.1100	1.1200	1.1300	1.1400	1.1500	1.1600	1.1700	1.1800	1.1900	1.2000
2	1.0201	1.0404	1.0609	1.0816	1.1025	1.1236	1.1449	1.1664	1.1881	1.2100	1.2321	1.2544	1.2769	1.2996	1.3225	1.3456	1.3689	1.3924	1.4161	1.4400
3	1.0303	1.0612	1.0927	1.1249	1.1576	1.1910	1.2250	1.2597	1.2950	1.3310	1.3676	1.4049	1.4429	1.4815	1.5209	1.5609	1.6016	1.6430	1.6852	1.7280
4	1.0406	1.0824	1.1255	1.1699	1.2155	1.2625	1.3108	1.3605	1.4116	1.4641	1.5181	1.5735	1.6305	1.6890	1.7490	1.8106	1.8739	1.9388	2.0053	2.0736
5	1.0510	1.1041	1.1593	1.2167	1.2763	1.3382	1.4026	1.4693	1.5386	1.6105	1.6851	1.7623	1.8424	1.9254	2.0114	2.1003	2.1924	2.2878	2.3864	2.4883
6	1.0615	1.1262	1.1941	1.2653	1.3401	1.4185	1.5007	1.5869	1.6771	1.7716	1.8704	1.9738	2.0820	2.1950	2.3131	2.4364	2.5652	2.6996	2.8398	2.9860
7	1.0721	1.1487	1.2299	1.3159	1.4071	1.5036	1.6058	1.7138	1.8280	1.9487	2.0762	2.2107	2.3526	2.5023	2.6600	2.8262	3.0012	3.1855	3.3793	3.5832
8	1.0829	1.1717	1.2668	1.3686	1.4775	1.5938	1.7182	1.8509	1.9926	2.1436	2.3045	2.4760	2.6584	2.8526	3.0590	3.2784	3.5115	3.7589	4.0214	4.2998
9	1.0937	1.1951	1.3048	1.4233	1.5513	1.6895	1.8385	1.9990	2.1719	2.3579	2.5580	2.7731	3.0040	3.2519	3.5179	3.8030	4.1084	4.4355	4.7854	5.1598
10	1.1046	1.2190	1.3439	1.4802	1.6289	1.7908	1.9672	2.1589	2.3674	2.5937	2.8394	3.1058	3.3946	3.7072	4.0456	4.4114	4.8068	5.2338	5.6947	6.1917
11	1.1157	1.2434	1.3842	1.5395	1.7103	1.8983	2.1049	2.3316	2.5804	2.8531	3.1518	3.4785	3.8359	4.2262	4.6524	5.1173	5.6240	6.1759	6.7767	7.4301
12	1.1268	1.2682	1.4258	1.6010	1.7959	2.0122	2.2522	2.5182	2.8127	3.1384	3.4985	3.8960	4.3345	4.8179	5.3503	5.9360	6.5801	7.2876	8.0642	8.9161
13	1.1381	1.2936	1.4685	1.6651	1.8856	2.1329	2.4098	2.7196	3.0658	3.4523	3.8833	4.3635	4.8980	5.4924	6.1528	6.8858	7.6987	8.5994	9.5964	10.6993
14	1.1495	1.3195	1.5126	1.7317	1.9799	2.2609	2.5785	2.9372	3.3417	3.7975	4.3104	4.8871	5.5348	6.2613	7.0757	7.9875	9.0075	10.1472	11.4198	12.8392
15	1.1610	1.3459	1.5580	1.8009	2.0789	2.3966	2.7590	3.1722	3.6425	4.1772	4.7846	5.4736	6.2543	7.1379	8.1371	9.2655	10.5387	11.9737	13.5895	15.4070
16	1.1726	1.3728	1.6047	1.8730	2.1829	2.5404	2.9522	3.4259	3.9703	4.5950	5.3109	6.1304	7.0673	8.1372	9.3576	10.7480	12.3303	14.1290	16.1715	18.4884
17	1.1843	1.4002	1.6528	1.9479	2.2920	2.6928	3.1588	3.7000	4.3276	5.0545	5.8951	6.8660	7.9861	9.2765	10.7613	12.4677	14.4265	16.6722	19.2441	22.1861
18	1.1961	1.4282	1.7024	2.0258	2.4066	2.8543	3.3799	3.9960	4.7171	5.5599	6.5436	7.6900	9.0243	10.5752	12.3755	14.4625	16.8790	19.6733	22.9005	26.6233
19	1.2081	1.4568	1.7535	2.1068	2.5270	3.0256	3.6165	4.3157	5.1417	6.1159	7.2633	8.6128	10.1974	12.0557	14.2318	16.7765	19.7484	23.2144	27.2516	31.9480
20	1.2202	1.4859	1.8061	2.1911	2.6533	3.2071	3.8697	4.6610	5.6044	6.7275	8.0623	9.6463	11.5231	13.7435	16.3665	19.4608	23.1056	27.3930	32.4294	38.3376
21	1.2324	1.5157	1.8603	2.2788	2.7860	3.3996	4.1406	5.0338	6.1088	7.4002	8.9492	10.8038	13.0211	15.6676	18.8215	22.5745	27.0336	32.3238	38.5910	46.0051
22	1.2447	1.5460	1.9161	2.3699	2.9253	3.6035	4.4304	5.4365	6.6586	8.1403	9.9336	12.1003	14.7138	17.8610	21.6447	26.1864	31.6293	38.1421	45.9233	55.2061
23	1.2572	1.5769	1.9736	2.4647	3.0715	3.8197	4.7405	5.8715	7.2579	8.9543	11.0263	13.5523	16.6266	20.3616	24.8915	30.3762	37.0062	45.0076	54.6487	66.2474
24	1.2697	1.6084	2.0328	2.5633	3.2251	4.0489	5.0724	6.3412	7.9111	9.8497	12.2392	15.1786	18.7881	23.2122	28.6252	35.2364	43.2973	53.1090	65.0320	79.4968
25	1.2824	1.6406	2.0938	2.6658	3.3864	4.2919	5.4274	6.8485	8.6231	10.8347	13.5855	17.0001	21.2305	26.4619	32.9190	40.8742	50.6578	62.6686	77.3881	95.3962
26	1.2953	1.6734	2.1566	2.7725	3.5557	4.5494	5.8074	7.3964	9.3992	11.9182	15.0799	19.0401	23.9905	30.1666	37.8568	47.4141	59.2697	73.9490	92.0918	114.4755
27	1.3082	1.7069	2.2213	2.8834	3.7335	4.8223	6.2139	7.9881	10.2451	13.1100	16.7386	21.3249	27.1093	34.3899	43.5353	55.0004	69.3455	87.2598	109.5893	137.3706
28	1.3213	1.7410	2.2879	2.9987	3.9201	5.1117	6.6488	8.6271	11.1671	14.4210	18.5799	23.8839	30.6335	39.2045	50.0656	63.8004	81.1342	102.9666	130.4112	164.8447
29	1.3345	1.7758	2.3566	3.1187	4.1161	5.4184	7.1143	9.3173	12.1722	15.8631	20.6237	26.7499	34.6158	44.6931	57.5755	74.0085	94.9271	121.5005	155.1893	197.8136
30	1.3478	1.8114	2.4273	3.2434	4.3219	5.7435	7.6123	10.0627	13.2677	17.4494	22.8923	29.9599	39.1159	50.9502	66.2118	85.8499	111.0647	143.3706	184.6753	237.3763
40	1.4889	2.2080	3.2620	4.8010	7.0400	10.2857	14.9745	21.7245	31.4094	45.2593	65.0009	93.0510	132.7816	188.8835	267.8635	378.7212	533.8687	750.3783	1051.668	1469.772
50	1.6446	2.6916	4.3839	7.1067	11.4674	18.4202	29.4570	46.9016	74.3575	117.3909	184.5648	289.0022	450.7359	700.2330	1083.657	1670.704	2566.215	3927.357	5988.914	9100.438

Illustrations Using Table A.2:
Present Value of a Single Amount ($1)

To use this table, locate the present value factor for the time period and the interest rate.

1. You want to begin a college fund for your newborn child; you hope to accumulate $30,000 by 18 years from now. If a current investment opportunity yields 7 percent, how much must you invest in a lump sum to realize the $30,000 when needed?

    The present value factor is 0.296; hence, the solution is $30,000 × 0.296, or $8880.

2. You hope to retire in 25 years and want to deposit a single lump sum that will grow to $250,000 at that time. If you can now invest at 8 percent, how much must you invest to realize the $250,000 when needed?

    The present value factor is 0.146; hence, the solution is $250,000 × 0.146, or $36,500. The present value of $250,000 received 25 years from now is $36,500 if the interest rate is 8 percent.

3. You have the choice of receiving a down payment from someone who wants to purchase your rental property as $15,000 today or as a personal note for $25,000 payable in 6 years. If you could expect to earn 8 percent on such funds, which is the better choice?

    The present value factor is 0.630; hence, the solution is $25,000 × 0.630, or $15,750. Thus, the present value of $25,000 received in 6 years is greater than $15,000 received now, and the personal note is the better choice.

4. You own a $1000 bond paying 8 percent annually until its maturity in 5 years. You need to sell the bond now, even though the market rate of interest on similar bonds has increased to 10 percent. What discounted market price for the bond will allow the new buyer to earn a yield of 10 percent?

    First, compute the present value of the future interest payments of $80 per year for 5 years at 10 percent (using Table A.4): $80 × 3.791, or $303.28. Second, compute the present value of the future principal repayment of $1000 after 5 years at 10 percent: $1000 × 0.621, or $621.00. Hence, the market price is the sum of the two present values ($303.28 + $621.00), or $924.28.

An alternative approach is to use a calculator to determine the present value, *PV*, of a single payment received some time in the future. The equation, which is a rearrangement of the future value Equation (A.1), is

$$PV = \frac{FV}{(1.0 + i)^n} \qquad \text{(A.2)}$$

where

$$
\begin{aligned}
PV &= \textit{Present Value of the investment} \\
FV &= \textit{Future Value} \\
i &= \textit{Interest rate per period} \\
n &= \textit{Number of periods the PV is invested}
\end{aligned}
$$

Table A.2 Present Value of a Single Amount ($1)

(Used to Compute the Discounted Present Value of Some Known Future Single Lump Sum)

n	1%	2%	3%	4%	5%	6%	7%	8%	9%	10%	11%	12%	13%	14%	15%	16%	17%	18%	19%	20%
1	0.9901	0.9804	0.9709	0.9615	0.9524	0.9434	0.9346	0.9259	0.9174	0.9091	0.9009	0.8929	0.8850	0.8772	0.8696	0.8621	0.8547	0.8475	0.8403	0.8333
2	0.9803	0.9612	0.9426	0.9246	0.9070	0.8900	0.8734	0.8573	0.8417	0.8264	0.8116	0.7972	0.7831	0.7695	0.7561	0.7432	0.7305	0.7182	0.7062	0.6944
3	0.9706	0.9423	0.9151	0.8890	0.8638	0.8396	0.8163	0.7938	0.7722	0.7513	0.7312	0.7118	0.6931	0.6750	0.6575	0.6407	0.6244	0.6086	0.5934	0.5787
4	0.9610	0.9238	0.8885	0.8548	0.8227	0.7921	0.7629	0.7350	0.7084	0.6830	0.6587	0.6355	0.6133	0.5921	0.5718	0.5523	0.5337	0.5158	0.4987	0.4823
5	0.9515	0.9057	0.8626	0.8219	0.7835	0.7473	0.7130	0.6806	0.6499	0.6209	0.5935	0.5674	0.5428	0.5194	0.4972	0.4761	0.4561	0.4371	0.4190	0.4019
6	0.9420	0.8880	0.8375	0.7903	0.7462	0.7050	0.6663	0.6302	0.5963	0.5645	0.5346	0.5066	0.4803	0.4556	0.4323	0.4104	0.3898	0.3704	0.3521	0.3349
7	0.9327	0.8706	0.8131	0.7599	0.7107	0.6651	0.6227	0.5835	0.5470	0.5132	0.4817	0.4523	0.4251	0.3996	0.3759	0.3538	0.3332	0.3139	0.2959	0.2791
8	0.9235	0.8535	0.7894	0.7307	0.6768	0.6274	0.5820	0.5403	0.5019	0.4665	0.4339	0.4039	0.3762	0.3506	0.3269	0.3050	0.2848	0.2660	0.2487	0.2326
9	0.9143	0.8368	0.7664	0.7026	0.6446	0.5919	0.5439	0.5002	0.4604	0.4241	0.3909	0.3606	0.3329	0.3075	0.2843	0.2630	0.2434	0.2255	0.2090	0.1938
10	0.9053	0.8203	0.7441	0.6756	0.6139	0.5584	0.5083	0.4632	0.4224	0.3855	0.3522	0.3220	0.2946	0.2697	0.2472	0.2267	0.2080	0.1911	0.1756	0.1615
11	0.8963	0.8043	0.7224	0.6496	0.5847	0.5268	0.4751	0.4289	0.3875	0.3505	0.3173	0.2875	0.2607	0.2366	0.2149	0.1954	0.1778	0.1619	0.1476	0.1346
12	0.8874	0.7885	0.7014	0.6246	0.5568	0.4970	0.4440	0.3971	0.3555	0.3186	0.2858	0.2567	0.2307	0.2076	0.1869	0.1685	0.1520	0.1372	0.1240	0.1122
13	0.8787	0.7730	0.6810	0.6006	0.5303	0.4688	0.4150	0.3677	0.3262	0.2897	0.2575	0.2292	0.2042	0.1821	0.1625	0.1452	0.1299	0.1163	0.1042	0.0935
14	0.8700	0.7579	0.6611	0.5775	0.5051	0.4423	0.3878	0.3405	0.2992	0.2633	0.2320	0.2046	0.1807	0.1597	0.1413	0.1252	0.1110	0.0985	0.0876	0.0779
15	0.8613	0.7430	0.6419	0.5553	0.4810	0.4173	0.3624	0.3152	0.2745	0.2394	0.2090	0.1827	0.1599	0.1401	0.1229	0.1079	0.0949	0.0835	0.0736	0.0649
16	0.8528	0.7284	0.6232	0.5339	0.4581	0.3936	0.3387	0.2919	0.2519	0.2176	0.1883	0.1631	0.1415	0.1229	0.1069	0.0930	0.0811	0.0708	0.0618	0.0541
17	0.8444	0.7142	0.6050	0.5134	0.4363	0.3714	0.3166	0.2703	0.2311	0.1978	0.1696	0.1456	0.1252	0.1078	0.0929	0.0802	0.0693	0.0600	0.0520	0.0451
18	0.8360	0.7002	0.5874	0.4936	0.4155	0.3503	0.2959	0.2502	0.2120	0.1799	0.1528	0.1300	0.1108	0.0946	0.0808	0.0691	0.0592	0.0508	0.0437	0.0376
19	0.8277	0.6864	0.5703	0.4746	0.3957	0.3305	0.2765	0.2317	0.1945	0.1635	0.1377	0.1161	0.0981	0.0829	0.0703	0.0596	0.0506	0.0431	0.0367	0.0313
20	0.8195	0.6730	0.5537	0.4564	0.3769	0.3118	0.2584	0.2145	0.1784	0.1486	0.1240	0.1037	0.0868	0.0728	0.0611	0.0514	0.0433	0.0365	0.0308	0.0261
21	0.8114	0.6598	0.5375	0.4388	0.3589	0.2942	0.2415	0.1987	0.1637	0.1351	0.1117	0.0926	0.0768	0.0638	0.0531	0.0443	0.0370	0.0309	0.0259	0.0217
22	0.8034	0.6468	0.5219	0.4220	0.3418	0.2775	0.2257	0.1839	0.1502	0.1228	0.1007	0.0826	0.0680	0.0560	0.0462	0.0382	0.0316	0.0262	0.0218	0.0181
23	0.7954	0.6342	0.5067	0.4057	0.3256	0.2618	0.2109	0.1703	0.1378	0.1117	0.0907	0.0738	0.0601	0.0491	0.0402	0.0329	0.0270	0.0222	0.0183	0.0151
24	0.7876	0.6217	0.4919	0.3901	0.3101	0.2470	0.1971	0.1577	0.1264	0.1015	0.0817	0.0659	0.0532	0.0431	0.0349	0.0284	0.0231	0.0188	0.0154	0.0126
25	0.7798	0.6095	0.4776	0.3751	0.2953	0.2330	0.1842	0.1460	0.1160	0.0923	0.0736	0.0588	0.0471	0.0378	0.0304	0.0245	0.0197	0.0160	0.0129	0.0105
26	0.7720	0.5976	0.4637	0.3607	0.2812	0.2198	0.1722	0.1352	0.1064	0.0839	0.0663	0.0525	0.0417	0.0331	0.0264	0.0211	0.0169	0.0135	0.0109	0.0087
27	0.7644	0.5859	0.4502	0.3468	0.2678	0.2074	0.1609	0.1252	0.0976	0.0763	0.0597	0.0469	0.0369	0.0291	0.0230	0.0182	0.0144	0.0115	0.0091	0.0073
28	0.7568	0.5744	0.4371	0.3335	0.2551	0.1956	0.1504	0.1159	0.0895	0.0693	0.0538	0.0419	0.0326	0.0255	0.0200	0.0157	0.0123	0.0097	0.0077	0.0061
29	0.7493	0.5631	0.4243	0.3207	0.2429	0.1846	0.1406	0.1073	0.0822	0.0630	0.0485	0.0374	0.0289	0.0224	0.0174	0.0135	0.0105	0.0082	0.0064	0.0051
30	0.7419	0.5521	0.4120	0.3083	0.2314	0.1741	0.1314	0.0994	0.0754	0.0573	0.0437	0.0334	0.0256	0.0196	0.0151	0.0116	0.0090	0.0070	0.0054	0.0042
40	0.6717	0.4529	0.3066	0.2083	0.1420	0.0972	0.0668	0.0460	0.0318	0.0221	0.0154	0.0107	0.0075	0.0053	0.0037	0.0026	0.0019	0.0013	0.0010	0.0007
50	0.6080	0.3715	0.2281	0.1407	0.0872	0.0543	0.0339	0.0213	0.0134	0.0085	0.0054	0.0035	0.0022	0.0014	0.0009	0.0006	0.0004	0.0003	0.0002	0.0001

Illustrations Using Table A.3:
Future Value of a Series of Equal Amounts (an Annuity of $1 per Period)

To use this table, locate the future value factor for the time period and the interest rate.

1. You plan to retire after 16 years. To provide for that retirement, you initiate a savings program of $7000 per year in an investment yielding 8 percent. What will the value of the retirement fund be at the beginning of the seventeenth year?

   Your last payment into the fund will occur at the end of the sixteenth year, so scan down the periods (n) column for period 16, and then move across until you reach the column for 8 percent. The future value factor is 30.32. Hence, the solution is $7000 × 30.32, or $212,240.

2. What will be the value of an investment if you put $2000 into a retirement plan yielding 7 percent annually for 25 years?

   The future value factor is 63.250. Hence, the solution is $2000 × 63.250, or $126,500.

3. You are trying to decide between putting $3000 or $4000 annually for the next 20 years into an investment yielding 7 percent for retirement purposes. What is the difference in the value of investing the extra $1000 for 20 years?

   The future value factor is 41.0. Hence, the solution is $1000 × 41.0, or $41,000.

4. You will receive an annuity payment of $1200 at the end of each year for 6 years. What will be the total value of this stream of income invested at 7 percent by the time you receive the last payment?

   The appropriate future value factor for 6 years at 7 percent is 7.153. Hence, the solution is $1200 × 7.153, or $8584.

5. How many years of investing $1200 annually at 9 percent will it take to reach a goal of $11,000?

   Divide the future value of $11,000 by the lump sum of $1200 to find a future value factor of 9.17. Look down the 9 percent column to find 9.200 (close enough). Read across the row to find that an investment period of 7 years is needed.

6. If you plan to invest $1200 annually for 9 years, what rate of return is needed to reach a goal of $15,000?

   Divide the future value goal of $15,000 by $1200 to derive the future value factor 12.5. Look across the row for 9 years to locate the future value factor of 12.49 (close enough). Read up the column to find that you need an 8 percent return.

   An alternative approach is to use a calculator to determine the total future value, *FV*, of a stream of equal payments (an annuity). The equation is

$$FV = \frac{[(1.0 + i)^n - 1.0] \times A}{i} \tag{A.3}$$

where

$$
\begin{aligned}
FV &= \textit{Future Value} \text{ of the investment} \\
i &= \textit{Interest} \text{ rate per period} \\
n &= \textit{Number} \text{ of periods the } PV \text{ is invested} \\
A &= \textit{Amount} \text{ of the annuity}
\end{aligned}
$$

Table A-3 Future Value of a Series of Equal Amounts (an Annuity of $1 Paid at the End of Each Period)
(Used to Compute the Compounded Future Value of a Stream of Income Payments)

n	1%	2%	3%	4%	5%	6%	7%	8%	9%	10%	11%	12%	13%	14%	15%	16%	17%	18%	19%	20%
1	1.0000	1.0000	1.0000	1.0000	1.0000	1.0000	1.0000	1.0000	1.0000	1.0000	1.0000	1.0000	1.0000	1.0000	1.0000	1.0000	1.0000	1.0000	1.0000	1.0000
2	2.0100	2.0200	2.0300	2.0400	2.0500	2.0600	2.0700	2.0800	2.0900	2.1000	2.1100	2.1200	2.1300	2.1400	2.1500	2.1600	2.1700	2.1800	2.1900	2.2000
3	3.0301	3.0604	3.0909	3.1216	3.1525	3.1836	3.2149	3.2464	3.2781	3.3100	3.3421	3.3744	3.4069	3.4396	3.4725	3.5056	3.5389	3.5724	3.6061	3.6400
4	4.0604	4.1216	4.1836	4.2465	4.3101	4.3746	4.4399	4.5061	4.5731	4.6410	4.7097	4.7753	4.8498	4.9211	4.9934	5.0665	5.1405	5.2154	5.2913	5.3680
5	5.1010	5.2040	5.3091	5.4163	5.5256	5.6371	5.7507	5.8666	5.9847	6.1051	6.2278	6.3528	6.4803	6.6101	6.7424	6.8771	7.0144	7.1542	7.2966	7.4416
6	6.1520	6.3081	6.4684	6.6330	6.8019	6.9753	7.1533	7.3359	7.5233	7.7156	7.9129	8.1152	8.3227	8.5355	8.7537	8.9775	9.2068	9.4420	9.6830	9.9299
7	7.2135	7.4343	7.6625	7.8983	8.1420	8.3938	8.6540	8.9228	9.2004	9.4872	9.7833	10.0890	10.4047	10.7305	11.0668	11.4139	11.7720	12.1415	12.5227	12.9159
8	8.2857	8.5830	8.8923	9.2142	9.5491	9.8975	10.2598	10.6366	11.0285	11.4359	11.8594	12.2997	12.7573	13.2328	13.7268	14.2401	14.7733	15.3270	15.9020	16.4991
9	9.3685	9.7546	10.1591	10.5828	11.0266	11.4913	11.9780	12.4876	13.0210	13.5795	14.1640	14.7757	15.4157	16.0853	16.7858	17.5185	18.2847	19.0859	19.9234	20.7989
10	10.4622	10.9497	11.4639	12.0061	12.5779	13.1808	13.8164	14.4866	15.1929	15.9374	16.7220	17.5487	18.4197	19.3373	20.3037	21.3215	22.3931	23.5213	24.7089	25.9587
11	11.5668	12.1687	12.8078	13.4864	14.2068	14.9716	15.7836	16.6455	17.5603	18.5312	19.5614	20.6546	21.8143	23.0445	24.3493	25.7329	27.1999	28.7551	30.4035	32.1504
12	12.6825	13.4121	14.1920	15.0258	15.9171	16.8699	17.8885	18.9771	20.1407	21.3843	22.7132	24.1331	25.6502	27.2707	29.0017	30.8502	32.8239	34.9311	37.1802	39.5805
13	13.8093	14.6803	15.6178	16.6268	17.7130	18.8821	20.1406	21.4953	22.9534	24.5227	26.2116	28.0291	29.9847	32.0887	34.3519	36.7862	39.4040	42.2187	45.2445	48.4966
14	14.9474	15.9739	17.0863	18.2919	19.5986	21.0151	22.5505	24.2149	26.0192	27.9750	30.0949	32.3926	34.8827	37.5811	40.5047	43.6720	47.1027	50.8180	54.8409	59.1959
15	16.0969	17.2934	18.5989	20.0236	21.5786	23.2760	25.1290	27.1521	29.3609	31.7725	34.4054	37.2797	40.4175	43.8424	47.5804	51.6595	56.1101	60.9653	66.2607	72.0351
16	17.2579	18.6393	20.1569	21.8245	23.6575	25.6725	27.8881	30.3243	33.0034	35.9497	39.1899	42.7533	46.6717	50.9804	55.7175	60.9250	66.6488	72.9390	79.8502	87.4421
17	18.4304	20.0121	21.7616	23.6975	25.8404	28.2129	30.8402	33.7502	36.9737	40.5447	44.5008	48.8837	53.7391	59.1176	65.0751	71.6730	78.9791	87.0680	96.0217	105.9306
18	19.6147	21.4123	23.4144	25.6454	28.1324	30.9057	33.9990	37.4502	41.3013	45.5992	50.3959	55.7497	61.7251	68.3941	75.8364	84.1407	93.4056	103.7403	115.2659	128.1167
19	20.8109	22.8406	25.1169	27.6712	30.5390	33.7600	37.3790	41.4463	46.0185	51.1591	56.9395	63.4397	70.7494	78.9692	88.2118	98.6032	110.2846	123.4135	138.1664	154.7400
20	22.0190	24.2974	26.8704	29.7781	33.0660	36.7856	40.9955	45.7620	51.1601	57.2750	64.2028	72.0524	80.9468	91.0249	102.4436	115.3797	130.0329	146.6280	165.4180	186.6880
21	23.2392	25.7833	28.6765	31.9692	35.7193	39.9927	44.8652	50.4229	56.7645	64.0025	72.2651	81.6987	92.4699	104.7684	118.8101	134.8405	153.1385	174.0210	197.8474	225.0256
22	24.4716	27.2990	30.5368	34.2480	38.5052	43.3923	49.0057	55.4568	62.8733	71.4027	81.2143	92.5026	105.4910	120.4360	137.6316	157.4150	180.1721	206.3448	236.4384	271.0307
23	25.7163	28.8450	32.4529	36.6179	41.4305	46.9958	53.4361	60.8933	69.5319	79.5430	91.1479	104.6029	120.2048	138.2970	159.2764	183.6014	211.8013	244.4868	282.3618	326.2368
24	26.9735	30.4219	34.4265	39.0826	44.5020	50.8156	58.1767	66.7648	76.7898	88.4973	102.1741	118.1552	136.8315	158.6586	184.1678	213.9776	248.8075	289.4945	337.0105	392.4842
25	28.2432	32.0303	36.4593	41.6459	47.7271	54.8645	63.2490	73.1059	84.7009	98.3471	114.4133	133.3339	155.6196	181.8708	212.7930	249.2140	292.1048	342.6035	402.0424	471.9811
26	29.5256	33.6709	38.5530	44.3117	51.1135	59.1564	68.6765	79.9544	93.3240	109.1818	127.9988	150.3339	176.8501	208.3327	245.7120	290.0883	342.7626	405.2721	479.4305	567.3773
27	30.8209	35.3443	40.7096	47.0842	54.6691	63.7058	74.4838	87.3508	102.723	121.0999	143.0786	169.3740	200.8406	238.4993	283.5688	337.5024	402.0323	479.2211	571.5223	681.8527
28	32.1291	37.0512	42.9309	49.9676	58.4026	68.5281	80.6977	95.3388	112.9682	134.2099	159.8173	190.6989	227.9499	272.8892	327.1041	392.5027	471.3778	566.4808	681.1116	819.2233
29	33.4504	38.7922	45.2188	52.9663	62.3227	73.6398	87.3465	103.9659	124.1354	148.6309	178.3972	214.5827	258.5834	312.0937	377.1697	456.3032	552.5120	669.4474	811.5228	984.0679
30	34.7849	40.5681	47.5754	56.0849	66.4389	79.0582	94.4608	113.2832	136.3075	164.4940	199.0209	241.3327	293.1992	356.7868	434.7451	530.3117	647.4390	790.9479	966.7121	1181.882
40	48.8864	60.4020	75.4013	95.0255	120.7998	154.7620	199.6351	259.0565	337.8824	442.5925	581.8260	767.0914	1013.704	1342.025	1779.090	2360.757	3134.522	4163.212	5529.829	7343.856
50	64.4632	84.5794	112.7969	152.6671	209.3480	290.3359	406.5289	573.7701	815.0834	1163.908	1668.771	2400.013	3459.507	4994.522	7217.714	10435.65	15089.50	21813.09	31515.33	45497.17

A-9

Illustrations Using Table A.4: Present Value of Series of Equal Amounts (an Annuity of $1 per Period)

To use this table, locate the present value factor for the time period and the interest rate.

1. You are entering into a contract that will provide you with an income of $1000 at the end of the year for the next 10 years. If the annual interest rate is 7 percent, what is the present value of that stream of payments?

   The present value factor is 7.024; hence, the solution is $1000 × 7.024, or $7024.

2. You expect to have $250,000 available in a retirement plan when you retire. If the amount invested yields 8 percent and you hope to live an additional 20 years, how much can you withdraw each year so that the fund will just be liquidated after 20 years?

   The present value factor for 20 years at 8 percent is 9.818. Hence, the solution is $250,000 ÷ 9.818, or $25,463.

3. You have received an inheritance of $60,000 that you invested so that it earns 9 percent. If you withdraw $8000 annually to supplement your income, in how many years will the fund run out?

   Solving for *n*, $60,000 ÷ $8000 = 7.5. Scan down the 9 percent column until you find a present value factor close to 7.5, which is 7.487. The row indicates 13 years; thus, the fund will be depleted in approximately 13 years with $8000 annual withdrawals.

4. A seller offers to finance the sale of a building to you as an investment. The mortgage loan of $280,000 will be for 20 years and requires an annual mortgage payment of $24,000. Should you finance the purchase through the seller or borrow the funds from a financial institution at a current rate of 10 percent?

   $280,000 ÷ $24,000 = 11.667. Scan down the periods (*n*) column to 20 years and then read across to locate the figure closest to 11.667, which is 11.470. The column indicates 6 percent; thus, seller financing offers a lower interest rate.

5. You have the opportunity to purchase an office building for $750,000 with an expected life of 20 years. Looking over the financial details, you see that the before-tax net rental income is $90,000. If you want a return of at least 15 percent, how much should you pay for the building?

   The present value factor for 20 years at 15 percent is 6.259, and $90,000 × 6.259 = $563,310. Thus, the price is too high for you to earn a return of 15 percent.

   An alternative approach is to use a calculator to determine the present value, *PV*, of a stream of payments. The equation is

$$PV = \frac{[1.0 - 1.0 / (1.0 + i)^n] \times A}{i} \tag{A.4}$$

where

$$PV = \textit{Present Value of the investment}$$
$$i = \textit{Interest rate per period}$$
$$n = \textit{Number of periods the PV is invested}$$
$$A = \textit{Amount of the annuity}$$

Table A.4 Present Value of a Series of Equal Amounts (an Annuity of $1 Received at the End of Each Period)
(Used to Compute the Discounted Present Value of a Stream of Income Payments)

n	1%	2%	3%	4%	5%	6%	7%	8%	9%	10%	11%	12%	13%	14%	15%	16%	17%	18%	19%	20%
1	0.9901	0.9804	0.9709	0.9615	0.9524	0.9434	0.9346	0.9259	0.9174	0.9091	0.9009	0.8929	0.8850	0.8772	0.8696	0.8621	0.8547	0.8475	0.8403	0.8333
2	1.9704	1.9416	1.9135	1.8861	1.8594	1.8334	1.8080	1.7833	1.7591	1.7355	1.7125	1.6901	1.6681	1.6467	1.6257	1.6052	1.5852	1.5656	1.5465	1.5278
3	2.9410	2.8839	2.8286	2.7751	2.7232	2.6730	2.6243	2.5771	2.5313	2.4869	2.4437	2.4018	2.3612	2.3216	2.2832	2.2459	2.2096	2.1743	2.1399	2.1065
4	3.9020	3.8077	3.7171	3.6299	3.5460	3.4651	3.3872	3.3121	3.2397	3.1699	3.1024	3.0373	2.9745	2.9137	2.8550	2.7982	2.7432	2.6901	2.6386	2.5887
5	4.8534	4.7135	4.5797	4.4518	4.3295	4.2124	4.1002	3.9927	3.8897	3.7908	3.6959	3.6048	3.5172	3.4331	3.3522	3.2743	3.1993	3.1272	3.0576	2.9906
6	5.7955	5.6014	5.4172	5.2421	5.0757	4.9173	4.7665	4.6229	4.4859	4.3553	4.2305	4.1114	3.9975	3.8887	3.7845	3.6847	3.5892	3.4976	3.4098	3.3255
7	6.7282	6.4720	6.2303	6.0021	5.7864	5.5824	5.3893	5.2064	5.0330	4.8684	4.7122	4.5638	4.4226	4.2883	4.1604	4.0386	3.9224	3.8115	3.7057	3.6046
8	7.6517	7.3255	7.0197	6.7327	6.4632	6.2098	5.9713	5.7466	5.5348	5.3349	5.1461	4.9676	4.7988	4.6389	4.4873	4.3436	4.2072	4.0776	3.9544	3.8372
9	8.5660	8.1622	7.7861	7.4353	7.1078	6.8017	6.5152	6.2469	5.9952	5.7590	5.5370	5.3282	5.1317	4.9464	4.7716	4.6065	4.4506	4.3030	4.1633	4.0310
10	9.4713	8.9826	8.5302	8.1109	7.7217	7.3601	7.0236	6.7101	6.4177	6.1446	5.8892	5.6502	5.4262	5.2161	5.0188	4.8332	4.6586	4.4941	4.3389	4.1925
11	10.3676	9.7868	9.2526	8.7605	8.3064	7.8869	7.4987	7.1390	6.8052	6.4951	6.2065	5.9377	5.6869	5.4527	5.2337	5.0286	4.8364	4.6560	4.4865	4.3271
12	11.2551	10.5753	9.9540	9.3851	8.8633	8.3838	7.9427	7.5361	7.1607	6.8137	6.4924	6.1944	5.9176	5.6603	5.4206	5.1971	4.9884	4.7932	4.6105	4.4392
13	12.1337	11.3484	10.6350	9.9856	9.3936	8.8527	8.3577	7.9038	7.4869	7.1034	6.7499	6.4235	6.1218	5.8424	5.5831	5.3423	5.1183	4.9095	4.7147	4.5327
14	13.0037	12.1062	11.2961	10.5631	9.8986	9.2950	8.7455	8.2442	7.7862	7.3667	6.9819	6.6282	6.3025	6.0021	5.7245	5.4675	5.2293	5.0081	4.8023	4.6106
15	13.8651	12.8493	11.9379	11.1184	10.3797	9.7122	9.1079	8.5595	8.0607	7.6061	7.1909	6.8109	6.4624	6.1422	5.8474	5.5755	5.3242	5.0916	4.8759	4.6755
16	14.7179	13.5777	12.5611	11.6523	10.8378	10.1059	9.4466	8.8514	8.3126	7.8237	7.3792	6.9740	6.6039	6.2651	5.9542	5.6685	5.4053	5.1624	4.9377	4.7296
17	15.5623	14.2919	13.1661	12.1657	11.2741	10.4773	9.7632	9.1216	8.5436	8.0216	7.5488	7.1196	6.7291	6.3729	6.0472	5.7487	5.4746	5.2223	4.9897	4.7746
18	16.3983	14.9920	13.7535	12.6593	11.6896	10.8276	10.0591	9.3719	8.7556	8.2014	7.7016	7.2497	6.8399	6.4674	6.1280	5.8178	5.5339	5.2732	5.0333	4.8122
19	17.2260	15.6785	14.3238	13.1339	12.0853	11.1581	10.3356	9.6036	8.9501	8.3649	7.8393	7.3658	6.9380	6.5504	6.1982	5.8775	5.5845	5.3162	5.0700	4.8435
20	18.0456	16.3514	14.8775	13.5903	12.4622	11.4699	10.5940	9.8181	9.1285	8.5136	7.9633	7.4694	7.0248	6.6231	6.2593	5.9288	5.6278	5.3527	5.1009	4.8696
21	18.8570	17.0112	15.4150	14.0292	12.8212	11.7641	10.8355	10.0168	9.2922	8.6487	8.0751	7.5620	7.1016	6.6870	6.3125	5.9731	5.6648	5.3837	5.1268	4.8913
22	19.6604	17.6580	15.9369	14.4511	13.1630	12.0416	11.0612	10.2007	9.4424	8.7715	8.1757	7.6446	7.1695	6.7429	6.3587	6.0113	5.6964	5.4099	5.1486	4.9094
23	20.4558	18.2922	16.4436	14.8568	13.4886	12.3034	11.2722	10.3711	9.5802	8.8832	8.2664	7.7184	7.2297	6.7921	6.3988	6.0442	5.7234	5.4321	5.1668	4.9245
24	21.2434	18.9139	16.9355	15.2470	13.7986	12.5504	11.4693	10.5288	9.7066	8.9847	8.3481	7.7843	7.2829	6.8351	6.4338	6.0726	5.7465	5.4509	5.1822	4.9371
25	22.0232	19.5235	17.4131	15.6221	14.0939	12.7834	11.6536	10.6748	9.8226	9.0770	8.4217	7.8431	7.3300	6.8729	6.4641	6.0971	5.7662	5.4669	5.1951	4.9476
26	22.7952	20.1210	17.8768	15.9828	14.3752	13.0032	11.8258	10.8100	9.9290	9.1609	8.4881	7.8957	7.3717	6.9061	6.4906	6.1182	5.7831	5.4804	5.2060	4.9563
27	23.5596	20.7069	18.3270	16.3296	14.6430	13.2105	11.9867	10.9352	10.0266	9.2372	8.5478	7.9426	7.4086	6.9352	6.5135	6.1364	5.7975	5.4919	5.2151	4.9636
28	24.3164	21.2813	18.7641	16.6631	14.8981	13.4062	12.1371	11.0511	10.1161	9.3066	8.6016	7.9844	7.4412	6.9607	6.5335	6.1520	5.8099	5.5016	5.2228	4.9697
29	25.0658	21.8444	19.1885	16.9837	15.1411	13.5907	12.2777	11.1584	10.1983	9.3696	8.6501	8.0218	7.4701	6.9830	6.5509	6.1656	5.8204	5.5098	5.2292	4.9747
30	25.8077	22.3965	19.6004	17.2920	15.3725	13.7648	12.4090	11.2578	10.2737	9.4269	8.6938	8.0552	7.4957	7.0027	6.5660	6.1772	5.8294	5.5168	5.2347	4.9789
40	32.8347	27.3555	23.1148	19.7928	17.1591	15.0463	13.3317	11.9246	10.7574	9.7791	8.9511	8.2438	7.6344	7.1050	6.6418	6.2335	5.8713	5.5482	5.2582	4.9966
50	39.1961	31.4236	25.7298	21.4822	18.2559	15.7619	13.8007	12.2335	10.9617	9.9148	9.0417	8.3045	7.6752	7.1327	6.6605	6.2463	5.8801	5.5541	5.2623	4.9995

Appendix B

Estimating Social Security Benefits

The Social Security Administration (SSA) provides basic benefits for your retirement, for a period of disability, or for your survivors. To qualify, you must have earned the number of credits required for each benefit program. Once you qualify, the level of benefits received is based on your income in past years that was subject to the Federal Insurance Contributions Act (FICA) taxes, commonly known as Social Security taxes. Benefits increase each year based on a cost of living adjustment (COLA) announced by the SSA each October for the following year. Over the past ten years, COLA adjustments have averaged 2.6 percent. The discussion and Table B.1 provide the authors' estimates of Social Security benefits for 2006 for various income levels using calculators found at www.ssa.gov/planners/calculators. htm. The amounts are for a 30-year-old worker but would not differ significantly for workers ten years older or younger.

Social Security Retirement Benefits

To qualify for Social Security retirement benefits, any worker born after 1928 must have earned 40 **credits** of coverage. As noted in the text, it is possible to receive a maximum of four credits per year. In 2004, a worker would earn one credit for each $900 of income subject to Social Security taxes (this figure is adjusted upward each year for inflation and is estimated to be $940 in 2006). Dependent children, spouses caring for dependent children, and retired spouses at age 62 (including former spouses if the marriage lasted at least ten years) may also collect benefits based on the eligibility of the retired worker.

You can use Table B.1 to estimate a person's Social Security retirement benefits in today's dollars, assuming the retiree worked steadily, received average pay raises, and retired at the full benefit retirement age. If more than one person would receive a benefit under the retiree's account (retiree and spouse, for example), the amount of the second person's benefit would be one-half of the retiree's benefit, giving a couple a total benefit 50 percent higher than the individual figure listed in Table B.1.

Social Security Disability Benefits

Social Security will pay disability benefits to an insured worker, dependent children up to age 18 (or 19, if the child is still in high school), a spouse caring for a dependent child who is younger than age 16 or disabled, and a spouse (even if divorced, but not remarried, provided that the marriage lasted ten years) aged 62 or older. The benefit amount depends on two factors. The first factor is the eligibility of the disabled worker. To qualify for disability benefits, workers need at least 40 credits of coverage under Social Security, with at least 20 of the credits attained in the previous ten years (depending on year of birth). A worker younger than age 31 must have attained at least six credits or one more than one-half of the total credits possible after age 21, whichever is greater. (For example, a 26-year-old worker would have five years, or 20 credits, possible and would need 10 credits of coverage.) The second factor affecting benefit levels is the predisability income of the covered individual that was subject to the FICA tax.

You can use Table B.1 to estimate an individual's Social Security disability benefits, assuming the disabled person worked steadily and received average pay raises. To obtain figures more specific than those given in Table B.1, contact the Social Security Administration to obtain your personal earnings and benefit estimate statement as described in Chapter 18, or log on to www.ssa.gov/mystatement/ or www.ssa.gov/planners/calculators.htm.

Social Security Survivor's Benefits

Social Security will pay benefits to surviving children younger than age 18 (or 19, if the child is still in high school), to a surviving spouse (even if divorced from the deceased, but not remarried) caring for surviving children who are younger than age 16, and to a surviving spouse (even if divorced, if the marriage lasted at least ten years) aged 60 or older. Two factors are important in such cases. The first factor is the eligibility of the covered worker. The deceased worker must have accrued at least 40 credits of coverage to be "fully insured," depending on his or her year of birth. Workers who have earned at least as many credits of coverage as years since turning age 21 will be fully insured as

Appendix B   Estimating Social Security Benefits

well. Other individuals may be considered "currently insured" if they have six credits of coverage in the previous 13 calendar credits. The survivors of currently insured workers receive limited types of benefits compared to those available to fully insured workers. The second factor is the covered worker's level of earnings, as indicated in Table B.1.

You can use Table B.1 to estimate monthly survivor's benefits from Social Security in today's dollars for eligible surviving family members. The table assumes that the deceased worker worked steadily and received average pay raises.

Table B.1 Estimates* of Social Security for the Three Major Social Security Programs

	Present Annual Earnings					
	$25,000	$35,000	$45,000	$55,000	$70,000	$85,000
Monthly Retirement Benefits at Age 67 in Today's Dollars						
Per month	$ 1,072	$ 1,352	$ 1,575	$ 1,752	$ 1,950	$ 2,146
Per year	$12,864	$16,224	$18,900	$21,024	$23,400	$25,752
As a percentage of income	51.5%	46.4%	42.0%	38.2%	33.4%	30.3%
Monthly Disability Benefits If You Became Disabled in 2006						
Individual benefit per month	$ 988	$ 1,234	$ 1,480	$ 1,665	$ 1,839	$ 2,012
Individual benefit per year	$11,856	$14,808	$17,760	$19,980	$22,068	$24,144
As a percentage of income	47.4%	42.3%	39.5%	36.3%	31.5%	28.4%
Maximum family benefit per month	$ 1,680	$ 2,098	$ 2,516	$ 2,831	$ 3,126	$ 3,420
Maximum family benefit per year	$20,160	$25,176	$30,192	$33,972	$37,512	$41,040
Monthly Survivor's Benefits If You Died in 2006						
Individual benefit per month†	$ 761	$ 953	$ 1,147	$ 1,269	$ 1,405	$ 1,540
Individual benefit per year	$ 9,132	$11,436	$13,764	$15,228	$16,860	$18,480
As a percentage of income	36.5%	32.6%	30.6%	27.7%	24.1%	21.7%
Maximum family benefit per month	$ 1,759	$ 2,338	$ 2,683	$ 2,964	$ 3,280	$ 3,596
Maximum family benefit per year	$21,108	$28,056	$32,196	$35,568	$39,360	$43,152

*Authors' estimates in today's dollars for a 30-year-old worker using Social Security Administration website calculators.
†A surviving spouse aged 65 or older would receive a retirement benefit approximately one-third higher than these figures.

Index

Note: Boldface type indicates key terms that are defined in text.

A. M. Best Company, 350
Above-the-line deductions, 103
Abstract, 255
Acceleration clause, 187
Accident insurance, 314
Account executive, 450
Account reconciliation, 141
Accredited financial counselor (AFC), 50
Accrual-basis budgeting, 69
Ackley, Dennis R., 518
Acquisition fee, 217
Active investor, 368
Activities of daily living (ADLs), 316
Actual cash value, 282
Actual-cash-value (ACV) formula, 282
ACV formula, 282
ACY, 469
Add-on loan, 195
Add-on interest method, **191,** 192–194
Adjustable life insurance, 337
Adjustable-rate CD, 147
Adjustable-rate loan, 186
Adjustable-rate mortgage (ARM), 247–248
Adjusted capitalized cost (adjusted cap cost), 216
Adjusted gross income (AGI), 103
Adjustments to income (adjustments), 103
ADLs, 316
Adoption tax credit, 110
Advance directive, 550–552
Advice from experts
  budget deficits, 80
  buying online, 210
  check endorsement, 139
  choosing a professional adviser, 51
  credit card, minimum payment trap, 173
  credit card debt, 197
  DRIP, 388
  estate planning, 551
  fun money, 442
  health care plan, 311, 314–315
  income tax, home ownership, 120
  income tax, sideline business, 104
  inflation, 12
  large-loss principle, 275
  life insurance, 348
  managed funds *vs.* index funds, 430
  managing retirement accounts, 529
  money mantras, 14
  option contracts, 495
  overdraft fees, 140
  private mortgage insurance, 254
  retirement benefit, divorced spouse, 510
  retirement savings, 518

  selling an investment, 386
  stockholder's background, 455
  student loan, 184
  used car, purchase of, 222–223
  zero-coupon bonds, 411
AFC, 50
Affinity card, 165
After-tax dollars, 112
After-tax money, 514
After-tax return, 376
After-tax yield, 118
Aftermarket, 395, 449
Agency issues, 410
Aggregate limits, 310
Aggressive-growth fund, 427–428
Aggressive investment philosophy, 367–368
AGI, 103
AIP, 348
Alhabeeb, M. J., 197
All-in-one account, 145
All-risk (open-perils) policies, 278
Alpha, 466
Alternative dispute resolution programs, 224
Alternative lenders, 189
Alternative minimum tax (AMT), 108
Alternative mortgage loans, 248–251
AMA, 145–146
American Century, 146n
American Stock Exchange (AMEX), 451–452
Ameritech, 385
AMEX, 451–452
Amortization, 192, 242
Amortization schedule, 242, 243
AMT, 108
Andersen, Jan D., 275
Annual percentage yield (APY), 143
Annual report, 437, 464
Annuitant, 534
Annuity, 17, 534
  future value, 19–20
  present value, 20–21
  retirement, 534–535
Antilock brakes, 215
Any-occupation policy, 319
Approximate compound yield (ACY), 469
APY, 143
Arbitration, 224
ARM, 247–248
As is, 218
Asked price, 452
Assessed value, 252

Assessing financial progress, 46–47
Asset, 36–37
Asset allocation, 380
Asset management account (AMA), 145–146
Asset-to-debt ratio, 44–45
Association of Independent Consumer Credit Counseling Agencies, 197–198
Assumable mortgage, 249
ATM, 77, 133
ATM transaction fee, 133
Automated teller machine (ATM), 77, 133
Automatic funds transfer agreement, 140
Automatic investment program (AIP), 348
Automatic overdraft loan agreement, 140
Automatic premium loan, 345
Automatic reinvestment, 431
Automobile bodily injury liability, 283
Automobile insurance, 283–290
  buying, 287–290
  collision insurance, 286–287
  liability insurance, 283–285
  losses covered, 283–287
  medical payments insurance, 285–286
  rental cars, 286
  uninsured/underinsured coverage, 286
Automobile medical payments insurance, 285–286
Automobile physical damage insurance, 286–287
Automobile property damage liability, 283–284
Automobile safety, 215
Automobiles/major purchases, 203–228
  comparison shopping, 215–219
  complaints, 224
  fixing expenditures into budget, 212–214
  golden rules, 205
  leasing *vs.* buying, 216–218
  making the decision, 221–223
  negotiation, 220–221
  new vehicle financing, 212, 216–218
  planned buying, 204–206
  prioritizing wants, 206–207
  research, 208–211
  service contracts, 219
  used car, purchase of, 222–223, 223–224
  warranties, 218–219
Average-balance account, 137
Average-cost basis method, 440
Average daily balance, 174
Average share cost, 383
Average share price, 383
Average tax rate, 96

Back-end load, **434**
Back-end ratio, **238**
Bad check, **140**
Bad check fees, 140
Balance sheet, **35**–39
   assets, 36–37
   liabilities, 37
   net worth, 37
   obtaining information, 43
   samples, 37–39
Balance transfer, **165**
Balanced fund, **427**
Balloon automobile loan, **218**
Bank credit card, 164–165
Bank credit card account, **164**
Bank Insurance Fund (BIF), **130**
bankrate.com, 47
Bankruptcy, **198**–199
Barron's, 438
Basic form (HO-1), **278,** 280
Basic liquidity ratio, **44**
Basic principles. *See* Golden rules
Basic retirement benefit, **508**
BEACON score, 161
Bear, **378**
Bear market, **378**
Bearer instrument, **139**
Beaver bonds, **406**
Beneficial Finance Corporation (BFC), 188
Beneficiary, **340, 546**
Beneficiary designation, **432**–433, **546**
Beneficiary designation form, **516**
Benefit period, **318**
Berra, Yogi, 511
Best buy, **214**
Beta, **401, 467**
Beta coefficient, **401**
Bid price, **452**
BIF, **130**
Big Board, 451
Big-ticket items. *See* Automobiles/major
   purchases
Billing cycle, **170**
Binder, **276**
Biweekly mortgage, **249**
Blank endorsement, **139**
Bloomberg, 465
Blue-chip stock, **403**–404
Boeing, 404
Bond, **395,** 405–416
   book-entry form, 406
   callable, 406–407
   characteristics, 405
   corporate, 407
   current yield, 413–414
   decisions to make, 415–416
   golden rules, 393
   government, 407–411
   interest rates, 411–412, 413
   Internet, and, 405
   junk, 395
   municipal, 410–411

   premium/discount, 412
   quotations, 459
   registered, 406
   secured/unsecured, 406
   selling price formula, 412, 414
   taxes, 416
   YTM, 414–415
   zero-coupon, 411
Bond fund, **426**
Bond quotations, 459
Bond rating, **407,** 408
Bond rating directories, 407
Bond-selling price formula, **412,** 414
Book-entry form, **406**
Book value, **398**
Book value per share, **399**
Bounce protection agreement, **140**
Break-even price, 495
brm.com, 47
Broad form (HO-2), **278,** 280
Broker/dealer, **452**
Brokerage firm, **448,** 453–454
Brokered certificates of deposit, **147**
Broker's commission, **257**
Budget, **60**
Budget controls, 77–80
Budget estimates, **70**–74
Budget exceptions, **79**
Budget surplus, 81
Budgeting, 60–82
   cash-basis *vs.* accrued-basis, 68
   cash-flow calendar, 75
   classifying income and expenses, 68–69
   control phase, 77–80
   decision-making phase, 70–74
   defined, **60**
   estimates, 70–74
   evaluation phase, 80–82
   financial statements, 61
   goal setting, 61–66
   golden rules, 60
   implementation phase, 74–76
   inflation, 70
   organization phase, 66–69
   phases in process, 61
   recordkeeping, 66–67
   revolving savings fund, 75–76
   variance analysis, 81
Buffett, Warren, 454
BuildaWill.com, 544
Building blocks of financial success, 5–7
Bull, **378**
Bull market, **378**
Bump-up CD, **147**
Bunching deductions, **121**
Business cycle, **8**–9
Business-cycle risk, **372**
Business risk, **365**
Business Week, 11, 434, 439
Buy-and-hold, **379**
Buy term and invest the rest, 348
Buyer protection plan, 219

Buyer's agent, **240**
Buyer's order, **223**
Buying and selling securities, 447–478
   brokerage firms, 453–454
   day trading, 454
   ECNs, 452
   golden rules, 449
   indexes, 461–462
   insurance, 453
   margin trading, 470–473
   market movements, 378
   newspaper price quotations, 458–460
   on-line resources, 465–466
   organized stock exchanges, 451–452
   portfolio tracking, 466
   primary market, 449–450
   rate of return, 466–470
   SEC, 453
   secondary markets, 450
   selling short, 473–474
   sources of information, 462–466
   stock order, 456–457
   taxes, 471
Buying long, **473**
Buying online, 210
Bypass trust, **549**

Cafeteria plan, **113**
Calculating your income taxes, 99–111
   adjustments, 103
   AMT, 108n
   balance due/refund, 111
   gross income, 100–101, 102–103
   itemized deductions, 105–107
   overview, 100
   personal exemptions, 107
   standard deduction, 104
   tax credits, 109–110
   tax liability, 108–109
   total income, 99–102
Calculator, 21n, 466
Call option, **492**
Callable, **406**–407
Campolo, Anthony J., 104
Canceled check, **137**
Capital assets, **36**
Capital gain, **101, 365,** 534
Capital gains distributions, **425**
Capital improvements, **485**
Capital loss, **101**
Capitalized cost reductions (cap cost
   reductions), **216**
Car insurance. *See* Automobile insurance
Card registration service, **135**
Career-related money decisions, 21–25
   compare salary/living costs in different
      cities, 21–22
   FSA, 22–23
   HSA, 23
   maximizing benefits from retirement plan,
      24–25
   retirement plans, 23–24

Carrigan, Martin, 311
Cars. *See* Automobiles/major purchases
Cash account, 453
Cash advance, 165
Cash-balance plan, 521
Cash-basis budgeting, 69
Cash dividends, 397–398
Cash equivalents, 129
Cash flow, 485
Cash-flow calendar, 75
Cash-flow management
   budgeting, 60–82. *See also* Budgeting
   couples/married persons, 82–86
Cash-flow statement, 35, 39–43
   expenses, 40–41
   income, 40
   obtaining information, 43
   sample statements, 41–43
   surplus (loss), 41
Cash loan, 185
Cash machine, 133
Cash surrender value, 344
Cash value, 332
Cash-value life insurance, 334–340, 352–353
Cashier's check, 142
Catch-up provision, 519
CCA, 197
CD, 147
Central asset account, 145
Certificate of deposit (CD), 147
Certificate of insurance, 307
Certificate of title, 255
Certified check, 142
Certified financial planner (CFP), 50, 351
Certified public accountant (CPA), 50
CFP, 50, 351
Chapter 7 bankruptcy, 199
Chapter 13 bankruptcy, 198
Charge card, 164–166
Chargeback, 173
Charges. *See* Fees/costs
Charitable remainder trust (CRT), 550
**Chartered financial consultant (ChFC),
   50,** 351
Chartered life underwriter (CLU), 50,
   277, 351
Chartered property and casualty underwriter
   (CPCU), 277
Chattel mortgage loan, 187
Check card, 133
Check Clearing for the 21st Century Act,
   137
Check endorsement, 139
Check register, 136
Check truncation, 137
CheckFree.com, 132
Checking account, 77, 135–138
ChFC, 50, 351
Chicago Board of Trade, 496
Chicago Mercantile Exchange, 496
Child and dependent care credit, 110
Child tax credit, 110

Children
   college tuition, 62, 115
   guardian, 545
   money sense, 86
Children's college tuition, 62
Claims adjuster, 296
Claims ratio, 314, 315
Cliff vesting, 520
Closed-end credit, 180. *See also* Installment
   credit
Closed-end investment company, 423
Closed-end lease, **216**
Closing, 241
Closing costs, 251
Closing date, 170
CLU, 50, 277, 351
CNNMoney, 465
Co-branded credit card, 165
COBRA rights, 311
Coca-Cola, 402
Codicil, 544
Coinsurance, 274–275
Coinsurance clause, 309
Collar, 493
Collateral, 186
Collateral installment loan, 187
Collateralized credit card, 165
Collectibles, 489–491
Collection agencies, 196
College savings plan, 115
Collision insurance, 286–287
Commercial banks, 130
Commercial properties, 481–482
Commission, 376
**Commission-only financial planners,
   49**
Common stock, 393–394
Community property, 548
Community property laws, 548
Community property states, 144
Comparison shopping, 215–219
Complaint procedure, 224
Compound interest, 16
Compounding, 16–17
**Comprehensive automobile insurance,
   287**
Comprehensive health insurance, 313
**Comprehensive personal liability
   insurance, 291**
Compu-Serve, 438
Computer software. *See also* Websites
   budgeting, 66
   income tax preparation, 47, 99
   investment portfolio, 381
   personal finance, 47
   retirement planning, 530
   will preparation, 544
Computerized ledgers, 66
Conditional sales contract, 187
Condominium (condo), 233
Condominium form (HO-6), 279, 281
Confirmation statements, 432

Conservative investment philosophy, 367
Consolidated statements, 432
Consumer credit, 163–164
Consumer finance company, 188–189
Consumer Information Center, 208
Consumer loans, 185–187
Consumer price index (CPI), 11
Consumer Reports, 208, 209, 351, 434, 439
Consumer Reports Buying Guide, 208
Consumer statement, 163
Consumption, 5
**Contents replacement-cost protection,
   283**
Contingency clause, 239
Contingent beneficiary, 340
Contingent (secondary) beneficiary, 546
Continuous-debt method, 184–185
Contract for deed, 250
Contributory plan, 517
Convenience check, 165
Conventional mortgage, 247
Convertible adjustable-rate mortgage, 248
Convertible term insurance, 333
Cooperative (co-op), 233
Coordination-of-benefits clause, 310
Copayment, 309
Corporate bonds, 407
Corporation, 393
Corpus, 548
Cosigner, 186
Cost index, 352
Cost-of-living adjustments, 319
Costs. *See* Fees/costs
Countercyclical stock, 401, 404
Counteroffer, 239
Coupon, 405
Coupon bonds, 406
   retire, 406
Coupon rate, 405, 406
Coupon yield, 405
Coverdell education savings account,
   62, **115**
Covered option, 492
CPA, 50
CPCU, 277
CPI, 11
Credit, 109
Credit application, 159
Credit approval process, 159–161
Credit bureau, 160
Credit card, 164–166
Credit card blocking, 156
Credit card disclosure information, 167, 168
Credit card insurance, 170
Credit card liability, 169
Credit clinic, 198
Credit controlsheet, 78–79
Credit counseling agency (CCA), 197
Credit disability insurance, 170
Credit discrimination, 159
Credit history, **159,** 161–162
Credit investigation, 159

Credit life insurance, 170
Credit limit, 164
Credit rating, 160
Credit receipt, 172
Credit repair company, 198
Credit report, 160, 162–163
Credit reporting bureaus, 162
Credit reputation, 161–163
Credit risk, 407
Credit scoring, 160, 161
Credit shelter trust, 549
Credit statement, 170–175
Credit term life insurance, 333
Credit unemployment insurance, 170
Credit union (CU), 131
Credit use and credit cards, 153–178
    bank credit card, 165
    billing statement, 170–175
    closing credit card account, 166
    consumer credit, 163–164
    credit approval process, 159–161
    credit history, 161–162
    credit report, 162–163
    credit reputation, 161–163
    credit statement, 170–175
    disclosure requirements, 167, 168
    disputing items on billing statement,
        173–174
    divorce, 163
    downside of credit, 156–157
    fees/charges/penalties, 169, 170, 174
    getting out of debt, 196–198
    golden rules, 155
    installment credit. *See* Installment credit
    insurance, 170
    line of credit, 166
    lost/stolen cards, 169
    overindebtedness, 194–199
    preapproved offers, 169
    retail credit card, 165
    service credit, 166–167
    T&E card, 166
    teaser rate/default rate, 167, 169
    why used, 155–156
Creditor concessions, 197
Credits, A-13
Credit statement, 170
CRT, 550
Crude annual rate of return, 491
Cude, Brenda J., 210
Cumulative preferred stock, 394
Current income, 365
Current liability, 37
Current rate, 344
Current yield, 413–414
Currently insured, 508
Custodial account, 62
Custodial care, 316
Cyclical stock, 404

Daily Stocks, 405
Day order, 457

Day trading, 454
Dealer holdback, 220
Dealer rebate, 220
Dealer sticker price, 208
Death. *See* Estate planning
Death benefit, 342
Debenture, 406
Debit card, 133
Debt collection agencies, 196
Debt-consolidation loan, 156, 195
Debt limit, 180–185
Debt management plan (DMP), 197
Debt payments-to-disposable income
    method, 181–182
Debt payments-to-disposable income ratio,
    45–46
Debt service-to-income ratio, 45
Debts, 369
Decision making, 12–15
    bonds, 415–416
    budgeting, 70–74
    income tax, 14–15
    investments, 368–370
    marginal analysis, 13–14
    opportunity costs/trade-offs, 13
    time value of money, 16–21
Decision-making worksheet
    automobile insurance, 290
    disability income insurance, 318
    home-buying *vs.* renting, 235
    mortgage refinancing, 246
    needs approach to life insurance, 330
    new vehicle financing, 212, 217
    retirement savings goal, 512
Decker, Lorraine R., 551
Declarations, 341
Decreasing term insurance, 333
Deductible, 274–275, 309
Deed, 255
Deed of bargain and sale, 255
Deeded timesharing, 482
Deep discount bonds, 411
Default rate, 167
Default risk, 407
Defensive stock, 404
Deferred annuity, 535
Deferred-compensation plan, 522
Deferred load, 434
Deficiency balance, 187
Deficit, 39
Defined-benefit retirement plan, 520–521
Defined-contribution retirement plan,
    114–115, 517–520
Deflation, 9
Deflation risk, 372
Demand deposits, 136
Dental expense insurance, 313
Deposit insurance, 131–132
Depository institutions, 130
Depreciation, 486
Designations/credentials, 50
Diamonds, 430

Did you know?
    alternative lenders, 189
    automobile safety, 215
    bonds and interest rates, 413
    budget surplus, 81
    cafeteria plan, 113
    check writing, 137
    college students, insurance coverage, 294
    computer software, 47
    credit card balance, 175
    credit discrimination, 159
    divorce, effect on credit, 163
    employer's retirement plan, 523
    FICO score, 160–161
    fundamental analysis, 403
    interest rate, monetary asset accounts, 146
    life insurance commissions, 340
    lotteries, 17
    marriage, life planning issues, 34
    mortgage, qualifying for, 237, 238
    mortgage rate, credit score, 241
    mutual fund commissions, 436
    mutual fund returns, 429
    new Treasury securities, 409
    ownership of accounts, 144
    payment instruments for special needs,
        142
    real estate agents, 240
    retirement plan contribution credit, 517
    rollover penalty, 530
    second mortgage loans, 250
    securities markets regulation, 453
    shareholder rights, 402
    stock dividend, 399
    stock split, 399
    surviving spouse, rights of, 548
    technical analysis, 403
    vehicle ownership, 288–289
    voluntary repossession, 195
    women and retirement planning, 506
    workers' compensation, 312
Differential, 454
Direct deposit, 134
Direct ownership, 481
Direct sellers, 277
Direct Stock Purchase Plan Clearinghouse,
    385
Disability benefits, 520
Disability income insurance, 317–320
Disabled tax credit, 110
Discharged, 198
Disclosure statement, 134
Discount bond, 148
Discount brokers, 454
Discount method, 191, 194
Discount yield, 408
Discounted cash-flow method, 484
Discounted value, 20
Discretionary income, 70
Disposable income, 70, 181
Disposable personal income, 45
Disposition fee, 217

Distribution fees, 435
Diversification, 373, 379
Dividend, 365, 397–398, 534
Dividend payout ratio, 398
Dividend per share, 398
Dividend-reinvestment plan (DRIP), 385
Dividend yield, 398
Divorce, 163, 510
DJIA, 461
DMP, 197
Dolan, Liz, 411
Dollar-cost averaging, 381–384
Domestic-relations order, 510
Donor, 548
Dow Chemical, 404
Dow Jones averages, 461
Dow Jones Industrial Average (DJIA), 461
Dow Jones News/Retrieval Private Investor
    Edition, 438
Dread disease insurance, 314
Dreyfus, 146n
DRIP, 385
Dual-earner household
    debt limit, 185
    health care benefits, 304
    mortgage, 238
Due-on-sale clause, 249
Dunning letters, 174
DuPont, 404
Durable power of attorney, 550–551

Early termination charge, 217
Early termination payoff, 218
Earned income, 96
Earned income credit (EIC), 109–110
Earnest money, 239
Earnings per share (EPS), 400
Earnings yield, 400
Eastman, 404
eBay, 402
EBT, 134
ECN, 452
ECOA, 159
Economic contraction, 9
Economic cycle, 8
Economic environment, 7–12
    business cycle, 8–9
    future direction of economy, 9
    future interest rates, 12
    inflation, 9–11
    state of the economy, 8–9
Economic growth, 8
Economy, 8
EDGAR, 465
Education IRA, 62, 115
Education savings account, 62, 115
Edwards, Phil, 462
EFA, 430
Effective marginal tax rate, 96
EFT, 132
Eighth, 454
Elderly (disabled) tax credit, 110

Electric vehicle credit, 110
Electronic banking, 132–135
Electronic benefits transfer (EBT), 134
Electronic check processing, 137
**Electronic communications network
    (ECN), 452**
Electronic funds transfer (EFT), 132
Electronic Funds Transfer Act, 134
Elimination period, 318
Emerging market fund, 428
EMPIRICA score, 161
Employee benefit, 21
**Employee Retirement Income Security Act
    (ERISA), 516**
Employee stock option (ESO), 394
**Employee stock-ownership plan (ESOP),
    522**
**Employer retirement savings account
    (ERSA), 526**
Employer-sponsored qualified retirement
    plans, 23–24
**Employer-sponsored retirement plan,
    516–523**
Employer-sponsored tax-sheltered spending
    accounts, 22–23
Encyclopedia of Associations, 463
Endorsements, 139, 341
Endowment life insurance, 337
Envelope system, 79–80
Episode limits, 309
EPS, 400
Equal Credit Opportunity Act (ECOA), 159
Equifax, 162
Equities, 242, 369
ERISA, 516
Ernst & Young Tax Guide, 99n
ERSA, 526
Escheat, 545
Escrow account, 251
ESO, 394
ESOP, 522
Estate, 542
Estate planning, 541–555
    advance directives, 550–552
    beneficiary designation, 546–547
    CRT, 550
    defined, **542**
    estate tax, 552
    executor, 544–545
    golden rules, 543
    guardian, 545
    inheritance tax, 552
    intestacy, 545–546
    joint tenancy, 547
    living trusts, 548–549
    living will, 550
    payable-at-death designation, 547
    power of attorney, 550–551
    probate, 543, 546
    testamentary trust, 549
    trusts, 547–549
    will, 544

Estate tax, 552
Estimated taxes, 98
ETF, 430
Etradebank.com, 132
Evaluating financial progress, 46–47
Excel, 66
Excess liability insurance, 291–293
Exchange fee, 431
Exchange privilege, 431
Exchange-traded fund (ETF), 430
Exclusion amount, 552
Exclusions, 102, 311, 341
Exclusive insurance agents, 277
Executor, 544–555
Excmption, 107
Exemption trust, 549
Exit fee, 434
Expansion, 8, 9
Expenditure, 74
Expense ratio, 436
Expense reimbursement account, 114
Expenses, 39, 40
Experian, 162
Experian/Fair, Isaac score, 161
Expert advice. *See* Advice from experts
Expiration date, 492
Exposures, 269
Express warranty, 218
Extended warranty, 219
ExxonMobil, 385, 404

Face amount, 332
Face value, 405
Factory-direct rebate, 211
Fair Credit Billing Act (FCBA), 173
Fair Credit Reporting Act (FCRA), 162
Fair Debt Collection Practices Act (FDCPA),
    195–196
Fair market value, 36, 252
Family auto policy (FAP), 284
Family trust, 549
Fannie Mae, 410
FAP, 284
Farcast, 438
FCBA, 173
FCRA, 162
FDCPA, 195–196
FDIC, 130
Federal agency debt issues, 410
**Federal Deposit Insurance Corporation
    (FDIC), 130**
Federal estate tax, 552
Federal funds rate, 12
Federal government securities, 407–411
Federal Home Loan Mortgage Corporation
    (Freddie Mac), 410
**Federal Housing Administration (FHA),
    253**
Federal National Mortgage Association
    (Fannie Mae), 410
Federal Reserve Board (Fed), 11, **412**
Fee-based financial planners, 49

Fee-offset financial planners, 50
Fee-only financial planners, 49
Fees/costs
   ATM, 133
   checking accounts, 136–137, 138
   credit cards, 169, 170, 174
   home ownership, 251–256
   installment credit, 190–194
   investments, 376–377
   mutual funds, 433–437
   overdraft fees, 140
   selling a home, 257–258
   stockbroker, 454
FHA, 253
FHA-insured mortgage, 253
FICA taxes, 506–507
FICO score, 160–161
Fidelity, 146n, 530
Fidelity Investments, 431, 439
Filing status, 104
Fill-or-kill order, 457
Final-average plan, 520
Final expenses, 326
financenter.com, 47
Financial calculators, 21n, 466
Financial compatibility checklist, 85
Financial Engines, 530
Financial goals, 33–35
   budgeting, 61–66
   long-term goals, 62–63
   precautionary goals, 65
   short-term goals, 63–65
Financial happiness, 6
Financial information providers, 405
Financial literacy, 3
Financial loss, 274
Financial Planners Association, 50
Financial planning, 29–56
   choosing an adviser, 51
   defined, **31**
   example, 32–33
   fees/costs, 49–50
   financial goals, 33–35
   financial strategies, 35
   golden rules, 31
   professional advisers, 49–50, 51
   professional designations/credentials, 50
   values, 33
Financial ratios, 44–46
   asset-to-debt ratio, 44–45
   basic liquidity ratio, 44
   debt payments-to-disposable income
      ratio, 45–46
   debt service-to-income ratio, 45
   investment assets-to-total assets ratio, 46
   savings ratio, 46
Financial records, 47–49
Financial responsibility, 3
Financial risk, 365
Financial security, 6
Financial services industry, 130
Financial statements, 35

   balance sheet, 35–39
   budgets, 61
   cash-flow statement, 39–43
Financial strategies, 35
Financial success, 6
Financing lease, 187
First dollar protection, 313
First-to-die policies, 342
Fixed expenses, 40
Fixed income, 369
Fixed interest rate, 186
Fixed maturity, 369
Fixed-time deposits, 139
Fixed yield, 412
Flat-fee brokers, 240
Flexible premium variable life insurance,
   339
Flexible spending account (FSA), 22–23,
   114, 308
Flipping, 195
Floater policies, 294
Floor broker, 455
Forbes, 9, 434, 439
Ford Motor Credit, 188
Forecasting, 7
Foreclosure, 195, 242
Form 1040-ES, 98
Form 1040-X, 97
Form 4868, 97n
Form 8822, 97
Form W-2, 100
Form W-4, 98
Fortuitous loss, 273
Fortune, 434, 439
Forward price/earnings ratio, 400
401(k) plan, 23, **114, 519**
403(b) plan, 519
457 plans, 519
Fox, Jonathan, 495
Frailey, Fred W., 434
Freddie Mac, 410
Free credit, 156
Front-end load, 434
Front-end ratio, 238
FSA, 22–23, 114
Full-benefit retirement age, 508
Full-service general brokerage firms, 453–454
Full warranty, 218–219
Fully insured, 507–508
Fun money, 442
Fundamental analysis, 403
Fundamental principles. *See* Golden rules
Future inflation rates, 11
Future interest rates, 12
Future value, 18, A-2
   annuity, 19–20, A-8–A-9
   series of equal amounts, A-8–A-9
   single amount, A-3–A-5
Futures contract, 496–497

Gap insurance, 210
Garnishment, 195

GDP, 9
GEM, 249
General brokerage firm, 453–454
General Electric, 404
General Motors Acceptance Corporation, 188
General partner, 483
Generation-skipping transfer tax, 549
Generation-skipping trust, 549
Generic products, 206
Getting out of debt, 196–198
Gibson Greetings, 402
Ginnie Mae, 410
Global fund, 428
Goal-setting process, 63
Goals. *See* Financial goals
Goals worksheet, 64
Golden rules
   automobiles/major purchases, 205
   budgeting and cash-flow management, 60
   buying and selling securities, 449
   credit use/credit cards, 155
   estate planning, 543
   health care planning, 303
   housing expenditures, 230
   income tax, 92
   installment credit, 181
   investment fundamentals, 362
   life insurance planning, 326
   monetary asset management, 129
   mutual funds, 424
   personal finance, 4
   property/liability insurance, 268
   real estate and speculative investments,
      481
   retirement planning, 504
   risk management, 268
   stocks and bonds, 393
Good-faith estimate, 240
Good-til-canceled (GTC) order, 457
Goodman, Jordan E., 348
Goods and services dispute, 174
Gordon, Gail M., 184
Gorham, Linda, 385
Government health care plans, 306–307
Government National Mortgage Association
   (Ginnie Mae), 410
Government savings bonds, 119, 148
Grace period, 143, 172, 319, 343
Graduated-payment mortgage, 248
Graduated vesting, 519–520
Grantor, 547
Greninger, Sue Alexander, 510
Griffith, Reynolds, 386
Gross capitalized cost (gross cap cost), 216
Gross domestic product (GDP), 9
Gross income, 100–101, **102**–103
Group health care plan, 303
Group term life insurance, 333
Growing-equity mortgage (GEM), 249
Growth and income fund, 428–429
Growth fund, 427
Growth stock, 402

GTC order, 457
Guaranteed insurability option, 346
Guaranteed level-premium term insurance, 332
Guaranteed minimum rate of return, 344
Guaranteed renewable policies, 319–320
Guaranteed renewable term insurance, 332
Guardian, 545
Guarino, Dave, 431

H.D. Vest Financial Planning, 99n
Haggling, 220
Hand, Learned, 111
Hardship withdrawal, 25
Have Nots, 5
Haves, 5
Hayhoe, Celia, 5
Hazard, 272
Hazard reduction, 275
H.D. Vest Financial Planning, 99n
Health care plan, 302
Health care planning, 301–323
    COBRA rights, 311
    dual-career families, 304
    golden rules, 303
    government plans, 306–307
    HMOs, 305
    insurance. *See* Health insurance
    Medicare/Medicaid, 306–307
    sources of benefits, 303–307
    taxes, 308
    workers' compensation, 312
Health insurance, 305–316
    accident insurance, 314
    comprehensive, 313
    coverage limitations, 310–311
    dental expense insurance, 313
    dread disease insurance, 314
    general terms and provisions, 307–308
    hospital coverage, 312
    long-term care insurance, 315–316
    major medical coverage, 312–313
    major medical expense insurance, 313
    medical expense coverage, 312–313
    payment limitations, 308–310
    policy limits, 309–310
    surgical coverage, 312
    traditional insurance, 305–306
    vision care insurance, 314
Health maintenance organization (HMO), 305
Health reimbursement arrangement, 114n
Health savings account, 308
Health savings account (HSA), 23, 308
Healthdyne, 402
Heir, 544
Hewlett, John P., 184
High-balling, 208
High-risk investments, 480, 489–497
    collectibles, 489–491
    futures contracts, 496–497

option contracts, 492–495
    precious metals and stones, 489–491
High-yield bonds, **395**
HMO, 305
HO-1, 278, 280
HO-2, 278, 280
HO-3, 278, 280
HO-4, 278–279, 281
HO-6, 279, 281
HO-8, 279, 281
Home-buying process, 234–241
Home Depot, 385
Home-equity conversion loan, 250
Home-equity installment loan, 250
Home-equity line of credit, 167, 250
Home warranty insurance, 255–256
Homeowner's association, 233
Homeowner's fee, 233
Homeowner's general liability protection, 278
Homeowner's insurance, 255–256, 277–283
    buying, 279–283
    coverages, 277–278
    defined, **277**
    types (HO-1 to HO-8), 278–279, 280
Homeowner's no-fault medical payments protection, 278
Homeowner's no-fault property damage protection, 278
Homeownership. *See* Housing expenditure
Hope Scholarship credit, 109
Hospital (hospitalization) coverage, 312
Hospital expense insurance, 312
Hospital indemnity insurance, 312
Hospital-service-incurred (fee-for-service) plan, 312
Household Finance Corporation (HFC), 188
Housing expenditure, 229–263
    attorney fees, 256
    buy *vs.* rent, 230–234, 235
    closing, 241
    costs/fees, 251–256
    financing a home, 241–251. *See also* Mortgage loan
    golden rules, 231
    home-buying process, 234–241
    home warranty insurance, 255–256
    negotiating a purchase, 239
    points, 254–255
    prequalifying a mortgage, 237–238
    real estate agents, 240
    selling a home, 257–258
    taxes, 236
    taxes and insurance, 251–252
    title insurance, 255
How to . . .
    account reconciliation, 141
    automobile insurance, 288
    bond selling price, 414
    budget setup, 72
    children, money sense, 86
    close credit card account, 166

employee health care benefits, 304
    financial compatibility checklist, 85
    financial statements, 43
    goal-setting process, 63
    insurance policy, 273
    Internet and investment, 405
    margin call stock price, 473
    net worth, 38
    option contracts, 493
    privacy, 158
    property and liability insurance, 292
    real rate of return, 377
    savings, 364
    security deposit, 232
    taxable *vs.* after-tax yields, 118
    term insurance policies, layering, 334
H&R Block's Kiplinger Tax-Cut, 99n
HSA, 23
HUD mortgage programs, 253
Hunts, Holly, 315
Hybrid loan, 248

I Bonds, 409
"I" statements, 84
IACI, 353
IANPI, 353
IBC/Donoghues Mutual Funds Almanac, 438
IBM, 404
Identity theft, 158
IJH, 430
Image statement, 137
Immediate annuity, 535
Immediate vesting, 519
Implied warranty, 218
Important insurance, 271
Impulse buying, 204
In-force illustration, 344
Income, 39, 40
Income and expense statement, 35. *See also* **Cash-flow statement**
Income shifting, 119–120
Income stock, 401
Income tax, 90–126. *See also* Tax considerations and consequences; Taxation
    calculating your taxes, 99–111. *See also* Calculating your income taxes
    decision making, 14–15
    filing a tax return, 96–97, 111
    golden rules, 92
    investments, 376
    pay as you go requirements, 98
    payroll withholding, 98
    progressive nature, 93
    real estate investments, 486–488
    recordkeeping, 122
    reduction strategies. *See* Reducing income taxes
    refund, 97, 110
    state taxes, 109n
    tax rates/tables, 93–96

Income tax (*cont.*)
 taxable *vs.* after-tax yields, 118
 taxable *vs.* tax-free income, 376
Incontestability clause, 342
Indemnity, 274
Indemnity plan, 305
Indenture, 406
Independent insurance agents, 277
Index fund, 430
**Index of leading economic indicators
 (LEI), 9**
Indirect investment, 481
Individual account, 144
**Individual practice organization (IPO),
 305**
**Individual retirement account (IRA), 115,
 524**–525
Industry-oriented investment publications,
 463–464
Inflation, 9
 budgeting, 70
 CPI, 11
 effect of, 10–11, 12
 estimating future rates, 11
 investments, 377
 measuring, 11
Inflation risk, 372
Information about industries, 462–463
Information about specific companies and
 funds, 464–465
Inheritance tax, 552
Initial public offering (IPO), 449
Insolvent, 38
Installment-certain annuity, 535
Installment credit, 163, 179–202. *See also*
 Credit use and credit cards
 bankruptcy, 198–199
 calculating installment loan payment,
 185–186
 consumer loans, 185–187
 debt limit, 180–185
 defined, **180**
 FDCPA, 195–196
 finance charges, 190–194
 getting out of debt, 196–198
 golden rules, 181
 installment purchase agreement, 187
 overindebtedness, 194–199
 secured/unsecured loans, 186–187
 sources of loans, 187–190
Installment purchase agreement, 187
Instinet, 452
Insurable interest, 274
Insurance, 272
 automobile, 283–290. *See also* Automobile
  insurance
 basic elements, 276
 brokerage firm bankruptcy, 453
 coinsurance, 274–275
 college students, 294
 credit card, 170
 deductible, 274–275

deposit, 131–132
disability income, 317–320
filing a claim/collecting, 295–296
floater policies, 294
health. *See* Health insurance
homeowner's, 277–283. *See also* Homeowner's insurance
insurable interest, 274
large-loss principle, 275
life. *See* Life insurance
malpractice, 291
mortgage, 253–254
personal liability, 291
retirement plan, 521
saving money, 292
title, 255
umbrella, 291–293
Insurance agents, 277, 351
Insurance claim, 296
Insurance dividend, 534
Insurance dividends, 342
Insurance policy, 272, 273
Insurance rate, 276
Insured, 272, 276, **340**
Insurer, 272
Insuring agreements, 341
Intel, 402
Interest
 calculating, 16
 compound, 16
 defined, **12,** 365
 retirement planning, 534
 savings account, 142–143
 simple, 16
Interest-adjusted cost index (IACI),
 352–353
**Interest-adjusted net payment index
 (IANPI), 353**
Interest-earning checking account, 136
Interest point, 254–255
Interest rate
 bonds, 411–412, 413
 estimating future rates, 12
 market, 412
 mortgage, 245
 preferred stock, 394
 rising, 12
 short-term monetary assets, 146
 tiered, 136
Interest-rate cap, 247
Interest-rate risk, 372–373, **412**
**Interest-sensitive life insurance,
 338**–340
Intermediate care, 316
Internal Revenue Code, 92
Internal Revenue Service (IRS), 92
International fund, 428
Internet banks, 132
Internet-based bill-paying services, 132
Internet websites. *See* Websites
Intestate, 545–546
Introductory (teaser) rate, 167

Investment, 5
 basics, 360–390. *See also* Investment
  fundamentals
 bonds, 405–416
 buying and selling securities, 447–478
 mutual funds, 421–446
 real estate, 481–491
 speculative, 489–497
 starting early, 363
 stocks, 393–405
 why people invest, 362–363
Investment assets, 36, 37
Investment assets-to-total assets ratio, 46
Investment banking firms, 449
Investment Companies Yearbook, 438
Investment company, 422
Investment Company Institute, 439
Investment fundamentals, 360–390
 active *vs.* passive investor, 368
 commissions/transaction costs, 376–377
 decisions to make, 368–370
 golden rules, 362
 income taxes, 376
 inflation, 377
 investment philosophy, 367–368
 investment plan, 364
 investment returns, 364–365
 investment strategies, 377–386. *See also*
  Investment strategies
 leverage, 374–376
 prerequisites to investing, 363
 risk, 366, 371–374
 short *vs.* long-term investments, 369–370
 starting early, 363
Investment-grade bond investments, 395
Investment philosophy, 367–368
Investment plan, 364
Investment profits, 351
Investment ratings publications, 465
Investment research, 462–466
Investment returns, 364–365
Investment risk, 366, 371–374
Investment scams, 466
Investment strategies, 377–386
 asset allocation, 380
 buy-and-hold, 379
 dollar-cost averaging, 381–384
 long-term investing, 384–386
 market timing, 378–379
 Monte Carlo simulation, 380–381
 portfolio diversification, 379
 retirement, 528, 529
Investor's Business Daily, 438
Invoice price, 220
IPO, 305, 449
IRA, 524–525
Irrevocable living trust, 549
IRS, 92
iShares, 430
Island, 452
Item limits, 309
Itemized deductions, 105–107, **308**

J. K. Lasser's Your Income Tax, 99n
JCPenney Credit Corporation, 188
Johnson, Alena C., 80
Johnson & Johnson, 404
Joint account, 144
Joint-and-survivor annuity, 535
Joint and survivor benefit, 521
Joint tenancy (joint tenancy with right of survivorship), 144, 255, 547
Jordan, Ronald R., 254
Junk bonds, 395

Keogh, 525
Key principles. *See* Golden rules
Keynes, John Maynard, 111
Kiddie tax, 119
Kiplinger's Personal Finance Magazine, 9, 11, 47, 147, 351, 434, 439, 440

Land contract, 250
Lapsed policy, 343
Large-cap stock, 404
Large-loss principle, 275
Law of large numbers, 276
Lawrence, Frances C., 120
Leading economic indicators (LEI), 9
Lease, 231–233
Lease factor, 216
Lease rate, 216
Leasing, 216
Ledger, 66
Legal guardian, 545
Legazoon, 544
LEI, 9
Lemon (car), 224
Lemon laws, 224
Lender buy-down mortgage, 248
Lesser-known growth stock, 402
Letter of last instructions, 545
Level of living, 5
Level-premium term insurance, 332–333
Leverage, 494
Leverage, 374–376, **486**
Liabilities, 36, 37
Liability insurance, 269
Lien, 187, 242
Life-cycle fund, 429
Life insurance, 324–357, **325**
  buying, 346
  calculating need for, 328–331
  cash-value, 334–340, 352–353
  choosing an agent, 351
  defined, **325**
  golden rules, 326–328
  interest-sensitive, 338–340
  policy, 340–346
  sales commissions, 340
  taxes, 350
  term insurance, 332–334, 352
  universal life insurance, 339
  variable-universal life insurance, 339–340

  whole life insurance, 336–337
  why needed, 325
Life insurance application, 341–352
Life insurance policy, 340–346
Lifeline banking account, 136
Lifetime learning credit, 109
Lifetime savings account (LSA), 526
Limit order, 456–457
Limited partner, 483
Limited partnership, 483
Limited-pay whole life insurance, 336–337
Limited power of attorney, 551
Limited warranty, 219
Line of credit, 167
Lipper's Mutual Fund Profiles, 438
Liquid assets, 36
Liquidity, 44, 129, 372
Liquidity risk, 372
Listed securities, 451
Listing agreement, 257
Living benefit clause, 345
Living costs, 21
Living trusts, 548–549
Living will, 550
Load, 433–435
Load fund, 434
Loan commitment, 241
Loan preapproval, 211, 241
Loan-to-value ratio, 244, 486
Lockheed, 404
Long-term care insurance, 315–316
Long-term gain (loss), 101
Long-term goals, 62–63
Long-term investing, 384–386
Long-term liability, 37
Long's Drug Stores, 402
Loss control, 271
Loss frequency severity, 270
Loss reduction, 275
Loss severity, 270
Lost/stolen credit cards, 169
Lottery, 17
Low-load fund, 434
Lowballing, 222
Lown, Jean, 85, 430
LSA, 526
Lump-sum distribution, 530
Lynch, Peter, 384, 464

Magellan Fund, 440
Magnuson-Moss Warranty Act, 218
Maintenance agreement, 219
Maintenance margin, 472
Major medical expense insurance, 313
Major purchases. *See* Automobiles/major purchases
Malpractice insurance, 291
Managed care plan, 305
Managed fund, 430
Management fee, 435
Management of monetary assets. *See* Monetary asset management

Manufactured housing, 234
Manufacturer's suggested retail price (MSRP), 208
Margin account, 470
Margin buying, 470
Margin call, 472
Margin rate, 470
Margin trading, 470–473
Marginal analysis, 13–14
Marginal cost, 13
Marginal tax bracket (MTB), 93
Marginal tax rate, 14, 93, 96, **376**
Marginal utility, 13
Marital deduction, 552
Market interest rates, 412
Market making, 452
Market movements, 378
Market order, 456
Market risk, 373, 467
Market timers, 378
Market timing, 378–379
Market-to-book ratio, 399
Market-volatility risk, 372
Marketability risk, 372
Marriage
  community property laws, 548
  life planning issues, 34
  money management, 82–86
Martin, Allen, 455
Matching contributions, 115, 518
Maternity benefits, 311
Maturity date, 395
Maximum capital gains fund, 427–428
Maximum taxable yearly earnings (MTYE), 507
McDonald's, 385
Mediation, 224
Medicaid, 307
Medical expense coverage, 312–313
Medical information bureau, 314
Medical payments coverage, 285–286
Medical power of attorney, 550
Medicare, 306–307, **509**
Medicare Part A, 307
Medicare Part B, 307
Medicare supplement insurance, 306n
Medicare tax, 507
Medigap insurance, 306n
Member firms, 451
MFCC, 50
MGIC, 253
Micro-caps, 404
Microsoft, 402
Microsoft Excel, 66
Microsoft Money, 47, 66, 132n
Mid-cap stock, 404
Millionaire, 25
Minimum-balance account, 137
Minimum payment, 164, 172, 173
Minor's account, 144
MMDA, 145

MMMF, 145
Mobile homes, 234
Moderate investment philosophy, 367
Modern portfolio theory, 380
Modified life insurance, 337
Monetary asset management, 127–152
  checking accounts, 135–138
  defined, 129
  deposit insurance, 131–132
  electronic banking, 132–135
  golden rules, 129
  long-term savings instruments, 146–148
  money market accounts, 143–146
  ownership of accounts, 144
  providers of services, 130–132
  savings accounts, 138–143
Monetary assets, 36
Money, 9, 147, 351, 434, 439
money.com, 47
Money factor, 216
Money income, 10
Money mantras, 14
Money market account, 143–146
Money market deposit account (MMDA),
  145
Money market mutual fund (MMMF), 145
Money order, 142
Money-purchase plan, 522
Monitor unexpected balances, 79
Monte Carlo simulation, 380–381, 529–530,
  531
Month order, 457
Moody's Investors Service, 405, 407
Moral hazard, 272
Morale hazard, 272
Morningstar, 465
Morningstar Mutual Funds, 438
Morningstar No-Load Funds, 438
Mortgage broker, 240
Mortgage fund, 427
Mortgage Guaranty Insurance Corporation
  (MGIC), 253
Mortgage insurance, 253–254
Mortgage interest tax credit, 110
Mortgage loan, 230, 242–251
  alternate loans, 248–251
  amortization, 242–243
  amount borrowed, 243, 245
  applying for, 240–241
  ARM, 247–248
  conventional mortgage, 247
  insurance, 253–254
  interest rate, 243
  length of maturity, 245–246
Mortgage lock-in, 241
Mortgage refinancing, 245, 246
Moss, Joan Koonce, 51
Motley Fool, The, 465
Motor vehicle insurance. *See* Automobile
  insurance
Motor vehicles. *See* Automobiles/major
  purchases

MSB, 131
MSRP, 208
MTYE, 507
Multiple indemnity clause, 343
Multiple listing service, 240
Multiple-of-earnings approach, 328
Municipal bond (tax-exempt) fund, 426–
  427
Municipal government bonds (munies),
  119, 410–411
Mutual fund, 132, 421–446
  automotive investment/reinvestment, 431
  balanced objective, 427
  beneficiary designation, 432–433
  closed-end funds, 423–424
  defined, 422
  fees, 433–437
  fund families, 431
  golden rules, 424
  growth and income objective, 428–429
  growth objective, 427–428
  income objective, 426–427
  index fund, 430
  load, 433–435
  managed fund, 430
  NAV, 425
  open-end funds, 424
  past performance, 439–441
  purchase and sale, 429, 457–458
  quotations, 460
  recordkeeping, 432
  sources of information, 437–439
  switching privileges, 431
  taxes, 440
  volatility, 439
  withdrawal plans, 433
Mutual fund asked price, 460
Mutual fund bid price, 460
Mutual fund chartered counselor
  (MFCC), 50
Mutual fund dividends, 425
Mutual fund expense charges, 435
Mutual fund family, 431
Mutual fund fees, 433–437
Mutual fund fund, 429
Mutual fund offer price, 460
Mutual fund quotations, 460
Mutual Funds Magazine, 439
Mutual Funds Update, 438
Mutual savings bank (MSB), 131

n-ratio method, 193
Naked option, 493
Named-perils policies, 278
NASD, 452, 455
NASDAQ, 452
NASDAQ 100 Index, 430
NASDAQ Composite Index, 461–462
National Association of Investors
  Corporation, 461
National Association of Personal Financial
  Advisors, 50

National Association of Securities Dealers
  (NASD), 452, 455
National Credit Union Administration
  (NCUA), 131
National Credit Union Share Insurance
  Fund (NCUSIF), 131
National Foundation for Credit Counseling,
  198
National Highway Traffic Safety
  Administration (NHTSA), 215
National Real Estate Investors Association,
  485
National Trade and Professional Associations,
  463
NAV, 425
NCUA, 131
NCUSIF, 131
Necessary insurance, 271
Necessary Losses (Viorst), 83
Need, 206
Needs approach, 329–331
Negative amortization, 247
Negotiable instrument, 136
Negotiable order of withdrawal (NOW)
  account, 136
Negotiating, 220–221
Net asset value (NAV), 425
Net cost, 353
Net gain, 39
Net income, 39
Net loss, 39
Net surplus, 81
Net worth, 36–38
Net worth formula, 37
Net worth statement, 35. *See also* Balance
  sheet
Netbank.com, 132
New-vehicle buying service, 220
New vehicle financing, 212, 216–218
New York Commodity Exchange, 496
New York Mercantile Exchange, 496
New York Stock Exchange (NYSE), 451
New York Stock Exchange Composite, 461
Newcomb, Cora, 140
Newspaper price quotations, 458–460
Newsweek, 9
NHTSA, 215
Nike, 402
Nikkei Dow, 462
No-load fund, 434
Nominal income, 10
Non-probate assets, 546
Non-probate property, 544
Noncancellable policies, 320
Noncontributory plan, 517
Noncumulative preferred stock, 395
Nondeeded timesharing, 483
Nonforfeiture values, 344–345
Noninstallment credit, 164
Nonparticipating policies, 342
Nonrefundable tax credit, 109
Not insured, 508

NOW account, 136
Nursing home care, 316
NYSE, 451

Odd lots, 454
Offer to purchase, 239
Older home form (HO-8), 279, 281
On-line financial calculators, 466
On-line investment club, 461
On-line investment resources, 465–466
On-line investment scams, 466
On-line investment screening, 465–466
Open-end lease, 216
Open-end mutual fund, 424
Open-ended credit, 164
Open enrollment period, 303
Open-listing service, 240
Open order, 457
Open-perils policies, 278
Opportunity cost, 13
Option contracts, 492–495
Option holder, 492
Option premium, 492
Option writer, 492
Optional insurance, 271
Optionally renewable policies, 319–320
Oracle, 402
Ordinary income dividend distributions, 425
Ordinary life insurance, 336
Organized stock exchange, 451–452
OTC market, 452
Over-the-counter (OTC) market, 452
Overdraft fees, 140
Overindebtedness, 194–199
Overwithholding, 98
Own-occupation policy, 319
Owned housing, 232–233
Owner, 340
Ownership of accounts, 144

P/B ratio, 399
P/E ratio, 400
Paid-at-65 policies, 337
Paid-up policies, 337
PAP, 284
Par value, 405
Participating policies, 342
Partnership theory of marriage rights, 548
Passbook savings account, 139
Passive investor, 368
Pawnshop, 189
Pay as you go requirements, 98
Pay-day lenders, 189
Pay yourself first, 141
Payable-at-death designation, 144, 547
Payment cap, 247
Payout ratio, 314
Payroll withholding, 98
PBGC, 521
Pension, 520

Pension Benefit Guarantee Corporation (PBGC), 521
Pentecost, Eve, 12
Peril, 270
Periodic rate, 174
Periodic statement, 134, 170
Periodic tenancy, 232
Permanent insurance, 334
Personal auto policy (PAP), 284
Personal exemption, 107
Personal finance, 4
    computer programs, 47
    golden rules, 4
    periodicals, 9
    why studied, 4–5
Personal finance software, 47
Personal financial goals, 33. *See also*
    Financial goals
Personal financial planning, 5. *See also*
    Financial planning
Personal financial success, 5–7
Personal identification number (PIN), 133
Personal inflation rate, 11
Personal injury protection (PIP), 285
Personal Journal, 438
Personal liability insurance, 291
Personal line of credit, 167
Personal loss, 274
Personal representative, 544
Personal residence. *See* Housing expenditure
Personal retirement account (PRA), 526
Personal retirement accounts, 524–526
Physical hazard, 272
PiggiBills.com, 132
PIN, 133
PIP, 285
PITI, 251
Planned buying, 204–206
PMI, 253, 254
Point, 254–255
Point-of-sale (POS) terminal, 133
Point-of-service (POS) plan, 305
Policy illustration, 344
Policy limits, 274
Policy loans, 345
Policyholder, 340
Political risk, 373
Portability, 516
Portability option, 311
Portfolio, 361
Portfolio diversification, 379
Portfolio tracking, 466
POS plan, 305
POS terminal, 133
Postnuptial agreement, 86
Postpone income, 121
Power of attorney, 550–551
PPO, 306
PRA, 526
Prawitz, Aimee D., 223
Preapproved credit card offers, 169
Preauthorized payment, 134

Precautionary goals, 65
Precious metals and gold fund, 428
Precious metals and stones, 489–491
Preemptive right, 402
Preexisting conditions, 310
Preferred provider organization (PPO), 306
Preferred stock, 394–395
Premium, 272, 412
Premium conversion plans, 308
Premium-only plans, 114
Premium quote service, 352
Prenuptial agreement, 86
Prepaid educational service plan, 115
Prepaid tuition plan, 115
Prepayment fee, 257
Prepayment penalty, 193
Present value, 20–21, A-2
    annuity, 20–21
    series of equal amounts, A-10–A-11
    single amount, A-6–A-7
Preservation of capital, 367
Preshopping research, 208–211
Prestige card, 165
Pretax conversion plans, 114
Pretax dollars, 22
Pretax income, 112
Pretax money, 514
Price appreciation, 485
Price/earnings ratio (P/E ratio), 400
Price-level-adjusted mortgage, 248
Price-to-book ratio (P/B ratio), 399
Price-to-sales ratio (PSR), 400–401
PricewaterhouseCooper's, 530
Primary-care physician, 305
Primary insurance amount, 508
Primary market, 449–450
Principal, 17, 164, 242, 395
Principle of indemnity, 274
Prioritizing wants, 206–207
Priority worksheet, 207
Privacy, 158
Private mortgage insurance (PMI), 253, 254
Probate, 543, 546
Probate court, 543
Probate estate, 544
Probate property, 544
Prochaska-Cue, Kathleen, 139
Professional advisers, 49–50, 51
Professional designations/credentials, 50
Professional liability insurance, 291
Professional shoppers, 220
Profile prospectus, 464
Profit-sharing plan, 522
Progressive tax, 93
Promissory note, 185
Property insurance, 269
Property report, 482
Prospectus, 426, 464
Provider sponsored association, 306
Provider sponsored network (PSN), 306
Proxy, 402

PSN, 306
Purchase contract, 239
Purchase loan, 185
Purchase offer, 239
Purchasing power, 10
Purchasing power risk, 372
Pure risk, 268, 371
Put option, 492

QDRO, 510
QQQ, 430
Qualified domestic-relations order
    (QDRO), 510
Qualified retirement accounts, 103
Qualified retirement plan, 23
Qualified tuition (section 529) programs,
    115
Quicken, 47, 66, 132n, 530
Quinn, Jane Bryant, 442
Quitclaim deed, 255
Quotation board, 453
Quotecom, 438

Random risk, 373
Rate of return, 365
Ratio analysis. *See* Financial ratios
Ratio of debt-to-equity, 183–184
Raw land, 482
RBC Centura, 132
Re-enter provision, 332
Real estate, 481
Real estate broker (agent), 240
Real estate investment, 481–491
    advantages/disadvantages, 484–489
    direct ownership investments, 481–483
    golden rules, 481
    indirect ownership investments, 483
    REIT, 483
    taxes, 486–488, 490–491
    valuation, 484
Real estate investment trust (REIT), 483
Real estate property taxes, 252
Real estate syndicate, 483
Real estate transfer taxes, 258
Real income, 10, 11
Real rate of return, 377
Rebate, 211
Recession, 8
Reconciling budget estimates, 72–74
Record date, 440
Recordkeeping, 47–49, 66
    budgeting, 66–67
    home files, 48
    income tax, 122
    mutual funds, 432
    safe deposit box, 48, 49
Recurring clause, 310
Redemption charge, 434
Redress, 224
Reducing income taxes
    buy a home, 120
    employer, 113–115

example, 116–117
income shifting, 119–120
lunch deductions, 121
pension plans, 114–115
postpone income, 121
real estate investment, 122
recordkeeping, 122
sideline business, 104
tax deductions, 121–122
tax-sheltered investments, 112–113, 115,
    119
Reduction-option loan, 248
Refundable tax credit, 109
Regional stock exchanges, 452
Registered bonds, 406
Registered investment adviser (RIA), 50
Regressive tax, 93
Regular income plan, 198
Regular IRA, 524
Regulation M, 216
Reinvestment risk, 372
REIT, 483
Release, 296
Remainder beneficiaries, 548
Remarriage, 84–86
Renewable policies, 319–320
Rent, 365
Rent-to-own program, 189
Rental cars, 286
Rental reimbursement, 287
Rented housing, 231–233
Renter's contents broad form (HO-4), 278–
    279, 281
Repairs, 485
Repossession, 187, 195
Research reports, 465
Residential lot, 482
Residential units, 481–482
Residual clause, 319
RESPA, 240
Restrictive endorsement, 139
Retail charge account, 166
Retail credit card, 165
Retirement, 505
Retirement nest egg, 511
Retirement plan contribution credit, 517
Retirement plan insurance, 521
Retirement planning, 502–540
    annuity, 534–535
    big mistakes, 527
    cash-balance plan, 521
    deferred-compensation plan, 522
    defined benefit plan, 520–521
    defined contribution plan, 517–520
    divorce, 510
    early withdrawals, 532–533
    employer's plans, 516–523
    ESOP, 522
    golden rules, 504
    insurance, 521
    investment strategy, 528, 529
    IRA, 524–525

Keogh, 525
money-purchase plan, 522
Monte Carlo simulation, 529–530, 531
part-time work, 535
personal retirement accounts, 524–526
profit-sharing plan, 522
proposed new accounts, 526
questions to ask, 523
retirement needs, 511–514
rollover penalty, 530
savings, 528
SEP-IRA, 526
Social Security benefits, 506–510,
    A-12–A-14
tax-sheltered retirement accounts,
    514–516
taxes, 517, 534
thrift and savings plan, 522
women, 506
Retirement planning computer software
    programs, 530
Retirement plans, 23–24
Retirement savings account (RSA), 526
Retirement savings contribution credit,
    110
Retirement savings goal, 511
Return, 365
Reuters Money Network, 438
Reverse mortgage, 250–251
Revocable living trust, 549
Revolving credit, 164
Revolving savings fund, 75–76
RIA, 50
Riders, 341
Risk, 267
Risk avoidance, 270
Risk management, 268–272
    estimate risk/potential losses, 270
    gather information to identify exposures,
        269–270
    golden rules, 268
    strategies, 270–271
Risk-management process, 268–272
Risk of dying too soon, 347
Risk of living too long, 347
Risk of premium, 366
Risk pyramid, 371
Risk reduction, 271
Risk retention, 270–271
Risk scoring, 160
Risk tolerance, 371
Risk transfer, 271
Rollover, 530
Rollover IRA, 530
Rollover mortgage, 249
Roth IRA, 115, 525
Round lots, 454
RSA, 526
Rule of 72, 18, 19
Rule of 78s method, 193–194
Running Paws Cat Food Company, 396–397
Russell 2000 Index Fund, 430

S&P 500 index, 461
Safe-deposit box, 48, 49
Safety, 129
SAIE, 131
Salary-reduction plan, 517
Sales contract, 239
Sales credit, 185
Sales finance company, 188
Sallie Mae, 410
Same as cash plans, 156
Saver credit, 110
Saver's tax credit, 517
Savings, 5
    categorizing, 69
    how to save, 140–142, 364
    retirement, 528
Savings account, 138–143
Savings account interest, 142–143
Savings and loan associations (S&Ls), 131
Savings Association Insurance Fund (SAIE), 131
Savings incentive match plan for employees IRA (SIMPLE IRA), 519
Savings ratio, 46
Scams, 466, 490
Scudder, 146n
Sears, Roebuck and Company, 385
SEC, 453
Second mortgage, 249, 250
Secondary beneficiary, 546
Secondary market, 395, 449, 450
Section 529 college savings plan, 62
Sector fund, 428
Secured bond, 406
Secured credit card, 165
Secured loan, 186
Securities, 361. *See also* Buying and selling securities
Securities and Exchange Commission (SEC), 453
Securities Industry Association, 405
Securities market indexes, 461–462
Securities markets, 378
Securities Transfer Association, 385
Security deposit, 231
Security Investors Protection Corporation (SIPC), 453
Self-directed retirement plan, 517
Seller-financed second mortgage, 250
Seller financing, 250, 258
Seller's cost, 220
Selling short, 473–474
SEP-IRA, 526
Separable property, 548
Serial bonds, 406
Series EE savings bonds, 119, 148
Series HH bonds, 148
Series I savings bond, 119, 148
Service contract, 219
Service credit, 166–167
Settlement options, 343–344
Settler, 548

Share draft account, 136
Shared-appreciation mortgage, 249
Shareholder, 393
Shareholder rights, 402
Shareholder's equity, 398
Short selling, 473–474
Short-term gain (loss), 101
Short-term goals, 63–65
Short-term liability, 37
Signature card, 144
Signature loan, 186
Simple interest, 16
Simple-interest method, 191, 192
SIMPLE IRA, 519
Simplified employee pension-individual retirement account (SEP-IRA), 526
Single-family dwelling, 233
Single-premium life insurance, 337
Singletary, Michelle, 14
Sinking fund, 406
SIPC, 453
Skilled nursing care, 316
S&Ls, 131
Small-cap fund, 428
Small-cap stock, 404
Small-capitalization fund, 428
Small claims court, 224
Small-loan company, 188
Smart card, 134
Smart Money, 9
Social Security benefits, 506–510, A-12–A-14
Social Security blackout period, 327
Social Security credits, 507
Social Security disability benefits, A-13
Social Security disability income insurance, 317
Social Security retirement benefits, A-13
Social Security rider, 319
Social Security statement, 510
Social Security survivor's benefits, 327, A-13—A-14
Socially conscious fund, 429
Software packages. *See* Computer software
Sold "as is," 218
Special endorsement, 139
Special form (HO-3), 278, 280
Special warranty deed, 255
Specialist, 455
Speculative companies, 403
Speculative risk, 268, 371
Speculative stock, 402–403
Split-definition policies, 319
Spousal consent, 521
Spousal IRA, 525
Spread, 452
Spreadsheet program, 66
Springing power of attorney, 551
Standard & Poor's, 405, 407, 438, 465
Standard deduction, 104
Standard deviation, 439
Standard of living, 5

Standardized expense table, 436
Startup capital, 393
State income taxes, 109n
State of economy, 8–9
Stated interest rate, 405
Statement date, 170
Statement savings account, 139
Steps to personal finance success, 5–7
Sticker price, 208
Stock, 393–405
    blue-chip, 403–404
    cap size, 404
    common, 393–394
    countercyclical, 404
    fundamental *vs.* technical analysis, 403
    golden rules, 393
    growth, 402
    income, 401
    Internet, and, 405
    numeric measures, 397–401
    preferred, 394–395
    quotations, 458–459
    speculative, 402–403
    value, 404
Stock, bond, and mutual fund advisory services, 465
Stock brokerage firm, 132
Stock dividend, 399
Stock exchange, 451
Stock option, 492
Stock orders, 456–457
Stock quotations, 458–459
Stock screener, 405
Stock split, 399
Stockbroker, 450
Stockholder, 393
StockScreener, 405
Stolen credit cards, 169
Stop order, 457
Stop-loss order, 457
Stop-payment order, 137
Stored-value card, 134
Straight annuity, 535
Straight bankruptcy, 199
Straight life insurance, 336
Street name, 450
Striking price, 492
Student Loan Marketing Association (Sallie Mae), 410
Student loans, 162
Stuhlman, Donald, 173
Sub-prime market, 241
Subleasing, 232
Subordinate budget, 79
Subrogation rights, 285
Substitute check, 137
Suicide clause, 342
Sum of the digits method, 193
Super NOW account, 143, 145
Surgical coverage, 312
Surgical-service-incurred (fee-for-service) plan, 312

Surplus, 39
Surplus/deficit formula, 41
Surrender charge, 340
Survivor's benefit, 521
Sweat equity property, 482
Sweeps, 146
Switching privilege, 431
Systematic risk, 373, 467
Systematic withdrawal plans, 433

T-Bills, 408
T&E card, 166
T. Rowe Price, 146n, 530
Tangible assets, 36
Tax avoidance, 111
Tax basis, 101
Tax considerations and consequences. *See
    also* Income tax
    buying and selling securities, 471
    charitable remainder trust (CRT), 550
    health care planning, 308
    income-producing real estate investment,
        490–491
    life insurance planning, 350, 416
    mutual funds, 440
    purchasing a home, 236
    reducing incoming taxes, 116–117
    retirement planning, 534
    saving for children's college, 62
Tax credit, 109–110
Tax-deductible expenses, 104–107
Tax-deferred, 113, 514
Tax evasion, 111
Tax-exempt bonds, 410
Tax-exempt income, 15
Tax-free bonds, 410
Tax-free exchange, 488
Tax liability, 97, 108–109
Tax losses, 122
Tax planning, 91
Tax-rate schedules, 94
Tax refund, 97, 111
Tax-sheltered, 112
Tax-sheltered income, 15
Tax-sheltered investments, 112–113, 115,
    119
Tax-sheltered plan, 23
Tax-sheltered spending accounts, 22–23
Tax-sheltering, 503–504
Tax tables, 94, 95
Taxable income, 91
TAXACT, 99n
Taxation
    computer software, 47
    estate tax, 552
    FSA, 22
    generation-skipping transfer tax, 549
    home ownership, 251–252
    income tax. *See* Income tax; Tax consid-
        erations and consequences
    inheritance tax, 552
    retirement plans, 23, 517

Teaser rate, 167, 247
Technical analysis, 403
10-K report, 464–465
Tenancy by the entirety, 144
Tenancy for a specific time, 232
Tenancy in common, 144
Tenant rights, 232–233
Tenneco, 385
Term life insurance, 332–334, 338, 352
Testamentary trusts, 548
Testator, 544
The Motley Fool, 465
Thrift and savings plan, 522
Tiered interest rate, 136
Tiered pricing, 161
Time, 9
Time deposits, 139
Time horizon, 372
Time period limits, 310
Time risk, 372
Time value of money, 16–21
    compounding, 16–17
    future value, 18–20
    present value, 20–21
    questions to ask, 16
Time Warner, 404
Timesharing, 482–483
Timing the market, 378–379
Title, 255
Title insurance, 255
Title search, 255
Total income, 99–102
Total return, 365
Towing coverage, 287
Trade association, 463
Trade-off, 5
Traditional IRA, 524–525
Trailing commissions, 435
Transaction date, 172
Transitionally insured, 508
TransUnion, 162
**Travel and entertainment (T&E) card,
    166**
Traveler's check, 142
Treasury bills, 408
Treasury Direct account, 409
**Treasury inflation-protected securities
    (TIPS), 148, 409**–410
Treasury note, 409
Treasury Securities, 407–410
Treasury security issues, 148
T. Rowe Price, 47, 146n, 530
Trust, 144, 547–549
Trustee, 144, 517, 547
Trustee account, 144
Trustee-to-trustee rollover, 530
Trustor, 548
Truth in Lending Act, 195
Truth in Lending Act, 190
TurboTax, 47
12b-1 fee, 435
20-pay life policies, 336–337

20 percent withholding rule, 530
Two-party check, 139
Two-step mortgage, 248

ucr, 312
Ultraconservative investors, 366
**Umbrella (excess) liability insurance,
    291**–293
Underinsured motorist insurance, 286
Underwriting, 276
Underwriting profits, 350
Unearned income, 62, 97
Unfair discrimination, 159
Uniform settlement statement, 241
Uninsured motorist insurance, 286
U.S. government savings bonds, 119, 148
U.S. News & World Report, 9, 439
Universal default, 169
Universal life insurance, 339
Unmanaged fund, 430
Unrealized capital gains, 425
Unsecured bond, 406
Unsecured loan, 186
Unsystematic risk, 373
Upside down, 210
Use assets, 36
Use-it-or-lose-it rule, 23, 114
Used car, purchase of, 222–223
Used-car trade-in values, 210
Usual, customary, and reasonable (ucr), 312
Utility, 13

VA mortgage insurance, 253–254
Value fund, 427
Value Line, 465
Value Line Mutual Fund Survey, 438
Value stock, 404
Values, 31, 60
Vanguard S&P 500 Index, 430
Vanishing premium life insurance, 337
Variable annuity, 535
Variable expenses, 40
Variable life insurance, 339
Variable-rate certificates of deposit, 147
Variable-rate loan, 186
Variable-rate mortgage, 247
Variable-universal life insurance, 339–340
Variable value, 412
Variance analysis, 81
Vehicle ownership, 288–289
Vesting, 519–520
Viatical companies, 346
Viorst, Judith, 83
VIPERs, 430
Vision care insurance, 314
Volatility, 439
Voluntary repossession, 195
Voting rights, 402

Wage earner plan, 198
Waiting period, 318
Waiver of premium, 346

Wal-Mart, 385, 402
Walkway lease, 216
Wall Street Journal, 11, 438
Want, 206
Warranty, 218–219
Warranty deed, 255
Warranty of fitness, 218
Warranty of merchantability, 218
Weagley, Robert O., 442
Wealthy, 6
Websites
  bonds, 405
  budget, 72
  financial information providers, 405
  financial planning tools, 47
  HUD mortgage programs, 253
  insurance companies, 350

investment information, 465
investment returns, 381
lemon (car), 224
life insurance, 352
Monte Carlo simulation, 530
mortgage prequalification, 238
munies, 411
new vehicle buying service, 220
on-line investment club, 461
portfolio tracking, 466
real estate investment, 485
tax tables, 94
wills of famous people, 544
Week order, 457
Well-known growth stock, 402
Westinghouse Electric, 404
Whole life insurance, 336–337, 338

Will, 544
WILLPower, 544
Wilshire 5000 Index, 430, 462
Withdrawal plans, 433
Withdrawals, 514, 515, 532–533
Workers' compensation insurance, 312
Worth, 439
Wray, David, 529

Yield, 365
Yield to maturity (YTM), 414–415
"You" statements, 84
Your Federal Income Tax: For Individuals, 99
YTM, 414–415

Zero-coupon bonds (zeros), 411
Zero-sum game, 497